Praise for Introduction to Management Fourth edition

'A classic and authoritative text, admirably suited to those students who are not studying management within the traditional "business studies" arena but who need an introduction that reflects current thinking and practices, and which uses cases and examples which are topical and relevant to them. This fourth edition is not only thoroughly revised and updated but incorporates new material on critical management issues like risk, globalisation, innovation, leadership and corporate governance. As someone who teaches management principles to a wide range of students as part of their degree programmes, this text – with its focus on developing management skills – provides an excellent all-round introduction to the subject. Highly recommended.' – David Gillingwater, Senior Lecturer, Department of Civil and Building Engineering, Loughborough University, UK

'This very readable account of the basics of management is highly topical, with clear discussions of current issues and with relevant case studies. It comprehensively combines theory and practice in a structure that will appeal equally to students of business and management and to practising managers in all sectors. For someone new to the study of management this book will provide a thorough grounding in every area, and will be a 'must have' to support them throughout their managerial career.' – Dr John Taylor, Senior Lecturer, Canterbury Christ Church University, UK

'A book with good coverage on the syllabus and packed with relevant facts for the students.' – Professor Gin Chong, Southampton Solent University, UK

'I think Richard Pettinger has done an exceptional job. This is a text which is comprehensive in its approach and is written in a "reader friendly" fashion. The wide variety of examples and international cases provided allows a clear appreciation of management issues. It is obvious that this text is centred on teaching and unlike other texts is not short in coverage of the depth and breadth of the management discipline.' – Dr John Chelliah, Lecturer, School of Management, University of Technology, Sydney, Australia

'This is an excellent book for learners and their facilitators across a wide range of levels. It's suitable both for dipping into topics and for more detailed information about theory and its application. The structure and clear layout allows readers to access information quickly and easily. I would advise and encourage students to buy a copy.' – Andrew G. Holmes, Academic Co-ordinator, Work-Related Learning Centre for Lifelong Learning, University of Hull, UK

'The new edition of Pettinger's *Introduction to Management* is an accessible, up-to-date and wide ranging text which gives proper recognition to the importance of managing people as a key resource, whilst ensuring that critical elements of modern management such as corporate governance, ethics, and globalisation are given due prominence. Management as a combination of science, profession and art is explored in a balanced and direct style. The section on management practice underpins the extensive use of short, focused real world examples helping to embed the theory in context, whilst the use of one wider case study on the Body Shop to illustrate different facets of management, provides an excellent thread across the range of management activity. Comprehensive, in a no nonsense style, there is no better introduction to management than this for either undergraduate or postgraduate students.' – David Banner, Senior Lecturer in Management Development, Harrow Business School, University of Westminster, UK

Introduction to Management

Fourth edition

Richard Pettinger

First edition 1994
Second edition 1997
Reprinted 5 times
Third edition 2002
Reprinted 4 times
Fourth edition 2007
Published by
PALGRAVE MACMILLAN
Houndmills, Basingstoke, Hampshire RG21 6XS and
175 Fifth Avenue, New York, N.Y. 10010
Companies and representatives throughout the world

PALGRAVE MACMILLAN is the global academic imprint of the Palgrave Macmillan division of St. Martin's Press, LLC and of Palgrave Macmillan Ltd. Macmillan® is a registered trademark in the United States, United Kingdom and other countries. Palgrave is a registered trademark in the European Union and other countries.

ISBN-13: 978–0–230–00038–4
ISBN-10:   0–230–00038–X

This book is printed on paper suitable for recycling and made from fully managed and sustained forest sources.

A catalogue record for this book is available from the British Library.

A catalog record for this book is available from the Library of Congress.

10   9   8   7   6   5   4   3   2   1
16   15   14   13   12   11   10   09   08   07

Printed and bound in China

Contents

Figures

Tables

Management in focus boxes

Preface

> Everywhere in the world there is a revolution going on, a transformation of business and of the services needed and wanted by people. At the heart of this revolution is management. This is underlined by a realisation that, whatever the merits of how things were conducted in the past, new ways and new methods are essential for the future; above all, this means a better understanding of what management actually is.

These words formed the opening paragraph of the first edition of this book, published in 1994. All of this remains true today, though clearly some of the outputs of this revolution and transformation were not foreseen. For example:

- Tesco has grown from being an 'improving' supermarket chain, to the largest retailer in the UK, and the second largest in the European Union.
- In 1994, low-cost air travel was little more than an idea. While it had been proven to work successfully in the United States, nobody really thought that it would be possible in the UK and EU.
- In the early 1990s large corporate losses were so rare as to become headline news. Today, large corporate losses are reported by companies in all sectors.
- The privatisation of public services, utilities and infrastructure organisations has sought to create 'markets' for much that was hitherto provided by the state as a part of its core responsibilities.
- Corporate scandals have become much more widespread.

The revolution and transformation in organisational activities and management practices has been driven by economic, social, political, legal and technological advances. The combined effect of these advances has been to enable organisations to establish activities anywhere in the world that they choose; to take advantage of deregulation in labour laws, trading practices, and the opening up of new markets. The expansion of the European Union, and the opening up of market, product and service opportunities in China, India and other parts of south-east Asia, continue to provide opportunities for all aspects of organisational activity: the supply side, manufacturing and service delivery, investment and returns, and new market development.

All of this has in turn sharpened up and crystallised what ought to constitute the body of skills, knowledge, attitudes, behaviour and expertise that all expert managers should have. At the core of this is the demand for a professional commitment on the part of all of those who aspire to management positions.

The cornerstone of managerial expertise is: achieving profits and effective performance; delivering the required performance; achieving things through people; knowing and understanding the environment and markets; knowing and understanding customers, clients and suppliers; establishing behavioural and attitudinal standards; taking a personal commitment to active responsibility and accountability; and transforming from administrative management to leadership.

The body of knowledge, understanding and expertise has been greatly enhanced in both volume and quality by the proliferation of media coverage of business and management matters, and by the range and variety of business and management publications and books now available. Business and management publications and books seem to fall into the following categories:

- text books that form the basis for studying the areas of skills, knowledge and expertise required, and whose importance is emphasised by the range of higher education courses now available at certificate, diploma, undergraduate and postgraduate levels
- managerial and organisational biographies and histories, identifying (in the best cases) where and why things went right, and where and why things went wrong
- critiques of organisational practice, especially where things have gone wrong
- expansion in the trade press sector, resulting in increased volumes of magazines, journals and periodicals both for industries and for public services
- research activities, resulting in the publication of substantial studies relating to all aspects of organisation practice.

For both the student of management and the practising manager therefore, there is a great range of material to read and study, and upon which to draw. The experiences of others, written up in each of the above ways, provides further opportunities for development of professional knowledge, understanding and expertise.

This edition orders the whole field of management, its professionalisation, discipline and expertise into four parts.

Part I considers the foundations of management, establishing that the cornerstone is the need to achieve profits and results, to deliver performance, and to achieve things through people. This part has chapters on performance, the environment, change and globalisation.

Part II is concerned with the strategy, direction and priorities of organisations. It has chapters on strategy, marketing, product and service development, finance, quantitative aspects, product and service development, and the creativity of management.

Part III is concerned with organisational behaviour. It has chapters on culture, attitudes and values, communication, technology, and human resource management.

Part IV is entitled 'Management in action', and deals with the delivery of expertise in organisational and operational situations. This part has chapters on leadership, motivation, power and influence, conflict and corporate governance. There is also a chapter entitled 'Management in practice', which deals with the ways in which daily problems and issues ought best to be handled.

There is a short introduction to each part, so that those who read the book can see how the whole is built and developed. There is also a continuous case study running throughout the book. This concerns The Body Shop, the organic cosmetics and gift retailer founded by Anita and Gordon Roddick 30 years ago. The Body Shop has for a long while been an iconic organisation, excellent and effective to study in terms of observing the main lessons of leadership and management in practice.

The Body Shop is of particular value at this stage, as Anita and Gordon Roddick withdraw from executive positions within the organisation, so requiring it to establish a corporate identity and existence.

The result is to ensure that the whole area of managerial knowledge, skills and expertise is introduced and covered comprehensively. As well as The Body Shop case, each chapter makes extensive use of examples from all organisations, industries, locations and sectors, and from many countries around the world. These examples are used to illustrate the different ways in which expertise is applied and the range of outcomes that are delivered.

Each chapter has a set of learning objectives, especially related to the understanding of knowledge, and the capability to apply this when faced with working issues. At the end of each chapter, there are discussion questions, and a case study for developing management skills and expertise to illustrate further the main points raised in the chapter and to set these in an operational context.

The primary target audience for this book is those on undergraduate courses in business and management, and those on undergraduate courses where business and management forms one part of their field of study (e.g. civil engineering with management, construction management, European studies with management, or languages with management).

The book is additionally of value to those already in work following certificate and diploma courses in management programmes. It is essential background reading for those following the professional studies courses of institutions such as the Chartered Institute of Personnel and Development, accountancy bodies, the Chartered Management Institute, and those related to specific disciplines, for example administrative management, marketing, education and healthcare.

The book has an additional purpose of being a comprehensive introductory text for those coming to postgraduate courses never having studied management before, for example those with engineering, technology and humanities degrees who now wish to pursue MBA programmes and others with a strong management element. The book is also of value to those in managerial and supervisory positions looking for a concise, comprehensive, and easy-to-read text which is related directly to examples from all the above areas of activity.

Richard Pettinger
University College London

Acknowledgements

The genesis of this book lay in the undergraduate Management Principles course of the Bartlett School of Architecture, Building, Environmental Design and Planning, University College London. In the pursuit and completion of this project, therefore, special thanks and acknowledgement are due to Graham Winch, then of University College London, now of the University of Manchester Institute of Science and Technology.

Since the first edition, this book has developed much further along the way; for that I wish to thank Andrew Scott, Linda Hesselman, Paul Griseri, Peter Antonioni, and all of the staff at the UCL Management Studies Centre; Bev Nutt, David Kincaid, David Woolven, Graham Bailey and David Coles of the UCL Bartlett School; and Stephen Gruneberg of the University of Reading.

Many other people have also contributed and given their support. Stephen Rutt and Ursula Gavin at Palgrave Macmillan have been a constant and positive source of help and guidance throughout. Chris Carr of Curran Publishing Services provided excellent and expert guidance at the proof stage. I am especially grateful for the support of: Kelvin Cheatle of Broadmoor Hospital; Jacek Klich of the Jagiellonian University, Krakow, Poland; Ram Ahronov; Jim and Margaret Malpas, and Sandra Madigan; David Scott; and to Rebecca Frith who, once again, typed and edited the manuscript. I am also grateful to Frances Kelly, Keith Sanders, Ken Batchelor, Michael Hutton, James Pollock, and Roger and June Cartwright for their constant support and encouragement over the years.

The Cary Grant dialogue on page 388 is a scene the author vividly remembers; if any reader can identify the film he would be very grateful.

Richard Pettinger

Part one

The foundations of management

● Introduction

Historically, management was always thought of as a combination of art, science and profession, and many used to take the view that management was no more than common sense. Developments over the recent past now make it clear that this only tells a part of the story. The principles, practices, profession and discipline of management have evolved into an ever more apparent body of knowledge, understanding, expertise and skills that have to be taught and learned, and which must be capable of application in whatever situation aspiring and practising managers find themselves. Studies, analyses and evaluations of organisations and their managers in the public and private sectors, in fields of activity as diverse as healthcare, airlines, shipping, transport, education, Internet, retail and wholesale, supermarkets and groceries, all clearly indicate that the differences between success and failure lie in the quality and expertise of management at all levels. For example:

● The commercial success of Tesco is due to the leadership and direction given to the company by Terry Leahy, and the strength and expertise of management at all levels – the stores themselves, the supply side, shelf and stack layout, shelf filling, product ranges and customer services.
● The commercial success of Ryanair, the budget airline, has been driven by the expertise, commitment and involvement of Michael O'Leary; and again, this has involved expert management in all parts of the company's activities – route networks and destinations, the purchasing of airliner fleets, high levels of staff training and attention to passenger demands.

Nobody ever forced anyone to use Tesco or Ryanair. Tesco has grown from having less than 10 per cent of UK supermarket sector market share, to over 30 per cent. Until the advent of Ryanair and easyJet, the received wisdom of the air travel industry was that this was an expensive activity, dependent upon high levels of charges. Ryanair and the other low-cost airline operators had to face initial scepticism and hostility, and the dominant perception that 'because they are cheap, they must therefore be unreliable and unsafe.'

Each of these companies operates in sectors where there are many companies, all of whom have varying degrees of success. At the core of these 'varying degrees of success' is management; and while expert management will never make a bad idea work, bad management can, and does, destroy organisations that have otherwise excellent, and highly desired and demanded products and services.

The purpose here, therefore, is to identify and illustrate the foundations on which are built the leadership, executive and managerial expertise that is delivered so effectively at organisations such as Tesco and Ryanair. In order to be fully effective in these or any other spheres of activity, the key priorities of profit and effectiveness, working with, and for, people, and delivering results have to be known and understood, and these are addressed by way of introduction in the first chapter. The ability to operate within a changing, turbulent and uncertain environment is dealt with in Chapter 2. The need for effective performance is introduced in the first chapter, and developed in detail in Chapter 3. The problems of uncertainty and volatility are developed further in Chapter 4, in the context of identifying and evaluating risk. The need to relate organisational performance, activities, products and services to given standards is covered in Chapter 5, which introduces the field of management and ethics. The need to see the environment in its entirety, to be able to take advantage of opportunities it presents and to work within its constraints is dealt with in Chapter 6. The final foundation stone is that of globalisation and internationalisation of organisations, management, products, services and activities (Chapter 7); and globalisation is dealt with as a foundation issue because of the need to be able to operate in fields of activities that now almost invariably include overseas competitors, suppliers and providers of products and services.

Chapter one

Introduction

'Julius Caesar never asked anyone to do anything that he was not willing to do himself.'
Gaius Suetonius, *The Twelve Caesars*.

'My staff – my people – were so fresh and full of enthusiasm.
It would have been criminal to drill this out of them.'
Shigeru Kobayashi, Sony (1961), at the opening of the company's first factory.

'Everyone wants instant success. No one is prepared to put in the hard work.'
David Cork, London Leisure Services Ltd, March 2000.

'If you don't like people, leave now.'
Tom Peters (1986), *The World Turned Upside Down*, Channel 4.

Chapter outline

- Introduction
- Summary of management expertise
- The professionalisation of management
- Management as a field of study
- Management research and literature
- The foundations of modern management
- The search for excellence
- Conclusions

Chapter objectives

After studying this chapter, you should be able to:

- begin to understand what management is, and what it is not

- understand the key management tasks and concerns

- understand the personal and professional qualities necessary to be a successful manager

- understand the nature of the professionalisation of management

- understand the piecemeal nature of the development of the body of knowledge of modern management, and the contribution of each accidental and individual step along the way to the present stage of understanding

- understand the foundations on which the expertise and practice of modern management are built.

● Introduction

The purpose of this chapter is to identify the range of general and universal concepts and elements that ought to be present in any worthwhile study of the subject of management. These are highlighted in themselves and then drawn together in so far as this is possible. However, many of these elements are disparate or divergent, and it is essential to recognise them as such.

There are many definitions of management; each tackles a part of the answer, and it is most useful to see these as complementary rather than conflicting. Henri Fayol, in the early twentieth century, defined it as the process of 'forecasting, planning, organising, commanding, coordinating and controlling'. E.F.L. Brech (1984) called it 'the social process of planning, coordination, control and motivation'. Writing in the 1980s, Tom Peters defined it as 'organisational direction based on sound common sense, pride in the organisation and enthusiasm for its works'. More recently still, Graham Winch of University College London described management as 'coping with change and uncertainty' (Winch, 1996). It is clear that management is partly the process of getting things done through people; and partly the creative and energetic combination of scarce resources into effective and profitable activities, and the combination of the skill and talents of the individuals concerned with doing this.

Management is conducted in organisations; and organisations operate in their environment. Organisations are variously described as: 'systems of inter-dependent human beings' (D.S. Pugh, 1986), or a 'joint function of human characteristics, the task to be accomplished and its environment' (H. Simon, 1967). Organisations may be seen as combinations of resources brought together for stated purposes. They have their own life, direction, permanence and identity; and are energised by people.

● The foundations of management

Management is a body of knowledge, skills and expertise which must be applied in ways demanded by the particular organisation in which the individual manager is working; and in ways demanded also by the particular environment in which activities are being conducted. The knowledge, skills and expertise required are as follows:

- achieving things through people
- achieving things for people
- making a profit
- delivering performance
- using scarce resources
- improving and developing things
- coping with change and uncertainty.

Achieving things through people

Achieving things through people is a key priority, because no managerial activity takes place in isolation from staff and their expertise. People's capabilities have to be harnessed in ways that are of value to the organisation, and their willingness to work has also to be engaged. The managerial task, and therefore the expertise demanded, is to engage, energise and harmonise the organisation's staff in pursuit of the stated goals, targets, aims and objectives. To do this effectively requires a knowledge and understanding of organisational, collective and individual human behaviour, with especial reference to how people act and react in particular situations and circumstances; and how people act and react in response to crises, emergencies and change (see Management in Focus 1.1).

MANAGEMENT IN FOCUS 1.1

STEW LEONARD

Stew Leonard Inc. is a small supermarket company based in Norwalk, Connecticut, USA. The company was founded by Stew Leonard, and each of the three stores is run by one of his children; his son. Stew Leonard Junior is the CEO. The company is the highest performing supermarket in the world in terms of income per square metre, income per product line, and income per product cluster.

The following are illustrations of the attention to detail that the company pays to operations and activities overall, and to the engagement and commitment of their staff.

- *Employees*: all employees are sent out on a regular basis to observe other companies in action. The companies observed may be from any sector or industry – the employee draws their examples from a hat. Employees then visit the company and observe its activities. Employees must then return from their visit

with at least one example of something that the other company does better than Stew Leonard Inc., and that could possibly be implemented at the shop.

- *Retail environment*: the company carries out regular consultations with customers, and all staff have to participate. One customer said: 'The fish that you sell is not fresh. It is always hygienic because you shrink-wrap it and you keep it on ice. But from time to time, I would like to be able to buy it fresh off the ice.' The company implemented this. The company lost no sales of shrink-wrapped fish. It gained sales of fish straight off the ice worth between $15,000 and $50,000 per week depending on the season.

- *Product and service quality*: Stew Leonard Junior tells the following story. 'We were having consult-

ants in to advise us on operational development. I asked dad if there was anything that I should take up with them. Dad replied: "Yes. I bought some vegetables for tea last night and they were not fresh." I said, "No dad, you misunderstand. The consultants are here to talk about product and operations development, merchandising and presentation. Is there anything you want me to ask them?" Dad replied: "Yes. I took some vegetables home for tea last night and they were not fresh." From that point onwards, the first problem for the consultants to solve was how to get the vegetables on to the shelves as early as possible. By getting the staff engaged, in the end we cut down delivery times by about three days.'

- *Staff management*: the store offers security of employment, training in product knowledge and retailing management, and a variety of tasks to anyone who expresses an interest. The company reinforces this with a presence in the community as a good employer and sponsor of local events and festivals. All staff are expected to become involved; those who do not, do not stay with the company.

- *Health and safety*: to date, the company has had no staff accidents or food safety scares. The company offers food across the entire price and quality range as an alternative to the big supermarket chains in the neighbourhood. On each, the company view is absolute: it cannot afford either accidents or food hygiene disasters, and so gears everything up to ensure that these do not happen.

The main lesson here is to illustrate the possibilities inherent in this and in every situation, in terms of getting the people who work for the organisation actively engaged, not just in their job, but in the present and future well-being of the organisation.

Source: T. Peters (1992), *Liberation Management*, Pan.

Achieving things for people

Achieving things for people, in particular meeting and responding to the legitimate demands and expectations of customers, suppliers and shareholders, is the next key priority. Each of these groups has particular requirements of every organisation. These requirements must be satisfied, or else the customers will go elsewhere, suppliers will seek other outlets for their materials, and backers will seek alternative organisations and ventures into which to put their funds.

Customers require confidence in the products and services on offer. They require that their demands for quality, durability and volumes of products and services are met. They expect to be able to return to the company or organisation for product and service upgrades, maintenance and repairs. The implication is therefore that successful organisations are managed for the long-term as well as to give immediate satisfaction.

Suppliers require steady and assured volumes of business; and so they will gravitate towards those organisations that meet this need. Again, the clear implication is the need to be confident that organisations being supplied will remain in existence over the long-term.

Shareholders require assured levels of returns, both in share values and in dividend payments, as a prerequisite to investment; otherwise they will move their investments elsewhere.

Overall therefore, achieving things for people is based on perceptions and understanding of expectations, assurance and permanence which, together with the delivery of good quality products and services, all add up to immediate and enduring confidence. Confidence in managerial terms is hard to define more precisely. The presence, knowledge and understanding of confidence is an absolute priority in achieving things for people; and it is also the case that, where confidence is lost or not fully assured, organisation decline quickly sets in (see Management in Focus 1.2).

MANAGEMENT IN FOCUS 1.2

ACHIEVING THINGS FOR PEOPLE IN PUBLIC SERVICES

In UK public services in the twenty-first century, the equivalent of customers, suppliers and shareholders, and their demands, are as follows.

- Customers are the users of services of education, health and social care, transport, policing and security. As the result of politicisation, restructuring (including privatisation) and extensive media coverage, general user expectations have been raised without a clear plan for how these expectations are to be met. The result has been increased pressures on managers and professional service staff (e.g. nurses, teachers, doctors, social workers) to respond to demands without always being fully clear about what these demands are.
- Suppliers include those providing health, educa-

tion, social services; and transport, equipment and materials. The supply side increasingly also involves the provision of information services and databases, finance and investment. This has led to uncertainties in the structures, remits and priorities of the public service organisations themselves.

- The 'shareholders' of public services are the statutory bodies, organisations and government departments responsible for service delivery. As the result of the politicisation and restructuring referred to above, there is now a lack of full confidence or general understanding of the levels, coverage and quality of services, the circumstances under which services ought to

be provided, and who is entitled to them. Especially there is no longer any clear understanding of who funds the services, who pays for them, and what the levels of prices and charges ought to be.

Lessons

The key application of managerial expertise here is the removal of uncertainty. In the UK public services overall, and in the individual institutions, schools, hospitals and other bodies which deliver them, there can be no clarity, progress or improvement until the priorities and structures are agreed, and until the expectations and demands of customers, users and backers are made clear. Until this happens, what is being delivered and achieved for people is set to remain uncertain.

Making a profit

All managers must 'make a profit'. 'Profit' needs to be defined by all organisations and their managers in their own terms. This definition requires attention to the following.

- Surplus of income over expenditure. A version of this is calculated by law for all organisations on an annual (and increasingly on a half-year and quarterly) basis. The managerial discipline additionally requires knowledge and understanding of product and service surpluses and losses on an individual basis; and 'individual' means surpluses and losses per location and per customer, as well as per product and service unit, product and service cluster and in terms of overall output.

- Increasing organisational reputation and confidence, as a result of the ways in which products and services are delivered, as well as attention to absolute expectations in meeting product and service volume and quality demands. Increasing reputation and confidence feed people's expectations and perceptions of products and services, and increasing quality and demand for products and services feed reputation and confidence.
- Costs, cost effectiveness and cost efficiency. There is a key organisational and managerial issue here, in that efficient and effective cost management can lead to a much greater income margin per product and service. The problem occurs when cost management is the only, or overwhelming, driving force towards profit; and this can then go seriously wrong (see Management in Focus 1.3).
- The 'profit' delivered by public service organisations is a function of the speed, effectiveness and completeness of service delivery, as well as the ability to stick within financial and other resource constraints. It is also, in practice, a function of the ability to respond to political directives, raise funds from external sources (e.g. hospitals selling flowers and books for the patients and other relatives), and develop their services according to particular local and environmental needs (e.g. schools providing evening classes, sports clubs and playgroups outside normal hours).
- The profit delivered by not-for-profit organisations and charities is a function of the extent to which they can, and do, raise the levels of funding and resources required to serve the particular client bases. As above, not-for-profit work ultimately takes place in a competitive environment; consequently those responsible for the management of foundations and charities have to arrive at a clear view as to whether they are competing with other charities (e.g. 'If people give to me, they will not give to others'), or whether people will give anyway (e.g. competing for customer's disposable income overall).

Resources

Managers are required to organise, prioritise, use and consume – and produce a return on – those resources that are placed at their disposal. All resources are ultimately finite; and even where resources are plentiful and assured for the present and foreseeable future, they should be used and consumed as efficiently and as effectively as possible. This gives a lead to every organisational and managerial activity to ensure that everything is valued; it provides a discipline for the use and consumption of scarcer and more valuable resources; and it is also the case that even plentiful resources can, and do, become expensive (e.g. oil in the 1960s, 1970s and early twenty-first century).

Organisation production, service and information technology, property, premises and equipment are resources with capital and operational values. Each represents a part of the total organisational investment, and the returns required and demanded must be known, understood and accepted. Organisations and their managers need to know, understand and be clear about the need for all technology and equipment, the returns required, and whether circumstances might change and affect the nature, levels and spread of returns.

Staff expertise, willingness and commitment are the primary organisational resources. Expertise and commitment are both required, neither is effective in isolation from the other. Organisations that have expertise and commitment, targeted at

MANAGEMENT IN FOCUS 1.3

FROZEN FISH

Helmont Ltd is a fish processing and cannery company located at Walsall, West Midlands, UK. Until recently, it took its supplies of fresh and frozen fish from Ocean Going Trawlers Ltd, a fishing fleet based in Liverpool. Helmont Ltd was a very successful and profitable company and supplied to all of the main brands, including John West, Bird's Eye and Ross. Helmont also supplied fresh, frozen, canned and processed fish products to the supermarket chains for sale under its own brand names.

Following new quota arrangements introduced by the EU, the prices of the landed fish catches in the UK rose by 10 per cent. Accordingly, Helmont decided to look around for alternative supplies. After extensive research, the company found that the port and fishing fleet of Cadiz, Spain, were prepared to supply them with the volumes of fish and the regularity of deliveries required.

Helmont unilaterally cancelled the contract with Ocean Going Trawlers of Liverpool and took up with Cadiz. The catch prices in Cadiz were 53 per cent lower than those in Liverpool; and

the full cost, including transport, worked out at 38 per cent cheaper than the Liverpool supplies.

The key lesson is that there is a simple cost advantage, and this is apparent to all. However, Helmont's previous suppliers were barely 100 miles away, and it was therefore much easier to manage any difficulties if things did go wrong. The new suppliers would be over 1000 miles away, and consequently, there was a much greater propensity for things to go wrong. All of this in practice has to be paid for out of the cost advantages.

This venture failed, because everything that could go wrong did go wrong. Refrigeration units on the lorries broke down. There were strikes and disputes involving the border authorities between France and Spain, with the result that the lorries were held up on their journeys (in spite of the fact that the EU is notionally an open market, the Spanish in particular retain an active border presence). There were hold-ups at the Channel ports in northern France. The lorries were then faced with the problems of negotiating the overcrowded UK motor-

way network, in particular the M25 around London and the M6 through the West Midlands, before they could get back to the company's headquarters and factory.

Helmont tried to reschedule deliveries to meet its own new limitations, and to ensure that the customers would remain satisfied. However, the customers – the branded goods and the supermarket own brands – had contracted with Helmont in good faith, and now did their best to hold them to the agreement. In order to remain viable, Helmont now had to return to Ocean Going Trawlers in Liverpool and to do their best to renegotiate the contract. This they did, but the conditions in the contract were now to be very much more onerous.

Clearly not every cost-saving exercise goes wrong; many indeed are very successful. However, as the result of seeking to engage in an extensive cost reduction exercise, Helmont found itself faced with operating losses for nearly two years into the future.

Source: adapted from P. Griseri (2004), *Foundations of Management*, UCL.

known, understood and agreed priorities, out-perform those that do not. Organisations that have expertise but no commitment lose staff to other organisations where there is a greater sense of overall purpose; and these organisations tend to retain staff because of their commitment to themselves and their own individual interests, rather than to the organisation and its products and services (see Management in Focus 1.4).

Improvement

Everything that is done in organisations and by people is capable of improvement. Customers, clients and product and service users expect improved and enhanced quality and volumes of what they require and demand. Staff expect improved wages, salaries, terms and conditions of employment; improvements in the quality of their working environment and working relationships; and improved opportunities and interest in their job and careers. Shareholders expect improved returns on their investments, and will seek out organisations in which to invest that promise or give a clear understanding of improvements in these areas.

Meeting the requirements and demand for improvement is a fundamental human need, as well as a priority placed on organisations and managers. Managers

MANAGEMENT IN FOCUS 1.4

RESOURCES, CAPABILITY AND WILLINGNESS IN THE FOOTBALL INDUSTRY

An international footballer greatly enhanced his reputation as the result of his performances in one of the international championships. After this, the leading clubs in the world of football queued up to take him on. He eventually chose one of the very top brand clubs in world football. The club were delighted; they offered him very high wages, and looked forward to his excellent performances continuing in their interests.

The relationship failed. The footballer quickly realised that he was a commodity to be bought and sold. The high levels of wages merely underlined this. He had, in addition, moved his family thousands of miles away from their home, and his wife was homesick. The footballer therefore settled down to ensure that he picked up the very high wages that were on offer for the duration of the contract (which was three years) before moving on.

The club never did understand what they had done wrong. They offered very high wages, as mentioned, and in addition provided a luxury house and car. They knew that the player was a good footballer; his subsequent international performances continued to underline this. The club continued to try to get him to play for two further years before they changed their management team, and sold the player on.

The lesson here is to underline and emphasise the relationship between resources, capability and commitment. In any industry or sector, each of the three elements has to be present. Failure to ensure that this is so leads to resources being squandered, and this in turn leads to enduring underperformance.

must therefore know and understand the full range of activities carried out in their domain and how these activities interact with each other; and from this, seek to improve processes, attitudes and behaviour, as well as products, services and outputs.

Change and uncertainty

Coping with change and uncertainty requires a full and dispassionate knowledge and understanding of the organisation; its products and services; its staff and their priorities, hopes, fears and expectations. It also requires a full and detailed knowledge and understanding of the external, economic, social, political and operating environment, and of the forces that are present within it. It is essential to know and understand, and be able to respond to, the effect of the following:

- Natural disasters including earthquakes, floods and drought. While it is never possible to predict the precise dates or locations in which these will happen, it is absolutely certain that each will occur at some time; and so the key is to be prepared and be able to respond when they do occur.
- Terrorist attacks. Again it is not possible to predict when and where these will happen; it is certain that they will occur and so again, it is essential to be able to respond at these times.
- Economic crises brought on by, for example: stock market crashes; runs on particular currencies (and upward valuations of others); oil crises (as above); energy shortages.
- Political crises and uncertainties, which are at their most visible in war-torn regions of the world, but which can occur anywhere (e.g. it took Germany nearly four months to form a government in late 2005).
- Market crises brought about by losses in consumer, wholesaler and investor confidence, which are increasingly set to be brought about as the result of macro market choices to invest either in India or China, or in Western Europe, North America and Japan, but not both.

The above are all macro issues that affect the activities, operations, effectiveness – and performance – of organisations when they do occur. That is not to say that each will occur, or occur on a regular basis. It is for managers to know, understand and be able to respond when they do.

At a micro level, the ability to respond depends on the overall efficiency and effectiveness of product and service delivery, and of organisational processes, attitudes, values and behaviour. For example:

- A competitor's new technology may render that of other organisations obsolete; or it may appear to do so; or it may not do so (however attractive it may look at first sight). The need therefore is to be able to take a fully informed view as to whether or not the competitor's technology requires that all other organisations in the sector replace their technology, rather than jumping to the conclusion that it does.
- A new entrant to a particular market may gain immediate share, and cause concern among existing players. Whether the new player sustains and develops the market for itself is very much up to the ability of the existing players to respond (see Management in Focus 1.5).

MANAGEMENT IN FOCUS 1.5

VIRGIN COLA

In 1990, the Virgin Organisation introduced a cola drink. As with all Virgin products and services, it was produced to the best possible quality in order to fill market niches in the UK and elsewhere which were not served fully by Coca-Cola, Pepsi-Cola and supermarkets' own brands.

All soft drinks companies conduct extensive consumer research. Part of this entails 'blind tests', in which volunteers are asked to taste the particular drink without knowing what it is, and rate it for taste and quality against alternatives. In blind tests conducted by Coca-Cola and Pepsi-Cola, the Virgin product was found to taste the best, better than all of the products of the two larger organisations. This caused initial concern at Coca-Cola and Pepsi-Cola; and the concern was deepened when they found themselves unable to respond quickly.

However, the problem passed. Coca-Cola and Pepsi-Co. already had marketing and branding strategies and campaigns in place, and these continued to deliver the results demanded. In spite of the fact that the Virgin product tasted best, it became clear that it was the full brand delivery that customers required, and that Coca-Cola and Pepsi-Co. could deliver this provided that the present product quality remained assured.

Change and uncertainty remain constant features in the employment of staff. The stability, commitment and engagement of the staff and workforce can only be assured so far, however good the wages, terms and conditions, and managerial and supervisory style and relations. The key issues for all organisations to be aware of as employers of staff are: the effects of new employers (especially large employers) moving into the area; the effects of large employers leaving the area; increases in demand for relatively mobile staff (e.g. professionally qualified people) elsewhere; and gaining and losing road, rail and air infrastructure and transport connections.

Alongside this, it is essential for managers to know and understand every aspect of the bond between organisation and staff, and to be fully aware of the strengths, and especially the shortcomings, present. Organisations and their managers must know and understand that in some cases individuals will move on for their own reasons. Organisations and their managers must also know and understand that if there are demonstrable known and understood weaknesses in the bond between employer and employee, they ultimately have a clear choice to make between remedying these issues, or managing the constant problems each time they arise.

A summary of the foundations of management in this way clearly illustrates the range of skills, knowledge, understanding and expertise involved. For those who aspire to be truly expert managers, delivering effective products and services in whatever organisation and circumstances they may find themselves, there is no substitute for acquiring and developing this range of skills, knowledge, understanding and expertise. The sheer complexity has driven others to seek quick, easy and assured solutions to problems, development, enhancement and improvement through the adoption of faddish approaches (see Management in Focus 1.6).

MANAGEMENT IN FOCUS 1.6

FASHIONS AND FADS

The opposite to the rigour of developing expertise and a body of knowledge is to take a prescriptive approach. 'Fashions and fads' is a useful way of describing directive, prescriptive and simplistic approaches to management issues and problems. Some current issues are as follows.

- *Job evaluation*: the analysis of job and work activities according to specific criteria in order to rank them in importance, status, values and place on the pay scale. In practice, job evaluation tends to be rigid, inconsistent and divisive.
- *Business process re-engineering (BPR)*: attention to administration, supervision and procedures for the purposes of simplicity, clarification and speed of operation. The premise is that improvements are always possible. In practice, business process re-engineering tends to be applied prescriptively to all functions without reference to organisational effectiveness or wider aspects of operations.
- *Total quality management (TQM)*: attention to every aspect of organisational practice in pursuit of continuous improvement, the high-

est possible standards of practice, products, services and customer service. In practice, TQM tends to be prescriptive in approach and dominated by paperwork and administration systems rather than attention to products and customers.

- *Right first time, every time*: this rolls easily off the tongue/pen; it is a direct contradiction of the view that everything can be improved.
- *Benchmarking*: benchmarks set standards of activity against which other activities can be compared and rated; benchmarking also applies to placing people on salary scales, activity scales, job importance scales and other matters to do with status. In practice, it is usually rigid, inconsistent and divisive. Some organisations also seek to benchmark their salaries, terms and conditions against other employers; while this is useful knowledge to have, ultimately all organisations have to be able to stand alone and independently.
- *Virtual organisation*: organisation structures based on technology rather than physical pres-

ence. A useful concept that tends to get drowned, either by cost-cutting or technological processes, or by conventional, adversarial supervision.

- *Outsourcing*: especially the practice of outsourcing manufacturing, production and service delivery activities to locations in Central America, the Pacific Islands, southeast Asia, and the Indian subcontinent. The driving force behind this form of outsourcing is to take advantage of the reduced labour costs and less stringent labour laws in these locations. The downside of this form of overt cost saving is that it is a lot harder to manage and resolve problems and issues when they arise in a rural location thousands of miles away, than if the same problems and issues arise on the spot.

The major contribution of each and all fashions and fads is to broaden the debate on management issues, and to get people thinking about progress and improvement. Their weakness is apparent when they are grasped as perfection, the absolute truth, and instant solutions to all-round management problems.

● The professionalisation of management

Management is variously defined as science, profession and art. The truth of its status lies somewhere between the three, and there are strong elements of each.

There are precise, scientific and exact aspects that have to be learned and assimilated. Any manager must have a good grasp of certain quantitative methods and financial and statistical data, as well as certain less scientific, but well tried and tested, elements such as human motivation and the effect of different payment systems on the performance of different occupations.

Management is a profession in so far as there is a general recognition that there are certain knowledge, skills and aptitudes that must be assimilated and understood by anyone who aspires to be a truly effective manager. Management is not a true or traditional profession in the sense that it is not a fully self-regulating occupation, and nor is there yet a named qualification that must be achieved before one is allowed to practise. However, pressure to be both educated and qualified is growing universally. There is a recognition also of the correlation between this and expert and effective practice.

Management is an art in the sense that within these confines and strictures there is great scope for the use of creativity, imagination, initiative and invention within the overall sphere of the occupation. The scientific methods and body of knowledge referred to must be applied in their own way to each and any given situation, issue or problem. This is the creative aspect of the manager's role and function; and anyone in a managerial position who seeks for prescriptive solutions to organisational problems is likely to fail.

The best managers are committed and dedicated operators; highly trained and educated; with excellent analytical and critical faculties. Beyond this, there is a body of skills and aptitudes, knowledge, attitudes and behaviour that the effective manager must have and be able to draw upon.

The personal qualities required include:

- ambition, energy, great commitment, self-motivation
- job, product and service knowledge
- drive and enthusiasm
- creativity and imagination
- a thirst for knowledge
- a commitment to improvement
- a commitment to continuous development, both personal and professional
- the ability to grow and broaden the outlook and vision of the organisation concerned
- a positive and dynamic attitude, self-discipline, empathy with the staff
- a love of the organisation and pride and enthusiasm in the job, its people, its products, its services, its customers and clients (see Management in Focus 1.7).

These personal qualities provide the springboard for the successful and professional operator. A good general knowledge, understanding and grasp of basic economics is necessary, including the relationship between organisations and their environment, current issues and affairs, and constraints on the ability to conduct business. It is also necessary to understand:

- strategy and policy
- marketing
- finance

- behavioural sciences
- personnel and industrial relations
- the use and management of information and statistics
- the use and management of technology
- production, operations, systems, service, projects and facilities management
- the management of initiative and innovation.

Currently, much of this is formalised and achieved through the study of business at school, college and university. This is by no means a universal requirement, however – there have been countless successful managers who never had this benefit, although their success was undoubtedly based on their own ability, however gained, in these areas.

Management is a global activity and lessons can be learned from everywhere in the world. This includes Western Europe, North America, Japan, Korea, the Philippines, Malaysia, Indonesia, the Middle East, Australia, New Zealand and South Africa, where managerial practices are well documented. This will inevitably be changed and transformed again as the economies of central and eastern Europe become integrated within the EU. Additionally, growth in the Middle East, South and Central America, south east Asia and Russia, while uncertain and far from assured, is certain to affect management practices. There is substantial growth already in India, China and Northern and Southern Africa; and this too continues to affect and develop the outlook and attitudes of organisations and managers in the most developed economies. It must be recognised, finally, that management is currently being conducted in a changing and turbulent environment. This has itself changed over the period since 1945 and the reconstruction of the world damaged by the Second World War. Then, everything was arranged to try and bring order, stability and performance steadiness to business, service and the markets and spheres in which they operated. Today all that has gone and the processes of technological advance, management education, automation, social change and political development, together with the globalisation of business and commerce, ensure that all concepts of management are in turn subject to continuous change and revision. Truly expert and committed managers will always ensure that they keep themselves up-to-date with everything that impinges on both their job and their chosen profession. Many managerial institutions now insist that their members keep records of all continuous professional development activities that they undertake and, indeed, insist on this as a condition of continuing membership (see Management in Focus 1.7).

Management research and literature

There is a great range of management research and literature – textbooks, how-to books, personal and organisational histories, professional and commercial journals and periodicals, computer-based packages, databases, leaflets, checklists; and also university and commercial research programmes, monographs and learned papers. This can be broken down as follows:

- Some of it is intellectually extremely challenging. The ability both to under-stand and to be an effective practitioner in certain aspects of the managerial sphere requires a high degree of intellectual capacity, higher education, and a basic grasp of some mathematical and economic theories as well as behavioural and operational matters.

MANAGEMENT IN FOCUS 1.7

PROFESSIONS

The 'classical' professions are medicine, law, the priesthood and the armed forces. The following properties were held to distinguish these from the rest of society:

- *Distinctive expertise*: not available elsewhere in society or in its individual members.
- *Distinctive body of knowledge*: required by all those who aspire to practice in the profession.
- *Entry barriers*: in the form of examinations, time serving, learning from experts.
- *Formal qualifications*: given as the result of acquiring the body of knowledge and clearing the entry barriers.
- *High status*: professions are at the top of the occupational tree.
- *Distinctive morality*: for medicine, the commitment to keep people alive as long as possible; for law, a commitment to represent the client's best interests; for the church, a commitment to godliness and to serve the congregation's best interest; for the armed forces, to fight within stated rules of law.
- *High value*: professions make a distinctive and positive contribution to both the organisations and individual members of the society.
- *Self-regulating*: professions set their own rules, codes of conduct, standards of performance and qualifications.
- *Self-disciplining*: professions establish their own bodies for dealing with problems, complaints, and allegations of malpractice.
- *Unlimited reward levels*: according to the levels of charges that the professionals choose for themselves and that members of society are prepared to pay for their services. For example, unlimited and self-set rewards are available to those army officers who make themselves available as mercenary soldiers, and those clergy who establish free and non-denominational churches.
- *Life membership*: dismissal at the behest of the profession; ceasing to work for one employer does not constitute loss of profession.
- *Personal commitment*: to high standards of practice and morality; commitment to deliver the best possible in all circumstances.
- *Self-discipline*: commitment to personal standards of behaviour in the pursuit of professional excellence.
- *Continuous development*: of knowledge and skills; a commitment to keep abreast of all developments and initiatives in the field.
- *Governance*: by institutions established by the profession itself.

Notes

1. In absolute terms 'management' falls short in most areas. Formal qualifications are not a prerequisite to practice (though they are highly desirable and ever more sought after). Discipline and regulation of managers is still overwhelmingly a matter for organisations and not management institutions. There is some influence over reward levels and training and development. Measures of status and value are uneven. Management institutions act as focal points for debate; and they also have a lobbying function. They do not act as regulators.

2. There is a clear drive towards the professional-

isation of management. This is based on attention to expertise, knowledge and qualifications, and the relationship between these and the value added to organisations by expert managers.

3. In 1995, Charles Handy proposed that all business school graduates should be required to take the equivalent of the Hippocratic Oath, thus committing themselves to best practice and high standards and quality of performance.

If management is viewed in this way, it is a highly professional activity and one that demands a set body of expertise and a large measure of commitment on the part of its practitioners.

In traditional terms, management falls short of the full status of profession in that the elements outlined here do not constitute yet a formal entry barrier (in medicine, the law, the clergy and the military, it is essential to have the stated qualifications before being allowed to practice).

- Some of the literature addresses precise or defined issues that have a direct bearing on the business sphere. This is especially true of the areas of leadership, motivation, perception, the formation of attitudes, standards and values, which have their own body of knowledge in their own right, and which then require translation into particular managerial situations in different ways.
- Some of it dwells heavily on empirical research, case histories and anecdotal examples. This enables studies of the relationships between variables in given situations to be undertaken and assimilated, and 'what if' and other hypothetical discussions to take place in relation to real events of the past, but in what are at present overtly 'safe' situations. The body of the general knowledge and experience of the manager is thus developed and extended, as are his or her critical faculty, awareness and overall view of the sphere.
- Some of it illustrates particular successes and failures; this is especially true of the swelling array of books produced by successful business people. The lessons to be drawn here are often in the mind of the reader. Such books tend to reinforce certain aspects only of the whole managerial sphere. They provide a very useful library of what has worked in practice for comparison against a theoretical or academic base, although one by-product of this has been to create and develop a faddish approach.

Over the years, management research and literature has concentrated heavily on all aspects of organisational and managerial performance, and the skills, knowledge and expertise required of those placed in management positions and responsibilities. To date however, there remains no firm, understood and agreed body of knowledge, skills or expertise; nor, as noted above, are there any qualifications required, as a condition of appointment, of those who come into managerial and executive positions.

That there is even any consideration that such a body of knowledge, skills and expertise might exist at all is overwhelmingly the result and impact of the work that came to be known as 'The Excellence Studies'.

● Excellence

The genesis of the work that subsequently grew into the management concept of 'excellence', was a review carried out in the latter part of the 1970s by McKinsey, the international management consulting firm, of its thinking and approach to business strategy and organisation effectiveness. This review was itself founded in a dissatisfaction with conventional approaches to these matters.

The approach adopted was to study both businesses and managers of high repute and/or high performance, and to try and isolate those qualities and characteristics that made them so. A model (the 7-S model; see Figure 1.1) for the design and description of organisations was also proposed. Those working on the study also identified those attributes that they felt ought to be present in such organisations and persons, and tested them against those studied.

In all, 62 organisations were studied. They were drawn from all sectors of US industry and commerce, and included many global firms (e.g. Boeing, McDonald's, Hewlett-Packard, 3M).

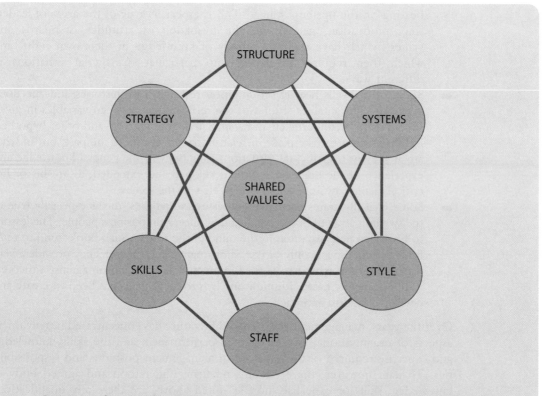

Purpose: a configuration of organisation, pattern and design that reflects the essential attributes that must be addressed in the establishment and development of an excellent organisation.

Figure 1.1 The 7-S framework

Source: Peters and Waterman (1982)

The concept of excellence applied to organisations

'High performing' took on a variety of meanings:

- ensuring appropriate levels of profitability
- a global organisation such as IBM
- a strong positive image such as that of Tesco
- a strong domestic organisation (Sainsbury's in the UK or 3M in the USA)
- a strong player in a slumped or declining market
- a strong general image for the organisation, its products and services
- strong levels of customer confidence, leading to assured levels of repeat business
- strong levels of staff and customer loyalty.

Peters and Waterman (1982) identified eight characteristics of organisational excellence; they went on to state that in all organisations, locations, sectors and industries, each of these ought to be a managerial priority for attention, development and improvement. These characteristics are as follows:

1. The leadership and management of business organisations requires: *vision*, energy, dynamism and positivism; the placing of customers and their needs and wants at the centre of the business; and the ability to change and improve as a permanent organisational feature.
2. The closeness of the relationship between the *organisation* and its *customers* and clients must be maintained; if this is lost the customers will go elsewhere.
3. The commitment, motivation, ability, training and development of all *staff* at all levels of the organisation are critical to the continuation of its success; closely related to this is a shared vision or shared values to which all members of the organisation must ascribe; staff must be held in high respect and well rewarded.
4. *Supervision* levels, hierarchies, and regional and head office establishments must be kept to a *minimum*; the purpose of these establishments is to service those who generate business for the organisation and not to impose a superstructure on them; such establishments should also be flexible and responsive and not hierarchical and inert.
5. Organisations must stick to their *core business*, to what they are good at and what is profitable and effective.
6. Organisations must constantly *innovate and improve*, update working practices, staff abilities, technology, customer response times and methods. They should constantly seek new applications and new markets for their existing products and services.
7. Organisations must be *receptive* to ideas and influences from outside, and be able to evaluate them for use and value to themselves in their own circumstances.
8. The bias of the organisation must be towards *action* not procedure.

Peters and Waterman went on to define the essential nature of organisation culture, and the importance of macro-organisational analysis, as critical bases on which overall organisational knowledge and understanding must be built. Their findings are summarised below.

The essential nature of organisation culture

In the organisations studied, organisation culture, values and attitudes were found to be very strong, positive and cohesive. The components of this strength and cohesion were found to be a set of corporate beliefs, as follows:

- a belief in being the best
- a belief in the importance of the staff and individuals as well as in their contribution to the organisation
- a belief in, and obsession with, quality and service
- a belief that organisation members should innovate and have their creative capacities harnessed
- a belief in the importance of excellent communication among all staff
- a belief in the concept of simultaneous loose–tight properties – measures of control that allow for operational flexibility
- a belief in the continuous cycle of development
- a recognition that there is always room for improvement
- attention to detail – the necessity to ensure that whatever the excellence of the strategic vision, it must always be carefully and accurately carried out
- a belief in the importance of economic growth and profit motive.

The importance of macro-organisational analysis

Macro-organisational analysis is the term used to define the need to know and understand everything about the organisation's characteristics, activities, behaviour and performance.

Essentially, this is dependent upon the strength and style of leadership – the drive, determination, core values and strategic vision necessary to energise and make profitable the organisation's activities. In time, this becomes 'the way things are done here'. Managers underpin this through their day-to-day activities – the issues they concern themselves with, the matters on which they spend resources, the people with whom they spend time. It is therefore a combination both of what they do and of how they do it, and messages are given off by this to the rest of the organisation. Above all, the leader of the organisation expresses the true organisational value through the means by which s/he conducts her/himself in all activities.

These values become an integral part of the structures and systems of the organisation that affect all of its activities. If the management style is energetic and positive, this is reflected in the ways in which senior managers wish to have things done.

The study also looked at the particular performance indicators of the organisation. These came from all areas of activity, including asset growth and returns on capital invested. The organisations studied and from which the lessons were drawn had rates of return on these factors of between 10 and 60 times the sectoral average. Absenteeism was another factor studied. In a US steelworks studied by Peters he found an uncertificated sickness rate of two-fifths of 1 per cent – against a national average of 6 per cent and a sectoral average of 9 per cent. Organisation reputation was another factor assessed. This was conducted across all of an organisation's activities – marketing, human resource policies, customer care and customer relations, equality of opportunity – and also across its wider general reputation in the environment and community, in which it invariably perceived itself to have a direct stake, interest and wider responsibility.

The work of Peters and Waterman caused many others to produce their own studies of organisational excellence. Different studies concentrated on different aspects of organisational leadership, direction, strategy, structure and performance (see Management in Focus 1.8).

MANAGEMENT IN FOCUS 1.8

CRITERIA FOR EXCELLENCE

- High growth of assets, value, turnover and profits.
- Consistent reputation in sector as leader and pioneer.
- Solid and positive reputation with customers, community and general public.

Source: W. Goldsmith and D. Clutterbuck (1990).

- Professional organisations are lean and empowered.

- Professional staff require flat structures and autonomy for effective performance.
- Processes and procedures are speedy, simple and effective.

Source: C.B. Handy (1984).

- Excellence is performance thousands and thousands of percentage points over sectoral norms.

Source: T. Peters and R. Waterman (1982).

- Innovation and development leading to maximisation and optimisation of the human resource.
- Innovation in quality of working life.
- Promotion of full and genuine equality of opportunity.
- Models of good practice offer their example to the world, and are pleased and proud to be studied.

Source: R.M. Kanter (1985).

Superficially, the result and outcomes of the Peters and Waterman study, and those which followed it, appear to simplify the range, expertise and environment of management. However, further consideration of the findings and conclusions of these studies underlines the complexities of the managerial task, the range, quality and depth of expertise required, and the extent of knowledge and understanding on which this expertise must be based.

The continuing professionalisation of management

The continuing professionalisation of management has led to attempts to classify the disciplines involved, as well as to crystallise the body of skills, knowledge and expertise required. This has led in turn to the rise of summary classifications, as follows:

- *The reflective practitioner.* The 'reflective practitioner' approach emphasises the ability to think things through, and to know and understand why things turned out in particular ways. This requires analytical and evaluative capabilities and expertise, as well as a detailed and comprehensive body of knowledge and understanding, so that for any given set of circumstances, a detailed and precise critique can be conducted.
- *The thinking performer.* The 'thinking performer' approach was developed by the Chartered Institute of Personnel and Development, the Chartered Management Institute, and the Association of MBAs, to attempt to summarise the expertise required under the following headings:

- personal drive and effectiveness, which requires individuals to set out their own personal as well as professional objectives
- people management and leadership, requiring capabilities in the management and leadership of people and the expertise that goes with it
- business knowledge and understanding, of the specific needs and wants of whatever organisation is being served at the time
- professional and ethical competence, and a commitment to serve the standards of all professional bodies of which the individual is a member. Handy (1996) proposed that all managers ought to be required to take the equivalent of the medical 'Hippocratic Oath', and to establish the same level of commitment to management as doctors do to medicine
- continuing learning, a discipline required of all those in the traditional professions of law and medicine, and a personal commitment of anyone who aspires to excellence in any field at all
- analytical and creative/intuitive thinking, to develop the capability to evaluate any situation, proposal, venture or initiative, and to be able to implement what is intended in the particular given set of circumstances
- customer focus, a commitment to serve to the best of one's ability all those who seek to take advantage of the particular professional and expert capability
- strategic capability, the capability to see the wider interests and ranges of issues, as well as being able to respond to specific requests
- communication, persuasion and interpersonal skills; this includes active listening as well as the ability to communicate actively, early, positively and with integrity.

Such approaches have reinforced the crystallisation of 'foundational management', which may be summarised as the basic body of knowledge, skills, expertise and understanding, as above. Many professional managerial bodies now run their own certificate and diploma level qualifications, management education schemes, foundation programmes and introductory courses, so that those who seek to join them and to practise in their name are known and understood to have an agreed level of competence; and this also applies to many organisation-based management training schemes.

⬤ Conclusions

The overall purpose here has been to illustrate the complexity, range and scale of the subject matter that is to be considered, the widely differing standpoints from which it has been tackled, and its progression as a field of study. The balance of the material quoted reflects the particular concern with it over the period since 1945 and its emergence as an area critical to both business and economic success, and also the wider prosperity of society at large.

It is not at all an exhaustive coverage. However, it does attempt to itemise major staging posts and fields of enquiry, and to illustrate the variety of studies that have been undertaken. Each study indicated addresses different parts of the business and management sphere. Each makes its own particular contribution to the whole field; none provides a comprehensive coverage of it. What is clear, however, is that it is an ever-broadening sphere. The works illustrated here demonstrate just how far this has developed and the variety of approaches that have been taken in the pursuit of it.

There is no doubt that there has been a shift in approach to regard management as an occupation in its own right. What has been less certain is what the actual composition of this occupation and profession is. This chapter has attempted to illustrate the basis of this and to introduce some of the major concepts, studies and ideas that have contributed to the state of its development.

Some more specific conclusions can also be drawn from this material. Management direction and leadership are separate from the functions, operations and activities of the organisation. Ability to generate confidence, loyalty, trust and faith of all those in the organisation is essential. It is necessary to establish the identity of a common purpose to which everybody in the organisation can aspire and to which all the resources of the organisation are concentrated. People must be rewarded in response to the efforts that they put into the achievement of the organisation's purposes. Both the organisation and its managers must have knowledge and ability to operate in the chosen environment and to influence this as far as they possibly can. Within particular constraints, organisations establish their own ways of working, cultural norms, procedures and practices, as part of the process of making effective their daily operations. There is the recognition that business and managerial practice takes place in what is both a global and turbulent environment. The ability to operate within this is critical to continuity and success.

This, then, represents the backcloth against which the rest of the book is set. It enables a broad understanding of where the current state of the management art/science/profession is drawn and where the current matters of importance and concern within it lie. It also indicates the range and complexity of the qualities and capacities required of the manager.

CRITICAL THINKING, ANALYSIS AND EVALUATION

1. Identify organisations where there is little evidence of humanity in managerial practice, yet (on the face of it at least) great evidence of economic success. What are the reasons for this? What effects do you think the addition of humanity to drives for productivity would have on these organisations?
2. What were the major influences of Tom Peters, and the other writers on excellent organisations, on the development of principles of management?
3. Why do so many excellent professionals (e.g. doctors, lawyers, teachers, nurses, sales people) find it necessary to take promotion into managerial positions? What are the advantages and disadvantages of this?
4. Identify those principles of management that have endured through the ages; and contrast these with those that have only recently been identified.

DEVELOPING MANAGEMENT SKILLS AND EXPERTISE

POTTER'S GLASS LTD

Potter's Glass Ltd is a medium-sized manufacturer of industrial glassware. It is situated near the southern entrance to the Blackwall Tunnel in East London. Its core business is to produce sheet glass and finished window units for the construction industry.

The company employs a total of 190 staff, of whom 130 are engaged on glass manufacturing, 35 on sales, and 25 on management and administration.

The company has recently experienced a downturn in its order book, and at present has the capacity to produce 20 per cent more than it can sell. The company Chief Executive, Nicholas Potter, has run the company successfully for the past 25 years. He has managed to avoid any redundancies or lay-offs in spite of the recessions in the UK building industry in the 1980s and 1990s. This time however, matters are more serious, because he understands that he is being undercut on both price and productivity by alternative suppliers from mainland Europe.

He has accordingly held meetings with two firms of management consultants. The first, a major City of London institution, charged £8000 for a two-day fact-finding exercise. When the consultants presented their report, they recommended an immediate reduction in the workforce of 25 per cent, and a reduction of the number of sales staff to 20.

The second firm of management consultants, a small company owned by a friend of Nicholas' brother and operating out of Dartford in Kent, 20 miles away, spent a week analysing the factory. This company's recommendation was that Potter's should maximise the productivity and sales efforts, and fight the continental opposition on price, value and reliability.

Nicholas Potter has both reports in front of him. He is just wondering what to do, when his secretary walks into the room. She asks him what he is studying. When he tells her, she replies: 'Yes, I've been thinking about this to. Why don't we go into the production of glass ornaments?'

'What?'

'I said, go into the production of glass ornaments. We could do it. I've done a little bit of research, and the people on the factory floor tell me that there is no reason why the machinery cannot be re-jigged to produce excellent, high quality, durable glass ornaments for the gift shop sector.'

● Questions

1. Briefly evaluate the information that you have been given. What further information do you require to arrive at an informed judgement?
2. On the basis of what you have been told, identify a much broader range of alternative courses of action open to Potter's Glass Ltd.

Chapter two

Managing in a changing environment

'We never had time to do anything properly.
Consequently, we always had to find time to do it twice.'
Marcus Aurelius, Roman Emperor, 120 AD.

'My people are getting more and more out of less and less; and we need this just to survive.'
Ken Lewis, Dutton Engineering Ltd.

'Fewer than half the firms that have downsized since 1990 have seen
long-term improvements in quality, profitability or productivity.'
American Management Association Report, 25 January 1999.

'The key to success in the twenty-first century is the management of knowledge and expertise.'
Peter Drucker, *Management Challenges for the 21st Century* (2000).

Chapter outline

- Introduction
- The drive for change and development
- Barriers to effective change
- Changing cultures and structures
- Change catalysts and agents
- Other factors
- The present and future of management
- Conclusions

Chapter objectives

After studying this chapter, you should be able to:

- understand the need to be able to change and develop within the constraints of the environment

- understand the key driving forces behind organisational and managerial change and development

- understand and be able to identify the operational and psychological barriers to change

- understand the pressures on organisation structures, cultures and strategies

- understand and recognise the effectiveness of particular approaches to the management of change

- understand and be able to identify the conflicting demands of particular stakeholders, lobbies and vested interests.

● Introduction

As stated in Chapter 1, a key managerial task and expertise is to be able to operate effectively within the constraints of a changing environment. The changes that have impinged on society over the period since 1945, and more particularly since the 1960s, have deeply affected the management of organisations. These changes may be summarised as:

● *Technological*: affecting all social, economic and business activities; rendering many occupations obsolete and creating new ones; and opening up new spheres of activity, bringing travel, transport, distribution, telecommunication, industry, goods and services onto a global scale; the development of fledgling virtual industries; the development by companies of virtual activities (see Management in Focus 2.1).

MANAGEMENT IN FOCUS 2.1

LASTMINUTE.COM

Lastminute.com was founded in 1998 by Brent Hoberman and Martha Lane Fox, as a virtual/Internet travel ticketing and gift company. It was floated on the London stock exchange in March 2000, and capitalised at £850 million. This floatation took place in the full glare of the media spotlight. Brent Hoberman and Martha Lane Fox became business celebrities. In April 2000 Martha Lane Fox was described by *Management Today* magazine as the fifth most powerful woman in Britain.

For all the huge capitalisation, and volume of money raised, the company was unable to translate its Internet activity into viable levels of sales. By the end of the year 2000, the company had generated just £1.6 million in turnover. In March 2001, it announced that it was going into partnership with Thomas Cook, the high-street travel agency, so that both companies would be able to benefit from each other's expertise.

Over the period 1996–2002, the value of the Internet as a business medium generated a great deal of financial, academic and commercial speculation. The ability of organisations and their managers to turn the vast amount of information and access available on the Internet into sustainable commercial or public service activities remains unproven. To date, the most successful companies trading on the Internet are those that have established an Internet branch alongside their mainstream activities –

e.g. Tesco.com, Ryanair.com. These companies, and others like them, are able to sustain commercially viable Internet activities only because of their physical presence and identity elsewhere.

The key lesson is therefore that technological advance is not an end in itself. It still has to be related to the opportunities and constraints of the operating environment, and to the behaviour of customers. While it is true that customers are now much more used to the Internet as a vehicle for commercial activity, the ability to take advantage on an individual organisational basis is still dependent upon sufficient volumes of customers using it to generate sufficient volumes of business to ensure that it remains commercially viable.

- *Social*: the changing of people's lives, from the fundamentals of life expectancy and lifestyle choice, to the ability to buy and possess items; to travel; to be educated; to receive ever-increasing standards of healthcare, personal insurance and information; to be fed; to enjoy increased standards of social security and stability, increased leisure time and choice of leisure pursuits; and all commensurate with increases in disposable income and purchasing power, and choices of purchase.
- *Economic*: pressures to change and develop are brought about by the ability of organisations to locate production and service delivery functions in the locations of their choice, based on their own priorities (especially cost reduction); the opportunities to develop markets in hitherto unfamiliar locations; and the opportunity to recruit staff from an international pool. Economic change also refers to fluctuations in currency exchange rates, interest rates and inflation rates, and these in turn are reinforced by the ability of organisations to trade with those whom they choose, anywhere in the world.
- *Macro-political*: the creation and expansion of the EU; the expansion of hitherto national currencies to become the currency of choice elsewhere (e.g. the US dollar is now the currency of choice in Ecuador); and these and similar moves have led some countries to be able to advance and enhance their political influence, with a clear implication that there is a commercial advantage to be gained for their own organisations, and therefore their own domestic economies.
- *Eco-political*: the creation and development of the Euro and Euro-zone; the priority of the EU in creating and adapting supernational laws and directives, and the single market; the collapse of the communist bloc and the former USSR; the fragmentation of the former Yugoslavia into its component states; the emergence of Taiwan, South Africa, Korea and Viet Nam as spheres of political and economic influence; the rapid expansion of China and India as spheres of economic, and therefore political, influence; the potential for Africa, Russia and Central and South America to develop along similar lines.
- *Expectational*: the development and enhancement of people's expectations as the result of their increased ability to gain access to products and services from all over the world; what was previously acceptable is now very often superseded by the presence and availability of substitutes and alternatives from a much wider range of organisations.

In order to achieve the degrees of permanence, order and stability essential to sustain long-term commercially viable products and services, and effective public services, the turbulent and changing environment has to be accommodated. The result is that pressures on managers for change, development, enhancement and improvement come from the following sources:

- the changing nature of markets, and their size, scope, scale and location
- the changing nature of technology, combined with the ability to locate it and use it effectively anywhere in the world
- the changing nature of work patterns, again in relation to the ability to locate and source workforces anywhere in the world
- the drive to maximise the return on investment on indigenous and domestic workforces, through the creation and implementation of flexible and non-traditional patterns of work
- the changing nature of competition, recognising that competitive pressures, products and services can come from any organisation, anywhere in the world.

● The drive for change

The main drive for change is concerned with maximising and optimising returns on investment. This in turn requires that organisations get a greater return on the investment that they make in premises, technology and expertise in the pursuit of producing and delivering effective products and services. This has to be delivered in the context of changes in the economic, social and political environment mentioned above, and within the constraints of the changing nature of market demands, and the pressures to produce and deliver public and other services.

The drive for change has also to be seen in competitive terms, meaning that even excellent and high performing organisations will lose their edge if they fail to constantly adapt and develop, and so leave themselves at the mercy of those that do (see Management in Focus 2.2).

MANAGEMENT IN FOCUS 2.2

THE DEMISE OF GOLDEN WONDER

In January 2006, Golden Wonder, the premium brand and manufacturer of crisps and other savoury snacks, called in the receivers.

This marked the end of a brand and organisation that had once dominated this particular market with 48 per cent of total sales in the sector.

The company enjoyed a reputation for producing and delivering excellent products. However, a series of bad decisions about market development, advertising and branding activities increasingly left the product range open to alternative products and brands, provided that smaller companies could promise to deliver those benefits and advantages of value to the customers.

In 1995, Walkers, a local English brand, engaged Gary Lineker as its advertising icon. Mr Lineker, an ex-professional footballer, enjoyed an excellent reputation for honesty, integrity and strength of character. The company used this to build and develop a strategic approach to the branding of its products, and to use Mr Lineker in its television advertisements.

The inability of Golden Wonder to respond to this meant that Walkers' sales began to grow; and as they developed their advertising and marketing campaigns, Walkers began to enjoy a very high recognition rate among customers and potential customers.

Over the period 1999–2003, Walkers grew their sales at an average of 12 per cent per annum; and nearly all of these sales over this period were at the expense of Golden Wonder. By the end of 2005, Walkers enjoyed 47 per cent of the market, while its once-dominant rival's market share had slipped to 10 per cent. Golden Wonder were no longer able to sustain a viable or profitable business at this level of market share, and so in early 2006 they called in the receivers.

The key lesson is that any organisation is vulnerable to others using their resources to better advantage in terms acceptable to the customer base.

● **Barriers to effective change**

Barriers to effective change, and the ability to respond to organisational, environmental and market pressures may be classified as either operational or behavioural.

Operational barriers

These are:

- *Location*: this is a barrier when, for whatever reason, it becomes impossible for the organisation to continue to operate in its current premises. Relocation has consequences for the resettlement of families, retraining and organisation development. Even where the new premises are close by, it may affect access, work and attendance patterns. For greater distances, the consequences of widespread disruption have to be addressed. As well as personal consequences, this includes attention to organisation culture and structure.

- *Tradition*: this is a problem where there has been a long history of successful work in specific, well-understood and widely accepted ways. This may be underlined where a whole community has grown up around a particular industry or organisation and where this is a major provider of employment and prosperity (for example, coal mining, iron and steel, shipbuilding, engineering). If this has been steady for long periods, there are strong perceptions of stability and permanence.

- *Success (and perceived success)*: if the organisation is known or perceived to be successful in its current ways of doing things then there is a resistance based on: 'Why change something that works?' This is especially true if there is a long history of stability and prosperity. It is often very difficult in these circumstances to get workforces to accept that technology, ways of working and the products themselves are coming to the end of their useful life.

- *Failure*: this is a barrier to change where a given state of affairs has been allowed to persist for some time. The view is often taken – by both organisations and the staff concerned – that this is 'one of those things', a necessary part of being involved in a given set of activities. Resistance occurs when someone determines to do something about it – again, upsetting an overtly comfortable and orderly status quo.

- *Technology*: this is a barrier for many reasons. It is often the driving force behind jobs, tasks, occupations and activities. Their disruption causes trauma to those affected by the consequent need for job and occupation change, retraining, redeployment – and often redundancy. Technological changes may also cause relocation to more suitable premises. Technological changes, in turn, cause changes to work patterns and methods. It has been one of the driving forces behind the increase in home working where employees can be provided with all the equipment necessary to work without the need to come together at the employer's premises; and part-time working where the demands for maximisation on investment in technology and increases in customer bases have led to extended opening and operational hours. Technological change disrupts patterns of identity. It has led to flexible working, away from traditional job titles, restrictive practices and demarcation. It has also disrupted traditions of representation and belonging to trade unions, and professional and occupational bodies. This has occurred as jobs and occupations have become obsolete, causing both the individuals and the bodies concerned to seek new roles.

- *Vested interests*: needs for organisational change are resisted by those who are, or who perceive themselves to be, at risk. Vested interests are found in all areas. They include senior managers threatened with loss of functional authority, operational staff faced with occupational obsolescence, people in support functions no longer considered necessary, and those on promotional and career paths for whom the current order represents a clear and guaranteed passage to increased prosperity and influence (see Management in Focus 2.3).

MANAGEMENT IN FOCUS 2.3

LOBBIES AND VESTED INTERESTS

Lobby groups and vested interests are present in all organisations, for example trade unions and management cluster groups; and they exist also within the environment in which activities are carried out, for example the green lobby, consumer groups. Lobbies and vested interests have to be managed whatever the present state of the particular organisation. It is essential to recognise the nature and extent of the influence of lobbies and vested interests, and where, when, why and how they are able to exert this influence.

The main lobbies and vested interests that have to be managed within a changing environment are as follows:

- *Management groups*: as stated in the text above, especially where their own interests and priorities are threatened.
- *Trade unions*: especially when faced with loss of influence in workforce representation.
- *Shareholders' representatives, stockbrokers and other financial interests*: when, for example, a change of ownership or direction is mooted or strongly indicated.
- *Customer, consumer and environmental groups*.
- *Over-mighty and over-influential individuals, groups, departments, divisions and functions*: especially where organisational restructuring or changes of direction mean that this influence is to be diluted or lost.
- *Environmental lobbies*: concerned with the effect of activities or proposed activities on the quality of the environment. Examples include: the effect of construction blight when road-building schemes are considered; the ability to dispose effectively of toxic waste and effluent; concerns for environmental blight brought about by noise, lighting and dust.
- *The media*: managing the media involves the ability to respond effectively to questions raised, both legitimately and otherwise.

The lesson here is that each of these groups expects to have its concerns addressed. In most cases, the concerns raised are legitimate, even if delivered from a biased or partial point of view. Those responsible for managing in a changing environment need to understand this. It is additionally the case that the response to concerns raised by such groups has to meet their expectations; an inability to respond adequately calls into question the strength, probity and integrity of what is proposed.

- *Managerial resistance*: the managerial barrier is a consequence of 'the divorce of organisation, ownership and control', where there is a divergence between the organisation's best interests and need for long-term survival, and the needs of individuals and groups of managers to preserve their own positions. Existing patterns of supervision may again provide both general order and certainty, and specific career and promotion paths.
- *Bureaucracy*: the bureaucracy barrier occurs where patterns of order and control have grown up over long periods in the recording and supervision of activities and in the structuring of organisational functions. The problem is worst where the bureaucracy is large and complex, and accounts for a significant part of the total range of activities.
- *Redundancy and redeployment*: this is referred to above. It is a barrier in its own right because in the current context any proposed change carries redundancy and redeployment as possibilities and because these have so often been the consequences of other changes.

Behavioural barriers

The main barriers are as follows:

- *'It cannot be done'*: this is a barrier both to confidence and understanding and is based on a lack of true, full and accurate information about the matters which the organisation is proposing.
- *'There is no alternative'*: this comes in two forms. First, it is adopted by the workforce and interest groups in and around it (for example trade unions) that have a vested interest in the maintenance of the status quo either because it is familiar or because any change will result in loss of influence. This is especially true where business has been conducted in an effective and productive steady-state for a long period of time. The other side of this is where directorates and managers adopt it as the one and only explanation for a change that is to take place. Conducted in isolation 'there is no alternative' simply becomes a challenge for others to think of alternatives. The matter requires explanation and communication in order to demonstrate to all those affected that alternatives have indeed been considered and that what is now proposed represents the chosen strategic direction.
- *Lack of clarity*: if organisations have not sorted out the basis of the changes that are proposed, neither staff nor customers will go along with them with any degree of confidence or understanding; aims and objectives must be clearly understood as the prerequisite to successful and effective change, and communicated to those concerned in their own terms.
- *Fear and anxiety*: these are human responses to concepts and situations that are unknown or uncertain, and are often the initial response (or part of it) to any change that is proposed. If allowed to get out of hand, they can become an exercise in the devising and promulgation of hypothetical scenarios that could in certain circumstances become problems on the changing landscape. Not only does this constitute a waste of organisational resources and a diversion from actual purposes, but such interaction among the staff feeds on itself, generating negativity and unnecessary internal turbulence.

- *Perfection*: at the point at which change is proposed suddenly everything about the status quo becomes 'perfect'. Anything that is proposed as an alternative has therefore to address this barrier. It is another manifestation of familiarity and comfort, and faced with the loss of this, retaining such elements come to be seen as very desirable.

For all barriers, the main issue is to avoid leaving a vacuum. Organisations have therefore to understand where the proposed changes are to lead and what their consequences will be. Early communication is essential for the benefit of all concerned. The best employers give every opportunity to their workforce to be a part of their future before casting around outside for new staff and expertise.

In most cases most of these barriers, operational or behavioural, are present.

The influence of each barrier depends upon the particular situation, the nature and extent of the changes to be made, and whether they are strategic, operational, locational, attitudinal, structural or cultural. Whichever is present, the keys to effective and sustainable progress are the following:

- Integrity and directness, coupled with a clarity of direction. Above all, people always suspect a partial interest when phrases such as 'economies of scale' or 'synergies' are used.
- Clarity of purpose, strategy, direction and priority, easily understood by all affected.
- Clarity of communication. This includes sustaining the directness of communication over the period of change.
- Clear monitoring, review and evaluation processes, so that problems and teething troubles are addressed as soon as they become apparent.
- Consultation, counselling and support for individuals and groups that know, believe or perceive themselves to be most at risk from particular changes.
- A capacity for addressing specific problems, issues, quirks and anomalies as these become apparent.

Changing cultures and structures

Effective, lasting and operationally successful change is achieved only if attitudes, values and beliefs are addressed with the same strength and priority as operational and technological factors. They all impinge on each other: for example, the introduction of an automated production line leads to new job requirements, which leads to new job descriptions, which leads to new ways of working, which leads to revised staff handbooks and work agreements – and so on. Consequently, the attempts to introduce an operational change in isolation (for whatever reason – and a common one in the UK used to be trade union pressure) simply results in the old stance being conducted less effectively on the new machine. While there may be a short-term gain in terms of expediency in the avoidance of a labour dispute; in the longer-term, both operation and production will suffer.

It has to be recognised that what is currently in place is undesirable for a variety of reasons. The desired state of affairs must be articulated; and a strategic approach adopted to ensure that the required conclusion is reached.

There are two standard approaches as follows:

- *Unfreezing–transforming–refreezing* (see Figure 2.1). It is important to recognise that the idea of 'refreezing' incorporates aptitudes of flexibility, dynamism and responsiveness.
- *Force field analysis* (see Figure 2.2). This is where the forces that drive change and those that restrain it are separated out. The drivers are then energised and pushed on; the restrainers are either removed, neutralised or else re-energised in ways productive to the required outcome.

Unfreezing	*Transforming*	*Refreezing*
● Consultation ● High-quality open information ● Getting people used to the idea	● Introduction of new technology, work patterns, products, services, attitudes	● The new becomes the steady-state and familiar ● Note the danger of becoming rigid or set anew

Figure 2.1 Unfreezing–transforming–refreezing

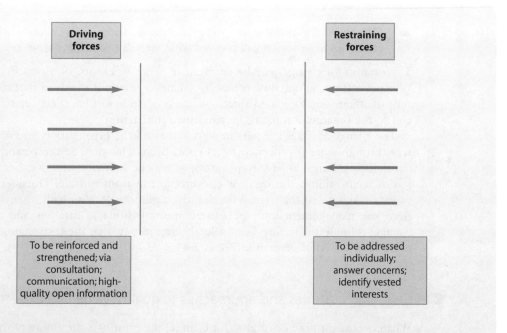

Figure 2.2 Force field analysis

The key problems with both the unfreezing/refreezing and the force field approaches are that:

- The history of organisation development indicates that structures are easier to put in place than they are to change, dismantle or rearrange.
- The need for change, as we have seen, may be neither apparent nor recognised.
- The structure has often provided a career progression path through the organisation that has been one of the attractions of working in it and staying in it.

Change catalysts and agents

In response to the pressures, drives and constraints outlined above, organisations create their own opportunities for change, development and improvement. These approaches may be:

- *Structured and strategic*: in which clear catalysts and agents are sought for something that is already to be implemented.
- *Opportunistic*: in which the senior management of organisations is sufficiently expert to take advantage of opportunities, when they present themselves, to engage in wider programmes of change.
- *Ad hoc*: in which changes, developments and enhancements are conducted in isolation from the overall purpose and direction of the organisation.

Whichever is chosen, the change process must be capable of being summarised as answers to the following questions:

- 'Change from what, to what, when, where, how and why?'
- 'Is this possible or feasible in the given state of the organisation and its environment?'
- 'Are there any possible or potential circumstances or conditions which may change or arise which will prevent what we want to achieve from occurring?'

The catalyst for change may be an event or series of events, or a person or group. Whichever it is, the outcome is that for whatever reason it is agreed that the present state of affairs is no longer adequate. Progress of some sort has therefore to be made, and so the organisation has to be galvanised into action.

The change agent is the person who galvanises the organisation into action, and sees through what is proposed to its conclusion. This may be the person who has decided that things do have to progress, or may be someone who is either given the job of seeing things through, or else brought in from outside. Outsiders may be experts taken on to the payroll for the given purpose. Additionally, many organisations use management and specialist consulting firms as catalysts and agents of change; though it is vital to be absolutely clear about what the consultants are there to achieve (see Management in Focus 2.4).

Changing attitudes and approaches to quality, value and expectations

Whatever the purpose or catalyst for change, the priority is the ability of the organisation and its managers and agents of change to concentrate on quality, value and

MANAGEMENT IN FOCUS 2.4

CONSULTANTS

Consultant-bashing is huge fun. The incomparable Stanley Bing, a real executive at a real, but unnamed, large US company recently wrote his regular column in *Fortune* magazine on: 'Why consultants generally suck. It's nothing personal. It's just that we know you are out to kill us.'

Whenever I write about management consultants, readers send me their anti-consultant stories and very entertaining they are too. If I attempt to redress the balance and say something positive, I am told not to be so silly.

They are snake-oil merchants. Their only strategy is slash and burn. They get between top management and the rest of the workforce, spreading fear and mistrust. They do not know the first thing about the businesses they are trying to advise. They cost too much.

The tirades make not a wit of difference. Consultancy remains impervious. The latest quarterly survey from the Management Consultancies' Association, which represents the largest consulting firms in the UK, shows a rise in the number of consultants employed, higher fee rates and growth in new business. Confidence is high, and clients are buying as never before.

Moreover, management experts and consultants have created a culture of reliance and dependence. Too many companies seem afraid to help themselves, with too many senior managers preferring to abdicate responsibility rather than face difficult issues themselves. This has been encouraged by the consultants themselves who have created proprietary brands of management voodoo – of which business process re-engineering (BPR) is perhaps the best example.

BPR's message is that organisations need to identify key internal processes and 're-engineer' them to become more efficient. That is, stripping out unnecessary steps in the organisation structure to streamline operations. This requires hard work and attention to detail; there is no black art involved. But consultants would have us believe that this requires the help of expensive outsiders. BPR has consequently been a prodigious money-spinner for the big consultancies, and have grown fat on advising companies about how to implement it.

Moreover, consultants will sell you only what they know. They latch on to the latest high-profile fad, and persuade their clients that this is the one true approach. When re-engineering was first defined by Michael Hammer and James Champy in *Re-engineering the Corporation* (1994), they stated unequivocally that the alternative to re-engineering was to close the doors and go out of business. The choice, they stated, was 'that simple and that stark'.

For all the hype, fad-based management relying on a consultant's recommendations usually fails to deliver. Quality programmes are launched with great fanfare, then fade away. Cutting management layers often disrupts internal communications. Moreover, the overwhelming impression is given that any managers who fail to follow the latest fad – regardless of its relevance to their own organisation – risk being thought unprofessional. Beyond this, management gurus encourage firms to believe that all fixes are not just easy to implement but quick to take effect: quality programmes will produce rapid declines in defect rates; re-engineering will swiftly revitalise paralysed processes; making use of subcontractors will instantly clear clogged production lines. When the promised benefits fail to appear managers – especially senior managers – quickly lose heart, and this is why most re-engineering and quality initiatives eventually break down.

More generally, many people in business have been surprised by the extent to which a clever, clear-headed colleague has come under the seductive power of management consultants. Some become dependent, seemingly unable to make even banal decisions without checking with their favourite guru. Others appear to turn their back on received wisdom and MBA training to pursue wacky, modern, airhead ideas favoured by the more controversial consultants.

There appear to be two main causes for this often bizarre behaviour. First there is the need to reconcile two overtly contradictory matters.

It may be that consultants were hired at great expense but did not produce the results desired. Many organisations and managers therefore redefine the results and point out how good the consultants were at diagnosing the real problems, and going on to implement long-term solutions. And the more the consultants cost and the greater the disappointment, the stronger the need to rationalise the mistake. On the other hand, stressed, bewildered, workaholic managers need a confidant, part confessor, part friend, part sounding board, a second opinion – in short a psychotherapist. Someone outside the business to whom they can talk about a range of issues.

This is a formidable cocktail to the rejected, ignored, despised business manager. And it gets better and stronger over time. A good business consultant knows that he/she is in the relationship business and that it is the support that gives the courage for business people to act decisively.

Sources: Alison Eadie, 'Management Matters', *Daily Telegraph* (15 June 2000); Des Dearlove, 'The Changing Business', *The Times* (5 November 1998); 'Instant Coffee as Management Theory', *The Economist* (25 January 1997); Adrian Furnham, University College London (15 June 2000).

expectations in all areas. All organisation stakeholders have presumptions of the quality and value that they are to gain from the organisation, and expectations that their own collective and individual aims will be met.

Customers expect improved ranges and quality of products and services. Shareholders and backers expect improved share values, returns on investment and dividend payments. Staff expect better pay and rewards, and greater opportunities for recognition and advancement. It is important to note that these expectations are not always met. Quick-fix approaches that have the purpose of increasing share values in the short term (e.g. outsourcing of functions) very often end with systems settling back to previous levels as the particular matter becomes institutionalised (and in some cases, operational problems start to emerge). Re-branded and re-designed products and services have to deliver additional benefits of value to the customers, otherwise they will be dismissed as fashionable, faddish or merely transient, not suitable to meet enduring needs and wants. Staff restructuring rarely delivers increased opportunities or rewards for staff; indeed, most staff expect that restructuring will lead to job and opportunity losses, and reduced career paths. If the above concerns are to be answered, meeting the demands of quality, value and expectations in managing within a changing environment requires that the following priorities are addressed by the change agent, leader or director:

- Obsession with customer satisfaction in terms both of the products or services offered, and of the ways in which they are delivered by the organisation. This must cover the whole process from the acceptance of orders through delivery and dispatch to after-sales service. In many cases, this is instrumental in the generation of repeat business. There is thus a strong element of long-term investment inherent in any true approach and attitude that has quality at its core.

- Obsession with staff excellence in terms of their expertise, skills and knowledge. This must be underpinned, however, by a commitment to them that ensures that they are instilled with the attitudes necessary to deliver this expertise in the ways that the organisation and its customers require. They must be paid and rewarded adequately. They must have their expectations and aspirations accommodated in the intention and pursuit of excellence. Again, this is regarded as a long-term, mutual investment and commitment between staff and organisation. It is not regarded as a purely instrumental or functional approach, or concept of employment.

- Obsession with constant improvement: the recognition that each and every aspect of the organisation, its products and services, its practices, procedures and operations, can be made to work better and more effectively in the pursuit of quality and excellence. Levels of investment in production methods and capacities, standards and life span of production plants and equipment will also be the subject of this commitment. Only the best equipment will do: that which has all the attributes required to meet the output levels required in terms of speed, reliability, perfection, regularity and universality.

The maintenance of operations at a continuing high-quality level is underpinned by both procedures and processes. The procedures include inspection, random sampling, testing and monitoring of products as they come off the line, and of the lines themselves during planned maintenance periods. The processes reflect the concept of continued improvement and must include work improvements and quality improvement groups addressing both product and production methods (see Management in Focus 2.5).

Current managerial issues

Those responsible for managing within the constraints of a changing environment have to be able to deal with the following.

Technological advance

This brings opportunities in terms of: increased opportunities for production, quality and durability; speed and flexibility of response to customer demands; and the capability to organise and develop workforces in ways that were simply not possible beforehand. Additionally, organisations have been under both operational and cultural pressures to develop e-business and Internet activities wherever they can; there is a widely held perception that not to have a website or Internet activity is demeaning to an organisation.

Investment

The best organisations are increasingly taking the view that much greater attention is required. Investment in technology is viewed as a continued commitment, together with

MANAGEMENT IN FOCUS 2.5

DUTTON ENGINEERING LTD

Dutton Engineering Ltd employs 600 staff in the design, manufacturing and delivery of plastic and metal office furniture and equipment, specialist parts for the motor car industry and components for the aircraft industry.

In 1996, faced with ever-increasing staff, employment, manufacturing and energy costs, the company's majority shareholder and Managing Director, Ken Lewis, undertook a total restructuring.

He organised the production crews into autonomous work teams. As well as being responsible for the output of their particular products, production crews would now set their own targets, work schedules and quality assurance processes. Production crews would be responsible for the attraction, recruitment and retention of new staff as and when they were required. The crews would ensure that their own paper-

work was accurate, answering directly to Mr Lewis and the Board of Directors in case of errors and omissions.

Production would be scaled back so as to manufacture only in response to orders, which were to be turned around within timescales demanded by customers. The emphasis here was to ensure that sales teams concentrated on existing customers with the purpose of generating repeat business, and on potential customers who were reassessed as being very likely or strongly likely to place orders.

Payroll was outsourced to a specialist firm. This cost the company a mere £50 per month, and prevented the need for employing up to four clerical staff to process time sheets, shift and productivity payments. These responsibilities were additionally handed to the production crews and sales teams.

Staff were shifted from

regular daily patterns of work to a system of 'annualised hours', in which staff were responsible for attending at work, and being able and willing to do so, at times of heavy workload pressures. This was to ensure that the priority of meeting deadlines was absolute.

Over the period 1996–2000, business volumes doubled. Over the period 2000–04, they doubled again. Staff productivity bonuses averaged 50 per cent of total salary over the period. Additionally, faults and rejects fell by 85 per cent.

All of this was achieved in response to the increases in costs, and market constraints outlined above. By concentrating on quality, value and expectations, and in particular ensuring that staff expectations were addressed, product quality, service levels and customer satisfaction were assured.

the need to change technology almost overnight if and when radically new approaches are invented. Investment in the production and maintenance of high-quality staff is a prerequisite to long-term and continued customer service and satisfaction, and therefore, to long-term organisational well-being (see Management in Focus 2.6).

Culture, attitudes and values

The best organisations and their managers are increasingly taking advantage of the changing environment to ensure that their staff adopt distinctive ways of doing things. These include:

MANAGEMENT IN FOCUS 2.6

INVESTMENT IN CHANGE

The apocryphal tale is told of two groups of managers, one British and one Japanese, who each ran a production line employing 20 people.

A machine was invented that could do the work of this line but which only needed one person to operate it. The British managers went home with heavy hearts because they knew they would have to make 19 people redundant.

The Japanese managers went home with glad hearts because they were going to get 20 new machines; they were going to expand output by a factor of 20; all the staff were going to get re-training and a fresh place of work; and they would not be adding to the wage bill.

The lesson for managers is that the way an opportunity is exploited is very much a matter of individual choice. Neither of the above approaches is right or wrong, except in the capability of the particular organisations to recognise investment as an opportunity, and ensure that it is maximised, whichever line is taken.

- supporting the organisation's own distinctive and considered view of how it should conduct its affairs
- being capable of accommodating the differing, and often conflicting, interests of the employees
- transcending local cultural pressures, meaning that both products and the ways in which they are produced and offered must be of a fundamental integrity, so that they are acceptable wherever business is conducted
- creating a basis of long-term mutual commitment serving the interests of the organisation, its customers, the wider community and its staff
- generating experience and expertise in managing across cultures, sectors, markets and locations.

Strategy

The Dutton Engineering example (see Management in Focus 2.5 above) shows how organisations can use change to develop greater clarity, awareness and understanding of the strategic aspects of business and management. This in turn makes it easier for all staff to acquire the following capabilities and expertise:

- Reconciling a range of conflicting pressures.
- Learning global and general lessons from successes and failures
- Investment and commitment to the long term in terms of technology, markets, customers and employees.
- Flexibility and responsiveness in the immediate term in the face of changing customer demands.
- Generating staff loyalty and commitment through a determination to invest in their long-term future. This above all, means attention to training and development. It constitutes a mutual and continuous obligation. The view is also

increasingly taken that long-term customer satisfaction can only be achieved through a commitment to staff excellence.

Flexible patterns and methods of work

Flexibility is needed to respond to the demand to maximise and optimise investment in production and other technology on the one hand, and changing patterns of customer requirements on the other. This has led, for example, to longer factory, shop, office, public and private facility opening hours, based in turn on the recognition that customers will use organisation services when it suits them. As organisations have extended their activity times, so they have found that extra customers have come to them and also that there is a great demand for short hours and other forms of part-time working and job opportunities on the part of employees and potential employees.

Ethics

There is a realisation that there is a much greater propensity for consumers to use organisations in which they have confidence and that they can trust. This is based on the expectation of a long-term and continuously satisfactory relationship – and on the knowledge that, if this is not forthcoming with one organisation, it can be found with many others. There is also a much greater demand for work and staff relationships based on honesty and integrity rather than bureaucracy, barriers, procedures – and in many cases duplicity. If an organisation promises lifetime job security, then its first duty is to remain in being for that lifetime, and to do this, it must take a view of itself based on integrity rather than expediency.

Concern for the environment

This is a matter of universal, political, economic and social priority at present; and is likely to become more vital in the future. It has direct implications for business and managers. It is also plainly related to the investment concept detailed above. It ultimately affects all aspects of the business sphere. Globally, there is a balance that must be struck between developing, economic and business activities in order to support a world population that is expanding at a great rate (the population of the city of Cairo goes up by 1 million every seven months, for example), and which has short-term needs, and on the other hand preserving the world so that it may support life and a quality of life further into the future.

At an organisation level there is a necessity to consider the effect of operations on the environment, in relation to all business aspects. Marketing policies and activities, for example, may demand levels of packaging to preserve the product, to demonstrate it to its best possible advantage, and to meet public and sectoral expectations. On the other hand, both the packaging itself and the technology used to produce it may be consumptive of resources themselves and also create high levels of pollution or waste. Production and operations and the technology related to this also create drains on the world's resources. They create waste and effluent that also have to be managed and disposed of. Human resource policies in certain parts of the business sphere (for example the UK) provide high-quality, prestige cars to go with particular occupations; these cars are very often resource-intensive in production and highly consumptive of fuel.

The net result is that strategies and policies for managing the environment have to be devised globally, sectorally and organisationally. This requires organisations and their managers to place the environment at or near the top of their list of priorities. It requires them to take a much wider view of the true cost of operations. Related activities may therefore include reorientation of marketing and product presentation, and a parallel re-education along these lines as part of the total strategy aimed at changing customer expectations in this way (and reconciling this with positive, persuasive wider marketing activities). It also requires organisations to take a longer-term view of production processes. The approach required is one that relates to both responsibility for, and the adoption of, procedures and practices which truly address the problems of the disposal of waste and effluent and for which organisation provision must be made in strategic, operational and investment terms.

The changing nature of public services

Demands on resources, and political drives for greater efficienct, have led to the restructuring, privatisation and commercialisation of many services that were tradition-ally delivered only by public bodies. The standpoint is the stated need to revitalise and regenerate these services, to restructure them, to improve the quality and effectiveness of their management and to make them more efficient. This is all based on the prem-ise that it can be achieved only if the organisations responsible are freed from bureau-cratic, state or other authority control. Managers will in turn be free to conduct and provide and order these services in the ways in which their expertise directs. This is of a special importance when the nature of these services is considered – they are the primary, critical, health, social and education activities that are ever more in demand, ever-expanding and the object of ever-higher social and public expectations. The same thinking has been applied to public utilities and strategic state industries. In the UK, gas, electricity, water, transport and telecommunications and some research have all been privatised or transferred from government to shareholder ownership. Other services, including the post and also parts of education, health and social care, are either already being restructured or else to be tackled very soon.

Conclusions

All of the factors and issues raised in this chapter concentrate on the drive for busi-ness and organisational quality, effectiveness and excellence. They reflect the fact that these constitute the major concerns of the business sphere in the last decade of the twentieth century and the first of the new millennium. They are further underlined by the relationship that is drawn between the existence of these qualities in organi-sations and the success, effectiveness, growth and profitability that are considered to arise from the fact that they either operate in these ways or exhibit these qualities.

The greatest mistake that anyone could make, however, is to believe that these improvements constitute an end in themselves; that, once they are achieved, an organisation is guaranteed permanence and eternal profitability. This is not so. At their highest level (and if one is offering or preaching perfection) these concepts represent threads and strands that ought to run through the core of any organisation or undertaking; they constitute a standard of ethic, aura, belief and pride in the organisation that are increasingly recognised as the sound foundations on which business success must be built. They also represent the obsession with top quality of products and services, the critical importance of recognising the central position of the customer in the activities of any undertaking. Such foundations require constant attention and maintenance, as do the organisations and their structures, cultures and practices which are built on them. This is also the basis from which the next developments of the business and management sphere, and of managerial expertise, are to come. It has taken the composition of the expertise and reality of management that is currently recognised thousands of years to develop this far; and this includes the globalisation of experience and practice.

The ability to operate effectively and respond to pressures within the changing environment is a critical part of management expertise (see also above, Chapter 1). Products and services have to be capable of effective delivery whatever the present and envisaged constraints of the environment. As well as maintaining a steady-state, opportunities for business development and advancement have also to be created.

The processes, qualities and expertise of business and management outlined here, and their interaction and interrelationship both among themselves and with the wider business sphere and environment, are having great and lasting effects on business practices. The transformation effected is to generate the creative and energetic aspect in the business sphere and to develop the nature and level of expertise in as many ways as possible. Management is thus no longer a straitjacketed or bureaucratic process; above all, it is not the equivalent of administration. Both business and management are ever-developing concepts, phenomena and realities. Their progress and transformation are limited only by the capacities and capabilities of those who work in them, in whatever sector or aspect.

Finally, these constitute global and universal activities and it follows from this that 'good practice is good practice wherever it is found.' It is ever more obvious that this is so and that any true expertise, whenever it is found and from wherever it is drawn, provides an increase in both understanding and in the fund of knowledge, skills and capabilities of the expert manager. Professional and expert managers have therefore to bring above all to their chosen profession a willingness, openness and capacity to learn and develop. Managers must be prepared to draw lessons from wherever they may become apparent and to assimilate these lessons in regard to their own expertise. This covers the whole spectrum of business and managerial activity, with opportunities afforded in all sectors across the whole world. This is the scale and scope of the range and potential offered to the truly expert manager. The whole field therefore opens up opportunities that are truly exciting, challenging and adventurous for anybody who wishes to take advantage of them and who has the qualities, capacities and personal attributes to do so.

CRITICAL THINKING, ANALYSIS AND EVALUATION

1. For the organisation of your choice, identify: a) a change that was particularly successful; and b) the main reasons for this. What steps could or should have been taken in order to build on the successes and minimise the failures?

2. Identify and discuss the cultural barriers that have to be overcome by retail and banking organisations when they establish activities in countries other than those of their origin.

3. What steps should organisations take to ensure that their managers and staff do not constitute a barrier to change as a vested interest?

4. Under what circumstances would you recommend that organisations use external consultants as change agents; and under what set of circumstances would you recommend that they do not use external consultants as change agents?

DEVELOPING MANAGEMENT SKILLS AND EXPERTISE

THE HOLLYOAKS HOTEL, MARGATE

The Hollyoaks Hotel is situated on the cliff tops at Margate in Kent overlooking the sea. It is about 100 years old and has always enjoyed a reputation for peace and tranquillity. Its core business is the provision of weekend breaks for couples. It has 80 rooms, each with full facilities; a swimming pool and fitness centre; and a large dining room where the food is consistently good. It is highly recommended by the English Tourist Board; both the AA and RAC have accorded it three stars.

For the past 50 years, the hotel has been owned by the Casper family. It was bought by Brian Casper; and he subsequently handed it on to his son Colin, who has run it with his wife Beryl for the past 20 years.

The hotel has always been prosperous and enjoys a consistently high reputation among its visitors. However, Colin and Beryl have noticed a gradual decline in bookings, and especially, a lack of young people coming to Margate for weekend breaks. As well as declining therefore, the clientele is also ageing. This has meant that over the past five years, while the hotel has continued to enjoy a good living, desirable refurbishment work has not taken place. Some of this is now beginning to become essential, and the gentility of the hotel is beginning to fade.

The hotel employs 60 staff – waiters and waitresses, chamber and room cleaning staff, chefs and kitchen staff, and maintenance staff. Unemployment in the area remains high, and were the hotel to go out of business they would have little prospect of work elsewhere.

Ever mindful of this, Colin and Beryl have recently been to meetings with the Chamber of Commerce, and the County Council, to explore ways in which the business might be developed. The response from the local Chamber of Commerce could offer little – other than undertaking to consider the possibility of holding conferences and meetings at the hotel, it was able to provide little in the way of business prospects. However, the County Council was much more promising, and suggested to Colin and Beryl that they look into the possibility of turning the hotel into a major conference centre. A Council official suggested that up to £50,000 might be available for refurbishment by way of grant support, provided that jobs could be guaranteed for an unspecified period.

The Caspers have always taken a pride in the business, and are keen to ensure that it continues if at all possible, and they wish to increase the level of turnover so that they can hand it on to the next generation when their children grow up. At the back of their minds however, is the knowledge that they could sell the site for redevelopment (subject to planning permission) into retirement flats.

One afternoon, during a quiet period, they sit down, determined to work out their options.

Questions

1. Conduct a force field analysis for the hotel, identifying drives and restraints, barriers and opportunities, for the hotel in its current situation.
2. Identify the vested interests that have to be satisfied by the direction that the Caspers ultimately choose.
3. On the basis of your answers to (1) and (2) above, outline the advantages, disadvantages, opportunities and consequences of each course of action open to them.

Chapter three

Organisational and managerial performance

'No more than 7.5 prisoners per 1000 are to be allowed to escape.'
Performance target, Scottish Prison Service (1993).

'All I ever set out to do was to feed my children.'
Anita Roddick, *Body and Soul,* Ebury Press (1992).

Interviewer: 'So then – you don't make mistakes. You get everything right first time, every time?'
Response from UK Managing Director, Panasonic Electronics: 'Of course we make mistakes.
I make them – lots of them – every day. The important thing – the reason why we are so
successful – is that we acknowledge them and learn from them.'
Radio 4, *The Today Programme* (26 June 1999).

Chapter outline

- Introduction
- Prerequisites for successful and effective performance
- Components of successful performance
- Information
- Responsibilities
- Stakeholder considerations
- Priorities, aims and objectives
- Qualitative assessment and judgement
- Priorities
- Conclusions

Chapter objectives

After studying this chapter, you should be able to:

- understand the context in which effective performance is delivered, measured and assessed

- understand the need for a variety of approaches and perspectives in all organisations in measuring and evaluating performance

- understand the range of performance measures that are available to managers in particular circumstances

- understand the need to choose, justify and apply specific measures to specific sets of circumstances

- understand the advantages and shortcomings of relying on quantitative methods alone

- understand the advantages and shortcomings of relying on qualitative and contextual measures.

● Introduction

Organisational and managerial performance is only measurable against what was intended or planned. It follows from this that organisational and managerial performance is a combination of priorities, aims and objectives, together with the capacity, capability and willingness on the part of everyone involved to do their best to achieve and to deliver what was intended. This has in turn to be seen in the context of whether performance is achievable in the present markets, locations and environment, with the present levels of staff and technology, and whether changes in all, or any, of these are required and desired; or conversely whether changes in any, or all, of these would render it impossible to deliver what was intended.

In general terms, all organisations in every sphere of activity are concerned with the same things:

● maximising customer, client and user satisfaction of their products and services over the long term
● maximising the confidence of everyone involved or affected by the organisation over the long term
● maximising long-term owner/shareholder value – i.e. getting the best possible return on investment over the long term (this applies to public services as well as commercial undertakings)
● securing the long-term future and well-being of the organisation
● working within this context and environment, with especial recognition of functions inside and outside the organisation's control.

This all applies to private and commercial companies, public sector and service organisations, and the not-for-profit sector (see Management in Focus 3.1).

● Prerequisites for successful and effective performance

Effective performance is only achievable if the following key elements are present:

● *Agreed aims and objectives, priorities, purposes and outcomes, as discussed above*: so that everybody knows and understands what is intended by the organisation as a whole, and what the collective and individual contributions to this core purpose are to be.
● *Clarity of purpose and direction*: knowing where you are going and how to get there; understanding the full implications and commitment necessary to achieve this.
● *Adequate levels of resources*: investment; information; technology; staff capability; expertise; willingness and commitment.
● *Knowledge and understanding*: of the markets in which activities and operations are to take place, and what customers and clients want and expect from them; of what the organisation's total capacity is; what it can and cannot achieve; and any operational implications arising; of the total environment in which activities are to take place.

This gives the broad context in which performance is measured. It cannot be measured effectively if this is not fully understood.

MANAGEMENT IN FOCUS 3.1

THE CONTEXT OF DEVELOPING EFFECTIVE ORGANISATIONAL PERFORMANCE: EXAMPLES

- People buy cars from a garage on the basis that any faults can be put right in the future; and that the garage will maintain and service the car during the period of ownership. People buy groceries from a super-market on the basis of its reputation for selling good food, and the assurance that if for some reason an item is not good, it can be taken back and replaced. People would not buy from either the garage or the supermarket if they knew or perceived that neither would last long into the future, or if they had no general feeling of confidence in those organisations' ability to sustain themselves. The context of effective organisational perform-ance in these circum-stances is therefore to know and understand customer expectations, and to commit as a prior-ity to meeting them.

- In public services, the approach is similar. People do not send their children to school where there is no confidence in the quality of education being offered. If it is announced that a school is to close, even if this is not to take place for a year or two, there is a rush to find alternatives with a more secure future. If there is no confidence that a hospi-tal can treat a particular condition effectively, or if there is to be a long wait before it is able to do so, people will again seek alternatives – as witness the burgeoning UK private health care sector. The priority therefore is to know and understand people's expectations of particular public services; to commit to meeting these as far as is reason-able and practicable; and to know and understand the nature of problems, issues and complaints that are likely to arise if these expectations are not met.

- In the not-for-profit sector, people give to the causes represented by individual charities because they want their money to go to those whom it represents, or in whose interest it oper-ates. They find other outlets for their giving if they have no confidence that particular charities have a future, or that their money is not being spent directly on the cause or client group. This is reflected in the ways in which the larger charities – Oxfam, NCH, NSPCC, RSPCA – have spent large amounts of resources on strengthen-ing their institutions and identity. While this is not always to the satisfaction of long-term regular supporters, they are nevertheless securing their long-term existence in order to be able to operate more effectively in the future.

⬤ Components of successful performance

Organisational and managerial performance is measured in the following areas:

- *Market standing*: overall organisational reputation; reputation of products and services; reputation of staff and expertise; size of market served; location of market served; specific needs, wants and demands.

- *Market position*: actual market position in relation to desired position; the costs and benefits of maintaining this; opportunity costs; returns on resources; returns on investment.

- *Innovation*: capacity for innovation; desired and actual levels of innovation; time taken for new products and ideas to reach the market; attitudes to innovation; percentages of new products and ideas that become commercial successes.

- *Creativity*: expertise of staff; versatility and ability to diversify; capability for turning ideas into commercial successes; new product/service strike rates; attitudes to creativity; other related qualities, above all flexibility and responsiveness.

- *Resource utilisation*: efficiency and effectiveness; balance of resources used in primary and support functions; wastage rates; resource utilisation and added value.

- *Managerial performance*: total managerial performance; performance by function, department, division, group; performance at different levels of management – director, general manager, senior, middle, junior, supervisory, first line (see Management in Focus 3.2).

- *Management development*: areas of strength and weakness; progress and improvement; desired expertise and capability; actual expertise and capability; development of specific skills and knowledge; desired and actual attitudes and behaviour; priority of training and development.

- *Staff performance*: areas of strength and weakness; progress and improvement; attitudes and willingness to work; degrees of commitment; desired expertise and capability; actual expertise and capability; development of specific skills and knowledge; desired and actual attitudes and behaviour; attention to work patterns; commitment; extent and priority of training and development; targeting of training and development; attitudes to staff suggestions; specific positive and negative features.

- *Workforce structure*: core and peripheral; flexibility in attitudes and behaviour; multi-skilling; work patterns; general employability; continued future employability; relations between organisation and workforce; relations between managers and staff; length and strength of hierarchies.

- *Wage and pay levels*: relationships between pay and output; relationships between pay, profits and performance; local factors and conditions; industrial factors and conditions; relationships between pay and expertise; pay as incentive; economic rent; known, believed and perceived areas of over and underpaying.

- *Organisational culture*: the extent to which this is positive/negative; identifying and removing negative factors; accentuating the positive; motivation and morale; staff policies; industrial relations; staff management; designed, emergent, strong, weak, suitable, unsuitable, acceptable, unacceptable aspects of organisation culture.

- *Key relationships*: with backers; with staff; with suppliers; with distributors; with customers; with community (see Management in Focus 3.3).

MANAGEMENT IN FOCUS 3.2

MANAGERIAL PERFORMANCE: THE PADDINGTON RAIL DISASTER

On 5 October 1999, two trains collided outside Paddington railway station in West London. Thirty people were killed.

It quickly became apparent that the disaster was caused by a combination of inadequate maintenance of the track and signalling systems, and signals that did not work properly. The company responsible, Railtrak Plc, undertook to put everything right.

However, continued media interest in the state of the railways ensured that the actions of Railtrak were kept constantly in the spotlight. Accordingly, on 21 October 1999, the Commercial Director of Railtrak, Richard Middleton, said to the media: 'It is time for the hysteria around rail safety to be calmed down. Rail is a safe mode of transport.'

This provoked outrage among the families of the 30 victims. Furthermore, on 6 November 2000, there was another serious accident, when a train travelling at high speed was derailed at Hatfield, to the north of London. It quickly became apparent that the cause of this crash was a faulty stretch of track, and that in spite of the fact that the company had known for months that it needed replacing, no action had been taken.

The lesson is knowing and understanding where the priorities lie. Effective rail transport is only possible if there is absolute security on the railway itself, and if the rail network is of a sufficient quality to deliver the services promised. The outcome of this disaster was clearly a failure to provide either quality or reliability in the rail network. It does no good for any organisation or its managers to produce responses like those above to legitimate questions concerning immediate and enduring organisational performance.

- *Public standing*: the respect and esteem in which the organisation is held in its markets, the community, among its staff, customers and suppliers; confidence and expectations; general public factor coverage.
- *Profitability*: levels of profits accrued; timescales; means of measuring and assessing products; scope for enhancement and improvement.
- *Ethical factors*: the absolute standards that the organisation sets for itself; what it will and will not do; its attitudes to its staff, customers, clients, suppliers and communities; the nature of the markets served; standards and quality of the treatment of staff; management style; attitudes and approaches to customer complaints; attitudes and approaches to suppliers; quality of public relations; quality of community relations.
- *Other factors*: general efficiency and effectiveness; product and service quality and value; areas for improvement; areas where complaints come from; opportunities and threats; crises and emergencies (see Management in Focus 3.4).

Many of the above areas overlap. In some cases the same phrases are used under different headings. Without doubt, different words and phrases could be used to convey the same meanings. The mix and balance varies between organisations.

MANAGEMENT IN FOCUS 3.3

STAKEHOLDERS

A stakeholder is anyone who has a particular interest in any aspect of the organisation. Stakeholders include:

- shareholders, backers, financiers and financial institutions and their representatives
- stock markets, stockbrokers and financial advisers
- organisation directors and shareholders' representatives
- public service governors and those charged with responsibility for gaining finance and backing for public ventures and enterprises
- the organisation's functional directors, managers, staff and their representatives
- suppliers and distributors
- customers, clients and end-users
- industrial and commercial markets

- the communities in which activities take place
- the media, business, financial and management journalists and media analysts
- pressure groups, lobbies and vested interests.

Organisations inevitably have dominant stakeholders – those whose interests must be served above all else; or, more insidiously, those whose interests are served as a priority, whether or not this is the correct course of action for the particular organisation. The financial interest is invariably to be found as a dominant stakeholder; the best organisations also place their staff, suppliers and customers at this level. It is also true that any group that has cause to raise legitimate concerns about the organisation and its activities should be treated as a dominant

stakeholder until its problems have been resolved.

Serious problems can arise when the interests of the dominant stakeholders are served in spite of conflicting or divergent concerns from less influential sources.

The lesson is to know and understand which interest is being served. In particular, it is essential to know and understand whether specific interests are being served at the expense of others; or whether every interest is being served as far as possible. It is additionally essential to know and understand that, whichever line is taken, there are opportunities and consequences that are certain to affect both performance itself, and also the ways and means by which performance is achieved.

However, every element is present in all situations to a greater or lesser extent. Initial lessons can therefore be drawn.

There is no single effective measure of performance in any situation or organisation. Even if a supervisor is working to a single daily production target, he/she must have: the right staff, adequately trained and motivated; the right volume and quality of components; and somewhere to put the finished items. And given the normal nature of work – all work – all this has to be available on a steady and continuous basis.

A large proportion of the elements indicated are qualitative not quantitative. The main qualities necessary to evaluate such factors properly are therefore judgement and analysis. Success and failure are value judgements that are placed on events and

MANAGEMENT IN FOCUS 3.4

CRISES AND EMERGENCIES

The following are examples of the management of crises and emergencies:

- In 1990, the Hoover Company offered vouchers that could be exchanged for airline tickets as part of its Christmas promotion. These vouchers were issued with every sale of a Hoover product during the period September–December 1990. For the price of an electric kettle, it was possible under the terms of the promotion to obtain an air ticket for the United States. When the scale of this marketing crisis became apparent, the company first tried to deny that it was a serious promotion, and then simply ignored requests from customers with vouchers for their airline tickets. It took the company six months to admit its mistake; indeed, it only did so after extensive adverse media and television coverage of the promotion. Not until 1997 did all those customers who were entitled to free air tickets get them.

- Pan Am, the American airline undertook a security operation after it became worried that its staff were stealing miniature bottles of whisky from its aircraft. The company wired up an alarm clock inside the drink's cabinet of one of the airliners. The clock was so arranged that it would stop whenever the door was opened. This, they said, would reveal the exact time of the theft. Naturally, the company management did not tell the cabin crew. On a flight between New York and Dubai, one of the stewardesses heard the clock ticking and assumed that there was a bomb on board. She alerted the pilot, and the plane made a forced landing at Berlin. In the inquiry afterwards, it became clear that the thefts had amounted to little more than petty pilfering. The emergency landing cost the company £16,500.

The lesson from these examples is: to be clear about what is intended, and to recognise the full range of possible outcomes. If this is not possible, then it is essential to tolerate and accommodate what has been delivered, and to ensure that lessons are learned for the future, so that the same mistakes are never made again.

activities on the basis of high levels of knowledge and expertise. Seldom, if ever, is success or failure self-evident except in the immediate or very short-term.

It follows, in turn, that the main attributes of those who measure business and managerial performance are knowledge, expertise and understanding of results, of the environment, of people, of customers and the market, of the product/services offered and of the organisation's general position.

It is also the case that any situation can be turned to the organisation's ultimate advantage if it and its managers choose to do so. Provided that the cause is not negligence or criminal activity, organisations can turn simple errors and omissions into profitable and effective ventures, by ensuring that what has happened is fully analysed and then used as a vehicle for learning and development (see Management in Focus 3.5).

MANAGEMENT IN FOCUS 3.5

COCK-UPS CAN HAVE A SILVER LINING

Many organisations, and especially their top managers, find themselves unwilling to admit where, when or why mistakes are made. Invariably, they rather look for scapegoats, or else are inclined (if allowed to do so) to put failure down to 'factors outside their control' or 'volatile market conditions'.

Yet the theory of managerial cock-ups is the orphan of management studies. Innumerable books have been written on strategic triumphs and tragedies, but nearly all assume that the heroes or villains knew what they were doing. By contrast, the 'cock-up' theory holds that management moves, not from one considered coordinated ploy to the next, but by isolated lurches. These are governed, not by deep analysis and optimisation of resources, but by impulse and unguarded optimism.

The 'cock-up' theory holds that problems always prove much greater than anyone expects. Financially, the potential killer is cost. If actual earnings fail to cover the true cost of capital and other resources used in particular ventures, the value of the company becomes eroded. Cock-ups might well be fewer therefore, if top managements were penalised when acquisitions, changes of direction, and other supposed brainwaves generated negative returns. Bonuses and long-term remuneration for directors and senior managers ought to be reduced in direct relationship to these negative returns. That is, after all, how many chief executives use remuneration systems to pressurise subordinates. What is sauce for the geese should surely apply to the ganders. But the 'cock-up' theory holds that this is where the

whole bungling process begins – with the lack of checks and balances on over-mighty corporate rulers.

Cock-ups teach invaluable lessons. Management that has had its nose rubbed in the realities of the market and economic conditions tends to ensure that false assumptions are replaced by true facts. Necessary changes in people and policies are clearly indicated. Instead of indulging in corporate hand-wringing, there is a clear opportunity to assess why things went wrong, and from this, to take steps to ensure that specific, useful and practical measures of performance are instigated at the outset of any venture or initiative.

Source: Robert Heller, *Management Today*, October 1998.

● Information

Effective performance measurement and assessment is never possible without full, or at least adequate, information covering each of these areas and this must be constantly gathered and evaluated. Markets, technology, expertise are all constantly changing, and organisations that do not respond have at the very least to recognise the effects that such a lack of response will, or may, have.

Full information enables organisations and their managers to reduce uncertainty, analyse levels of risk, maximise chances of success, minimise chances of failure and assess the prospects and likely consequences and outcomes of following particular courses of activity. It enables projections to be made for the organisation as a whole and for each of its activities. Summary positions are often established under the headings of strengths, weaknesses, opportunities, threats; and these are most effective when related to the organisation as a whole, to its markets, to its backers and stakeholders, and to its competitors.

Effective planning is also based on full information. The value of planning is at its greatest when it allows organisations:

- to see the future as it unfolds, recognising possible, likely and (more or less) certain developments
- to assess the continued performance of all activities and operations
- to assess the ways in which other people and organisations, especially competitors, are operating.

Effective planning is a process, the purpose of which is to arrive at and retain continued clarity of direction. It involves: analysis of the information; thinking it through, testing ideas; examining what is possible and what is not.

More specific schedules, practices, operations, activities, aims and objectives all then come from this body of knowledge and the understanding which arises from analysing it. Implementation and execution are then handed on to different people, functions, divisions and departments within the organisation.

It should be apparent from this that there is a world of difference between planning and plans. Dwight D. Eisenhower, the United States General and President, once said: 'Planning is everything, the plan is nothing.' At their best, corporate and organisational plans are statements of what is now proposed as the result of information available; and subject to change, modification and, when necessary, abandonment as and when circumstances change.

At their worst, plans are detailed statements covering the way that the world is certain to be extending into the far-distant future. No such position is sustainable now – indeed, it probably never was in the past. This does not prevent large corporations, both public and private, and the policy units of public services drawing these up. At best, they are an irrelevance. More usually, they constitute a waste of organisational resources that would be better used elsewhere. At worst, they are indeed slavishly followed in the teeth of a changing world and competitive environment with immense adverse consequences for the organisation.

Responsibilities

Organisational responsibilities

Specific organisational responsibilities exist in the following areas:

- *Anticipating the future in terms of the changing environment*: anticipating changes in customer demands and perceptions; recognising changes in the nature of competition; recognising changes in production and service technology; recognising and anticipating changes in the nature of people attracted to work for the organisation and the sector; recognising and anticipating changes in the customer base.
- *Investment as a continued commitment*: in the areas of product development; quality improvement; management and staff training and development; production and service technology; the well-being of the customer.

- *Organisation development*: in terms of its skills, knowledge, capabilities, attitudes and expertise; in terms of customer awareness and satisfaction; in terms of processes and procedures; in terms of supplier and distributor relations; in terms of its culture and structures.
- *Training and development*: of both management and staff in the skills, qualities, attributes and expertise necessary to secure the future; and in the key attitudes of flexibility, dynamism, responsiveness, willingness and commitment.
- *Recognition of the fact that all organisations currently operate in a changing and turbulent environment*: that historic and current success, efficiency, effectiveness and profitability is no guarantee that this will extend into the future. From this comes an obligation to ensure that all staff are capable of existing in this environment and that they are equipped with the resources and capability to do so.
- *Openness*: people respond to uncertainty and turbulence much better if they understand its extent and why they must constantly update and develop. Organisations therefore have a clear duty to inform, consult and provide detail on all aspects of performance in general; and in more detail, concerning things which directly affect specific members and groups of staff.
- *Ethics*: long-term existence, the ability to secure the employment of staff, and establishing a regular and profitable customer base are enhanced by taking, accepting and understanding a view of the world as it really is. There is therefore, a moral, as well as commercial, commitment.

Managerial responsibilities

Specific managerial responsibilities exist in the following areas:

- To develop (and be developed in) capabilities and expertise required by the organisation; those required by the nature of professional management as it develops; and those which involvement in the particular business, industry or service requires.
- To take a personal commitment to organisational success as well as that of the department, division or function for which the individual is responsible. High levels of personal commitment are required of all professions and professionals in all spheres of activity and expertise, and this is also true of management and managers.
- To develop the full range of managerial skills and qualities required by the profession of management. This currently means being able to solve problems; manage people; set standards of performance; understand where the manager's domain fits into the wider scheme of things and total organisational performance; use resources efficiently and effectively; set and assess budgets; recognise the constraints under which operations have to be carried out; and generate a positive, open and harmonious culture and attitudes.

At the heart of all organisational and managerial responsibility is the need to produce goods and services in the required volume and quality, at the right price, in the right place (see Management in Focus 3.6). This can only be achieved through having top quality, expert and highly motivated staff. This is the critical factor in which the long-term future of the organisation is secured and all effective measures of organisation and managerial performance have this at their core.

MANAGEMENT IN FOCUS 3.6

INTERNET COMPANIES AND PERFORMANCE MANAGEMENT

Reflecting on the events of the past five years, and especially the capital volumes invested in Internet companies, it becomes clear that very few ever considered in any detail the nature and level of returns on capital employed that could be anticipated. Neither did most Internet companies pay any attention to measures of managerial performance in relation to staff motivation and morale, customer service and satisfaction, or frequency, availability and accessibility to the people who worked at the company.

As examples, Boo.com had no customer helpline until a fortnight before it was liquidated; LastMinute.com had nobody responsible for staffing matters for the first two years of trading.

Clearly, much of the fault lies with the companies. However, there are lessons to be learned by all. Each of the above issues was neglected by those backing the companies. In many cases, backers simply failed to ask where the returns would actually be coming from – they acted simply on an assumption that customer volumes would exist once the website was up and running.

Stakeholder considerations

Both organisations and their managers have to recognise that their performance is going to be measured and assessed by a variety of different people and in a great range of different ways. Everyone who comes into contact with an organisation assesses it in one way or another. The stakeholders and their perspectives may be summarised as:

- *The staff:* all those who work for, and in, the organisation and who are therefore dependent upon it for their income and spending power; this also applies to subcontractors and other retainers and potential staff.
- *The customers:* for continued satisfaction and service.
- *The communities:* the environments in which staff and customers live and work, and in which the organisation operates.
- *Social customers:* for example, charities, schools and hospitals which may approach the organisation for sponsorship and support.
- *Backers:* shareholders, contributors, bankers, loan makers, venture capitalists, sponsors, city institutions, stock markets and public funds.
- *Suppliers of components and raw materials:* these have a vested interest in the success of the organisation in terms of their own continuity of activity and profitability.
- *The community sectors and markets:* in which the organisation offers its products and services for sale and consumption.
- *Distributors:* relying on their own position between the organisation in question and the end users of the products or services for their continued existence.

- *Trade unions, market and employers' federations and associations*: that are active in the particular field.
- *Competitors and offerers of alternative products and services*: as part of their own quest for knowledge and expertise in the given field.
- *Lobbyists and vested interest groups*: related to the location of activities, the nature of activities and the ways in which those activities are carried out.
- *Media*: especially business and financial journalists. Organisations and their managers also receive wider local and media coverage as the result of particular initiatives and ventures undertaken, and as the result of crises and disasters (see Management in Focus 3.3 above).

Performance is measured by each of these groups according to their own particular interest. For example, brilliant commercial performance may be rated very highly by consumers but not by shareholders if this brilliant performance does not result in rises in the share prices.

It is measured continuously by each of the groups indicated. It is punctuated by formal and semi-formal events: annual reports; interim reports; staff, production and service performance appraisal; production and sales figures; pay rises and pay rounds; activity levels; budget efficiency and effectiveness.

Priorities, aims and objectives

All performance has to be measured against what was intended, as noted above; and this is the reason for setting priorities, aims and objectives. Aims and objectives occur at different levels, and again, are set or inferred by each of the above groups to satisfy their particular points of view:

- *Corporate*: reflecting the overall scope of the organisation; how it is to be run in structural and financial terms; how resources are to be allocated.
- *Competitive/business level*: how the organisation is to compete in its different markets; which products and services should be developed and offered; the extent to which these meet customer needs; monitoring of product performance.
- *Operational*: how different functions of the organisation contribute to total organisational purpose and activities.
- *Behavioural*: related to the human interactions between different parts of the organisation; and between the organisation, its customers and the wider community.
- *Confidence*: the generation of confidence and reputation among all those with whom it comes into contact.
- *Ethical*: meeting specific standards that may be enshrined in policy; the ability to work in certain activities, in certain locations; the attitude taken towards staff, customers and others with whom the organisation comes into contact.

Aims and objectives should be a combination of the precise:

- *specific* – dealing with easily identifiable and quantifiable aspects of performance
- *measurable* – devised in ways so that success and failure can be identified
- *achievable* – striking a balance so as to maximise/optimise resources and output without setting standards so high that targets are unattainable and therefore unvalued

- *recognisable* – understood by all concerned
- *time constrained* – so that a continuous record of progress and achievement may be kept and problem areas identified

and the imprecise, continuous and proactive:

- reconciling these differing and often conflicting pressures
- attending to all aspects of organisational performance
- providing distinctive measures of success and failure
- enhancing the total performance of the organisation
- where necessary, reconciling the different and conflicting demands of particular stakeholders and interested parties
- being prepared to adjust or alter direction and priority if the situation demands
- establishing procedures for monitoring, reviewing and evaluating all aspects of performance, and acting on the results.

Aims and objectives are required for the organisation as a whole, and for each and every department, division, function, work group, location and individual. It is therefore impossible to set generic objectives. All aims and objectives must be drawn up against the organisation's specific context and background if they are to have any meaning. Whatever they refer to, they must reflect the following questions:

- What contribution does this activity/set of activities make to total organisational performance? Where does this fit into the broader objectives of the department, division or function concerned? Where does this fit into the wider purpose of the organisation?
- What resources, equipment, information, technology and expertise are needed to carry it out successfully?
- What specific restraints are there? For example: can it be done straight away? Are there other things that must first be done? How long does it/will it/must it take?

Aims and objectives therefore attend to both the broad and the precise.

This is the broad context in which measuring all aspects of organisational and managerial performance takes place. It is not possible to do this effectively or successfully in isolation – and the fact that some organisations nevertheless attempt this does not make it right. Unless this basis is understood, neither quantitative and qualitative performance measures will have any meaning to those who are allocated more specific performance targets. Lack of any context is also one of the main reasons why staff, product and service performance appraisal and measurement schemes fall into disrepute. Whatever is done must be understood, acceptable and valuable to those involved. Acceptability springs from understanding, and this in turn is based on effective communication of the right and required information to those involved.

Qualitative assessment and judgement

It is clear from the above that business and managerial performance measurement is largely qualitative (see Management in Focus 3.7). This is because organisations are created and staffed by people, and because their customers, clients and users are also

PERFORMANCE MEASUREMENT: EXAMPLE

To illustrate the point, a 35 per cent increase in sales is an overtly easy and straightforward measure of performance. There is a precise target to aim for, and whether or not it is achieved is easily quantifiable. However, the following elements have still to be addressed:

- The time period over which the increase is to take place.
- Whether the 35 per cent increase is required from every unit across the board, or whether an overall increase of 35 per cent will do.
- Whether the 35 per cent would be covered by a one-off purchase or windfall.
- Whether, if the 35 per cent increase is fulfilled the following week, the target will be revised for the future.
- Whether this is a reflection of the capacity and capability of the rest of the organisation.
- Whether this is within the workforce's capability, whether overtime will have to be worked, or whether new staff will have to be taken on.
- Any questions of location. Are there any questions of specific market/localised constraints? To what extent is it related to relative levels of prosperity in the market?
- The wider state of the market; the activities of competitors; whether the market is capable of sustaining this (or any other level of increase).
- Whether the 35 per cent increase represents an increase in the total market, or whether it means taking market share from competitors.
- Finally, where does the figure of 35 per cent come from? Who decided it and on what grounds?

Once this form of judgement and evaluation has been made, the behaviour of customers, consumers and clients has to be considered. For example, the buyer may come into the establishment, not receive instant attention, and turn round and storm out. Or a salesperson may be so busy giving excellent service to one customer that other customers are delayed, leading to dissatisfaction on their part. Or they may be dealt with by a good salesperson who has nothing to offer that really meets their needs; or by a bad salesperson, who in such a situation nevertheless persuades the customer to buy, leading to an instant sale but subsequent dissatisfaction.

The key lesson is therefore that the process cannot possibly be completely objective or rational; nor can it be quantified in isolation from the need to apply judgement. Effective qualification and judgement of performance effectiveness and success therefore relies on each of the following, even if one is delivering a numerical target and outcome:

- recognising the human signs of buyer behaviour and attitudes
- recognising the human signs of organisational behaviour and attitudes
- recognising the convergence and divergence of priorities and objectives
- recognising the importance and influence of stakeholders and participants.

The best approach is to identify the most likely outcome in the most sets of circumstances; and to concentrate primarily on this; and to deal with exceptions as and when they arise.

people. Moreover, the most overtly mathematical and precise measures of performance have to be seen in the context in which they are established and then judged and evaluated by those responsible.

Priorities

Ideally, priorities are established to ensure concentration of organisational resources to best commercial or service advantage in the pursuit of long-term customer, client and user satisfaction. In practice, it is rarely possible to achieve everything desired or required. Two basic approaches are possible (see Figure 3.1).

There is nothing intrinsically right or wrong with either approach indicated in Figure 3.1. The main issue at the outset is to know which approach is being taken and the opportunities and consequences of that choice.

Objectives

Objectives are:

- *Organisational*: reflecting the overall purpose and direction of the department/ division/function, the contribution that each is expected to make to the whole.
- *Managerial*: reflecting the contribution that different managers are expected/anticipated to make to the overall direction.
- *Professional/occupational*: reflecting the need for professional and occupational satisfaction in different staff and work categories.
- *Personal*: reflecting more general needs, especially those of job security, enhanced reward and prosperity, and advancement.
- *Present priorities*: from whatever source they are driven.
- *Future priorities*: those that begin to become apparent as a result of knowing and understanding the organisation's preferred future direction.

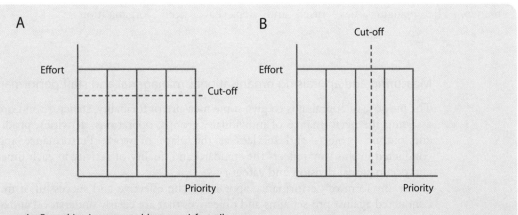

A Everything is attempted, but unsatisfactorily
B Those things that cannot be completed satisfactorily are not attempted

Figure 3.1 Establishing priorities

MANAGEMENT IN FOCUS 3.8

SUBJECTIVE AND PREJUDICIAL CONVERGENCE AND DIVERGENCE OF OBJECTIVES

It is essential to recognise the existence of these differing objectives. The best and most successful and effective organisations harmonise personal, professional and occupational objectives with those of the organisation as a whole. Where this is not possible, a certain amount of dysfunction/malfunction occurs.

For example, a manager charged with responsibility for introducing a new education policy knows that this will take several years to evaluate for success. The manager's political masters want tangible results within three months. The next promotion in the manager's career is dependent upon the satisfaction of the political masters with his/her performance. The manager has

therefore to reconcile the following:

- delivering the initiative professionally
- advancing his/her own career
- doing the work to the satisfaction of the political masters.

It is clear that doing the job properly requires persuading the political masters that a three-month measure is neither feasible nor legitimate in the circumstances. It is also clear that, on the face of it, there exists a real discrepancy between doing the job properly and receiving personal reward, recognition and advancement.

The greatest success is achieved where the potential problems have been recognised and steps have been

taken to harmonise and integrate these different forms of objectives.

The lesson is that failure is likely where little or no recognition exists of the problem. Where it is not possible to integrate organisational and personal/professional objectives, recognition of the effects on performance (especially long-term performance) is essential. Problem areas for the future can then at least be more clearly identified.

Moreover, levels of motivation and morale are normally much higher where objectives in each category are harmonised. Where objectives do diverge and conflict, people always pursue their personal and professional objectives rather than those of the organisation.

Measuring and appraising organisational, managerial and staff performance

The purpose of appraisal is to give some measure of formality, structure and order to assessing the performance of individuals, groups, operations, activities, production and output, projects and services at the place of work. Performance appraisal conducted in this way reflects the standard and quality of activity in each functional and occupational division and category.

For any form of performance appraisal to be effective and successful, it must be conducted against pre-set aims and objectives that are clearly understood and agreed by all concerned. These aims and objectives should be prioritised with deadlines for achievement. Performance targets need to be realistic and achievable, balancing the need for effective and improved performance against what is possible in the given environment and within any organisational constraints. If targets are unrealistic they will be ignored; if they are too easy, they set a wider agenda for the lowering of performance standards.

Performance appraisal needs to be a combination of regularised formal reviews, together with a continuous assessment of what is happening, based on effective and open staff management relationships. The most effective forms of appraisal are fully participative, in particular identifying problems and issues early, and taking steps to remedy matters which have arisen

The measurement of production and service activities is chiefly designed to check that everything remains on course, and where there are deviations, to identify these early, understand them, and either accommodate them and work within them, or else change direction to ensure that what is required, can still be delivered.

All performance measurement approaches can fall into disrepute if:

- They are neither believed in nor valued.
- They do not contribute to the wider success of the organisation.
- They are bureaucratic or mechanistic.
- It is the scheme and its paperwork that are important, and not the process.
- The reviews are too infrequent or missed altogether; or what is promised in them (e.g. pay awards, training, promotion, development), is not delivered in practice.

They also suffer from performance criteria being identified in general terms only. This leads to inconsistency in application, which leads in turn, to unevenness and unfairness in the measurement of staff performance, and a lack of clarity and precision in the measurement of organisational performance.

The best approach to performance measurement is to be completely open. Monitoring, review and evaluation activities are conducted on the basis of mutual understanding, trust and honesty. If staff are required to declare shortcomings in their own or departmental performance, they must be able to do so from the point of view of remedying matters. Punishments and sanctions should only be considered where there is positive evidence of negligence, persistent incompetence or a regular inability to meet agreed performance targets. Even then, other remedies ought to be considered, before turning to punishments and sanctions.

It therefore follows that there is a necessary body of skills and knowledge required of senior managers in the establishment of effective performance measurement. This has to be underpinned by the presence of positive attitudes and a determination to measure performance accurately and make improvements where required, rather than finding fault. Communication, articulation, target and objective setting, consultation, counselling, support, trust, dependency and assertiveness are all clearly necessary. If this is the basis on which performance is to be measured, there is plenty of scope for picking up genuine poor performance, whatever its cause or source.

Confidence and expectations

Everyone who comes into contact with an organisation expects to have confidence in it – confidence in the strength and quality of the overall relationship; confidence in its products and services; confidence in its continuity, reliability and stability; confidence in its continuing success and effectiveness.

People join and work for organisations, make purchases, and avail themselves of services, with certain expectations in mind. They anticipate that their expectations will be fulfilled. Problems occur when these expectations are not fulfilled. Levels of expectation are set by a variety of needs:

- *For staff*: there is the need to be well rewarded; to gain job satisfaction, fulfilment, development and achievement; to be associated with a positive and prestigious organisation or occupation; to be valued, respected and esteemed.
- *For shareholders and backers*: there is a need to receive regular positive returns on investment – to receive specific dividends and other benefits as the result of investment.
- *Customers, consumers, clients and users*: expect satisfaction and utility from the products and services; in many cases, they also expect esteem, respect and value to be enhanced.
- *Communities*: expect to feel pleased and proud to have certain organisations established and working in among them.

MANAGEMENT IN FOCUS 3.9

PERFORMANCE TARGETS IN PUBLIC SERVICES

The main problem to be addressed lies in the establishment of a valid standpoint from which to measure the performance of these services. This has to be reconciled with immediate short-term needs, drives and directions of politicians and service managers. There are also often historical biases, resource constraints and social pressures which all have to be accommodated.

The knowledge, expertise, judgement, attributes and qualities of the public service manager become critical. These form the context in which the following broad and narrow perspectives can be taken.

- *Broad*: the state of the work environment – the school, classroom, library, hospital ward, laboratory, prison; the availability, use, value, quality and appropriateness of equipment to service users and consumers; cleanliness, warmth and comfort; general ambience; professionalism of staff; currency of professional expertise; interaction of staff with consumers; prioritisation of activities; resource effectiveness, efficiency, adequacy and usage.
- *Narrow*: application of absolute standards of service delivery; speed of response to consumers; nature and content of response to users; nature and volume of complaints, failures and shortcomings; attitudes of service users to providers and vice versa; acceptance of professional responsibility for standards; commitment to professional development; personal commitment.

This is the context for setting specific aims and objectives in public services. It requires concentration on the output of specific services – and has no reference to inter-functional comparisons or league tables. This is the best basis of judgement and evaluation of performance for such services. It is to be carried out by service experts and analysts (in the same way as commercial and business analysts and experts carry out the evaluation of private sector company performance).

Problems arise when a lack of confidence sets in and when expectations are not met. Part of the wider assessment of managerial performance is therefore to understand what the nature of confidence is and what the expectations of the particular stake-holders and interested parties are, and take steps to ensure that, as far as possible, these are satisfied.

Conclusions

Each of these elements and factors is an essential and legitimate area for managerial inquiry when assessing either total organisation performance or parts and features of it. Most of these elements and factors are interrelated. Several appear under different headings. Others are directly consequential – for example, it is impossible to have good and positive organisational attitudes without having clear standards established by top management. Taken all together they reflect the fact that the performance of every organisation, and every department, division and function within it, can always be improved.

This also underlines the complexity of measuring performance successfully. This is true even where supposedly simple or direct targets have been set – for example, a simple increase in the outputs of a production line. Before such a decision can be taken, it has to be ensured that adequate volumes of components and supplies are available (or can be made available); that they can be stored; that any additional staff or overtime can be paid for; and that the increased output can be packaged, stored, distributed – and sold. It may be that such an increase adversely affects morale (for example, the need for additional production may be the latest in a long series of crises); or it may send morale sky-high, and this may subsequently lead to complacency if a positive yet realistic approach is not maintained.

So the role of the professional manager – whether chief executive officer, director, top, middle, junior or front line and supervisory – is to understand this, and to continue to attend to each of the elements and factors indicated. This is equally important when things are going well, as the reasons why success is being achieved can be fully explained and understood. When things do go wrong, and problems begin to arise, they can be identified early and nipped in the bud. This, in turn, is best achieved if all managers understand the full range of inquiry that they need to make, and that nothing happens in isolation.

The measurement of organisational and managerial performance is complex and requires a high level of contextual knowledge and understanding, as well as the capability to choose the right qualitative and quantitative measures, and the required points of inquiry.

From this, managers are able to identify what contributes to successful, effective and profitable performance for their own organisation, and that part of it for which they are responsible. They can also pinpoint:

- those activities that contribute to effective, successful and profitable organisational performance; the extent and nature of that contribution; and their effects upon each other
- those activities that do not make any direct contribution to performance
- those activities that detract from successful and effective performance, that destroy and damage it, that dilute its effectiveness

- diversions from purpose, blockages and barriers to progress
- the proportion and balance of steady-state activities with crisis handling.

It is necessary to recognise the range of parties, both internal and external, who have a legitimate interest in the organisation, who measure it for success or failure, and the measures that they bring to bear from their own point of view. Long-term viability is much more likely where the concerns of each group can be addressed and reconciled successfully. One of the main tasks of top managers is to recognise the nature and legitimacy of the interests of the different stakeholder groups and interested parties, and to take steps to see that these are widely understood and satisfied as far as possible.

From this approach to performance, assessment and measurement comes a clear understanding of what the organisation and its managers can control and influence, and what cannot be controlled or influenced. For example, it may not be possible to suppress a glut of bad or negative publicity and adverse media coverage. However, organisations can influence future coverage by responding as positively as possible in the circumstances, and by using this as a springboard to generate long-term positive interest.

Similarly, it is not possible to control particular social, legal, economic and political constraints; but it is possible to recognise and understand the extent of their influence, and to work within them. It may also not be possible in the short to medium term at least, to influence the size or nature of markets served; but again, it is possible to recognise these specific constraints, and to provide products and services as successfully, effectively and profitably as possible within them.

CRITICAL THINKING, ANALYSIS AND EVALUATION

1. Outline the advantages and disadvantages of using performance league tables for schools and hospitals. What, in your view, are the right measures of performance measures for these organisations; and how should such measures be implemented, monitored, reviewed and evaluated?
2. Discuss the view that the shareholders and the financial interests are the only stakeholders with legitimate views on the performance of organisations.
3. For the organisation of your choice, choose a set of performance indicators. Measure the performance of this organisation using the company annual report and any other information that you are able to obtain. Compare and contrast this with the statement by the Chairperson or Chief Executive Officer in the annual report. What conclusions can you draw?
4. Using a high profile public project as an example (e.g. the Channel Tunnel, the Millennium Dome, Concorde) state how, when, where and by whom this venture should be measured for success.

DEVELOPING MANAGEMENT SKILLS AND EXPERTISE

BUILDING SERVICES GROUP PLC

'I am delighted to be able to report another busy, successful and fulfilling year for BSG with profits increasing from £2.9 million to £4.3 million.

The value of work performed increased from £200 million to £290 million, an increase of 45 per cent. Adjusted earnings per share increased by 48 per cent to 13.97p from 9.43p.

An interim dividend of 1.5p per share was paid last April, and a final dividend of 2.5p per share has been recommended. Subject to its approval at the Annual General Meeting on Thursday, 2 December, the final dividend will be paid on 6 December to all shareholders on the register on 12 November.'

Strategic development

'Growth of the group this year has been focused on three areas: to develop our facilities management capability by acquisition; to grow the interior fit-out and refurbishment business organically; and to establish ourselves as a credible force in the professional new build construction management market. Starting last February, we have made a number of significant acquisitions. This includes H. Waters and Company, a northern-based property management company specialising in the leisure, transport and health sectors. Last May, we acquired the London-based property management and advisory company, Walker, Sun and Packman.

Since the year end, we have made our largest acquisition yet of the multidisciplinary facilities management services provider, Care Services Ltd. Care is a national company employing over 1700 staff offering a broad range of facilities support services.'

Trading

'Despite the global economic concerns of the past two years, demand for our services has been high. This has grown by over 25 per cent in volume, winning many of the largest and most prestigious fit-out projects available. These include the new HQ for West LB valued at £50 million, the new £12 million Mobil HQ and most recently, in a joint venture, the expanded HQ of a global investment bank in London. In Europe, the new management team has been redefining the business and has identified a number of major opportunities. Since the year-end, a £10 million project for Level 3 Communications in Dusseldorf has been awarded.

We have therefore achieved critical mass with a number of major projects under way.'

Staff development

'We measure the level and quality of service that we deliver. This has increased again this year. This is a measure of the level of commitment, positive attitudes and willingness of all the staff to continuously improve and embrace new ways of working. Their enthusiasm is a major asset to the business and once again, I want to thank them sincerely. Encouraging and maintaining the values-driven culture that has been so important in the development of the Group so far is a major priority. The Group's in-house training facility, the Academy, will continue to play its role in helping us integrate our culture and invest in our people'.

Prospects

'With the acquisition of Care completed, we will be concentrating on the integration of new businesses and realising some of the considerable potential for cross-selling available within the group. We have started the new financial year positively with the order book at a new high. Fee income margin growth will be a key objective this year, as well as expanding into new sectors and territories. With the economic outlook more stable than last year and with most of our acquisition work completed, we will now concentrate on improving the quality and visibility of our earnings. Fundamental changes are occurring in the delivery of total occupancy services and ISG is in a strong position to benefit from these changes and we look forward to the future with enthusiasm and optimism.'

David King
Chairman and Chief Executive

Source: Adapted from: ISG Plc, the building services and property maintenance group of companies.

Questions

1. Study this statement from the point of view of all stakeholders. Which groups are likely to be encouraged by the statement and why; and which are not likely to be encouraged by the statement and why?
2. Identify the areas where performance has been measured precisely; and where performance has not been measured precisely. From this, identify a set of precise performance measures that you feel would be appropriate to this particular company.
3. What further information would you need in order to be able to arrive at a fully accurate evaluation of the company's performance for this year?

Chapter four

Risk

'The greater the risk, the greater the rewards.'
Universal myth and fallacy.

'The one thing we will not risk or compromise is passenger safety.'
Michael O'Leary, Chief Executive Officer, Ryanair (2003).

'The Olympic games can no more have a deficit than a man can have a baby.'
Jean Drapeau, Mayor of Montreal, three weeks before the
City declared a $1 billion loss on the 1976 Olympics.

Chapter outline

- Introduction
- Risks and rewards
- Internal colloquy
- External colloquy
- Strategic risk management
- Operational risk management
- Theft and fraud
- Dirty tricks
- Factors outside the control of the organisation
- Accidents
- Single events and errors
- Applying risk management
- Early warning systems
- Dealing with crises and emergencies
- Other aspects of risk management
- Conclusions

Chapter objectives

After studying this chapter, you should be able to:

- understand the wide-ranging coverage of risk management

- understand the importance and value of risk management to effective organisational performance

- understand how risk management techniques may be applied in particular situations

- understand the need to evaluate consequences of particular courses of action

- understand the importance of risk management as a part of professional managerial expertise.

● Introduction

The purpose of this chapter is to introduce and illustrate that part of organisational, managerial and environmental knowledge and understanding that is concerned with those things that can, and do, go wrong from time to time.

The nature of risk is a reflection of the amount that is known and understood about a particular situation, or as a precursor in deciding to do something. High levels of risk are incurred when little is known or understood; the more that is known and understood, the lower the level of risk because everybody knows and understands what they are letting themselves in for, and the opportunities and consequences that are likely to arise. Uncertainty exists where there is no knowledge of the particular situation. As a direct consequence, risk is insurable, uncertainty is not. The level of risk involved in something is therefore dependent upon the completeness of knowledge and understanding about it; and this knowledge and understanding is then used to present the fullest range of outcomes possible in the given set of circumstances. In particular, a full evaluation is required of best and worst outcomes, so that those involved know and understand the opportunities and consequences of both success and failure before anything is undertaken.

Uncertainty exists where there is no knowledge or understanding. One key part of managerial expertise is coping with uncertainty (see Chapter 1). The first step towards coping with uncertainty is to gather as much knowledge, information and understanding of what is not presently known or understood. This is to move the collective levels of expertise at least to relative familiarity, and from this to begin to build again so as to know and understand the risks involved in whatever is contemplated, and to take active steps towards minimising and, where possible, eliminating them.

● Risks and rewards

'The greater the risk, the greater the reward' is a cosy, easy and exciting mantra for organisations and managers to adopt. It is also dangerous nonsense. The best managers relate the assurance of rewards directly to the elimination of risks so far as is possible in the circumstances (see Management in Focus 4.1).

The correlation between risks and rewards is therefore dependent upon seeing risks as obstacles to progress. These obstacles have either to be circumvented or removed. Their effects on what is intended require full acknowledgement and understanding as above; and if the obstacles cannot be removed, then there is a question of whether or not what is proposed should go ahead at all (see Management in Focus 4.2).

● Internal colloquy

It is essential to realise that even when a venture has been fully evaluated, and steps taken to minimise the risks involved or inherent, this is only the first step in strategic and operational risk management. Before a detailed evaluation and implementation plan can be considered, the capability, expertise and willingness of staff have to be assessed. Existing processes and systems have to be capable of delivering what the new proposal or venture requires; or else new systems and processes have to be designed and integrated with what exists already.

MANAGEMENT IN FOCUS 4.1

RICHARD BRANSON AND THE VIRGIN ORGANISATION

We took incredible risks when we first went into the airline industry. We knew that we would be up against everything that the established airlines, the national flag-carriers, could throw at us. They tried to affect everything, from the availability of take-off and landing slots, to questioning our quality or commitment, or reliability – indeed, the very stability of the company as a whole.

(Branson, *The Money Programme Lecture* – BBC 1998)

The picture that Branson paints is of a highly risky and very exciting venture. The perception, excitement and adventure surrounding the whole of the Virgin organisation is enhanced by the very high profile adventures in which Branson himself has been involved in the past. For example, he has made three attempts to circumnavigate the world in a hot air balloon, as well as being shipwrecked in the Atlantic Ocean, before going on to claim the Blue Riband for the fastest Atlantic crossing by boat.

Lessons

Branson's statement should be rewritten to make clear that, because they knew that there would be risks, the company would take (and did take) active steps to ensure that each of these eventualities had been fully known and understood before the services were introduced. Consequently, the 'incredible risks' described by Branson were fully recognised, acknowledged and understood as a prelude to ensuring that they were minimised so that the Virgin Organisation would be able to operate within the given limits and constraints. It should also be noted that Branson took every step possible towards minimising the risks involved in his ballooning and boating adventures so as to ensure that these too would have the greatest possible chance of success (ibid.).

Collective and individual staff perceptions have to be managed. This is less of a problem where there is a collective cohesive and positive culture (see below, Chapter 16). However, fundamental questions have to be addressed as to whether the new venture is known, believed and perceived to be glamorous and prestigious; whether it is a necessary evil (or a necessary good); and whether ultimately it represents a step on the road to progress. Fundamental issues of where the resources are coming from, and especially whether these are to be taken away from existing work, must be made clear; and if the staff do not understand or support this, then they may resist the idea itself.

● External colloquy

A detailed understanding is required of what external stakeholders are to make of what is proposed. Detailed knowledge and understanding is required of the likely

MANAGEMENT IN FOCUS 4.2

OPULENCE: THE NEXT GLOSSY MAGAZINE

Opulence is the working title of a proposed new glossy magazine. The magazine is to be 160 pages long and presented in the same style, format and approximate size as *Vogue, Cosmopolitan* and *FHM*.

The style therefore clearly draws from glossy magazines pitched presently at both men and women; and indeed, the magazine's proposed uniqueness and selling and branding point is to be the fact that it is to attract both male and female readers. The received wisdom is that this has never been tried before in the magazine trade, though it does work in other aspects of publishing. For example, Colin Forbes, the thriller writer, states that his readership is divided evenly between the sexes; and indeed, about half the people who buy *The Sun* newspaper are women.

Opulence is to be published monthly at £4.95. The proposed content of the magazine is as follows:

- editorial – 4 pages
- celebrity interviews – 25 pages
- book and music reviews – 10 pages
- travel – 25 pages
- finance – 6 pages
- property – 6 pages
- exclusive news scoops – 6 pages

- advertising – 30 pages.

This leaves a certain amount of leeway for other features, editorial, advertorial and other matters that are certain to turn out to be of importance to the proposed readership.

Opulence is the brainchild of Graham Edwards. Graham has worked in the publishing industry for the past ten years on a series of glossy magazines in London and New York. His last post was as assistant managing editor of *Vanity Fair* in New York. Accordingly, he has experience of managing mass-circulation, glossy, high-value/high-brand/high-cost magazines for a wide variety of markets.

For several years, he has identified, as a gap in the market, the fact that there is no glossy magazine for men and women. In spite of the fact that, as stated above, the received wisdom of the industry is that it cannot be done, *Opulence* is to fill the gap. Specifically, it is to be pitched at: men and women with disposable income of £40,000 each or £60,000 per couple. These men and women hold professional jobs in banking, retail, law and management within these sectors, and also in engineering, travel, transport and public services.

The intended circulation is 120,000 per issue. At £4.95 per sale, the intended circulation brings in £594,000 per issue.

The minimum viable circulation is 60,000. At £4.95, the minimum circulation brings in £297,000. It is unviable to go below 60,000 because production costs rise as follows:

- 20,000 copies – £2 per copy
- 50,000 copies – £1.50 per copy
- 60,000 copies – 80p per copy
- 120,000 copies – 50p per copy.

Additionally, the advertising revenues drop sharply if circulation falls below 60,000. At above 60,000, a single page advertisement can be charged at £8000 per page; below 60,000, the charge drops to £3000. Over several months, Graham met with six venture capitalists to seek their backing, all of whom turned him down. Overall, there was a generally favourable response to the idea, but the crunch came on editorial and especially the market – on Graham's own admission, nobody had ever tried to produce this kind of magazine for a male/female split market.

The key lesson is that the risks have been known, understood and evaluated in full detail before the proposal or venture has gained life. Edwards himself therefore knows and understands where the risks lie; and he will be able to explain this if, and when, he ever gets backing for this particular product. In particu- lar, both he and anyone who can be persuaded to back the venture, will know and under- stand the barriers and obsta- cles to progress. Their first commitment is therefore to ensure that these barriers and obstacles can be overcome, otherwise there is no point in pursuing the venture at all. In particular, pitching the maga- zine at both male and female readers is in direct contrast to the past history of success- ful magazine launches. This means that there is addition- ally the question of where to locate the magazine on retail- ers' shelves, which tend to be divided on gender lines. This too is a critical question that has to be addressed.

and possible ranges of customer, client and end-user responses, not only for the new venture or proposal, but also in terms of the response to the existing range of products and services (see Management in Focus 4.3).

Shareholders have also to be satisfied that their returns will continue, ideally because of the new venture or proposal, and at least in spite of it. Shareholders need to know and understand the worst possible consequences; and they normally need to be satis- fied that they will at least get their money back over the long term. To that end they are entitled to see detailed forecasts and projections (see below, Chapters 12 and 13), to have questions answered, and any doubts and fears addressed. In particular, share- holders are entitled to be absolutely certain that their funds are not to be used in glam- orous, exciting and untargeted ventures and adventures, without additionally being satisfied that there are commercially viable prospects and returns available also. This is the full basis and context in which strategic and operational risk management is then learned in detail, and put into practice. It is increasingly usual to separate out the discipline of risk management into strategic and operational issues as follows:

● Strategic risk management is concerned with creating the conditions, attitudes and expertise for defining the organisation's approach to risk; identifying those areas of risk with which the organisation is, or may be, faced; and ensuring that the desired approach is undertaken.
● Operational risk management is concerned with the detail of risk management in everyday activities. This means addressing all of those things that can, and do, go wrong, and ensuring that steps are then taken to reduce, minimise and, where possible, eliminate risk from specific activities.

● Strategic risk management

A strategic approach to risk management requires that the components of risk and uncertainty that can, and do (or may possibly), affect the organisation and its envi- ronment must be studied so as to ensure that anyone in a top, senior or executive position understands the full range of issues that must be considered for any situa- tion that could conceivably arise. In particular, a strategic approach to risk management requires the following:

MANAGEMENT IN FOCUS 4.3

MARKS & SPENCER'S ENTRY INTO THE YOUTH MARKET

In the mid-1990s, following a period in which there were many changes in the leadership and direction of the company, Marks & Spencer Plc – the UK's premium brand quality clothing and food retailer – decided to enter the youth fashion clothing market.

At first glance the idea was attractive. Marks & Spencer's customer base, while more or less stable, was ageing. The company had a worthy but dull reputation, and had spare store capacity. The youth clothing market was booming, especially in the good-quality and value ranges where other stores such as Top Shop, New Look and Gap were expanding.

Marks & Spencer consequently launched its Per Una range of fashion clothing; and this launch was reinforced by using David Beckham, the then England football captain, fashion icon and role model, in marketing and advertising campaigns.

There were high levels of all-round media interest, and this was followed by initial commercial success. However, over the medium term (1998–2002), sales of all products fell away. External audits by the company concluded that:

- The company gave prominence to the new products rather than to the steady-state and assured ranges demanded by the core customer base.
- The core customer base drifted away, feeling that Marks & Spencer was now a youth outlet and no longer for them.
- The youth market persisted in seeing Marks & Spencer as the shop to which their parents went. Once they saw that the new ranges were good, but not unique, exceptional or highly desirable, the younger customers went back to their familiar and assured outlets.

Over the period 2002–05, Marks & Spencer further repositioned itself at the centre of what it knew and understood to be its assured market, only to find that this market had moved on. Tesco and Asda now produced their own clothing ranges, and they and the other supermarket chains (Sainsbury, Morrisons and Waitrose) now also produced food ranges of a quality comparable with that previously exclusive to Marks & Spencer.

In 2005 and 2006, Marks & Spencer consequently undertook a further re-positioning offering a centre-of-town alternative to the big supermarket chains, which were now concentrating their core activities on out-of-town retail parks. Marks & Spencer also further consolidated their position by developing food-only outlets in city and town centres, concentrating on what the core customers would buy and on the circumstances under which they would buy it.

The lesson is that the company based its initiative on perception rather than reality. The company consequently endured almost a decade of uncertainty and volatility, essentially because it failed to tackle the problem of external colloquy and customer response when it entered into an overtly glamorous new venture. Glamorous or not, new ventures must still be capable of delivering enduring levels of profit.

- *Assessment of sectoral trends*: whether the sector is growing or declining, either in size or prosperity; whether these trends are likely to continue; the nature of factors that are affecting particular trends at present; and the nature of factors that could conceivably affect these trends in the future.
- *Knowledge and understanding of substitutes and alternatives*: evaluating the possibilities of whether customers, consumers and clients could, or might, change their buying habits as an alternative to what the particular organisation provides; and whether it is necessary, both now and in the future, to have a range of responses available.
- *Knowing and understanding social, political and economic issues, drives and restraints*: in particular this means knowing and understanding the likely, possible and potential effects of changes in interest and exchange rates, credit squeezes, and overall purchasing power (which may be affected by such things as taxation increases, or increases in charges for transport, fuel, energy, gas and electricity).
- *The constitution of the organisation*: this is assessed and evaluated from the point of view of capability and willingness to undertake present ranges of activities in their present volumes; proposed ranges of activities in proposed volumes; and changes to internal structures and systems.
- *Evaluation of outcomes*: at a strategic level, this means that all initiatives, ventures and proposals require evaluation from the point of view of:
  - identification of the best, medium and worst outcomes
  - analysis and evaluation of any critical obstacles or incidents
  - evaluating the capability to extricate oneself from the particular situation (or not) and the consequences of having to do this
  - assessment of the full range of costs and benefits, to the organisation and all its stakeholders.
- *Other behavioural and perceptual issues*: in particular the comfort and commitment which the staff are going to bring to present and envisaged ranges of activities, products and services; this is an especial problem where mergers and takeovers are proposed, or where there are radical shifts into new products and services.
- *Early warning systems*: early warning systems are based on the collective capability of the organisation and its managers to have at their disposal the fullest possible data concerning the nature of organisation activities, the quality and volume of products and services, and the present levels of activity within the markets and environments served. In particular, organisations ought to be able to know, understand and evaluate the likely, possible and potential effects on the overall ability to conduct business of: epidemics; strikes and disputes; wars and terrorist attacks; major incidents and disasters; and sudden unavailability of supplies, raw materials and information. Internally, there needs to be a strategic approach to organisational processes, databases and information systems.

At a strategic level also, there are specific issues that have to be covered in terms of theft and fraud, and of dirty tricks.

Theft and fraud

All organisations are susceptible to theft and fraud, both petty pilfering, and also on a large scale.

An organisational view is required of what constitutes petty pilfering. This normally comes out in the extent to which the organisation is prepared to tolerate the de facto theft of consumables such as pens and paper by staff; and also the extent to which the organisation is prepared to tolerate the use of its telephones and computers for personal convenience. This sounds petty and trivial; however, it is essential to realise that small thefts can, and do, grow into grand larceny if not checked; and that the problems can, and do, grow as a consequence, and may become unmanageable if rules are not made clear and enforced (see Management in Focus 4.4).

Fraud on a grand scale may be carried out on an individual or institutional basis. In both cases, it is the institution and employees that suffer; and this invariably leads to suffering also on the part of staff, shareholders and backers, and suppliers. In many cases also, wider reputation is lost through adverse media coverage; this can, and does, affect supplier confidence and the willingness of potential staff to come and work for the organisation. This reinforces the need for clear and absolute sets of standards, behaviour and performance. Each of these have to be reinforced by the presence, implementation and enforcement of rules and procedures, reporting relations, and standards of conduct; and each of these in turn, has to be underpinned by sanctions when broken (see Management in Focus 4.5).

MANAGEMENT IN FOCUS 4.4

SMALL PROBLEMS

In the 1970s, the CIA issued all of its staff with American Express cards. The stated purpose was to ensure a speedy processing of small purchases made by its staff for operational purposes. Having the cards and sending the statements directly to CIA Headquarters was to remove the lengthy and expensive process of checking, verification, agreement and signing-off that had been in place at the time. This process itself was becoming increasingly complex as the result of ever-greater internationalisation of the Agency's activities.

The system was discontinued in 1996. The US Treasury found itself unable and unwilling to divulge the amounts of money that had been lost as the result of payments simply being paid automatically. Anecdotal evidence subsequently emerged over the period 2002 to 2004, that the CIA issue cards had been used by staff to purchase, among other things, cars, houses (including property abroad), holidays, and school and college fees. Anecdotal evidence produced over the same period also pointed to the reason for the whole

process having got to this pitch: that no purchases made on these cards were ever questioned.

The lesson is that strategic management systems have to be made to work. It is additionally the case that there was never any collective conscious intention to defraud the CIA; this emerged at a later date. Furthermore, responsibility for checking expenditure was never allocated. The end result was that there was a strong and rigorous system in place; however, it was simply not used, but rather just assumed to be working.

MANAGEMENT IN FOCUS 4.5

LARGE-SCALE THEFT AND FRAUD: THE EXAMPLE OF BARINGS BANK

Barings Bank had existed for over 300 years when it chose to employ Nick Leeson to go to Singapore, and head up its Far Eastern operation.

Nick Leeson was a successful trader in financial instruments, currency transactions and foreign exchange. He was chosen as a high flier; and chosen also because he had a sense of adventure and cultural understanding which was required when relocating thousands of miles away. When he arrived in Singapore, he was given a clear reporting line to managers in corporate headquarters in London, and he was expected to keep them informed of progress. From time to time, he would be visited by headquarters' staff from London to check on progress.

There was however no supervision of his daily activities. Nor was there any close scrutiny of the currencies and commodities in which he and his staff traded.

For a while everything went well. However, over a three-month period, Leeson himself engaged in a series of bad trades, and he also sanctioned the involvement of his staff in these trades. As the result of lack of full knowledge and understanding, the position quickly became a crisis. Without proper supervision, Leeson opened a 'phantom account' and apportioned the losses to this.

This crossed from a lack of knowledge and understanding into fraud when he reproduced another organisation's letterhead in order to give substance to the phantom account. This was then submitted as a summary of trade to the Singapore authorities, and to his own headquarters in London. When the account was finally inspected formally it was found to be £600 million in deficit. The authorities asked for their money and Barings foreclosed. The company was subsequently sold for £1 to ING, the Dutch finance house.

The example illustrates *in extremis* what can happen when staff work practices, and production and service performance, are not closely scrutinised or monitored. It is essential for all managers, in every organisation, whatever their sector or location, to know and understand the potential for this kind of activity to take place, and the potentially catastrophic consequences if systems are not in place and also enforced rigorously.

Dirty tricks

All organisations engage in competitive practices. These practices exist in all areas of organisational and managerial activity, and are not simply confined to product and service delivery and performance. Organisations compete for assurances on the supply side, for technological advantages, for key staff and expertise, and for customer knowledge, understanding, acceptance and engagement. Companies and organisations engage in marketing and public relations, and some of this can be targeted at denigrating the competition and alternatives, as well as building up one's own position.

Problems arise when, again individually or institutionally, the line is crossed between legitimate competition (however aggressive) and criminal activity. Thus for example:

- It is legitimate to offer potential staff inducements to come and join a particular organisation; it is not legitimate to induce them to breach their existing contractual duties and obligations.
- It is legitimate to market aggressively to potential customers and clients; it is not legitimate to tell lies about their present product and service providers.
- It is legitimate to transfer funds between budget headings within an organisation; it is not legitimate to pay individuals bonuses out of these transfers at the expense of the future well-being of the organisation and the rest of its staff.
- It is legitimate for top and senior managers to pay themselves (and be paid) bonuses in accordance with the constitution of the organisation; it is not legitimate for those same managers to use the organisation as a personal bank account, effectively to be looted for personal gain at the expense of the rest of the staff and stakeholders.

By the same token, it is additionally essential to guard against the risks inherent in talking up an organisation's product, service, staff or share performance to the point at which it is neither sustainable nor true. This becomes a form of 'dirty tricks' when the organisation, its managers and staff, start to believe their own rhetoric, and to act as if their own rhetoric were actually the truth.

These forms of behaviour are often illegal; and they are always unethical (see below, Chapter 5). The risks involved are wide-ranging, as follows:

- Some may be trivial, normally consisting of passing media commentary on a blemish to the organisation; these are normally quickly forgotten if the matter is clearly a single aberration in an otherwise excellent organisation.
- A series of events and issues may become known and cause the media and other stakeholders to take an active interest in the organisation's conduct and performance.
- Staff demotivation and demoralisation can be caused by known, believed and perceived sharp practice within the organisation; this problem is compounded where these issues are known, believed or perceived to be allowed to exist and continue.
- There will be loss of customer, supplier and stakeholder confidence if the errors and crises persist; again, the problem is compounded where it becomes known and understood that the organisation is not tackling these issues.

The key lesson is to know and understand the full range of risks, outcomes and consequences which can, or might, occur as the result of choosing to go down such paths; or of doing nothing when it becomes clear that some organisation functions are acting in these ways on their own initiatives.

An organisation-wide approach to theft, fraud and sharp practice is therefore clearly essential so as to minimise the chances of things going wrong, as described above, and additionally so as to be able to take remedial action quickly when problems do occur.

● Factors outside the control of the organisation

Addressing factors outside the control of the organisation is essential for effective strategic approaches to risk. Addressing factors outside the control of the organisation means knowing and understanding the likely, possible and potential effects of events and actions which include the following.

● Political instability, war and terrorist attacks, and their effects on the ability of the organisation to conduct business, and on the confidence of customers and consumers.

● Changes in the weather and consequent changes in customer and consumer behaviour; a very hot summer, for example, may cause a serious loss of trade to local businesses as customers go overseas for their holidays; or the same thing may cause a glut of trade if customers choose to stay at home. It is not possible to predict absolutely which way events such as these will turn out; it is essential to take active steps to find out the likely outcome so as to be as well prepared as possible.

● Changes in currency values and exchange rates and their effects on consumer propensity to spend; and changes in interest rates and their effects on consumer confidence.

The result of a strategic approach to risk, and detailed consideration of the market and environment, criminal activities, and factors outside the organisation's control, ought to be a detailed knowledge and understanding of the worst possible set of circumstances in which the organisation might conceivably be required to operate. This reinforces the need for absolute standards and priority areas of attention, and the need to enforce proper conduct and behaviour with clear policies drawn up and implemented to meet the particular concerns of the organisation. This fundamental approach is then translated into action through operational approaches to risk management.

● Operational approaches to risk management

At an operational level, the priority is to know and understand which events are most likely to occur, where and why. It then becomes a priority for all managers, supervisors and section heads to take active steps to prevent these events occurring so far as is reasonably practicable. The following areas for attention vary between, and within, organisations, departments, divisions and functions. The key areas for attention are as follows:

● patterns of behaviour
● accidents
● single events and errors.

Patterns of behaviour

Risk management of patterns of behaviour means that it is essential to be aware of the potential for, and effects of, bullying, victimisation, harassment and discrimination. Each is damaging and ultimately destructive to motivation and morale if not stamped out immediately it becomes apparent. Each becomes more and more difficult to deal with the longer it is allowed to persist (see also below, Chapter 20). The outcome internally is that resources and energy are consumed in dealing with these cases. Externally, customer and consumer confidence can be affected, especially when it becomes clear that such problems are endemic or institutional. People would rather not deal with organisations that conduct themselves in these ways.

Bullying, victimisation, harassment and discrimination are extreme examples of collective and individual behaviour. As well as these extremes, operational risk assessments are required to ensure that overall standards of conduct and behaviour within departments, divisions and functions are assured and enforced. The need is to know and understand the effects on staff cohesion and working relations of allowing, and de facto condoning, different patterns of behaviour. It is essential to know and understand that there is a direct relationship between behaviour and performance; and to know and understand that failure to manage behaviour always affects performance adversely. It is therefore essential to be able to assess the likely and potential consequences of allowing particular patterns of behaviour to persist unchecked (see Management in Focus 4.6).

Accidents

Accidents occur everywhere. From an operational risk management point of view, the need is to ensure that accidents are kept to an absolute minimum. This part of risk management requires attention to the nature and quality of the working environment, patterns of work, specific health and safety aspects, and the use of technology. Health and safety management normally requires that all staff are trained and briefed in every aspect of the operational environment, especially in relation to technology usage and emergency procedures. It is impossible to eliminate the chance of accidents occurring; it is essential to take steps to ensure that they occur as infrequently as possible. An isolated accident is a cause for concern all round, but normally carries little subsequent long-term risk. Regular accidents are damaging to morale and performance, as discussed above, and expensive in terms of resources and energy when they have to be dealt with, investigated and evaluated.

Single events and errors

Single events and errors are impossible to manage; they will always occur. The operational management priority is to ensure that the risk is kept to a minimum. This is achieved through the creation of the right quality of working life and environment, patterns of activities and behaviour, that ensure that overall risk is minimised. The whole is then enforced through inspection and supervision systems and procedures (see Management in Focus 4.7).

Analysing risk

Analysing risk requires the consideration of two key elements:

- What is the risk of particular events and circumstances occurring?
- What is the probability of the particular events and circumstances occurring?

The outcome of expert, comprehensive and effective risk analysis is the ability to take and implement informed decisions. This is so that whether things succeed or fail, those involved will know and understand the reasons, and can use this knowledge and understanding to better inform future decisions, proposals and initiatives.

MANAGEMENT IN FOCUS 4.6

ROBERT ARCHER AND THE INFORMATION SYSTEMS DEPARTMENT

Robert Archer was recently appointed manager of the information systems division at a large firm of business technology consultants. Robert has taken over from Jack Webb, who retired six months ago after working for the firm all his life. In between, there was a period of eight weeks when the division was run by Malcolm Smith, another long-serving employee. Malcolm Smith made it his business to impose himself and his ways of doing things on the rest of the staff. Smith was not popular; and most of the staff evidently continue to fear and hate him. There have been rumours that he has hit two other individuals in recent weeks. There are a total of 20 staff in the information systems division, 8 men and 12 women, each with an individual cubicle and workstation. Individuals may leave their workstations at any time provided that it is for no more than five minutes. In addition, everyone gets half an hour for lunch; the manager is entitled to one hour.

Morale is low. Two members of staff, Shenaz Ali and Rachel Ling, have recently had a stand-up argument over 'a personal matter', and it is clearly only a matter of time before they come to

blows. Some of the other staff are quite looking forward to this and seem to be egging them on. Another member of staff, Paul French, is awaiting investigation over the alleged sending of obscene e-mails; the notes have been sent from his e-mail address, but he vigorously denies the allegation and alleges that someone has cracked his password and is out to make trouble.

Because of the eight-week delay in Robert's appointment, all staff have missed out on productivity bonuses and commissions for the past nine weeks. The longest-serving member of staff, David Jones, has quite openly given up altogether; he feels very strongly that he should have been given the manager's job when the previous incumbent retired, so that his own pension would be enhanced when he himself retires in two year's time, and so that he could have his own office and bit of peace and quiet.

Robert Archer has now been in post for two months. He is wondering what course to take. His own manager, Harriet Green, now wants to know what Robert is going to do, when and how. Harriet was very keen for Robert to be appointed to the post;

indeed, he was her preferred candidate. Robert is 32 years old and well qualified. Before his appointment, he had been with the firm for six months as an information systems analyst. His information systems work was excellent, and he was deemed to have shown 'managerial potential'. In particular, the appointment of Robert was to get the division to look forward rather than backwards.

This illustrates the complexities of behaviour that ought to be addressed from an operational risk management point of view. In particular, it illustrates the sort of disruptions and divisions that can quickly arise in any organised situation when patterns of behaviour and conduct are not strictly established or enforced. This has allowed a combination of other adverse perceptions to grow up including:

- the idea that the manager's job should provide peace and quiet, and an enhanced pension
- the idea that rumours of fighting and assault are allowed to persist without being directly managed
- the idea that specific incidents are not investigated

immediately they become apparent.

The clear implication is that, as the result of the situation described above, sustained effective work is impossible.

There is therefore a risk to the organisation in terms of:

● continued ability to deliver required levels of performance
● continued ability to

satisfy customers, clients and end-users of the services provided by this particular division
● and an unwillingness to do anything about it.

The techniques available for effective risk analysis are as follows:

● *Specific factor analyses*: in which a particular issue or factor is entered into a given scenario, proposal or set of circumstances, and its likely and possible outcomes and effects evaluated. Specific factors can be considered in either linear or complex terms. it is certain that anything which is finally implemented following specific factor risk analyses, will have to survive in a complex and changing set of circumstances.

● *Random factor analyses*: in which single or multiple issues and factors are entered by chance or at random into a given scenario, proposal or set of circumstances, and their possible and potential outcomes evaluated. Random factors can be introduced either by choice or by chance; or they may be drawn from a list using random number tables.

● *'What if?' approaches*: which are simpler to introduce because they can be started by a simple statement, using any or all of the questions above. This approach is often limited, however, by personal, professional, collective or institutional lack of capability or willingness to consider the fullest possible range of issues and factors that could conceivably occur (see Management in Focus 4.8).

Each approach depends for its effectiveness on the quality of the information available at the time of risk assessment; this in turn is dependent on the overall understanding of the organisational and operating environment, and the circumstances that may cause this to change.

Each of these approaches can then be used to assess the probability of particular outcomes occurring. The establishment of probability or likelihood then needs further managerial evaluation and analysis to determine whether or not the outcome is mathematically certain or not. Where it is not (as in the overwhelming majority of cases), managerial debate is then required. This then leads to an informed and expert judgement on which particular decisions can be taken; the risk of undertaking particular initiatives and proposals can be assessed; and organisations and their managers additionally develop an aspect of professional discipline which enhances their own detailed expertise and understanding in this critical area of activity (see Management in Focus 4.9).

● Applying risk management

Strategic and operational risk management is only effective if it is enforced. The Confederation of British Industry stated that over the period 1985–2005, the number of organisations with risk management policies had risen from 30 per cent

MANAGEMENT IN FOCUS 4.7

SINGLE EVENTS AND ERRORS: EXAMPLES

- During routine maintenance, a paint scraper worth 30p was accidentally dropped into the torpedo chamber of the USS *Swordfish*, an American navy nuclear submarine, and jammed the loading piston for the torpedoes. For a week, divers worked to try to free the piston while the submarine was waterborne, but all attempts failed. The submarine had to be dry-docked. Subsequent repairs cost nearly £100,000.

- The *Mariner 1* space probe was launched from Cape Canaveral with the purpose of orbiting the planet Venus. All calculations were checked and double-checked; this was to ensure that the extremely complex and precise programme that had to be followed was fully accurate. The programme required that after 13 minutes of flight, a booster engine would give acceleration of up to 25,000 miles per hour to *Mariner 1*. After 44 minutes, 9800 solar cells would unfold to provide further energy. After 80 days, the computer would calculate the final course corrections; and after 100 days, the space probe would circle Venus. Four minutes after take-off, *Mariner 1* plunged into the Atlantic Ocean. Inquiries later revealed that a minus sign had been omitted from the instructions fed into the computer.

- Another example of such an error was the Pan Am security operation that triggered a bomb scare, as described in Management in Focus 3.4.

The lesson is that each of these events, rationally considered, could have been prevented. If the programmes had been rationally managed, computer programmes for the space probe would have been checked again; additional decking would have been provided on the submarine; and the crew of the airliner would have been called to account, if necessary directly, rather than taking such a heavy-handed approach. Each of the examples does however indicate the propensity for things to go wrong by chance. When chance occurrences such as these occur, it is essential that steps are taken to ensure that they do not occur again. However, as stated in the text above, it is impossible to eliminate every eventuality from working situations.

to 92 per cent (CBI, 2005). However, this has occurred alongside a combination of organisational, institutional, strategic and operational errors which have nevertheless continued, and which the examples in this chapter illustrate.

The need therefore is to ensure that standards of conduct, behaviour and performance are related to the strategic and operational approaches to risk outlined above. Also as stated above, standards need to be enforced and this requires that sanctions are applied to those who breach them. This is only achievable if the organisation's top and senior managers know and understand that it is in their interests to do so. They then need to take the additional step of ensuring that risk management is also an operational priority. Additionally, whoever is to be responsible for risk management within the organisation requires genuine influence and authority, and the

MANAGEMENT IN FOCUS 4.8

FUEL COSTS IN THE AIR TRANSPORT INDUSTRY

In 2005 and 2006, the price of all fossil fuels rose steeply. This was variously blamed on:

- the oil companies, who saw the global political instability as a way of driving up energy prices and therefore securing short and medium-term price and income advantages for themselves, as a hedge against the day when prices would start to fall
- oil market traders, who were using the media reportage of high prices together with the political uncertainty to drive prices higher
- political initiatives undertaken by the United States and EU, which were deemed to drive prices up
- the huge and increasing demand for fuel and energy in the emerging markets and economies of India and China
- the use of fuel supplies by many of the main supplying countries (especially Russia and the Middle Eastern states) as a bargaining chip to secure political advantages.

Each is worthy of analysis. However, from an organisation management point of view, the main priority is the capability and willingness to assess how high fuel prices might rise, and then to extrapolate further still to try and assess how high they might conceivably go if crude oil prices continue to rise ever further, the point at which they will cause a crisis for the organisation itself, and the point at which this one factor would drive the company or organisation out of business. This then informs the risk assessment of entering into new ventures, investing in technology, or operating any plant or machinery. It will also help to inform transport costs and delivery charges, and may also give indications of possible upward changes in the costs incurred through heating and lighting for premises, and energy charges for activities.

ability to impose sanctions for particular breaches of rules for conduct, behaviour and performance. Such persons also require the ability to impose delays and investigations on operational proposals and initiatives when the matters of risk relate to the competitive environment, and new product and service development. There is an overall general need for all managers to know and understand that they operate within a risky environment, from the point of view of risk minimisation as well as remedying adverse events and incidents.

Early warning systems

Managers at all organisational levels require early warning systems. Such systems are required in each of the areas of environmental assessment and organisational understanding mentioned above. Early warning systems include:

- Regular professional updates on the state of markets, the economy, product and service performance, the activities of competitors and alternatives, and technological advances and developments.

MANAGEMENT IN FOCUS 4.9

MATALAN

In early 2006, amid difficult retail trading conditions, Matalan, the good-value clothing and household goods chain, announced that it was having to make a special payment of £20 million to offset the shortcomings and under-performance of its computer-based operational and management information systems. This system had been installed on the advice of Kurt Salmon Associates, an information systems and management consultancy practice. In May 2006, Matalan considered suing Kurt Salmon in order to try to recoup some of the losses.

The lesson is that any risk assessment and analysis carried out in advance of the installation ought to have considered:

● What could possibly go wrong with the installation and implementation?
● What costs and charges could this possibly or conceivably cause?
● What would be the consequences of having to consider legal action against the consultancy?
● What it would then take to put matters right?

Such an approach would have helped to inform the choice of system made by the company, as well as providing a much clearer understanding of the basis on which the consultancy was being engaged, and the key results required.

● Regular scouring of the business, professional and news media so as to be aware of the events that they suggest are, or might be, important to the future. This is not to say that these events *will* be important in the future, but expert managers will be able to use this knowledge to help form their own judgements.
● Early signs of dissatisfaction among staff about something. Again this may, or may not, be important, but knowing and understanding that there is a bit of trouble or grumbling is again useful information
● Early signs of increases in individual grievances and disputes, absenteeism and staff turnover.
● Early indications of organisational costs beginning to rise in particular areas without apparent reason.
● Early signs of rising levels of customer complaints.
● Early signs of hold-ups and disputes on the supply side.
● Early signs of malfunction in information and administration systems and processes.

The overall outcome is to ensure that managers know and understand every aspect of their domain; and in the context of risk management, they build their knowledge and understanding of where things can, and do, go wrong; and immediately, where things might be about to go wrong. Managers faced with these issues then construct a series of priorities designed to ensure that they are aware of the potential problems, and have a range of approaches that can be taken according to whether things do in fact occur, and how, when and where they do so (see Management in Focus 4.10).

MANAGEMENT IN FOCUS 4.10

EARLY WARNING SYSTEMS AT GEC

When he was the Chief Executive at GEC, Arnold Weinstock used to either meet with or telephone his top managers on a weekly basis. During these conversations, he would question each manager closely about the performance of his/her division, and this would always include matters to do with costs, sales, staffing and supply-side issues. Failure to give precise assurances was always unacceptable; and this failure did, from time to time, result in some staff being 'transferred'.

The process had two clear outcomes. The first was that Mr Weinstock always knew well in advance where troubles might occur, and so he could work through the matters with top managers, and endorse their preferred lines of approach. The second outcome was that top managers knew and understood that they were expected to do this and that failure to do so would always be a major omission, and could get them transferred elsewhere.

By the time of Mr Weinstock's departure from the company, he had generated a cash surplus of £2.5 billion, partially at least through ensuring that both he and his top managers paid constant attention to what could possibly go wrong and took early steps to remedy matters whenever they could.

Dealing with crises and emergencies

All organisations from time to time.face crises and emergencies caused by:

- combinations of circumstances
- series of accidents and chances
- 'one of those things'
- as well as by ineptitude, incompetence, negligence, fraud and other criminal activity.

The managerial priority is to face the crisis or emergency; and a very fine balance has to be struck between providing a quick and effective response, and taking time to gather enough information to provide the actual response required.

Much of the work ought to have been done in advance through knowing and understanding the range of risks inherent in the particular situation, and having systems and procedures in place to respond as and when things do occur. The manager then deals thoroughly with whatever has occurred.

The organisational, managerial and human priority in all crises and emergencies is to ensure that whatever is done in response is clear, honest and effective as far as possible. People expect to be treated honestly in response to their legitimate concerns. Failure to do so, and inability or unwillingness to do so, leads to an enhancement of organisational and institutional risk. This is because people do not, and will not, trust the managerial response to the crisis or emergency, nor do they trust the managerial capability to resolve the matter (see Management in Focus 4.11).

MANAGEMENT IN FOCUS 4.11

HURRICANE

In June 2005, the city of New Orleans was hit by a Category 5 hurricane. Overall, the city was used to dealing with violent storms. This one would have been little different except for the fact that the force of the storm breached one of the levees (protection banks) holding back the waters of the Mississippi River. This breach caused the city to flood.

Instead of responding to the legitimate concerns of people who had lost everything, and especially addressing questions about the potential for pollution and disease, the US authorities concentrated on defending the strength of the levee and the fact that it should not have breached. Only following the resignation of top officials did it become clear that the levee was only constructed to withstand Category 3 storms, and that the city had in fact been at risk of flooding for many years.

In early 2006, the decision was taken to rebuild the levee to withstand a Category 4 hurricane. An absolute approach to risk management, so as to minimise absolutely the risk of the crisis ever happening again, would be to rebuild it to withstand a Category 8 storm, and then to see that it was fully maintained on a regular basis.

Other aspects of risk management

Clearly, things can, and do, go wrong in every aspect of organisational and managerial performance and activity. Of particular concern to managers in all spheres and areas of activity ought to be the following:

- Technology performance, including the consequences of technology crashes and the loss of information about product and service delivery. Alongside technological performance is the question of suitability and capability in terms of what the organisation expects it to deliver.
- Managing over distances, which refers to the risk inherent in devolving responsibility, authority and accountability to persons working in remote locations (see the Barings example above).
- Ensuring that drives for expansion into new products, services, ventures, markets and locations (including overseas ones) are driven by organisational capability and willingness, and the prospects of profitable and effective activities; above all, managers must be sure that these ventures are not driven solely by the excitement of the venture or the prestige of being international.
- Ensuring a rigorous approach to new product and service development, again so that the drive is concentrated on commercial potential rather than pure creativity.

Conclusions

It is clear from the above that the effective management of risk requires involvement in all aspects of organisational structure, activities, behaviour and performance.

If anything goes wrong in any area, there is the potential for a knock-on effect that may ultimately affect every aspect of the organisation. Serious problems can, and do, lead to loss of confidence in the organisation and its products and services; this in turn is certain to lead to downturns in performance, and can lead to bankruptcy.

It is therefore essential that everyone in the organisation knows and understands the importance of constant attention to activities, behaviour and performance. This is a key part of the personal commitment and professional discipline required of managers in all organisations, in every aspect of business, industry and public services. This has to be tempered by knowing and understanding that it is impossible to plan for every eventuality; it is however necessary to learn from these eventualities when they do arise, so as to ensure that the same thing never happens again, and so as to develop a broader understanding of the potential for problems in every area of activity.

CRITICAL THINKING, ANALYSIS AND EVALUATION

1. Identify the full range of costs incurred as the result of having to deal with the aftermath of a disaster or serious accident.
2. Outline the approach to risk management required for a not-for-profit organisation such as Oxfam, when assessing the environment of the early twenty-first century.
3. Where do management responsibilities lie in response to the single events outlined in Management in Focus 4.7 above? What is the nature of these responsibilities; and how should these responsibilities be discharged for the future?
4. Identify the risks that are incurred by organisations when they outsource production and service functions in countries in the emerging world.

DEVELOPING MANAGEMENT SKILLS AND EXPERTISE

A380: THE AIRBUS SUPER-JUMBO JET

In April 2005, the *Airbus A380* took off on its maiden flight. It was the largest airliner ever built. Structured as a complete double-decker, the airliner has the capacity to carry 850 passengers. Some airlines, however, when expressing their initial interest, identified the possibility of installing 550 seats in the lower deck. The upper deck would be equipped with all of the facilities necessary to make long-haul international travel as pleasant as possible. Airlines that made this choice therefore proposed a range of facilities on the upper deck ranging from restaurants, bars, nightclubs and casinos, to gymnasiums and saunas.

The airliner was developed and built by Airbus Industrie SA, and Aerospatiale SA, in Toulouse, southern France. However, it was very much an international collaboration. While the assembly and finishing work were carried out in Toulouse, many of the parts were made elsewhere. There was extensive strategic and operational collaboration between Airbus, Aerospatiale and companies in Great Britain, Germany and Spain. Some of the facilities on board are very specialised, and are to be provided by companies from Sweden, Norway, Denmark and Italy, as well as from France, Great Britain, Germany and Spain.

The *A380* is envisaged to have two core markets. The first of these is on long-haul, intercontinental routes. The second is on short-haul and internal routes in China, India and south-east Asia, as well as in the United States. For both of these proposed markets, the great strength of the *A380* is its ability to ferry large numbers of passengers between two major destinations, thus reducing the number of airliners required, and the consequent pollution, traffic jams, queues and delays on airport runways.

Questions

1. Identify the risks inherent in each aspect of the Airbus A380 project.
2. Identify the wider lessons to be learned by managers in all organisations and situations where this level, scope and scale of activity is present.

Chapter five

Ethics

'It does exactly what it says on the tin.'
Advertisement, Cuprinol Plc.

'Our staff are our greatest asset.'
Tarmac Plc, Annual Report (1995) –
a year in which they had made 2200 members of staff redundant.

'What was wrong with Marks and Spencer was that its senior management,
notably the man at the top, reported in the general press as regarded as a bully
by some colleagues, failed to realise that they were the shareholders' servants.'
David Thomas, *Writers' News* (March 2001).

Chapter outline

- Introduction
- Survival
- Relationships with employees
- Responsibilities and obligations to staff
- Conduct
- Relationships with suppliers
- Relationships with customers
- Relationships with communities
- Relationships with shareholders and backers
- Conclusions

Chapter objectives

After studying this chapter, you should be able to:

- understand the relationship between ethical standards and the effectiveness and delivery of businesses and public services

- understand the effects of ethics on all aspects of organisational and managerial performance

- understand the personal, professional, occupational and human responses to variations in standards of ethics, morality and integrity

- draw conclusions about the relationship between ethical standards and sustainable organisational performance.

Introduction

Ethics in management is concerned with those parts of organisational, operational, occupational and professional conduct that relate to absolute standards and moral principles. Establishing standards of conduct requires reference to questions of what is right and wrong in absolute terms, the desired ends and outcomes, and the ways and means by which the ends and outcomes are achieved. There are additional factors of:

- the nature of working, professional and personal relationships
- attention to the quality of working life
- compliance with the law
- working effectively within the constraints of social, cultural and religious customs.

Below are a variety of views and perspectives on the relationship between ethics, business and management.

Sternberg (1990) states:

Business ethics applies ethical reasoning to business situations and activities. It is based on a combination of distributive justice – that is, the issuing of rewards for contribution to organisation goals and values; and ordinary common decency – an absolute judgement that is placed on all activities.

Johnson and Scholes (1994) state:

Ethical issues concerning business and public sector organisations exist at three levels. At the macro level there are issues about the role of the business in the national and international organisation of society. These are largely concerned with addressing the relative virtues of different political/social systems. There are also important issues of international relationships and the role of business on an international scale. At the corporate level the issue is often referred to as corporate social responsibility and is focused on the ethical issues facing individual and corporate entities (both private and public sector) when formulating and implementing strategies. At the individual level the issue concerns the behaviour and actions of individuals within organisations.

Adams, Hamil and Carruthers (1990) identify a series of factors and elements as measures against which the performance of organisations could be measured in ethical terms. These factors are:

- the nature of business; Adams, Hamil and Carruthers identify contentious industries such as tobacco, alcohol, chemicals and armaments
- the quality, integrity, availability and use of information
- participation, consultation, employment relationships, the recognition of trade unions, means and methods of representation
- relationships with emerging economies and markets
- marketing and selling initiatives, again with reference to contentious products and services as above
- connections with governments – especially where these were considered to be undesirable or where the regime in question was considered to be unethical itself (see Management in Focus 5.1).

MANAGEMENT IN FOCUS 5.1

THE HUNGER BUSINESS

There is mounting evidence to suggest that much of the effort carried out in the emerging world by charities and voluntary organisations (including the United Nations) is extensively manipulated by the governments of the people that they are supposed to be aiding.

General 'Michael' Ojukwu, President of the Nigerian enclave of Biafra in 1967, stated:

We were fighting a civil war with the Nigerian government. We needed support from the outside world, otherwise we would have been massacred. We therefore took a television news crew to a small enclave of the region where people were starving. These pictures were then transmitted around the world. The result was that donations from the Western public, and assistance from the big charities, came pouring in.

As a condition of receiving this aid, we were able to insist that the big charities also flew in armaments and other military equipment that could be used in order to sustain our campaign.

(Mangold, 2001)

In 1995 and 1996, there was a very brutal civil war in the African state of Rwanda. In 1999, trouble flared up again; and there was a mass exodus of the people of Rwanda to neighbouring countries. Refugee camps quickly became unmanageable, and their population swelled to about two million.

Representatives of all the big international charities went on television to announce an imminent humanitarian disaster. Each spokesperson tried to outbid all of the others in his/her description of the numbers of people likely to starve to death. One figure

extensively used was that there were over one million persons at risk of starvation or disease.

In the event, 192 people died in the camps before there was a mass return by the people to their homelands in Rwanda. Of those who died, two were stillborn babies. One was killed as the result of a domestic dispute. The other 189 were all killed in inter-tribal and inter-gang fighting within the camp. There was no humanitarian disaster.

The purpose here is to illustrate the ways in which organisations and their products and services can be compromised in their operations within the given environment, and especially in their dealings with particular governments. The 'hunger business' examples are especially contentious because the organisations concerned were (and are) delivering literally the difference between life and death.

There are additional issues to be considered as follows:

- compliance with the law, as noted above
- general approaches and attitudes to staff and customers
- attitudes to the communities in which the organisation operates
- attitudes to environmental issues – especially waste disposal and recycling, replanting, and the ways and means by which scarce resources are consumed
- business relationships with suppliers and markets
- product testing, where this involves the use of animals
- product testing, where the outcomes are not fully known, understood or evaluated (see Management in Focus 5.2).

MANAGEMENT IN FOCUS 5.2

GENETICALLY MODIFIED (GM) CROPS

Scientists believe that they have found ways to improve the quality and durability of agricultural crops, through modifying the genes of particular plants. This has caused extensive political, social and media debate and argument – on the one hand the need to enhance global food production is recognised; on the other, many concerns about long-term damage to the food, agricultural, and environmental infrastructure have been voiced.

The key problem here is lack of openness, quality and integrity of information. The companies responsible for producing genetically modified crops have found themselves under attack from powerful consumer and environmental lobbies, and have therefore retreated within themselves, concentrating on their existing markets and those that they are able to dominate, rather than opening up a higher quality of debate. Politicians, while recognising the need to enhance the quality and volume of food production, have equivocated on the environmental issues. Environmental lobbies have sought to simplify the debate into a single issue – the general rights and wrongs of 'tampering with nature'.

The net result is an entrenchment of position – resulting, in turn, in a hysterical and ill-informed exchange of views, arguments and insults. The chief sufferers of this are the public at large, who to date have not been told the true merits and demerits of each side as part of the case.

Drucker (1955) stated:

> The more successfully the manager does their work, the greater will be the integrity required. For under new technology the impact on the business of decisions, time span and risks will be so serious as to require that each manager put the common good of the enterprise above self-interest. Their impact on the people in the enterprise will be so decisive as to demand that the manager put genuine principles above expediency. And the impact on the economy will be so far reaching that society itself will hold managers responsible. Indeed, the new tasks demand that the manager of tomorrow root every action and decision in the bedrock of principles so that they lead, not only through knowledge, competence and skill, but also through vision, courage, responsibility and integrity.

Payne and Pugh (1970) identified the relationship between the absolute standards of the organisation and its 'climate'. They stated that: 'Climate is a total concept applying to the organisation as a whole or some definable department or subsystem within it.' It is descriptive of the organisation. There are four main aspects of climate:

- degrees of autonomy given to particular individuals, groups, departments, divisions and functions
- the degree of structure or flexibility imposed on work positions
- the reward orientation, both in terms of individual satisfaction and overall organisational achievement
- the degree of consideration, warmth and support; the human aspects of staff-management relationships.

There is clearly no common agreement on what constitutes an absolute body of knowledge and expertise in the area of business and managerial ethics. Some useful initial conclusions may however be drawn as follows:

- It is essential to take a long-term view, as well as satisfying immediate interests and demands.
- Absolute standards are required relating to organisational policies, aims and objectives.
- Common standards of equity, equality, honesty and integrity are required; if they are not established, they will, de facto, emerge anyway.
- There is a relationship between organisation standards and integrity, the delivery of performance, and the distribution of rewards.
- There are key relationships between means and ends, and actions and motives (see Management in Focus 5.1 above).
- It is important to establish where conflicts of interest lie, and the reasons for their existence.

● Survival

Survival is the main ethical duty of the organisation, to its staff, customers, communities and other stakeholders. In order to survive over the long term, a long-term view must be taken of all that this means. For business and companies, profits must be made – over the long term; for public services, this means effectiveness – over the long term. This is the basis on which confidence and an enduring and continuous positive relationship with customers (or service users) are built and developed. This is also the only ground on which an effective and satisfactory organisation for the staff is to be created.

Short-term views, expediency, the need for triumphs – all detract from this. Especially, there is a serious problem in this area with some public services. For example, the output of education can take 15–20 years to become apparent. Health and social services have similar extreme long-term requirements and commitments. Yet those responsible for their direction (both service chiefs and cabinet ministers) need to be able to show instant results to be presented before the electorate, or before the selection panel for their next job.

This is not wholly confined to services. For example, pressures from bankers and other financial backers in some sectors (especially loan makers) lead to companies being forced or strongly encouraged to sell assets during lean periods in order to keep up repayments or show a superficial cash surplus over the immediate period. This happened with the UK construction industry over the early 1990s when there was a great decline in work brought on by recession and general loss of confidence. Short-term cash gain was made through the sale of assets (especially land banks). Long-term survival was threatened because these assets would not be present when any upturn in confidence and activity came about.

However, this again has to be balanced with matters of general confidence and expectation. If backers expect to see a series of short-term positive results then these have to be produced, especially if backing may be withdrawn if these are not forthcoming or do not meet expectations. This implies re-educating backers into the long-term view. It also means seeking out others who are disposed to take the long-term view.

Relationships with employees

This refers to the nature of participation and involvement, and the point of view from which this is approached. Basic integrity in employee relations stems from the view taken of the employees, their reasons for working in the organisation, their reasons for being hired to work in the organisation and the absolute levels of esteem in which they are held.

Confrontational or adversarial styles of employee relations are always founded on mistrust and reinforced by offensive and defensive positions adopted by the two sides concerning particular issues. The phrase 'the two sides' confirms and underlines this. Resources are consumed in this way to the detriment both of organisation perform-ance and of resource utilisation – resources used in these ways cannot be put to better use elsewhere (see Management in Focus 5.3).

Adversarial employee relations is therefore normally unethical. On the other hand, greater or full participation and involvement is only ethical if the point of view adopted is itself honest – if a genuine view of respect and identity is taken. This is made apparent – or not – in the continuity and enduring nature of this relationship. It is underlined by the volume, quality and relevance of information made available to the staff, the means by which problems are addressed and resolved, the prevalence of equality of treatment and opportunity, and the development of staff.

It also refers to the attention to the standards set to which employees are to conform and the reasoning and logic behind this. It covers all aspects of the traditional personnel area – recruitment and selection, induction, performance appraisal, pay and reward, promotion and other opportunities for development and advancement. Above all, at its core, lies equality of treatment for everyone.

Responsibilities and obligations to staff

The general responsibilities and obligations to staff consist of providing work, remaining in existence, equality and fairness of treatment, compliance with the law and the specific regulations of training and development. The basis on which this is established is discussed below.

It is essential to acknowledge the range of pressures and priorities that exists in the lives of everyone, including health, family, social, ethical and religious factors, as well as those related to work. The outcome of this is understanding and not interference or imposition. It sets the relationship between work organisations and people in context. It indicates areas where stresses and strains are likely to arise. It indicates the relationship between organisation and individual priorities, where these coincide and where they diverge. It indicates areas for accommodation and for regulation.

Extreme human concerns and conditions have to be dealt with. This refers to personal crises – serious illness, death, bereavement, divorce, drink and drug prob-lems. The concern is to ensure that the organisation gives every possible support to people facing these issues so that a productive and profitable relationship is main-tained even through such times. Individuals can, and should, be referred to outside professional support services and agencies for these matters with the full backing of the organisation (see Management in Focus 5.4).

Ultimately, however, organisations do not have the right to pry into people's personal affairs. Individuals may be referred for counselling or other expert help and

MANAGEMENT IN FOCUS 5.3

EMPLOYEE RELATIONS AND PROBLEM SOLVERS

Many large industrial, commercial and public sector organisations have extensive human resource management departments and functions. In this context, an especial problem concerns those that have responsibility for employee relations.

These companies and organisations hire employee relations specialists to devise policies for the effective management of staff and resolution of conflict, and to resolve problems when they arise.

Serious organisational problems can, and do, arise when these employee relations staff are rewarded on the basis of the problems that they solve. If emphasis is placed on the ability of employee relations staff to solve problems, then they will find problems to solve. For example:

A large London radio station was going through a period of extensive restructuring. Two programme-producing departments were required to restructure their workforce, terms and conditions of employment and hours of work. The manager of one of these departments saw the problem early; and, by engaging in extensive consultation and discussion with the staff, avoided all problems. The matter was resolved smoothly and without any disputes.

The manager of the other department did nothing about the matter until the weekend before the changes were due to take place. In the period immediately preceding this weekend, staff morale plummeted, and there was an increase in the number of disputes and grievances. Accordingly, the manager commanded all of the staff to attend a weekend briefing, consultation and crisis resolution session immediately before the changes were due to take place. The matters were resolved at this weekend meeting.

The radio station's senior management, who were very familiar with the situation and the mounting crisis, looked on with admiration as, at the end of the weekend, all of the staff trooped out and announced themselves satisfied with the new arrangement. Because of his crisis management skills, the particular manager was rewarded. The manager who had tackled the problems early received no reward or recognition for the ways in which she had managed the situation.

advice if they give their consent, unless the matter is adversely affecting their work performance beyond a fair and reasonable extent, or where they constitute a real or potential threat or danger to their colleagues or the activities of the organisation.

Problems related to drug or alcohol use or addiction always fall into the latter category and are therefore always a matter of direct concern. Organisations set absolute standards of handling and using equipment, carrying out activities and dealing with the public. Addiction and abuse problems directly affect each of these. The individual is therefore to be removed from these situations and supported through rehabilitation.

MANAGEMENT IN FOCUS 5.4

ORGANISATIONAL AND MANAGERIAL RESPONSIBILITIES AND STAFF BEREAVEMENTS

One of the world's big oil companies had to manage two bereavements affecting members of its staff.

A senior finance executive, working at the company's London office, suffered the loss of his wife in childbirth. This was quickly shown to have been the result of medical negligence. He was given three months' paid leave of absence from the company in order to get over his bereavement, and to sort out childcare and domestic arrangements for the newborn baby, and for his other two children.

At about the same time, a female member of staff in her mid-fifties lost her 22-year-old son, who died as the result of a drug overdose. The female member of staff worked as a forecourt cashier at one of the company's 800 filling stations. She was given three days' paid leave immediately following the death; and paid time off to attend her son's inquest and funeral only. Any other time off she was required to take either as annual or unpaid leave. The company held her job open for her until such time as she felt able to return to work.

It is essential to preserve confidentiality and integrity in all dealings with staff. This is the cornerstone on which all effective staff relationships are built. Where confidences are not kept, where sensitive personal and occupational information becomes public property, the relationship is tainted and often destroyed. Confidentiality also encourages people to be frank, open and honest themselves, and this leads to a genuine understanding of issues much more quickly. It also enables managers and supervisors to address matters of concern – for example, declines in standards of performance and behaviour – directly and immediately they are observed (see Management in Focus 5.5).

It is essential to respect individuals for the value of their contribution to the organisation. If they bring no value, they should not be there in the first place. Ideally therefore, the fact of their employment (in whatever capacity) equates to high and distinctive value – and where it does not, stress and conflict invariably occur.

This respect extends to all aspects of the working relationship; and includes attention to the current job, future prospects, continuity of working relations, creation of suitable working environments, creation and maintenance of effective occupational and personal relationships, creation and maintenance of effective management and supervisory styles (see Management in Focus 5.6).

The traditional or adversarial view of this approach to responsibilities and obligations was that it was soft and unproductive, and diverted attention away from production and output. Organisations could not afford to be 'nice' to their employees while there was a job to be done.

The reverse of this is much closer to the truth. The acknowledgement, recognition and understanding of the full nature and range of complexities and conflicting

MANAGEMENT IN FOCUS 5.5

INTEGRITY IN DEALINGS WITH STAFF

This incident happened to a senior and extremely capable bank employee. He was assigned an urgent project with very high priority that involved designing a new product in a very short period. He worked 18-hour days for weeks. He treated weekends just like weekdays. He only went home to sleep. The project was completed on time, and the employee's boss, was congratulated heartily by the bank's executives. The next week was time for the individual's performance review.

The review meeting took five minutes. The manager sat the employee down and said: 'I think you may be a little disappointed with the rating I have given you. Generally speaking, you have been working well. However, there are two problems which you have that need to be addressed. First, I have never seen you go a whole day without unbuttoning your shirt and loosening your tie. Second – and this is more important – you have a habit of stretching out at your desk and kicking your shoes off. Frankly, that is offensive. If it weren't for these problems, you would rate a solid "competent". As it is, you are scruffy and I'm afraid that means you are "developing".'

Source: Scott Adams (1999), *The Joy of Work*, Macmillan.

pressures on individuals is the first step towards effective and profitable activities. By engaging in a basis of honesty, confidentiality, trust, support and integrity – rather than coercion, confrontation, dishonesty and duplicity – a long-term positive relationship can be established. The interests of organisation and individual are bound up with each other, especially over the long-term. Ultimately therefore, their interests coincide. A critical part of this approach is concerned with creating the basis on which this can be built.

Relationships with suppliers

There used to be a received managerial wisdom, that it was good and effective practice to create 'a multiplicity of suppliers', because this would 'keep suppliers on their toes', and 'keep suppliers loyal'. In practice, companies that adopt this approach actually show no loyalty to suppliers; they simply shop around, taking either the short-term view that they will accept deliveries from the lowest-priced suppliers at the particular moment, or the expedient view that particular suppliers may be changed at will. This especially applies where there is an over-supply of particular commodities, components, and primary and raw materials.

By the same token, companies and organisations may know, believe or perceive themselves to be held to ransom by those who supply rare or highly sought-after primary resources and components.

Wherever either of these two extremes exists, the relationship has to be managed with integrity, if long-term security of purpose and business is to be achieved. Indeed, any business or managerial relationship where there are dominant and dependent

MANAGEMENT IN FOCUS 5.6

STAFF LOYALTY AND REWARDS

In the City of London, the nature and size of bonus payments comes in for criticism, because of the disparity that exists in the size of bonuses awarded, and between those who receive them, and those who do not. Amanda Lote, Manager of Badenoch & Clarks corporate finance team, stated:

> Some corporate financiers with as little as four years experience are receiving between 300–400 per cent of salary as bonus, creating a considerable imbalance between them, and others in the banks who work within what are regarded as cost centres rather than revenue generators. This creates a highly remuneration-orientated culture that is not necessarily productive, and certainly overvalues skills, especially in the current [2001] candidate-led market.

In many cases, high bonus levels have evidently become the crucial factor in decisions about careers. A survey carried out by CityPeople.com, a city online recruitment and remuneration consultancy, showed the overwhelming supremacy of bonus awards when financiers chose companies for which they were going to work. A third of those questioned said that if their bonus was less than expected, they would start looking for another job. With a key skills shortage at present, the City could be creating a serious dilemma for itself by paying big bonuses, in spite of the fact that these neither buy nor guarantee loyalty.

Similar problems abound in the football industry. One top international star at a wealthy London club had his salary doubled between the years 1998 and 2000; and still left in 2001, claiming that he was undervalued. Another joined a top Spanish club in 1996 on a guaranteed salary of £72,000 per week for a 3.5-year contract, and subsequently failed to perform to expectations. Another was transferred between English, Spanish and French clubs for a net value of over £50 million; at each club, the particular individual criticised supporters for failing to show him the respect that he felt he was due. In each case, the clubs felt bound to pay the salary levels demanded, regardless of any relationship to individual or club performance.

At the core of both examples is the (almost incredible) managerial dilemma, centring on whether loyalty can be bought, or whether it has to be earned.

Source: Wendy Ledger, 'The Bonuses that Create Millionaires Overnight', *Evening Standard*, 20 February 2001.

partners must be considered from the point of view of the business requirements, rather than the imbalance of power which exists.

It is also true that those organisations that secure themselves medium and long-term contracts to supply large public and commercial institutions may take advantage of this security of relationship. For example, those supplying management consultancy services and medical supplies to the UK National Health Service have, in many cases, secured for themselves premium-priced contracts in return for stability and security of supplies. Organisations engaged in public–private partnerships and other forms of contracting out of particular activities normally found in the public service domain have been able to get themselves fully underwritten by the government, in case of changes in the business relationships or strategic and political directions of particular services. Similarly, those organisations providing subcontracted specialist products and services to industries such as civil and mechanical engineering, building and construction, and information technology have also been able to charge premium rates at the times when their particular expertise is required.

This has caused many organisations and their managers to take a fresh look at the nature of the desired relationship with the suppliers. At the core of this must be attention to the short, medium and long-term organisational and business demands, and also to the nature, value and frequency of the supplies required. This is certain to change with technological advances, the opening up of new markets, and increased availability of supplies of components, materials and information from different parts of the world (see Management in Focus 5.7).

Relationships with customers

This is the basis of the commercial or service provision: the respect and value in which the customers and clients are held. From this springs the drive for product quality, presentation and offering; of public relations and other customer management and service activities; and of handling complaints.

It also impinges on the staff. Where staff know that high standards of customer service and top-quality products are being offered, the relationship between organisation and staff is also reinforced. The converse is also true – where these standards

---

MANAGEMENT IN FOCUS 5.7

RELATIONSHIPS WITH SUPPLIERS

Three years ago, as part of a schools–industry liaison project in south-east England, a small group of schoolteachers spent two weeks work shadowing the staff of a large fruit and vegetable farm. During the course of their placement, the teachers found out that over 90 per cent of their produce was sold to a major supermarket chain. One of the teachers, a man in his forties, was perturbed by this. He asked the farm General Manager: 'Isn't that a bit risky?'

'What do you mean?' replied the General Manager.

'Well – what if the department store chain were to go out of business? Or to stop selling food? Or to change its suppliers?'

'Oh, that will never happen', replied the General Manager. 'We have supplied this company for over 20 years. They know us and understand us; and we know and understand them. Why on earth would they want to change their suppliers?'

Some time later, the particular teacher was driving past the farm. The vegetable greenhouses were clearly not being used; and in one corner of a field, there was a huge pile of rotting apples. He drove on to the farm gate. At the gate was a 'for sale' sign. The farm was clearly closed.

The schoolteacher noted the name of the estate agents, and made contact. He asked them what had happened. He was told: 'The company that bought all of the farm's produce changed its supplier at 24 hours notice. They found themselves a supplier in France who would deliver the same quality and volume of fruit and vegetables at a lesser cost.'

are low or falling, or where it is known that poor products and services are being offered, the integrity of the relationship between organisation and staff is also compromised.

This affects all production, output and sales activities, especially in terms of attention to product quality, the terms under which the product is offered, its uses and availability and recognition of the levels of satisfaction that are required by the customers. In the long term, if this is not present, confidence is lost (see Management in Focus 5.8). While it is possible to identify areas where short-term gain has been made without integrity (for example, in the sale of building products, home improvements, life assurance and pensions, and poor quality Christmas presents), there is no (or reduced) likelihood of repeat business occurring. This also fails to satisfy either the long-term criteria or the requirement of confidence on the part of the employees; above all, there is no integrity of relationship. This way of conducting business is therefore also unethical.

MANAGEMENT IN FOCUS 5.8

PRODUCT, QUALITY, INTEGRITY AND WHOLESOMENESS: BARBIE

The Barbie phenomenon illustrates much of the complexity surrounding the quality and value of products to customers and consumers, and their fundamental integrity and wholesomeness.

Barbie dolls are overwhelmingly played with – consumed – by urban and suburban small girls; they are bought for them, also overwhelmingly, by their mothers, grandmothers, elder sisters and aunts. The product is constantly being developed and enhanced; new doll designs, clothing and accessories are brought onstream every week. The product and brand are further reinforced by extensive advertising campaigns, and also a range of complementary books, comics and films.

The product has existed for over 50 years. It is one of the most recognised products and brands in the world. A Barbie product – either doll or accessory – is sold every 11 seconds. At present, turnover of Barbie products continues to exceed £1 billion per annum; and this is in spite of incursions into this market by Bratz (which has continued to be much more up to date and immediately fashionable) and Burkha, a range of dolls produced specifically for the Muslim community.

A part of the success of the product development refers to the number of different jobs and occupations that Barbie has had. These include: schoolteacher, doctor, nurse, dentist, astronaut, fashion model, show-jumper and financier. The doll has been presented in a variety of different ways including: walking, talking, disabled, dark-haired, fair-haired, short-haired, long-haired, and from various perceived different ethnic origins.

The core of the debate around the fundamental wholesomeness and integrity of the product however, centres on the core presentation of the doll. It is deemed to enhance unethical and unacceptable perceptions of womanhood by the world at large, and to contribute greatly to the early attitudes formed by young girls of society's broad expectations of them.

This also refers to attention to the marketing activities undertaken and the point of view adopted. Creative and imaginative presentation is highly desirable as long as this underlines (and does not misrepresent) the quality, desirability and image of the particular product or organisation. Again, where integrity is missing, the relationship is invariably short-term and terminated by loss of confidence in the organisation and loss of regard for its products and services. This applies to all aspects of marketing – promotion and advertising, packaging and presentation, direct sales and distribution (see Management in Focus 5.9).

Relationships with communities

The complexities of organisational and managerial relationships between companies or public service bodies and the communities within which they operate has to be addressed. The factors that have to be considered are as follows.

Communities expect the provision of long-term, enduring work and the prosperity that this brings to communities. One of the major problems that was not

MANAGEMENT IN FOCUS 5.9

MARKETING: CONTENTIOUS EXAMPLES

The following are worthy of consideration.

- *Benetton*: in the mid-1990s, Benetton, the Italian clothing company, created its United Colours of Benetton advertising and marketing campaign. Two controversial images used were photographs of human foetuses and new-born babies, which were presented as stark images on white backgrounds, with the slogan United Colours of Benetton underneath; and wounded soldiers photographed during the Bosnian civil war of 1993–94, with the same

slogan underneath. These were roundly condemned by advertising lobbies and pressure groups concerned with maintaining standards of probity and integrity. They were deemed by the Benetton company to have been a major contributory factor in doubling company turnover in the clothing market during the period 1993–98, and the campaign was revived again in 2001 with similar success.

- *Marlboro*: Phillip Morris Inc., the company which manufactures and distributes Marlboro cigarettes world wide, has settled without prejudice many

claims brought against it by persons who have contracted serious diseases, including heart disease and lung cancer, as the result of using the company's products. As the major sponsor of Formula 1 motor racing, the company is able to secure for itself, a minimum of six hours multi-channel television promotional exposure each time a Formula 1 race takes place. Marlboro is the most universally recognised cigarette brand. It is also, of all the cigarette brands in the world, that which enjoys the greatest universal customer loyalty.

managed in the UK during the recessions of the 1970s and 1980s, and the job losses that accrued as a result, was the provision of substitute or alternative sources of work, and therefore economic support, for communities at large. This had an enduring social effect on attitudes to work in certain areas of the country. Moreover, there is plenty of evidence to suggest that this part of the transition process is seldom addressed. Examples include the extensive job losses and community deprivations that have occurred in the former East Germany as the result of reunification, and in countries such as Poland, the Czech Republic and Viet Nam, as the result of the fall of communist regimes.

Community confidence is founded in general feelings of social well-being that accrue as the result of having particular organisations located in specific communities. This may bring with it particular ethical dilemmas – for example, there is a conflict that has to be addressed in areas where nuclear power stations are located. These stations provide large volumes of high-value and well-paid work to the communities, and this has to be reconciled with continuing concerns and perceptions about radiation pollution.

There are concerns about pollution and environmental damage, especially the disposal of waste and effluent, noise and lighting blight, and the effectiveness of waste and effluent management by organisations. Closely related to this are more general concerns surrounding the health and safety aspects of specific operations that are located in particular areas. Much of this is compounded by a failure to pin down global and corporate responsibilities for particular activities, as well as legislative inadequacies and a lack of executive powers on the part of statutory executives.

Community disruption is caused, for example, by construction and civil engineering activities, which bring with them 'building blight' for the duration of their activities. They may also leave 'residual blight' if those responsible for drawing up the contract have not ensured that the particular construction or civil engineering firm concerned has been made responsible for the restoration and enduring quality of the broader environment in which the work was carried out.

Exploitation is a key issue, when organisations move into particular areas as the result of the cheapness and perceived plentiful supply of labour and other resources. This was a problem that successive governments tried to address in the 1970s and 1980s in the UK through the use of regional aid and other development grants in areas of high unemployment. This is less of a problem now in the UK; however, there are enduring concerns about the wholesomeness and integrity of those organisations that source their manufacturing operations in the poorest parts of the world, purely because labour is cheap, plentiful, and unregulated (see Management in Focus 5.10).

Social dominance and dependence comes in three main forms:

- Where a large organisation moves into a particular location and is able to poach staff from others already working there, by virtue of its economic ability to provide substantially superior terms and conditions of employment.
- Where large firms are able to insist on specific development activities, to the known, believed or perceived detriment of the rest of the economic community. Of specific concern here is the development of out-of-town industrial and retail centres that are believed to damage or destroy the economic viability of centre-of-town activities.

MANAGEMENT IN FOCUS 5.10

ETHICAL ISSUES IN OUTSOURCING INITIATIVES

The outsourcing by Western companies of manufacturing activities in the garments and electrical goods industries, and of customer relations management in financial services, is well established in practice. The priority is to be clear, in advance of implementing any outsourcing venture, about the reasons for outsourcing; the choice of location, again with reasons; and the results that are anticipated. This gives a focus for the nature of investment that is undertaken, and the desired relationship with the outsource location. It also gives a clear indication of attitudes to staff (both those who remain in the country of origin and those in the new location). It additionally indicates the length of the outsource relationship, and whether or not this might lead to further ventures and initiatives – either the outsourcing of other functions (which has implications for working rela-

tionships in the organisation as a whole) or developing the relationship with the particular outsource provider, so long as agreement can be reached.

Western companies bringing outsource ventures to emerging economies have conflicts of interest to be resolved (see above). The governments of the emerging world countries need hard currency, and the companies bring this with them. The locations often need work as a fundamental prerequisite of further economic development. Western companies can (and often do) exploit their sheer size and financial influence to drive down wages and other terms and conditions of employment, and to flout any employment, production or environment laws that may exist.

Western companies bringing outsource ventures to emerging world economies are likely therefore to be met

with a combination of fear and loathing, and certainly a feeling of mistrust. Western companies will gain workforces and compliance only because of the absence or otherwise of work in the locality. This antipathy continues to be reinforced by the emergence of stories and scandals about forced overtime, child labour and abuse of staff in the clothing and electrical goods industries, and by the contempt with which highly educated workforces are treated in financial services.

The key lesson is that all of this needs to be fully evaluated in advance of any initiative being undertaken. The one-dimensional economic advantage that is overtly present is, in practice, quickly dissipated if aims and objectives are not made clear, and if the ethical, social and moral issues are not also managed effectively.

● The economic ability of large organisations to transcend their central responsibilities, by ensuring that they have powerful political and economic support. In these cases, they are able to build and operate what they want from their own point of view and narrow self-interest, rather than what is in the wider interests of the particular community.

These are the main relationships upon which successful and effective organisational performance is built and developed.

● Means and ends

Crimes are not annulled by altruistic motives even though those motives may arouse human sympathy. For example, where a hungry person robs a rich person just to get food to eat, a crime is still committed. Robin Hood was a robber, whether or not he gave the proceeds of his robberies to the poor. The sale of cocaine on the urban streets of Europe and North America is wrong even if it provides the means of economic survival to the people of South America.

This applies to organisation practices also. If a manager dismisses an employee to make an example of him/her, and if the employee did not deserve dismissal, then a wrong act is committed even if it brings the remaining staff into line. If the organisation secures its long-term future through gaining a contract by offering a bribe to a major customer, then again a wrong act is committed. In each of these cases, in practice the stated ends are very unlikely to be secured anyway because there is no integrity in the relationship. In the first case, the staff will look for other ways of falling out of line (but without risking further dismissals); in the second case, the corruption may come to light and the relationship be called into question or cancelled as a result.

Organisations must recognise and resolve conflicts of interest (as discussed above). The first step is to acknowledge the legitimacy and certainty of these. From this, steps can be taken to ensure a resolution which benefits the long-term future of all concerned. Conflicts of interest arise between all organisation stakeholders, and among individuals within and between departments and divisions. These conflicts may be based on divergence of aims and objectives, as well as on general professional and expert disagreements as to the best interests of the organisation (as well as matters of in-fighting and operational and personality clashes).

The ethical approach is bound up in the integrity and visibility of management style and working relationships, and the early recognition of operational, professional and personal problems. These are then addressed when they arise and before they are allowed to fester and become a part of organisation folklore. What is to happen as the result of these matters arising can then be transmitted early, and it can be demonstrated why this is in the best interests of the organisation (see Management in Focus 5.11).

● Conclusions

The ethical approach is not altruistic or charitable, but rather a key concept of effective long-term organisational and business performance. The commitment to the staff is absolutely positive. This does not mean any guarantee of lifetime employment. It does mean recognising obligations and ensuring that staff, in turn, acknowledge their obligations. These obligations are to develop, participate and be involved; to be flexible, dynamic and responsive. The commitment of the staff to the organisation and of organisation to staff is mutual. This also extends to problem areas – especially the handling of discipline, grievance and dismissal issues, and redundancy and redeployment – and the continuity of this commitment when these matters have to be addressed.

Organisations must structure decision-making processes in ways that consider the range and legitimacy of ethical pressures. This also means understanding where the

MANAGEMENT IN FOCUS 5.11

GOOD ETHICS IS GOOD BUSINESS

Although ethical conduct is not sufficient to assure business success, and business success is no guarantee of ethical conduct, distributive justice and ordinary common decency do typically enhance long-term owner value. They do so in many ways. Chief of these is obviating the difficulties of operating without them. Stakeholders who doubt the good faith of companies and organisations, or of their colleagues, are more likely to spend time in protecting their backs than in performing their functions. Time, resources and energy that could be spent more productively and rewardingly are consequently diverted to basic self-preservation, with a direct opportunity cost to the business. Decent treatment, in contrast, permits and encourages stakeholders to get on with the job and to conduct business effectively and profitably.

The costs of disregarding ordinary decency and distributive justice are far-reaching. In a business characterised by lying, cheating and stealing this illusion of low morale typically replaces initiative and enthusiasm; teamwork becomes difficult at best, and long-term commitments counter-productive. When exertions on behalf of a business are rejected or penalised, rather than encouraged and rewarded, they are unlikely to be repeated. Distributive justice and a modicum of decency are therefore essential for any business to operate. Without them, the best business is unlikely to attract the best people or their best efforts. But when they are respected, the business will normally be characterised, not only by responsibility and integrity, but by maximum long-term owner value.

Source: E. Sternberg (1995) *Just Business*, Warner.

greater good and the true interests of the organisation lie, and adopting realistic steps in the pursuit of this. An ethical assessment will consider the position of staff, the nature and interrelationship of activities, product and service ranges, mixes and balances, and relationships with the community and the environment (see Figure 5.1).

Organisations are not families, friendly societies or clubs. By setting their own values and standards, and relating these to long-term effectiveness, they become distinctive. These values are almost certain to be at variance from those that are, and would be, held by natural families and clubs. Problems that arise are clouded therefore, where the organisation does indeed perceive itself to be 'a big happy family'. Families are able to forgive prodigal children; organisations may not be able to afford to do so however, if they are to maintain long-term standards, or if substantial damage has been done to customer relations for example. Organisations exist to provide effective products and services for customers while families and clubs exist to provide comfort, society and warmth. For organisations these elements are by-products, they are not the core.

Organisations are not obliged to provide employment at all except in so far as they need the work carried out. They will select and hire people for this on the basis of capabilities and qualities. They have no obligation to take staff from the ranks of the unemployed (though they may choose to do so). They have no obligation to locate for all eternity in particular areas (though again they may choose to do so).

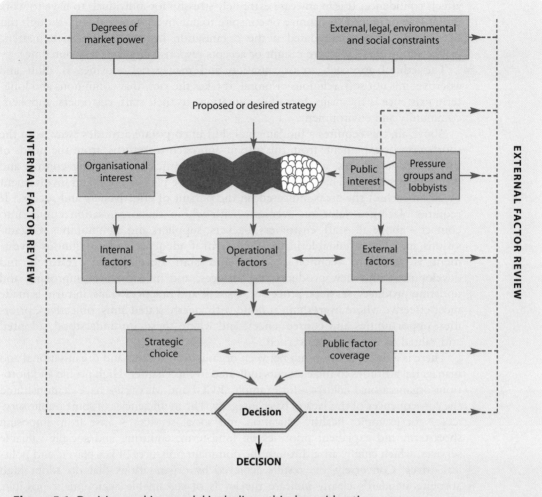

Figure 5.1 Decision-making model including ethical considerations

Organisations that pursue high ethical standards are not religious institutions, nor do they have any obligation to reflect any prevailing local traditions, values, customs, prejudices – or religion.

Japanese organisations setting up in the UK were, and remain, successful precisely because of this. Rather than trying to integrate their activities with the traditions of their locations they brought very distinctive and positive values with which people who came to work for them were required to identify.

Organisations must distinguish between right and wrong. Lying, cheating, stealing, bribery and corruption are always wrong and can never be ethically justified.

This has to be set in the context of the ways in which business is conducted in certain sectors and parts of the world. If a contract is only to be secured by offering a bribe the relationship is corrupted and based on contempt. If and when prevailing views change, the total relationship between organisation and customer is likely to be called into question, and any scandal or adverse publicity that emerges invariably affects confidence. It is in any case extremely stressful for individuals to have to work in this way or indeed to connive or conspire to any overt wrong-doing (though this may clearly be accommodated if the organisation institutionalises such matters, protects individuals who are caught or accepts responsibility for every outcome).

The ethical approach to organisation and managerial activities is adult and assertive; it is not soft, religious or moral. It takes the view that continuous and long-term existence is the main duty of organisations to their staff, customers, suppliers, community and environment.

Above all, this requires a fundamental shift in corporate attitudes away from the short-term or expedient, from the instant approach to returns, from the needs of the influential figures, and from wasteful and inefficient budgeting control and production systems. This is to be replaced by active participation and involvement by all, in each of the areas indicated, in the pursuit of effectiveness and success. It requires placing a value on everyone with whom the organisation comes into contact – above all, staff, customers, backers, suppliers and communities. Organisations are only sustainable in the long term if adequate and continuous investment is made in technology, staff and staff development; research and development into new products and services; and in constantly improving and updating products, services, processes, systems and practices. This, in turn, is made most effective where everything is done with clearly stated aims, objectives, priorities, opportunities and consequences, and where these are understood, adopted and valued by everyone concerned.

There is a direct relationship between organisation success and organisational and managerial attitudes to the elements indicated in this chapter. High profile and notorious organisational failures – for example, BCCI and Maxwell – have demonstrated the consequences of this lack of basic integrity. The inefficiencies of some public services – for example, health, education and social services – arise from imposing short-term and expedient priorities on long-term, enduring and socially valuable services, which chiefly arise through the dominant pressures of key players and political drives. Conversely, the results achieved by organisations that do adopt high absolute standards clearly indicate the levels of sustainable achievement possible, whatever the industrial, commercial or public sector considered.

CRITICAL THINKING, ANALYSIS AND EVALUATION

1. Under what circumstances, if any, may organisations legitimately be dishonest with their staff, customers, markets, community or environment? What are the short-term and long-term benefits and consequences?
2. Outline the legitimate reasons for the existence of the armaments and tobacco industries. Of all their activities, which may be considered ethical? Which may be considered unethical, and why?
3. Discuss the ethical implications surrounding the statement made by many organisations that: 'We are an equal opportunities employer'.
4. An individual is accused of theft. He vehemently denies the accusation. The organisation conducts an inquiry, and satisfies itself that he was indeed guilty. It dismisses him. The fairness of this dismissal is upheld at a subsequent employment tribunal hearing. Much later, it comes to light that the individual was indeed innocent. What action, if any, should the organisation take, and why?

DEVELOPING MANAGEMENT SKILLS AND EXPERTISE

SHANGRILA

The ShangriLa project is a hi-tech social, commercial and industrial community to be constructed on a new site in southern India. The project has been devised by an American company, Catalytic Software, which has produced plans for a self-sustaining community of concrete domes that will house 4000 software engineers, as well as 300 sanitation, police, fire and other support personnel.

The chief employer in this new city will be Catalytic Software itself. The company will supply contract software engineers for high-level technical projects around the world. It will also produce technology support systems, and industrial, commercial and leisure computer software.

The project is being driven by a directorate of three: Stefan Engstrom, Swain Porter and Christopher Phillips. The total cost of the project is expected to reach £250 million. All aspects of the project – work, leisure and social – are to be housed within a series of giant domes. The site is to include multi-storey office domes, swimming pools, tennis courts, football and baseball pitches, and an ice rink. As employees, members of the community will be entitled to live in shelters ranging from 800 to 2400 square feet in size. They will not be required to pay for their accommodation; they are to receive salaries competitive with these sorts of activities in the software and hi-tech consulting industries; they will also be entitled to share options in Catalytic Software.

The buildings have been designed to ensure that they are earthquake resistant; this is of especial importance following recent major disasters in the region.

Building a techno-city in India is designed to save Catalytic Software from having to import workers to other sites, especially the United States. It is envisaged that the overall quality of life in ShangriLa may help the company retain job-hoppers. There are also broader social issues, which the company is determined to consider. On previous visits to India, Stefan Engstrom had witnessed barefoot women hammering rocks at construction and civil engineering sites. Catalytic Software are determined to change all this. Engstrom stated: 'We wouldn't feel good doing business in India if we didn't have a hand in raising the standard of living.'

Questions

1. Comment on the ethical approaches stated and implicit in the ShangriLa project. On balance, is the approach ethical and wholesome or not?
2. What other factors have to be in place in order to ensure the long-term success of this venture? From the material in this chapter, identify the key ethical considerations that have to be addressed, and the consequences should any of these fail.
3. What specific problems do you foresee for this project in the medium to long term?

Chapter six

Globalisation

'We will deliver anything, anywhere in the world.'
Mission Statement, DHL.

'Anyone can use us, anywhere in the world.'
Sergey Brin, co-founder of Google.

'We are moving from being the world's best energy company,
to being the world's best company.'
Kenneth Lay, CEO, Enron, immediately before the company collapsed.

Chapter outline

- Introduction
- Globalisation
- The foundations of globalisation
- Drives for globalisation
- Other factors in globalisation
- Developing a global presence and influence
- Organising and managing in a global environment
- Organising and managing across cultures
- Organising and managing expertise and technology
- Dominance, dependence and responsibility
- Conclusions

Chapter objectives

After studying this chapter, you should be able to:

- know and understand the main organisational, managerial and environmental issues that have to be considered when seeking, establishing and maintaining a global and international presence

- identify the specific responsibilities that have to be addressed by organisations seeking a global or international presence

- recognise and understand the need for financial resources, technology and expertise that are capable of being used anywhere in the world

- recognise and understand the main problems and pitfalls that are likely to arise as the result of the decision to go global or international.

Introduction

The question of globalisation is dealt with in the context of the foundations of management because the nature of the operating environment requires attention to, and understanding of, global and international social, economic, political and competitive forces, and because the potential for all organisations to expand outside the borders of their own immediate locality is growing all the time. This has come about as the result of greatly enhanced supply, transport and distribution infrastructures; through access to the Internet for trading purposes; and through political drives to make trading blocs which transcend national boundaries. The other side of the coin is the ability of large organisations to command and direct the financial, staffing and technology resources on scales which allow activities anywhere and everywhere in the world; and this is reinforced by the mobility of individuals which enables them to act either on their own behalf, or in the name of a given organisation, anywhere in the world.

Globalisation

Globalisation is the capability and willingness to act and operate anywhere in the world according to circumstances, market presence and potential, and the demand for the given range of products, services and expertise. It is however necessary to develop this approach in more detail at the outset.

Genuine globalisation is very rare. Only two companies, ABB, the engineering concern, and Microsoft, the technology and software provider, have operated in every country of the world. Most of the major national airlines claim to be able to get passengers to any destination in the world, either themselves, or through their onward ticketing systems and alliances. Companies such as Amazon, the online retailer, and DHL and UPS, the high-value transport and distribution organisations, state that they will deliver their products and services anywhere in the world. Google claims to be able to provide information anywhere in the world. Other distribution and information systems management are dependent upon subcontracting and onward delivery systems created and agreed by large international organisations that do not themselves have a truly global reach.

There is additionally a more or less globally recognised range of brands and business icons. Coca-Cola is available in 180 countries of the world, and yet the logo is more or less universally known. McDonald's trades in 170 countries, and the company's 'Golden Arches' logo is (apparently) more widely recognised than the cross of Jesus Christ, and so is the most recognised symbol or 'icon' in the world.

Beyond this coverage, many organisations have nevertheless a truly international presence, especially in the areas of present and envisaged commercially viable activities. Many such organisations seek only the opportunity to carry out their activities and expertise.

It is however important to recognise that the mere existence of transport and distribution infrastructures, and an Internet presence, do not by themselves secure a genuinely global position (see Management in Focus 6.1).

MANAGEMENT IN FOCUS 6.1

CLAIMING TO BE GLOBAL

The fact of having conducted activities overseas does not deliver a genuinely international or global presence. For example:

- Tarmac Carilion claims to be a global operator in spite of the fact that 19 of its 40 offices are in the UK. This therefore is a UK company with overseas and international interests.
- Lastminute.com claims

that it is seeking to be 'The world's leading provider of last minute gifts and travel'. This is in spite of the fact that it only operates in ten countries.

The lesson is that it is one thing (often very admirable) to have a general attitude of internationalisation and globalisation, of seeking a position of commercial viability, rather than feeling restrained or tied

to national or local boundaries. However, making such a statement does not give the presence; a truly global or international presence requires investment, cultural knowledge and understanding, as well as managerial awareness of the full opportunities and constraints of the environment and other societies as a precursor to giving substance to any claims of being truly global.

● The foundations of globalisation

Genuine globalisation is founded in one or more of the following:

- *Global presence*: as stated above, a genuine and comprehensive global presence is very rare. Global presence has therefore to be attached to the capability and willingness to go anywhere in the world if circumstances, product, service and market potential demand.
- *Global technology*: this refers to the ability to use technological capacity anywhere in the world in the pursuit of serving product, service, information and market demands. This is not to be confused with general capability however; anyone with an e-mail address has a notionally global reach, but this does not make that individual a global operator.
- *Global influence*: global influence is based on product and service quality and value, and on project and project-based delivery. Thus for example:
  - The dominant, and therefore global, leaders in the airliner industry are Boeing and Airbus, because they set the absolute standards of performance, quality and durability, as well as because they command 97 per cent of the world's airliner industry.
  - The dominant, and therefore global, leaders in the electrical goods industry are Panasonic, Sony, Toshiba and Samsung, because they set the standards of reliability, quality and durability which others must aspire to if they are to maintain a presence in these markets.
  - The dominant, and therefore global, players in the car industry are Ford, General Motors and Chrysler by virtue of the sheer volumes of cars that they produce; and Toyota and Nissan, also because of the sheer volumes

of cars produced, as well as the aspects of quality, reliability and durability which set the standards for the others to follow.

- *Financial size* is required for a global presence; this has to be underpinned by the capability to command the sheer volume of financial resources necessary to maintain and develop a global presence.
- *Command of technology*: production, service delivery and information systems are essential so as to be able to assure control and influence of the usage of technology in the name of the organisation and the pursuit of its own interests. Technology must be capable of being used anywhere in the world that the organisation chooses. Information systems and databases must be capable of being made secure anywhere in the world where it is chosen to use them.
- It is additionally necessary to be able to *influence markets*, and where necessary dominate them, so as to provide an effective and viable range of products and services, either competing directly with what is presently on offer, or else creating new markets for those products and services where none previously existed.
- Globalisation requires the ability to command *expertise*, to attract and retain the nature and levels of skills necessary to deliver the organisation's purposes anywhere in the world where this may be required. It is additionally the case that, alongside capability, there is a cultural awareness and personal and professional comfort that is a precondition to particular individuals being capable of delivering their expertise in the given context, and not in isolation from it.
- Global organisations have the ability to *move quickly* in order to respond to market opportunities wherever these may occur. This does not always sit easily with organisations of the sheer size and complexity that a global presence demands.
- The ability to command *supply* and *distribution* chains and resources wherever these are required is also essential. Genuinely global organisations have also to ensure that the sheer volumes of resources required, as well as the resources themselves, are again available when required.
- It is essential to be capable of engaging workforces of the right quality, volume and duration wherever and whenever required. Where local workforces are recruited for particular purposes, it is essential that they operate in the organisation's best interests, as well as their own (see Management in Focus 6.2).

Drives for globalisation

Rationally, the drive for globalisation ought to be centred on market need, scope, scale and potential, together with the ability to deliver the products and services and expertise required. This drive is further fuelled by the physical presence of volumes of customers and consumers not presently being served. Additionally, the organisation needs to have the collective capability and willingness to go overseas, together with the production and service delivery capacity in order for the idea to look favourable from all points of view at the outset.

The strength of the driver to go overseas then requires testing; and a series of questions have to be addressed and answered as follows:

1. What is the attitude of the proposed new location to incomers? If favourable, what are the opportunities? If unfavourable, how do we work our way around this?

MANAGEMENT IN FOCUS 6.2

THE LESSONS FROM JAPAN

When Japanese manufacturing companies first established a presence in Western Europe and North America in the 1970s, they took the view that, if they were to become and remain commercially viable in these locations, certain commitments had to be fulfilled.

Accordingly, the large Japanese corporations adopted philosophies of lifetime employment and with very few exceptions, have managed to practise this up to the present day in their activities in Western Europe and North America.

Japanese companies set their own standards of behaviour and performance. This was based on conformity, and this conformity was based in turn upon a cornerstone in employment practice of 'high levels of wages in return for high levels of commitment and high levels of high quality output'.

Japanese companies placed emphasis on the long term, rather than immediate returns, in their overseas activities. This was reinforced through investment in staff training at all levels of the organisation. For example, Nissan spent millions of pounds and dollars training production operatives in Washington, Tyne and Wear, in the UK, and Smyrna, Tennessee, in the United States, before switching on the production lines. As well as the high quality of the finished product, the returns were, and remain, measurable in terms of employee commitment, positive attitudes, identity with the organisation and minute levels of absenteeism.

The Japanese approach was to retain overall executive corporate control at head office. However, in terms of managing localities, divisions and functions, there was a concentration on, and commitment to, the development of managers and supervisors. This was of especial importance in the areas of staff management and problem solving. The high levels of conformity required managers to recognise and solve problems early, rather than institutionalising them.

In the management of staff relations, most of the Japanese companies entered into 'single status workplaces' and 'no strike agreements'. However, the Japanese approach was to place the onus and responsibility on managers to remove status differentials and to ensure that they did not subsequently resurface; and to remove also the reasons why employees might conceivably want to go on strike at all.

All of this was underpinned by high and enduring levels of commitment and especially investment in the areas of new product and service development, creating distribution networks, and sales and service outlets.

In summary therefore, the Japanese manufacturing companies created employment products and services that were of value to the particular locations served. Taking each of the above steps, and committing themselves for the long term, ensured that the companies quickly became respected and valued members of the particular localities in which they established themselves.

2. What are the present attitudes to what we intend to provide? If favourable, what will cause the local population to change their behaviour and use us? If unfavourable, what will it take to persuade the local population of the benefits of doing business with us?

3. What is the initial scale and value of the market? What is the potential scale and

value of the market? What is the scale and value of the market likely to be in six months/one year/five year's time? Do these represent enduringly viable levels of business? How might markets be developed in the future?

4. What are the wider economic and political issues that have to be faced? What is the level of investment required to face these issues?

5. What are the social and cultural issues that have to be faced? Are we prepared to face these?

6. Where do our particular products and services come in the order of priority of the particular markets targeted? Is it possible to influence this in our favour? If so, how; and how much investment is required; and when might returns be seen?

7. What are the legal constraints within which we are required to operate? Are these onerous or a barrier to progress or not? How well do we know the particular locations? What are the perceptions and preconceptions of the location? What are the best ways of providing knowledge and information of a professional standard in order to inform any decision to go there?

This distinctive line of questioning is then followed up alongside detailed market, social, cultural and environmental research; this in turn normally involves establishing a physical presence in the country, region or locality (see Management in Focus 6.3).

Having carried out this detailed assessment, the organisation should now have a clear knowledge and understanding of the opportunities and constraints of going

MANAGEMENT IN FOCUS 6.3

THE UK CONSTRUCTION INDUSTRY IN MALAYSIA

Just how strong the need is for a detailed pre-investigation of markets, locations, cultures and perceptions may be illustrated by an example from the UK construction industry as it sought a presence in Malaysia.

One of the large UK construction companies gained access to the Malay Ministry of Works. The company, a major player in the UK domestic construction industry, accordingly sent a senior manager to meet with top executives at the Malay Ministry of Works, with a view to generating contracts worth many millions of pounds.

The director of the company sat down and began telling the executives of the Ministry of Works what needed to be built for the good of Malaysia, which materials were to be used, and how the contract ought to be structured. The Malay officials looked bemused. They stated: 'But this is not the way in which we do things here.' The director replied: 'This is the way in which we do things in the UK. The UK construction industry sets standards for the rest of the world to follow.'

The conversation carried on in this way until the UK manager, becoming exasperated, finally asked the Malay officials: 'Can you even name ten UK construction companies?' The most senior official present replied: 'No. Can you name ten Malay construction companies? Because if you cannot, it is clear that you do not know or understand the operating environment here, and it is also clear that you do not understand either the ways in which we do things, ahead and opening operations and activities in the chosen location. In some cases, the choice will be not to go ahead; investing time and resources only to pull out before activities commence is one of the consequences and obligations of aspiring to be (or being) international and global. In practice, the truly global or international organisation will have many of these investigations going on at the same time; and as it grows in international experience, it ought to become better able to target those areas of likely potential, and to edit out more quickly those areas where there are few prospects.

Axes of globalisation

A physical presence is the key to market, economic, social, political and cultural knowledge and understanding. Organisations that aspire to enduring global and international influence therefore require a physical presence in the dominant areas of economic and commercial activity. At present, this means having and maintaining a presence in the United States, EU and Japan; and it will increasingly mean extending that presence to India and China. In the longer term a physical presence will also be required in the Middle East, Southern Asia (including Australia and New Zealand), Russia and Central America; and eventually, this presence will be required in Africa and South America.

Organisations develop their global presence further by spreading out from the axis positions into locations close by; and this normally results in the development of sub-axes, created by organisations to establish, maintain and develop their own distinctive spheres of influence in their own ways.

Establishing, developing and maintaining a physical presence along these lines normally follows one or more of the following approaches:

- The purchase of land and premises to set up a distinctive and independent presence.
- Buying up or taking over a local company, provider or partner; the advantage of this approach is the speed of completion. This approach is not normally a problem for the global organisation because of the resources at its command.
- Entering into joint ventures with local providers; this has the advantage of providing access to experience and knowledge and understanding of the locality without the full commitment of resources required for a permanent presence, at least at the initial stage.
- Buying up companies on the supply and distribution sides so as to be able to influence local operations directly; such companies have the added advantage of influencing the rate of supply, and the structure and priorities of supply and distribution in the sector or locality as a whole.
- Buying up or taking over local expert or specialist firms, and using their expertise and reputation as a vehicle for full commercialisation and development in the interests of the global or international organisation.
- Using involvement in project work to gain local knowledge, understanding, experience and reputation; this is of especial value to construction, civil engineering, and information and telecommunications infrastructure projects.
- Outsourcing specific activities to overseas providers; examples include call centres for the financial service industries, clothing and garment manufacture, specialist component manufacture and electrical goods.

Whichever is chosen, the advantage to the global or international organisation is gained as the result of its ability to use its financial and other resources to choose where to go (and therefore, where not to go). How the organisation then uses its presence and influence, having established its initial position, is a matter of individual choice (see Management in Focus 6.4).

Other issues in globalisation

As stated above, the priority in all drives for globalisation ought to be the ability to develop markets and sell products and services. It is essential however to be aware of the other drives that are also present.

Industrial and commercial peer pressure is a major driving force. This form of peer pressure operates when organisations feel themselves to be forced or heavily pressurised into developing overseas activities simply because everyone else in the sector is doing so (or appears to be doing so). This has led many western banks and financial houses to establish call centres and customer service operations in India, South Africa, Central Europe and elsewhere, partly at least because it is the industrial norm (see Chapter 1 above); this also applies to garment manufacture, in which smaller operators feel pressurised to follow the top brands in sourcing their products overseas.

Organisational prestige has to be recognised as a factor in globalisation. Organisations, and their top and senior managers, gain a believed and perceived cachet following globalisation or internationalisation. Such organisations buy into new ventures, products, services and locations so as to be able to appear and describe themselves as international or global; and the results are not always positive (see Management in Focus 6.5).

MANAGEMENT IN FOCUS 6.4

INDIVIDUAL CHOICE: EXAMPLES

The following examples illustrate the range and nature of choices available to large, dominant, global and international companies.

- *The Body Shop* uses its international position and global reputation (for its distinctive ethical position in trading) to ensure that it pays Western prices for the crops and other supplies purchased from the emerging world.

- *Oil companies* take advantage of the lax pollution and environmental laws in West Africa to dump untreated oil production effluent into the Niger Delta in large volumes.

- *Microsoft* continues to maintain its global presence and dominance of information systems through the use of its software, by ensuring that its quality, reliability and security remain universally acceptable (rather than technologically the best).

MANAGEMENT IN FOCUS 6.5

POWERGEN IN BRAZIL

In 1998, Powergen, the UK's electricity supply and infrastructure company, was awarded a contract to build a power infrastructure network across the Brazilian hinterland. This was an extremely prestigious contract, the largest ever awarded to a UK commercial organisation in South America for anything except defence contracting.

When the contract commenced, it quickly became apparent that there were problems that Powergen had no experience of tackling or resolving. The company was an expert provider of electricity and power infrastructure in a small country (the UK). Powergen had no experience, in particular of the sheer vastness of the terrain, the mountains, the forests, or the savannah grasslands that cover so much of the Brazilian hinterland. The company found it impossible to recruit and retain the levels of local expertise needed, nor were they able to provide the expertise from the UK.

After four years, the company pulled out of the contract, and was forced to pay compensation to the Brazilian government. Powergen had to write off £250 million, as well as the loss of the contract value, as the direct consequence of becoming involved in this work in this way.

Preconceptions have to be tackled as an issue, and the overwhelming preconception to be managed is: 'Because something works in one place, it will work elsewhere.' This has caused organisations in such diverse industries as toys, soft drinks, clothing and fashion accessories to put large volumes of resources into hitherto untapped markets on the assumption that because there was no activity at present, activities could be developed if only the global or international company could get in. For example:

- Mattel Inc., the toy company, opened up toy shops in Romania and Bulgaria because they thought themselves to be well known throughout the globe. The children who were to buy the toys however had no idea of what they were for or how to use them. The levels of poverty presently existing in these countries meant that there were far more important things in life than playing with toys.
- Sophie Mirman, the founder of Sock Shop, developed a fully commercial and very successful UK operation by opening retail outlets in railway stations selling socks, stockings, underwear, scarves and hats. Following this success, Ms Mirman opened retail outlets in the railway stations of New York and elsewhere in the United States. Sock Shop spent heavily on these ventures, only to lose everything. The reason the US ventures failed was because there was no history, tradition or expectation of needing or wanting to buy socks and underwear at railway stations, and Sock Shop failed to change this perception.
- *Vogue*, the international glamour magazine, sought to open an edition to take advantage of the new-found prosperity in post-communist Russia. The magazine was to be delivered in Moscow exactly as elsewhere – the universal structure, full of glamorous features and photographs, localised for Russia in

exactly the same way that other editions were (and are) localised for London, New York, Paris, Tokyo and elsewhere. The Russian venture failed; post-communist prosperity turned out to be a myth; and even those who could afford to buy the magazine chose not to do so, preferring to guard their resources against further economic collapses, hardships and chaos.

Political pressure is an issue; and political pressure as a force for globalisation and internationalisation comes about as the result of political drives to develop preferred national spheres of influence. There are two main approaches as follows:

- The government of a country makes it easy for overseas corporations to enter and establish a presence. This process is called inward investment. Inward investment is normally due to political drives to develop and increase volumes of employment in depressed areas. At present, this form of incentive is being given by governments in Asia to encourage manufacturing, service and oil exploration firms to come in. It is also the device that has been used by UK governments among others to encourage Japanese and Korean car and electrical goods firms to establish themselves in the UK since the 1970s.
- The other approach that is used is where the government of one country wants an economic sphere of influence in other countries. It therefore encourages its largest, most powerful and influential companies and organisations to set up in the preferred locations. The most extreme example at present is the way the US government provides commercial and revenue incentives to giant US corporations to open subsidiaries and enduringly viable activities in Iraq. Again however, the process is not new and has been observed since the establishment of trading stations (and piracy) by European governments in the sixteenth century in North and South America, and subsequently in India, the Dutch East Indies, French Indo-China and many other areas.

Developing a global presence and influence

Once the decision to develop a global and international range of activities and operations has been taken, a further series of choices is required. At the hub of these choices lies addressing the key question of whether to:

- think global/act global, in which the organisation's policy is to impose its own preferred ways of working wherever activities are to take place
- think global/act local, in which the organisation seeks to match its own strengths with local customs, habits and values, and in particular with locally preferred ways of working.

Neither is right or wrong in itself; each brings its own opportunities and consequences; and so a further set of decisions is required:

- Think global/act global ought to mean that the organisation's own standards of conduct and performance are so high as to transcend anything that may be present anywhere. Organisations that think global/act-global do however use their size and command of resources to impose their own ways of working and patterns of conduct on particular locations, exploiting them, closing down and moving on to the next place. Standards of management practice in health and safety, staff supervision, hours of work, training, wages and salaries are imposed from outside; and while some global and international organisations invest high levels of commitment in those areas, others do not (see Management in Focus 6.6).

● Think global/act local is superficially more wholesome and therefore intrinsically attractive. However, this also brings its own responsibilities. Organisations bringing UK or EU wage levels, working practices and overall standards to other locations need to consider the effects that paying staff in such ways may have on the structure and stability of the local and wider economy of the chosen locations. Organisations that establish consultative and participative styles of management can, and do, meet resistance because local workforces do not always have any knowledge or understanding of such approaches and do not expect them from places of work. There is a responsibility therefore to ensure that investment is made from the outset in training, educating and briefing staff of the ways in which activities are to be carried out. Additionally, if local managers are recruited and given executive responsibility, they need to be able to deliver productivity and output from the locality in ways acceptable to the organisation as a whole.

The need therefore is to choose which of the two lines to go down, and then undertake to accept and discharge the full range of responsibilities that accrue as a direct result. This is a major management discipline in globalisation and internationalisation, and it occurs as the direct result of taking the decision to go global or international. This decision is not always fully appreciated or understood. It is

MANAGEMENT IN FOCUS 6.6

GARMENT MANUFACTURE FOR THE GLOBAL CLOTHING INDUSTRY

In the recent past, there have been many scandals over the conditions under which branded and fashionable clothing, footwear and sportswear are manufactured for consumption in the West and developed markets by those working in sweatshop conditions in south-east Asia, Central America and the islands of the Pacific Ocean.

Originally, without doubt, the problem was not malevo-lently created. However, faced with organisation and shareholder pressures to drive costs down, customer pressures to drive up quality and volumes, and macro-commercial and economic pressures to drive up sales volumes and profit margins, the clothing and sports goods companies have found the supply side the easiest part of the operating environment to dominate, influ-ence and pressurise. This has resulted, in some cases, in low and declining levels of wages, increased hours and compulsory overtime for those in the factories, and ever-increasing productivity, output and quality targets. The result has been a general perception that this is how all clothing is made; and this has caused others to look to the developing world to source their garments also.

additionally the case that organisations who seek to undertake and discharge their full range of responsibilities and obligations can, and do, find themselves facing severe pressure from elsewhere (see Management in Focus 6.7).

MANAGEMENT IN FOCUS 6.7

FAIRTRADE

Fairtrade is both an organisation and a brand. The Fairtrade organisation inspects and assesses the ways in which organisations from the developed world conduct themselves in every aspect of their dealings with emerging-world suppliers. The key criteria on which these assessments are made are:

- the treatment of staff
- prices paid
- length of trading relationship
- variations in contracts
- quality assurance.

Organisations that satisfy each of these criteria are allowed to use the 'Fairtrade' logo; this gives a form of branding reflecting the strength and integrity of the trading relationship, based on the above criteria.

The approach is not new. During the eighteenth and nineteenth centuries, many European trading companies sought to ensure longevity, consistency and assuredness of supplies through ensuring that emerging world suppliers continued to want to trade with the Western organisations. The Fairtrade brand and approach arose from a combination of pressures from the United Nations, World Health Organisation, and other transnational bodies in response to concerns that prices in the emerging world were being driven down. Companies such as The Body Shop, Twining's Teas and many of the branded coffee retailers pioneered the approach as they pursued the greatest possible range and quality of ingredients for their particular products. In particular, when she was travelling the world and looking for new ingredients, Anita Roddick of The Body Shop promised the farmers with whom she came into contact, and from whom she agreed to buy, that she would pay Western prices for their crops.

A further boom in Fairtrade was driven by the Western coffee shop explosion of the 1990s and early twenty-first century. Starbucks especially undertook to pay 'fair' prices for the crops that they bought, both for their premium retail offerings and also for their standard products. Accordingly, Starbucks were given the Fairtrade logo to display. Starbucks continue to run a high-added-value, high-brand organisation, selling a wide range of coffees and other drinks and snacks at premium prices. The variety of coffees, the need to source them from different parts of the world, and the Fairtrade logo and endorsement, all add to the knowledge and perception of high quality.

Those that enter into genuine Fairtrade arrangements face constant questions from shareholders and other backers, demanding to know why managers are choosing to pay over the odds for supplies and commodities that can be obtained for a fraction of the present cost elsewhere. The question is not always easy to answer; and not always easy to justify in the short term, when shareholders are seeking quick and assured returns in volatile stock markets. However, it should be noted that each of the examples referred to above is a high-quality brand, delivering high-value-added products and services to niche markets; and at present, these are both able and willing to bear the additional cost on the supply side.

Organisational and management aspects

Whatever the approach taken, as above, there are some universal issues that have to be addressed. These are as follows:

- organising and managing across distances
- organising and managing across cultures
- organising and managing expertise and technology
- developing an organisational ethos of globalisation.

Organising and managing across distances

Whatever the approach taken, the need for global presence, influence and reach requires the establishment of regional and local offices and facilities. The decision is then required as to whether to staff them with locals or from headquarters, or a combination. Whichever is chosen, systems of reporting relationships, progress checks and controls are required, and these must be culturally acceptable and technologically compatible, as well as functionally deliverable.

It is also the case that from time to time remote locations will need to be visited by somebody from head office for operational reasons; and in any case they ought to be visited by those from head office on a regular basis in order to preserve and develop an active identity and mutuality of interest. There is then a question of how long it takes in fact to get from head office to the remote location, how long it may be necessary to stay there, how easy it is to get back afterwards how long it will take to do so.

Organising and managing across cultures

Effective organising and managing across cultures requires attention to the behavioural aspects of creating and developing effective working relations. One key part of this is to recognise the question of physical access and presence as above. Additionally, as stated above, it is clearly open to organisations either to impose their own ways of working, or to try and work in harmony within the local prevailing culture, customs, habits and social pressures.

Whichever is chosen, it is essential to commit to learning, knowing and understanding the local customs and patterns of behaviour. If the organisation is going to choose to impose its own way on the particular locality, it will then be fully aware of where the cultural and behavioural clashes are going to occur. Conversely, if the organisation is going to work within the local customs, it will then be fully aware of the constraints under which it is going to have to deliver commercially viable products and services. In either case, it is going to need a clear idea of where the pressures on head office staff are going to come from, and the nature of these pressures. It is consequently going to have to develop a deep level of knowledge, understanding and expertise about the local environment.

From this level of knowledge and understanding comes a much clearer capability to decide whether commercially viable activities are sustainable in the given set of circumstances. This ought then to be further considered, and a direct set of questions can be posed as follows:

- Does this location actually need or want us? And if so, why and under what conditions? And if not, why not; and is there anything that we can do to change this view?

● Where do the local sources of power and influence lie? What is the nature of the relationship that should be developed with them? How ought this power and influence be harmonised with what we have to offer? How might this power and influence work against us if we do not get the relationship right?

The result of addressing these questions ought to be a detailed evaluation of the ways in which the cultural knowledge and understanding already gained are then likely to affect, both positively and negatively, the potential for effective activities (see Management in Focus 6.8).

MANAGEMENT IN FOCUS 6.8

ACN INC. AND THE TELECOMMUNICATIONS REVOLUTION

ACN provides a range of discounted utilities, products and services. Founded in Chicago in 1989, it has grown to establish a presence in the United States and Canada, 18 countries in Western Europe and Australia. The company headquarters is in Chicago, and it has regional head-quarters in Amsterdam and Sydney.

Products and services

The discounted utilities, products and services sold by the company in different regions consist of the following:

● North America: telecom-munications, gas, elec-tricity and water.
● Australia: telecommuni-cations.
● Western Europe: tele-communications, mainly landline but with some mobile telecommunica-tions in some countries.

The core product and service is landline telecommunica-tions. For all the products and services, the basis for business is to acquire capacity from particular utility providers, and then sell this capacity on to individual consumers at rates fractionally below the local provider's prices and charges. Thus for example, in France, ACN acquired the right to buy landline telecommunications capacity from France Telecom at 1 cent per minute. France Telecom sells to customers at 2.5 cents per minute; and so ACN will sell at 2.2 cents per minute. In the United States, ACN acquired the right to buy energy from the electricity generating companies at 0.5 cents per kilowatt hour (kWh); the rate charged to customers by other providers is 1.5 cents per kWh, and so ACN sells to customers at 1.3 cents per kWh.

The product is sold as a niche brand immediately below the rates available on the mass market from established providers.

Developing the business

The company gained its initial momentum through taking advantage of the deregulation of the US telecommunications and energy markets. When-ever, and wherever, particular markets have been deregu-lated, the result has been to attract entrepreneurs, pioneers and business developers (and sharks) to provide competition for the existing public monop-oly or near-monopoly. ACN was one of many such compa-nies at the time. The position was replicated in deregulated sectors in the UK and else-where. In the UK telecommu-nications sector, BT was ordered to give up part of its landline monopoly. This led to Mercury and others being able to offer landline services. Companies such as OneTel and Unix were able to buy landline capacity from BT and sell it on at their own preferred rates and ranges of costs and charges.

ACN entered the UK telecommunications market in 2002, buying capacity from BT and selling it on at its own preferred charge levels, coming in as usual at just below BT rates.

Developing the French market

ACN entered the French telecommunications market in early 2004. The company followed its usual pattern of buying capacity from the national monopoly, in this case France Telecom. It then set about selling to the French population.

The sales method

ACN have always used a form of multi-level marketing (MLM). MLM is a method of product and service distribution that relies on one individual finding a number of customers to sell to, and these customers then find another number of customers to sell to, and these customers then find another number of customers to sell to, and so on. A web or network is created.

This method has been used in various sectors to distribute a variety of products and services. Some have been successful and are well established in different locations and cultures. For example, Avon

has a high reputation and well-established network of this form of selling in the UK; Tupperware also used this approach, and only failed or began to lose its position of pre-eminence because supermarkets and other retail outlets started selling equivalent products.

Others have been less successful and more contentious. Some operations have led to accusations of pyramid selling. Pyramid selling is very similar to MLM, but the products and services have to be bought and paid for in full by individuals who are then faced with sole and independent responsibility for selling on. This is strictly illegal in the UK.

ACN and MLM

ACN use an adopted format. The difference between ACN's method and other MLM (or pyramid selling) is that there are no products or inventories to hold. CAN service is sold by independent associates who are rewarded for finding new customers and signing them up, and for their subsequent volume of telephone usage. Further rewards are gained when the those new customers then sign up customers of their own. Each level of customer thus contributes both to their own prosperity and, in particular, to the prosperity of those above them.

The market

Since deregulation there have

been many entrants into these markets, as stated above, but the main providers of telecommunications services have remained the big national companies – AT&T, BT, FT. Deregulation has forced each to improve its product and service quality. In general, each has been able to use its dominant market position and enduring brand recognition to do this effectively.

At the margins, new providers have been able to grow successful, profitable and effective businesses; the sheer volume, size and service usage in the telecommunications sector makes this both possible and, for good providers, highly profitable.

ACN target the core markets, those served by BT/FT, rather than attempting to get people who already have other providers to change again.

This is an American company opening up operations in Western Europe, and with the potential for starting operations elsewhere in the world also. It is essential to recognise that there is a physical distance between the United States and Western Europe that has to be managed effectively; and there are cultural barriers also. In this case, these may be summarised as: an American company, using English expatriate staff, to develop a business presence, products and services in France and Spain.

Organising and managing expertise and technology

Any organisation seeking a global presence or influence has to equip itself with communication, information and telecommunications technology that is capable of being used anywhere in the world. This is to ensure that the key managerial functions of coordination, communication, progress chasing and reporting can be conducted from anywhere, at any time, in response to the full range of circumstances, markets and activities in which the organisation is involved.

It is also likely that product and service delivery technology are going to be required; this too must be capable of full and effective operation wherever it is located, and capable of harmonisation and integration with the organisation's other production, service, delivery and information systems.

Expertise requires further consideration. Those who have expertise which can be delivered anywhere in the world must be both willing to do this, and also capable of fitting in to particular cultures and locations (see Management in Focus 6.9).

MANAGEMENT IN FOCUS 6.9

SCHLUMBERGER AND OIL PROSPECTING ENGINEERS

Schlumberger, the French oil engineering and exploration company, undertook extensive staff profiling to ensure that those who applied to work in remote locations were not only expert but also personally and culturally suited to the work.

The profiling approach consisted of a detailed series of examinations and tests conducted over the course of one week. The purpose was to establish strength of character, capabilities and resourcefulness, and response to crises and emergencies. Each of these capabilities was required in addition to high levels of education in geological and mining engineering.

The desired outcome of the profiling was to ensure that those selected for the work were able to complete 24-month tours of duty without leaving the company. Key characteristics identified which gave the greatest possible chance of success in meeting this objective were as follows:

- age range 28–36
- high levels of academic and educational achievement from the age of ten
- single persons of either gender
- the provision of career opportunities once tours of duty have been completed.

It was additionally established that the maximum compulsory tours of duty in a single location ought to be of no more than six months; after this, it should be up to the individual to choose whether to stay in the particular location or to move on. It was additionally necessary to provide regular flights from remote locations to places where normal and familiar human contact could take place. The company also undertook to ensure that all staff working in remote locations visited head office in Paris for at least one week every year.

The result was to cut down staff turnover in these activities from 70 per cent per annum to 12 per cent per annum.

Developing an organisational ethos of globalisation

Global managerial expertise is at least partly dependent on personal attitudes, approaches and aspirations, as discussed above. These attitudes, approaches and aspirations are a function of specific personality traits that include tenacity, a love of the unknown, determination to explore and thirst for adventure, together with a professional commitment to do the job and deliver the expertise in the ways that the particular location demands, operating within its constraints.

This clearly indicates that international and global organisations need to make extensive investment in the development of both expertise and character of those staff who are to be posted overseas (see Management in Focus 6.9 above). As well as high levels of education and skills and expertise development, there needs to be a structured series of placements and secondments in order to build cultural awareness, and the capability of dealing effectively with workforces, customers and suppliers in their own domain.

By the same token, a view is required of how to train, develop and make expert and effective those staff recruited from particular localities. A view is required as to whether staff recruited from particular localities are to be given the full range of opportunities afforded to those from head office and from the organisation's land of origin.

There is additionally the need to create and develop those capabilities in the people who are to become the future generations of top, key and senior organisation management. Leading and directing a global organisation from a given location requires extensive travel, the ability to understand situations very quickly, acceptability in all locations, and expertise in taking effective strategic decisions, quickly in many cases, according to the constraints of the particular situation.

● Dominance, dependence and responsibility

Global and international organisations moving into new areas normally have the economic, financial and resource capability to dominate individual locations. This dominant position gives rise to a further series of decisions that must be taken:

- whether to use the dominant position to exploit the particular location, take what can be taken and then leave, or to develop a position of corporate citizenship and use the resource capability for social infrastructure and other development as well as a commercial basis
- whether to adopt and impose absolute head office standards and customs, or to harmonise with the particular locality (as above)
- whether one approach is to be used in all locations, or whether each location will be considered on its own merits.

The position arrived at is one of active responsibility. The outcome is knowledge, understanding and acceptance that the organisation is using its resources in prescribed and predetermined ways.

At operational and functional levels, clear decisions are then taken in the following areas:

- whether to treat staff in all locations with absolute standards, or to allow standards to vary

- whether to use the dominant position to drive down wages and drive out competitors
- whether to use the dominant position to engage in production and service flooding and dumping, driving out local providers and others
- whether to use the dominant position to buy up property, suppliers and distribution channels, or to use these on an independent basis.

Again, a clear set of decisions is then arrived at. In some areas, there are moral dimensions that have to be considered, and these are never easy to resolve. Each of these considerations forms a key priority for all those who aspire to be global and international organisations. Those who become international managers need to be able to take these decisions, and to be prepared to justify and defend them clearly and unequivocally.

● Conclusions

The purpose of this chapter has been to outline and illustrate the main issues, responsibilities and obligations that managers have to face when the decision is taken that their organisations are to expand into global and international markets. This also reflects the operating environment for those managers who find themselves working in organisations that are already global and international.

Adopting this kind of approach also means that key questions are constantly addressed. Of primary importance are the following:

- The ability to manage across distances and cultures; and the ability to deliver the organisation's core purposes within the given constraints. Of primary importance is the need to ensure the absolute standards and quality of: communications and information systems; transport, supply and distribution networks; and product and service delivery volumes.
- Knowing and understanding that whatever can, and will, go wrong is certain to be compounded by the physical and cultural distances that have to be covered.
- Knowing and understanding that a physical presence is required and demanded in particular sets of circumstances; and again, the distance issue may mean that this is not always easy to achieve in the longer term.

Managing in these conditions, and creating and developing the expertise required, is certain to be an organisational and managerial priority for as long as the present approaches to globalisation instituted by Western companies exist. The material covered in this chapter indicates the nature, range and applications of this expertise, both to ensure that the overall viability of the organisation is maintained, and to be able to address problems as and when these do arise.

CRITICAL THINKING, ANALYSIS AND EVALUATION

1. Identify the cultural and distance issues that have to be addressed by a company exporting its products from south-east England to north-eastern France and Belgium.
2. Identify the advantages and disadvantages of buying in supplies on a 'Fairtrade' basis.

3. What form of cultural evaluation should take place on the part of a western organisation seeking to open activities in Malaysia? How would this differ, if at all, if the company were to change its mind and open activities in Latvia?

4. Because of a production hold-up, a western manager running a production operation in Pakistan now has to get his/her staff to work during a religious festival. What options are open to him/her?

DEVELOPING MANAGEMENT SKILLS AND EXPERTISE

SPORTS GOODS

One of the major branded sports goods companies had a problem with a supplier. The supplier, a wholly owned subsidiary factory in rural Malaysia, contacted head-quarters to state that there was a problem with wholesale distribution.

A senior production engineer was dispatched to go and see the problems for himself. He left head office and arrived for a full briefing the following day in Kuala Lumpur. The regional manager could tell him little more than 'there was a problem'. Because of the remoteness of the location, the transport difficulties and the short-comings in the communications infrastructure, it was very difficult to get real information.

The senior production engineer accordingly set out the following day to visit the factory. A four-hour flight in a small plane was followed by a four-hour drive to the factory. The road was uncertain, flooded in places and rutted throughout. On the drive to the factory, the manager passed two lorries obviously struggling to cope with the conditions.

At the end of the third day out from headquarters, the senior production engineer arrived at the factory. Tired and travel-lagged from the flight and drive, he was greeted by the entire factory staff who had put on a special welcome for him. After the festivities which ran on well into the following day, the factory manager did his best to explain that everything was going exactly as scheduled. The only problem was the fact that it was very difficult to get lorries into the factory during the present season; and consequently, there were hold-ups with product discharge and delivery. As well as the present range of products in question, the factory manager pointed proudly to the array of cricket gear for the Australian, Indian and Pakistani markets, all of which had been beautifully produced, and which were just waiting for lorries to take them away. There were, however, certain to be hold-ups with these products also.

After a short rest, the senior production engineer debated the matter with the factory manager. In particular, he asked for the factory manager's opinions on the earliest date that products could be got to Kuala Lumpur and Penang for shipping onwards. The factory manager did not know; it depended on the lorries; and he knew only that the roads were bad as he had said before.

For the next four days, the senior production engineer was unable to leave. He therefore used the time to do his best to consider the options open to him, concentrating on how to get the products out as quickly as possible once they were manufactured.

The factory was by local standards a good one, paying relatively well, and giving the staff fully regulated rest breaks and periods away. Education was provided for child staff up to the age of 16. On the one hand therefore, the company was proud both of the integrity and effectiveness of its operation, and of the quality of goods provided. On the other hand, locational issues meant that, from time to time, the problems now faced by the senior production engineer were certain to arise again in the future.

Questions

1. Identify the courses of action open to the senior production engineer in the pursuit of getting the goods to market as quickly as possible.
2. Identify possible longer-term approaches that could be taken by the organisation so as to get the goods to market when required.
3. Identify the range of lessons for managers and students of management from this situation.

Chapter seven

Organisations, managers and the environment

'The reasonable man adapts himself to the world.
The unreasonable man persists in trying to adapt the world to himself.
Therefore all progress depends on unreasonable men.'
George Bernard Shaw, *Man and Superman* (play 1903).

'We predict an inflation rate of no more than 5 per cent.
We also predict an interest rate of no more than 5 per cent.
It is therefore impossible that the Channel Tunnel will run over-budget.'
UK Treasury Briefing Paper, 1986.

'The Titanic is unsinkable.'
Universal myth, 1911–12.

Chapter outline

- Introduction
- The environment of business and management
- Analysing the environment
- Setting priorities, aims and objectives
- Decision making
- Management style and priorities
- Limitations
- Conclusions

Chapter objectives

After studying this chapter, you should be able to:

- understand the main organisational and environmental pressures and constraints that have to be accommodated

- understand the need for environmental analysis as a foundation of managerial expertise

- identify specific organisational forms, and the particular constraints under which they have to operate

- identify both opportunities and problems associated with decision making and organisational progression and development

- understand the specific opportunities, consequences and pitfalls that are present in organisational and managerial attitudes and approaches to their environment – especially those relating to decision-making processes.

● Introduction

Organisations are created on the basis that more can be achieved by people working in harmony and towards a stated purpose than by individuals acting alone. It is also more efficient and effective to specialise in seeking to serve or fulfil a given set of wants or needs. Resources – technology, expertise, information, finance and property – can then be commanded and ordered for the stated purpose, within the constraints of the environment.

The result of this is that society is more or less founded on a highly complex and all-pervading network of organisations, each of which serves a given purpose and all of which serve the entire range of purposes required. Organisations pervade all aspects of life – economic, social, political, cultural, religious, communal and family. They serve needs and essentials – food, shelter, health, education, water, energy, transport and communications – as well as wants and choices – cola, cinema, football. They serve these needs and wants from before the cradle, through every aspect of life until the grave.

An organisation is any body that is constituted for a given purpose, and which then establishes and conducts activities in pursuit of this purpose. Managers are then employed by the owners and directors of organisations to run them on their behalf.

For those who work in them, organisations form a distinctive and significant part of their society. Human beings generally need, want and enjoy the company of other people. Organisations fulfil social as well as technical, occupational and professional needs.

There is therefore a great complexity in the relationships between organisations, between organisations and their wider environment, among those who work within them, and between organisations and those who come to them for products and services.

It is now necessary to consider in more detail the factors and components that affect these relationships. These relationships in turn form the basis of: designing and implementing effective organisation strategies, policies and direction; creating and developing effective behaviour in organisations; and providing a focus for the leadership, direction and top management.

● The nature of the environment

The environment in which organisations operate, and in which managers have to manage, is ever-changing and complex. In order to stand any chance of being successful, managers have to be able to operate within the constraints and complexities present. It is therefore essential to know and understand the forces that are present within the environment as a whole, and to be able to assess and evaluate these forces in detail, in the context of the given organisation, its products and services, and markets served, in order to respond to stakeholder demands and interests.

The environment in which organisations and managers have to operate may be summarised under the headings of:

- ● external factors
- ● the immediate environment
- ● internal factors.

External factors

The external factors and forces that have to be understood are the economic, social, political and legal constraints which form the basis of the wider overall operating environment. These forces include: the present and evolving nature of the trading environment; the nature of competition and rivalry; and whether the given markets are expanding, stagnant or contracting. This has to be seen in the further context of: inflation and interest rates, and currency exchange rates; wider volumes of economic activity; degrees of confidence in the trading environment; and the ways in which political, financial and economic interests manage change and develop each of these elements.

Economic forces are directly affected by the actions of government and the central banking system through the use of interest rate and currency valuation policies, changes in rates of taxation, and specific initiatives such as regional development (see Management in Focus 7.1).

Wider social issues refer to the mobility of the population, availability or scarcity of skills and expertise, pay and reward levels in given sectors, and the volumes of jobs and occupations available. This is related to and influences absolute levels of prosperity and relative levels of prosperity by occupation and location; this also influences the capability and willingness to spend money on goods and services.

The population structure and demographics have to be considered. It is usual to evaluate this through reference to age structures, cultural and social issues, and the wider general expectations and perceptions of what the society ought to provide. Social issues are additionally affected by taxation levels, as mentioned above, and related also to the capability and the willingness of the population to pay taxes and compulsory or near-compulsory charges for public services and utilities.

MANAGEMENT IN FOCUS 7.1

GOVERNMENT ACTIONS AND INFLUENCES

In the early twenty-first century, it became clear that the UK consumer population as a whole was heavily in debt. Statistics showed that the average UK citizen had debts of approximately £5000 on consumer goods alone. Moreover, these debt levels were rising; this was being fuelled by rapid increases in property prices and values, and by allowing people to take enhanced capital value out of their homes, and spend it on consumer goods.

Over the period 2003–05, the Bank of England increased interest rates by a total of 2 per cent in six stages. This had the effect of making borrowing much more expensive.

The immediate result was to kill the property market. While property values did not fall, transaction volumes in property sales and purchases fell, meaning that the values could not in practice be realised. This led to a wider effect on general spending, leading to downturns in all areas of activity, as people were forced to service their debts at new higher levels, and as they began collectively to look much harder at what they were spending, and the reasons.

Legal issues refer to the present state of the law, and to envisaged changes in it. Of particular present concern to organisations and managers are the ever-greater protection for staff at work, and the strengthening of health and safety legislation, including the possibility of introducing corporate manslaughter for negligence at disasters. Other areas of present and enduring concern relate to advertising and marketing, the materials used in production and packaging, and strengthening demands for accurate descriptions of products and services (see Management in Focus 7.2).

The other parts of the external environment that require continued assessment and consideration are: technology, information and telecommunications infrastructures; the strengths, opportunities and constraints of the transport and distribution networks and infrastructure; and the energy charges that arise as the direct consequence of having to use these infrastructures.

The immediate environment

Knowing and understanding the immediate economic, social, political and legal environment requires taking the wider concerns outlined above, and relating them directly to the location or locations where activities are taking place. Particular priorities are:

- availability of staff skills and expertise
- property and transport prices in particular localities
- competitive demands for staff skills and expertise from others in the area
- competition for supplies and the distribution network in the immediate area
- the quality of the energy, transport and telecommunications infrastructure in the immediate area

MANAGEMENT IN FOCUS 7.2

THE OBESITY CRISIS

Faced with evidence that up to half the UK population is either overweight or obese, both government and health lobbies targeted the fast food industries and snack providers as the cause. Of particular concern was the fact that the take-away food industry did not have to display the composition or ingredients of its products, unlike off-the-shelf grocery and supermarket purchases. Legislation is therefore widely anticipated in response to this.

This is a legal/political response which will certainly force organisations and their managers in these sectors to redesign their packaging and presentation, and this will incur cost. A full evaluation of the consequences of these and similar moves ought to include: possible upturns, as well as downturns, in product consumption; demands for new ingredients; changes in sales volumes of what is presently on offer; and the loss of reputation of some of the products.

It additionally needs to be noted in passing that the obesity problem is not confined to the UK. The United States admits to having an equally serious problem; and there are concerns also in France, Germany, Holland, Belgium, Italy and Spain.

● specific issues concerning replacement, maintenance and upgrades of all organisational technology, equipment, expertise and resources.

There is additionally the question of the overall aura or climate of the organisation and its industrial or commercial sector (see Chapter 5), which can, and does, affect the capability of organisations to attract and retain staff and expertise. In many cases, this capability is not so much a function of competition for staff and expertise from other organisations, but rather a wider malaise within the sector that cannot easily be remedied (see Management in Focus 7.3).

Internal factors

The internal environment of the organisation is a reflection of capability and willingness to operate within the wider external and immediate forces present, to create effective working relationships and conditions, and to deliver products and services whatever the constraints. Priorities for managers include the capability and willingness to:

● improve cost bases so as to be able to remain effective at times of rising energy and fuel costs, interest and transaction rates, and budget constraints
● respond to changes in employment production and service law while keeping disruption to a minimum
● respond to the arrival of new employers into the area.

MANAGEMENT IN FOCUS 7.3

ATTRACTING AND RETAINING STAFF IN THE NHS

In its primary functions of medical care, sickness and emergency treatment, and overall healthcare provision, the UK NHS continues to experience difficulties in attracting, recruiting and retaining staff to work in its core professions of medicine, surgery and nursing. These problems have been caused in part by depressed salary levels which have resulted in nursing and junior medical staff not being able to afford to buy property, and partly by the extremely stressful working conditions that are generated by staff shortages and lack of medical technology resources.

The problems have been compounded, however, by continued restructurings in the NHS overall; and by the consequent pressures on local managers as the result of having to constantly change their aims and objectives to meet the latest rounds of political targets.

The net result is that for individual hospitals and other health service facilities in many areas, it is impossible to attract any staff at all to train or work in these professions. Local managers have therefore to find alternative solutions to the particular problems.

The wider lesson for all managers and students of management is to know and understand the fact that these extreme constraints can apply within any sector, and to use whatever influence they have to structure work as effectively as possible within these extreme constraints. It is additionally the case that anyone working within these constraints will always have operational problems, whatever the location or nature of the organisational and operating environment.

The professional management discipline required is therefore to know and understand where the pressures and forces are likely to come from, and to create the conditions within the organisation, departments, divisions and functions that enable the required responses to be made. It is therefore in turn necessary to be able to conduct each of the following activities effectively:

- analyse the environment
- set effective priorities and targets
- take effective decisions, and create effective series of decisions
- form the basis for an effective management style
- understand the wider constraints of the limitations present.

● Analysing the environment

The normal basis for analysing the environment is to be able to identify, separate out and classify the forces present.

The standard way of approaching this is to use the PEST approach (see Chapter 8) in which political, economic, social and technological pressures are analysed and evaluated.

For the specific purposes of developing the discipline of analysing the environment in full, and to ensure the maximum completeness of coverage, Cartwright (2001) proposed the SPECTACLES approach. He argued that it was not enough to limit consideration to political, economic, social and technological issues (the PEST elements), and developed the wider view required under the acronym SPECTACLES as follows:

- *Social*: changes in society and societal trends; demographic trends and influences.
- *Political*: political processes and structures; lobbying; the political institutions of the UK and EU; the political pressures brought about as the result of, for example, the Social Charter and market regulation.
- *Economic*: referring especially to sources of finance; stock markets; inflation; interest rates; government and EU economic policy; local, regional, national and global economies.
- *Cultural*: international and national cultures; regional cultures; local cultures; organisational cultures; cultural clashes; culture changes; cultural pressures on business and organisational activities.
- *Technological*: understanding the technological needs of business; technological pressures; the relationship between technology and work patterns; the need to invest in technology; communications; e-commerce; technology and manufacturing; technology and bioengineering; technological potential.
- *Aesthetic*: communications; marketing and promotion; image; fashion; organisational body language; public relations.
- *Customer*: consumerism; the importance of analysing customer and client bases; customer needs and wants; customer care; anticipating future customer requirements; customer behaviour.
- *Legal*: sources of law; codes of practice; legal pressures; product liability; service liability; health and safety; employment law; competition legislation; European legal pressures; whistle blowing.

- *Environmental*: responsibilities to the planet; responsibilities to communities; pollution; waste management; farming activities; genetic engineering; cost benefit analyses; legal pressures.
- *Sectoral*: competition; cartels, monopolies and oligopolies; competitive forces; cooperation within sectors; differentiation; and segmentation.

Cartwright states that his intention is:

> to widen the scope of analysis that needs to be carried out in order to include a more detailed consideration of the environment and culture within which an organisation must operate, the customer base, competition within the sector, and the aesthetic implications, both physical and behavioural, of the organisation and its external operating environment.

This approach requires managers to take a detailed look at every aspect of their operations within their particular environment and niche. It requires managers to understand fully the broadest range of environmental constraints within which they have to conduct effective operations. It is also much more likely to raise specific, precise, detailed – and often uncomfortable – questions that many managers (especially senior managers) would rather not have to address (see Management in Focus 7.4).

● Setting priorities, aims and objectives

A full understanding and analysis of the environment, and classification of the pressures and constraints present, establishes the context in which priorities, aims and objectives are set. Establishing effective and achievable priorities, aims and objectives is the foundation for measuring and assessing all aspects of organisational and managerial performance (see Chapter 3).

Drucker (1955) summarised this as 'management by objectives'. To be fully effective, management by objectives required the establishment of specific targets and priorities that were capable of achievement within the constraints of the operating, competitive and wider environment. This clarity of approach, and attention to the environment, was essential, whether establishing overarching goals and targets for organisations as a whole, or establishing specific achievements and results desired and demanded of particular departments, divisions, functions, groups and individuals.

Within these constraints, the establishment of priorities, aims and objectives, concentrates on the following:

- key tasks, key results and performance standards
- work improvement plans, setting key tasks against action plans, target dates and intended outcomes
- regular performance reviews based on participation
- attention to future directions, as well as assessment of the present
- previewing and reviewing the potential of staff, products, services and inventions.

For each of these to be effective, management information systems are required; these have to be kept fully up to date at all times. Information has additionally to be capable of delivery in ways that are usable by those who have to take decisions for

MANAGEMENT IN FOCUS 7.4

THE MILLENNIUM DOME

In order to celebrate effectively the second millennium of Christianity in the year 2000, the Millennium Dome was conceived by the UK government in 1994. The Millennium Dome was to be built on a former naval site on the south bank of the River Thames at Greenwich, southeast London. As well as celebrating 2000 years of Christianity, the Dome would provide an exhibition and demonstration of everything that was best about the British way of life.

The project failed. The visitor numbers (projections were estimated at 30,000 per day every day for the year 2000) never materialised; the quality of the exhibitions and presentations was variable; and transport access and egress was never fully resolved.

From the point of view of analysing the environment in this way, the best that could be said for the project was: the micro-environmental issue was addressed, because the pollution present on the site had to be cleared up before the Dome could be built; and from an aesthetic point of view, the Dome was a particularly distinctive design.

From every other point of view, there were shortcomings however. Society had changed, and people would only visit such an exhibition if it was both of a high quality and convenient for them to do so. The political issues, especially in terms of who was to take responsibility, were never fully evaluated; neither were the economic questions of cost, nor the cultural, aesthetic and customer demands for quality

and variety of actual presentation and exhibition content. Wider environmental and sectoral demands in terms of the quality of the transport infrastructure, or specific questions of what constitutes 'a good day out' for those visiting London were not addressed. It was additionally the case that the Millennium Dome was located many miles away from the majority of tourist attractions, the rest of which are in central London.

A full SPECTACLES analysis, conducted in this way, would therefore either have concluded that the Millennium Dome should never have been built in the first place, or if it was to be built, that specific barriers had to be identified and addressed if it was not to turn out as a political, social and organisational failure.

the future; this refers both to those at the top of organisations and to those with specific responsibilities at more junior levels.

Establishing priorities, aims and objectives in this way enables the tangible and high-profile aspects of organisational performance to be addressed. These areas are:

- market standing, reputation and position
- sales performance
- innovation, enterprise, pioneering, research and development
- productivity and output levels
- assessments of resource utilisation: premises, technology, capital goods and equipment, expertise and the human resource.

Assessing these areas in this context ought to lead additionally to developing the capability to address and assess the less tangible areas of organisational cohesion and performance: managerial performance and development, staff performance and attitudes, and the nature of responsibility and accountability towards the public and the wider environment.

Approaching priorities, aims and objectives in these ways gives a basis for the judgement of likely overall profitability and effectiveness, and also for assessing the value and actual profitability and effectiveness of activities presently in hand.

To be fully effective, attention is necessary in each area. While the balance clearly varies between organisations, neglect in any one area is likely to weaken the whole. Setting priorities, aims and objectives additionally has the purpose of ensuring that the organisation is not blinded by extremes of performance in one area to the detriment of the others. For example, excellent sales performance may lead to feelings of complacency and lack of attention to the need for new products, or to any assessment of potential declines in sales, should environmental circumstances change.

Simon (1967) further highlighted the difficulties of establishing effective priorities, aims and objectives within the constraints of the environment; these constraints were related to the capability of the organisation to deliver sustained levels of excellent performance within the changing nature of the operating and competitive environment.

Simon identified three levels of performance:

- *Excellent*: sustained high achievement, output and quality, leading to high levels of profit, effectiveness and satisfaction; in reality achieved by very few organisation.
- *Unsatisfactory*: low levels of achievement, unacceptable to stakeholders, and leading to losses, inefficiency, ineffectiveness and dissatisfaction.
- *Satisfactory*: achieved by most organisations most of the time; satisfactory performance required producing acceptable levels of output, volume and quality, and leading to enduringly acceptable – and therefore satisfactory – levels of profit and effectiveness.

Simon found that the drive for satisfactory performance was influenced by a lack of capability to predict future pressures within the environment; and a lack of capability additionally to be able to respond effectively to changes in these pressures. Simon found that in many organisations and industries, there existed in practice therefore a consensus that satisfactory performance represented an acceptable level of achievement; that in practice, the top priority of senior managers was to ensure that satisfactory levels of performance were achieved. Simon also found that this approach was a major influence on decision-making processes.

Decision making

Whatever the size, nature or purpose of the organisation and the management style adopted, effective decision-making processes are required. Decisions are taken at all levels – strategic and policy; operational, divisional and departmental; managerial and supervisory; and individual. Whatever the level, there are certain fundamental considerations to be considered if the process is to be effective and successful. There are also different stages that have to be understood and followed.

This is the context in which elements and process are considered as follows (see Figure 7.1).

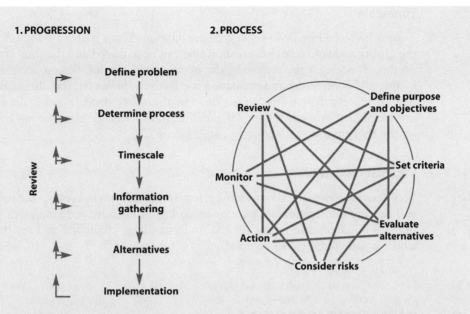

Purpose: to draw the distinction between the two elements of progress and process. The former is a schematic approach; the latter is that from which the former arises, and which refines it into its final format. Effective and successful decision-making requires the confidence that is generated by continued operation of the process.

Figure 7.1 A decision-making model

● Decision making, organisations and their environment

The key features are discussed below.

Problem or issue definition

Issue definition is the starting point of the process. Once this is defined, the likely effects and consequences of particular courses of action can begin to be understood. Failure to do this may lead to considerable waste of time, effort and resource. It is therefore essential to establish clear, achievable and acceptable objectives, and relate these to the full context.

Process determination

Determining the process largely depends on the culture and structure of the organisation or department involved, and the environmental and other pressures on it. It also depends on ways of working and the personalities and groups involved. There may also be key groups – staff, customers, vested interests, pressure groups – who must be consulted on particular matters. Not to do this, in spite of the fact that the decision may be 'right', is likely to minimise or even nullify the whole effect.

Timescale

Time is involved heavily in process determination. There is also a trade-off between the quality and volume of information that can be gathered and the time available to do this. The longer the timescale, the better the chance of gaining adequate information and considering and evaluating it effectively. However, this also increases the cost of the eventual course of action. On the other hand, a quick decision may involve hidden extras at the implementation stage if insufficient time has been spent on the background (see Management in Focus 7.5).

Information gathering

Very few decisions are taken with perfect information; conversely, decisions made without any information are pure guesswork. Both quality and volume of information are required, and means for the understanding, evaluation and review of that which is gathered are also essential.

MANAGEMENT IN FOCUS 7.5

TIMESCALES

Organisation and managerial time is viewed from a variety of points of view, as follows:

- *Steady-state*: the total time frame required in order to engage in, produce, deliver, develop and enhance activities.
- *Productive/non-productive balance*: the amount of time that is actually taken on productive activities; the amount of time that is taken on non-productive activities; the balance of this; and the reasons for this.
- *Maintenance time*: in which periods of equipment and technology maintenance are in-built to organisational activities.

- *Downtime*: in which activities are not taking place. It is again essential to establish the reasons for this.
- *Development time*: as a proportion or percentage of total time available to the organisation; this should be subject to continuous monitoring, review and evaluation.
- *The primary function/ non-primary function balance*: in which organisations assess the volume of total time available to them, in terms of the amount of time spent on dealing with production, service and customer management activities on the one hand, and the

amount of time spent on administration and support on the other.
- *Wasted time*: all organisations have this, and it is essential that this part of time management is assessed in order to understand the reasons for wastage, and where it can be reduced.

These act as a general discipline for the organisation and as specific performance constraints on groups and individuals. Timescales also have to be considered when specific decisions are being taken and implemented; whatever is considered must be capable of achievement and implementation in the time allowed.

The alternatives

The result of the process is that alternative courses of action become apparent. At the very least there is always the choice of doing nothing.

Implementation

This is the point of action. It arises as the result of working through each of the previous elements. The choice made affects future courses of action; as well as the choice, the reasons for which it was made should be understood.

One key part of implementation is the need to provide a basis and rationale for courses of action that sometimes do not appear to be fully logical. At the point of implementation, it is therefore essential to recognise where the non-rational elements lie and, in recognising these, how they can best be accommodated. It is not a prescription for providing perfect decisions. It is rather, the means by which opportunities and consequences of following particular courses of action may be understood, assessed and evaluated.

Stakeholder pressures

Effective understanding and evaluation of the environment, setting priorities, aims and objectives, together with the decision-making processes involved, ought to ensure that there is a sound basis and context for organisational activities. Once preferred courses of action are determined however, it is necessary to know and

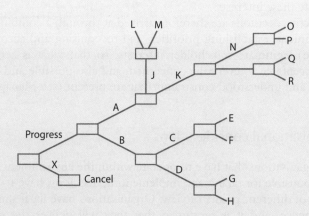

Purpose: to illustrate proposed courses of action, and likely and possible outcomes of them, from a given starting point.

In this particular example, option X – Cancel – is evidently not on the agenda, as the consequences of this are not extrapolated.

What is illustrated are the ramifications that accrue once the decision is taken to progress; and assuming two positive choices (i.e. other than cancellation) at each stage.

The tree is a useful illumination of the complexity and implications of the process, and of the reality of taking one decision.

Figure 7.2 The decision tree

understand, and be able to respond to, the pressures, concerns and legitimate interests of all stakeholders.

It may therefore be necessary to consider:

- staff interests, capability and willingness to implement what has been determined and carry it out to the best of their ability
- shareholder pressures, concerned with the extent to which what has been chosen is capable of delivering the rewards that they seek
- top and senior management interests, in terms of fulfilling their own aims and objectives (which may, or may not, be in harmony with those of the organisation)
- the demands and interests of suppliers, in terms of the volumes and regularity of business that they seek
- the demands and interests of customers and consumers, in terms of the range, volume and quality of products and services that it has been decided to deliver
- economic, social and political groups, including consumer groups, environmental lobbies, other special interest groups, as well as local and public authorities, public agencies and statutory bodies, industrial lobbies and staff representative bodies.

Public services have additionally to be capable of satisfying political demands, drives and restraints, and to be able to respond to changes in those drives and restraints, often at very short notice.

The effective management of stakeholder interests invariably requires some form of organisational adjustment. Organisational adjustment is needed where analysis of the environment shows that decision-making processes are limited or constrained by the interests and influences of the different stakeholder groups. The normal result is that the organisation alters, adjusts or limits its activity in some way, so as to be able to satisfy these interests.

Effective decisions are therefore arrived at through a combination of analysing the environment, establishing priorities, and recognising and accommodating (as far as possible) legitimate stakeholder interests, so that what is actually implemented is both acceptable to everyone concerned, and also possible and achievable within the known and understood constraints that are present (see Management in Focus 7.6).

Organisational considerations

The organisations that have to operate within the environment, and whose managers are responsible for taking and implementing decisions, have to be considered from a variety of different points of view. Organisations have legal status, a presumption of permanence, and it is presumed that they will deliver the products and services stated.

The legal status of organisations refers to their constitution and composition. The main forms of legal status are:

- *Commercial organisations*: sole traders, partnerships, private limited companies and public limited companies (Plc). Each of these organisation forms may additionally be: local, regional, national, international or global; part of a joint or multi-venture; a specialist subsidiary; or an organisation constituted for the purposes of delivering a single project, after which it is disbanded.

MANAGEMENT IN FOCUS 7.6

STARBUCKS IN NORTH LONDON

Starbucks, the high brand international coffee shop chain, identified the potential for opening a retail outlet in Highgate, north London. The company identified premises that could be converted and upgraded in keeping with its overall preferred image. The company's standard forms of market and environmental assessment also concluded that this would be a profitable venture, in harmony with the overall retail environment in the locality.

However, a small but influential pressure group objected. The chief concerns of the pressure group were as follows:

- There were no international brands present in the retail environment.
- Opening a Starbucks would drive out both sole-trade coffee shop operators and the local brands – Costa and Aroma.

Additionally, the group did not want the incursion of a single Starbucks to lead to total domination through the subsequent opening of further Starbucks outlets.

The lobby raised its objections at the planning stage; and was initially turned down. However, it used the resulting publicity to gain support from powerful and influential members of the community. These included merchant bankers, senior civil servants, and stars of film and television. The lobby was therefore able to use the media connections of its new members to gain a much wider coverage of their concerns, and the result was that Starbucks withdrew the application. What was right from a business point of view, was wrong from the point of view of wider concerns, and the decision to pursue this particular venture had to be cancelled.

- *Friendly or mutual societies or cooperatives:* in which the profits and rewards are shared among members.
- *Public bodies and public corporations:* these organisations are the institutions of central, regional and local government that normally have the remit of providing essential public services, providing for civil and military defence, and maintaining the desired and anticipated quality of life on the part of the nation, region or part of society concerned.
- *Non-governmental organisations:* non-governmental organisations are autonomous entities funded by government and constituted for a particular purpose; this includes the constitution of bodies for the independent regulation of specific activities.
- *Churches and other religious foundations:* this category includes charities which are funded by donations and other receipts for stated purposes; these funds are then distributed in the areas with which the charity is concerned.
- *Transnational organisations:* transnational organisations include the United Nations (UN), World Health Organisation (WHO), and International Monetary Fund (IMF); these and other bodies have a general influence on the ways in which organisations operate and interact with their environment; they may, from time to time, make specific pronouncements, recommendations and interventions in given locations, directly affecting the activities of other organisations in those areas.

It is essential to note that the legal status of organisations can, and does, change. Governments privatise public services; commercial organisations undertake merger and takeover activities, and open and close subsidiaries. Changes of legal status can, and do, also occur as the result of changes in international, corporate and company law.

Beneficiaries

The beneficiaries of an organisation are those people for whom the organisation is especially constituted, and whose interests it seeks to serve.

The primary beneficiaries of an organisation are normally its staff, customers, clients, shareholders and suppliers, and these may also be its *ultimate* beneficiaries. However, problems do occur when top and senior managers and (in public services) powerful political interests use organisations in practice for their own ends. Powerful and influential figures and groups tend to disrupt the effectiveness of organisations in the interests of pursuing their own position and reputation. Short-term share-holder drives disrupt the long-term effectiveness of commercial organisations, and political ambitions disrupt the enduring effectiveness of public services.

Changing beneficiaries occurs when organisations change their status. Newly privatised public services have suddenly to run under the financial regimes of the new owners, and a proportion of the funds raised will be redistributed in the form of share dividends rather than going straight back into the services. Mergers and takeovers mean that staff, customers, shareholders and suppliers of the previous organisations have to get used to new ways in which they are to be dealt with, and any or all of these groups may cease to benefit from the new organisation (though these groups are also often replaced by new beneficiaries who find the new organisation attractive to them).

Non-beneficiaries are present where organisations do not deliver what they promise, and where customers and clients do not receive the expected products and services. Attention to non-beneficiaries is a prime concern when changing or varying the quality, range and coverage of all public services, and in ensuring that customers continue to receive adequate quality of supplies following the privatisation of infra-structure and essential commodities of life, especially water, gas, electricity, heating and lighting.

● Management style

The nature of the operating environment, the priorities identified and established, decision-making processes and the legal status of the organisation, all impact heavily on the management style of the organisation. Effective delivery of products and serv-ices depends upon managerial expertise, capability and willingness to operate within these constraints; and this leads to the design and emergence of preferred approaches to staff, workloads, priorities and decision making.

In this context, the key to an effective management style is founded in the approach chosen to the staff of the organisation. This approach is normally one of the following:

- *Unitary*: in which the aims, objectives, hopes, fears, aspirations and ambitions of the individual must be harmonised and integrated with those of the organisation

– and where necessary subordinated so that the overall purpose of the organisation remains the main driving force.

● *Pluralist*: in which the organisation recognises the divergent and often conflicting aims, objectives and drives of the people who work for it. Organisations that take this view normally include opportunities for personal and professional (as well as organisational) fulfilment. The basis is that by recognising this divergence and attending to all needs, organisation needs will be satisfied.

● *Radical*: in which it is recognised that there can be no long-term productive effort and harmony unless everyone involved is given a substantial and meaningful stake in the organisation. This used to be regarded as the Marxist approach, and has therefore fallen into some disrepute. However, many organisations take the view that by offering staff substantial shareholdings in the company for which they work, or substantial profit-sharing arrangements, they engage the direct interest of the staff in their own future and economic prosperity. For example, John Lewis, the department store, divides 15 per cent of its retained profits among its staff, while Semco assigns 23 per cent of its retained profits to its staff.

● *Mutual*: the mutual organisation is normally based on the abolition of status and rank in favour of occupational and organisational effectiveness; however, this normally only works where there is full openness and availability of information, knowledge of activities and understanding of the value of every contribution.

● *Cooperative*: in which the organisation establishes a psychological and behavioural basis of partnership and involvement based on the value of the contribution that everyone is to make.

● *Confrontational*: an adversarial approach to staff. This is based, at best, on the recognition that harmony of objectives is impossible leading to the creation of systems and processes for the containment and management of conflict. At worst it is based on mistrust and coercion, often stemming from a lack of genuine value placed on staff.

Psychological contract

Organisations may be viewed in terms of the nature of the psychological contract that they engage in with their staff. This is the result of implications and expectations that arise as the result of organisational, occupational, professional and personal relationships in specific situations. They vary between all organisations and situations, and may be summarised as follows:

● *Coercive*: whereby the relationship between organisation and staff, and also organisation and customer, is founded on a negative. An example of this is prison – the prisoners are there against their will. It is also present where sections of the community are forced or pressurised into using a monopoly or near-monopoly for an essential commodity or service – examples are electricity, telecommunication, petrol and fuel. It also can be present in institutions such as schools and colleges where the children or students attend because they are required to do so by society.

● *Alienative*: whereby the relationship between staff and organisation is negative. This has traditionally applied to large and sophisticated organisations and especially to those staff working on production lines and in administrative hierarchies where they have no or very little control over the quality and output of work.

- *Remunerative*: whereby the relationship between staff and organisation is clearly drawn in terms of money in return for efforts and attendance. It is normally to be found as the dominant feature where there is also a low level of mutual identity between staff and organisation.
- *Calculative*: whereby the staff have a low commitment to organisation goals and high commitment to current levels of earning and satisfaction. It is again a key feature of the wage–work bargain for production and administrative staff. For those with high levels of professional and technical expertise, the calculative relationship is based on the ability to practise, and the need to find an employer and outlet for those skills and individual drives to serve and become expert.
- *Normative*: whereby the individual commitment to organisational purpose is very high. This is found in religious organisations, political parties and trade unions. It is also increasingly found in business organisations and public service bodies when a normative as well as an economic approach to the wage–work bargain is taken; and in the majority of cases, the normative approach here means 'a committed quarrel' – an ever-present roundelay of arguments (quarrels) over pay and terms and conditions of employment. It is effective as long as the wage–work bargain itself is sound and the organisation accepts a range of obligations and responsibilities to ensure that it is maintained.
- *Internalised*: whereby individual and collective commitment to organisation purpose, activities, attitudes and values is unquestioning.

Viewing organisations from a variety of positions in these ways indicates the background against which aims and objectives are to be drawn up. It also indicates the source of some of the limitations and constraints that have to be taken into account when considering the capabilities of organisations and the nature and relationship of these with the purposes that are to be pursued.

This also gives rise to conflicting and divergent aims and objectives, as those with managerial responsibility either seek to reconcile these divergences, or else prioritise some (often their own interests rather than those of the organisation) at the expense of others (see Figure 7.3).

Limitations

The limitations on both management style and organisation effectiveness are encountered where the context is not fully evaluated or understood. Further problems arise when the elements discussed below are either dominant or not capable of being reconciled with overall purpose.

The first of these is awarding priority to the drive for volume of work rather than quality or effectiveness. This is exacerbated where rewards are given for volume. This is satisfactory only as long as competitive position can be maintained on the basis of volume and as long as some level of profit is achieved. It is invariably unsatisfactory in the long term unless accompanied by drives for quality and effectiveness.

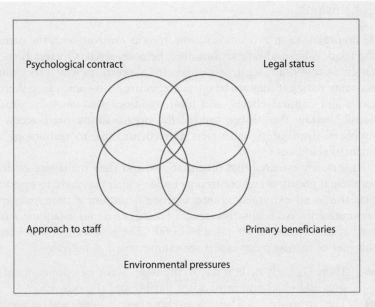

Psychological contract

Legal status

Approach to staff

Primary beneficiaries

Environmental pressures

Figure 7.3 The foundations of management style

Second is a lack of attention to supposedly non-quantifiable aims and objectives – especially for managers, administrators and support functions. At its most positive this gives those categories of staff considerable latitude to exercise judgement, initiative, creativity and enthusiasm, and these are the usual excuses cited by organisations that fail to address the problem of establishing effective aims and objectives for these categories of staff. More usually, however, it is a symptom of failure to structure and direct these activities in the organisation's best interests and to harness the qualities indicated in this pursuit. The invariable result is that managers set and pursue their own agendas, achieving high rewards for themselves and minimum-to-satisfactory levels of success for the organisation.

Displacement occurs where the work itself becomes the overriding aim. Attention becomes focused on length rather than effectiveness of attendance; volume rather than quality or purpose of work; day-to-day activities, clearing the in-tray and invariably the backlog; attention to immediate tasks and requests; attendance at meetings.

The operational and political influence of interest groups increases at the expense of their productive output. This tends to put pressure on resources and stress on individuals and groups. Internal competition for resources becomes itself a resource-consuming process and an objective in its own right.

Adherence to and operation of procedures and rule books becomes a goal in itself. Focus is therefore placed on compliance and conformity rather than effectiveness.

Compliance is not achieved. This is either because the required attitudes and standards are not recognised or valued, or because those working in the organisation place no value on the overall purpose, and the work is not carried out in its pursuit.

● Conclusions

As no organisation exists in isolation from its environment, the nature and extent of the relationship and interactions must be considered. Organisations are subject to a variety of economic, legal, social and ethical pressures which they must be capable of accommodating if they are to operate effectively. In some cases, there are strong religious and cultural effects, and local traditions that must be capable of effective harmonisation also. More specifically, organisations need access to workforces, suppliers, distributors, customers and clients, and to technology, equipment and financial resources.

It is clearly essential that organisations, and their managers, understand the environmental pressures and constraints under which they have to operate. It is also clear that this is an extremely complex process, requiring time, energy, resources and commitment. As a result, this aspect of managerial understanding is often not considered at all, or else not attended to in full. The position is further complicated when this part of management expertise is summarised as follows:

- There is clearly no best way to organise; as the environment changes so systems, aims and objectives must adapt flexibly and responsively.
- The environment changes in both predictable and unpredictable ways; it changes in ways that can be controlled and influenced and in ways that cannot be controlled and influenced. The problem for managers lies in the extent of their understanding of their environment and in their ability to anticipate the unexpected by building systems that are capable of accommodating these pressures.
- Because of the nature of the relationship with the environment, organisations need to spend time on external issues, assessing and understanding the environment, and the changes and turbulence within it.
- Decision-making processes have to be both structured and effective within the context and environment in which they are undertaken. No decision can be taken in isolation from either internal or external pressures.
- Each input–process–output cycle changes the nature of the organisation's social and technical resources, presenting an opportunity to strive for optimisation and improvement.
- Above all, the environment is dynamic and not static or rigid, allowing for limitless opportunities for change to occur; investment in environmental adaptation and transformation are as essential to success as investments in capital, equipment and staffing. The more complex and turbulent the environment, the more essential this form of investment becomes.
- Environmental, technological, market and competitive pressures, as well as social changes, are the primary causes and inspiration for organisational improvement, development, enhancement and change.
- Social, legal and ethical constraints constitute the main limitations placed on the activities of organisations. These require that specific approaches are adopted to all aspects of activities in order to meet standards prescribed by law or laid down by the prevailing values and morals of society.

The purpose of this chapter has been to summarise and indicate the various forms of organisations, the different points of view from which they may be considered and the wider context in which they operate. No organisation operates in isolation from, or without reference to, its environment. The environment provides staff, customers, resources, technology and equipment, and also confidence and expectations – the context in which successful and effective activities take place.

CRITICAL THINKING, ANALYSIS AND EVALUATION

For a city hospital, waste disposal organisation, airport, mass production car factory and Internet-only bookseller:

1. Summarise the environment, pressures and constraints that are imposed and have to be accommodated.
2. Identify the timescale pressures that are present in each case. What are the implications for managers in these organisations?
3. What steps should each of these organisations take to create, maintain and improve harmonious relationships with their community and environment? What specific problems are the managers of these organisations likely to have to address?
4. To what extent does each of these organisations dominate its environment? And to what extent is each dominated by its environment?
5. Who are the ideal primary beneficiaries and likely primary beneficiaries of each? What specific pressures does this produce for managers in these organisations?

DEVELOPING MANAGEMENT SKILLS AND EXPERTISE

BURROUGHS WELLCOME AND AZT

The prevalence of the HIV virus, and its increase among the populations in all societies of the world, has generated intense and highly pressurised activities among pharmaceutical companies to find an immunisation, vaccine or other treatment for those who have contracted the virus, and in whom this has developed to full-blown AIDS.

Burroughs Wellcome produced AZT in response to this during the 1980s. Huge levels of investment were made, and initial results among users of the drug were encouraging, in spite of the fact that it had serious side effects – including severe diarrhoea, dehydration, weight loss and skin rashes.

The drive to get it on to the market came from the usual areas of need to get returns on investment. There were also overwhelming social, political and community drives. Moreover, from the point of view of the industry, the company that could demonstrate itself the first to produce a vaccine or cure for this infection would generate a sustained long-term market advantage. Burroughs Wellcome was besieged by patients' groups, and AIDS and HIV charities, and subjected to a sustained period of media and vested interest group lobbying.

This was reinforced by the promotional culture and aspects that are all-pervasive in the healthcare, drug and pharmaceutical sectors. Promotions range from notepads and pens issued by drugs and medical equipment companies, to the medical equipment itself. Anything provided by the companies carries logos, brands, and other distinctive identity marks. This is all provided in hospitals, clinics and doctors surgeries. According to Eric Clark (1988):

> Doctors are subject to the most intense sales promotions and pressures in the community. As much as 25 per cent of the sales effort may be sent on promotions. In the United Kingdom, each doctor is the target for over £5,000 worth of promotion a year ... which falls better into place when another [figure] is added – the £58,000 worth of drugs that the average British GP prescribes each year.

AZT was promoted in exactly this way, and quickly gained a huge general familiarity as a believed landmark in the fight against the disease, which was – and remains – incurable. This was reinforced by extensive media coverage of drug trials, in which those with both the HIV virus and full-blown AIDS clamoured to take part.

Trials of the drug went on for an initial period of five years, and subsequently a further three. Then, in 2000, the results of the trials were finally published. The conclusions were as follows:

- There was no difference in timescales in which the HIV virus developed into full-blown AIDS, whether the patient took AZT or not.
- It was more likely that the general state of health and well-being of patients who did take AZT would be worse than those who did not, because of the severe side effects.

Questions

1. What were the effects of the environmental pressures on Burroughs Wellcome to produce a cure for HIV/AIDS? Why do you think these pressures arose? What should the company have done to manage them?
2. On the basis of the information given, what was the company's absolute corporate responsibility in this situation? How should this have been managed?
3. What lessons are there to be learned by all organisations from this example?

The Body Shop

When I opened the first Body Shop in Brighton in 1976, I knew nothing about business; my sole object was simply to survive, to earn enough to feed my kids. If it had not worked, I would have found something else to do. But it did work. And I'm glad. Today, The Body Shop is an international company rapidly expanding around the world, and in those intervening years, I have learned a lot.

Anita Roddick, the founder of The Body Shop, stated that survival was the primary drive that led her to set up The Body Shop. She goes on:

I started with a kind of grace which clung to the notion that in business you didn't tell lies. My motivation for going into the cosmetics business was irritation: I was annoyed by the fact that you couldn't buy small sizes of everyday cosmetics and angry with myself that I was always too intimidated to go back and exchange something if I didn't like it. I also recognised that a lot of the money I was paying for a product was being spent on fancy packaging which I didn't want. So I opened a small shop, to sell a small range of cosmetics made from natural ingredients in five different sizes in the cheapest possible plastic containers.

I did not deliberately set out to buck the trend – how would I even know what the trend was? It turned out that my instinctive trading values were diametrically opposed to the business practices of the cosmetics industry in just about every area:

They were prepared to sell false hopes and unattainable dreams; I was not. From the start, we explained to customers in simple language everyone could understand what a product would do and what it wouldn't do.

They sold through hype; I was so innocent, I didn't even know what hype was.

They thought packaging was important; I thought it was totally irrelevant. We happily filled old lemonade bottles with our products if a customer asked.

They tested on animals; I was repulsed by the practice and made it clear that I would never sell a product that had been tested on animals.

They spent millions on market research; we simply said to our customers: 'Tell us what you want and we will try to get it for you.'

They talked about beauty products; I banished the word 'beauty'.

They worshipped profits; we did not. In all the time I have been in business we have never had a meeting to discuss profits – we would not know how to do it.

Finally, and most importantly, they thought it was not the business of business to get involved in wider issues, in the protection of the environment or involvement with the community; I thought there was nothing more important.

In Anita Roddick's own words, this is the basis on which The Body Shop was founded. From this position in 1976, The Body Shop now has activities in 38 countries around the world, and draws supplies from many others. To date, the company has consistently sought to trade on the above basis, and to ensure that the profits made would continue to be divided up between the organisation, employees, the wider community and environmental causes.

At the outset, the company found itself hindered by the institutional and structural unwillingness of the UK financial sector to back an idea formulated on this basis. From the beginning, the company sought to be a force for social change, reminiscent of the eighteenth and nineteenth-century 'middle class ideal' of using profitable and effective business to provide institutions and facilities for the wider well-being of society. From the outset also, the company acknowledged a specific responsibility to suppliers. The crops used in the manufacture of the company's products were all bought in from countries in the third and emerging world, and The Body Shop committed to paying fully commercial prices; this continues to the present.

The company has grown from a single store in Brighton, UK, to its present position of having 740 stores across the world. The Body Shop commands only 0.05 per cent of the global cosmetics industry; however, it consistently features in the top 20 companies when viewed from the point of view of corporate social responsibility, contribution to the environment, supply side management and employment practices. It is important to note also that much of this was achieved during recession in the UK, Western Europe and North America.

Sources: A. Roddick (1992) *Body and Soul: The Body Shop Story*, Ebury Press; www.anitaroddick.net; www.thebodyshop.com.

Questions

1. Identify and summarise the main obstacles that Anita Roddick and The Body Shop had to face when establishing the business. What lessons can be drawn from this by managers in other organisations?
2. How, when, where and by whom should the performance of The Body Shop be measured and evaluated for success or failure?
3. What global and international barriers had to be faced by The Body Shop when seeking to take their distinctive and unique range of products overseas? What are the key lessons to be drawn from this by managers in other organisations?
4. Identify the external, economic and social factors that might possibly hinder the future viability of The Body Shop as a commercial organisation.

Part two

Strategy, policy, direction and priorities

Introduction

> Some of this stuff is just plain facile. Know what you are going to do, why you are doing it, how to do it, make good products and services, support them well, and make large amounts of money (Tom Peters, 1986).

Stripped of its complexity, this is what strategy, policy, direction and the creation and development of effective products, services, projects and activities is about, and the above statement is a very useful summary to be learned and applied.

The best, most profitable and most effective organisations are those that are clear about what they are doing; how, when, where and why they are doing it; and what they intend the results to be. This can only be achieved however, if a clear core or foundation position for activities is established, because everything else emerges and is developed from the core or foundation position.

For the sake of clarity, organisations and their managers need to establish and agree this foundation; this is because if those who are responsible for the direction of organisations are not themselves clear, they cannot expect anyone else to be either. The clarity of position emerges essentially from one of the following positions:

- Cost leadership and cost advantage, in which products and services are produced to the maximum/optimum cost-effective position; investment is in securing and developing the cost advantages; marketing and promotion concentrates on the cost (and often price) advantages; and new product and service development is driven by further ensuring and enhancing this position.
- Brand leadership and brand advantage, in which everything is driven by the need to secure a set of brand values. Brand values normally consist of: developing knowledge, understanding and perceptions of quality; products and service benefits that are of value to the given customer base; and a position of identity with the particular products and services on the part of customers. Marketing and promotion are a priority, and are driven by building, developing and enhancing the brand; giving clarity and consistency; and by the consequent ability to charge premium prices. The top brands are invariably the most expensive products and services in their sectors; this is because the marketing, promotion and presentation activities reinforce and enhance the quality and values associated by customers with the brand.

Something else: if it is not possible to secure cost advantage or brand leadership, customers must have their own clear reasons for nevertheless continuing to deal with a particular organisation and its products or services. This 'something else' that an organisation may offer is normally one of the following: providing a local product or service, providing specialist products and services, absolute convenience to customers, absolute assurance of response, or subcontracting to one or two dominant customers or clients. The 'something else' position is inherently brittle, in that if the distinctive standards and benefits provided either start to fall or are no longer of value to the particular set of customers, then those customers will gravitate either to the cost leader or to those providing brand advantage.

This clarity of position requires detailed knowledge and understanding on the part of top managers, and this must be reflected in the ways in which all activities are organised. Failure to do so means that effort is diluted, and this invariably leads to resources being not used to maximum advantage. Real clarity of position additionally informs the effectiveness of marketing campaigns and new product and service development, as described above; and each of these areas is dealt with in the chapters in this part of the book. It is additionally the case that managers need to be able to develop and harness their own creativity in response to all aspects of this part of management, and this is dealt with in the final chapter of this part.

Chapter eight

Strategy, policy and direction

'What are we going to do, Sir?'
'Why, soldier, we are going to advance and win the war. That is what we are going to do.'
R.C. Sheriff, *Journey's End* – on the First World War military deadlock of 1916.

'I've always worked terribly hard.'
Anita Roddick, founder, The Body Shop.

'Unless you are motivated with determination to succeed, you will not be able to go
past obstacles. When passion and desire become so strong as to rise out of the
body like steam, and when the condensation of that which evaporated occurs
and drops back like raindrops, problems will be solved.'
Kazuo Inamori, quoted in Peter Senge, *The Fifth Discipline*, Century Business (1992).

Chapter outline

- Introduction
- Business policy and strategy
- Sources and development of strategy
- Internal and external factors
- Core and peripheral activities
- Strategic approaches – cost, focus, differentiation, withdrawal, acquisition, pioneering, incremental
- Strategic analyses – SWOT, STEP, Five Forces, customers, competitors
- Conclusions

Chapter objectives

After studying this chapter, you should be able to:

- understand the overall conception of organisational business and public service strategy, policy and direction

- understand the opportunities and consequences that accrue as the result of pursuing particular directions and initiatives

- understand the importance of relating desired and required directions and activities to what is possible in the context and environment

- understand strategy, policy and direction as part of the process of securing long-term organisational viability.

● Introduction

The overall purpose of strategy is to guide and direct the inception, growth and change of organisations as they conduct their activities (see Management in Focus 8.1). The purpose of this chapter is an introduction to the essentials of corporate policy and strategy; the form that it takes in different types of companies; the variations in strategy between companies, public services and other sectors; the issues involved in devising policy and strategy; and the development, implementation and evaluation of policy and strategy.

A clearly articulated, accurate and well-understood strategy is at the hub of all successful commercial and public activities; where success is not forthcoming, it is often where this clarity of purpose is also not present. This clarity additionally gives a standpoint for the need and capability to manage resources effectively and efficiently; this continues to be intensified by requirements for greater accountability in both public and private sectors.

● The development of strategy, policy and direction

Corporate strategy is the outcome of a series and pattern of decisions that: determine the organisation's aims, objectives and goals; produce the plans and policies required to ensure that these are achieved; define the business in which the organisation is to operate; and define how it intends to conduct this business and what its relations

MANAGEMENT IN FOCUS 8.1

WHAT STRATEGY IS NOT

The aim of all industrial, commercial and public service sector organisational strategies, policies, purposes and directions should be:

'long-term existence in a competitive and turbulent world.'

Anything that does not contribute to this should not be contemplated.

Strategy therefore is not:

● a product of focus groups, contemplating what would happen in a hypothetical or imperfectly modelled set of circumstances

● a statement of blandness or general intention that binds nobody to anything

● about prestige, triumphalism, vanity or image – except where these factors can also be translated into successful, profitable and enduring activities.

These approaches invariably lead to the avoidance of the real issues of: matching opportunities with resources; accepting the consequences of particular choices; concentrating on one group of stakeholders at the expense of others; determining to satisfy all groups of stakeholders as far as possible; and above all, ensuring that everything is driven by the required and desired volumes and quality of product and service delivery.

with its markets, customers, staff, stakeholders and environment will be (see Management in Focus 8.2).

Operational policies are based on the choices made within the overall strategic view. They are based upon: a continuous appraisal of current and potential markets and spheres of activity; the ability to acquire, mobilise and harmonise resources for the attainment of the given aims, objectives and goals; and the actual means of conduct, including philosophical and ethical standpoints and the meeting of wider social expectations (see Management in Focus 8.3).

Effective strategy development requires that the following are understood and assessed in detail:

- the level of finance and capital required in order for the operation to be established and maintained successfully

MANAGEMENT IN FOCUS 8.2

THE INTERNET REVOLUTION

An inability to attract, retain and serve customers on an enduringly commercial basis is a fundamental, invariably fatal, weakness of the vast majority of Internet companies at present. Overwhelmingly, the vast amounts of capital drawn into Internet company start-ups were driven by:

- fashionability and faddishness, based on extensive media coverage and public relations activity surrounding what was perceived to be 'a new generation' of entrepreneurs
- the perceived technological supremacy of the Internet, and its infallibility as a commercial medium
- environmental pull – in which those who were known, believed or

perceived not to be at 'the cutting edge' of technology were deemed to be obsolete or boring
- failure to consider the customer, consumer, client or end-user aspect in any detail
- failure to consider how the levels of investment made in Internet organisations was to generate returns, or where and when these would arrive.

The problem was also compounded by the attitude adopted by many of the new venturers and entrepreneurs when their companies ceased to trade. One virtual shoe retailer stated: 'It was a lovely place to work, and we still can't think of anything we have done wrong.'

Another, the head of a virtual cookery and recipe production company, stated:

'We assumed that further investment funds would be forthcoming, on exactly the same basis as they had been before.'

Those organisations that have succeeded in using the Internet as their hub of activities are those that have concentrated on the enduring commercial drives in this context. Amazon, the online retailer, continues to sustain business viability through high-volume/low-profit-margin approaches to sales. Google, the search engine company, makes its profits through its ability to sell advertising space alongside search results. Supermarket and department store chains generate Internet sales largely as the result of customer familiarity with their products and services, gained over many years of traditional retail shopping.

MANAGEMENT IN FOCUS 8.3

THE RISE OF SOCIAL ENTREPRENEURING

Social entrepreneuring arose out of the high levels of unemployment that came about in the UK as the result of the collapse of traditional primary and heavy engineering industries in the 1970s and 1980s. The concept was adopted by the Prince of Wales, who sought to make a real contribution to the quality of life of those to whom this would not otherwise be available. He generated funds and business support, using his royal social position.

The success of projects generated and supported by the Prince's Trust caused others to pay attention, though the total economic output, as a percentage of gross domestic product, remains small. However, substantial contributions have been made to communities that have been encouraged to take responsibility for their own economic well-being, and to relate this to the social, ethical, cultural and traditional elements with which they are surrounded. Initiatives supported by the singer Bob Geldof, and the sportsmen Duncan Goodhew and Geoff Thompson, have led to substantial regeneration of small parts of south-east and north-east London. Elsewhere, similar activities have been generated in seeking to turn parts of south Wales, the southwest of England, and central Scotland into tourist attractions using the previous historical heritage as the base for this.

By the beginning of 2006, there were more than 15,000 social entrepreneuring ventures; and this figure looks set to rise.

- the levels of income, surplus and profit that the organisation needs to make and wishes to make
- the structure of the organisation that is appropriate for those operations to be carried out
- the management style that is to be adopted and the style of leadership, direction and supervision
- the priorities that are to be placed on each of the operations; the markets and sectors in which business is to be conducted.
- the timescales involved, especially where these are long-term, and therefore difficult to predict (see Management in Focus 8.4).

Figure 8.1 models the sources and development of organisation strategy.

Internal strategies and policies

Effective and successful organisation strategy is dependent upon integrated and complementary internal policies as follows:

- *Financial, investment, budgeting and resourcing strategies:* concerned with both the underwriting and stability of the organisation, and also the maintenance of its daily activities.
- *Human resource strategies:* designed to match the workforce and its capabilities with the operational requirements of the organisation; and related policies on

MANAGEMENT IN FOCUS 8.4

STRATEGIC DEVELOPMENT AND TIMESCALES: EXAMPLES

The long-term nature of strategic development, essential if the overriding aim of long-term viability and existence is to be achieved, is often in direct conflict with financial, competitive and other stakeholder drives for short-term, indeed immediate, financial results and advantages. Timescale issues have to be known and understood however, if strategy development is to be successful. For example:

- *The airline industry*: it was not until the 1930s, a generation after the first manned flight took place, that anyone was able to produce a sustainable, commercially profitable airline operating on a regular schedule of routes. The concept of flight as a means of mass travel took 35 years to develop into something that was commercially viable. The airline industry has time constraints around each one of its core operations. It is only possible to change route networks and destinations during periods when landing and take-off slots are made available. It then takes time to build a customer base, brand recognition, and confidence in the viability and permanence of the new routes. There are timescale issues at departure and arrival points (the need to check-in early for security reasons; the need to wait for baggage to be delivered to the arrival halls). It is additionally the case that new generations of airliners take many years to develop. The *Airbus A380*, the largest plane ever built and capable of carrying up to 800 passengers, took ten years from conception to delivery. Demand for medium-size airliners capable of travelling long distances without refuelling has also led to commitments of between five and ten years on the part of both Boeing and Airbus, which remain the world's dominant suppliers of commercial planes. These constraints go directly against the short-term pressures for financial results. It is true that both Boeing and Airbus deliver continuing adequate financial results, in the form of continuing sales of existing products. The need to commit to the level of resources required over the long term to ensure that the industry and companies are able to sustain themselves and produce the next generation of products remains however an essential feature of the industry; and those responsible for backing strategic development have to know, understand and accept this, or else move their funds elsewhere.

- *Mergers and takeovers*: when organisations are taken over by others, there is normally an instant financial advantage to shareholders and other backers. For those concerned with strategy development and long-term business activities, there are additional pressures to get results out of the newly acquired 'asset', and these are very often not realisable in the immediate future.

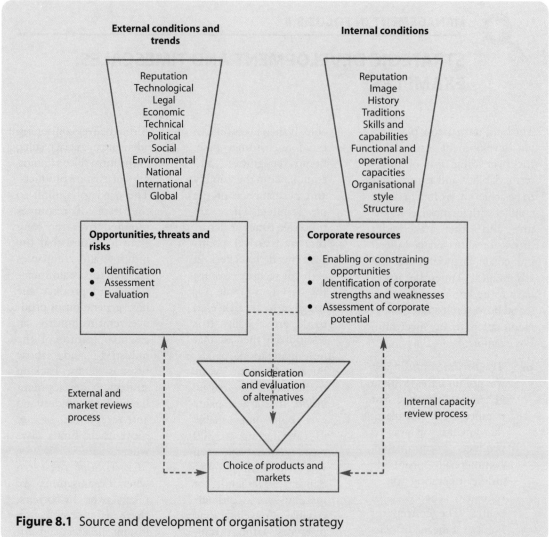

Figure 8.1 Source and development of organisation strategy

ensuring the supply of labour, effective labour relations, and the maintenance and development of the resource overall.

● *Marketing strategies*: designed to ensure that the organisation's products and services are presented in such ways as to give them the best possible impact and prospects of success on the chosen markets.

● *Capital resource and equipment strategies*: to ensure the continued ability to produce the required value and quality of output, to the standards required by the markets; and to be able to replace and update these resources in a planned and ordered fashion (i.e. including research and development and commissioning of new products and offerings).

● *Communication and information strategies*: both for the organisation's staff and its customers/clients, designed to disseminate the right quantity and quality of information in ways acceptable to all.

- *Organisation, maintenance, development and change strategies*: for the purpose of ensuring that a dynamic and proactive environment is fostered, along with a flexible and responsive workforce, and an environment of continuous improvement and innovation.
- *Ethical factors*: including establishing overall standards of attitude and behaviour; absolute standards in dealings with customers, suppliers and the community; specific approaches to the environment, corporate citizenship; the nature and quality of leadership.
- *Subjective elements*: reflecting collective and individual preferences and priorities; also acknowledging matters of expediency and organisational politics, including the need for triumphs, and the pursuit of individual whims and fancies.

Core and peripheral activities

Core activities

Core activities reflect primary purpose and may be assessed in terms of:

- *Volume of activity*: what most people do, or what most resources are tied up in.
- *Profit and income*: where most of the money comes in from.
- *Image and identity*: that which gives the organisation its position, status and prominence in the sphere in which it operates.

Peripheral activities

These are the other activities in which the undertaking gets involved. They must not be at the expense of the main or core activities, nor should they be a drain on resources. Rather they should enhance the core activities, or reflect niche or segment opportunities that exist as the result of the core business. Such activities will nevertheless be essential, expected and extremely profitable. A hospital is not 'in business' to sell food, sweets, newspapers, books, cards, fruit and flowers; nevertheless it is essential for a variety of operational and social reasons that these activities be undertaken. Similarly, a car company will invariably make additional parts for the replacement, service and spares sectors; these simply require some form of repackaging or 'differentiation' to generate additional business, in an obvious and profitable area of activity.

Strategic approaches

All effective organisation strategies must have the following components:

- *performance targets*, in whatever terms these are to be measured (e.g. income, volume, quality, but set against measurable, understandable and achievable targets)
- *deadlines that are achievable*, that have been worked out in advance and that represent a balance between commitment, resources and contingencies
- *contingencies* built in, to cover the unlikely, and the emergency

- consideration of the *long-term effectiveness* of the organisation
- consideration of the organisation's *products and services* in terms of value and quality, and utility to customers, clients, consumers and end-users.

All effective organisation strategies must have additionally a core foundation or generic position on which to base these considerations, performance targets and deadlines.

MANAGEMENT IN FOCUS 8.5

STRATEGIES FOR FAILURE

While it is impossible to predict with absolute accuracy where success and failure are likely to occur – especially if a rigorous approach is not taken – it is possible to indicate likely causes of failure. The usual way of expressing this is as follows.

- *Increased price/standard value*: risks loss of market share, especially where lower price, undifferentiated alternatives are available of the same quality and value.
- *High and increasing prices/low value*: this is unlikely to be sustainable in the long term in anything but a monopoly situation. Where perceived quality and value for money are not forthcoming, customers and clients will change from using such organisations if they have any choice in the matter at all.
- *Low value/standard price*: in these cases, customers and clients perceive that they are over-paying for a reduced or basic level of benefits

and satisfaction. Especially where there is no cost advantage, organisations finding themselves in this position are at immediate risk from either others who improve quality and value levels, or from those who reduce prices in order to reflect existing levels of quality and value.

A strategic approach that is based on any of these is sustainable only so long as there is a relatively captive medium to long-term customer and client base. For example, petrol retailing manages to secure medium to long-term advantages under the heading of 'increased price/standard value' simply because the product is such a fundamental commodity of the present state of civilisation. Some privatised health and social care organisations are able to sustain themselves under 'increased price/low value' and 'low value/standard price' because of the political drive to place clients of these organisations, and because the activities are

underwritten to some extent by government policy and willingness to pay. Nevertheless, serious disadvantage is certain to be reached if there is ever a political drive to improve the quality and value aspects.

In recent years, as the result of the Internet revolution, a further indicator of likely failure has become apparent:

- *Standard price/low convenience*: in which customers and clients are required to search for products and services on the Internet. Even assuming that the correct company website can be found, problems are often compounded by the fact that while this is technologically brilliant, it is customer and end-user unfriendly. It is also increasingly apparent, at least in commercial-consumer transactions, that it is essential that the virtual presence is reinforced by help lines, or increasingly, an access to a physical presence alongside it.

⬤ Generic strategies

Porter (1980, 1986) identifies three generic positions from which all effective and profitable activities arise. These are:

- *Cost leadership*: the drive to be the lowest-cost operator in the field. This provides the absolute ability to compete on price where necessary. Where this is not necessary, higher levels of profit are achieved in both absolute terms and also in relation to competitors. To be a cost leader, investment is required in 'state of the art' production technology and high-quality staff. Cost leadership organisations are lean in form, with small hierarchies, large spans of control, operative autonomy, simple procedures and excellent salaries and terms and conditions of employment. The drive for cost leadership and cost advantage is essential in any strategic approach that seeks mass market/mass volume products and services for which price is the overriding benefit to customers, and public services and utilities delivery.
- *Focus*: concentrating on a niche and taking steps to be indispensable. The purpose is to establish a long-term and concentrated business relationship with distinctive customers, based on product confidence, high levels of quality, utter reliability and the ability to produce and deliver the volumes of product required by customers when required. Investment is necessary in product technology and staff expertise. It is necessary to understand the nature of the market and its perceptions and expectations. It is also necessary to recognise the duration of the market, where developments are likely to come from, and the extent to which these can continue to be satisfied.
- *Differentiation*: offering homogeneous products on the basis of creating a strong image or identity. Investment is required in marketing, advertising, developing brand strength and loyalty, and outlets and distribution. Returns are generated over the medium to long term as the result of cost awareness, identity, loyalty and repeat purchase.

Porter argues that the common factor in all successful strategies is clarity, and that this stems from adopting one of these positions. Organisations that fail to do this do not necessarily fail outright; they do however fail to maximise and optimise resources. They lay themselves open to loss of competitive position from those who do have this clarity. They tend towards a proliferation of management systems and processes that dilute effective efforts.

Outcomes

Outcomes should be pre-evaluated in terms of the following (see also Figure 8.2):

- *Best*: what is the greatest level of success that we can possibly gain by following this course of action?
- *Worst*: what is the worst level of failure that can be achieved (if that is the right word) if everything that can go wrong does go wrong?
- *In between*: a range of outcomes under the general heading of 'medium' or 'acceptable'.

In particular, the level of bare acceptability of the outcome of a particular strategy should be assessed at the stage of devising strategy.

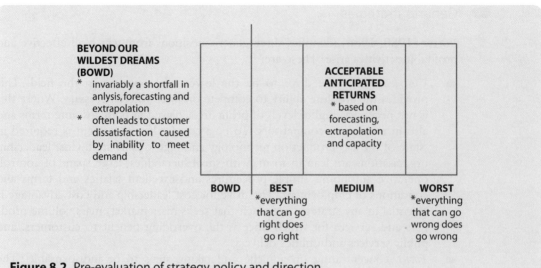

Figure 8.2 Pre-evaluation of strategy, policy and direction

Outcomes should be extrapolated from each of these positions to try and envisage the following stage of the organisation's activities and the wider implications for the short, medium and long term.

Having established the need for a core foundation or generic position, the main approaches to strategy, development and implementation are as discussed below.

Growth strategies

Growth is measured against pre-set objectives, whether in terms of income, profit margins, shareholder value, reputation enhancement, income per customer, income per location, income per product, market share, sales volume or new products and services. Required, expected or anticipated measures of growth, and the reasons and timescales for these, must be stated in advance. How such strategies are to be supported, financed and resourced, and the implications of this, must also be clearly stated and understood. The staff concerned must know this and the implications for them.

Acquisitions, mergers and *takeovers* are all variations on the theme of growth. Again, these approaches must be taken against pre-set objectives, and with the overall aim of enhancing the profitability and/or quality of the business (see Management in Focus 8.6). In support of this, what may actually happen is to introduce the organisation into new geographical areas, to increase the sectoral position; this may also help to defend and protect the organisation's own position.

Such activities may also include the acquisition of suppliers and distributors and sources of raw materials; this is known as 'vertical integration'.

They may also provide niche opportunities, the ability to get into new and profitable market sectors, or to purchase the client list, resource or base of a competitor, or parallel operator.

MANAGEMENT IN FOCUS 8.6

ACQUISITIONS EXAMPLE: SONY AND MATSUSHITA

In 1989 the Sony Corporation paid $3.4 billion for Columbia Pictures, a Hollywood TV and film studio. In 1990, Matsushita paid $6.1 billion for MCA, the American music, video and entertainment company.

The lessons to be drawn in both cases stem from an assessment of the strengths and direction of the organisation in question. In general, any growth, diversification or acquisition strategy will be based upon an estimation of what the new business will bring to the existing one and how this will strengthen both the overall portfolio and its operational capacities.

The rationale behind each takeover was that the acquiring companies had expertise and capabilities in electrical and electronic technology that could usefully and profitably be translated into the new spheres, and that there would be measurable commercial returns on the amounts paid. The acquisitions would also lead to new market opportunities in the United States and in the entertainment sectors, and would give each of the companies a further foothold and reputation in the West.

Both decisions were criticised at the time as being acquisitions for their own sake, pushed on by the desire of the companies' managements to gain a stake in a glamorous and high-profile industry, and by companies that had more cash than they knew what to do with. There was also perceived to be an element of competition between the two organisations – and especially their chairmen (Akio Morita of Sony and Konosuke Matsushita of Matsushita).

The flaws in both these two cases and in the wider sphere of mergers and acquisitions have subsequently been extensively researched. Reports published by the London Chamber of Commerce and Industry (1998) and the American Management Association (2001) strongly support the view that almost 90 per cent of mergers and acquisitions lead to increased costs, declining performance in the short and medium term, and extensive staff and customer uncertainty, dissatisfaction and stress. This is because mergers and acquisitions are almost exclusively driven by a short-term dominant stakeholder interest or undertaken for reasons of prestige and triumph, rather than in order to secure long-term commercial or public service advantage.

Retrenchment

Retrenchment usually takes the form of a withdrawal from niche or peripheral activities, sale of assets and concentration on the core activity. It need not have negative connotations; for example an organisation may sell off its lorry fleet and lease lorries at a time of credit squeezes and high interest rates. On the other hand, where there are negative connotations, effective retrenchment will have the overall purpose of protecting the core business and the certain markets (in so far as there are any), at the expense of the niches in which the organisation has been operating.

Retrenchment in relation to core activities may need to occur as the result of changes in market demands, and customer needs and wants. Retrenchment from core activities becomes serious when it calls into question the overall viability of the organisation's primary ranges of products and services; if this is truly necessary, organisations normally need to have something with which to replace these.

Retrenchment activities in public services are very often the cause of operational crisis, because there has to be every attempt to maintain the level of service against a declining budget provision.

Diversification

This is where organisations take the conscious decision to move into new markets and activities, very often in spite of the fact that they have no particular expertise in the new chosen field. Such organisations must acquire expertise and assimilate the new field's modus operandi if they are to be successful.

In practice, most effective and successful diversification strategies follow the vertical integration pattern, moving into new sectors that are clearly indicated by the current core business. For example, the Murdoch organisation moved into satellite television; it had no particular expertise in television or satellite technology but, looked at from a different standpoint, was a major player in mass media and communications). Consider Management in Focus 8.7.

MANAGEMENT IN FOCUS 8.7

THE VIRGIN GROUP

The move by the Virgin Group into the fields of airline operation, financial services and railways from music, video and record distribution was, and remains, successful; but to do it required extensive research, projections, expertise acquisition and market understanding on the part of what was hitherto essentially a chain of shops. The group perceived that it had certain assets of which it could take advantage as it moved into other areas – a large customer base, strong UK image, reputation for quality and public confidence. However, these qualities had

in practice to be refashioned by the new airline for itself. Moreover, any failure on the part of the new venture would have had serious consequences for continuing and future confidence in the rest of the group's activities.

The Virgin Group's approach to involvement in new ventures is based on some basic principles:

● The proposed new sector of activities must already be well established and served by other providers.

● The service provided by

other organisations must fall short in some way – especially perceived customer satisfaction.

● There must be commercial and profitable potential for engagement in 'the Virgin way'.

● There must be potential for developing the sector using the existing Virgin customer base.

● There must be a sense of fun and adventure.

Provided that any proposal meets at least four of these points, the company will consider it seriously.

Price leadership

The organisation aiming for price leadership sets out to be the market player with the lowest prices, and to ensure that everyone who purchases from the organisation knows this. This will not be entirely at the expense of quality; products and services still have to be good enough to attract people to purchase in the first place.

Some price leadership activities are spectacularly successful, such as the sale of petrol by British and European supermarket chains. Supermarkets in Europe and North America do adopt 'pile it high, sell it cheap' strategies, but this is generally limited to certain products. 'Do-it-yourself' chains will generally have some products at good prices for the consumer. The concept is most widely developed as 'loss leadership', rather than as price leadership. The IKEA furniture chain, however, is making attempts at present to expand across the countries of the EU, on the premise and image that all its prices are low and represent better value than the indigenous competition.

Branding strategies

Branding strategies concentrate on using a combination of marketing, operational, technological and professional activities in order that an instant perception of the company product or service in question is fixed in the mind of customers or clients (and also the community at large) immediately they see the brand name. A strategic approach to branding usually considers one or more of the following points of view.

- *Global branding*: examples are McDonald's and Coca-Cola, which present a set of core business drivers – in McDonald's case, quality, value, cleanliness and convenience – in ways that will generate the maximum response from the particular location in question.
- *National*: in which particular marketing strategies are devised to generate the required responses among particular nations of the world.
- *Organisational*: in which the organisation seeks to attach organisational values to any line of business or activity into which it chooses to go. For example, Virgin attaches a single name – its own – to its airline, music, bridal wear, publishing and high-tech activities; Heinz attaches a single name to its food products, whether they are for babies, children or adults, and whether they are standard, good value, healthy option or high value. Supermarkets also offer extensive ranges of their own brand products, though with very few exceptions they sell these alongside other branded goods and thus offer the maximum range of consumer choice.
- *Organisational diversity*: in which organisations adopt different brand names according to different product lines and/or different markets served. For example, Sony offers high-quality, high-value, premium-price ranges of electrical goods under its own name; in order to serve medium-quality, medium-value, medium-price ranges it has devised the name AIWA for its products. Similarly, Matsushita offers commercial electrical goods under its own name, and consumer electrical goods under the name Panasonic.
- *Local*: in which smaller organisations seek to gain a local presence and reputation through being corporate citizens, model employers or high-quality, high-value servants of local markets.

Market domination

Strategies aimed at market domination normally adopt and adapt components from each of the above to ensure a dominant position. Domination may be by sales volume, assets, derived income, largest number of outlets, or outlets in the most places (or a combination of some or all of these). It may also arise as the result of being the majority supplier (i.e. holding more than 50 per cent of the market); the largest single player, though with less than 50 per cent; or one of an oligopoly of operators (in some countries and sectors, this may be organised into a cartel, though this is illegal in many sectors and many countries).

It is still quite rare to find massive majority dominators of sectors, though there are exceptions. For example, British Airways and Ryanair each handle about 30 per cent of UK short and medium-haul British air traffic, while easyJet handles about another 28 per cent. Tesco handles about 31 per cent of food and grocery sales, Asda about 18 per cent, and Morrisons and Sainsbury's about 14 per cent each. Domination otherwise is limited to gas, electricity, water, telecommunications, and public road and rail transport. Commercial oligopolies are also found in media, newspapers, cars, and oil and petrol sales.

Incremental strategies

The view of strategy as incremental is popular with those who argue for a rational approach to long-term business and public service sustenance. The reasoning is that a genuine long-term strategy is actually impossible to achieve, given the sophisticated structure of organisations and the turbulence and instability of markets and sector activities, without paying constant attention to direction and purpose. A successful approach to long-term viability has therefore to be seen as being constantly influenced by changing environmental, social, political and economic circumstances.

The starting point for future strategies is therefore the position of the organisation today. From this, the organisation moves forwards in small steps or increments. As each of these steps is successful, the next becomes apparent. If a mistake is made, it is easy to retrace the step and seek other directions from the previous position. The status quo and present levels of performance are clearly identified; and these are then taken as the correct starting point for the next step or 'increment'. If costs are reduced or if profits have gone up in relation to last year, this is a good general measure of satisfactory performance. If costs have risen or profit has declined in relation to the previous period, this becomes a cause for concern.

Opportunities arise from the fact that the organisation is moving slowly enough to recognise and evaluate those situations that present themselves before rushing in headlong, or rejecting out of hand.

Measurement and evaluation

Measurement and evaluation are carried out against the pre-set aims and objectives of the particular strategy. Assessments should be quantifiable wherever possible so that areas of particular success or shortfall will become apparent, contributing to the organisation's expertise in the field and ensuring further improvement in the strategic and planning processes for the future.

Beyond this, evaluation is both a continuous process, and the subject of more formalised regular reviews at required and appropriate intervals. This process sets a framework against which the strategy is to be judged.

The following can then be assessed:

- To what extent is the strategy *identifiable*, clearly understood by all concerned, in specific and positive terms? To what extent is it unique and specifically designed for its given purpose?
- Is it *consistent* with the organisation's capabilities, resources and aspirations; and the aspirations of those who work in it?
- What levels of *risk* and *uncertainty* are being undertaken, in relation to the opportunities identified?
- What *contribution* will the proposed strategy make to the organisation as a whole over the long term?
- What are the likely market *responses* and *responsiveness*? What degrees of market captivity or choice exist?
- What are the effects – *positive* and *adverse* – of dominant stakeholders, driving and restraining forces, and product, service and project champions?

These questions can be answered as part of both the continuous evaluation and the regular review process.

Implementation of strategy

The determination of strategy is therefore a combination of the identification of the opportunities and risks afforded by the environment; the capabilities, actual and potential, of the organisation, its leaders and top management; and issues of ethical and social responsibility. Turning this into reality requires that the following are addressed:

- *Key tasks* must be established and prioritised, effective decision-making processes drawn up, and systems for monitoring and evaluation of strategic process devised.
- *Work* and *workforce* must be divided and structured to a combination of functional and hierarchical aspects, designed to ensure the effective completion of the tasks in hand; this must include relevant and necessary project coordination activities by committees, working parties and steering groups (see Figure 8.3).
- *Information* and other management systems must be designed and installed; control and constraint systems must be a part of this, to include financial, human resource, production, output and sales reporting data.
- Tasks and actions to be carried out must be *scheduled* and *prioritised* in such a way as to be achieved to given deadlines. As well as establishing a background for precise work methods and ways of working, scheduling provides the basis for setting standards against which short and medium-term performance can be measured.
- The *required technology* must be made available, and staff trained to use it.
- *Maintenance* and *repair* schedules must be agreed and integrated with other activities.
- *Research and development*, improvement and enhancement schedules must be incorporated with the rest of activities. This includes making financial,

technological and staff resources available as a key part of organisation product and service development.

● *Monitoring, review* and *evaluation mechanisms* and *procedures* must attend to hard aspects of market responses, sales figures and product and service usage, and to soft aspects of meeting customer, client, consumer and end-user satisfaction and expectations.

● *Actual performance* must be *measured* against forecast, projected or budgeted activities.

● *Staff management* and *human resource polices* must be assessed for: effectiveness and quality; the extent and prevalence of conflict, communication blockages, disputes and grievances; the effectiveness of pay and reward systems; the application of rulebooks and specific procedures.

● *Financial returns* must be assessed in line with projections and forecasts. A key feature of strategy implementation is the ability to compare overall returns, costs of sales, product and service delivery, with projections; and to gauge the effects of unforeseen circumstances on particular activities.

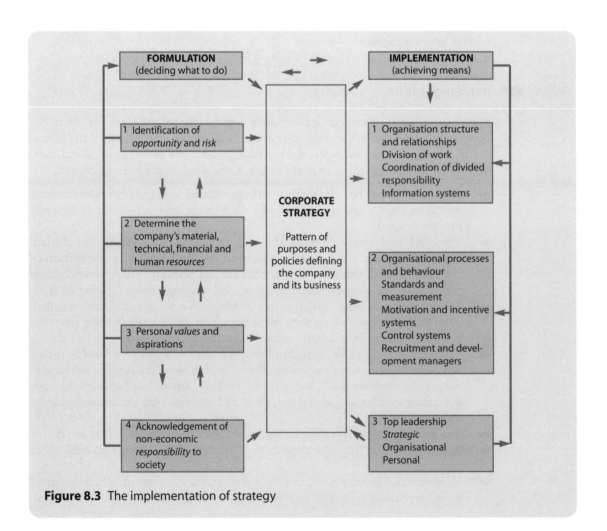

Figure 8.3 The implementation of strategy

Each of these aspects provides a critical element for effective monitoring, review and evaluation activities (see Figure 8.4).

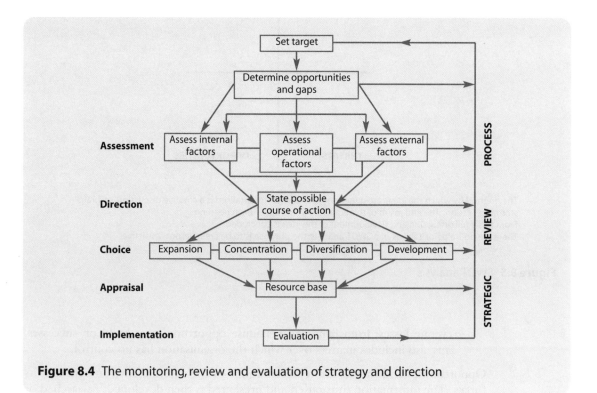

Figure 8.4 The monitoring, review and evaluation of strategy and direction

● Strategic analyses

Strategic analyses are conducted to ensure that each aspect of the organisation, and its competitive and general environment, are clearly understood. The approaches used are as discussed below:

Strengths, weaknesses, opportunities, threats: SWOT analysis

In this activity, issues are raised, highlighted and categorised under four headings:

● *Strengths*: the things that the organisation and its staff are good at and do well; that they are effective at; that they are well known for; that make money; that generate business, and reputation.
● *Weaknesses*: the things they are bad at, or do badly; that they are ineffective at; that they are notorious for; that make losses; that cause hardships, disputes, grievances and complaints; that should generate business, but do not. This aspect requires a degree of candour.
● *Opportunities*: the directions that they could profitably go in the future. These may arise because of strengths or the elimination of weaknesses.
● *Threats*: from competitors; from strikes and disputes; from resource and

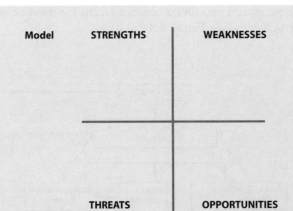

Model	STRENGTHS	WEAKNESSES
	THREATS	OPPORTUNITIES

The method by which the ideas are generated and compartmentalised is a creative discussion, or 'brain-storming' session. The end result of this is a list of items under each heading.
From this a full discussion and development of the idea is concluded.
There are no 'holds' or 'taboos' in a SWOT analysis: the purpose is to be creative, not restrictive.

Figure 8.5 SWOT analysis

revenue losses; from failing to maximise opportunities or build on successes. This also includes matters over which the organisation has no control.

Opportunities and threats are representations of the external environment and its forces. The information thus raised and presented is then developed, researched or investigated further. SWOT analysis can be done for all business and managerial activities, and to address wider global and strategic issues. It is an effective means of gathering and categorising information, of illustrating or illuminating particular matters, and for gathering or articulating a lot of information and ideas very quickly.

Social, technical, economic, political: STEP analysis

The purpose of STEP (or, sometimes, PEST) analysis is also to help organisations learn, but the material that arises relates much more to the analysis of the wider strategic situation, and the organisation in its environment:

- *Social*: the social systems of the workplace, departmental and functional structures, work organisation and working methods. Externally this considers the relationship between the organisation and its environment in terms of the nature and social acceptability of its products and services, its marketing, and the regard with which it is held in the community.
- *Technological*: the organisation's technology, the uses to which it is put, and its potential uses; and the technology that is potentially available to the organisation and others operating in the given sector.
- *Economic*: the financial structure, objectives and constraints (e.g. budgets and budgeting systems) at the place of work. Externally this considers the market

position, levels of economic activity, and commercial prospects and potential of the products and services offered.

- *Political*: the internal political systems, sources of power and influence, key groups of workers, key departments, key managers and executives. Externally, this considers particular considerations in the establishment of markets, by product, location, ethics and values.

Again, the information thus raised can be further analysed and evaluated. STEP analysis establishes in more detail the wider background against which particular product or service initiatives are to take place, and raises wider issues or concerns that may in turn require more detailed resource and analysis.

Industry structure analysis

Industry structure analysis is based on evaluating and analysing the 'five elemental forces of competition' identified by Michael E. Porter. The five elements are:

1. *The industry competitors*: the nature and extent of rivalry among those organisations currently operating in the field and the implications of this for the future (for example, reduced profit margins where price wars occur, or reduction in capacity where there is over-provision).
2. *Suppliers*: the extent to which they dominate the sector either through the supply of a key, critical or rare component; their ability to integrate forwards into the market itself; the range of choice of suppliers available, and the ability to use alternative supplies; the overall bargaining position of the suppliers.
3. *Buyers*: the extent to which they dominate the sector either because they purchase high volumes from it, or because they control the final outlet of the product in question; their ability to integrate backwards into the market itself; the number and type of operators in the buyer group; and the ability to generate and supply alternative buyers; the overall bargaining position of buyers.
4. *Potential entrants*: the extent to which organisations operating in other sectors have product, technology and staff capacities to gain entry to the sector in question; and the extent and nature of the entry barriers that surround the sector.
5. *Substitutes*: the extent to which the organisation's product is a matter of choice on the part of the buyer; the extent to which equivalent benefits can be gained from a product that is similar, but not the same (see Figure 8.6).

Competitor analysis

Competitor analysis involves an assessment and evaluation of the other players in the field. It considers the initiatives that they may themselves take to promote their own strategic advantage, and also measures their likely responses to such initiatives on the part of the organisation in question (see Figure 8.7).

The components of a competitor analysis are:

- the strategy of the competitor, its driving and restraining forces
- its current business operations, capacities, strengths and capabilities
- the assumptions held about both the competitor and the industry itself
- a detailed profile of the competitor: its current satisfaction with its existing

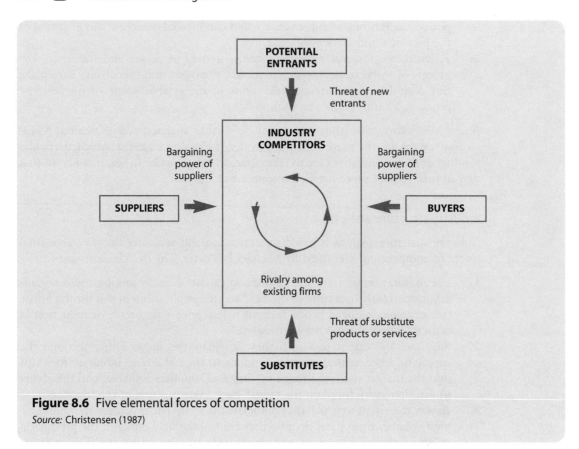

Figure 8.6 Five elemental forces of competition
Source: Christensen (1987)

position; its likely moves and responses to moves; its position in the market; its under or over-capacity.

This constitutes a detailed discussion to be devised and conducted by sectoral and corporate strategy specialists and experts. It can be used as the basis on which both offensive and defensive strategic moves are made. Presentation to an organisation's top management and directorate will normally be limited to the matters arising, the results of analysis, the conclusions and recommendations drawn from a detailed competitor analysis.

Customer and client analysis

The purpose of conducting customer and client analyses is to ensure that the business or public service relationship is considered from the point of view of customers, clients, consumers and end-users. It should form a major component of strategic analysis. This is necessary in order to:

- test assumptions and received wisdom concerning the attitudes of customers and clients to the particular organisation, its products and services
- ensure that these assumptions are not being taken as absolute fact
- assessing the extent to which organisational direction is being based on

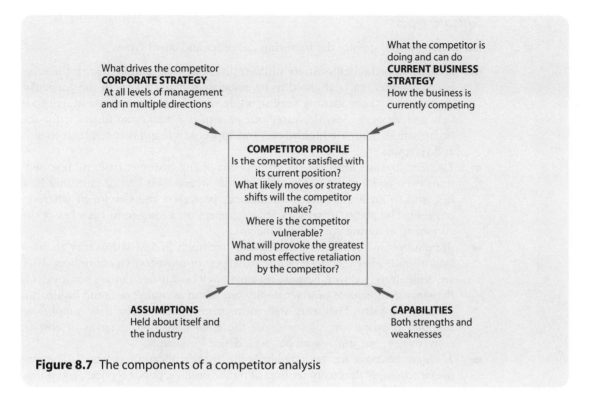

Figure 8.7 The components of a competitor analysis

generally favourable responses and attitudes, rather than real customer and client demands

● ensuring that customer behaviour is not being taken for granted.

In order to build up as much understanding as possible, it is necessary to make detailed enquiries along the following lines:

● Why do customers and clients use us/why do they not use us?
● Why have customers and clients increased/decreased the value or volume of business that they conduct with us?
● Why have customers started using us/stopped using us?
● Where does our product or service come in the customer's order of priority? Do we serve wants or needs?
● Under what circumstances would customers use us more/use us less? Under what circumstances would customers increase/decrease the value and volume of their business with us?
● What are the alternatives available to customers if they do not do business with us?
● What do competitors provide that is better than us? What do competitors provide that is worse than us?
● Why do customers use us/why do customers use our competitors?

These are direct and precise questions, requiring accurate answers. In particular, if the answer to any question is either available in general terms only, or is simply not known, then lines of enquiry should be opened as a matter of urgency.

Customer types

Cartwright (2000) defines the following customer and client types:

- *Apostles*: apostles demonstrate ultra-loyalty. They are delighted with the service or product, and delighted to be associated in any way with the particular organisation. They identify very strongly with the organisation and its products and services. Apostles carry out part of the marketing function for the organisation. They are highly loyal and appreciative, and they tell their friends and relations.

- *Loyalists*: loyalists form the key component of any customer base. All organisations need to be able to accurately identify where their loyalist customer base lies, and to ensure that it is maintained, preserved and developed wherever possible. The ability to satisfy loyal customers on a long-term basis lies at the core of all enduring commercial success.

- *Mercenaries*: mercenaries are the hardest customers to deal with as they are basically a-loyal. They tend to go for the cheapest or most convenient option. They are difficult to deal with because they may well be satisfied but are not loyal. Or they may demonstrate product loyalty but brand a-loyalty; or brand loyalty but supplier a-loyalty. They may well move from brand to brand or supplier to supplier. If asked why they moved, the answer may be in terms of cost or convenience, but it may well be just a desire for change.

- *Hostages*: hostages are the individuals that make up 'captive markets'. They are overwhelmingly the customer base of public utilities, public services, and public transport. Hostages are also found in isolated communities where, for example, there is only one convenient shop, garage, pub or restaurant.

- *Defectors* and *terrorists*: these are customers who once used a particular organisation, but now do not do so. Defectors may move from a position of loyalty because there is now a much better or more convenient alternative source of supply; or they may move because they are actively dissatisfied with what has previously been on offer, but have simply said nothing about it.

    Terrorists however, tend to have been extreme loyalists or apostles, and therefore, when they switch their allegiance, are determined to make sure that everybody knows. Cartwright states that: 'Many of those who appear on consumer affairs television programmes have been previous apostles. On being let down, they have no problem in letting the world know about it.'

To this list others may be added, as follows:

- *Browsers and window-shoppers*: those who have a general interest in what particular organisations have to offer, and who may make unconsidered occasional purchases from time to time.

- *Passing trade*: in which particular customers and clients find themselves confronted with something which they are interested in purchasing by chance.

- *Convenience customers and clients*: who use a particular organisation purely because of its overwhelming convenience to them in their own terms. This is especially important in the case of business-to-business activities, when organisations become the clients of suppliers purely because of the quality of relationship between themselves and the suppliers' representatives (see Management in Focus 8.8).

MANAGEMENT IN FOCUS 8.8

CUSTOMER AND CLIENT TYPES

It is also possible to distinguish the following types of customers and clients, and customer and client behaviour.

- *Passive loyalists*: those who think very highly of particular organisations, but who seldom or never use their products and services.
- *General loyalists*: those who think very highly of particular organisations, but who only use those organisations once, or very, very infrequently (this is an especial problem in the luxury goods and services industries, and also in the medium, high and top-quality holiday package industry).
- *Passive apostles*: customers and clients who always used to use an organisation, its products and services, but who do so no longer – either because they no longer need it, or because it is no longer convenient to get to. They nevertheless continue to praise the organisation, often years

after they have last used it (N.B. this was an especial problem in the decline of Marks & Spencer; everyone whom the company asked about the reasons for declines in sales, continued to speak very highly of the company as an entity, and so the problems of product sales were never addressed).

- *Loyal mercenaries*: customers who come to an organisation for the first time as mercenaries may be translated into loyalists, so long as the product or service quality can be demonstrated. This was the basis on which the Japanese car and electrical goods manufacturers built their industrial base in the UK, United States and Western Europe in the 1970s and 1980s. Customers and clients had no particular affinity for the Japanese (indeed many still had vivid memories of brutal treatment at the hands

of the Japanese military during the Second World War). Nevertheless, when the product and service quality was demonstrated, they were persuaded to change their buying habits.

- *Anticipatory terrorists*: this is an enduring present problem for those needing to avail themselves of public services. Because of media coverage that gives the overwhelming impression of the decline in quality of healthcare, education and social services in the UK, clients of these services use them on the basis that they are going to receive poor-quality service, badly delivered. They therefore tend to look for the bad rather than the good in the service; and this gives rise to a culture of client complaint and compensation. So far the strategic management of these services has not begun to address this issue.

This approach provides an easy-to-understand explanation of where and why customers and clients come to particular organisations; and why they start to come, cease coming, and change their attitudes and behaviour. The approach may be shown as a matrix, as in Figure 8.8.

Customer and client analysis is a key task of strategic management, and a critical component in the determination of policy, direction and priorities. It is also more complex than organisational or environmental analysis, because it requires time, energy and resources to be consumed in understanding the precise nature and requirements of those with whom the organisation is to do business. It therefore becomes very easy to neglect this, to take customer and client attitudes on trust, or to understand them in general terms only. Specific points of enquiry are required in order to establish precise understanding of:

- the price that customers are willing to pay for particular products and services
- the value and quality that they expect from particular products and services
- making products and services as convenient as possible to the customer and client bases served
- length, frequency and intensity of usage
- depreciation/appreciation and re-sale aspects
- maintenance, repair, replacement and upgrade elements
- personal feelings of esteem and worth that accrue from ownership and usage
- fashionable and faddish elements (especially important in clothing, cars, computers and furniture)
- feelings of exclusivity, luxury, desirability
- returns on financial and emotional investment
- particular demands and requirements of individual customers.

Much of this is clearly subjective. Purchases made by different customers of the same item, for the same purpose, for the same price may result in widely differing levels of satisfaction.

Conclusions

A successful strategic approach can only be achieved if the ways in which the particular sector operates are fully understood and analysed. This analysis must also depend on gaining as full an understanding as possible of customer and client behaviour, demands, wants and needs.

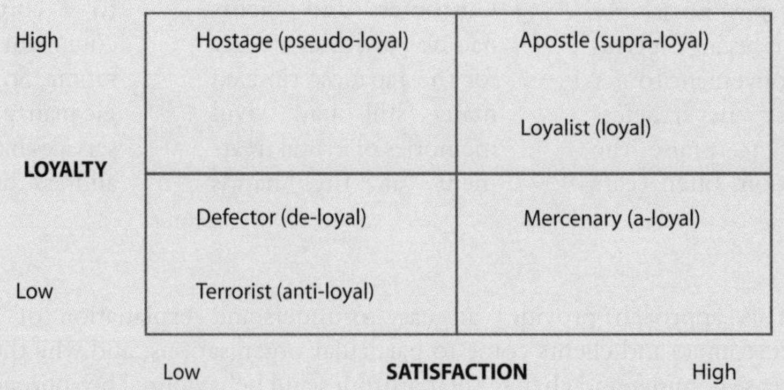

LOYALTY	SATISFACTION	
High	Hostage (pseudo-loyal)	Apostle (supra-loyal)
		Loyalist (loyal)
	Defector (de-loyal)	Mercenary (a-loyal)
Low	Terrorist (anti-loyal)	
	Low High	

Figure 8.8 The loyalty matrix

Ideally, the main outcome of these analyses is an informed base for those responsible for organisational direction. This should consist of a full understanding of the wider environment and general pressures that exist, as well as the more specific aspects indicated.

It is important in the process of educating and informing all managers, and especially top managers, to think strategically, as well as operationally, and to relate the two directly. All of the approaches and models indicated should cause managers to look beyond their operations, activities and areas of responsibility to the wider context, and from the short to the long-term. They also act as initial indicators of opportunities and threats. Areas of risk and uncertainty should start to become apparent and points of stress and strain that may be created by following certain directions should also be indicated, especially if the full environment has not been analysed.

These activities are not ends in themselves. The key to successful strategic management lies in how the information gained is evaluated and used, how accurately the particular position of the organisation is assessed. Organisations must be able to translate this into effective activity based on their own strengths of flexibility, dynamism, responsiveness and commitment. They must also be able to recognise potential weaknesses and pitfalls, and take whatever steps are necessary to address these.

CRITICAL THINKING, ANALYSIS AND EVALUATION

1. Analyse the state of the market for petrol in the UK, using the SWOT and STEP models. What conclusions can be drawn from this? What are the likely effects on car companies, the oil companies and consumers of: taxing motorway driving; doubling the price of crude oil; the production of medical evidence proving that both petrol and diesel fumes are potentially lethal health hazards to car users?

2. Conduct a customer analysis for the top UK football club of your choice. Identify:
   a) who the customers and clients of the club are, and their place in the order of priority in the club's interests
   b) the nature of satisfaction expected and anticipated as the result of buying the club's products and services (including tickets to matches and season tickets)
   c) what causes apostle and loyalist customers to become a-loyal or even terrorists in this industry.

3. Choosing a particular strategic initiative with which you are familiar, and which is deemed to be a failure, identify the reasons why it failed. Identify the points at which failure could have been reasonably anticipated. Identify the remedial action that could, should or might have been taken to ensure its success, and the circumstances in which the particular venture should have been cancelled.

4. Addressing the particular questions of price, quality, value and convenience, identify the actions necessary for an Internet venture, if it is to stand any chance of success.

DEVELOPING MANAGEMENT SKILLS AND EXPERTISE

MARKS & SPENCER IN THE TWENTY-FIRST CENTURY

In 1998, Lord Marcus Sieff retired from the Board of Directors of Marks & Spencer. This represented a severance of the last link between the company's founding fathers and the present day (Lord Sieff was the great-grandson of Michael Marks). At the same time, the beginnings of decline in the company's fortunes began to be apparent. The company, which had prided itself on high-quality, high-value sales of clothing and food products to middle-class customers, began to build a reputation for being out of touch with present customer demands. The company went through various short-term initiatives. These included:

- changes in top management (the company had two chief executives in nine months)
- changes in the supply chain, shifting sources of clothing away from traditional suppliers in England and Scotland, and buying overseas to perceived better value operators in the emerging world
- attempts to 'modernise' the ranges of clothing for women
- attempts to move into the youth market.

Business analysis carried out in the early twenty-first century produced the following conclusions:

- Sales of underwear (especially female underwear) by the company remained buoyant; customers found that these were both of high and enduring quality, and sufficiently fashionable to suit a wide range of tastes.
- Sales of food remained buoyant; again, the quality was perceived to remain high.

The company recruited high profile designers, including Julien Macdonald, 'to add some much needed glamour to its clothing range for both men and women'. The company also introduced the designer ranges Autograph and Per Una, to drive up perceived product quality and durability, and again, to give a more fashionable and current image.

However, both ranges consistently under-performed following their introduction in the early twenty-first century, as did new menswear ranges. The overwhelming problem was that of customer perception. A survey carried out at the company's Kensington store concluded that there was neither product nor price differentiation between what Marks & Spencer had on offer and what was offered at specialist designer stores. Additionally, Tesco introduced its good-value, medium-quality range of clothing under the name Cherokee. Asda followed in 2003 when it took the George range of clothing on as its own and undertook a huge marketing campaign, which in 2005 resulted in George becoming the largest selling range in the UK. This meant that for the first time ever, Marks & Spencer was no longer the largest single clothing retailer.

The company therefore determined upon the following courses of action:

- an internal campaign called 'fight back' in which a corporate will was expressed to counter the current bad publicity and adverse media coverage

- a bonus and incentive scheme to motivate all store staff
- job cutting in the company's head office – the loss of 300 jobs, mainly in the information technology, administration and financial management areas
- closure of the company's 20 stores on mainland Europe.

Questions

1. Produce a customer analysis for the company, based on the details given in the case study above.
2. To what extent do you think that the strategic approach indicated at the end of the case study above is appropriate? What are the problems faced by the company? How should these be tackled?
3. Assuming that the company is to go into the designer clothing market, what further strategic initiatives are necessary in order to ensure that this is successful?

Chapter nine

Investment appraisal

'We cannot succeed in the long run if we are focused only on the short term.'
Bill Ford, CEO, Ford Inc., 2006.

'The predictions of the world's economic forecasters are confounded on a regular basis.'
Anatole Kaletsky, London School of Economics.

'Everything takes twice as long as you think, and it costs twice as much.'
J.E. Firth, farmer in south-eastern England.

Chapter outline

- Introduction
- The complexity of investment appraisal
- Costs
- Returns on investment
- Acquisitions, mergers and takeovers
- Capital projects
- Public services
- Conclusions

Chapter objectives

After studying this chapter, you should be able to:

- understand the complexities of investment appraisal

- understand the forces and influences which affect the outcome of particular decisions

- understand the barriers and assumptions that are made when determining and implementing investments

- understand the importance of cost management in particular circumstances.

Introduction

Investment appraisal is considered to be a primary managerial expertise for two reasons. The first reason is because financial considerations affect all aspects of organisation size, strength, performance, effectiveness and profitability; and the second is because a detailed understanding of the implementation of strategic and other activities in financial terms is essential as a part of the enduring effectiveness and strength of the organisation as a whole.

Effective investment appraisal is complex because it requires a full assessment of every factor that can possibly affect the outcome of resourcing or supporting a particular initiative. This in turn means considering the full range of organisation and environment pressures and constraints present: stakeholder demands and drives for returns; technology capacity; staff capability, willingness and commitment; the relationship between what is intended and the organisation's core foundation or generic position; and the relationship between what is intended and what actually happens.

In this context, investment appraisal is a managerial discipline and expertise that relates the commitment of resources to results and outcomes. Conducted rigorously and effectively, investment appraisal makes a critical contribution to effective decision making, strategy development, productivity and service delivery capability, and long-term profitability, viability and effectiveness.

The complexity of investment appraisal

The purpose of investment is to gain returns, and these are normally expressed in financial terms. The required, desired and demanded levels of returns must be made explicit at the outset.

For example, if returns of 30 per cent per annum are required, then investments must be concentrated in areas where these levels are possible. Conversely, if an organisation is determined to remain in particular activities even though they only normally produce returns of 3 per cent per annum, then this represents a key constraint which has to be understood and managed.

It is however impossible to predict with absolute certainty the outcome of specific initiatives. It is therefore usual to define boundaries of acceptability, or margins against the target which are agreed to represent success and achievement in context.

The purpose additionally needs timescales and timeframes, in all circumstances. Timescales and timeframes also require understanding and acceptance at the outset, at the point at which resources are committed to particular initiatives. Timescales can be changed, extended or contracted as the result of changing circumstances within the environment, changes to market, product and service demands, and as the result of changes in the priorities of key stakeholders.

Additionally, it is increasingly the case that people's expectations have to be managed. As awareness is raised that it is indeed impossible to predict with absolute certainty the outcome of particular decisions, it becomes essential to ensure that all those with an interest in the investment are kept informed of progress at every stage. The final part of this complexity is managing the interests of dominant stakeholders. Dominant stakeholders are those who, for whatever reason, are able to drive the particular investment, initiative or venture in their own preferred direction. They hold the overriding position of influence because of one or more of the following:

- their knowledge and expertise
- their position of power and status
- their command of key resources (usually finance)
- the nature of the backers who appointed them to their position of dominance.

Once this is understood, it becomes possible to plot both the position of the dominant stakeholder and likely problems and issues on a grid as shown in Figure 9.1.

Understanding this complexity forms the basis on which pre-investment groundwork is carried out.

Pre-investment groundwork

Pre-investment groundwork is carried out with the purpose of gaining satisfactory knowledge and understanding of the context in which investments, initiatives and ventures are being considered. The issues that normally have to be covered are as follows:

- the range of returns possible, both positive and negative, expressed in financial terms
- the range of returns possible, both positive and negative, expressed in non-financial terms
- determination of primary aims and objectives for the particular initiative
- determination of secondary or subsidiary aims and objectives for the particular initiative
- assessment of the risks involved, related to both primary and subsidiary aims and objectives
- definitions of success and failure, known and understood by all parties (it is essential to remember that a true evaluation of success or otherwise can only be effective if conducted against what was intended in the first place).

It becomes clear from the above that investment appraisal is a process, and that this process is not linear. At the core of all effective investment appraisal are the financial considerations; however, much of the complexity involved is non-financial, relating to the priorities, drives, aims, objectives and demands of all those involved, and in particular the demands of dominant or key stakeholders. It is therefore necessary to consider the barriers that have to be addressed and overcome if investments are to gain the returns desired and required.

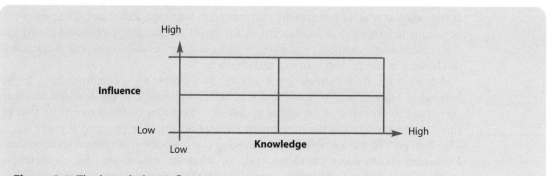

Figure 9.1 The knowledge–influence spectrum

● Barriers

Barriers and assumptions exist wherever economic and financial information is requested, where forecasts and extrapolations are demanded, and in assessing the ranges of outcomes possible when considering particular initiatives. A simple model of this can be seen in Figure 9.2.

Figure 9.2 represents a simple form only; the problem is compounded every time more complex information is required or where it is requested from a variety of sources. The initial lesson, therefore, is to ensure that full and effective liaison is established between investment information experts and decision-making bodies to ensure that the assumptions and barriers are broken down. This, in turn, leads to a much greater mutual understanding of the real range of pressures and priorities (see Management in Focus 9.1).

This represents the overall context in which all investment decisions are taken and in which the following approaches are used.

Time

It is usual to distinguish three timeframes:

- *Short-term*: which is attractive to all concerned, because the outcome and returns on a particular venture are easier to predict with a greater degree of certainty than when the time period is extended. It is also a favoured strategy of those concerned with the assessment and management of risk to reduce, as far as possible, the time-frame involved in calculating returns on investment because, again, acceptable rates of return can be calculated with a greater degree of certainty.

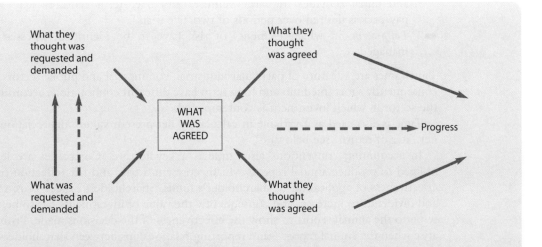

Each full arrow represents an area where misunderstandings occur, each broken arrow indicates the assumption that the job was perfectly carried out.

Figure 9.2 The nature of barriers and assumptions

MANAGEMENT IN FOCUS 9.1

'WE BASED THE DECISION ON THE BEST INFORMATION THAT WE HAD AVAILABLE'

This statement is almost invariably untrue. In practice, there is always sufficient information available on which to base decisions about the long-term viability of ventures (or not), or to predict with a fair degree of certainty the range of possible outcomes of a particular venture.

The problem lies in the understanding and assessment of the information, and of the other forces present when the decision is taken. In practice, most decision makers consider the information in the context of satisfying short to medium-term shareholder or owner interest, or (in the case of public ventures) political drives and initiatives, and budget constraints.

The process is therefore normally tainted by:

- *Partiality*: in which one party either wishes the venture to go ahead, or else wishes that the venture does not go ahead, and therefore uses the information in support of this preordained point of view.
- *Over-mightiness*: in which the interests of one dominant party become the overriding reason for it to go ahead.
- *The interest of short-term gain*, which is especially fuelled by the fact that any consultants, lawyers or investment analysts see their returns at the inception of the venture and not its completion.

- *Medium-term*: which normally covers the period of commitment to purpose, and initial activities for large ventures and fixed-term ventures (e.g. when pay-back is desired over periods of two–five years).
- *Long-term*: in which elements of risk have to be identified, assessed and managed.

Timeframes are a feature of particular industrial, commercial and public sectors, and consequently short, medium and long term have different connotations according to the sector in which investment is contemplated.

Time is also used as a variable in calculating net present values, depreciation and net rates of return (see below).

In accounting conventions also, time is a key feature. Companies are legally obliged to produce annual reports which represent a true and fair reflection of the effectiveness of application of shareholder's funds. Shareholders expect share values and dividends to increase, and consequently the value of investments has to be written into the annual report to show the effectiveness of the decisions made. Problems arise when the annual report – and reporting relationships between shareholders and decision makers – become the driving force for the assessment of investments and other work in progress.

In the public sector, there are also problems of this nature with annual budget cycles. Those who invest in public services may therefore find themselves unable to proceed with the venture as they would prefer; the archetype model of public availability of funds is given in Figure 9.3, and this still remains the norm.

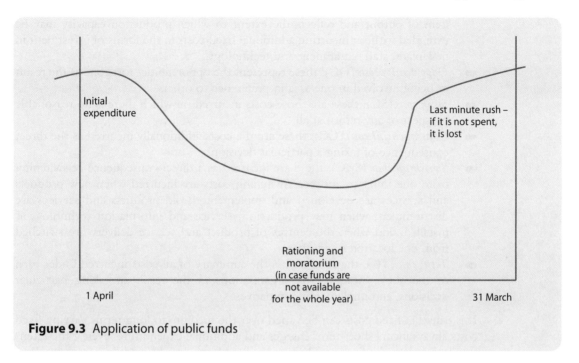

Figure 9.3 Application of public funds

Finally, money itself has a time value. A present unit of currency is valued more highly than at some time in the future, but lower than at a time in the past. This is largely because inflation is an ever-present factor in modern economies. This erodes the value of money as a means of exchange, and as a reckoner of value. Inflation reduces purchasing power, and the extent to which a currency is at risk of inflation (i.e. the rate at which it is losing its value) also causes questions of confidence. For example, over the period 1998–99, the Turkish lira lost half its value, and similar problems were encountered with currencies in the Far East in the period 1997–98.

The consequence is that both individual and corporate investors prefer to have their money now, or failing that, as quickly as possible. Again, this is because the value of the money, and its purchasing power, can be predicted with a greater degree of certainty the sooner it is received.

● Costs

It is usual to distinguish between the following:

- *Fixed costs* (FC): these are the costs incurred by organisations whether or not any business is conducted. They consist of capital charges, the costs of premises and staff, and administrative, managerial and support function overheads.
- *Variable costs* (VC): these are the costs incurred as a result of engaging in activities. They consist of raw materials, packaging and distribution costs, and also relate to the frequency and density of usage of equipment (e.g. production technology, telephone and information systems).
- *Marginal cost* (MC): this is the cost incurred by the production of one extra

item of output and reflects the extent to which production capacity may be extended without incurring additional fixed costs in the forms of investment in new plant, staff, equipment and technology.

- *Opportunity costs* (OC): these represent the opportunities foregone as the result of being involved in one area in preference to others.
- *Sunk costs* (SC): these are those costs incurred on which there is no reasonable prospect of any return at all.
- *Consequential costs* (CC): these are the costs additionally incurred as the direct consequence of taking a particular decision.
- *Switching costs* (SwC): these are incurred as a direct consequence of switching from one thing to another. Switching costs are incurred when new products and services are developed and implemented; old products and services are discontinued; when new production, service and information technology is installed; and when the centres of product and service delivery are switched from one location to another.
- *Total cost* (TC): the total cost is the summary of all costs incurred under each of the above headings by organisations as the result of taking particular decisions, and implementing initiatives.

It is true that fixed costs can be varied over the medium to long term. Varying fixed costs always incurs short-term charges and additional expenditure, even if the intention is to reduce the fixed cost base in the long term. Involvement in new technology or projects always involves an initial outlay. The sale of further shares normally includes discounts to existing shareholders. Redundancies always increase costs because they mean that in the short term people are to be paid additional amounts to leave their jobs. Sales of assets – residual products, technology, property – normally mean that these items have to be written down; there is usually a substantial difference between the value placed on these items, and the real returns that accrue when they are sold.

Producing additional items out of the existing cost base is extremely attractive; the greater the ability to get as near as possible to 100 per cent productivity or potential, the greater the returns on the capital and assets employed. Problems arise where the '100 per cent' is miscalculated. This means that either output and venture facilities are over-extended causing stresses and strains, or else they break down altogether which requires investment in either maintenance, refurbishment or replacement.

There are also problems with the management of opportunity costs. Once it becomes apparent that funds, resources and expertise are available to invest in new ventures, it is possible to become bogged down in extensive consultation and research processes, with the result that any opportunity initially apparent may be lost. Thist also introduces the point that it is impossible to take perfect decisions. While it is necessary to understand the range of opportunities that are on offer at a particular time, once the decision to go with one of them is taken, this must represent commitment to purpose (see Management in Focus 9.2).

The costs of capital

Commercial organisations draw their financial resources from:

- the sale of shares either to family, friends and colleagues, or else on stock markets

MANAGEMENT IN FOCUS 9.2

CONSIDERATION OF COSTS

Labour costs

Many consider labour costs to be variable. This is almost always untrue. The nearest that companies and organisations can genuinely get to a variability in labour costs is either to relate performance directly to productivity and effectiveness (for example through the use of performance-related or profit-related pay schemes), or else to put employment out to tender and subcontract (in which case, there will be a fixed price for the labour once the contract is agreed). Moreover, when variations in the labour force are required through redundancy, retraining, redeployment or redevelopment, there is an immediate additional cost to be borne. Job evaluation also brings additional costs related to the engagement of consultants, the consideration of cases, and the resolution of anomalies. The only variation

therefore in the price of labour, in the short to medium term at least, is upwards.

Technology and equipment costs

While these may be depreciated over periods of time by accountants quite legitimately through the use of accounting conventions, in practice:

● The purchase of equipment may be required immediately, whether or not the previous technology has been fully written off or depreciated.

● Also the equipment may become obsolete overnight, again whether it has been fully written off or depreciated.

There is therefore a clear distinction between the accountancy and managerial approach to investment in technology and this needs always to be maintained.

A behavioural view of costs

Observations carried out by McKinsey in the 1980s led the researchers to conclude that whenever a company found itself in short to medium-term financial difficulties, it would engage in any or all of the following:

● confrontational relationships between itself and any recognised trade unions

● cutbacks in training and development activities, especially for those lower down the organisation

● the removal of tea and coffee-making facilities and machines, and the removal of flowers and magazines from the reception area.

Source: T. Peters (1986) *The World Turned Upside Down*, Channel 4.

● the sale of loan notes and debentures, which may be described as short-term or fixed-term capital and which must be repaid on the date specified
● government grants and incentives, issued either in the form of regional aid, start-up and pump-priming funds, and guarantees, or else in return for undertaking government contracts
● retained income, surpluses and profits from activities carried out
● bank and finance house loans on which interest is repayable over the period of the loan.

Different sources of capital incur different kinds of cost.

- Share capital has a perceived or indicated cost attached to it, in that shareholders expect a dividend commensurate with the levels that they have been led to anticipate. They also expect ventures to be conducted in such a way that the commercial value of the shares will rise.
- Loans have contracted charges in the form of interest repayments or – in the case of debentures – a deadline on which the money outstanding has to be repaid.
- Retained income surpluses and profits have managerial and expertise charges placed on them to ensure that this part of the resource is used as effectively and profitably as possible so that it becomes less necessary for further share or loan funds to be sought.

Gearing

Gearing is the relationship between bank loans and other sources of finance. The convention in the West is that gearing should be as low as possible, meaning that the balance of financial resources should depend as little as possible on bank loans.

Gearing may be expressed as the following ratio:

$$\text{Gearing} = \frac{\text{Bank Loans}}{\text{Share Liabilities}}$$

Percentages can then be calculated, and assessed for suitability and viability.

The higher the level of capital gearing, the greater the risk associated with the company. The gearing ratio should always represent a key point of inquiry in the assessment of risk.

High levels of gearing may have implications for cash flow, in that interest charges are a contracted cost of capital and have to be paid when required. In long-term capital ventures, this may bring the additional cost of having to provide extensive overdraft facilities.

When high profits are being made, high gearing provides shareholders with high returns on their investment. This is because interest charges are written out of the equation before the profit on which the dividends and returns to be paid are calculated.

Borrowing is also attractive when inflation is high – especially when it is higher than the percentage rate of interest required. If a company borrows money at an interest rate of 5 per cent per annum, and inflation is running at 5 per cent per annum, then the funds are effectively free of charge. If inflation is any higher than this, then it is effectively being subsidised in its venture by the loan maker.

Other costs and charges that have to be written in are:

- liability for taxation over the duration of the venture
- servicing inflationary pressures, where the value of one of the currencies being used is declining steeply in value
- assessing maintenance upgrade and replacement charges for each aspect of the venture.

This involves the creation of capital cycles as follows:

- *Taxation cycles*: taxation volumes, frequencies and regularities of payments demanded by government (or governments if the venture is a multinational or international one). This is also a key issue for those investing in small business ventures in the UK where taxation for the current year is pre-assessed by the Inland Revenue on the basis of the previous year's trading (and any tax credits that become subsequently due are paid a year in arrears by the Inland Revenue).

● *Inflation cycles*: underwriting or insuring against the effects of inflation is extremely difficult to achieve; and this is a further problem when conducting long-term ventures, because long-term inflation rates are extremely difficult to predict. Again therefore, this becomes a key point of enquiry when assessing the risk involved in particular ventures.

● *Replacement cycles*: replacement cycles are concerned with the operational aspects of investment. Referring especially to technology and expertise, replacement cycles have to be calculated in order to obtain the best possible returns on technology before it reaches the end of its useful life; establish pay and reward rates that are likely to attract, retain and provide incentive to those with the expertise required.

● *Crisis replacement cycles*: these must also be in-built into this part of the process so that breakdown of equipment, or the sudden loss of key expertise, can be addressed quickly.

● Assumptions

Effective consideration of barriers, costs and returns is certain to bring about a series of assumptions that have to be made. It is assumed that:

● the perceptions present have been tested and understood by everyone involved
● the complete range of likely and possible barriers and their effects are fully understood
● the costs involved have been accurately assessed and classified
● the initiative, venture or proposal still remains viable in the terms in which it was originally conceived
● overall returns on the particular investment are still possible.

These assumptions have then to be tested.

Clarity of the role, function, aims and objectives of everyone involved must be continuously ensured to at every stage. In particular, those who are asked to accept as their primary responsibility the key elements of risk or uncertainty must be content to do this.

Working relationships must be capable of addressing the problems and issues that are certain to arise. Working relationships when developing and implementing investments, ventures and initiatives are often not clearly defined, and this invariably leads to problems along the way. Problems are compounded when the core issue of return on investment begins to vary; and problems become more serious still if it becomes apparent that the desired or demanded returns are not now to be achieved.

The aims and objectives of individuals involved can and do change. These changes may come about as the result of any personal, professional or occupational circumstance. When this is the case, some individuals leave their jobs or change their roles and so are no longer involved; other individuals are brought into the roles associated with the particular venture or initiative, and are certain to bring different perspectives and points of view.

The circumstances of the organisations involved can and do also change. Both upturns and downturns in other activities within the organisation affect the priority and viability of particular ventures. Provisions for cancellation, downgrade and upgrade of the particular initiative ought always to be made available. Identifying and testing assumptions is therefore a key part of the process of appraising and implementing investment and capital expenditure effectively. It is essential that the professional managerial discipline relating to using organisational resources as efficiently and effectively as possible remains at the core of everything that is undertaken; and a key part of this professional discipline is ensuring that everything that is assumed is rigorously challenged when it arises (see Management in Focus 9.3).

● Returns on investment and returns on capital employed

Calculating returns on investment and on capital employed is overtly straightforward. The formula is as follows:

$$\frac{\text{Income Generated}}{\text{Investment/Capital Employed}} \times 100 = \text{Percentage rate of return}$$

Problems arise with this however if the capital employed in the venture is not precisely defined, or if the real level or value of the investment to all parties concerned is not realised. This is exacerbated by promised and 'certain' predicted rates of return, which often come to be accepted as 'the truth' as a result of the barriers and assumptions indicated above, and as a result of calculations carried out and analysed from a narrow perspective only.

Real and projected rates of return are also distorted when resources from outside the direct investment are used in pursuing it, but then not included in the return on investment or capital employed calculations. It is necessary to distinguish between gross and net return on investment and return on capital employed; while it is usual to present this as net, whichever is the case needs to be made clear.

There may also be derived returns, and these can be both positive and negative. From a positive point of view, this is the enhancement of reputation, better than anticipated returns, and the opportunity to pursue new ventures. Negative rates of return include provision for bad debt, loss of reputation, unsuccessful ventures, or changes in priorities that have taken place during the course of completion of the project.

Returns on investment calculations may also be subject to time constraints, especially the pressures of the annual report. This again is a particular problem in long-term ventures, where, because of the nature of the investment made, shareholders may not receive anticipated dividends or the desired level of increase in the value of their shares.

Expected and anticipated returns on investment and on capital employed reflect the nature and extent of expectations and anticipations of shareholders, other backers, stakeholders and vested interests. Managerial approaches to projections of returns therefore tend towards the lowest common denominator because anything above this is then normally perceived to be a huge success.

Returns on capital employed are most useful as comparators between desired and actual performance. This should provide a key point of inquiry when evaluating the

MANAGEMENT IN FOCUS 9.3

TESTING ASSUMPTIONS

There are two priority areas where assumptions should always be tested. These are denial and decision making.

Denial

The problem of denial exists when an initiative or venture which looks overwhelmingly attractive, is suddenly faced with a key barrier. The problem of denial has to be addressed when any, or all, of the following occur:

- denial on the part of a dominant or influential backer or sponsor of what is proposed
- denial on the part of the individual or group responsible for producing the initiative or venture
- denial on the part of those responsible for implementing the initiative or venture.

The problem is compounded by having to attend to the human and behavioural aspects. For example, if one of the above interests is also strident in manner, prone to unpleasantness when confronted, or used to over-riding any concerns raised,

confronting the particular barriers then becomes a test of personal courage as well as professional discipline. For example, when Richard Greenbury became CEO of Marks & Spencer, he proposed a series of initiatives to redevelop the business. Many of these initiatives were opposed on an individual basis by a majority of the company's top and senior management. However, when Greenbury asked for formal decisions in his favour in boardroom and top management meetings, none of these decisions ever went against him.

Decision making

There are two key approaches to decision making in investment appraisal:

- evaluating the information, testing the assumptions, and then arriving at fully informed decisions
- taking the decision, and then fitting the facts to what has already been decided.

Clearly, in an ideal world, the first of these should be the only approach that is ever used. In practice, the second approach

is at least as prevalent as the first. Again, this ought to give rise to the engagement of the professional discipline of testing assumptions, especially when the presentation of information, and the case for investment as a whole, has been skewed by some form of subjectivity or irrationality. For example, many UK and US banking and financial services organisations have taken the decision to outsource customer services and customer information management functions to locations in India and other parts of the Far East. The organisations that pioneered this approach did so on the basis of known, believed and perceived reductions in labour force and technology costs that could be achieved by establishing activities in these places. Many of those organisations that simply followed the trend assumed that these cost reductions would also be available to them; they went ahead and established their own activities in these locations also, without having tested the assumptions in terms of their own interests, organisation structures or required standards of service delivery.

success or failure of activities and ventures. It may also identify particular inefficiencies of resource utilisation.

Inflation, interest and retail prices indices can also serve as general benchmarks on which to assess their returns for basic acceptability.

Returns on capital employed should always be seen in terms of the nature of actual returns in the particular industrial, commercial or public service sector in question.

Returns on investment must also be seen in terms of the size and value of the particular venture, and of the other opportunities available. For example, simply carrying out the calculations in isolation, without consideration of the broader context, might lead a venturer to conclude that a 15 per cent return on £1000 over a five-year period was more attractive than a 14 per cent return on £5000 over a twenty-year period.

● Net present values

The net present value of an investment can be defined as 'the value today of the surplus that the company makes, over the future period of time that the surplus is made'. This is based on two considerations:

● first, that the company has assessed its lowest acceptable rate of return on investment
● second, that the investment itself has a better or more assured chance of achieving that rate of return than the next most overtly profitable venture available.

This may be summarised by the formula shown in Figure 9.4. Provided that the information fed into the formula is based on real research and venture assessment, and that contextual and situational factors have been taken into account, the calculation provides a useful indication of likely rates of return.

The calculation can then be carried out for best, medium and worst outcomes (see Figure 9.5).

While this provides a measure of substantial quantitative information on which investment decisions can be taken, the problem lies in the fact that anything in between the two extremes indicated will nevertheless become acceptable. In other words, provided any form of positive outcome to the venture can be envisaged the decision is likely to be taken to go ahead with it. If the medium-acceptable rate of return envisaged is attained, then inefficiencies and ineffectiveness present in the inception and completion of the venture may not be fully considered because the overall rates of return are well within the margins of acceptability.

Net present value calculations may also be used to assess the relative merits of continuing ventures and activities. They can be used to analyse products and service portfolios in terms of:

● those which attract investment, and which attract buyer and consumer interest
● those which people buy, which contribute to particular volumes of sales as a percentage of the total
● those on which the greatest margins are achieved, and those on which the greatest margins can be projected.

They also make possible a calculated assessment of those ventures that are coming to the end of their useful life, and those on which the desired or required rates of

$$\text{Net present value} = \frac{A}{1+R} + \frac{A}{(1+R)} + \frac{A}{(1+R)} + \text{------} + \frac{A}{(1+R)^n} - I$$

Where:

A = the net cash flow in the particular year
n = the point in time when the project comes to the end of its life, representing the total number of years in which the project has been conducted
R = the firm's annual rate of discount
I = the initial cost of the investment

Figure 9.4 Net present value formula

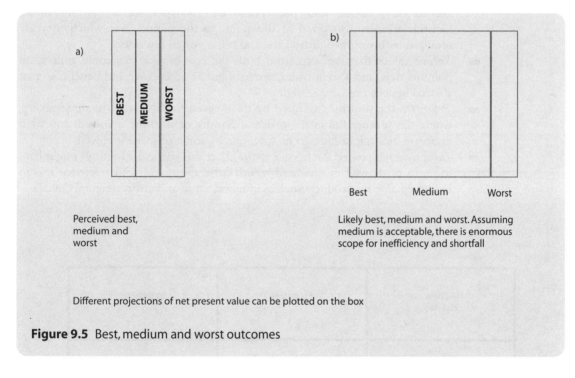

Different projections of net present value can be plotted on the box

Figure 9.5 Best, medium and worst outcomes

return are no longer forthcoming. This is likely to provide a basis for discussion as to whether particular products, projects and ventures should be continued or divested.

Again however, this has to be seen in the broadest context. Especially the attract/sell/make-money approach needs to be seen as a whole rather than as parts. For example, the divestment of a product or venture which is attractive but does not produce returns must be seen in terms of the knock-on effects that it may have on the rest of the activities.

● Cost–benefit analysis

Cost–benefit analysis is a quick and easy, ready-reckoner method of establishing a basis on which a given initiative might be feasible or profitable (in whatever terms that may be measured), and of identifying those elements that require further more detailed consideration before it is implemented. It simply requires itemising all the costs and charges that could possibly be incurred in the venture, and setting them against all the values and benefits that the completed item, project or product might bring.

Cost–benefit analysis is used widely in the consideration of public sector projects, and those commercial ventures that bring with them real or perceived social benefits. Cost–benefit analysis involves consideration of nine related areas (see Figure 9.6).

The approach is as follows:

● *Action choices*: the meaning of the costs and benefits of alternative courses of action in relation to each other.
● *Timeframes*: short, medium and long term – the time periods over which costs are to be incurred and the results and benefits are to be measured. Consideration is also given at this point to the period over which they are required by investors and backers, and other vested interests.
● *Values*: values that are seen from both the economic and income generation point of view, and also in wider terms, of public acceptance and benefit, so that a social benefit can be assessed.
● *Priorities*: the priorities ascribed by all involved to the particular undertaking; where the venture lies in the order of priority of all those involved; and what opportunities might have to be foregone by some of those involved.
● *Initiatives*: with especial reference to the effect that particular ventures might have in terms of derived income and wealth generation; and with reference also to less acceptable by-products such as effluent, waste and environmental damage.

Action choices	Priorities	Initiatives
Short, medium long term	Strategic aspects	Risk
Relative valuation	Income expenditure	Value

Figure 9.6 Cost–benefit analysis model

- *Risk and uncertainty*: consideration of the aspects of risk must be built into this form of evaluation of any venture.
- *Strategy*: strategic aspects and overview will take account of all aspects of political, economic and social costs and benefits as well as the direct financial demands and implications presented.
- *Relativity*: the relative valuation of different costs and benefits in terms of all those involved in the venture; in terms of the frequency and intervals at which they occur; and how they are to be reconciled when they occur at different points in time, or in relation to the different priorities brought by all those concerned to the venture.
- *Income and expenditure*: related in particular to values that accrue to those on different incomes; to those dependent on the completion of the venture for continued employment; and to questions of political, and other, reputation and enhancement.

Cost–benefit analysis has normally been used as one key method of assessing the viability of public and politically driven projects and initiatives.

It is however of increasing importance that commercial ventures consider their investments – especially large and long-term projects – from this broader perspective, because of legal constraints continually being imposed in matters of employment protection, and environmental awareness and responsibility. Those seeking to become involved in private finance initiative ventures, and the delivery of services hitherto part of the public domain, also need to consider the cost–benefit perspective if they are to fully understand the situation in which they are being asked to operate in the future. Figures 9.7, 9.8 and 9.9 give examples of this.

Each venture can be seen in this way from the narrow perspective of maximising investment, or the broader perspective of accepting the responsibilities and consequences of that investment. This will not necessarily mean that those involved will

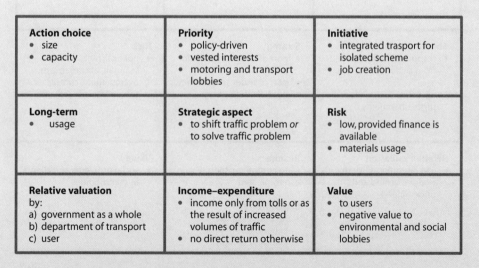

Action choice	Priority	Initiative
• size • capacity	• policy-driven • vested interests • motoring and transport lobbies	• integrated trasport for isolated scheme • job creation
Long-term • usage	**Strategic aspect** • to shift traffic problem *or* to solve traffic problem	**Risk** • low, provided finance is available • materials usage
Relative valuation by: a) government as a whole b) department of transport c) user	**Income–expenditure** • income only from tolls or as the result of increased volumes of traffic • no direct return otherwise	**Value** • to users • negative value to environmental and social lobbies

Figure 9.7 Cost–benefit analysis model for a motorway scheme

Action choice	Priority	Initiative
• size • capacity • projected length of useful life • resale value	• buy/lease • construct	• market aimed at ability and propensity to pay
Short-term • familiarity, confidence **Long-term** • market size	**Strategy** • niche • competition from other holiday packages • returns on volume sales	**Risk** • local publicity • accidents and tragedies both to this venture and others would cause loss of overall confidence and demand
Relative valuation • low to consumers, part of very high choice sector	**Income** • steady, long-term **Expenditure** • high initial • steady long-term	**Value** • ability to brand and differentiate • perceived value

Figure 9.8 Cost–benefit analysis model for a cruise liner

Action choice	Priority	Initiative
• to privatise	• to reduce public expenditure(!) • to offer choice(!) • political and expedient	• to address a long-term social and political problem
Short-term • responsibility is removed from public service **Long-term** * problem remains	**Strategy** • part of wider privatisation policy • part of wider social policy • not fully defined	**Risk** • political: high, due to scandals, abuse, abuses, overcharging, contractor can unilaterally pull out
Relative valuation • low – problems like this are under-invested and undervalued	**Income** • to contractor: high, economic rent **Expenditure** • no public capital expenditure • charges are high	**Value** • social problems and clients as commodities

Figure 9.9 Cost–benefit analysis model for a privatised children's home

not proceed purely from the narrow point of view. However, it does indicate some of the obligations and responsibilities inherent in different types of venture; it also indicates the fact that eventually someone will be called to account for these.

Conclusions

The purpose of this chapter has been to identify and illustrate the complexities of investment proposals, to demonstrate the need for managerial expertise in this area, and to underline the importance of this form of approach in the pursuit of effective decision-making processes.

It is clear that there are no universal criteria for the effective measurement of investment. This is a matter for consideration by those seeking to enter into particular ventures and initiatives; and decisions have to be taken on the basis of evaluating each proposal or initiative on its own merits. Different approaches to similar ventures and initiatives may produce very different results. This underlines the need for full evaluation and effective decision making in response to each proposal.

Investment appraisal is often dominated by the demands of dominant and key shareholders, backers and driving forces. From a macro-organisational point of view, the key priority remains maximising short to medium-term shareholder value, and share value enhancement. This remains true despite the fact that every other drive is towards long-term sustainability and viability in the provision of products and services. This underlines the need for professional discipline and evaluation. Any managers wishing to depart from the line of maximising short to medium-term shareholder value have to be capable of presenting the ways in which they calculate the likelihood of success or otherwise of particular initiatives, and to get this accepted by those with both knowledge and influence.

Failure to maintain this professional discipline invariably leads to inadequate criteria for the measurement of investment performance being established at the outset. This in turn leads to a tendency to stick to simplistic approaches, rather than addressing the complexities involved.

Effective performance criteria must be related to each of the areas covered, and the possibilities and prospects of delivering what was intended. The need to address the full range of complexities is illustrated in Figure 9.10.

Finally, the effective implementation and delivery of investment lies in managing the diverse and conflicting interests, and reconciling the different results required by particular stakeholders from ventures and initiatives. For anything to be successful, it is essential that the conditions are created in which effective groundwork can be carried out in advance of ventures and initiatives going ahead. It is essential to recognise this as a barrier to effective progress, and it is also essential to jump this hurdle as a prerequisite to generating full support from all those involved, and to ensuring that adequate levels of resources are considered and evaluated, and then commanded. It is certain that those who appraise ventures, investments and initiatives from the broadest perspective are more certain to secure long-term and enduring success, and the confidence that goes with this, than those who do not.

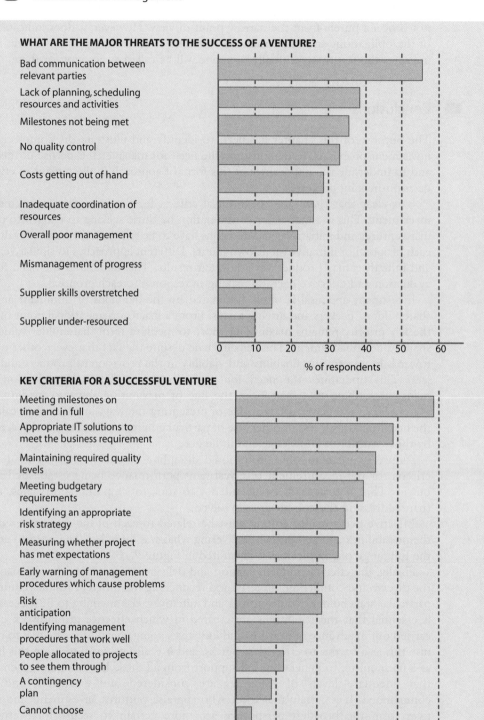

WHAT ARE THE MAJOR THREATS TO THE SUCCESS OF A VENTURE?

KEY CRITERIA FOR A SUCCESSFUL VENTURE

Figure 9.10 Key criteria for venture success

CRITICAL THINKING, ANALYSIS AND EVALUATION

1. Identify the range of benefits that ought to accrue as a result of investing in information technology upgrades. Identify the barriers that have to be addressed.
2. By what criteria may the construction of the Channel Tunnel be deemed to have been a success; and by what may it be deemed to have been a failure?
3. Identify the range of costs that have to be evaluated by a UK company when it is considering establishing factory facilities in Hungary and the Czech Republic.
4. Conduct a cost–benefit analysis for the construction of an edge-of-town retail park, for which planning permission has already been granted. Identify and prioritise the costs and benefits; and from this, make recommendations for the possibility of other similar developments in the future.

DEVELOPING MANAGEMENT SKILLS AND EXPERTISE

COOPER'S CLOTHES: MANAGERIAL AND STRUCTURAL RESISTANCE TO CHANGE

Research carried out by the Cranfield Institute in three retail clothing companies identified the extent to which managerial and structural resistances to change could affect both profitability and performance in spite of the fact that there was a clear collective understanding on the part of all of those involved that changes needed to take place.

One of the companies investigated was Cooper's; a wholesale producer of children's and youth clothing for both the school uniform and the leisurewear market. The company sought to move out of this sector to a strategy based on younger, more fashion-oriented clothing, and to expand upwards into the 'young male' sector where it thought that the future lay.

This approach centred on the view that Cooper's success in recent years was due to its merchandising strength. In particular, merchandising and the policies associated with it were such that those within the firm came to see that changes in fashion were not important since Cooper's were concentrating on commodity rather than market merchandising. Indeed, such was the perceived prowess at merchandising that Cooper's failed to undertake any form of market assessment and evaluation, environmental analyses, or market testing. The collective view was that the company thought that it knew enough about retailing to retail anything, to anyone, anywhere.

Then performance at Cooper's declined dramatically. However, this was blamed on the economic recession at the time, loss of consumer confidence, and the need for people to buy on credit. School uniform sales were declining because unifoms were perceived to be 'un-cool'. Cooper's response was to engage in a cost-cutting and product-standardisation programme rather than examining and re-examining the market, the operating environment and the proposition of moving from school uniforms into clothing for older age ranges.

The initial efforts failed to make an impact. There was further response along the same lines. Finally, the company engaged in major cost-cutting through massive redundancies.

The company then engaged a new marketing director, who was given the brief of establishing in detail what Cooper's ought to do next. The new director presented findings that pointed to outdated conceptions of the clothing market on the part of the existing senior management. He proposed returning to the core market and building a fundamental business strength on developing and extending the school uniform provision.

However, this did not go down well. There was heavy resistance to the report that the marketing director presented. It was seen as a political attack on those who were running the company, and a jockeying for political position on the part of the new marketing director. This led to the existing management questioning his expertise and experience.

Questions

1. Taking an investment appraisal approach to the decision to appoint a new marketing manager, answer the following questions:
   How is the appointment to be judged for success and failure?
   What other factors needed to be taken into account?
   What assumptions needed to be tested?
2. Identify where the priorities for the company now lie, the nature of investment required to address those priorities, and the ranges of outcomes possible. On the basis of your evaluation, what do you recommend that the company now sets out to achieve?
3. How are you going to gauge returns on investment (ROI) on:
   - the marketing manager?
   - the investments you propose for question 2 above?

Chapter ten

Marketing

'All this marketing is such a bore.'
Alec Douglas-Home (1963), during the run-up to
the general election of that year. He lost.

'I will make Britain great again.'
Margaret Thatcher, Conservative leader,
during the 1978 election campaign. She won.

'We used a £400 photograph; and we bought £8.5 million worth of advertising.'
Michael O'Leary, CEO of Ryanair, on the controversial use of a
photograph of Pope John Paul II in a company advertisement.

Chapter outline

- Introduction to marketing and its importance in all sectors and activities
- The marketing process
- Marketing mixes
- Marketing strategies
- Product and service lifecycles
- Public relations

Chapter objectives

After studying this chapter, you should be able to:

- understand what marketing is, and why it is so important to managers and organisations

- understand managerial priorities and responsibilities to the integrity and presentation of products and services

- understand the importance and value of marketing and market research

- understand how the different marketing strategies and activities may best – and worst – be applied.

● Introduction

The purpose of this chapter is to introduce and illustrate the priorities and principles required for a full understanding of marketing.

Marketing is the competitive process by which goods and services are offered for consumption at a profit. Marketing combines product and service substance with effective presentation, convenience and acceptability to engage the interest and commitment of customers, consumers and clients, and the public at large (see Management in Focus 10.1).

MANAGEMENT IN FOCUS 10.1

MARKETING: SOME INITIAL EXAMPLES

The quality of marketing very often makes all the difference to the viability of particular organisations and industrial and commercial sectors. For example:

- *Nuclear electricity generation*: in the face of enduring public uncertainty and lack of overall confidence in the long-term safety of this industry, its managers have concentrated the presentational side of their activities on what they can do well. The marketing of nuclear electricity therefore concentrates on two key features: the bringing of work into remote and isolated communities – in the UK all of the nuclear electricity generating stations are situated on the coast, away from centres of population; and education – above all for schoolchildren, but also for anyone who is interested; this has led to most stations opening up visitor centres. These are supported with archive material, brochures and a general publicity programme that emphasises the enduring benefits of an industry that nevertheless has a very long-term and difficult challenge in the management of its waste effluent and radioactive residue.

- *The tobacco industry*: this industry has managed to secure for itself major sponsorship of high-profile global sporting events in order to counteract the bans that exist throughout most of Western Europe and North American on direct advertising and sales efforts. Concentrating especially on Formula 1 motor racing and the Indie circuit in North America, tobacco companies have created for themselves a position in which the global sport of motor racing cannot exist in its present form without them. This gives them a television audience of between six and ten hours per channel, per country every fortnight for ten months of the year. Government-sponsored anti-smoking promotions that are intended to counter this publicity consist largely of small and under-produced leaflets distributed in schools, public libraries and doctors' surgeries. This is so ineffective that the commercial producers of products that counteract the effects of smoking have had to assume direct marketing responsibility for their own products, rather than coordinating their efforts with government anti-smoking campaigns.

Marketing processes and activities are normally classified as follows.

- *Consumer marketing*: which comes in two basic forms:
  - unconsidered purchases, leading to instant satisfaction (or dissatisfaction)
  - considered, high value purchases, leading to ensuring satisfaction (or dissatisfaction).
- *Industrial and business-to-business marketing*: unconsidered purchases (e.g. the office coffee), and considered purchases (e.g. capital goods, access to information), which are based on the development of relationships so that considered purchases carry trust and confidence, as well as enduring utility.
- *Public services marketing*: an area in which substantial development is required, particularly in response to political drives to engage commercial interests in these activities.
- *The not-for-profit sector*: advantages gained by engaging interest, sympathy and, above all, action from those targeted.
- *Internal marketing*: activities designed to build mutuality of interest and confidence, and enduring workplace relations, across organisations.

A core outcome of the marketing process is the development of relationships between the organisation and its customers and clients. Every interaction between the organisation, its staff and customers makes a contribution to the development of these relationships. This is a function of generating customer loyalty, and of getting customers to relate that loyalty to purchasing and consumption activities.

Relationships and loyalties are built, maintained and developed through the combination of product and service quality on offer, immediate and after-sales activities, and the continued ability of the customers to buy, use and consume the products and services in ways that are of value to them (see Management in Focus 10.2).

MANAGEMENT IN FOCUS 10.2

CUSTOMER NEEDS AND WANTS: THE PACKARD APPROACH

Packard (1957) sought to define the relationship between product, presentation and image, and customer and consumer motivation. The conclusions were that the most successful marketing of products and services arose when both the product and its presentation engaged one or more of the following responses among customers, clients, consumers and end-users:

- *Emotional security, comfort and confidence*: related to bulk purchases of food, safety features in cars, domestic security and insurance.
- *Reassurance of worth*: purchases must make customers feel good. This

means that customers have to be satisfied with the products and services on offer, and their use of the products and services must also be respected and valued by others around them.

- *Ego gratification*: anything that is sold to gratify the ego must meet the subjective demands of luxury, exclusivity and immortality. Products and services sold to gratify the ego include expensive luxury cars, exclusive holidays and vanity publishing.

- *Creativity*: products and services sold to feed the need for creativity put a critical value on the contribution of the customer or end-user to make the product effective. For example, cake mixes that required the addition of eggs were found to be more successful than those that simply required the addition of water, because there was a greater input on the part of the user or consumer.
- *Love objects*: this aspect may be summarised as: 'cuddly toy', 'dear little child' or 'sweet/cute little animal'. Andrex, the major suppliers of toilet tissue to the UK retail sector, has used labrador puppies as the central feature of its commercials since the 1970s. Children are used extensively in television commercials in the pursuit of engendering this sense of love and warmth; this

extends to the marketing of washing powder, grocery shopping, fast food, cars, holidays, central heating and double-glazing.

- *Power*: the power of the product or offering is reflected in the user of it. Nearly all automobile advertising and marketing is on the basis of power, performance and speed, as well as security. Power and strength are also strongly related to cigarette marketing, especially in Formula 1 motor racing, and also the sponsorship of cricket, rugby league, sailing and power boat racing.
- *Traditions and roots*: this is relating 'the good old days' to the modern era. For example, food promotions use phrases such as: 'just as good as mother used to make'; Rolls-Royce cars maintain the traditions of fittings and furnishings, and reliability and exclusivity on which their original reputation was built. Politicians exploit perceptions and visions of golden ages with calls for 'returns to traditional values' and 'back to basics' because there is a

very strong perception of 'the good old days' and association with historic success, order, stability and prosperity.

- *Immortality*: this is related to security, ego gratification and traditions and roots. Maintaining the illusion of immortality is an essential prerequisite to the effective marketing of housing, life assurance and other forms of insurance, loans and other financial products.

People buy products and services for the value, benefits and satisfaction delivered; and Packard sought to indicate that maximising the chances of delivering benefits and satisfaction required targeting at least one of the above points.

It is additionally the case, that by using a managerial approach to marketing and product and service presentation using the above criteria, it was much easier to target the subjective (rather than perceived or pseudo-rational) needs of customers, consumers, clients and end-users.

Source: Vance Packard (1957) *The Hidden Persuaders*, Penguin.

Marketing strategies

As stated in Chapter 8, all organisations require a core foundation or generic strategic position, and all effective marketing strategies consequently need to reflect the core foundation or generic position chosen. Marketing strategies are then used to build on that position as follows:

- *Pioneering or 'first in the field':* opening up new markets or new outlets for existing products, or new products for existing outlets; taking an original and distinctive view of the marketing process and devising new methods and campaigns.
- *'Follow the leader':* the great benefit of being second in the field is to learn from the mistakes and experience of the pioneer, and make informed judgements about the nature of the involvement to be taken based on their experience. Or it may be that the second organisation can see opportunities that were not exploited by the first.
- *'Me too' or 'all-comers':* where the market is wide open, entry to and exit from it are relatively easy, where the products and services in question are universal or general, and where there are many suppliers but where there are more buyers than suppliers.
- *Supply led:* where the product is produced because the organisation has complete faith in it and knows that, once made, it can be sold at a profit.
- *Technology led:* where the organisation finds itself in a particular line of business because it has at its disposal a particular type of technology which can be turned to productive and profitable advantage in a variety of sectors.
- *Staff led:* because of the skills, qualities and preferences of the staff of an organisation that happen to be gathered together, the products or offerings reflect these (very prevalent in the small business sphere).
- *Market led:* where the organisation looks first at a range of markets, then assesses their requirements, and finally decides which of these it can most valuably and profitably operate in and fill.
- *Moral or ethical marketing:* creating and developing a high-value reputation as the result of a distinctive moral or ethical stance, for example using Fairtrade ingredients (e.g. Starbucks), or using trading practices as a presentational feature (e.g. The Body Shop).

In relation to each of the above, marketing strategies may be either offensive or defensive. Offensive marketing activities seek to make inroads into the competitive position and customer and client bases of others. Defensive and responsive marketing activities are undertaken with the object of preserving the present position in response to the offensives of others (see Management in Focus 10.3).

Segmentation

Effective marketing demands that the needs and wants of customers and clients are defined as precisely as possible. It is therefore essential to be able to 'segment' or classify the population in some way. The normal approaches are social segmentation, market and social segmentation, and customer definition.

MANAGEMENT IN FOCUS 10.3

THE LEISUREWEAR SECTORS

The provision of products for the leisurewear sectors of Europe, Australia, New Zealand, South Africa and North and South America constitutes the ultimate in selling fast-moving consumer goods. The benefits that accrue to customers from their ventures into this area are to do with image, impression, distinctiveness, lifestyle, identity, the imitation of film, pop or sports stars, and personal esteem and comfort. Having gained all this for themselves, they wish to be held in positive and popular esteem by their peers, and to carry a wider label of status and prominence in the society in which they live. Niches for leisurewear may therefore additionally be identified by:

- *Age*: which ranges from birth virtually through to death and is often very precisely targeted in the areas in between. For example, the teenage sector can be further defined to target each of the teenage years (i.e. each of 13 through to 19) and any combination of them (e.g. 13–15, 14–18); and alongside the teenage sector are the pre-teen or tween (8-12) and post-teen (early 20s and even beyond) groups.
- *Sex, gender and sexuality*: and associated images.

- *Location*: regional, local and national variations on the particular products. This is compounded by that which is perceived either to be a leading location or one to be avoided at all costs.
- *Branding*: the quest for distinctiveness mirrored in the desire and ability on the part of the consumer to wear the badge and distinction with the given qualities of pride, identity and esteem and to gain the esteem, real or perceived, of others. Branding confers the ability to charge high prices.
- *Transience*: the new is not new for long. The moment the next distinctive offering comes along, the previous one is first passé, and then obsolete.

The importance of image must be reflected in both strategies and ways of working adopted by companies that seek to operate in this field. In particular, at the beginning of the twenty-first century, the leisurewear sector is dogged by ethical issues, and allegations of slave labour in the garment manufacturing factories. Nike, Reebok and The Gap, have all had to counter these allegations, and such issues remain an enduring problem for all those companies that draw supplies from the emerging world. Marketing and market research are therefore required to cover everything if a profit base is to be established. In particular, many companies that have relocated manufacturing to the emerging world are increasingly required to adopt a practice of close supervision of factory activities, in order to secure the total integrity of product manufacture and presentation. Staffing policies will ideally mirror this, drawing upon a range of qualities and levels of commitment that represent expertise, familiarity, understanding and a fundamentally ethical approach, as well as the ability to forecast in the area and to produce new, effective and targeted products quickly. Design is a critical facility in such companies. Marketing strategies concentrate on the differentiation aspects and use all media sectors, both mainstream and niche in the pursuit of this. The leisurewear sector is saturated, yet entry and exit barriers are low, affording plenty of opportunities in a business area in which the consumers of the entire world wish to participate, and which they will participate in provided that they have sufficient disposable income. This is the strategic base from which all players in this sector must operate.

Social segmentation

Social segmentation breaks down the population according to the occupation of the head of household as follows:

- *A*: aristocrats and upper middle class, including directors, senior managers, senior civil and public servants.
- *B*: middle class, such as lawyers, doctors, senior managers.
- *C1*: lower middle class, such as teachers, nurses, doctors, engineers, technologists, managers.
- *C2*: skilled working class, including some engineering and technology activities.
- *D*: working class.
- *E*: subsistence, including the underclass and unemployed.

Market and social segmentation

Market and social segmentation has existed in the UK since 1998, when the UK National Office of Population, Census and Surveys produced the following framework.

- *Class 1A*: large employers, higher managers, company directors, senior police, fire, prison, military officers, newspaper editors. The structure also included top football managers and restaurateurs in this section.
- *Class 1B*: professionals – doctors, solicitors, engineers, teachers. This section also included airline pilots.
- *Class 2*: associate professionals, journalists, nurses, midwives, actors, musicians, military NCOs, and junior police, fire and prison officers. This section also includes lower managers (with fewer than 25 staff).
- *Class 3*: intermediate occupations – secretaries, air stewards and stewardesses, driving instructors, telephone operators. This section also includes 'employee sports' players', e.g. footballers and cricketers.
- *Class 4*: small employers, managers of small departments, non-professional self-employed, publicans, plumbers, farm owners and managers. This section also includes self-employed sports players – e.g. golfers and tennis players.
- *Class 5*: lower supervisors, crafts and related workers, electricians, mechanics, train drivers, bus inspectors.
- *Class 6*: semi-routine occupations, traffic wardens, caretakers, gardeners, shelf stackers, assembly line workers.
- *Class 7*: routine occupations, cleaners, waiter/waitress/bar staff, messenger/couriers, road workers, dockers.
- *Class 8*: the excluded. This includes the long-term unemployed, those who have never worked, the long-term sick, and prison populations.

Customer definition

Customer and segment definition is defined according to one of the classifications above; this is further refined by identifying in detail the customers required by: age, sex/gender, status, aspiration, values, location, occupation and expectations. Marketing then concentrates on defining products and services in terms of the benefits of value to the given and precisely defined segments.

Additional approaches to customer definition produce the following information:

- type and class of buyers
- size of customer bases in given locations and niches
- the balance of quality, volume and price that customers expect
- the value of the product or service relative to other items available for consumption
- the value of the product or service relative to other items that the customer base either needs or wants to purchase
- patterns of spending among members of the niche or customer base, and the extent to which they use credit, credit cards, cash or cheque books
- the need for access to product and service after sales
- the ease of access to facilities and services
- the frequency with which a given product or service is to be used.

Social segmentation and customer definition are not exact sciences. They are however useful means of defining and classifying society for the purpose of targeting products and services as effectively as possible. They also provide a focus for understanding better the needs and wants of the particular segment targeted, so as to refine and improve product and service quality, and also the marketing effort in terms of the benefits that are of value to the given customer base.

Marketing mixes

Marketing activities are based on mixes of the elements described below. Each is present to a greater or lesser extent in all marketing activities, though the balance of each clearly varies between different products and services.

The 4Ps

- *Product*: variety, branding quality, packaging, appearance and design.
- *Promotion*: advertising, sponsorship, selling, publicity, mailshots.
- *Price*: basic, discounting, credit, payment method, appearance.
- *Place*: coverage, outlets, transport, distribution and accessibility.

The 4Cs

- *Customers*: directing marketing and presentational activities at the needs and wants of customers.
- *Convenience*: a combination of establishing the required and desired outlets, and of educating customers and clients to access the available outlets.
- *Cost*: the equivalent of price in the 4Ps, with the additional management discipline implicit that requires the balancing of cost and price with value and benefits.
- *Communication*: the production of advertising, sponsorship, selling publicity, mailshot and Internet material that is customer, client and consumer-friendly, rather than technically or visually brilliant per se.

Marketing mixes arise from combinations and interactions of each of these elements. Consumers of products and services – offerings – will normally hold one of the

MANAGEMENT IN FOCUS 10.4

THE COMPLEXITIES OF ETHICAL MARKETING: EXAMPLES

- *Barbie*: as noted in Chapter 5, the Barbie doll is an enduringly successful commercial product, having been in existence for nearly 50 years. This is in spite of the fact that it has been very heavily criticised as projecting unacceptable social, ethical and sexual images of young girls and reinforcing particular stereotypes. This did not prevent an exhibition, 'The Art of Barbie', being mounted to raise funds for the Elton John AIDS Foundation in 2000. For this exhibition, world celebrities were asked to lend or donate their Barbie dolls. In addition, a collection of 50 Barbie figures were dressed by artists and fashion designers including Stella MCartney, Alexander McQueen and Phillip Treacy. Some of the dolls were dressed in high fashion items; others were dressed as Princess Diana, punks and the homeless.

- *Charities marketing*: there is no question that at the core of the activities of all major charities is the fundamental drive to alleviate problems that exist in different parts of society, and different parts of the world. However, the drive for ever-greater access to sources of funds, as well as overall increases in funding, has led to questionable marketing and promotional activities on behalf of these charities. Many charities now blitz town and city centres with teams of subcontracted public relations staff. These teams stop passers by in the street, engage them in conversation, and then ask for covenanted or credit card donations in support of the particular cause. This is a clear direct sales approach, and would probably be unacceptable if it were for consumer or capital goods and services. However, the large charities point to the financial results of this approach – for example, in 2004, donations to War on Want rose by 27 per cent.

Each of these examples illustrate the complexities that have to be considered when seeking to adopt an ethical approach to marketing, and marketing for ethical reasons.

elements more important than the others. In turn, the forces and pressures of the markets in which the offerings are made also reflect their relative importance.

There are legal and ethical restraints on marketing activities in the Western world. In general, spurious or misleading claims may not be made for products, nor should misleading impressions be deliberately fostered – apart from anything else this is very bad for repeat business. Actual products must reflect the reality or impression given by both promotion and packaging. Products must also not be harmful or detrimental to their consumers; minimum standards of performance, manufacture, quality and safety have therefore to be met.

We will now consider each of the elements in turn.

Product

'Product' in this context is the term habitually used to describe anything that is offered to a market sector for consumption, including commercial and public services. The product mix is the range of products offered by an organisation. This is determined by the matching of the organisation's capabilities and capacities with the markets and niches to be serviced and by the scope and scale of its operations. People buy the benefits that they expect to accrue from a product or service as follows:

- *Quality and durability*: product and service quality and durability must be considered from the point of view of the balance required, and also in terms of customer demand (for example, there is no point in offering a highly durable product to the chosed market sector if that is not what the customers want).
- *Branding*: which gives credence and confidence, especially where the brand is well known and the consumer is content with what is offered and comfortable with the appearance of the name on the product.
- *Packaging*: used to present the product to its best advantage and to protect it up to the point of consumption. Packaging also reinforces the identity of all products and services – for example, Barbie (toys), Persil (soap powders) and brochure presentation (e.g. package tours).
- *Product and service benefits*: these should be seen in their widest context. The full offering often includes after-sales service, spare parts, help and emergency lines, call-out facilities, and product and service advice and familiarity sessions.
- *Product and service ranges and portfolios*: reflecting the total range. Ideally, the confidence and reputation of each feeds all the others. When one product or service is perceived to be bad or unreliable, it is likely to have a knock-on effect to all of the others. There are various different ways of looking at product and service portfolios and ranges. Examples are:
  - those which are advertised, those which sell and those which make money
  - yesterday's breadwinners, today's breadwinners, tomorrow's breadwinners, twinkles and sparkles, and dead weights (see Management in Focus 10.5 and Figure 10.1).

The product lifecycle

All products have a beginning, a middle and an end (see Figure 10.2). The concept of product lifecycle defines more precisely these stages and identifies the points at which specific marketing initiatives and activities might usefully be generated. There are four stages:

- *Introduction*: the bringing in and bringing on of the new product; this is the culmination of a period of both product and market research, the point at which the offering in question first comes on to the market.
- *Growth*: this is where the product takes off and its true potential (rather than that projected by research and modelling) begins to become apparent; sales and demand both rise where this is successful; unit costs decline.
- *Maturity*: the product is now a familiar and well-loved feature on the market; people are both happy and confident with it, and unit costs are low. The last part of the maturity stage is that of saturation; this is where the company seeks

MANAGEMENT IN FOCUS 10.5

PRODUCT AND SERVICE CLASSIFICATIONS: EXAMPLES

Ford, the car manufacturer, classifies its products, as follows:

- *Products to advertise*: high performance (e.g. Ford GT, S-Max) or high specification (e.g. top of the range models used in television advertising).
- *Products that sell*: Ka, Fiesta, Fusion, Focus; and also Mondeo and Galaxy – especially the mid-range; both the high specification at one end of the scale and the basic model at the other extreme sell less well than the mid-range.
- *Products that make money*: accessories, servicing packages, trade-in value, and finance plans.

Sony, the electrical goods manufacturer, classifies its product range as:

- *Yesterday's breadwinners*: the Walkman, sales of televisions, other electrical goods, video, audio and computer equipment and accessories.
- *Today's breadwinners*: music catalogues, mp3 players, DVD and other advanced computer, audio and video equipment.
- *Tomorrow's breadwinners*: developing the Vaio laptop and desktop computer ranges; developing high definition and flat screen television technology.
- *Twinkles and sparkles*: Playstation 3, commercial computer software, mini-disc potential.
- *Dead-weights*: very little – the company takes the view that even if something is a commercial failure, the knowledge and expertise gained as the result of its development should not be lost, but rather retained within the organisation.

to squeeze the last remaining possible commercial benefits from the item before it loses its commercial value.

- *Decline*: when the product is deemed to have run its course and no more value or profit is to be gained from it, it will then be withdrawn from the market.

Marketing interventions are made at each stage to ensure that the product potential is maximised. The product must take off so that the full range of benefits to be gained from the consumers are realised by the sector at which it is aimed. Then, as it reaches maturity, initiatives are taken to breathe as much new life into it as possible, using the whole range of promotional and advertising media; very often this means one advertising campaign too many before the product declines.

Products may also be rejuvenated through re-packaging, re-presentation and changing the quality or value emphases.

Price and cost

In simple terms, the price of an item covers at least the variable costs incurred in producing it. It also reflects the levels of perceived quality and value held by the customers, clients and consumers. Beyond this, organisations set price levels that enable them to generate sufficient income to keep shareholders and other

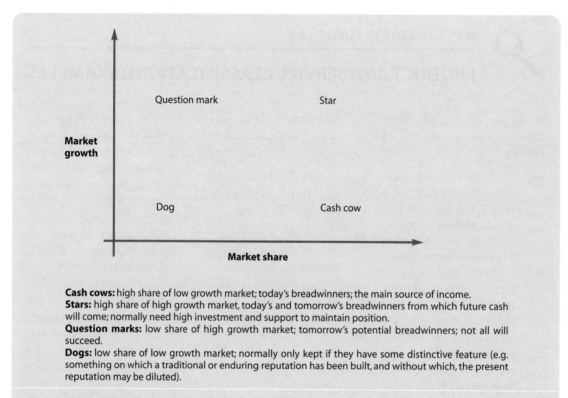

Cash cows: high share of low growth market; today's breadwinners; the main source of income.
Stars: high share of high growth market, today's and tomorrow's breadwinners from which future cash will come; normally need high investment and support to maintain position.
Question marks: low share of high growth market; tomorrow's potential breadwinners; not all will succeed.
Dogs: low share of low growth market; normally only kept if they have some distinctive feature (e.g. something on which a traditional or enduring reputation has been built, and without which, the present reputation may be diluted).

Figure 10.1 The 'Boston group' matrix

stakeholders happy and contented. They must further set prices to ensure that sufficient income is generated to ensure continuity of operations and to provide sufficient general cash flow to meet the needs of the organisation (above all, it must be profitable).

The price of an item must reflect both the willingness and capability of the customer to pay. If one is offering in niches where the customers and consumers always pay cash (as distinct from cheques, credit or debit cards or finance plans) then prices must reflect the volume of cash carried and must be sensitive to the competing demands on it. Management in Focus 10.6, 10.7 and 10.8 demonstrate crucial aspects of price setting.

Organisations need both an understanding of the full range of constraints on price, and also a measure of flexibility in its determination, enabling them to respond to competitive moves elsewhere in the market.

It is also necessary to consider what is actually included in the total price of an item or commodity. For example, when a car is bought the consumer achieves personal transport and mobility. However, the price paid may also include the concept of the 'lifetime of the car', including regular servicing, after-sales arrangements, emergency cover, insurance policies, and finance plans that cover the purchase of the car as well as the other accessories that may go with it. In addition, a relationship with the garage or dealer may be bought that takes all the worry out of

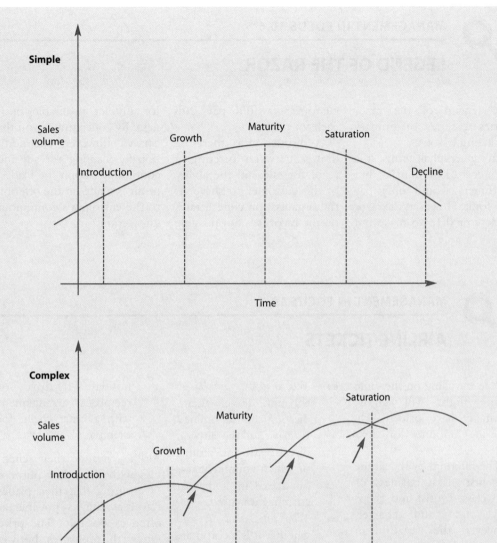

Purpose: the model indicates the conception, growth, regeneration, renewal and extension of the effective and profitable life of particular products and services. The figure also indicates relationships with successful and effective marketing activities.

Figure 10.2 Product lifecycles

MANAGEMENT IN FOCUS 10.6

LEGEND OF THE RAZOR

The legend of the razor carries a series of primary marketing lessons.

In apocryphal terms, the razor cost £1.00 to make, but customers would only pay 20p for it. However, the razor blade cost 0.1p to make but customers would pay 20p each for them.

A distinction is therefore drawn between offering a razor for sale and the ability of the customer to shave. If the organisation concentrates on the razor it is not possible to conduct profitable business. By concentrating on the 'shave', however, and additionally ensuring a steady and continuing supply of blades, profit is made on the offering to the customer's continuous satisfaction.

MANAGEMENT IN FOCUS 10.7

AIRLINE TICKETS

People travelling on the same airline flight will almost inevitably have paid widely differing amounts for their seat.

The offerings by the airline are: first class; business or club class; tourist and economy class and charter. However, the variation in price will depend on a much greater number of matters:

- *When the ticket was purchased*: airlines give discounts for purchases well in advance or right at the last minute (standby).
- *Where it was purchased*: through travel agent, discount house, online/Internet, at the airport, direct with the airline; or which country it was purchased in, and what currency was used.
- *Who purchased it*: and whether it is a corporate or personal expense.
- *Why it was purchased*: for business, pleasure or holidays.
- *Other factors*: especially concerning whether the trip is part of a package holiday, fly-drive or reciprocal arrangement with a hotel chain, for example.

Airlines arrange their schedules with the prime purpose of ensuring that their planes travel as full as possible as often as possible. The price range thus ensures both a variety of offerings and also many sources of passengers. More importantly from their point of view, the airlines thus maximise their chances of achieving their prime purpose.

motoring provided that you continue to patronise the establishment, to have the servicing and after-sales conducted by them, and possibly also to replace the car through them in a period of years hence. Customers and consumers may also be prepared to pay for convenience of access to products and services, provided that quality and satisfaction are assured.

MANAGEMENT IN FOCUS 10.8

THE 99p SYNDROME

The first use of price as a means of marketing in itself is ascribed to Marks & Spencer Plc of the UK in the 1970s. Instead of charging £5, £10 (or 5 or 10 local units of currency) the amount is reduced by one currency unit, to £4.99 or £9.99.

There is a strong perceptual message inherent in this, which must be considered at this stage. The customers receive change as well as the goods or service that they desire, assuming that they pay with the single currency unit. The message that they consequently receive is that they are paying less than a particular amount for the product. In addition, the price is related to the note value of the currency where possible – £4.99 is related to the UK £5.00 note, for example, and 99p to the £1.00 coin.

The price label thus becomes a feature of the presentation of the product or service itself, and becomes incorporated into the mainstream marketing activities generated.

This also acts as a check on the integrity of both staff and customers. It is very unusual to pay the exact price if it is so presented. This means that the staff have to use the till, and that the customer must be given a receipt.

Promotion to customers

Promotion is a combination of methods used to generate public awareness, identity, confidence, desire and conviction about a product, and ultimately its adoption and usage by the general public. The methods used in the pursuit of this are:

- advertising in all mass media including newspapers, television and radio; sponsorship of events, other products and activities
- sales-calling by organisational representatives to generate new business and general awareness and to maintain and service existing business
- brochures designed to generate the image required of the product and to demonstrate the features and benefits that its consumers are perceived to demand
- product placement, in which producers of films, brochures, magazines, novels, stories and television series are persuaded to adopt distinctive brands of product such as cars and clothing to be used and worn by their heroes and heroines, thus assisting in the generation of positive images and high level identity
- other publicity features such as general awareness-raising articles, news items and general interest stories, featuring particular products and services
- price, which may also be integrated into the promotional campaign adopted, and which is of critical importance in marketing at the extremes of luxury/ high-value products and services, and cheap/good value products and services (see Management in Focus 10.9).

Image and identity

In the early twenty-first century, in spite of all the social and ethical pressures to the contrary, the strongest, most enduring and effective promotional images remain:

- sex, especially female sexuality
- glamour and opulence, especially related to clothing lifestyle, cars and holidays
- sunshine and brightness, as the backdrop to the sales of any product or service, because these images are both socially and professionally perceived to be positive
- high-tech, to demonstrate the association between human brilliance and product and service usage
- celebrity endorsement, though this has to be approached in the context that many celebrities now lose their positive identity very quickly
- strong colours, especially black, red, crimson, purple and deep blue (the use of green in advertising and promotion is widely perceived to reinforce perceptions of ecological and environmental awareness, but there is no research to suggest that this enhances interest in, or desire for, consumer products and services, except in small niches of the population)
- enduring safety and security (again this is a double-edged sword, as customers and consumers at large expect products and services to be fundamentally safe and secure, and in any case, nobody likes to be reminded of their own vulnerability or mortality).

There has been extensive creative activity within the advertising and marketing industries to try and break the mould, or at least to use it differently. However, given that the overall purpose of these activities is to ensure that products and services remain in the mind and perception of actual and potential customers, consumers and clients, it remains absolute that, all other things being equal, images based on these factors are the most likely to carry out this function effectively.

MANAGEMENT IN FOCUS 10.9

CHEAP AND GOOD VALUE

All those with responsibility for marketing should understand that very few customers, consumers (or for that matter commercial clients) buy anything purely on price alone. Even mercenaries (see customer analysis, Chapter 8) who state that they buy on price alone, very often spend a lot of other resources (especially time and energy) in finding the perceived, cheapest or best-value option.

There is also a serious behavioural issue to address. Feelings of self-worth are affronted if consumers believe themselves to be forced into buying the cheapest option. Anything that is pitched at the low-price market should carry enduring perceptions of 'good value' because this is a reinforcement of self-esteem and self-worth ('I am getting excellent value for money'), rather than cheap, which gives negative feelings ('I am forced to buy this because I haven't any money').

In the capital goods and major projects sectors, where competition is overtly on price, the cheapest tender very often carries with it all sorts of hidden extras. In construction and civil engineering, there is a long history of a claims process at the end of a contract. The companies that have successfully tendered for the work have offered a superficially attractive price up front to the client, and have then sought to build on this by seeking to claim for extras that were either not built in to the original tender, or else have become apparent as the contract has been completed.

Place and convenience

The fourth element of the marketing mix is place; getting the products and services to the customers and clients. This means knowing who they are, where they are, how they want the products and services delivered, what the nature and level of their expectations are, and how these may best be satisfied. Part of the creative process involved in marketing is concerned with both meeting this requirement on the part of the customer and also generating an expectation that if they do go to a particular place then this particular need will be satisfied (see Management in Focus 10.10).

Location also reflects any sectoral or regional demands or desires or constraints. Hitherto, for example, there has been an expectation that each community would have its own school, its own library, its own hospital; these have become limiting factors in the offering of education and health services. The same is true for certain sports facilities. There is thus an onus placed on those responsible for organising, providing and managing these services, and constraints within which they have to work. If this is not the most efficient or effective way of providing the service, then part of the process of changing it must include a raising of public understanding – promotion of the benefits of the new proposed arrangement. People will go along with this if they see and understand that it is in their best interests to do so, and if they can see the benefits that will accrue to them (see Management in Focus 10.11).

MANAGEMENT IN FOCUS 10.10

THE INTERNET AS LOCATION

The use of the Internet as a marketing and organisational location has to be seen from a variety of often conflicting points of view:

● From the organisation's point of view, using the Internet means it has a presence – a location – on every computer screen in the country.

● From the point of view of customers and clients, the particular organisation has a general presence on every computer screen in the country. However,

this location is convenient to customers and clients only if the organisation website is easily accessible, and customer-friendly once accessed. This has especially to be borne in mind when it is remembered that speed and convenience of access (and also perceived speed and convenience of access) are key marketing functions.

● If the great strength of the Internet as location is its potential presence on

every computer screen, its great weakness is the lack of physical or human presence. This has to be seen in the context that the enduring success of all marketing activities is built on the expectations of customers and clients. This, in turn, is universally reinforced by the human interaction that also takes place in every traditional transaction – whether consumer, industrial, commercial or public service.

MANAGEMENT IN FOCUS 10.11

MARKETING PROFESSIONAL SERVICES AND LOCATION

The marketing of professional services is carried out according to the norms and expectations of the particular sectors. Those providing professional services – for example, private medical services, private education, architectural and other construction and civil engineering services, or for that matter marketing and public relations consulting – have to make themselves convenient to their potential customer and client bases. A major part of the investment in these cases is therefore the creation of communications links, public relations functions, customer and client services and management functions, and marketing and sales teams, in order to ensure that the 'location' is taken to existing and potential customers and clients.

Effective location marketing has been achieved by the supermarket, retail and shopping mall sectors in Europe and North America. People now go to edge-of-town and out-of-town locations, because the benefits of ease of access and having everything under one roof have been successfully demonstrated. Those responsible for the hypermarkets and the generation of business for shopping malls took steps to understand the nature of the requirements of their target customers, and the products and services they would require, and designed a consumer environment where all this could be satisfied. This has had a major impact upon the location of commercial activity, and those who continue to do business in the centre of towns have had to consider much more carefully the attractions of their particular location to the consumers that continue to come to them.

Marketing research and development

The purpose of such research is to identify and maximise opportunities that the product and marketing mix of the organisation affords. Essentially, this combines the need to seek alternative outlets for the products and technology that the organisation has at its disposal with the need to find out what customers' wants and needs are. Initiatives can then be proposed and generated with the view to satisfying these needs, and to the devising and initiating of further business opportunities. Properly structured market research also addresses the 'generally favourable response'. Once a generally favourable response is encountered, the customer or client group can be targeted. It then becomes essential that this is followed up in detail to establish exactly how often the product or service is to be bought, used and consumed, how much the particular segments are prepared to pay for this, and how often they are willing to pay it (see Management in Focus 10.12).

The process undertaken is concerned mainly with an understanding of the capabilities and capacities of the organisation on the one hand, and the requirements of

MANAGEMENT IN FOCUS 10.12

CUSTOMER PERCEPTION

Research conducted by the tobacco industry demonstrated that brand loyalty was almost entirely based on image and identity rather than the taste of the product. Tests were conducted on those who stated categorically that they only liked their own brand. Smokers could not differentiate between their usual brands and others of equivalent strength and similar tobacco when they were not given the packet from which to choose.

Research carried out by the Coca-Cola company through blind tastings of both its own Cola products and those of competitors gave initial cause for alarm. As mentioned in Chapter 1, in the blind tasting sessions, Virgin Cola was found to carry what the testers perceived to be the best taste. Initially alarmed by this finding, the company soon became comfortable with its products, when it was realised that, whatever the results of blind taste, the

customer-base at large would buy the Coca-Cola product anyway.

This also applies to other soft drinks; tea and coffee; bread, cakes and biscuits; butter and margarine; beer, wine and spirits. People are more positively disposed towards any of these products if they are told that it is of their preferred brand, whether it is or not.

Source: E. Clark (1988; 2002) *The Want Makers*, Corgi.

the market and environment in which business is conducted, on the other. This will address matters concerning general levels of confidence on the part of the market, customers' purchasing power, their needs and wants, their priorities and any other aspects (seasonal, for example), and relate these to the capabilities and capacities of the organisation. Other factors to be taken into account will include a more general assessment of the market and the products in question, the extent to which these are in expansion, decline or stability. Research will include competitor analyses and the extent to which alternative and substitute products are available in the broadest sense. It will consider the reputation of the organisation in question from a universal and general standpoint, as well as in the particular case of its own relationship with its own market sector. Customer assessments will also be conducted in order to gain a general understanding of customers' motives, desires, preferred images and identity with the particular product, or range of products, that is to be offered. Finally, modelling activities will need to be commissioned or conducted by the organisation with a view to assessing the extent of the profitability or effectiveness of the range of activities in question. Marketing research and development is thus an integral part of the success of wider strategic aspects, and critical to the determination of the organisation's future direction and instrumental in the determination of its success.

Public relations

The public relations or PR function is to ensure that the marketing wheels are kept oiled and that the organisation's marketing machine works smoothly and positively in order to fulfil the purposes for which it was designed. It has a maintenance and development function that mirrors the operational equivalent. Planned PR concerns identifying in advance any suitable initiatives and items that will generate good publicity, and placing them in the media where they will have the greatest positive effects. There is also remedial PR, which is where the organisation has to take responsive or other creative action to put right something that has gone wrong or to address a negative story about it that has appeared somewhere in the media.

Similarly the handling of the press, television and radio must be conducted in ways that ensure that an overall positive tone is maintained, and that when problems arise, the last and most enduring note of the story is of the progress that is now to be made.

Organisations will also engage in the placement of stories favourable to themselves in the media, in those parts of it where the greatest benefit to them will accrue. This is both as a counter to those occasions when problems do arise, and also as part of the more general process of building confidence, positive images and an aura of 'good corporate citizenship'.

Organisations may also engage in more general customer and market liaison activities as part of their PR effort. This usually takes the form of sending staff on high-profile and sectoral seminars and conferences, and taking stands at trade fairs and exhibitions. Part of the effort of the sales force may also be simply to ensure that customers, and potential customers, are kept aware of the organisation's continued existence and activities. The sponsorship of events also contributes to this general effort.

● Conclusions

Effective marketing management stems from the successful identification of a core or generic strategic position, and then relating this to the distinctive marketing strategic approach, whether that is first-in-field, me-too, all-comers, product or service-led, staff and expertise-led, or market-led.

From this, it is essential to develop effective marketing mixes of all products and services on offer, targeted at customer and client perceptions and expectations, with the appropriate connotations of quality, value, and convenience.

Alongside this, it is essential to develop images and impressions of the organisation as being safe and steady, full of confidence and strength. This is directly related to the current range of offerings, and also has implications for new products and future activities, and for the organisational culture and management style.

Effective marketing depends on determining the sectors in which products are to be offered, so that the benefit and satisfaction to be accrued through ownership and usage may be presented in ways that reflect customer and consumer needs. Activities created in support of this – including advertising campaigns, sales teams, brochures, information, help and support lines, websites, public relations activities, product placement and sponsorship – must reflect the hopes and aspirations of those targeted, as well as concentrating on the benefits of the specific products and services. Increasingly popular also are perceived and real relationships between organisations, their markets, and communities at large; this includes support for local groups, clubs, philanthropic and charitable activities, as well as precise attention to concerns about the particular products or services in question.

Market research and development are essential to ensure that high levels of mutual satisfaction and advantage continue to accrue. This is particularly critical in assessing likely and potential demand, opportunities to be gained and possible consequences of failure.

Product and service lifecycles have also to be continually assessed. This needs to be conducted both for individual items and for the total range. It is also essential to consider the effects of general organisational and management practice on the confidence in which particular products and services are held. Staff conduct is an essential marketing tool, both in the ways in which they deal with their customers, and also how they conduct themselves in the wider community. Accidents, spillages and pollution scares each contribute to the general public perception of particular companies and activities. In the public sector, stories – especially negative stories – about delays and waiting lists, each affect the expectations of those using the services.

Therefore, the management of marketing requires continued attention to all aspects and details. Activities that are acceptable and effective today have to be maintained, developed and improved in order to ensure that their value is retained into the future. The development of marketing strategies must be entwined with the wider aspects of organisational direction, purpose and priorities. Marketing, as with all functional activities, has to be directed and managed in support of this, in order to ensure that the presentation of the organisation, its products and services, remains as effective as the substance.

CRITICAL THINKING, ANALYSIS AND EVALUATION

1. What steps should those responsible for public services management take to enhance the reputation and standing of these services?
2. Why is cigarette marketing so effective? What are the main lessons to be learned from this by those working in sectors where marketing activities are less well developed – e.g. construction and civil engineering, the Internet or health promotion?
3. What are the main factors to be taken into account when deciding to use:
   a) a major celebrity
   b) controversial images
   in the marketing and promotion of goods and services?
4. Why does everybody consider themselves so familiar with the Virgin organisation? What are the implications of this for any change of ownership in this and similar companies that may occur in the future?

DEVELOPING MANAGEMENT SKILLS AND EXPERTISE

ETHICAL INVESTMENTS IN FINANCIAL SERVICES: FRIENDS PROVIDENT

Friends Provident, the mutual life insurer and financial services company launched the first ethical financial services lobbying unit in the UK in October 1998. The purpose of this is to put pressure on FTSE companies to amend their environmental policies, to include investments in:

- 'wholesome industries', rather than the safe and generally assured sectors of international infrastructure investment, defence, oil and energy, and gas and chemicals
- those that took active responsibility for waste and effluent management and disposal
- those that engaged in 'fair trading policies' with both emerging-world governments and the companies that managed the commodity output produced in those countries
- those that took active responsibility for infrastructure development in order to provide social as well as narrow, economic benefits for those areas.

The company stated that its ethical investment unit would employ six researchers and cost up to £1 million per year to run. This is estimated to be at least ten times the sum spent on ethical research by other companies in the industry. The unit will also lobby companies with whom it places investments, to improve their stance on pollution, human rights, equal opportunities and broader responsibility to the environment.

The purpose of the approach was to gain a greater share of the personal pensions market, and to be attractive to the unit trust markets also by offering a branded and differentiated alternative to what was already on offer through clearing banks and other financial services institutions. The company additionally wished to target the then lucrative organisational and occupational pensions market. Under its 'Stewardship' brand, Friends Provident manages over £2 billion worth of institutional and individual investments, and the company continues to state that this brand remains 'strong'.

Friends Provident's premise was that investors in each of these sectors, and especially occupational pension schemes, were looking at ways of giving members a choice over where their money was invested. However, the company has sought to reassure traditional investors by stating that the new range of activities would not alter the investment performance of any of the existing funds, and that the company would remain competitive, with all of its products.

Questions

1. In your view, how should such an ethical approach to investment be marketed? What are the benefits and pitfalls of the approach you have chosen?
2. What is going to cause investors to:
   a) be drawn to ethical investments
   b) be drawn away from ethical investments; in the medium to long term?
3. What other general marketing and public relations activities are required in order to make a venture such as this successful?

Chapter eleven

Managing operations and projects

'I always wanted to manufacture real products from real assets to be sold world-wide.'
Sir Denys Henderson, former Chairman of ICI (2000).

'The key to effective company and operations launches is
to refine your plan and assemble your team with care.'
Matthew Lynn, *Management Today* (May 2000).

'What in the world is a time clock? All we want is successful products and happy staff.'
Shigeru Kobayashi, Sony, commenting on the highly successful operations
management style at the Company's main factory in Japan (1986).

Chapter outline

- Introduction
- Location
- Health and safety
- Quality of working environment
- Scales of production and output
- Production capacity
- Managing the supply side
- Maintenance management
- Coordination and control
- Measures of success and failure
- The complexity of operations and project management
- Joint ventures and other cooperative efforts

Chapter objectives

After studying this chapter, you should be able to:

- understand the implications of different sized operational activities and demands made on managers in them

- understand the need for a wide range of skills, aptitudes and expertise when managing projects and operations

- understand the need for absolute universal standards in health and safety at work

- understand and be able to apply simple and universal scheduling methods.

● Introduction

The primary concern of operations and project management is the translation of strategy, policy and direction into productive, effective and profitable activities. To do this requires attention to internal and external demands and constraints, and proper design work of activities so that the desired returns on investment are achieved.

The nature and mix of operations and project activities varies between and within organisations. The purpose here, therefore, is to concentrate on those aspects that are universally found.

● Location

Location depends on the following factors:

- Sources, frequency and regularity of input deliveries, especially where this includes physically heavy or bulky resources. There must therefore be adequate access to transport and distribution infrastructures.
- Virtual location: this is less of a problem where the delivery of everything critical can be guaranteed through computer networks and via the Internet. Again however, it is necessary to ensure that the necessary staff have access to places of work. Where the 'place of work' is at home, at business centres, or on the road, the problem is reversed because managers and supervisors require convenient access to their staff working in these ways.
- Just-in-time inputs and deliveries mean that a lot of physical storage effectively takes place on the road; and again, the 'location' aspect has to ensure that there is sufficient infrastructure capacity for this to remain efficient and profitable.
- Location is also affected by political, social and cultural factors. For example, many transport, distribution and haulage companies, or multi-activity companies with transport, distribution and haulage fleets, are now looking at the best places to locate from the point of view of optimising their corporation and capital taxation allowances, as some countries load these elements much more heavily than others.
- Location was traditionally influenced by the nature of production processes. Industry tended to locate near its markets if the production process added weight to the product, and at the sources of materials if the processes detracted weight from the products.
- Location is affected by wider environmental support. For example, communities expect to have their own schools and social, health and hospital services, as well as commercial services, including supermarkets and banks.

For project work, location is dictated by where the work is required. The constraints of the environment have to be reconciled with the demands of the project. Building and civil engineering require consideration of effective access and egress. Information technology projects have to reconcile the demands placed on the particular system with the constraints of their physical location and the size of the environment in which they are to be implemented.

Organisations must choose their location on the basis that there is a sufficient volume of staff available; where too few staff can be found locally, those recruited from further away must be able to get to work through the use of commuter routes or public transport (see Management in Focus 11.1).

MANAGEMENT IN FOCUS 11.1

ACCESS TO WORK

Access to work is becoming a serious problem for those responsible for the location, management and delivery of public services. Solutions have to be found to problems caused by the inability of those in public services to afford local property because of the high prices of homes in relation to salaries offered. This is also an enduring problem for those on career paths in public services. In the overwhelming majority of cases, frustration and stress are caused by strong and enduring levels of commitment to the service itself, and to the client groups in question, set against the inability to afford to remain in the sector; or if staff do stay, then reconciling this with the high levels of fixed charges that accrue as a consequence and condition of remaining in the profession.

This has led to highly publicised, long-term and enduring shortages of teachers, nurses and social workers. Nor is this confined to the high profile cases; there is also a long-term and enduring shortage of those coming into the medical, legal and military professions, which always used to carry perceptions of high status and exclusivity, as well as excellent terms of employment and job security. The location of these activities, together with the enduring levels of stress and social dysfunction faced as the result, mean that:

- A better quality of life can be enjoyed in other occupations for the same level of qualification, salary, and expertise.
- Equivalent levels of personal, professional and occupational satisfaction can be gained without the locational dysfunction.

For example:

- A lawyer working within the military establishment found himself having to stay in London during the week for a period of two months. This was due to a combination of particular work pressures at the time, combined with the uncertainties of public transport. This meant that he was only able to return home at weekends, and this caused domestic stresses and strains, in spite of the fact that he had been married for over 15 years.
- A country GP in the south-west of England found himself working from any one of six locations. This was because he was required to cover his own surgery, a cottage hospital, two clinics, and two out-of-hours call centres and emergency surgeries. While this was a clearly stated and understood precondition of the job, it took nearly three years for the local health authority to agree to provide a mobile telephone, or a substantial medical emergency travelling kit.

●   Health and safety

'It is the duty of every organisation, so far as is reasonably practicable, to provide a place of work that is both healthy and safe.' (Health and Safety at Work Act, 1974 – Preamble).

The great strength of the Health and Safety at Work Act's approach is that it requires organisations to be fully aware of the contextual, environmental and operational pressures. From this, organisations are required to provide a place of work that is both healthy and safe, and to take an active responsibility for this, rather than to respond to a detailed set of legally stated criteria.

Health and safety at work in the UK is inspected and monitored by the Health and Safety Executive (HSE). The HSE is responsible for ensuring that standards are set and maintained, and for investigating accidents and emergencies.

This is underpinned with specific legislation in particular areas. Both the EU and the UK government have legislated to address particular operational issues, especially in the following areas:

● *Working time*: the establishment of a basic level of maximum hours that may be requested without gaining specific consent from employees. In the UK at the beginning of the twenty-first century, this is 48 hours per week. This may be varied in particular cases according to the nature of the work being carried out; where longer hours are required in some weeks, time off must be given in others to ensure that the average of 48 hours per week, over a reasonable period of time, is not exceeded.

● *Substances hazardous to health*: these must be registered, monitored, recorded and, when not in use, kept under lock and key. Such substances may normally only be used under supervision, or with the knowledge of someone else on the premises.

● *VDU screens*: it is normal practice not to allow anyone to work for longer than 2.5 hours at a VDU screen without giving them at least 15 minutes away.

● *Breaks*: it is usual to ensure that everyone who works for a continuous period of four hours is then given a break of at least 30 minutes. Anyone working longer than eight hours per day must be given a break of at least one hour.

● *Emergency procedures*: all organisations must have stated emergency procedures. These must be put in writing and made available to all staff and visitors to the premises, regardless of size of the organisation or complexity of operations.

● *Road haulage and transport*: anyone driving for more than four hours at a time is required by law to take a break of at least 30 minutes; anyone driving for more than ten hours, is required by law to take a break of at least two hours.

● *Waste and effluent disposal*: all organisations are responsible for disposing of any waste or effluent that their operations and activities produce.

The penalty for breaches in each of these areas is a fine. At the beginning of the twenty-first century, plans exist to introduce the offences of 'corporate negligence', 'corporate harm' and 'corporate manslaughter.'

The effectiveness of these statutory approaches to the management of health and safety in operations activities lies in:

● the acceptance of corporate responsibility, as well as the one-dimensional duty to work within the law

- the powers of the HSE, and levels of fines, in order to act as deterrent to corporate malpractice
- the relationship between being known as a healthy and safe employer, and levels of positive operational activity; and conversely, the effects of being known as an unhealthy and unsafe employer, and the detrimental effects on business and service operations.

Overall responsibility for health and safety at the place of work rests at the top management level in terms of setting standards and producing formal policies. However, all individuals at every level have a joint degree of responsibility to ensure that their own sphere and work environment are kept as far as possible both safe and healthy. The policy will identify any instruments for monitoring and assessment – such as safety representatives and the election or appointment of safety committees. This may also include training for both managers and operative staff. Finally, particular hazards will be indicated, as will the requirements to wear particular types of clothing, use particular types of equipment and follow particular procedures in dealing with particular hazardous or potentially unsafe situations and practices at the place of work. This includes the storage, handling and usage of restricted or supervised goods, chemicals and other equipment.

● Quality of working environment

The work environment must be organised in such a way as to be healthy and safe as far as possible, and to provide the required and acceptable standards of comfort and humanity. This includes:

- *Temperature levels*: proper training and clothing must be provided for those who have to work in extreme heat or cold.
- *Lighting*, which must be adequate to work without strains on the eyesight of the workforce.
- *Ventilation* of all work premises, where necessary through air-conditioning and filtration procedures.
- Suitable and sufficient *sanitary accommodation* for all, including separate conveniences for each gender and the disabled, and related provisions of washing and drinking-water facilities.
- *Machinery* must have in-built guards and cut-outs, and training must be given in usage and operation; these guards must be maintained in an effective state, and not be removed during operations.
- *Offices* must also be *maintained* in a safe way: telephone and computer wires must not be left trailing; fire doors must not be propped open or locked shut; passages and corridors must be clear and unobstructed.
- *Floors, stairs and passages* must be soundly constructed and maintained, and railings put on stairs and raised walkways.
- Specific *training* must be provided for all those who are required to lift *heavy weights*, or to work with *toxic or dangerous fumes or substances* (e.g. in laboratories, or work with chemicals and radioactive substances).
- *Records of accidents* must be kept; all accidents that result in fatality, loss of limb, or absence from work of more than three days must be notified to the Health and Safety Inspectorate.

- *Technology* provided must be capable of safe, effective, productive and profitable use; where necessary, training must be provided, and this applies to upgrades as well as the installation of new equipment (see Management in Focus 11.2).
- *Toxic and hazardous substances* must be kept locked; access to them must be via designated persons only.

MANAGEMENT IN FOCUS 11.2

TECHNOLOGY AND STAFFING

All technology should be provided on the basis that it is useful, valuable, effective, profitable and productive in the terms demanded by the organisation, as it produces products and services for the enduring satisfaction of its customers and clients. There are however, other points to be considered:

- No technology is ever effective on its own. Its value to the organisation is entirely dependent upon the capability of those operating it.
- The purchase of generic technologies – especially in production and information technology – must always be considered from the point of view of their precise suitability for the particular organisation. In particular, many off-the-shelf personnel information management systems have been found to be less than effective because they do not address the precise questions required by the

particular organisations that have purchased them. Similarly, many financial management information systems purchased by central government as an aid to the management of public services, and by multinational corporations as an aid to the management of international purchasing and distribution, have been found not to address the substantial and priority questions required by these institutions.

- Many technologies are produced to demonstrate the technological brilliance of the inventors and designers, rather than the requirements of the end-users.
- Many technologies have insufficient capacity for upgrade, maximisation, or changes in product and service specification.
- Many perceived revolutionary technologies have failed to deliver the benefits promised or

strongly indicated. This, above all, applies to commercial usage of the Internet, and this is not confined to dot.com companies. Many organisations have websites, purely because it is perceived that they must – that not to have one represents a lack of modernism, lack of current awareness.

- Many individuals, groups, departments, divisions and functions are fitted out with technology (especially computer technology), effectively as part of the reward package. For example, for managers or other perceived experts not to have a personal computer in their office or individual place of work is perceived as a loss of status or face; or there may be a perception that the reason that there is not one present is that the particular individual does not know how to use it.

- *Access and egress* must be arranged so that everyone can get to work and be accommodated, and where necessary or required, so that there is adequate provision for visitors and deliveries.

Scale of production and output

Woodward (1961) defined the following scales of production:

- *Jobbing or unit production*: the production of single, unique or specialist items; unique quality of service delivery; the ability to customise or make unique products and services according to customer and client demands (see Management in Focus 11.3).
- *Mass production*: organising work in order to produce high volumes of standard quality products and services. Traditionally, mass production has been the cornerstone of all consumer goods; the same principles apply to the output of consumer services (e.g. holidays, travel and transport, banking and financial services).

MANAGEMENT IN FOCUS 11.3

CUSTOMISED PRODUCTION AT LEVI STRAUSS

Levi Strauss conducted a project to test the feasibility of offering a customised service allowing customers to choose from a set of features, enabling them to have, within these constraints, the jeans of their choice. Levi Strauss has created a website page offering the range of features – including colour mixes, measurements around the hips, waist, thighs and ankles, choice of waist fasteners, and belt buckle options. Customers simply log on to the website, choose their precise requirements from the range on offer, and arrange to collect their jeans or have them delivered at their convenience. For those wanting more precise made-to-measure garments, a body scanning service is available. This comes through either:

- indicating precise measurements, where the individual customer know these, on the website
- attending a Levi Strauss outlet that has the body scanner facility
- attending another outlet which has the scanner facility available by arrangement with Levi Strauss.

Mass customisation was first piloted in the United States in the summer of the year 2000. This facility was then expanded so as to be made available across the UK, western Europe, and the Far East, by the end of 2003. This was achieved by companies offering the service out of their own shops and franchises and specialist clothiers. However, continued attempts by large retail chains and supermarkets (many of them successful) to drive down the prices of Levi Strauss products, without offering the customisation service, has meant that the Levi Strauss venture into mass customisation remains a niche (if very high value and exclusive) product to date.

Source: Costas Pringipas (2001) *Individual Customisation of Mass Offering Products*, UCL.

- *Process and flow production*: traditionally applied to oil, petrol, chemicals, plastic extrusion, steel and paper manufacturing – the output of commodities in a continuous stream or flow. This approach also applies to commercial and public services (see Management in Focus 11.4).
- *Batch production*: the output of medium volumes of products and services, normally based on the ability to re-jig production and service technology so

MANAGEMENT IN FOCUS 11.4

PROCESS AND FLOW IN COMMERCIAL AND PUBLIC SERVICES

Problems in both commercial and public services arise when managerial attention is concentrated on operational efficiency rather than quality of service, and customer and client satisfaction. For example:

- *Banking*: one major clearing bank went through a process of closing hundreds of small branches. The defining criteria was simply the volume of money held in each account. Accordingly, a tiny rural branch in which one or two wealthy people held accounts was kept open, while branches with a larger volume of accounts were either closed down altogether, or opened on a part-time basis only, because the particular branch did not serve a sufficient number of more opulent customers. The programme was subsequently rescinded, costing the bank a total of

£170 million. Paradoxically, the bank was the same one that greatly improved the effectiveness of service in the eyes of customers by introducing the single queue, in place of individual queues at each desk. Just as effectively, this was copied by, among others, post office, large estate agencies, and travel agents. Some banks are however, diluting the effectiveness of this part of their operations, by restricting the nature of services which can be provided through the cashier and customer service, and insisting that customers use machines for their particular service requirements, whether or not they wish to do so.

- *NHS*: the single operational criteria in the provision of hospital services is frequency of bed usage. Extremely efficient in narrow

terms, in that it is most unusual to find a bed unoccupied for more than an hour between patients, this has nevertheless led to ward closures and reductions in hospital capacity. This, in turn, has led to increases in waiting lists for hospital treatment that is deemed to be non-emergency or non-urgent; increases in times between admission through casualty, accident and emergency departments, and being found a ward bed; and, in extreme cases, the stacking up of patients on trolleys in hospital corridors, canteens, and other non-operational areas. In some cases, it is possible to observe a queue at the entrance to wards, where patients are waiting to go in before the previous bed occupant has actually been discharged.

that different inputs, processing and production methods can be accommodated and different outputs produced. Batch production is the standard form used in the manufacture of drugs and pharmaceuticals. It is also common in the package holiday sector, where companies buy up volumes of hotel bookings, airline seats and other facilities in advance that are then combined into distinctive batches of offerings.

● *Project production*: a combination of technology, expertise, information, resources and components for the purposes of producing substantial, unique, finished items. Project work is a major concern in all sectors, both internally (e.g. the installation of information systems), and externally, where market testing and feasibility may be conducted on a project basis. This is quite apart from those sectors that operate on a project basis – information systems, civil engineering and construction, defence, and electronics and robotics.

Whatever the set of circumstances, production capacity and productivity are a direct consequence of the nature of the available equipment and technology, and the quality of staff employed. Both the technology and the staff have to be capable of meeting the demands for product and service output, and project delivery, on an immediate and enduring basis. This means ensuring that a realistic and practical view of the nature and volume of demands on the organisation is undertaken. It is additionally necessary to reconcile the balance between getting adequate returns on technology and expertise on the one hand, and retaining both the flexibility and the spare capacity to undertake special activities when required on the other (see Management in Focus 11.5).

Confidence and feasibility

Projects, products and services must be the subject of wider assessment. This is to ensure that what is proposed fits in with all aspects of the nature and level of activities. If it is decided to proceed down a particular line in support of a new product, it must both have the support of the staff, and be complementary to the organisation's current range. If the new product is to replace an old one, the process must be a check that it will do so adequately. If it is to tap into a hitherto unexploited sector, the same criteria of confidence and feasibility will also have to be tested.

Schedules and timetables can then be drawn up. Project work requires establishing the earliest point at which all materials, resources, equipment, technology, staff, information and supplies can be gathered together for the particular purpose stated. Operations management requires that each of these is organised in order to meet the schedules demanded by production and service output processes.

Proper running timetables, charts, work flows and other processes can then be determined. Each includes the maximum and minimum completion and acceptable periods determined by the particular work in hand. This then forms one part of the basis for work arrangements and methods, and a key element of monitoring, review and evaluation processes. Actual timetables and schedules are compared against ideals; and remedial action taken where the two are out of harmony. Schedules must also be related to precise targets and sub-targets along the way so that work appraisal, operations and project development may take place at regular intervals and in relation to critical activities.

MANAGEMENT IN FOCUS 11.5

MEASURING PRODUCTIVITY: EXAMPLES

- *McDonald's*: McDonald's calculate that the average stay per customer in each of their restaurants is 12 minutes. This can lead the unwary into thinking that every seat in the restaurant can be filled five times an hour.
- *The National Health Service*: for many years now, the NHS has entered into extensive calculations designed to work out: costs per patient across the entire service; costs per patient in particular regions; costs per patient in particular hospitals; and costs per patient in other activities – clinics, day-care centres, doctors' surgeries, district nursing, and midwifery. This has led to

a system of service budgeting that was flawed from the outset.
- *Further education*: a further education college calculated the costs of using its classrooms at £130 per hour. A nearby hotel offered conference facilities at £80 per hour. It was not until extensive discussions had been held between the college authorities and the hotel management concerning the feasibility of renting rooms on a regular basis from the hotel that the college realised the fundamental flaw in its comparisons – that the calculation of costs and the payment of charges are only tenuously related in complex activities.

- *Semco*: 'One sales manager sits in the reception area reading the newspaper hour after hour, not even making a pretence of looking busy. Most modern managers would not tolerate it. But when a Semco pump on an oil tanker on the other side of the world fails, and million of gallons of oil are about to spill into the sea, he springs into action. He knows everything there is to know about our pumps and how to fix them. That's when he earns his salary. No one cares if he does not look busy the rest of the time' (Semler, 1993).

Managing the supply side

The principle here is to ensure that all materials, resources and information required are in place when necessary, while at the same time striking a balance against unnecessary storage costs and charges.

The main elements for consideration are:

- convenience of access, frequency and reliability of sources and deliveries, the flexibility or otherwise of production and project scheduling
- speed of obsolescence of components and information
- whether to bear the price of stockpiling as a comfort or necessity
- any specific demands of the particular range of operations, or project requirements
- the extent to which it is necessary to do things in accordance with the demands of suppliers

- specific issues on the supply side, especially the scarcity of expertise or raw materials
- storage costs and charges
- the need for specific storage facilities (large storage facilities become expensive in terms of land and capital resource usage; information may require storage in specific formats).

The sourcing of raw material, components, information and other supplies is based on the required balance of each of these elements.

Just in time

The just in time (JiT) approach to purchasing is attractive because it removes the need to use expensive premises for the storage of components and supplies. JiT is based on the ability to engage in relationships with suppliers requiring regular (daily and in some cases many times a day) deliveries to be made. This form of supply has always been the norm in the fresh foodstuffs industry. It has now been extended into many industrial and commercial areas, and public service activities.

When they are delivered, supplies go more or less straight into production areas. As long as it works well and supplies can be virtually guaranteed, JiT is both efficient and effective. Its success depends entirely on the reliability of the suppliers. In practice, it also depends on the ability and willingness of the supplier (or suppliers) to vary the volumes, normally at short notice, to cope with sudden up-flows and down-flows in production.

Further developments are as follows:

- *Only when required*: in which the supplier has the capacity and willingness to provide what is required, when required, at instant or very short notice, in response to individual requests from purchasers.
- *Only when provided*: in which the supplier establishes a set pattern of frequent deliveries. This enables suppliers to schedule their own activities with a degree of certainty, and requires entering into relationships with purchasers to establish the enduring convenience of the 'only when provided' approach. From this it is possible to plan hourly, daily, or weekly schedules by arrangement (see Management in Focus 11.6).

Dominance and dependency

Dominance and dependency is a behavioural view of the relationship between purchaser and supplier.

Suppliers tend to dominate the relationship when they are the key or major source of a particular component or material, or when they are the only organisation able to respond to the specific needs in the ways required by a purchaser. It also occurs where they control a rare and much sought-after primary source of raw materials.

Purchasers tend to dominate the relationship when they are the major user of the materials or components. This is also the case when they are a sufficiently large customer that the loss of their business would be a threat to the well-being of the supplying organisation.

In the short term, on either side an advantage may be gained through dominating the relationship. In the longer-term, whichever side is dependent will seek to reduce its dependency.

MANAGEMENT IN FOCUS 11.6

'JUST IN TIME': EXAMPLES

- *DHL*: DHL is a fully flexible, high-quality, instant-response mail, delivery and courier service provider. The company undertakes to take and deliver anything, anywhere in the world, within three hours (local), six hours (regional), ten hours (national) and twenty-four hours (international) – subject only to the vagaries of long-haul air flights. The only leeway that they allow themselves in setting their standards concerns long-haul air deliveries – in these cases, specific terms of business are drawn up with particular clients, in order to establish reasonable parameters around scheduled air services. In return for this quality assurance, reliability, and flexibility of delivery, the company charges extremely high prices.

- *Harrods*: Harrods and other perceived exclusive providers of goods and services insist on full flexibility of response when dealing with those who supply them with exclusive, unique or customised goods and services. Again, the charges incurred in such a relationship are very high; and again, this is reflected in the price paid by individual customers for this quality of service.

- *Sandals*: Sandals, the exclusive travel and tour operator, had to change its West Indies weddings package from 'only when provided' to 'only when required', and accept any increase in costs that this brought about. This was because, on some days, couples to be married found themselves being rushed through due to the numbers being married on the same day. On other days, in contrast, it was impossible to provide the full range of services (e.g. video packages, priests of particular religious denominations) because the lack of volume demand meant that those subcontracted to provide these found it economically unviable to turn out.

It is important to recognise that each situation brings its own advantages, disadvantages, opportunities and consequences. If a durable and high-quality working relationship is to be established between suppliers and purchasers, then any potential pressures brought about by instant demands, short-term changes in quality and volume, and changes to production and service specifications must be addressed by those managers responsible.

Suppliers seek alternative outlets for their products and alternative uses for their technology. Purchasers seek alternative sources of components and may also redesign their offerings to avoid having to use the particular components or materials.

Maintenance management

The core purpose here is to ensure that all resources and equipment are in a state suitable for use when required and to provide a swift and effective remedy when things break down or go wrong. It is thus essential that maintenance activities are planned and scheduled and organised in the same way and from the same standpoint as anything else.

Two distinct factors emerge from this: that of planned maintenance and that of emergency response. Planned maintenance requires the ordering and rescheduling of activities designed to prevent things from going wrong – indeed it is often called 'preventive maintenance.' By conducting regular audits and checks of equipment, signs of wear and tear can be detected. Parts that are beginning to wear out can be replaced before they break down or cause malfunction; and equipment that is reaching the end of a production or operational period can be planned to be out of productive action while it is being serviced (see Management in Focus 11.7).

Coordination and control

Operational and project systems, procedures and processes must be sufficiently well ordered and also flexible enough to be improved where necessary. This is to ensure effectiveness in addressing the task in hand, and also gives the means of improving every aspect.

MANAGEMENT IN FOCUS 11.7

RAILWAY MAINTENANCE

Since the privatisation of railways in the UK, maintenance contracts and schedules have presented an enduring problem. This has centred around requirements for extensive investment in improvements and upgrades to the railway tracks themselves, and the demands of train operating companies to keep their trains running.

From the outset, this was at variance with the strategic priorities of Railtrak Plc., a company originally constituted to manage the railway network. In 2002, Railtrak Plc. was wound up, and replaced by Network Rail, a

company guaranteed by the government.

Railtrak Plc.'s ability to meet its maintenance demands were always hampered by its requirements to pay dividends to shareholders. When the company was wound up, and Network Rail took over, a maintenance strategy began to emerge. Prior to that, maintenance operations consisted purely of 'repair response', in which no action would be taken unless a fault was discovered. Preventative maintenance took place only as a matter of coincidence, where the 'permanent way' was in any case being refurbished or upgraded.

Problems were also caused by the incomplete nature of maintenance contracts, and the inability to find sufficient contractors to carry out the sheer volume of work required. This led to gaps in schedules and specifications for particular operations. For example, one maintenance contract failed to specify the requirement to replace the third electrical conductor rail, and this led to the particular stretch of line being shut for a further 48 hours during a busy operating period. Others contracts have failed to include provisions for delays caused by bad weather or a lack of access to supplies.

The following key points have to be addressed:

- *The slowest part of the process*: where this occurs; why it occurs; what if anything should be done about it; how it might be speeded up; the consequences of this on other activities.
- *The quickest part of activities*: together with any consequences. This especially becomes a problem if it results in staff or equipment operating to less than full capability.
- *Blockages*: where, why and how these occur; how often they occur; and the range of possible responses. Blockages occur as the result of the nature of production, service and output processes; shortage of specific facilities; stockpiling at the input and output locations. They cause stresses and strains on other parts of the process (see Management in Focus 11.8).
- *Volume, quality and time issues*: consideration of what is available, what is possible and what the customers, clients and consumers require.
- *Wastage rates*: these should always be attended to, and constantly assessed for acceptability or otherwise; the expense incurred requires calculation and evaluation; this may also increase concerns for, and volume of activities in, waste and effluent disposal.
- *Customer complaints*: traditionally, this is not regarded as being part of the sphere of operations management. However, it is essential to recognise that all customer complaints originate during production and output processes; and that therefore production and service functions require designing with this in mind. As stated elsewhere, many organisations now make their production functions responsible for managing customer complaints. Even where this is

MANAGEMENT IN FOCUS 11.8

BLOCKAGES IN THE NATIONAL HEALTH SERVICE

Regular, enduring and frequent blockages occur in the provision of effective patient services in many parts of the NHS. Specific blockages include:

- Those in casualty, accident and emergency departments, where patients often have to wait many hours for urgent and non-urgent treatment.
- Patients often have to wait many hours for admission to the correct hospital ward; in extreme cases, where a patient's urgent condition becomes an emergency, this has resulted in the need for a high-speed transfers to another hospital.
- Bed-blocking occurs when it becomes difficult to pass patients on to the form of care required next, or back into the community. This is an especial problem with elderly patients.

Each of these has a compounding effect on activities in the immediate future.

These blockages are caused by a combination of staff, equipment and bed shortages that have resulted from a lack of full understanding of or attention to the broader medical environment.

not the case, production and output processes require assessment for the potential for dissatisfaction and complaint.

- *Workforce morale*: there is a direct relationship between being able to operate in a good-quality working environment, and sustained high and satisfactory levels of volume and quality output. Attention to the working requirement requires:
  - a full assessment of the working environment, its strengths, weaknesses and shortcomings
  - a full assessment of the expectations of individuals and groups, and what they require to do the jobs properly and effectively
  - prioritising those areas that require attention
  - identifying those factors inside and outside the control of those involved
  - identifying accurately staff pressures brought about by the requirement to work, for example, in untidy, dirty, damp or draughty conditions; and recognising that these conditions may exist in any form of activity
  - recognising the particular health and safety constraints inherent, and taking all steps necessary to ensure that accidents, injuries, emergencies and illnesses are kept to an absolute minimum.
- Recognising the particular constraints placed by engaging in *different patterns of work*. Specific professional and occupational groups also require particular attention. Those with high degrees of specialisation or expertise, or who work away from the organisation or to non-standard patterns of work, require full organisational and managerial support if they are to remain effective for the long term. This applies to many occupations, for example:
  - professional health service staff working nights and weekends
  - sales staff working in the field for long periods of time, and in many cases, also working evenings and weekends
  - those who work twilight shifts, at times when senior management are likely not to be present
  - those on job and finish activities
  - those working for agencies, subcontractors, consultancies and other distinctive specialisms that are only required for short periods of time.

Measures of success and failure

Projects and operations are measured for success and failure as follows:

- *Specific aims and objectives*: whether these were met; the reasons why and why not; areas for improvement.
- *Derived aims and objectives*: the ability to take advantage of specific opportunities that occurred along the way.
- *Timescale*: whether the deadlines were achieved and if not, the reasons for this.
- *Budget and financial performance*: and the reasons for variances in these.
- *Acceptability*: of the finished project to those who commissioned it, and again the reasons for this (especially if it is not acceptable).
- *Durability*: of the finished project to those who now use it, or work in it or with it; the durability and continuing utility of the finished project to the community at large; the specific durability of information management projects to those now required to implement them.
- *Effects*: on the organisation (or organisations in the case of joint ventures) that

has agreed to carry out the work; these will be seen in terms of general changes, cultural effects and special effects upon the rest of the work (e.g. the extent to which one project is dominating the whole of an organisation).

● *Side effects and spin-offs*: opportunities, inventions and openings that occur as the result of carrying out the core activities or main project (see Management in Focus 11.9).

The complexity of operations and project management

Other matters relating to operations and project management must be addressed as follows:

● working out, and evaluating the effectiveness of, information flows in advance
● establishing the means of dealing with crises and emergencies
● the management of the financial aspects of the work, based on accurate, high-quality information that is available to, and understood by, everyone involved
● the management of the work and task schedules inherent in the work, including the establishment and acceptance of work methods and timescales, and of resource-gathering, problem-solving, maintenance and development functions
● the management of the personal and professional aspects, including identifying and addressing barriers to understanding and progress
● managing communications between everyone involved, with especial reference to organisational, occupational, professional, cultural and language difficulties
● attention to the demands of key individuals

MANAGEMENT IN FOCUS 11.9

CONCORDE

Concorde was developed in the 1960s as an Anglo-French joint initiative that was going to show the way forward to universal supersonic airline travel.

The project did not however succeed in generating universal supersonic air travel. The only supersonic airliners ever used commercially were the nine Concordes of British Airways and Air France. The airliners were all taken out of service in July 2000, when one of the Air France Concordes crashed on take-off. Since

then, the planes have been mothballed, or else given over to air museums and aircraft exhibitions.

However, there were some very advantageous side effects and spin-offs. The French government used the scale of investment, technology and expertise to develop their own airliner manufacturing capacity. This formed the foundation for Airbus Industrie; based in Toulouse in south-west France, Airbus Industrie is the largest airliner manufacturer in the world.

British Airways used their Concordes as an elite, top-brand and exclusive high-speed passenger service. The lessons of the service were additionally used to develop in-flight staff working practices and levels of service for the whole of the company's operations. British Airways additionally used Concorde extensively in its marketing campaigns, and used the airliner in ensuring that the strength of the company's brand was built, developed and enhanced.

- attention to all individuals involved, including making constructive use of the talent and expertise of all those involved
- the creation and adoption of a positive and dynamic management style, with especial concentration on the coordination and communication aspects; ensuring effective staff, supplier, customer and client liaison
- agreement of common aims and objectives that are understood, valued and accepted by all those involved, or at least capable of being harmonised in pursuit of the ultimate outcome
- the establishment of key and specific areas of responsibility and accountability, with procedures established for the resolution of any conflict of dispute.

The mix of this varies. In the management of computer or information-systems projects, for example, ultimate responsibility for its effectiveness lies with the clients, who must be able to communicate their precise requirements to the contractor. For civil engineering and building projects, responsibility lies with the contractors, who must be capable of translating the project requirements into something that is acceptable, using their design, building and environmental management expertise.

In certain public projects it may be necessary to develop the liaison process into a non-executive but highly authoritative steering group, because of the requirements or demands of the commissioning bodies, for example where these are municipal health authorities or instruments of national, regional and central government.

Constraints on projects and operations

All work is carried out within particular constraints. These are as follows:

- *Sectoral economics*: activities in every sector are limited by the rates of return available, and by the costs of technology and expertise required.
- *Schedules*: the speed at which operations and projects progress is, in part, dictated by the speed at which supplies, expertise and information can be made available.
- *Operational and project lifecycles*: relating to the length of useful life of the finished item (e.g. fashionable and seasonal goods and services have to be provided at very short notice; project work often requires substantial redesign in order to meet changing social, economic and technological pressures).
- *Resources, expertise and technology*: project and operations work is always affected when there is a sudden shortage of resources, technology and expertise due to matters outside the organisation's control. For example, finance may suddenly become unavailable because of wider economic changes (especially downturns); expertise may no longer be available when required (e.g. due to the UK recession in building and civil engineering in the early 1990s, much expertise was lost to these sectors altogether).

Conclusions

The effectiveness of the management of projects, operations and activities lies in the ability to understand the extremely complex set of principles indicated in this chapter and apply them to particular situations. There is no absolute set of rules that applies to all circumstances, and the balance and mix of these principles varies between organisations (even those in the same industrial, commercial or public service sector) and projects (even those concerned with the same ultimate output, e.g. a new motorway, a new information system).

Operations and project managers therefore need as full an understanding of their particular environment as quickly as possible. Currently, it is becoming increasingly the norm that anyone responsible for a set of activities or project must become an enthusiast in the particular field in which they are being asked to work. For example, the project manager who was responsible for the completion of the Twickenham rugby stadium in 1996 had never been to a rugby match, or had anything to do with the game, until he was asked to build the stadium. He subsequently became – and remains – an enthusiast and committed follower. For all the failings of the Inland Revenue database in 1999, the project manager responsible made it his business to understand the legal, social and operational intricacies of the UK tax system. All those who work on *The Big Issue* adopt personal commitment to the problems of homelessness, whether or not they have had any involvement before (see Management in Focus 11.10).

MANAGEMENT IN FOCUS 11.10

THE BIG ISSUE: COMMERCIAL AND SOCIAL DRIVE

The Big Issue was founded in 1996 by John Bird, a journalist. It is a foundation for the homeless, raising funds to purchase commercially accommodation, food, shelter and clothing for people in the UK who either have no home or live in sub-standard accommodation. The Big Issue is a company limited by guarantee, and accorded charitable status. It raises money through lobbying, covenanting and philanthropic donations. It employs homeless persons to sell its magazine – also called *The Big Issue* – as a means of getting them back into work, and away from all of the problems of homelessness.

Originally campaigning on the single issue of homelessness, it quickly became apparent that *The Big Issue*

magazine would have to appeal to a much wider audience if it was to be enduringly commercially successful. It was accordingly revamped at an early stage to include feature articles on controversial and more broadly campaigning issues. Some pages in each issue are devoted to the creativity of the homeless. There is also an extensive entertainments section.

The original project was designed to find an alternative route to tackling both the causes and effects of homelessness. However, it quickly became apparent that the operational side had to be enduringly commercially successful. The homeless people employed to sell the magazine have to be convinced that they are newsagents by any other

name, otherwise the work itself would have no intrinsic value. The operational side of the project is run on standard lines. Emphasis is given to those wishing to get into news media, journalism and other creative activities; otherwise the structure is exactly equivalent to that operated by mainstream magazines. The initial project has therefore developed into a long-term and enduringly viable operation. Regional issues are produced in different parts of the UK, and the magazine is sold in most towns with a population of over 10,000. It has attracted a strong following of loyal customers, especially in the major commuter areas; and also continues to attract a large amount of interest from browsers and passers-by.

It is also essential to recognise that the understanding and application of these principles requires constant development. For example, production and operational processes can be speeded up; blockages and barriers can be removed. Effective attention to these requires that managers are creative and visionary, as well as rigorous and focused – and this applies to all aspects of activities.

Effective project and operations management requires the ability to coordinate this level of application with a detailed understanding of the following in every particular set of circumstances:

- A strategic approach to operations and project management.
- Operational planning in detail; operational efficiency; operational effectiveness. Each of these applies in project as well as mainstream, activities. Each requires full attention. It should be noted that attention to one, at the expense of all the others, is certain to result in long-term operational and general management decline, to the detriment of customers, clients and end-users. For example, in the NHS, attention to operational efficiency – bed management, in which hospital beds are left unoccupied as little possible – has contributed greatly to the declining fortunes and reputation of the NHS. Narrowly efficient though this undoubtedly is, it is flawed because it is based on a perfect set of calculations, rather than human demand, and has also caused the other factors to be neglected.
- Whether in operations or project management, the importance of relationships cannot be overstated. Relationships with contractors, suppliers, expertise, customers and clients must be developed and maintained on a personal as well as a professional basis in order that the effectiveness of activities and mutuality of interest is established. Where this is not possible, or not seen as a priority, there is a loss of understanding of the precise requirements on the part of those involved. This leads to medium and long-term performance declines – especially when purchasers feel themselves able to switch suppliers at short notice, when subcontractors feel themselves able to produce substandard work for project managers, and when specific expertise is capable but not willing.

Finally, it is essential to recognise the broader context of operations and project management. It is perfectly possible to create, both from the point of view of the satisfaction of a narrow self-interest or key stakeholder drive. Anything that requires a more enduring basis must however be managed with the wider environment, other stakeholders and the long-term effects of particular activities in mind.

CRITICAL THINKING, ANALYSIS AND EVALUATION

1. A new management information system is to be installed into an organisation. What operational activities immediately become necessary as the result?
2. A medical research company has spent 20 years developing a cure for cancer. It now thinks it has the results, and these are positive. It has spent £600 million doing this. Identify the operational drives and restraints that now exist, stating where the overwhelming pressures are coming from, and the implications for those responsible for the management of operations.
3. A pottery production line can produce 500 mugs an hour. A blockage then occurs at the decoration stage, because each has to be painted by hand, except

where simple patterns and designs are required. Each member of staff responsible for painting mugs, can do six per hour. What is the nature of the blockage that exists, and what action, if any, should the managers of this situation take and why?

4.   When it was commissioned, a motorway project was expected to cost £63 million, and be completed in nine months. To date, it has cost £93 million, has so far taken 15 months, and is not expected to be ready for a further six months. What actions should those responsible for the project design, inception, management and delivery now be taking, and why?

DEVELOPING MANAGEMENT SKILLS AND EXPERTISE

EDINBURGH AT CHRISTMAS

For some years, the Scottish Executive, Edinburgh City Council and the Health Service have been taking part in discussions about a proposal to develop a site in Chalmers Street, at the side of the Edinburgh Royal Infirmary (ERI). When the discussion started, the site largely consisted of substandard housing, under-utilised space, car parks (owned by NCP) and depots and storage facilities for the university and ERI.

Eventually the three main parties came to an agreement, and a proposal was finalised to develop the site as follows:

- a ten-storey block of offices in which 3500 of the City Council's officials would be relocated
- an eight-storey block in which the ERI management and administration would be housed
- underground car parking beneath the two blocks for 700 cars, to be shared jointly by the city, ERI and the university
- the development, jointly between the university and the ERI, of an acute and serious injuries centre of excellence, adjacent to the two office blocks.

The development was to take place under a PFI/PPP arrangement. A preferred lead contractor, Cazeries Sarl (a large French civil engineering company based in Toulouse in southern France), has been approached. Cazeries are very keen to participate, because they need to expand into new markets, and they want to build up their own experience in this kind of work. They have proposed an arrangement as follows:

- The clearing and building work are to commence in February of next year, and to be completed in 30 months; this Cazeries estimate to cost £93 million.
- The facilities are to be finished and ready to use after a further six months; Cazeries estimate that this will cost £63 million.
- The facilities to be leased by Cazeries to each of the clients for an estimated £260 per square metre per annum, and for a minimum term of 25 years. The rental is to rise by 2 per cent per annum after an initial period of three years; this figure may be revised upwards to reflect commercial pressures on Cazeries brought about by inflation, interest rate changes, and any changes in value to the site itself.

- At the end of this period, either the site will pass to Cazeries to be redeveloped yet again, or it will be transferred to the clients for 'a fee that reflects the commercial value, factor utilisation elements, and general relationship' of the project.

Agreement was finalised on 30 November, and everyone involved was very keen to proceed. A skeleton organisation, Erigate Plc, was created to coordinate efforts and to be the formal client of Cazeries for this project. Erigate hired a top executive, Anthony Hague, from a small political consultancy in London, to be the venture's CEO and project leader. His deputy is Michael Brown, another Englishman. Hague and Brown have a high professional respect for each other, but do not otherwise socialise.

Hague was very keen to go ahead, and proposed to call a press conference for 3 January. At it he intended to announce that the venture would go ahead and would commence on time in February, and to publicly sign the agreement. Also, if the project were to be given the go-ahead at this point, Hague would hold a massive firework party and project celebration on the open ground at the back of the site. Hague himself will appear at this, introducing some of his many English pop-star friends.

Brown however, would like to know more about what he is letting himself and the clients in for. He accordingly asks you to address the following questions.

Questions

1. Briefly evaluate the assumptions and information that you have; identify gaps in the information, and what needs to be done about them.
2. Briefly summarise the environmental pressures and arrive at an initial view of the viability of the proposal as given.
3. Identify the broader issues that have to be considered if the strategic and operational approaches are to be successful.
4. Briefly identify the pressures, drives and restraints on the proposal; stakeholder positions and requirements; and the main elements that are likely to contribute to the overall success or failure of the venture.

Chapter twelve

Financial management

'The words "figures" and "fiction" both come from the same Latin word *fingere*. So beware!'
M.J. Moroney, *Facts from Figures*, Pelican (1963).

'If a company's sales are £2 million more than planned, is this necessarily a good trading result?'
Geoffrey Knott, *Financial Management*, Macmillan (1998).

'If we owed our backers £1 million, we would have a problem.
Because we owe them £10 billion, they have a problem.'
Alistair Morton, Chief Executive, Eurotunnel (1998).

Chapter outline

Chapter objectives

After studying this chapter, you should be able to:

- understand the difference between accounts and financial management

- understand the complex relationship between finance, accounts and financial management

- understand how accounts are constructed, and how managers should make use of them

- understand some of the different approaches used by organisations in the management of their finances

- understand and be able to apply the simple measures of finance to particular activities and operations, and to be able to evaluate these for success and failure.

● Introduction

Finance is the lifeblood of all organisations, in whatever sphere they operate. Companies in the private sector are required to make profits, to generate a surplus of income exceeding expenditure over a period of time that supports the continuation of the business and provides an adequate return to the backers. Public, social and health services, working to targets allocated by governments and other authorities, must use these resources to best advantage to satisfy the sectors that they serve, and to cope with any constraints under which they may be placed.

Accounts are kept and produced for three main reasons:

- As an essential check by the organisation on the state of its activities, income and expenditure in financial terms. This enables it to identify where resources are being consumed, in what volumes and the reasons.
- To present its financial state to stakeholders – staff, stock markets, stock and shareholders, banks, suppliers, customers, the community at large and the sectors in which it operates.
- In compliance with the law. Across the Western world, the law requires organisations to produce 'a true and fair' statement of their activities in financial terms, normally once a year, indicating the performance and state of the organisation in this way. This must be subject to external scrutiny and audit. Organisations have to pay tax, and the extent of liability for this arises as the result of these accounting activities.

● The context of financial management

Accounts are produced by qualified, professional accountants and other experts in accordance with legal requirements and their own rules, codes of conduct and conventions which govern the ways in which they carry out the work and produce results. Explanations and translations of these are often given in organisational, annual and other public reports, together with how these conventions have been applied. Detailed explanations of these are available from the professional bodies of the accounting industry.

The managerial approach to accounts and financial aspects is concerned with the use, evaluation, interpretation, analysis and judgement of the financial data, and with what it means for the present and future of the organisation. It is one of the points of information used as the basis for effective decision making. It enables a managerial assessment of current and recent performance in financial terms.

More specifically, effective and accurate accounts enable managers to pinpoint the following:

- *Costs*: it is usual to classify costs as in Chapter 6 above. Costs are assessed in order to develop an informed view of the effectiveness of usage of financial resources; whether or not they represent effective usage of the organisation's resources; whether the activities funds are assigned to are worth pursuing; whether improvements could/should/must/might be made in the given area.
- *Income*: this can then be assessed on the basis of adequacy overall. It also enables a picture of income per product, per product range, per outlet, per region and overall, to be built up.

- *Returns*: attention to returns enables the organisation to assess the extent to which the income being generated represents an excellent, adequate, satisfactory or unsatisfactory return on investment, activities and cost. This is seen in turn, from a variety of points of view: the organisation's own desired levels of return; the time period over which the returns are to be made; and the performance of products, services and activities in their pursuit.

- *Timescales and deadlines*: all financial performance has to be seen in terms of how long it takes to achieve particular aims, objectives, goals and targets. These can then be evaluated in terms of whether the desired or required returns were feasible in the circumstances, and the lessons that need to be learned as a result. It is also essential to realise that, where desired or required returns were anticipated, the actual returns need to be monitored, reviewed and evaluated:
  - where they were met more or less exactly, in order to understand the reasons why things were successful
  - where the results were seriously under-target, in order to understand what had gone wrong, or else had not been considered
  - where returns were seriously over-target, in order to be able to understand why this particular set of circumstances simply had not been considered in advance.

- *Wider expectations and perceptions of satisfaction*: based on sectoral norms and the interests of stakeholders. Specific attention needs to be paid to:
  - shareholder and backer demands – for dividends on their shareholdings, repayments and other financial returns, which must be paid on the deadlines anticipated and agreed
  - staff – the demand for steady and increasing levels of wages and salaries; the capability to earn commissions and bonuses where these are stated or clearly implicit in reward patterns
  - suppliers – the ability to establish a pattern of financial management that ensures that their cashflow management is adequate and effective
  - customers, clients, consumers and end-users – the hub of all financial management lies in the ability to charge prices for products and services that ensure the volumes of business necessary to sustain the organisation's financial requirements in the medium to long-term, and to provide adequate returns on the capital and other resources employed (see below)
  - media and financial analysts – unless carefully managed, the media and financial analysts are likely to arrive at their own view of the performance of a particular organisation, partly on their own soundness of judgement, and also on the demands of their own particular professions – especially if there is a potential for a controversial or sensational news story
  - vested interests, pressure groups, lobbies – that require a proportion of organisational finance to be spent in addressing their own particular concerns; of especial currency are the needs to put a proportion of resources into maintaining and improving the environment, quality of life and quality of working life.

- *Comparisons*: with the achievements of other organisations in the same or related sectors and activities. It is important to note here however, that all organisations are ultimately required to stand alone. While comparisons along these lines make easy reading, they do not always convey a total understanding of organisational financial performance, nor do they give anything other than a single and non-contextual means of comparison. For example, a company that had overtly under-performed others in its sector by 90 per cent may have done so because the majority of its contracts were in a sector of the world that had suddenly become volatile; or because one of its key suppliers had gone bank-rupt; or large numbers of a key market had suddenly lost their jobs due to closure of their own place of work – and the list could be more or less endless.

- *Departmental, divisional, functional and sectional performance*: these need to be assessed in the same terms. Again, it is important to recognise that it is very unusual to allocate resources purely on departmental headcount or nature of activities. Assessment is required according to specific needs. From a financial management point of view however, managers should be seriously concerned where it becomes evident that support functions are consuming larger and increasing volumes of resources and primary activities, especially where it is also apparent that the primary activities are declining as a result.

Sources of finance

Companies and commercial organisations draw their financial resources from the following:

- Sale of shares, either to family, friends and colleagues (if the company is small and private), or else to the general public and other institutions, on the stock markets of the world if the company is 'public'.
- Sale of loan notes and debentures which may be described as short-term or fixed-term capital and which must be repaid on the date specified.
- Government and EU grants and incentives issued either in the form of a company guarantee, or else in return for undertaking government and EU contracts, including private finance initiative and public–private partnership work.
- Retained income and profits from activities carried out.
- Bank loans on which interest is repayable over the period of the loan. The loan, itself is normally arranged under a form of contract and again, must be repaid at the stated time (or times).

Note: Gearing

Gearing is the relationship between bank loans and other sources of finance. The convention in the West is that gearing should be as low as possible, meaning that the balance of financial resources should depend as little as possible on bank loans. Conversely, Japanese companies tend to have very high gearing, though it should be noted that the majority of their loans come from nationalised banks underwritten and effectively guaranteed by the government; this is therefore seen as less of a problem in these circumstances.

Assets and liabilities

Assets

Assets may be defined as follows.

Capital and tangible assets

Capital assets consist of premises, technology, equipment, expertise and machinery to be used in the production of the organisation's offerings. They are sometimes referred to as fixed or tangible assets. Their acquisition is based on a combination of what the organisation can afford, the projected length of the asset's useful life and the uses to which they are best suited.

Capital expenditure is also undertaken on supplies (and suppliers) and the means of distribution, including vehicle fleets, containers, retail and other points of public contact outlets.

Intangible assets

Intangible assets consist of reputation, goodwill, confidence, identity and expectation levels. They reflect the basis on which people come to do business with a particular organisation. High levels of goodwill and expectation are normally expected to translate into high levels of repeated business, increased reputation, and enlarging of customer demands and customer bases.

This may, in particular, be applied to brand names and images. Strong brand names (for example, Coca-Cola, Nescafe, Barbie) carry high and continuing levels of value. They each also have a commercial value in their own right, and the owning companies could (if they so wished) put them up for sale.

Customer bases, the regularity and frequency of business, and the general perceptions which customers hold of particular organisations, may also be said to be intangible assets. This is often referred to as goodwill in company accounts, and also holds true for other major stakeholders, especially suppliers, the media, and the community at large.

Key figures

Also, somewhere in the asset base, account should be taken of the contribution of key figures. For example, the 'value' of Richard Branson to the Virgin Group is clearly considerable; yet it is very difficult to put a precise figure on this. It is also possible to infer from this that other stakeholders will write down the value of the group, once he leaves it, or should anything happen to him (see Management in Focus 12.1).

Short and medium-term assets

These take the form of acquisitions made specifically for a purpose. Building companies acquire land banks on the basis that they will be able to build on these in the near future. Glassware and china companies acquire designs to be used in future product development. Travel companies and agencies acquire banks of hotel rooms and airline seats to be sold on in the next season.

Long-term assets

These are acquired on the basis that the organisation is always going to need them. This especially applies to property and some forms of capital goods and production

MANAGEMENT IN FOCUS 12.1

KEY FIGURES: EXAMPLES

There are examples of key figures as organisational assets in all areas of activity. For example:

- *Once-family businesses*: some businesses previously owned by founding families, which are now in the hands of shareholders' representatives, continue to keep a family member on the board of directors. This is to ensure that the original identity is not completely lost, and to retain the sense of purpose with which the business was first built up. For example, there are still family members on the board of McAlpine (civil engineering), John Lewis (department store), Pichetschreider (BMW), even though overall control has long since passed out of the hands of the family.

- *Football*: many top clubs continue to employ former great players as consultants, advisers and directors. For example, Franz Beckenbauer (Bayern Munich), Gianni Rivera (A.C. Milan) and Bobby Charlton (Manchester United) are all executive directors of the clubs for which they used to play, and this gives an impression of continuity to both backers and club supporters.

- *Financial services*: someone who has made a real or perceived major contribution to the commodity performance of financial products, stocks and shares may be hired by a rival organisation in order to enhance their own prestige and confidence among their client base. For example, Nicola Horlick became an extremely valuable commodity in her own right once it became known that she was a very successful fund manager. She became even more valuable from an intangible/behavioural point of view when she became famous for also being a working mother with five small children.

equipment. However, at present production technology in all fields is being improved with such rapidity that it also may be necessary to discard expensive equipment even if it is only a fraction of the way through its useful life, if to sustain production using it would render the organisation uncompetitive. In the particular case of information technology, the demands from management information systems may be predicted with a fair degree of certainty; the capability of organisational websites certainly cannot. While the former is therefore clearly an asset, the latter has to be seen from a much broader perspective – on the one hand, not to have a website at all may be psychologically damaging, while on the other hand it may be actually commercially unviable to retain one.

Managerial assets

The concept of managerial assets takes the view that all elements of the organisation should, be viewed as assets. This especially concerns:

- *Staff,* especially where they have distinctive expertise and high and enduring reputation for quality, value and service; excellence in innovation, research and development activities; or rare and highly prized skills and knowledge.
- *Markets, customers and client bases,* especially those dominated by the particular organisation in terms either of volume of business conducted or high levels of reputation. However, this should be acknowledged in all areas in which the organisation operates, especially as even a bad reputation acquired in a small niche market may have substantial knock-on effects for the rest of its activities.
- *Command* of commodities, components or other valuable and highly sought-after scarce resources; command of key expertise; command of key outlets and points of distribution.
- *Excellence* and *expertise* of management and direction (see Management in Focus 12.2).

Liabilities

Liabilities are the obligations and charges that are certain to be incurred or that are present as the result of the company's current activities. They are as follows:

- *Regular and continuing costs and obligations:* of these the most regular and continuing is staff – all staff incur costs and have to be paid. Other regular liabilities include capital repayments; interest charges; supply, production and distribution costs; and other bills and charges incurred – especially fuel, electricity, rent, rates, heating and lighting.
- *Activity-related charges:* these vary according to the nature of the organisation. The most universal are marketing activities, maintenance charges, research and development, and other pioneering and prospecting work.
- *Short-term liabilities:* incurred, for example, by hiring extra or specialised staff or equipment to get over a particular problem and for which a long-term benefit is expected to accrue.
- *Intangible liabilities:* of these the most common is a bad reputation based on poor production, quality and volume; inability to meet deadlines; poor presentation; wrong and inappropriate images; or the loss of reputation or of a key figure.
- *Sudden liabilities:* these may be caused, for example, by the sudden obsolescence of products, sudden price drops, increases in the price of supplies or components, or production and other technology. When this occurs, the organisation has to decide very quickly whether it is going to try to rejuvenate that which it is already doing, or whether to remain in the sector or not. If it decides to remain, then it must meet the sudden liability as a consequence of this (see Management in Focus 12.3).

The relationship between assets and liabilities

Something that is bought as an asset can quickly turn into a liability. Production and information technology, bought as a long-term investment, may be rendered obsolete at any time by new inventions. Building companies that bought land banks find that these become a liability if the demand for buildings dries up or if the price of land falls. Projects for which capital goods have been bought may be cancelled if other costs or unforeseen problems make the project no longer worthwhile.

MANAGEMENT IN FOCUS 12.2

MANAGEMENT AS AN ASSET

Many organisations can confuse the value of management as an asset, and that of particular managers, with the price (i.e. salary, share options, bonuses, and perks) that they place on them. The value of management as an asset is something on which it is difficult to be precise; it is a reflection of a combination of:

- the relationship between the results that are desired and required and those that are achieved
- the difference that they as individuals have made to the performance of a particular organisation – and again, this is something on which it is very difficult to be precise
- the value brought to the organisation as the result of their name and past reputation – again, very difficult to measure
- the value accrued as a result of the consequences of particular actions. For example, managers that employ high-profile management consultants to make recommendations for business restructuring may accrue a short to medium-term increase in

the share price; however, this has also to be seen in terms of the long-term performance of the organisation
- the relationship between courses of action prescribed by managers, and opportunities foregone – which again are very often the subject of supposition or extrapolation only.

The problem is further compounded by the perceived need to pay high salaries for key individuals – and when senior figures and others are known, believed or perceived to be over-compensated for failure. For example:

- Announcing salary packages of between £80,000 and £120,000 per annum for those concerned with the crisis management of NHS funding shortfalls in 2005 and 2006, a spokesperson for the Department of Health stated: 'It is necessary to pay the market rate for key executives' (though it was not stated what the market rate actually was, nor why these particular figures had been arrived at).

- One major clearing bank doubled the pay package available to its Chief Executive Officer in order to secure the right person. This person subsequently left the company after three months because of cultural differences and boardroom in-fighting.
- A top-brand sports and leisurewear company paid off its Chief Executive after 13 months in post with a severance package worth £22 million.

From this, it is clear that organisations which are genuinely concerned about their long-term future are going to be required to take a much more precise account of what constitutes the relationship between the value of particular managers (and this is not just confined to top managers) and the price that ought to be paid for them. It is another clear indication that in the future there are going to be far fewer managers in organisations, with far greater precise expectations placed upon them, and levels of reward commensurate with achievement, rather than presentation.

MANAGEMENT IN FOCUS 12.3

SALES OF ASSETS

The item 'sales of assets' very often appears as a line in corporate balance sheets and profit and loss accounts. From a managerial point of view, this has to be viewed in one of two ways:

● The assets being sold are genuinely assets, but there is an overriding organisational reason for selling them on which is normally to get over a short-term crisis.
● The sale of assets is actually a sale of liabilities – the organisation is divesting itself of things that it no longer wants.

Once it becomes apparent that an organisation is divesting itself of a substantial volume of property, goods, databases or expertise that it no longer requires, it is important to recognise that the value of these on the market always declines. Other organisations know that these items have to be sold, and are therefore prepared to either wait for the price to drop, or to name their own lower price in order to secure the particular item at a discount.

From a managerial point of view also, it is essential to recognise that the sale of items that genuinely are assets is certain to do short and medium-term damage to the continuing viability of the organisation, and that some way is going to have to be found of replacing these assets as soon as operating conditions allow. The sale of liabilities should be conducted as quickly as possible in order to remove the necessity to consume resources on their continued upkeep and usage.

Depreciation

Depreciation is an accounting convention that shows the period of time over which an item is gradually paid for, paid for in instalments, or written off altogether. It is important to remember that it is purely an accounting convention and not a managerial tool.

For example, a piece of equipment may have cost £100,000. The organisation's accounting function may set out to depreciate it, quite legitimately from their point of view, at £20,000 per annum for five years. If it does become obsolete after two years, then the managerial stance must be to scrap it and replace it, whatever the accounting convention may say.

Financial commitments

Financial management is a continuous commitment, a direct condition and consequence of being in a particular sector. The specific nature of financial management varies between sectors and between organisations. However, in all sectors and activities, financial management must cover the following:

● staff expertise, training, improvement and development
● organisational capability, capacity, improvement and development
● systems improvement and development and refinement

- brand and other marketing assets, reinforcement, development and enhancement
- reputation, confidence and expectational enhancement
- technology improvement, development and replacement.

Financial management expertise is required in key areas of decision making as follows:

- whether to buy up stocks of supplies; whether to stockpile or to rely on frequent deliveries (just in time)
- whether to buy up or lease transport and distribution fleets and other vehicles
- whether to employ or subcontract specialist staff and expertise
- the vagaries surrounding the useful life of each of these elements and necessary actions that may have to be taken concerning them at any time
- whether to buy, rent or lease premises, staff, equipment and technology (see Management in Focus 12.4).

Profit and loss account and balance sheet

Once the data is collected it has to be made available to both the internal and external environments. The external environment in the UK requires the annual

MANAGEMENT IN FOCUS 12.4

PRODUCTS, SERVICES AND EQUIPMENT: TO MAKE, LEASE OR BUY?

This part of financial management is specifically concerned with whether organisations choose to:

- make their own products from components and raw materials, or buy them in ready-made and then re-package them and sell them on
- lease or buy capital goods and other equipment
- construct, own or lease their own databases
- employ or lease their own expertise.

It is a complicated series of decisions. However, overriding considerations will include:

- expenses, liabilities and charges incurred as the result of going down each path
- the relative availability of equipment, expertise, products and services should they only be leased or bought in when required
- the nature of any contractual and other legal obligations that may have to be met each time the product,

service or expertise is used.

It is also essential to recognise that even where there is a clear financial advantage, the decision will ultimately be taken on the basis of managerial choice. For all of the financial advantage, some organisations prefer to own their own assets so as to have full control over them; while others prefer to lease or charge out as much as they possibly can in order to reduce their fixed cost base. It is therefore not possible to arrive at this decision on the basis of any 'rational' approach.

presentation of a balance sheet, and profit and loss account. These are governed by accounting conventions, and must be subject to scrutiny and audit. The balance sheet is a financial snapshot of the company on a stated day. It shows assets and liabilities in balance, and what the components of each are; this enables the wider business and financial world to make an informed judgement on the company's inherent strength and stability. The profit and loss account is a representation of income and expenditure, showing a surplus or deficit (see Figure 12.1).

Company accounts must be countersigned as giving 'a true and fair reflection' of the financial state and performance of the organisation by an externally appointed auditor.

Profit and loss accounts and balance sheets are normally presented as part of the annual report. As well as the figures, the annual report also includes statements by the Chairman/woman and other top managers and directors concerning the well-being of the organisation, and the nature, content and volume of activities and future plans.

It is then possible to compare one year's performance with another, both overall and line-by-line. This is useful up to a point.

To gain a more complete picture however, it is much more useful to take the same view over a longer period of time – often five years. This approach is the same: to take overall and line-by-line comparisons. Taking this longer view enables identification of more genuine trends and directions. It also enables 'blips' – extraordinary items of sale and expenditure, share issues, special loans – to be set in context.

The balance sheet and profit and loss account are primarily for external consumption, though much useful information can be gathered by anyone.

From a managerial point of view, it is much more useful to be able to observe trends over longer periods of time, than simply comparing the current year's figures with the previous. Comparisons of performance over five years, both total organisational performance and line-by-line, give a much clearer indication of what has been changing in the long-term. The reasons for these can then be investigated in much more detail. One year's figures compared against another's give little more than the percentage increase or decrease; while this might be satisfactory to some managers, it is certain not to give a complete picture.

Moreover, the availability of this much more extensive information means that it is possible to assess whether something is truly effective. At an organisational level, trends in turnover, profit levels, costs and overheads can be assessed, and enquiries made, when it becomes apparent that these are changing steadily and substantially over periods of time. At a departmental level, the availability of financial information over such periods gives a much truer indication of, for example, whether budget and resource levels are adequate, where resources are being consumed, and the extent to which this is contributing to the effectiveness or otherwise of departmental performance. Consider Figure 12.2.

● Cost apportionment

Fixed and variable cost apportionment

Fixed and variable cost apportionment is a process devised by organisations for the purposes of identifying where these costs should be charged and apportioned. This is often known as the process of 'cost centring', and whatever is identified as having costs apportioned is called the cost centre.

Profit and Loss Account	0001 £ million	0000 £ million	
Income	3188	3097	
Operating cost	(2736)	(2771)	
Operating profit	452	326	
Interest	(27)	33	
Profit before tax	425	359	
Tax	(140)	(117)	(brackets indicate subtraction)
Profit after tax	285	242	
Dividend	(82)	(72)	
Retained profit	203	170	

Figures are then normally given for earnings per share and dividend per share

Balance Sheet	31 December 0001 £ million	31 December 0000 £ million
Fixed assets	2106	1996
Current assets	1109	1043
Short-term creditors	(771)	(890)
Net current assets	338	153
Total assets	2444	2149
Long-term creditors	(475)	(325)
Liabilities and charges	(299)	(359)
Net assets	1670	1465
Capital and reserves		
Share capital	1470	1000
Capital reserve	150	265
Other reserves	50	200
Total equity	1670	1465

Notes:

It is usual to give current and previous years' figures for purposes of comparison. Thus, the overall performance can be compared, and also the line-by-line movements and charges.

Figure 12.1 Profit and loss account and balance sheet: example

Many organisations are increasingly taking the view that the apportionment of fixed costs is not only operationally unnecessary, but also misleading when trying to assess the true costs of activities. The fixed cost base – overheads, staffing costs, interest charges, and shareholders' obligations – are taken as an organisational bill, that has to be paid as a condition of being in the particular line of activities at the time.

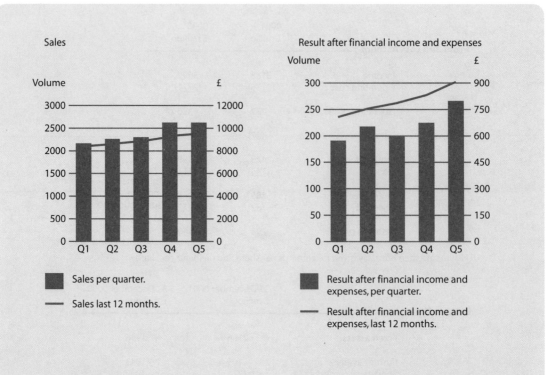

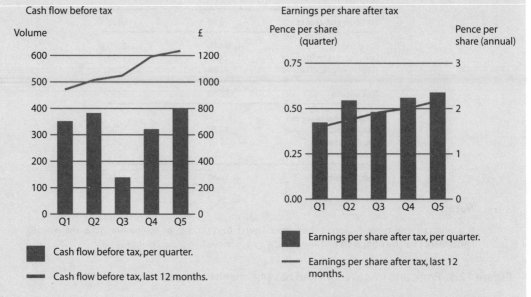

Notes: these diagrams emphasise the benefit of taking a longer view than simply comparing one year's figures with the previous year. In the above examples, it is possible to gain a much clearer view of trends over a longer period; and it is possible to see where particular blips may have occurred in the past.

Figure 12.2 Trends: example

Cost apportionment is limited to assessment of variable costs – those incurred as the result of the volume of activities conducted.

Break-even

This is the point at which the balance between costs and income is established (see Figure 12.3).

Profit apportionment

This is the converse of cost apportionment and is the organisation's method of ensuring the nature and sources of income generated by its various activities. This serves to identify profit centres in the same way as cost centres mentioned earlier.

Similarly also, while it is useful to be able to identify those activities that do make the greatest contribution to organisational viability, it is being increasingly recognised that there are limitations in assessing each activity narrowly as a profit centre. It is much more usual to take the total range of activities as being the basis on which profits are earned, even if profits are much higher for some products and services than others.

Asset valuation

The purpose of identifying, assessing and valuing the activities and resources as assets is as part of the means of measuring their total contribution and worth to the

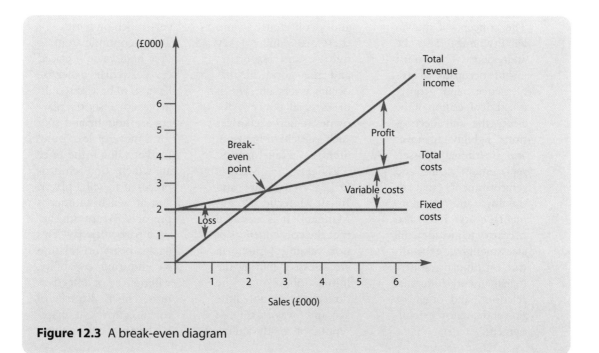

Figure 12.3 A break-even diagram

organisation. Management in Focus 12.5 shows the method adopted in such evaluation in response to the human resource. Equivalent approaches can be taken to 'hard resources' (production technology, capability, expertise, production volumes) and to 'soft' assets (reputation, goodwill and quality).

MANAGEMENT IN FOCUS 12.5

A MODEL OF HUMAN ASSET VALUATION AND ACCOUNTING

1. The 'base' to be adopted is employment costs, which are measured:
   - in total
   - by staff category
   - by operational division
   - in terms of the added value that each contributes
   - by sectoral factors.

2. Return on these bases may be measured and assessed in the same way as for any other asset. The concept of human liability must also be addressed. This must include occupational obsolescence and consequent depreciation of the asset; the full occupational liability; turnover and terminal losses; replacement costs; and refurbishment (that is, training and development) costs. It is also necessary to include a full assessment of expenditure on human resource management, industrial relations, and organisation and employee development.

3. The value that organisations place on collective and individual expertise requires careful assessment. Questions of profitability, effectiveness, and organisation and market development have to be assessed in terms of the results of having or of not having this expertise present. It is also necessary to consider the effects on organisational reputation and confidence, and therefore value, of key figures and expertise, and the goodwill that occurs as a result. This is of especial concern for owner/chief executives such as Richard Branson, Stelios Haji-Ioannou (easyJet), Michael O'Leary (Ryanair), and Julian Metcalfe (Pret A Manger). It is essential that the consequences of not valuing reputation are assessed. During the initial phase of the dot.com revolution, little account was taken of reputation or durability;

it was simply 'established wisdom' that dot.com companies would be successful. Any reputation that the entrepreneurs had was driven by the media, rather than by business viability and longevity. While it remains true that most dot.com entrepreneurs have fought very hard to make their businesses successful, the question of reputation was taken very much on trust.

4. The economic rent – very high value – placed on particular expertise has also to be assessed. In professional sports, players are bought and sold for a more or less 'pure' market value – the price at which one club is prepared to sell a player, and at which another is prepared to buy him/her on a particular day. This again, bears no relation to enduring capability, willingness or effectiveness. This is also true of top executives at shareholder-dominated

companies, where a particular chief executive officer is hired on the same basis as the professional sports player, and again without any regard for that person's enduring future value.

5. Gains and losses in organisational value as the result of acquisitions and divestments of particular expertise have also to be assessed. Again, whether the particular expertise is kept or allowed to leave, may be driven by short-term expedient or political motives. However, when assessing the enduring financial viability of the organisation as a whole, it is essential to take a strategic view of the required expertise, and of the specific individuals. Where it is likely that specific individuals will leave to the detriment of organisational value, the transitional period has to be extremely carefully managed.

● Ratio analysis

Ratios are used in financial management to identify, establish and measure particular performance aspects. The results and outcomes of the analysis of the ratios, and the level and quality of performance that they indicate, contribute to management knowledge and information, and become part of the process of assessment and evaluation. These ratios include:

Profit Ratio $\quad \dfrac{\text{Net Profit}}{\text{Total Sales}} \times 100$ Indicates percentage return

Selling Costs $\quad \dfrac{\text{Selling Costs}}{\text{Total Sales}} \times 100$ Indicates percentage consumed on sales costs

The same approach can be taken for energy, production, marketing, staff, distribution, research, development and capital goods as a percentage of sales.

The ratios provide distinctive measures of the particular activities. The information gained has to be seen in context however. For example, while a 'quick ratio' may show that a company could not easily cover its current liabilities, this does not matter if these are not to be called in. Similarly, different commercial and public sectors will have their own norms and expectations that have also to be taken into account – a 2 per cent return on capital employed may sound low, but it may be twice the usual rate in the industry concerned. There is also the wider environment to be considered, and any opportunities or difficulties, boom or recession.

The main purpose of identifying the nature of these costs and their extent in given situations is as the basis of managerial assessment and decision making. Costs should never become straitjackets outside which a department or function may not budget. It should always be remembered that the driving force of any organisation is its products and services and relations with its markets; costs and the management of them should never take the place of market imperatives. Only if this is achieved can a true assessment of the nature and extent of the effectiveness (in financial terms) of the organisation's activities be made (see Management in Focus 12.6).

Assets and liabilities	$\dfrac{\text{Assets}}{\text{Liabilities}}$	A general ready-reckoner

This may then be broken into:

a)	$\dfrac{\text{Long-term assets}}{\text{Long-term liabilities}}$	
b)	$\dfrac{\text{Current assets}}{\text{Current liabilities}}$	
c)	A quick ratio or 'the acid test'	$\dfrac{\text{Quickly realisable assets}}{\text{Current liabilities}}$
d)	Debtors and creditors	$\dfrac{\text{Debtors}}{\text{Creditors}}$ — Indicates whether an organisation is paying out its bills more quickly than it is receiving
e)	Return on capital employed (ROCE):	$\dfrac{\text{Profit before tax}}{\text{Capital employed}}$ — Gives rate of return on the investment Depends on what is included in 'capital employed' and 'returns'

Figure 12.4 Ratio analyses

⬤ Internal markets

Internal markets are present in holding company structures, multinational organisations and health and public services. They are a combination of the following elements:

- The first is the distinction between purchasers and providers for the purposes of establishing internally contracted arrangements as the basis on which the relationship between the two is to be carried out in the future.
- Second is the establishment of a price–service return and the ways in which everything is to be paid for, including the agreement of quantity/volume, quality and timescales/deadlines criteria. In multinationals this will generally be on a system of transfer pricing, using the most advantageous currency available; in other situations, a system of internal invoicing may be devised.

The emphasis of each element will vary; the overall constitution of any organisational internal market, however, must be such as to ensure an effectiveness of operation, and efficiency of resource identification, allocation and evaluation on the part of the control, administrative and support functions of the organisation.

MANAGEMENT IN FOCUS 12.6

FINANCIAL MEASURES OF PERFORMANCE FROM A MANAGERIAL POINT OF VIEW

The following are useful managerial financial measures of performance. Their application and emphasis varies between organisations.

Income/profit

- Per product; per product group or cluster; per product range; per activity; in total.
- Per employee: front line staff; support staff; in total.
- Per square metre; per outlet; per location; per region; per country.
- Per customer.
- Per hour/day/week/month/season/year.

Fixed variable and total cost

For each of these costs, calculations may be made:

- Per employee; per function; per activity; per department/division/section; per outlet; per location; per region; per country.
- Per square metre.

Marginal cost

Marginal cost is usually best calculated:

- Per product; per outlet; per employee (if overtime or time off is given).

Notes

1. Fixed and variable costs per customer can be calculated, but this is not normally very useful unless all customers are receiving the same regularity and level of service.

2. Identifying cost per function can be used as the basis for developing a cost–benefit analysis approach, in which the costs and benefits of (or returns on) a particular venture or initiative are weighed and balanced against each other. This is especially valuable when assessing the contribution of support functions and the effectiveness of primary (i.e. production and direct service) activities.

3. Assessing cost per customer is especially futile in considering public services, health care and transport because the cost of providing given levels of service is more or less fixed. A hospital must be able to cope with maximum volumes of patients at all times and be able to provide the maximum range of services stipulated. Trains, buses and aeroplanes must stick to their schedules. One view is that, especially for trains and planes, there are no variable costs; they must follow their schedules and it may even be necessary to move empty on one route or between two destinations, given that increased volumes of business are present further down the line.

Budgets

The budget is a plan (with sub-plans) that constitutes part of the process of managing the organisation, department, project or initiative. It aims to provide an accurate picture of where resources are being used, the speed and frequency of this, and the basis for making future judgements on the levels of finance required to meet particular targets (in terms of volume, quality and time).

The budget enables specific analysis and evaluation of the accuracy of the resource allocation process, and variances from it, and explanation of such variables.

Budgets normally identify the fixed costs associated with the department, division, function or activity in question. They must identify the variable costs, relating these to given volumes of activities and providing sufficient resources to ensure that the desired volume and quality of activities can be achieved. It is usual also to identify the marginal costs incurred by getting involved in one-off special and additional activities.

There is normally some form of time constraint imposed. The work of accountancy and resource allocation often requires an annual statement of budget/resource utilisation even if the budget is not being operated to the same deadlines.

There is also certain to be some form of budget reporting required from a managerial and directional point of view to enable judgement on the effectiveness of this form of resource allocation and utilisation to be made (see Management in Focus 12.7).

MANAGEMENT IN FOCUS 12.7

BUDGETS: THE PUBLIC SECTOR EXAMPLE

This is an illustration of the shortcomings of the budgeting process and of what happens when budgets, rather than activities, become the driving force.

In UK public services, resources are allocated on an annual basis to support various activities. At the end of each 12-month period, the last budget is cancelled and a new one put in place. Any resources not used up over the period are lost and returned to whoever and wherever is responsible for providing them. There is therefore no incentive to conserve resources for a time when they might become useful in the future. There is every incentive to spend the resources, whether or not the activities are useful. There are two further effects:

- *The budget cycle*: this works as follows. For the first three months of the cycle, activities are constrained while assessment of the resources in relation to activities is carried out. A steady-state is generated during the next three months based on this. Further restraints are applied during the third period of three months. The final quarter consists of a frantic attempt to use up everything not so far consumed because otherwise it will be lost.
- *Closures and shutdowns*:

under this system these occur when the budget is used up due to pressures outside the organisation's control before the end of the cycle. Under this system it becomes 'more cost effective' to have premises closed and staff and equipment idle, than to have them at work.

The very best that can be said for the system is that it can be seen where stated amounts of money have been spent. Apart from this, in virtually all circumstances, it is the wrong way to budget. It fails on all other counts, especially on that of devising budgets in support of real and desired levels of activities.

Managers should be aware of the three main prevailing corporate attitudes to budgeting:

- Where there is a close relationship between the resources required and the resources budgeted.
- Where there is some relationship between the resources required and the budget allocated.
- Where there is no relationship between the resources required and the budget allocated. This is an especial problem in the provision of frontline public services.

Two forms of budgeting should be noted:

- *Historic budgeting*: where the previous year's (or activity's or project's) budget is taken as the starting point for the current allocation of resources. To be fully effective, it assumes that everything was correct and adequate in the previous period.
- *Zero-based budgeting*: the opposite of historical budgeting, this assumes that a fresh approach and consideration is required for current and future activities and periods. It requires a proper examination of the current and future activities, proposals and time periods, rather than reliance on historic figures as the starting point.

There are prescriptive, consultative and participative elements involved in establishing and implementing an effective budgeting process. There should be not only a means of effective resource allocation and wage monitoring, but also the means of ensuring that all those involved in its implementation understand fully the resource obligations and constraints under which they have to work. Even in areas of severe constraint a better operational response will be generated if everyone concerned understands the nature and range of resource limitations (see Management in Focus 12.8).

It is also necessary to be able to reconcile control with flexibility, and with divergent and conflicting demands for resources. This, in turn, requires providing a measure of leeway for an otherwise productive initiative that needs a small extra resource in order for it to be fully successful, without at the same time destroying the credibility of the process. It follows from this that all budgets and budgeting systems must be specifically designed for the organisations, initiatives, operations, projects, staff and facilities in question. While general principles and standpoints hold good, these must be applied as required to particular situations; and therefore, a universal set of precise rules is not appropriate.

Conclusions

The main conclusion to be drawn is in recognising the difference between the work of professional accountants in producing figures, and that of managers in using, interpreting, analysing and evaluating them. In many ways, therefore, the work of the manager starts where that of the accountant finishes. Having said that, the manager must have proper knowledge and understanding of how figures are produced, what they mean, and what they state about the condition of the organisation as a whole and its particular activities.

MANAGEMENT IN FOCUS 12.8

SYMPTOMS OF DECLINING FINANCIAL PERFORMANCE

Whenever it becomes clear that 'the figures' are not going to be 'right' for the particular financial year, organisations require their managers to make budget cuts. This normally involves tackling the variable costs which have been incurred as the result of engaging in activities, rather than assessing the fixed costs that are likely to be contributing much more substantially to decline in performance or to the overall burden on the organisation. For example:

● A hospital faced with a £2.5 million deficit sent a memorandum to all its nursing and medical staff asking them to be 'especially careful' with the use of medical resources. Staff were especially exhorted not to use too many dressings, bandages or toilet rolls, in order to maximise efficiency of resources. A 'back of the envelope' calculation conducted by a senior registrar came to the conclusion that the hospital would have saved more money if it had not sent the memorandum than it was possible to save by 'using bandages wisely'.

● Faced with constraints from its parent company, a financial services organisation cut its training budget from £600,000 to £40,000. It then spent a substantial amount of the 'saving' on HR procedures; this became necessary in order to manage the large volume of grievances that occurred as the result. In particular, the parent company never explained to the financial services subsidiary how it was supposed to handle £500,000 worth of training that it had contracted to provide to its employees.

More general symptoms of declining financial performance are observable in peripheral activities. Peters (1986) states:

> You can always tell an organisation that is in difficulties. The free tea trolley stops coming round, and staff are asked to pay for their drinks out of machines. Flowers disappear from the reception areas. Corporate subscriptions to business and trade press are cancelled. Senior managers go to expensive locations for weekend think-tanks, and emerge with the news that staff have got to up their productivity, with no additional resources. Bonuses for all but senior staff are cancelled. Expense claims are either capped or rigorously checked.

Source: T. Peters (1990) *Thriving on Chaos*, Macmillan.

It is necessary to recognise that, because of legal constraints, professional accountants tend to work in annual cycles. Managers should not be hidebound by this. Some managerial cycles are much shorter; others are much longer. In particular, the establishment of annual budgets needs extremely close attention – this is not to say that annual budgets are necessarily wrong, but they must be seen in an operational as well as financial context – and the operational drive must be paramount. The archetypal public sector approach indicated above is wrong and should be avoided.

Effective financial management requires a high level of organisational and environmental knowledge and understanding, as a key part of the capability to choose the right approach to finance in any particular set of circumstances, and the right financial performance measures and the right means for the assessment of the financial aspects of management in particular situations.

Managers additionally need to know and understand the nature and levels of financial resources that they require in order to carry out effective and successful performance. They should be able to do this from at least two points of view:

- the nature and levels of finance required 'in a perfect world'
- the nature and levels available in the real world, and the pressures and constraints that these bring.

In practice, the financial aspects of management are often not helped by the resource allocation process that occurs within organisations. At its worst, this consists of lobbying for, and bargaining for, the levels of finance necessary in order to carry out even a barely adequate job. For some reason, many senior managers find this to be an acceptable and useful way of 'ensuring that resources go to the right department'. In absolute terms this is unacceptable; in the real world, there is a clear duty on shareholders' representatives, and other dominant stakeholders, to ensure that where this practice becomes apparent, it is stopped forthwith.

There is also an enduring problem for those responsible for managing finance in public services. The point is made above that many budgets are set without any relationship to the levels of finance required, or what they are to be spent on. This is likely to endure until the political dominance is removed from public services, and budget holders and other with financial management responsibility at the frontline of public services are allowed to use resources for the primary purpose of serving their clients.

It is also true that those who command financial resources are often placed under great pressure to divert these away from mainstream, steady-state activities into those that have a perceived instant, high-profile, expedient and triumphal return. The long-term integrity of steady-state activities is therefore compromised in pursuit of instant returns.

CRITICAL THINKING, ANALYSIS AND EVALUATION

1.   A departmental manager with a staff of 20 has suddenly received an additional budget of £40,000, which he is only allowed to spend on training for his staff. He has three months to spend it. What actions should he take – when, why and how? What overall courses of action are open to him?

2.   For the organisation of your choice, obtain a copy of the annual report. Without reading the Chairperson's statement, study the five-year organisational trends. Draw your own conclusions from these. Then read the Chairperson's annual statement, and compare and contrast your findings with his/hers.

3.   A department store operates in a city-centre location. It has four floors, of which the ground floor and first floor are the retail area; there is a customer restaurant on the second floor; and the company's offices are on the top floor. The company is going to redevelop the second floor, so that the restaurant space is reduced by two-thirds; the residual space is to be redeveloped to

provide additional retail capacity for high-quality, high-brand-value china and glass. Suggest two different ways in which costs might be apportioned, and draw conclusions as to the best way of going about this from a financial management point of view.

4.　How in your view should organisations manage sudden downturns in overall business performance? Identify as full a range of actions as possible that are open to them. From this, identify those which are likely to be most cost effective, and most likely to be implemented in the real world.

DEVELOPING MANAGEMENT SKILLS AND EXPERTISE

WHEATFIELDS AND THEIR TROUBLE WITH HOLIDAYS

Wheatfields is a single department store located in the city centre of Canterbury, Kent. It has always enjoyed a good reputation for customer service, employment practice and community contribution.

Last year it was taken over by a holding company located in London.

Prior to the takeover, and in spite of the vast tourist trade in the city, the shop was always shut for bank holidays, and also Christmas Eve and New Year's Eve. Now, however, the new owners want to change this. As a consequence, the following directive was issued to the store's general manager three weeks before Easter.

It has been decided to bring all areas of activity into line concerning the Easter trading period. In order to alleviate the excessive pressure on profit margins, Wheatfields will consequently remain open all day Good Friday and Easter Monday. All staff will be compensated by an increase of 1 per cent (15 per cent–16 per cent) in the staff discount allowance scheme. Moreover, please note that in future all staff will be required to work on Christmas Eve and New Year's Eve.

A week later, the holding company's personnel director heard from Wheatfields' general manager, that she had been inundated with staff complaints. She cited the following information:

- 20 per cent of staff complained on religious grounds.
- 15 per cent complained that their families would not enjoy the unique benefit of having Good Friday and other historic 'special days' together.
- Skeleton public transport and consequent congestion on the roads created difficulties for 20 per cent of staff who commuted in from the outlying villages.
- Part-time staff who did not receive the staff discount would not benefit, but would still be required to work if their hours came up on these particular days.
- Whenever staff had been asked to work on other bank holidays, they were normally paid double time; would this still apply?
- Staff also wanted to know whether the requirements to work on these extra days of the year would be compensated by being able to take additional days as part of their annual leave allowance.

Neither Wheatfields' general manager, nor the holding company's personnel director, had been consulted on the decision. Each independently fed the results back to the Chief Executive of the holding company. He was astonished at the reaction.

Wheatfields employs 200 staff. 140 of these work on the shop floor in contact with customers. A further 40 work in the storeroom area, unloading goods inwards and arranging for deliveries of goods to customers where required. The other 20 are all managerial – dealing with staff supervision, customer liaison (including complaints), and attending to specific requests from top-value clients. Purchasing, sales and marketing is now carried out centrally at the holding company.

The average wage on the shop floor is £7.00 per hour. The average daily sales value is £120,000; the average profit margin is 4 per cent.

Questions

1. On the basis of what you are told, identify the assets and liabilities present at Wheatfields. Of these, which assets are specifically declining in value, and what are the likely or possible effects of this on the enduring performance of the Wheatfields store?
2. What is the volume of business that it will be necessary for the store to conduct in order to break even for the bank holiday periods assuming that:
   – overtime is paid, and
   – the days worked are given as part of the annual leave allowance?
3. Identify a package of benefits designed to alleviate the concerns indicated above. Calculate as accurately as possible, the cost of offering these to all staff in order to address their particular concerns. What other actions might it be necessary for the holding company management, and Wheatfields' manager to take, and why?

Chapter thirteen

Quantitative methods

'Lies, damned lies – and statistics.'
Benjamin Disraeli.

'Data should always be collected with a clear purpose in mind.
Not only a clear purpose, but a clear idea as to the precise way in
which they will be analysed so as to yield the desired information.'
M.J. Moroney.

'I'm the number one fan of the data coming out of
Detroit and it's real simple – our cars don't work!'
Tom Peters, *The World Turned Upside Down* (1986).

Chapter outline

- Introduction
- Statistics
- Sources of information and data
- Presentation of data
- Accuracy of data
- Index numbers
- Probability
- Sampling
- Operational research
- Forecasting, extrapolation and inference
- Network analysis
- Proof and indication
- Management information systems
- Validity and reliability
- Information currency
- Conclusions

Chapter objectives

After studying this chapter, you should be able to:

- understand the range of mathematical and statistical approaches required by expert managers

- understand and be able to apply specific and precise forms of enquiry to particular situations

- understand the forms of enquiry that particular situations demand

- understand the need for accuracy of data, and the limitations where this is not possible

- understand the contextual features of statistical and mathematical approaches

- understand the importance of data in decision-making processes.

● Introduction

The purpose of this chapter is to introduce and outline the importance, use and value of the quantitative tools and methods that are available to the manager, and to indicate and illustrate their uses in different situations.

From the point of view of the manager, it is the ability to interpret and use statistical and financial data (rather than being a specialist in statistics or mathematics) that is important. It is this standpoint, therefore, that is taken.

Managers need to know why, when, how and by whom data was gathered. They need to be able to set data in context, and to know, understand and accept any constraints under which it was gathered. It is additionally the case that managers need to know and understand the reasons why data may be incomplete, or why it was not possible to gather the required amount of information in particular circumstances.

Data provides a quantitative basis for the evaluation of issues and situations; and this in turn informs the basis and strength of decisions, both from a qualitative and from a quantitative point of view. Even where it is possible to gather full information, and provide accurate statistics and other figures, this is not an end in itself. It is the use to which the evaluation of data is put that is of greatest value.

● Statistics

Statistics is the discipline that deals with the preparation, collection, arrangement, presentation, analysis and interpretation of quantitative data. The discipline can be divided into the study of probability (or mathematical statistics) and descriptive statistics, which deal with the compilation and preservation of data to provide information on which to base decisions, and to assist in forward planning and forecasting.

Primary and secondary data

Data can initially be categorised as primary or secondary data:

- *Primary data*: is obtained direct by organisations and individuals through observation, surveys, interviews and samples, using methods and instruments drawn up specifically for the stated purpose.
- *Secondary data*: comes from other data sources, such as official statistics, provided by government sources and sectoral data gathered by employers' associations and federations, and marketing organisations.

Uses of data gathered

The use of secondary data always involves taking information that others have gathered, and interpreting, analysing and using it for purposes different from those which the original gatherers designed or intended. There may also be variations in definition or coverage that have to be taken into account.

The decision about whether to gather primary data or use other sources depends on the nature of the information required, its availability from sources other than primary, its range and coverage, the nature of the fields of enquiry, and the accuracy required. It is essential to be able to reconcile completeness with timescales and deadlines. The shorter the timescale or deadline, the greater the reduction in accuracy likely.

Data is then classified into groupings or sections for the purposes of analysis, comparison and evaluation.

From the manager's point of view, gathering and assessment of data is to provide information that is accurate and quantifiable. This then becomes the basis for planning, forecasting, projected activities and decision making in the given set of circumstances; at strategic levels it serves to inform and reinforce decisions taken in the interests of the organisation as a whole.

Sources of information and data

The main sources of data are as follows:

- *Government statistics*: highly publicised in the media, and useful as general indicators of the state of national, business and economic confidence, direction and activity, and the direction that the economy is likely to take in general over the foreseeable future.
- *Sectoral statistics*: produced by trade federations, employers' associations and professional bodies for the support and enlightenment of member organisations, and to contribute to their knowledge and awareness of the global aspects and overview of their own sectors. This may contribute in great measure to policy formulation in particular sectors, in the setting of minimum and maximum wage, price and output levels, for example.
- *Market research organisations*: these hold data on vast ranges of issues that they promulgate and sell on a commercial basis to those requiring it. The main initial value of this is to indicate the general state of business, and the range of business opportunities that may be available, again as a prelude to organisations either conducting or commissioning their own future investigations.
- *Local government*: holds a wide range of general data on the composition, social state, occupational range and population structure of those who live in the UK; this is published in general terms by local government and municipal departments, and again is a useful precursor to more rigorous investigation.
- *Public enquiries and investigations*: these generate a great amount of information about particular initiatives (e.g. urban development, bypasses, power stations) that is often a useful initial point of reference for those planning to go into similar ventures in the future.
- *Organisational statistics*: gathered internally for specific purposes (see Management in Focus 13.1).

Presentation of data

Data must be presented in ways that are easily and readily understood by those on the receiving end. This is true both in the generation of overall impressions, and in the presentation of precise findings. The method of presentation must take into account the relative interest and capability of the audience, the time that is to be spent on it, and the purpose for which it is being presented.

It is essential that this is understood at this stage, because statistical surveys and

 MANAGEMENT IN FOCUS 13.1

ORGANISATIONAL STATISTICS AND MANAGEMENT INFORMATION

This may be classified as follows:

- *Human resource management*: wage levels (individual, departmental, divisional, functional total); staff turnover measured in terms of overall turnover; and by department, division, function and occupation; the turnover of individuals ought also to be assessed in terms of how long they have stayed in previous jobs, and how long people tend to stay in a given position before seeking or needing to move on; absence and absenteeism levels (individual, departmental, divisional, functional and total); strikes and disputes; levels of disciplinary and dismissal activity; grievances and other staff problems; ability/inability to recruit; qualifications and capabilities; training and development records; identification of potential; succession; variety of work and experience; total experience.
- *Public relations*: nature and volumes of complaints; sources of complaints; nature and volumes of media inquiries; general requests; dealings with the community and its institutions – schools, colleges, evening classes, clubs and societies; nature and volume of organisational coverage in the community and media; proportions of time spent on general public relations activities; proportions of time and resources spent on specific issues.
- *Marketing*: market assessment information; gathering of marketing information; use of information; information for using and evaluating the effects of marketing campaigns; effectiveness of the targeting of marketing activities; effectiveness of general marketing activities; effectiveness of the total marketing position
- *Sales*: by product; by product cluster; total range of product; by outlet; by location; volume and quality; demands for returns; after-sales demands; the number of times that guarantees are invoked; complaints; blockages

- *Production*: deliveries; product output volumes; product to market; time factors; quality factors; volume factors; number of complaints per site/factory/batch/unit/production run/location; blockages; supplier factors; distribution factors
- *Financial*: total costs; cost breakdowns – by site, division, department, function, location, occupation; fixed costs; variable costs and causes of variability; marginal costs; budget and budgeting processes
- *Administration*: staff records; financial records; budget usage; balance of activities; technology usage; technology life span; technology obsolescence; replacement programmes.

Sources of information are therefore clearly readily available. The effectiveness of the use of information depends on both the organisation's ability to gather and store this information, and on the capabilities of individual managers to identify what they want and when they want it, and to evaluate it in particular situations.

information systems now hold, and can generate, vast amounts of data on all aspects of business in relatively short periods of time. The data is of value, however, only if it can be understood and assimilated. For this to be effective, presentation must be in 'audience-friendly' or 'user-friendly' forms, meeting the audience's expectation as well as getting the required message across.

There are five main methods available (see Figure 13.1):

● *Tabulation*: where data is presented in tables devised against two axes or criteria.
● *Bar charts*: a more visual representation of tables, and usually presented against two axes or variables.
● *Pie charts*: where the data is represented in a circular or 'pie' format, with the slices representing the quantities or percentages given.
● *Graphs*: on which data is plotted, also against two variables (e.g. dates and volume; timescale and sales figures).
● *Pictures (pictograms)*: such as the use of a small picture of a person to represent a small number of unemployed and a larger picture to represent an increase in the figure recorded.

Accuracy of data

The accuracy of any data depends on the way in which it was gathered, the quality of the actual data gathering, and any rounding at the end of it. If a survey takes a sample, rather than dealing with everyone or everything concerned in a particular activity, the results may indicate particular conclusions very strongly, but they will only be proven if the entire sector is surveyed. If there is a flaw in the statistical methods used, or if the wrong questions are asked, the results will also be flawed and inaccurate. Finally, rounding of numbers is widely used and has also to be seen in context and as a limitation – balance sheet figures for multinational companies are given to the nearest hundred thousand pounds, or even million pounds.

Social survey and market research organisations consequently go to a lot of trouble to make their surveys both valid and reliable through the establishment of proper objectives, the design of questionnaires and other survey instruments, the provision of high-quality and rigorous training of surveyors, and the recognition, understanding and acceptance of any limitations present (see Management in Focus 13.2).

Decision making

The primary use of data and statistics to managers is as an aid to decision making. In particular, reliable and accurate data and information are required in the following areas:

● policy and strategy formulation, and the assessment of priorities
● marketing activities and initiatives, measurable in increases or decreases in sales of products and services
● output productivity and delivery
● identifying faults in particular aspects of products and services
● successes and failures in staffing issues, employee relations, recruitment campaigns and staff retention rates

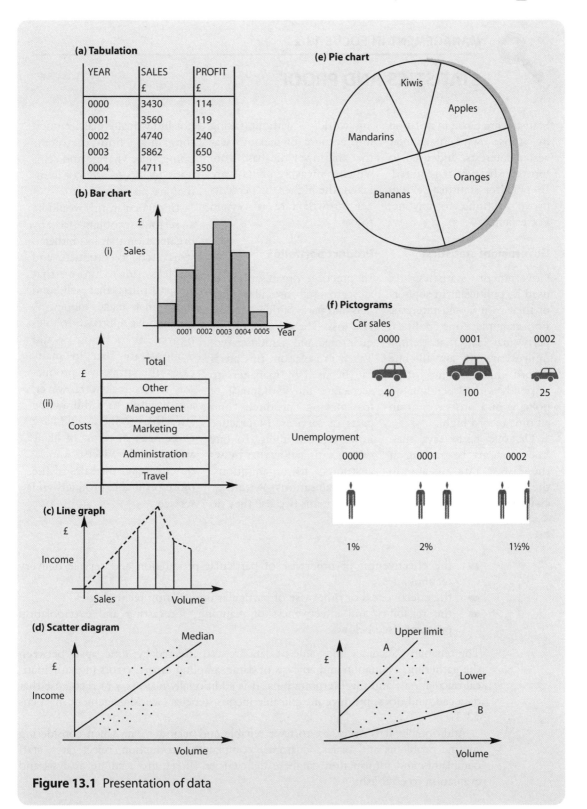

Figure 13.1 Presentation of data

MANAGEMENT IN FOCUS 13.2

STATISTICS AND PROOF

Statistics are taken in isolation by those with particular vested interests, and used to 'prove' whatever is required. In practice, statistics seldom prove anything to anyone. For example:

Government statistics

Government statistics are used by politicians in support of their own vested interests. For example, one political party may say that: 'crime figures are at an all-time record high.' The other responds with: 'spending on policing and prisons is at an all time record high.'

Or, one party says that: 'the economy is growing at the fastest rate of any in the world/Western world/ civilised world/EU/emerg- ing world' – without taking into account or making clear that the lower the base from which measurements are taken, the higher the percent- age growth rate is certain to be.

Product portfolios

In practice, organisations in all sectors sell particular prod- ucts and parts of their services at a loss. These losses can be quantified and demonstrated. Taken in isolation, this proof can be used by managers to accelerate the withdrawal of loss-making products and parts of services. In practice however, it is ability to buy overall satisfaction that draws customers to organisations. If organisations withdraw specific items because they do not individually make money, they may find customers going elsewhere; and this leads to loss of sales of items that are profitable.

In particular, this would be a serious problem to any organisation that has hitherto structured its products and services into those that attract, those that sell, and those that make money. A quantitative approach to sales figures in isolation would demonstrate that in many cases the attractive product was a loss maker. However, any attempts to withdraw the attractive product would have to be seen in terms of likely and possible adverse knock- on effects on the sales of the more profitable products and services.

- the effectiveness or otherwise of particular production and service delivery technologies
- the effectiveness or otherwise of particular information technologies
- the reliability and effectiveness of planning, forecasting and extrapolation processes (see below).

The reliability, accuracy and value of data are also affected by: time lapses between the gathering, evaluation and analysis of data; sampling errors; errors in mathemati- cal calculations; and misinterpretations. It is additionally necessary to recognise that data can, and does, produce inexplicable inconsistencies (see Management in Focus 13.3).

Additionally, it is necessary to have reliable and accurate data when considering specific problems and issues. Customer complaints, production, reject rates, staff complaints and information database deficiencies all require accurate analysis and evaluation to establish:

MANAGEMENT IN FOCUS 13.3

INEXPLICABLE INCONSISTENCIES

Supposedly inexplicable inconsistencies exist in practice in every area of activity; and the following examples reinforce the need for managers to analyse and evaluate all data in its full context before taking decisions:

Japanese cars and electrical goods

When the Japanese car and electrical goods manufacturing companies first arrived in the UK in the early 1970s, they were treated with scepticism and rejection. Data was produced by UK manufacturing associations that appeared to prove that local customers would continue to buy British, and this formed the basis for the 'I'm backing Britain' campaign. Data produced by the UK trade federations stated that up to 8 million customers would continue to buy British; and that they would never, in any circumstances, buy Japanese. When faced with the choice of UK and Japanese products, however, customers quickly found that the in-built reliability, quality and durability of the Japanese goods were of far greater value than a general pledge to continue to buy the indigenous product.

The privatisation hypothesis

Political drives in the UK and elsewhere to reduce the 'influence of the state', caused many nationalised industries and public utilities to be sold off to the private sector. Protagonists of the privatisation hypothesis stated that because these were essential industries and utilities, many organisations would be drawn into providing them, and this would lead to reductions in price and increases in quality. In practice, however, the reverse has occurred; the quality of utility provision has gone down, there are fewer companies involved than when the utilities were first privatised, and prices and charges have risen steeply.

The dot.com revolution

Quantitative analyses of Internet companies conducted over recent years have all come to the conclusion that for them to be enduringly viable, they had to offer products and services that would deliver separate and distinctive benefits not available through standard retail, wholesale and business-to-business outlets. None of this prevented rushes to invest in the fashion and fad of the 'Internet revolution' of the late 1990s; it still remains the case that any Internet initiative that looks viable will often gain support in advance of the production of a proven and quantifiable business case.

The ethical products hypothesis

Protagonists of the drive to provide 'ethical' products and services produced statistics to support the 'fact' that the overwhelming majority of the population would prefer to buy goods and services that have been produced by people working in companies that have the highest possible standards of employee relations, quality of working life and humanity of treatment. In practice, there remains no direct relationship between product and service consumption on the one hand, and the conditions under which the products and services were produced on the other. Asked to comment on this in early 2006, when introducing an 'ethical' range of clothing at Marks & Spencer, the company's Chief Executive, Stuart Rose, stated: 'This ethical range of clothing is an additional product, an additional string to our bow. Ethical products are not going to replace anything that we presently offer for sale.'

- the nature and frequency of the occurrence of defects and complaints
- the source of these defects and complaints – whether for example, they are all coming from one source, from one region, or spread across the entire board
- the time period over which the complaints have arisen, and any trends within these time periods – for example, whether complaints have suddenly started to be made, or whether they have risen or fallen on a regular basis, or whether the methods of logging them have changed (see Management in Focus 13.4).

Index numbers

Index numbers show at a glance the overall direction of changes in a variable over a period of time. These variables can be virtually any regularly produced statistic. Those most frequently referred to are: the Retail Prices Index (RPI), wholesale price index, unemployment rate, national output, The *Financial Times* Stock Exchange Indices of the top 30 and top 100 shares (FTSE 30 and 100), and exchange ratios. Industrial and commercial sectors also produce their own indices.

Bases are established, against which the subsequent movements are measured, in order to give accurate statistical variations. These bases are normally: time – a base year or date; percentage relatives – the most common of which are price, quantity or

MANAGEMENT IN FOCUS 13.4

CUSTOMER COMPLAINTS AND THE RAILWAY INDUSTRY

The UK railway industry has a bad reputation. While it is true that service levels, reliability, and quality have all declined at exactly the same time as prices have risen, there is no doubt that the volume of complaints received by the railway and train operating companies has been exacerbated by extensive negative media coverage and a series of high profile disasters.

This reinforces the need for structural investment, re-positioning of services, short-term attention to the specific complaints, and long-term strategic approaches to ensure that when the industry is renovated these complaints are removed altogether.

The railway operating companies have an extensive database of the nature and content of what causes customers to complain the most. In many ways, they have ignored the statistical evidence that they have available, and chosen to concentrate on what they can do. In the face of demands for reliability and services, and a basic level of comfort on the trains them- selves, they have chosen to do nothing until the railway infra- structure is renovated. This is likely to cause further upturns in the complaint volumes, and downturn in the perceived quality of service.

In linear terms, this may well be the right answer. In managerial terms, the problem is certain to be compounded by declining staff morale, the loss of good and committed members of staff, and the inability to attract the next generation to come and work in the industry.

value; and weighting – where more than one item or variable is used on one index. In the expression of indices, the base year, base percentage relative, and any base weighting are combined together and given a numerical value, a base number, against which future variations are to be expressed (see Figure 13.2).

Managers use indices produced by their own sectors to get information about wage rates and pay rises, marketing information, sectoral trends, wholesale prices, and energy, transport and distribution indicators. These are useful sources of information when looking at possible concerns and potential problems across the sector.

Managers use the various national indices as general sources of data and information. In particular, the annual rise in the RPI may give an indication of the level of wage rise likely to be demanded by the staff. Indices of wholesale price may be used as a starting point for a full investigation into the likely costs to be incurred over the coming period in the purchase of raw materials, or into inflationary pressures (usually) or sectors with which the organisation has trading and other commercial relationships. More generally still, the indices may indicate or imply such things as national or market confidence, recessionary pressures, or even 'green shoots' of recovery. Widely used in the media, indices are of limited value in practice (see Management in Focus 13.5).

Accuracy and approximation

As stated above, all data must be considered in the context of the method of collection, and any constraints present. The accuracy of the final data depends upon the soundness of the basis originally chosen. Other factors to be considered are time lag and rounding.

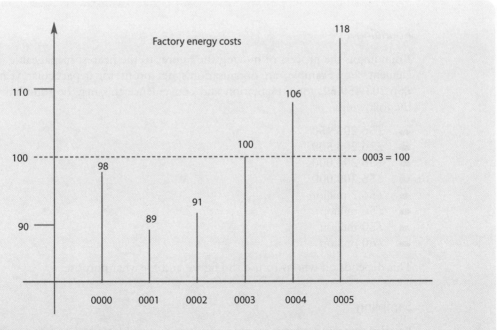

Figure 13.2 An index number

MANAGEMENT IN FOCUS 13.5

INDICES

Indices are used in general as 'evidence' to advance and support particular points of view. These points of view are usually partial, and the indices therefore misrepresented in support of a particular interest group. The Retail Prices Index (RPI) provides an example.

The Retail Prices Index and 'the going rate'

The going rate for pay rises is normally a reflection of the prevailing RPI. People in work require compensation for the loss in value of their earnings caused by inflation. People in work therefore use the RPI movement as the benchmark against which to judge whether or not they get a favourable pay rise. A pay rise above the present RPI is deemed to be a good one; a pay rise below it is deemed to be a bad one. Employees and their repre- sentatives consider that employers use the present RPI to keep pay rise levels as low as possible; employers and their representatives perceive that employees are using the RPI as a vehicle for driving levels of pay up.

The RPI does not measure inflation. It measures price movements in a standardised range of goods and services, giving a reflection and sample of price movements only.

Time lag

Time lag is the difference between the time when the information was collected and when it is to be used. Some statistics can therefore quickly become obsolete.

Rounding

Rounding is the process of moving the figures to the nearest manageable or useable element. For example, an organisation's net profit for a particular year may be £56,203,459.52; for presentation and convenience this may be rounded to any of the following:

- £56,203,450
- £56,203,500
- £56,204,000
- £56,200,000
- £56.2 million
- £56 million
- £50 million
- £60 million

This depends on who is to use the figure and for what purpose.

Sampling

In relation to most business activities it is impossible to gain perfect information; sound methods of sampling must be used if data of meaning and value is to be gathered. Effective sampling may be used to gain valid and accurate impressions of markets, products, volume and quality of work, the nature of the work being carried out, the complexities of it, the intensities of work activities, staff turnover and absenteeism, and the regularity and severity of accidents.

The purpose of sampling is to learn information about the whole from the study of a part, providing results that would mirror those that a full survey would produce.

Sampling methods

Any sample must be representative of the population, activity or product under consideration. This may be ensured by a variety of sampling methods.

- *Regular*: whereby each nth product is chosen for testing, or each nth person is chosen for survey of their his/her opinion.
- *Random*: whereby each person or product has an equal chance of being selected or tested. If a sample is chosen at random from a large group or collection, it will exhibit the same characteristics as the whole provided that both are sufficiently large collections in the first place. Random numbers may be used either as the starting point for this, or to select samples at each stage.
- *Stratified*: the grouping of populations and products into state or subgroups, according to the needs of the data being gathered. This may be by age, location, occupation, street, town, country, and urban or rural areas, for persons; or by date, time, shift and line, in the measurement of products.
- *Multi-stage*: the purpose of this is to provide a measure of checking on one sample, and to identify where bias and inconsistency may arise. In the normal course of events, the stages are:
  - piloting, to establish the fundamental soundness or otherwise of the methods to be used
  - the main survey, in which the main data will be gathered
  - a follow-up survey among those initially surveyed, to establish any inconsistencies, perceptual failings, anomalies and bias that may be present.
- *Non-random and the use of quotas*: this is most prevalent in street surveys, where an interviewer may be required to get the responses of 50 people on a particular day to a particular set of questions. It is subject to a substantial degree of error, being additionally limited by the perceptions of the interviewer, external pressures on interviewees, and other variables (e.g. was it carried out on a Sunday, was it in a town, city or village, where did the people interviewed come from?).

Questionnaire

Questionnaires are instruments for gaining information for particular purposes. They must therefore be designed with specific understood purposes, aims and objectives. If possible, they should be piloted or tested to check that they do fulfil these purposes, and to identify gaps and misperceptions.

The questions used may be open (see Management in Focus 13.6), where the subjects are invited to expand their responses in their own words or style on given matters. Such questions are led by words such as 'who', 'what', 'where', 'why', 'how' and 'when'. The responses to these may be limited by the use of rating scales which may be either numerical:

How important is it?   1   2   3   4   5
(please circle)

or verbal:

How important is it?   Very   Quite   Reasonably   Not very   Not at all
(please circle)

It is normal also to ascertain some background information on the respondents for the purposes of classification, and to indicate any bias or external factors that may be affecting responses. Otherwise, the questions will be closed, eliciting precise and definite answers from the respondents (see Management in Focus 13.6).

● Operational research

Operational research is the use of statistics and quantitative methods in informing approaches to problem solving. Operational research had its origins in military strategic planning, especially in relation to assessing acceptable levels of losses and casualties. In commercial and public service organisations, operational research is normally conducted by think tanks and quantitative analysis units. Problems are considered and models are constructed to represent the system or problem under consideration. Key variables are then introduced in order to present the quantitative aspects of a range of possible outcomes.

Operational research is of particular value in the following areas:

● *Blockage analysis*: blockages occur because organisational systems operate at the speed of the slowest part. Operational research is used to assess the effects of likely changes to the total process of the removal or repair of the blockage.

MANAGEMENT IN FOCUS 13.6

OPEN AND CLOSED QUESTIONS: EXAMPLES

Open

What do you like about Sweden?

Closed

(a) What I like about Sweden is: (tick box)

● the scenery   [ ]
● the public transport [ ]
● the food   [ ]

● other   [ ]
(please specify) . . . .
. . . .
. . . .
. . . .
. . . .
. . . .

(b) Do you like Swedish scenery?

Yes [ ]   No [ ]

This illustrates the range and limitation that can be placed on responses. The ways in which information is asked for can thus be varied according to overall need, and in order either to give the respondent maximum opportunity for self-expression, or to limit this to pre-set and predetermined areas.

- *Production*: operational research is used in ordering the sequences of work, tasks, jobs, machine pressures and loading, and order scheduling. It may also be used to model for profit maximisation, volume maximisation, income maximisation or market dominance.
- *Marketing*: the relationship between organisations and their markets; the consequences of introducing or reducing the volume and range of products available; the effects of steady-state activities – distribution; vehicle and mail shot scheduling; direct marketing activities. In more extreme cases, operational research may be used to model the effects of market saturation – or, at the opposite extreme, red-lining.
- *Queuing*: modelling the effects of increased customer flows, increased operations to reduce queues, and the effects such reductions will have on financial and other resources, and on the operations of the rest of the organisation. It is used to produce 'perfect models' of the optimum size of a particular part of the workforce concerned with managing and serving the queue.
- *Purchasing*: used to assess economic purchasing quantities; used to assess the differences between stockpiling and frequent regular deliveries; also used to assess the continuing relationship between the organisation and its sources of supplies.
- *Research and development*: used for example to produce analyses of the frequency with which new inventions become commercial products, of the effects of research and development on other activities, and of the priority of research and development activities.
- *Communication*: used to analyse the relationship between quality, volume and effectiveness of communications and other aspects – e.g. strikes and disputes, absence and turnover, accidents and misunderstandings. It may also be used to analyse the effectiveness of committee systems and meeting groups, and general quality of information dissemination.

The greatest problem with operational research methods and techniques is that they produce perfect models.

Managers must understand that in practice such perfection is never going to happen. A perfect model is only an indication of what would happen if everything was orderly and rational. In practice, nothing ever is. Again, therefore, the information thus produced is to be used, analysed and evaluated, not adopted as a certain prediction for future activities.

Forecasting, extrapolation and inference

Forecasting, extrapolation and inference are concerned with facing the future with as much certainty as possible in the circumstances. Each depends upon the availability of high-quality and usable information for its accuracy and reliability. Each brings a slightly different point of view to the same problem.

Forecasting is a prediction of the future based on knowledge and analysis of both the present and the past, and relating the two to the set of circumstances immediately foreseen. Forecasting further into the future is less certain. In managerial terms, it requires acknowledgement that business and commercial circumstances change and that operations and activities are affected by factors outside the managers' and organisation's control. These may include changes in customer behaviour and confidence, government activities, the entry of new players into the sector or the exit of players (especially a key player) from the sector, changes in production technology and changes in other technology.

Extrapolation is the linear projection of the future based on current and historic statistics. It is a key output of operational research. Its value is in identifying linear trends. These are produced by statisticians, economists and information scientists for use by managers in their decision-making processes. *It is not a decision-making process in itself.*

Inference is the assessment of the likely state of the future based on a lack of complete (sometimes a lack of adequate) information. Inference leans heavily on relating the experience of previous similar situations to the present, and using this as the basis for making judgements and choosing directions for the future.

Situational analysis (the basis of forecasting), the projection of statistics (extrapolation) and inference together form the quantitative basis for qualitative evaluation and analytical judgements to be made by managers when they consider future directions and activities. It follows from this that information must be as complete as possible and that managers must know how to use it. They must know what is proved by this information and what is indicated by this information, the difference between the two and the strength of that indication.

Above all, managers must recognise that just because something is forecast or extrapolated, that does not mean it will indeed come to pass. The probability of particular outcomes requires evaluation; and probability is normally supported by a fresh set of calculations and data analyses so as to predict the relative probabilities of each potential outcome from the range indicated. Additionally, serious problems always occur where forecasts are taken as future statements of absolute fact. Unwary managers, including senior managers, are always caught out when they allow themselves to be drawn into this way of thinking. Forecasts and extrapolations should be constantly updated, and changed in the light of changing circumstances, and especially environmental pressures.

Network analysis

Network analysis is the term used to summarise organisation scheduling, planning and control methods used in the ordering of complex projects and operational activities. The purpose is to identify in advance:

- the shortest possible time
- the longest possible time

in which activities or projects may be completed, or new products and services brought on-stream. From this, sub-schedules and activities are worked out to establish the nature and ordering of resources, staff, technology and other inputs that need to be present at given stages (see Figure 13.3).

The shortest and longest routes through such schedules are the critical paths. Critical incidents within the network will also be identified in advance. Incidents are normally classified according to such criteria as: difficulty; frequency; importance; value; scarcity and balance of resources; availability and conflicting demands on resources, expertise and equipment; and the consequences of delays on the critical incident to the rest of the schedule.

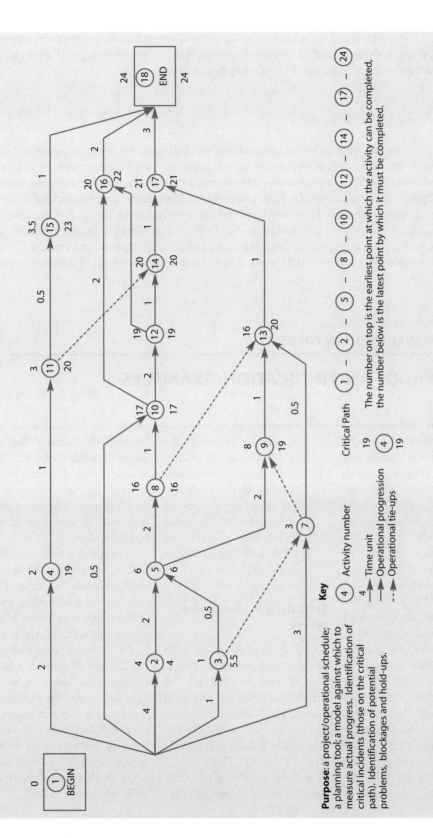

Purpose: a project/operational schedule; a planning tool; a model against which to measure actual progress. Identification of critical incidents (those on the critical path). Identification of potential problems, blockages and hold-ups.

Key

(4) Activity number

4 Time unit

→ Operational progression

--→ Operational tie-ups

Critical Path (1) – (2) – (5) – (8) – (10) – (12) – (14) – (17) – (24)

The number on top is the earliest point at which the activity can be completed, the number below is the latest point by which it must be completed.

Figure 13.3 A network diagram

Networks are used additionally as control mechanisms, progress monitors and progress chasers, and as a continuing method of monitoring and evaluating the whole series of activities and its component parts.

Proof and indication

Effective managerial use of information must distinguish between proof and indication. At one level, statistics can prove anything (see Management in Focus 13.2 above). This takes no account of the context or interrelationship between one set of figures, others, and the broader context (see Management in Focus 13.7).

From a managerial point of view, information and statistics are not therefore to be seen in isolation. They complete (or help to complete) a broader picture which consists at least in part of qualitative and behavioural aspects. Information, however complete, does not of itself make decisions or solve problems. Problems, especially,

MANAGEMENT IN FOCUS 13.7

PROOF AND INDICATION: EXAMPLES

- *Cars*: a car dealership which sells 10 per cent of its expensive models and 100 per cent of its cheap models must take into account the likelihood (and the extent of the likelihood) that it has only sold all of its cheap models because the customers were first attracted by the expensive.
- *Hospitals*: an indication of hospital workload is likely to be the number of patients treated. If this rises by 20 per cent it proves increased workload. Again, this cannot be seen in isolation, and factors which would always have to be considered include: the number of patients

returning for extended courses of treatment; for re-treatment following unsatisfactory treatment the first time round; and the number of patients attracted to the hospital following closure of other facilities elsewhere in the region.

Statistics and managerial action

A car dealership faced with the statistics indicated above, may choose to discount the unsold models, as proof of managerial action. Broader evaluation of whether the product is indeed price sensitive, whether there is a slowdown in the market for these models, and whether

there is an increase in competitive activity for the range of models of which this is one, would need to be carried out in advance of ascertaining whether price discounting was indeed the right decision.

A hospital whose workload had increased by 20 per cent might choose to extend its capacity by purchasing more trolleys, opening more wards and engaging more staff. This again demonstrates managerial activity. However, a fuller evaluation of why the workload had gone up by 20 per cent, and the components of the workload increase, would need to be evaluated in full detail, before ascertaining whether this was indeed the right decision to take.

are always bounded by a combination of information, deadlines and consequences – it is therefore certain that normally the solution to problems will be 'the best answer available on the day'. Information provides a basis (indeed part of the basis) for this approach. This is ultimately carried out on the basis of the manager's judgement, analysis, evaluation and choice. It does follow that the greater the volume of relevant and useful information available, the greater the propensity, rationally, for effective and successful analysis – and therefore accurate decisions and effective solutions to problems.

Management information systems

Management information systems exist to provide information that is as complete and as useful as possible in relation to organisation, collective and individual priorities and requirements. Management information systems are a combination of:

- data gathering, storage and retrieval facilities
- electronic capability, storage and transmission, including Internet and intranet access
- archives and filing systems
- library and data management services.

Management information systems are supported and developed through the use of enhanced technological and physical capacity. The content of the systems is enhanced and updated through constant flows of data and information to and from, and within, the organisation. As stated above, this information comes from a variety of sources.

Each of the above elements is more or less universally present, though the size, complexity and nature of the data stored clearly vary greatly according to the size and structure of particular organisations.

Management information systems are ultimately only effective and efficient if they can be used according to need and want by everybody concerned. This means ensuring that the mix of access and security is addressed and evaluated for each user and group of users; and this in turn means that:

- Technological and electronic systems have to be easy and convenient to use. Effective capability in using the system always requires support through staff training and development.
- Archives and physical storage of documents and papers must be made available to those who need them, without compromising the security of historic as well as current and recent papers.

It is certain that management information systems require enhanced capacity and upgrades from time to time. Critical choices are required as to the following:

- Whether to replace electronic systems, or to enhance the capacity of those presently in use. If existing systems are to be improved then there is the question of whether to integrate new elements with the existing ones, or to operate a separate system alongside what is currently present. There is nothing intrinsically wrong with either approach, provided that the opportunities and constraints are clearly understood before the decision is taken. The normal position is to ensure that everything is capable of full integration. However, this is not always feasible in practice especially if this means having existing systems out of action for some time.

- Whether to outsource data management and other information systems. The advantage of outsourcing is that, in return for a fee, there are no daily organisational and managerial issues that have to be handled; the disadvantage is that a measure of control over the integrity and security of the system is inevitably lost.

Whatever is implemented must be capable of use by all those involved. The normal approach is to provide generic technology and access systems both for electronic and paper information. This is underpinned by structures and requirements based on identity, passwords and electronic and physical access processes and procedures.

Management information systems require confidentiality and security procedures. These procedures exist to ensure that access to sensitive confidential material, especially concerning personal and financial records, is restricted to named and designated individuals.

Electronic and physical systems must be as secure as possible to prevent the prospect of hacking, theft and data corruption, both from outside and from within the organisation. Additionally, electronic systems require sufficient intrinsic stability to be able to withstand power cuts and surges.

Ideally, all management information systems should be designed to meet the specific demands of the particular organisation. Otherwise, off-the-shelf software and generic hardware each require full pre-evaluation, to ensure that it will be capable of being modified to suit the needs of the particular organisation once installed (see Management in Focus 13.8).

Validity and reliability

Managers need to know and understand the basis on which specific information has been gathered if they are to use it successfully and effectively. It is therefore necessary to know and understand what methods were used to gather, store, analyse and evaluate particular information, and any shortcomings that either were present at the time when the information was gathered, or have subsequently been found to be present. Managers therefore need to know and understand the strength of the data and information from the point of view of:

- *Validity*: the extent to which the data and information prove, imply or indicate what was intended; if the data is invalid, this means it cannot be used to prove, indicate or imply the conclusions drawn.
- *Reliability*: the extent to which the data supports a single set of results only; or the extent to which the data can be relied on to support the fact or belief that the results would have been the same, wherever and whenever the information was gathered.

The strength, reliability and validity of data and information require specific attention to the following:

- the basis on which the information was gathered and any specific constraints that were imposed, such as time pressures, size of samples and access/lack of access to sources of information

MANAGEMENT IN FOCUS 13.8

MANAGEMENT INFORMATION SYSTEMS AT CLARK AND CROSBY PLC

Clark and Crosby Plc is a medium-sized manufacturing company employing 1100 staff across six sites in the north of England. The company manufactures metal casings for white goods, filing cabinets, video cassette and DVD players, and safes and strongboxes.

Until three years ago, invoices were processed by hand using a team of six clerks. Each clerk would simply work through a pile of invoices so that customers were billed directly the goods were sent from the factory.

Three years ago, an electronic system was introduced. The capacity of the electronic system meant that it was only possible for each clerk to process 20 invoices per day. Within six months of implementation, a backlog amounting to two months' work had built up. This in turn meant that Clark and Crosby had to engage a further six invoicing clerks, and open new work-stations for each of them.

The system had been designed and implemented by IT consultants who had simply installed a generic system without reference to the volume of work required in the particular set of circumstances. Accordingly, Clark and Crosby suffered serious cashflow problems; this led to having to pay for an extended overdraft facility, as well as the employment of additional staff and the purchase of the new work-stations.

- the context in which the information was gathered – the extent to which it was directed or prescribed; what information has not been taken into account (for whatever reason); who requested the information and why; what, if anything, it is intended to prove or indicate; what it actually proves or indicates
- expert conclusions drawn by statisticians, mathematicians and information systems experts and their impact on managerial judgement, evaluation and analysis
- uses to which the information may legitimately be put; uses to which it may not legitimately be put; the extent to which it is legitimate to use for other purposes information that was gathered for one purpose
- the wider context – the general extent to which the information may be used; its place in the overall scheme of things; the effects – both positive and negative – of taking one piece of information in isolation from others (see Management in Focus 13.9).

It is also important to recognise the difference between what can and cannot be controlled. Where organisations have to deal with factors outside their control, the best approach is to gather as much information as possible, to know as much as possible about those factors that are outside their control, and to cover the range of possible outcomes on the basis of the spectrum shown in Figure 13.4.

MANAGEMENT IN FOCUS 13.9

THE GENERABLY FAVOURABLE RESPONSE

It is very easy to generate generally favourable responses (GFR). This is achieved as follows:

Example: marketing (upon the launch of a new product)

Interviewer: Do you like this product?

Subject: Yes

Interviewer: How would you rate it on a scale of 1-10, where 10 is the most favourable?

Subject: About 7.

Interviewer: Would you use it?

Subject: Yes, I would.

Asking questions in this way is comfortable and reinforcing. But it is fraught with danger. Not enough follow-up information is demanded. It is certain to be clouded by:

- perceptions of what the rating scale means – different to every individual
- the likeness – the subject will not wish to offend the interviewer

- the question: 'Would you use?' – very different from: 'Will you use?' and 'And if so, how often?'

Example: staff references

Many organisations send out pro forma questionnaires to previous employers of potential employees. A common question on these is: 'Would you re-employ?', to which there is a range of GFRs, including: yes, yes if a suitable vacancy were to arise, probably, possibly, maybe, and so on.

The question is never framed as: 'Will you re-employ?' or: 'Will you re-employ if a suitable vacancy comes up?'

The problem is bad enough in the latter case. In the former, the question is incapable of validation as it is based entirely on a set of personal perceptions (on the part of the responder) to a future hypothetical situation.

Example: questionnaire structuring

More insidiously still, GFRs are achieved through careful

combinations of ostensibly direct, but actually leading, questions. It is, for example, used by political parties in the pursuit of a vested interest as follows:

Question 1: Do you believe that crimes against children should be stopped?

Question 2: Do you believe that those who carry out crimes against children should be punished?

Question 3: Do you believe that society should clean up those who carry out these crimes?

Question 4: Will you support the death penalty?

The effect is at least threefold. It leads people down a particular direction involving them in the desired train of thought. It produces (in fact) subjective answers to (overtly) rational questions. It makes overtly rational, but actually spurious, connections between questions 1–3 and question 4. And it is the answer to question 4 (not 1–3) that is then used by the vested interest.

Information currency

The other main issue to be addressed is the currency of the information. In general, circumstances change rapidly and information quickly becomes obsolete. To be effective, systems have to be kept up to date so that whatever is withdrawn and analysed is current.

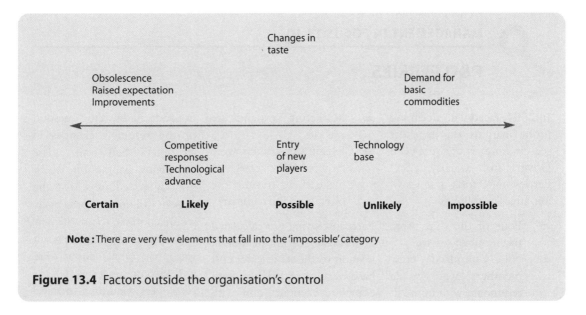

Figure 13.4 Factors outside the organisation's control

This applies in all spheres. A company may be overtaken in production design, capability and quality by its competitors, and the organisation needs to know this in order to be able to respond. Human resource systems must be kept up to date about qualifications, length of service, employee history and staff capability. Marketing information must reflect current, not recent, states of the segments and niches in which activities are carried out. Sales information must reflect the current state of activities if there is to be any chance of effective forecasting, extrapolation and inference for the future.

Otherwise, the main conclusion to be drawn here relates to the managerial constructs that are to be placed on the quantitative data and information. This consists of ensuring that both the information and the methods used to collect, store and present it are suitable for the purposes of the organisation and the needs of the managers also. All quantitative data is only of value if it is available in ways that the organisation and those within it can understand and use. This must include the behavioural and perceptual aspects of it as well as the quantitative material itself. Above all, managers must have confidence in both the budgeting information that they receive and the systems that produce it if these are to have in themselves any credence or organisational value.

● Conclusions

Hannagan (1998) states that: 'the principal function of statistics and quantitative approaches to management is to narrow the area of disagreement that would otherwise exist in a discussion, and in that way help in decision making.' The key areas are:

- the rigour with which data is gathered
- the purposes for which it is gathered; and this is a particular problem when using secondary data and non-specified sources of information
- the uses to which the data is to be put once it is analysed.

The problem for managers lies in their ability to be able to coordinate each of these

MANAGEMENT IN FOCUS 13.10

P&O FERRIES

In 2004, faced with declining profit margins on its short sea-crossing route between Dover and Calais, P&O Ferries undertook a series of initiatives as follows:

● Four of the ships were taken out of service.
● Nine hundred crew members were made redundant with immediate effect; with a further 900 to leave by the end of the following year.

● Marketing expenditure was cut.
● Existing customers were targeted in order to try to make them travel more often with the company.

Each cost saving was calculated in full detail. Income margins in relation to the new, lower cost base were projected, also with complete accuracy, and with reference to as full a range of possible outcomes as possible.

The one tiny flaw that was not addressed was the question of the resultant changes in customer behaviour. The underlying assumption, which nobody tested, was that the present volumes of passengers would continue to use the new and reduced service. The result was that while costs were indeed cut, income fell as passengers continued to travel at times suitable and convenient to themselves, rather than continuing to travel with P&O.

elements. If they are required to use data that is flawed, the first step must be to acknowledge its imperfections. This need not necessarily be a basis for not going ahead, but it should reinforce the need to constantly review and update data, as well as progression once the decision is taken.

The context in which data is gathered is also important. If people are asked what is wrong with something, they will tend to respond by seeking and reporting faults. If people are asked for their comments on something, unless they know the precise nature of the comments required, they will stick to blandnesses, rather than present something with which they are not entirely confident. If people want a particular result from statistical and quantitative analysis, they tend to ignore anything that dilutes or disproves the point. If statistics indicate a tiny flaw in a line of reasoning, then in practice this is often ignored (see Management in Focus 13.10).

Managers do not need to be mathematical experts. However, they are required to be experts in the analysis and evaluation of information, and in their ability to question that which they do not fully understand or recognise. They must also be receptive to those who are expert in these disciplines, when they explain the results. Above all, when statistical and quantitative analyses indicate the need for particular courses of action, managers should be prepared to engage in them.

CRITICAL THINKING, ANALYSIS AND EVALUATION

1. What statistical measures should be used by a department store to indicate that it had:
   - serious customer complaint problems

– serious problems with suppliers

      – serious staff morale problems?

2.   What primary research should be carried out in order to assess the reasons for reject rates on a food production line?

3.   What statistical measures should be used to assess the commercial viability of an organisational website? What would these measures show, and what would they not show?

4.   What are the dangers of having a) too little; b) too much information available in any set of circumstances.

DEVELOPING MANAGEMENT SKILLS AND EXPERTISE

LEVI STRAUSS

In recent years, Levi Strauss has looked at ways of diversifying away from its heavy dependence on a jeans market that it perceived to be saturated. The company has tried introducing shoes, shirts and socks. These sold quite well among people who were already buying Levi jeans. A more recent initiative was to move into the market for higher-priced clothes, in order to attract a new type of customer to the Levi Strauss brand. As menswear had always been the company's biggest seller, it was decided to concentrate on the male market first.

As the 'Type 2 Classic Independent' men fitted in with Levi's objective, a research company was asked to computer-analyse the findings so that the behaviour and attitudes of this specific group could be split out from the rest of the sample. The large total number of interviews made it possible to have confidence in the reliability of the data from this sub-sample. It emerged that Type 2 men wanted traditionally styled, perhaps pin-striped, suits; that they liked to buy through independent clothes shops or tailors, rather than at department stores; and that they liked to shop alone, whereas others liked having their wives/girlfriends with them.

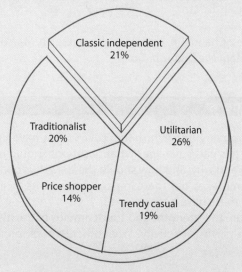

Menswear market segmentation

To tackle this segment of the market, Levi's decided to introduce 'Tailored Classics', a range of high-quality wool suits, trousers and jackets. The research showed that Type 2 buyers valued quality and fit rather than low prices, the company decided to price its range 10 per cent above that of the competition. To avoid direct product comparisons – and to ensure that not too large a sales force was needed – Levi chose to distribute through department store chains.

Having decided on this strategy, its acceptability to the target market was tested via a series of group discussions. These were conducted by a psychologist who was to look for the real motivations behind respondents' opinions or behaviour. The psychologist reported that the Type 2 men had two misgivings: first, they were concerned that the garments would be in standard fittings, and so would not provide the tailoring they wanted; second, although they could believe that Levi's could make a good suit, they still felt uncomfortable about the Levi name. One said: 'When I think Levi, I think jeans – if they're making suits I have to be convinced.'

Another felt that: 'If I went to work and someone said: "Hey, that's a good suit, Joe, who's it by?" – I wouldn't feel comfortable saying Levi'.

The company's marketing executives responded to this by deciding to concentrate on the separate jackets and trousers in the launch advertising, and let suits 'slipstream'. The Director of Consumer Marketing felt certain that:

> The thing that's going to overcome Levi's image for casualness as no other thing can is a suit that's made by Levi that doesn't look like all the other things we've made. Once that gets on the racks people will put an asterisk on the image that says: Oh, and they can also make a good suit when they put their mind to it.

Soon after this decision, salesmen started contacting retail buyers. After four months of selling to the trade, it was clear that the range's sales targets would not be met. Even a price cut did little to redeem the situation, and Tailored classics achieved only 65 per cent of its modest sales targets.

Levi's could only find consolation if they could learn why they went so badly wrong.

Sources: Channel 4: commercial breaks; Ian Marcouse (1990) *Business Case Studies*, Longman; *The Financial Times*.

● Questions

1. What primary research should Levi Strauss have undertaken before deciding to go down this particular line? What questions should have been asked, to whom, when, where and why; and how should the data thus gathered have been analysed?
2. What mistakes did the company make in its forecasting and extrapolating? How might these have been avoided?
3. What are the strengths and shortcomings of the market segmentation method used for this particular activity? What other form of segmentation might have been used?

Chapter fourteen

Product and service development and innovation

'We provide what people want, good quality, at reasonable prices.'
Michael Marks, Marks & Spencer, quoted in
M. Sieff, *Marcus Sieff on Management: The Marks & Spencer Way* (1990)

'We provide what people want at the best possible prices.'
Michael O'Leary, CEO of Ryanair, 2003.

'If it works, we learn from it and move on. And if it does not work, we learn from it and move on.'
Ricardo Semler, 2006.

Chapter outline

- Introduction
- Dreams and imagination
- Myths and legends
- Failure
- Research and development
- Market research and development
- New product and service development
- Innovation planning
- Monitoring, review and evaluation
- Attention to detail
- Conclusions

Chapter objectives

After studying this chapter, you should be able to:

- understand the position, priority and value of generating new ideas, products and services

- understand the nature of investment required to do this, both in financial terms and with reference to the need for other resources, including personal energy and commitment

- understand the position of research and development in terms of long-term organisational profitability, effectiveness and viability

- understand the importance of developing innovating and entrepreneurial attitudes in all organisations.

Introduction

All innovation, development and enterprise is dependent upon the combination of creativity, inventiveness and imagination, with professional knowledge, understanding and expertise, and the availability of, or potential for, sufficient resources to be gathered together. This applies equally to:

- new product and service developments in existing organisations
- new ventures and changes of market conducted by existing organisations
- product and service regeneration by those taking on moribund and under-performing companies, products and services and making them effective
- re-packaging and re-branding existing products and services
- design and presentation improvements in products and services
- research and development experts working in all fields, in both new and existing organisations and ventures
- translating the work of university research departments and other specialists into products and services that can be commercialised
- think-tanks and project groups charged with developing new initiatives and ventures
- technological and market transformations.

It is also essential that all managers and supervisors undertake to improve both the ways of working and the outputs of their own particular areas of responsibility. All managers are therefore required to have some measure of innovative expertise. Managers are also increasingly expected to be able to analyse and evaluate new ideas, proposals, initiatives – and daydreams – for potential, feasibility and commercialisation; this may be acceptable within the organisation, or it may have to be carried out in the face of extensive opposition (see Management in Focus 14.1).

New ideas and potential innovations and developments are the beginning of hard, targeted and thorough work, and not an end in themselves. This, in turn, is certain to lead to financial and other resource commitments. For example, Sony has always taken the view that once an idea is adopted, then it is pursued with 100 per cent commitment. If for any reason the venture is not fully realisable or a commercial success, Sony believes that nevertheless lessons will have been learned, expertise and technology developed, and a greater body of knowledge and understanding will exist within the corporation as a result, on which the next set of ventures and therefore the long-term future, will be built (see Management in Focus 14.2).

For all innovation and enterprise, whatever the organisation and sector, the following are required:

- dreams and imagination
- research and development activities
- market and marketing research and development
- product and service development, innovation, improvement and enhancement; including the more nebulous concept of 'idea development'
- business planning, to combine the disciplines of strategy, marketing, finance and operations
- administration planning, to combine the need for speed and quality of operations and processes, with deliverability to market
- champions, product, service and project leaders, and the drive, energy, leadership, enthusiasm and vision necessary to transform ideas into reality.

MANAGEMENT IN FOCUS 14.1

SWATCH

For centuries, the European wristwatch industry had been dominated by small factories and producers in Switzerland. Between them, these factories used to produce a large volume of differentiated products, heavily branded and relatively expensive.

The wristwatch industry was transformed by Seiko and Casio, two Japanese companies that produced calculators. The two companies found that they were able, with little difficulty, to adjust the technology used for calculator manufacture to make cheap wristwatches; and these wristwatches were fully accurate.

Seiko and Casio brought their watch range on-stream in the late 1960s. Within ten years, the Swiss watch industry had lost three-quarters of its market.

The Swiss watch industry created a consortium. With the backing of UBS, the Swiss bank, it appointed Nicolas Hayek to advise. Hayek, a Swiss national originally from Lebanon, assessed the whole industry. He concluded that the Swiss watch industry could be revived and that it could, and should, remain in Switzerland. He proposed:

● maintaining the top-value brands such as Piaget, and maintaining the mid-range brands, such as Omega
● creating a cheap/good-value brand as a basis on which to compete with Casio and Seiko.

The basis on which this would be achieved was to be created and developed in Switzerland. In spite of the extremely high land values and labour charges, Mr Hayek was confident that he could create production facilities that could compete effectively on cost with Casio and Seiko.

Unsure of this, UBS and the Swiss watch industry asked Mr Hayek to invest in the venture himself. There was an additional problem in that Casio and Seiko were now beginning to build factories in China, thus giving them an overtly even greater cost advantage.

Mr Hayek put up 50 per cent of the capital. The production technology was of a sufficient quality to produce fully accurate components, many of which were generic and could be used in every product range.

At the bottom end of the market, the presentation and delivery of the Swatch range was distinctively different from the digital appearance of Seiko and Casio. The Swatch range was developed using different materials, colour schemes, designs and decorations. Anyone wanting a cheap wristwatch had therefore a clear choice: if they wanted the digital presentation, they would continue to use Casio and Seiko; if they wanted anything else, Swatch provided a clear alternative.

Investment in top-quality, fully accurate and very productive component technology meant that the manufacture of the watches was cheaper in Switzerland than in the Far East. Through continued attention to branding and product development, Swatch quickly gained its own identity, and the mid-range and top range brands maintained both their identity and also their perceptions of exclusivity. By the early 1990s, the Swiss watch industry was fully revived, and able to compete in all sections of the market on price, cost, value and brand. The watches were also as accurate as those produced by Casio and Seiko.

Nicolas Hayek achieved this in the face of the doubts of UBS, as noted above; and he also successfully challenged the received wisdom that cost-effective production was only possible in the Far East. Subsequently, Swatch has opened production facilities in China; however, this has not led to any closures in Switzerland.

MANAGEMENT IN FOCUS 14.2

A NOTE ON THE DOT.COM REVOLUTION

Investment in Internet companies is driven by the real and perceived opportunity to take advantage of the huge volume of information available on the Worldwide Web on the one hand, and the equally vast potential access afforded by computer and telecommunications technology to customer bases on the other. Consequently, Internet companies operating over the period 1998–2000 were able to attract both corporate and individual investors to make substantial investments. For example, LastMinute.com, the online travel and airline ticket sales company, was able in March 2000 to attract investment of £850 million at a time when its annual turnover was £1.6 million with an annual operating loss of £24 million.

In 2004, LastMinute.com merged with Thomas Cook, the long-established and very traditional retail travel agent. LastMinute.com's products and services are now sold through Thomas Cook travel agency outlets, and Thomas Cook's products and services are now available on the Internet, using LastMinute.com's Internet reach and brand awareness.

This reinforces the need to have real customers, spending real money on real products and services.

Yet the pursuit of real customers, spending real money, on real products and services, came late to then Internet revolution. Anthony Impey, General Manager of Optimity Plc, stated:

Investment in Internet opportunities and the dot.com revolution represents 0.5 per cent of total investment volumes only. Of the first wave of companies floated on the stock exchange, 97 per cent are expected not to exist in their present form in five years' time. Many will fail; others will merge; others still, will be taken over. Of those that do still exist at the end of the period, a similar shake-out is expected over the following five years.

He went on to put forward the view that when – not if – a fall in values came around, it would be the entrepreneurs themselves and small private investors, not big institutions, who would lose their investment.

● Dreams and imagination

All ideas, great and small, start with imagination, or 'what if?' approaches – from 'What if I could reduce each task in the office by five minutes per day?' to 'What if I could operate my own shipping line?'

Most ideas are rejected at this stage; yet interest and creative processes have been aroused. The point is to ensure that all managers are encourage to think like this as a part of the pursuit of overall business organisational and operational excellence, and their own contribution to this. All managers should also be encouraging their staff to think in these ways.

Managers ought to think like this all of the time. All managers ought to have time and space available in their working schedules to work on improvements and developments; this is reinforced if they are given performance targets to achieve in this area.

Requiring this of managers creates a culture of advancement and development, and this is extremely effective when trying to convince others of the value of new ideas. Even small changes in office procedures are certain to be more acceptable if they respond to the staff's dream of a less stressful or more productive working day. This form of approach then becomes the basis for involving everyone in brainstorming activities, work improvement and suggestion schemes. These approaches should always lead at least to general discussions; they ought to lead to serious analysis and evaluation, projections and forecasts, leading in turn to acceptance or rejection (see Management in Focus 14.3).

● Myths and legends

Peters (1996) states that: 'all new ideas come from the wrong people, in the wrong location, in the wrong line of business, at the wrong time. If you thought about this rationally, you would never start.' It is certainly true that far too many organisations preach empowerment and development without practising it. Any attempt at genuine innovation is smothered by rank, status and hierarchy, or put into the corporate mill and never heard of again. At the other extreme, those with status and influence are known, believed or perceived to get pet schemes off the ground on the basis of being seen to have the ability to command resources, or because they have the need for a political triumph.

Breaking free of organisational myths and legends requires courage. For those who have genuine ideas that they wish to try and develop, the two main approaches are as follows:

● to work on the idea using as much time, flexibility and resources as the organisation will allow; and if the present organisation cannot, or will not, accommodate this, then to find one which will

● to establish the idea as a business – possibly at first as a hobby on evenings, weekends and free time until it becomes clear that the idea does have commercial

MANAGEMENT IN FOCUS 14.3

ACCEPTANCE AND REJECTION

People need to know and understand what has been accepted and rejected, and the reasons. Within all organisations, and whatever the idea, this first part of the process has to be conducted with absolute integrity. It is extremely damaging to motivation and morale, as well as long-term organisational commitment and operational well-being, if ideas are overtly rejected but actually stolen by those in higher authority and claimed as their own.

Many organisations run extremely successful suggestion schemes. These only work well if there is a tangible return when implemented to the person or group that dreamed them up. This also encourages others to adopt the same approach. Properly managed, this is an extremely valuable and effective method of organisation development and enhancement, because it involves everyone as a matter of course.

potential; or to establish a company straightaway, the purpose of which is to commercialise the idea, and which will clearly fail if the idea is not, or cannot be, commercially viable (see Management in Focus 14.4).

⬤ Failure

The fear of failure is a strong cultural and behavioural barrier, especially in the UK. This is quite apart from the fact that it clearly has economic consequences. People collectively do not like to have to admit to failure, and will seek excuses for it, above all to absolve themselves from any responsibility or contribution when things go wrong (see Management in Focus 14.5).

⬤ Research and development

Research and development comes in many forms. It is an essential feature of all innovation, progress and enhancement, and takes two basic forms:

- *Pure research and development*: to find out what exists, how and why things work, how and why they could be made to work better, the opportunities and consequences of combining elements, materials, matter, information and process in an infinite number of ways. The purity of this kind of research is maintained by ensuring that it is 'untainted' by any commercial or personal gain. It is then up to others to decide what the various results can be used for, whether they can be used at all, or whether they simply add to the fund of knowledge. This approach to research and development is becoming increasingly rare. Even university postgraduate and postdoctoral students are being increasingly steered in the direction of things that have a real or potential commercial spin-off.
- *Applied research and development*: where, at the very least, a commercial spin-off is anticipated. Applied research and development is now undertaken widely because there is known or strongly believed to be a direct opportunity to commercialise the results. The consequence of this is that the broader approach is often lost. For example, medical research is heavily concentrated on curing diseases rather than health promotion, because there is a ready and tangible market for the products that emerge as the result, rather than one that is nebulous and intangible, if still essential. Computer consulting is driven by the ability to solve particular problems, rather than concentrating on improved software design and capability. Management consultants depend heavily on their ability to sell business process re-engineering, total quality management, and other branded tangible solutions, rather than conducting rigorous organisational research to assess where problems truly lie.

⬤ Market research and development

Anyone wishing to commercialise anything that is genuinely or perceptually new must take whatever time and steps are necessary to ensure that there is an enduring

MANAGEMENT IN FOCUS 14.4

FOOL'S GOLD

The main pitfall at the early stage of any new product, service or venture development is that of 'fool's gold' or the 'absolute certainty'. Once an idea has been given life, it becomes 'an absolute certainty' that it will work, and that it will make a fortune. In practice however, there is never an absolute certainty, foolproof scheme or product and service without which people cannot do. The world existed before the new idea and will continue to exist after the particular venture has run its course.

This has not prevented the following from taking place:

● *Internet ventures*: many Internet ventures were based on little rigorous business or managerial analysis. Supported and fuelled by extensive media coverage, business legends claimed that: all you needed to do was design a website and people would queue to buy it for millions; if you were not in the Internet industry, you were nobody; the collapse of traditional ways of conducting business was both certain and imminent.

● *Football ventures*: following large increases in tele-vision and sponsorship money, business legends were that: all you needed to do was to buy the best players, hire the best coach, and the results would be forthcoming; if you were not in the football industry, you were nobody; the football industry was glamorous and high profile, and these features were ends in themselves.

In these cases, and others, the assumptions were substituted for rigorous business analysis. The result was that, with very few exceptions, the initiatives and ventures failed.

MANAGEMENT IN FOCUS 14.5

ATTITUDES TO FAILURE

Following the success of the London Millennium celebrations on 31 December 1999, it was determined to have a giant New Year's Eve party every year. However, during the autumn of the year 2000, it became apparent that there would be difficulties both with transport and with the provision of medical emergency and policing services.

On 1 December 2000, the government minister for London Transport, Keith Hill, announced that the party would have to be cancelled. Ken Livingstone, the Mayor of London, stated that the only reason that the festivities would have to be cancelled was because of the government's dislike of him personally; Keith Hill responded by saying that Livingstone was using his own personal popularity to whip up support for something that could not be carried out properly.

In this case, as in many others, individuals apportion blame to events or personalities outside their control, and so seek absolution for being associated with failure.

market, and that customers and clients will buy it because of the utility and benefit that it brings to them.

Most businesses and innovations that fail at an early stage do so because they do not fully assess their markets or the capability and willingness of customers to pay adequate price levels. The vast majority of dot.com company failures are directly attributable to the fact that they mistook genuine interest in the Internet for market certainty; yet they would be the first to understand that people who take a genuine interest in old steam engines seldom actually buy one.

This applies to all sectors. There is always room for those who bring real and differentiated alternatives to that which exists already, provided that:

● The benefits and utility offered are those that customers and clients want and are prepared to pay for.
● The location is sufficiently convenient to the proposed or target market.
● The wider behavioural issues are understood, especially in terms of the relationship between price, real and perceived quality and value, expectations and satisfaction.
● Customers get at least what they expect (even if they do not quite know what this may be until they get it).
● The product or service envisaged is capable of being presented and marketed in a real or perceived differentiated way. If this is to be done on price alone, then the particular organisation has to be absolutely certain that it can if necessary sustain a long-term price war with large, well-established existing players. If this cannot be done on price alone, then other approaches have to be taken (see Management in Focus 14.6).

Customer volumes have to be sufficient to allow the development of a loyal, active base capable of sustaining long-term, profitable, effective activity. Where a loyal base is not available, then others have to be considered. If passing trade is all that is available, then passing interest must be capable of development into active interest. If mercenaries are sought, then the price advantage must be capable of sustenance, without compromise on quality or value. If repeat business is sought or assumed, then the regularity, frequency and income volume per customer must be assessed on the basis of what is required and essential, what is likely, what is possible, and what circumstances may cause this to change. If one-offs only are being provided (e.g. once in a lifetime holidays) then there must be sufficient numbers of potential customers in this situation who can be turned into real customers on the regularity required.

New product and service development

New product and service development is normally targeted as follows:

● Existing products and services, differentiated by new organisations in the same and other sectors.
● New products and services for existing markets and sectors.
● Existing products and services for new markets. These may have to be differentiated in some way in order to preserve the satisfaction levels of existing customers and clients (see Management in Focus 14.7).

MANAGEMENT IN FOCUS 14.6

MARKET RESEARCH AND INNOVATION: EXAMPLE

When John Gray was made redundant from his job in the City of London, he and his wife Jane took a holiday in the New Forest. They loved the location, and with John's redundancy money could afford to move there. On the first day of their holiday, they drove around the area, and resolved to have fish and chips for their supper.

They found only one fish and chip shop. They queued for hours, only to receive a small, over-priced and poor-quality meal. Discussing the matter later, they decided there was a potential business opportunity. Accordingly, for the rest of their holiday, they worked – researching the market, alternative provisions, and above all, the cost of premises. They found that

there was indeed an insatiable demand among regular visitors, as well as locals, for high-quality convenience food of this kind. The only problem was the price of property, which made it overtly prohibitively expensive to open this kind of venture to any sort of quality.

However, further research strongly suggested that the product was highly quality sensitive – but not at all price sensitive. Holidaymakers had a high propensity to spend, provided that the quality could be assured.

Accordingly, some months later, John and Jane opened their fish and chip shop in a small town in the centre of the New Forest. Because of the need to make returns on their investment, the prices that

they charged were substantially higher than those offering alternatives in the area. However, they compensated for this by serving huge portions, well presented, and cooked to a high standard. During the main holiday seasons at Easter and the summer, people would drive from all over the New Forest, and were prepared to queue, just in order to receive an excellent meal.

Not long afterwards, the Grays were visited by a deputation from the local Chamber of Commerce. These people wanted to know how it was possible for such a business to 'buck the trend' at a time when all of their market research had suggested that everything was price sensitive.

Product and service extensions are also considered as follows:

- In products, for example after-sales, maintenance and finance plans; guaranteed trade-ins and upgrades; the ability to buy add-ons and accessories.
- In services, the provision of peripherals as standard and all-inclusive.
- Demonstrable improvements in quality, value, convenience and price. This has to be supported by precise market targeting, so that customers and clients know in advance what they are to receive in the future is better than in the past (see Management in Focus 14.8).

Once at least one of these conditions has been satisfied, a precise and rigorous evaluation of the proposal, product or service needs to take place. Again, this applies to new companies and ventures, new products and services from existing companies, and improvements to processes, procedures and functions. The initial line of enquiry consists of answering as many of the following questions as positively as possible.

MANAGEMENT IN FOCUS 14.7

NEW PRODUCT AND SERVICE DEVELOPMENT: EXAMPLES

● *Virgin*: Virgin has chosen to put its own brand name on everything that it does – whether music, air travel, bridal wear, publishing, financial services or mobile telecommunications. This has laid the company open to the charge of 'brand stretching' – trying to put the Virgin brand on so many different products that its intrinsic value is lost. This is refuted by Richard Branson, who states that the strength of everything that it does, in whatever sector, is due to the distinctive Virgin corporate approach.

● *Sony and Aiwa*: the approach taken by Sony in order to get into perceived lower-value markets was to re-brand those offerings pitched at non-premium customers. The company took the view that if it put the Sony name on lower-price, good-value products, it would dilute the expectations and perceptions of those who continue to buy the premium offering.

● *Fit with the market*: is there a real customer need? Are prices available that give good margins? Will customers and clients buy this product or service from this company? Do the products and services produce customer benefits that are clearly much greater than what is currently being offered? Are there cost-effective ways to get the presentation and the product or service across to customers? Is the customer and client base convenient? If not, can it be made so? If it cannot, do the benefits outweigh this lack of convenience?

● *The company*: are there good reasons to believe that the company will be excellent at the business? What is the nature of the profit required? What is the nature of income volume that has to be generated? Over what time period? How much money does the company want/need to make from this particular venture? Will this dilute or enhance other products, services and offerings?

Where else may this lead? What if the company succeeds beyond its wildest dreams? What if the product or service fails? What are the consequences of each? Will this lead to larger markets and higher growth? Will this lead to enhanced volumes of business from existing customers?

● *Those involved*: do they believe in the product or service? Do they have personal, professional and occupational commitment? Do they understand the potential customers and clients? Do they like, respect and value the potential customers and clients? Are they committed to serving the potential customers and clients?

● *Circumstances*: do the prevailing set of circumstances lend themselves to the commercialisation of the particular idea? Can a set of circumstances be envisaged in which this commercialisation could fail? If the product or service feels right, but the timing feels wrong or if market research and evaluation suggest that it is wrong, can a set of circumstances be envisaged or foreseen in which this may become effective at some time in the future?

MANAGEMENT IN FOCUS 14.8

CHILTERN RAILWAYS: 'THE FUTURE IS BETTER'

As part of the improvements in the UK railway system following privatisation, Chiltern Railways promised 'improved quality of service and attention to customer needs and wants.' What customers needed and wanted was comfortable, reliable trains. What they got was improvement in the quality and variety of on-board refreshments, while the regularity, frequency and reliability of the train services themselves declined.

Defending the position, Chiltern Railways stated that they were simply concentrating on those areas of their business that could be improved. Confronted with demands for greater reliability, regularity and frequency of services from the travelling public, Chiltern Railways were forced to state that these factors were outside their direct control and so could not be addressed independently of the wider constraints of the UK railway industry.

- *Business processes and organisation structure*: can these accommodate the idea as it exists? Do these need to be adjusted or changed? What are the consequences of each?
- *Business process innovation*: if changes in the ways in which things are carried out are being envisaged, what are the tangible benefits? What are the cost advantages? Are these effective in terms of: pure cost? Derived cost? 'Cultural and behavioural cost'? Are staff comfort and effectiveness enhanced or diminished? What are the consequences of each?
- *Support*: is the idea institutionalised? On whose support does it depend for success or failure? What are the consequences of this, especially if the supporters change their priorities or move on?
- *Resources*: is capital available? On what conditions? For how long? What are the consequences and advantages of this? Is expertise and technology available? If so, for how long? If not, does it have to be sought? If so, from where? Internally or externally? What are the consequences of this?
- *Benefits*: are the benefits tangible or intangible? Instant or long term and enduring? Who are the primary beneficiaries – staff, customers, backers, the innovator? What are the consequences of this? Are there social as well as commercial benefits? What is enhanced and diminished as the result of the venture? What are the consequences of this?

This may then be represented graphically as shown in Figure 14.1.

● Innovation planning

The innovation planning process crystallises the particular proposal as follows:

- by answering each of the above questions as accurately and positively as possible

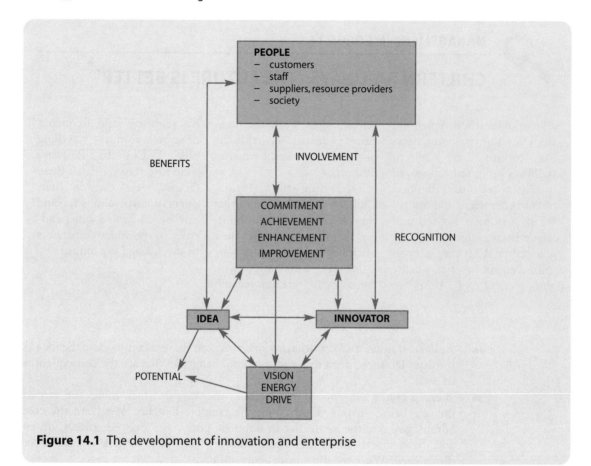

Figure 14.1 The development of innovation and enterprise

- by attending to the questions of strategy, marketing, finance and operations that have therefore to be engaged
- by harmonising these two aspects.

The nature of the venture, and how it is to be perceived and classified by others as well as those involved, is then ideally apparent.

Beyond this, any plan for the introduction of an innovation or advance must have the following attributes, and these must be made clear:

- It must be easily understandable, and capable of acceptance, on the part of all others involved.
- It must make clear the benefits that are to be achieved.
- It must make clear that alternatives have been considered.
- It must be capable of withstanding sceptical questioning; this above all, refers to any assumptions that have been made, or any steps proposed that are based on less than accurate or perfect information.
- It must pay particular attention to the question of finance. In the case of commercial innovations, this must include cash flow and profitability considerations. In the case of internal process innovations, this must include attention to cost savings, greater efficiency, and better returns on existing activities.

Where these conditions cannot be satisfied, or satisfied fully, there must be a substantial alternative reason for proceeding.

It is then necessary to:

- detail cash and other financial requirements and timing, in both the short and long term
- indicate accurately the extent of managerial, organisational and individual commitment
- indicate where assumptions have been made, and be prepared to justify why these have been found to be reasonable in the particular set of circumstances
- indicate wherever possible the range of best, medium and worst outcomes that have been considered, and the consequences of these
- indicate by name who is to be the innovation driver or champion.

Innovation and new product and service drivers and champions

Drivers and champions are those people who put their heart and soul, as well as expertise and acumen into the particular venture. It is essential that everything that is proposed has a single, named and identified individual who holds ultimate responsibility and authority for the venture, and is accountable as it unfolds, and also upon completion, success and failure. In these cases, committee structures do not work. For example, when Virgin went into the airline business for the first time, the company bought in expertise from all over the world to ensure that it was successful – but ultimate responsibility and accountability rested with Richard Branson.

The champion's job is to energise, enthuse and motivate, as well as coordinate and control. Champions must ensure that resources and expertise are gathered and used as required. This invariably means creative use of time, energy and existing technology as well as developing and enhancing the new product or service along the way as opportunities for this become apparent (see Management in Focus 14.9).

Potential problems arise whenever drivers or champions move on. They may do this for a variety of quite legitimate reasons – career moves, further opportunities elsewhere or the fact that they have taken the venture as far as they can. In these cases, somebody else must be available to take up the reins.

More insidiously, drivers and champions may be removed because the original backers have lost confidence. Drivers may be removed because new pressures and priorities have simply replaced the particular venture. Whatever the case, when this happens, it normally leads to at least a temporary loss of energy, vision and drive – and therefore confidence is called into question (see Management in Focus 14.10).

Monitoring, review and evaluation

Monitoring, review and evaluation processes are essential to effective product and service innovation and development. The overall purpose is to ensure that the viability (or otherwise) of ideas and innovations quickly becomes apparent. Once an innovation is proposed, this becomes the foundation for hard work, as stated above. Monitoring, review and evaluation processes are therefore created and implemented at the outset of any proposed innovation.

MANAGEMENT IN FOCUS 14.9

PRODUCT AND SERVICE CHAMPIONS AS PROJECT MANAGERS

The roles of product and service champion and project manager are very similar. Each is required to call on different resources and expertise as and when required, and to do everything possible to schedule these into some sort of priority or critical path order.

For each also there is a very fine line that divides healthy commitment from unhealthy obsession. It is not always easy to see where the line is. Art Fry, who developed the Post-it, only took up the challenge so that he could mark the pages in his church hymn book without the pieces of paper falling out.

The whole process took 12 years. Because the end result was the transformation of the office stationery industry, this clearly and obviously represents healthy commitment!

There are problems also when organisational authorities pressurise the champion to produce results. This leads, in many cases, to corners being cut or a lack of attention to finer detail. This lesson was learnt many years ago. The thalidomide drug was produced with the objective of reducing morning sickness suffered by women during pregnancy. Because it was not fully tested, and the total range of side effects was unknown, this led to the birth of several hundred babies with malformed legs and arms, and extensive social distress. The project was shortcut in this way because of pressures from the Distillers Company, the owners of the research, to get tangible commercial returns to satisfy their own financial interest. Elsewhere, a major reason why the loss of life on the *Titanic* in 1912 was so great was that there were insufficient lifeboats available on the ship. In spite of the fact that she was thought unsinkable, they should have been provided anyway.

Both that particular drug and that particular ship were supposed to transform the totality of their markets and produce greatly enhanced social benefits. Because of the lack of attention to detail, and the perceived commercial drives and pressures, both failed.

Once an innovation has been given the go-ahead, momentum and enthusiasm have to be maintained. This is often easier at the outset than during continued progress. This is especially the case where innovations in products, services and processes are constantly coming on-stream; what is fresh and new today quickly becomes commonplace and mainstream in such circumstances. This reinforces the need for named individuals to be identified whose remit is to see the particular innovation or venture through to completion.

Process innovations have to be capable of maintaining and developing the organisational relationships necessary to make them effective; and product and service innovations also normally require the creation of different relationships and new ways of working. A key part of monitoring, review and evaluation is therefore attention to the ways in which organisational, managerial and operating relationships are working, the extent to which these are effective, and the identification of any changes that may become apparent.

MANAGEMENT IN FOCUS 14.10

PROBLEMS WITH DRIVING FORCES

When innovation is being driven in these ways, and when problems do arise, one or more of the following is likely:

- A period of limbo or vacuum occurs, during which none of those involved quite know where they stand, and so they consume valuable time, energy and resources in trying to find out.

- Powerful or dominant individuals and groups try to take charge with varying degrees of success. They may also try and use the project for their own ends, for example to build their own reputations, or to have a high profile triumph.

- When confidence is called into question, the driver or champion may be removed on spurious or political grounds. For example, a person in charge of a major research initiative into the consequences of the private finance initiative at one of the 'new' London universities was removed after the initial phase on the grounds of 'cultural incompatibility'. This was a euphemism for 'we don't like you, and in any case, you are not producing the results we wanted'. Elsewhere, a man in charge of a computer software development at a plastics factory was removed on the grounds that 'he did not smile enough'. In each case, the particular innovation (both hitherto considered vital, pioneering and far-sighted) was dropped shortly afterwards.

More generally, when it becomes known, believed or perceived among top managers that the particular drive is going to cost more than forecasts and projections indicated, they seek cuts elsewhere to pay for it. These are invariably demoralising, petty, inadequate and drawn from other frontline activities, rather than from the support, administrative and head office functions. An early symptom of this is the removal of newspapers, magazines and flowers from reception areas. Other examples include:

- A hospital manager had to fund a £2.5 million deficit that he had incurred through being required to follow political drives to cut waiting lists. Accordingly, he wrote to all nursing managers and staff asking them to be careful about the number of bandages that they used. The flaw in this approach was discussed in Management in Focus 12.8.

- An Internet bookseller cut out the free Friday night champagne for all staff (cost approximately £80) as a step along the way to filling a £33 million shortfall.

Attention to detail

Processes should also ensure that every detail receives attention (see Management in Focus 14.11). Drivers or champions of particular ventures or innovations must ensure that, if they are unable to pay sufficient attention to details, then they have someone available who can do this on a daily basis. The adoption of a management style based on visibility, integrity and high-quality communication goes a long way

MANAGEMENT IN FOCUS 14.11

ATTENTION TO DETAILS: EXAMPLES

- The 1944 Arnhem paratroop landings failed because nobody in authority paid sufficient attention to three photographs that clearly showed fresh and well-equipped German troops in the designated landing zone.
- The Canary Wharf proj-ect took 12 years (rather than the projected 30 months) to become fully successful, because nobody considered the enduring problems with transport to and from the area to be a significant factor.
- Workforce restructuring at the Orion Insurance Company failed because no one took account of the public transport timetables from the places where many of the staff lived, and nobody thought to provide sufficient car parking, or company transport, as an alternative.

to ensuring that, when particularly adverse issues may arise, they can be addressed and dealt with immediately. Beyond this, all monitoring, review and evaluation must be punctuated with regular formal meetings involving all those concerned, so that those whose resources are being invested or consumed in the particular activity are satisfied that their own particular contribution is being used effectively.

Conclusions

All organisations depend on innovation and new product and service creation and development for their advancement. Much of this is dependent upon the imagination, creativity – dreams even – of individuals within organisations; and this extends to changes in business processes as well as the creation of new products and services.

However, this in itself is not enough. Once the decision has been taken to implement a particular initiative then hard work is required, and this work must be structured and ordered towards a clearly understood process (see Figure 14.2). Figure 14.2 indicates the main reasons why many organisations are resistant to change development and advancement, and why it takes so long to bring new products and services on-stream.

The hard challenge of carrying innovation through is one of the main reasons why many organisations are so resistant to change and advancement. Faced with the prospect of this level of commitment and energy required, they seek alternatives. For large complex organisations, and those that have substantial market share and capital resources, it seems overtly straightforward to take over smaller organisations so as to acquire their technology, customer base, inherent imagination and creativity and expertise. This is all very well provided that the acquiring organisation uses the new purchase for the purposes that were initially attractive. All too often, the innovative zeal (such as it is) is lost as it becomes easier and more straightforward to subsume

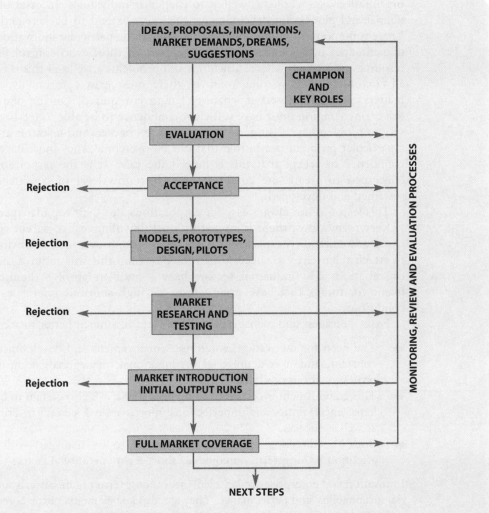

Figure 14.2 New product and service development

the new acquisition in the existing culture. Innovation and progress therefore become by-products, rather than the driving force.

It is also essential to ensure that the person put in charge of any innovation or development is given sufficient authority and responsibility, as well as resources. Again, in practice, it becomes expedient to find fault with developments when these are starved of resources and therefore given little strategic chance of success at the outset. This does not prevent organisations from choosing to pick on innovations and developments in times of crisis, rather than tackling the root causes – which are normally to be found in existing steady-state activities and organisation culture, rather than new ventures.

Innovation, enterprise, development and enhancement are dependent upon energy, ambition, enthusiasm, drive and commitment. This must extend to the organisation as a whole, as well as to particular individuals. In cases of entrepreneurial and pioneering development, this must extend to backers and investors. There is no point in going down such a route if the particular innovation or development does not command the full support of those who control finance and resources. Above all, where difficulties and problems arise (and this is universal in all circumstances from time to time) there must exist a forum in which such matters can be discussed at whatever length is required. On the one hand, the driver or champion must have sufficient confidence to be able to tell backers when serious problems are arising; on the other, when backers and investors are told that a particular problem is a hurdle that can be overcome, they must have sufficient confidence to accept that this is indeed the case. It is the responsibility of all concerned to create the conditions in which this level of confidence can be sustained and developed.

This lesson is not always easy for corporations and their top managers to learn. In very many cases, there is an institutional unwillingness to accept responsibility or accountability, especially for failure – though everyone is obviously eager to attach themselves to successes! In the past (and this still endures today) many organisations and industrial sectors have sought to absolve themselves from blame for things that have gone wrong through spurious references to global conditions.

From a business and managerial point of view, it is much better to accept that:

- The need for innovation, enterprise, enhancement and development remains constant, and it is a universal organisational, managerial, occupational and professional responsibility.
- This commitment is certain to bring hard work; it is also certain to bring problems, uncertainties and imperfections; moreover, it is certain to bring failures, as well as success.
- Both the direction and the process need to be managed with the same attention to long-term outcomes as short-term operational factors.

Innovation and enterprise are key elements of long-term organisational and managerial sustainability and performance. They are also key elements of the core functional activities of strategy development, marketing effectiveness, operational cohesion, and the management of financial resources, including the maintenance of cash flow, and enduring profitability. In order for this to be effective, the conditions in which innovation and enterprise can flourish have to be created. This is an enduring responsibility for:

- the most influential people in society, including financiers, backers and politicians, because the macro conditions have to be created in which positive attention, respect and value are accorded to those who have ideas for products and services that provide an enduring and positive contribution to society in general, and customer and client bases in particular
- directors and senior managers in organisations, who are required to take an enlightened view of what constitutes the best use of the resources available to them. Not to take an enlightened view of the benefits of innovation and enterprise means that organisations are invariably left behind by those that do.

1. Under what circumstances would it be right to withdraw organisational resources from innovations and development?
2. Why do organisations blame anyone but themselves when innovations go wrong? How might these attitudes be tackled?
3. What problems are faced by organisations when they need to 're-brand' themselves? Outline an effective strategic approach to get over the problems that you have identified.
4. Identify the lessons that may be learned from industrial and commercial companies by the public services, as they seek to enhance and improve the quality of health and education services.

DEVELOPING MANAGEMENT SKILLS AND EXPERTISE

ST GEORGE'S FARM SHOP

Many farmers are finding it increasingly difficult to continue supplying many of the large chains of supermarkets where prices are kept to the absolute minimum for the supplier without any financial benefit being passed on to the end consumer. Moreover, with competition from air-freighted imports produced more cheaply abroad, it is not surprising that many producers are looking for alternative markets that not only remove these problems, but also have the advantage that their customers are buying only the freshest locally produced goods.

Where once farmers and growers sold their produce at their local market, a growing number of them now see the farm shop as a reasonable alternative. By selling direct to the public locally, not only do they eliminate the logistics of transporting goods long distances, but they no longer need to be totally dependent on a market that does not operate in their favour economically. The farm shop also goes a long way to recreating the atmosphere, if not of the market of bygone days, then at least of the fast-disappearing village store.

When Susan and Edward James inherited their farm from Edward's parents in the early 1980s, they had already come to terms with the fact that they would need to diversify in order to make the farm survive as a commercially viable concern. As cattle farmers, Edward's family had farmed the land for over a hundred years, selling produce locally in East and West Sussex.

During the 1940s, a transport café known as the Union Jack had operated on land adjoining the James' farm. When the café and associated land came on the market in the early 1960s, the family bought it with the long-term view of selling produce direct to the public. It was not until 1984 however, when Edward inherited the land, that he and Susan were able to push ahead with their plans to diversify, little realising that it would take them 12 years to gain planning permission from the local council.

'We initially applied for planning permission in 1984 but our application was declined,' explained Susan, 'and we also lost on appeal. Even alterations to the plans so that the farm shop did not exceed the café's original size were at first rejected.'

It was only on further appeal that the James' were finally granted planning permission and the St George's Farm Shop opened its doors for business in December 1996. There was however one stipulation, and that was that 90 per cent of all the goods sold had to be home produced. How home produced was to be defined was never clarified, causing further bureaucratic nightmares. An enforcement officer from the local council's planning department gave them just two days in February 1997 to remove any goods that had not been produced on their own farm.

Susan found that she had to close the farm shop every Monday to devote the time needed to resolve this latest issue with the council. Local support though, including the signing of a petition, encouraged her to continue the battle. She is particularly grateful to the monks at the local monastery, St Hughes Charterhouse, who offered to buy all her unsold produce at the end of each weekend to help her stay in business during this period.

Now, several years further on, Susan and Edward have a thriving farm shop that sells fresh produce from the family farm and also provides a retail outlet for other local producers of items ranging from cheese, fresh vegetables and organic cream, to chutneys and home-baked cakes and biscuits. They also sell both fresh meat and meat products – sausages, bacon, ham, pate, lard and dripping. And the advantage to the local consumers is that, while producers and growers are paid the weekly recommended market price, any reduction in that market price is automatically passed on to the customer.

'Not only is it now rather like a small scale village cooperative,' says Susan, 'it is also helping to make shopping locally the social event it once was and this particularly appeals to my older customers. After all, how often do you see people chatting to each other, let alone smiling, in the supermarket?'

Source: taken from The Union Jack Farm Shop, Chates Cottage, Henfield Road, Cowfold, West Sussex, *Prime Health magazine* (February 2000).

Questions

1. Why did the negative attitudes to the farm shop on behalf of the local council exist in the first place? In general, how are such attitudes overcome?
2. What actions should Susan and Edward James now be taking in order to develop their customer base?
3. What circumstances outside the control of Susan and Edward James could conspire to place this particular venture at risk? How should they respond to these?

The Body Shop

The status quo says that the business of business is to make profits. We have always challenged that. For us the business of business is to keep the company alive and breathlessly excited, to protect the workforce, to be a force for good in our society and then, after all that, to think of the speculators. I have never kowtowed to the speculators or considered them to be my first responsibility. They play the market without much concern for the company or its values. Most are only interested in the short-term and quick profit; they do not come to our annual general meetings and they don't respond to our communications. As far as I am concerned, I have no obligations to these people at all.

This is Anita Roddick's statement of the priorities and obligations of The Body Shop as a company. She goes on:

I believe that if companies are in business solely to make money, you cannot fully trust whatever else they do or say. I do not understand why anyone would want to run a business like that. I see business as a renaissance concept where the human spirit comes into play. It does not have to be drudgery; it does not have to be the science of making money. It can be something that people genuinely feel good about but only if it remains a human enterprise.

How do you ennoble the spirit when you are selling something as inconsequential as a cosmetic cream? You do it by creating a sense of holism of spiritual development, of feeling connected to the workplace, the environment and relationships with one another. It is how to make Monday to Friday come alive rather than being a slow death. How do you give people a chance to do a good job? By making them feel good about what they are doing.

Not a single decision is ever taken in The Body Shop without first considering environmental and social issues. We do not sell products which consume a disproportionate amount of energy during their manufacture or disposal, cause unnecessary waste, use ingredients derived from threatened species or threatened environments, or adversely affect other countries particularly in the emerging world. We have a vigorous 'trade not aid' policy encouraging local communities in the emerging world to utilise their resources and trade with us to help alleviate poverty.

As the result of what we have learned, we have evolved a simple credo. It goes like this: you can run a business differently from the way most businesses are run; you can share your prosperity with your employees and empower them without being in fear of them; you can rewrite the book in terms of how a company interacts with the community; you can rewrite the book on emerging world trade and global responsibility, and on the role of educating the company customers and shareholders; finally, you can do all this and still play the game according to the city, still raise money, delight the institutions, and give shareholders a wondrous return on their investment.

Sources: A. Roddick (1992) *Body and Soul: The Body Shop Story*, Ebury Press; www.anitaroddick.net; www.thebodyshop.com.

Questions

1. Identify the core foundation or generic strategy of The Body Shop. What are the organisational and managerial responsibilities and commitments inherent in this position?
2. Comment on the view expressed by Anita Roddick in the above statement that it is 'possible to rewrite the book' on all aspects of business. Identify those elements of the business that The Body Shop genuinely conducts differently; and identify those areas in which the distinctions are perceptual rather than substantial.
3. Identify the strengths and weaknesses of the ways in which The Body Shop markets its products, services and brand. Why has the marketing of The Body Shop remained so consistently successful?
4. What actions are required by the present generation of managers to ensure that the success of the company's first phase of existence is consolidated, sustained and developed?

Part three

Organisational and behavioural aspects

Introduction

Organisations are composed of people; and organisations provide products and services for use and consumption by people. It is therefore essential for those in leadership, executive, key and managerial positions to know and understand collective and individual human behaviour. Managers need to know and understand the influences that cause behaviour to be modified and changed, and how people think, behave and react when faced with the variety and complexity of situations present or potentially present in organised business and managerial settings.

The context for knowing and understanding collective and individual human behaviour is capable of simple introduction. For example:

- If you prefer to work in a positive, cheerful and productive setting and organisation, then it is likely that most people will want to do so.
- If you prefer to be treated with honesty and integrity, then it is likely that most people prefer this also.
- If you expect an interesting and varied working life and career, then it is likely that most people expect this also.
- If you expect to be treated fairly and equally, free from discrimination and harassment, then it is likely that most people will expect this.

A key to learning and developing understanding of organisational behaviour is therefore empathy. Lack of empathy (sometimes described as lack of humanity) is always present when top and senior managers find themselves having to explain why organisations have wasted resources on ill-considered ventures, or when they have to make lay-offs, or when they have to explain collective organisational ineptitude or failure. This lack of empathy arises from a fundamental inability to recognise the legitimate concerns that everyone involved has when particular situations arise. Conversely, it is the ability to provide simple, direct and honest communication in response to any particular issue, that marks out successful and effective organisations, and the quality of their management. Understanding behaviour from the point of view of personal, professional and occupational empathy additionally gives a clear reference point for the range of likely, possible and potential outcomes when dealing with any situation in which people are involved. People need to know and understand where they stand on the full range of organisational issues. People need to have confidence in the actions and initiatives of those leading and directing the organisation; and people need a degree of permanence and order in their working lives.

From this position, the complexities of organisational collective and individual behaviour can then be understood. As indicated above, people respond clearly and positively to directness of communication and equality of treatment. This has to be capable of effective delivery in organisations of great complexity, wide cultural differences, and varying collective and individual aspirations. Organisations and their managers have to be capable of creating and developing effective patterns of behaviour so as to ensure that activities are carried out effectively. They have to be capable of harmonising and assimilating people into different roles and responsibilities, and ensuring that these are carried out. Organisations increasingly have to be able to manage across physical, psychological and technological boundaries, and they require systems and procedures that enable all of this to be done as effectively as possible.

This forms the basis for the study of organisational behaviour. The issues surrounding organisational culture, perceptions, attitudes and values are dealt with first. The need for effective communications, which underpins all effective organisational behaviour and cohesion, is then covered. The specific discipline of human resource management, and the relationship between organisational effectiveness and technology, are then also dealt with in this context.

The overall context for studying organisational and behavioural issues is to ensure that this part of the discipline of management is known and understood to make a critical contribution to the enduring profitability and effectiveness of organisations. It should especially be noted that lack of cohesion, or negative culture, attitudes and values, always contribute adversely to organisational performance, profitability and effectiveness; it should also be noted that the enduring success of organisations as diverse as Sony, Oxfam, Ryanair and Tesco, as well as The Body Shop, is ascribed largely to the success of those organisations in creating and maintaining a positive collective cohesion, attitudes, standards and values.

Chapter fifteen

Innovative, creative and entrepreneurial management

'If you have the talent and application, you can achieve anything.'
Dawn Airey, Managing Director, Sky Networks.

'If you don't enjoy it, don't do it.'
Philip Green, Chairman and Chief Executive, BHS.

'We are all measured by our failures.'
Mike Brearley, former England cricket captain.

Chapter outline

- Introduction
- The range and scope of innovative and creative management
- The foundations of entrepreneurial management
- Developing creative and innovative approaches
- Intrapreneuring
- Evolution
- Conclusions

Chapter objectives

After studying this chapter, you should be able to:

- understand the contribution to overall effectiveness made by creative approaches to different issues

- understand the value of creative and entrepreneurial approaches to the development of managerial expertise

- understand, and be able to apply, creative approaches to problem solving

- understand the need for mixing creativity with expertise

- begin to develop greater expertise in the detailed evaluation of organisations, products, services and the environment

- begin to develop greater expertise in dealing with workplace priorities and issues.

● Introduction

The purpose of dealing with creative and dynamic approaches to management, and the issues that managers have to face, is to underpin the need for rigorous and effective critical thinking as a core part of the overall expertise required.

The approach called 'entrepreneurial management' is founded on the premise that it is neither productive nor profitable to employ managers simply to operate and administrate processes, chase progress and fulfil an 'in-tray–out-tray' way of working. Each of these tasks is essential; yet for productive and profitable management, other skills, knowledge and expertise must be present.

Developing management in this way had its roots in the work of Reg Revans during the 1960s. He proposed an 'action-learning' and 'action-oriented' approach to management that required those in managerial positions to be constantly aware of where improvements, developments and enhancements could be made in all aspects of their operating environment; this included staff management aspects and the effectiveness of procedures and processes, as well as attention to product and service performance. Revans also recognised that such an approach fostered a creative, positive and dynamic spirit within all those affected by managers who operated in these ways. He pointed to the life and energy that came about throughout the organisation, both for the present and for the future, if an action orientation could be achieved (see Management in Focus 15.1).

● Developing the approach

Failure to develop this part of managerial thinking and expertise leads to collective and individual regimentation and inertia, in which managers have only a limited set of responses to whatever might occur. Increasing dependence on outsiders to come in and resolve serious problems and issues is expensive, as noted above. It results in an ever-decreasing pool of managerial capability and expertise, and this then makes the ability to fill managerial positions difficult and costly (see Management in Focus 15.2).

Peters and Waterman (1982) identified the basis for an effective approach. The core tenets of the 'Excellence studies' refer especially to 'a bias for action', and being 'hands on and value-driven'. The approach of Peters and Waterman additionally concentrates on productivity through people and closeness to the customer: that is, everything that is contemplated, generated or engaged must be in the ultimate interests of the performance of products and services and the satisfaction that they deliver to the customer. This can only be achieved through engaging the capability and willingness of the staff involved; and failure to do this means that products and services will not perform as well as they should, and this ultimately leads to a decline in performance.

Peters and Waterman also identify 'shared values', and especially positive shared values, as preconditions for the comfort, confidence and well-being of staff, again as a foundation for profitable product and service performance. This was reinforced by Pascale and Athos (1983). In their study of Japanese management principles, techniques and approaches, they found that the creation of a cohesive, inclusive and binding culture was seen as essential to excellence in business product and service performance. Referring especially to Japanese manufacturing organisations, Pascale and Athos found that this binding culture was based on: mutual confidence; mutual

MANAGEMENT IN FOCUS 15.1

CREATIVITY, MYTHS AND LEGENDS

As with many other parts of managerial disciplines and expertise, organisations have been reluctant to provide the commitment and resources required to make effective this part of management development.

Organisations and institutions have adopted phrases such as 'blue sky thinking' and 'thinking outside the box', to indicate at least that they are aware of the problem. However, giving such vague remits to project teams and externally appointed management consultants is normally seen as an abdication of responsibility. It is also damaging to the organisation in anything but the short term, since it means that its own managers are neither encouraged to develop this area of expertise, nor given any direct input into problem solving, product and service development, or organisation change and enhancement.

Blue-sky and outside-the-box approaches therefore invariably reflect organisational and collective sloppiness. Spending money on external agencies to produce creative and dynamic approaches is expensive from the point of view of losing the capability to develop expertise, as mentioned above; this in turn is bound to reduce the capability to face those problems and issues that are certain to occur in the future.

interest on the part of the staff, organisation and management; excellent working conditions; good to high levels of wages; inclusive and consensus-based employee relations and staff management practices; and a commitment to resolve problems rather than institutionalise them. Levels of investment in capital goods and production technology were, at the time, between 10 and 20 times greater than those found in Western Europe and North America.

Japanese organisations, and also those that followed similar approaches, consequently created all of the conditions required for sustainable, profitable and effective activities, products and services. The priority then became to ensure that creativity, invention and enterprise remain concentrated on the profitable cores of the business, while at the same time developing new products, services, ventures and procedures. It is not always easy to maintain the balance between sustaining historically effective and profitable activities on the one hand, and developing the nest generations of products and services on the other (see Management in Focus 15.3).

Intrapreneuring

Pinchot (1984) used the term 'intrapreneur' as a description of 'enterprising individuals working within existing organisations'. He distinguished between enterprising individuals working within organisations and entrepreneurs who created their own organisations in order to pursue their own vision of the future, independent of existing organisation constraints. Pinchot's approach set out to reconcile enterprise, management, organisation and the community. The requirement was for organisations to create the conditions in which progress, creativity, invention and innovation

MANAGEMENT IN FOCUS 15.2

THE FOOTBALL INDUSTRY

The football industry in the UK, Western Europe and South America has a serious problem in attracting, recruiting and retaining people who are going to be enduringly effective in top managerial and executive positions. The industry has a history and tradition of filling top positions from among the ranks of former players, substituting profile for capability. The industry has a history and tradition of finding money from the broadcasting media, sponsorship, sales of merchandise and wealthy patrons; much of this money has been squandered in attracting, appointing and then dismissing those who have failed to live up to the managerial side of the industry.

On the administrative and executive side, the industry as a whole is just beginning to realise that managerial expertise operating within the constraints of its particular environment is as necessary for this industry as for any other. Failure to understand and acknowledge this has led to a general absence from the industry of collective and structural capability in management. The clubs (the companies) that have bucked this trend have either done so from the point of view of ensuring that they are a successful and valuable local brand, or else have undertaken extensive and time-consuming restructurings. For example:

● *Local brand*: Leeds United were forced to re-position themselves as providing regular entertainment for their own locality following losses of £97 million which had been incurred in the pursuit of an illusory and unattainable high-profile status.

● *Restructuring*: for all of the millions of pounds poured into the club by Roman Abramovich, the restructuring of Chelsea Football Club, and its re-positioning as a major London brand (with aspirations to raise its international profile substantially), has cost over £500 million to date, and the club is not expected to show a profit until 2008 or 2009. This restructuring is therefore expected to take about ten years.

This is replicated in many of the strongholds of the football world. In Brazil and Argentina, the big clubs are dependent upon their continued capability to sell expert and promising players to the European parts of the industry in return for hard currency. In Germany, Borussia Dortmund is faced with the continuing need to service a £63 million charge for its stadium; in Italy, SS Lazio, the Rome club, is servicing a £138 million debt which had been incurred as the result of assurances of broadcasting income that were not fulfilled.

The problems and issues have arisen as the result of using capital resources for revenue expenditure. This underlines the structural and institutional lack of managerial expertise in all aspects of the industry.

could thrive and prosper, while at the same time ensuring a fundamental level of discipline, cohesion and commitment to the organisation. Pinchot stated:

> We have entered a world of constant change where certainties do not exist and productivity in innovation is becoming as important as productivity in production. But this is no

MANAGEMENT IN FOCUS 15.3

SONY

Sony was one of the first companies to publicly establish its long-term existence on the basis of creativity, innovation and dynamism. Sony's product, innovation and development rate is of the order of 15 new ideas and initiatives per day, and out of this enduring commitment has come the strength of its core range of electrical goods, music and film products.

In recent years however, the company has been hit by a series of failures. The company engaged in an expensive lawsuit with George Michael over the rights to the singer's back catalogue; while the judgement was in the company's favour, it led to sever-ance of the contract. Mariah Carey had her contract cancelled with the company for selling only $35 million worth of albums. The company produced its own differentiated DVD and micro-disc systems that could only be used on Sony equipment, and this caused people to look elsewhere, buying both DVDs and mini-discs that could be played on generic equipment. In the computer games area, there were glitches on the Playstation 2 when it first came out, and delays on Playstation 3; there was also additional competition in this field from the Microsoft Xbox.

Faced with the cost burden incurred, adverse media coverage and stock market expectations, the company was forced in 2005 to break its 60-year history of lifelong employment and no compulsory lay-offs. The company announced a total of 10,000 redundancies across its manufacturing units in the UK, Western Europe, North America and Japan. This in turn has called into question the enduring viability of the company's creativity and dynamism in product and service development, and the capability of top and senior management to find anything but a linear and rigid approach to stock market, media and financial pressures.

cause for alarm. Not only is the world of innovation more fun, but it is a world in which entrepreneurial and intrapreneurial talents can prove the decisive advantage. The vigour of the entrepreneurial spirit is a great business treasure.

The starting point for organisations engaged in intrapreneuring is the selection of intrapreneurial people capable of turning ideas into action. Many entrepreneurs and pioneers are excellent at building up businesses from scratch but have great difficulty in delegating responsibility to others; this becomes a serious problem when faced with success and growth. Managerial intrapreneurs, however, seek the opportunity to empower others, draw them into their sphere of influence, let them make their own mistakes, and use these as a vehicle for collective and individual development.

Organisational structures and systems have to be capable of accommodating and supporting such approaches and attitudes. This requirement is not always easy to reconcile with demands for steady and assured volumes and quality of products and services. Organisation culture, management priorities, and shareholder and backer demands do not lend themselves readily to supporting and resourcing often nebulous approaches that have general objectives only. On the other hand, when things do work out, organisations are then perfectly happy to accept the results (see Management in Focus 15.4).

The intrapreneur's ten commandments

Pinchot went on to produce ten commandments which reflected the dimensions, characteristics, qualities and commitment required:

1. Come to work each day willing to be fired.
2. Circumvent any orders aimed at stopping your dream.
3. Do any job needed to make your project work, regardless of your job description.
4. Find people to help you.
5. Follow your intuition about the people you choose and work only with the best.
6. Work underground as long as you can – publicity triggers the corporate immune system.
7. Never bet on a race unless you are running it.
8. Remember that it is easier to ask for forgiveness than for permission.
9. Be true to your goals and be realistic about the way to achieve them.
10. Keep your sponsors informed.

Pinchot's presentation is part idealistic, part fanciful, yet it has a key lesson for organisations and their managers, especially top managers and directors. In particular, commandment six relating to 'corporate immune systems' ought to be a major concern to all CEOs, general managers and functional directors. As illustrated in Management in Focus 15.4 below, organisations remain at the mercy of

MANAGEMENT IN FOCUS 15.4

THE RESULTS OF ENTERPRISE: EXAMPLES

- *3M*: the 3M company was very happy to take the Post-it innovation once Art Fry, the inventor, had taken 12 years of his own time to prove that it could work. 3M then used this to transform themselves into a major international supplier of stationery and office goods.

- *Bloomsbury Publishers Ltd*: the publishers were very happy to support J.K. Rowling once the Harry Potter series became successful, though they did not support her until after success was demonstrated in terms of book sales.

- *Ericsson, Nokia and Motorola*: the mobile phone manufacturers, used hearing aid technology to produce the present range of mobile phone headset connections. None of them supplied or supported the product development until the connection had already been demonstrated and proven by those working as specialists in the hearing aid industry.

someone else's work until the case is proven, and this can lead to major and institutional disadvantages. From refusing to create the conditions in which the developments in Management in Focus 15.4 have been produced, the corporate immune system now immunises itself against everything except inventing the next Post-It, Harry Potter or headset-technology equivalent, rather than creating and supplying the conditions necessary for the next wave of inventions to take place (see Management in Focus 15.5).

The organisational/individual mix

Creating the conditions in which this form of expertise development can flourish is not always easy. Not only may organisational structures and systems not easily accommodate such approaches as those discussed above, but also the organisation may have its own preferred ways of dealing with new product and service development, internal problem solving and changes in process with which it is presently perfectly happy. If this is the case, then creativity and organisational and management development have to take place within the stated, prescribed and understood confines.

Even if there is space, capability and willingness to enlarge the scope for creativity and development, a form of organisational assessment is required as follows:

- Does your desire to make things work better occupy as much time as your need to maintain things the way they are? Does the organisation have the collective will to make things work better?
- Do you get very excited about what you are doing at work? Is the organisation collectively and institutionally an exciting place to work? Is the organisation capable of harnessing people's enthusiasm and excitement?
- Do you continually think about new business ideas all of the time? Is the organisation receptive to new business ideas?
- Can you visualise concrete steps for action when you consider ways to make a

MANAGEMENT IN FOCUS 15.5

ERNST & YOUNG AND THE NINE-DAY FORTNIGHT

Ernst & Young, the international high-brand firm of management consultants, created and institutionalised the nine-day fortnight. The message was that staff would spend nine working days out of ten on their steady-state activities and projects. The other day – or 10 per cent of working time – was to be given over to development work. This could be anything, provided only that there was the prospect of tangibles for the business somewhere along the line. During this 10 per cent of time, staff were free to make any contacts, propose initiatives, chase up old or dormant leads – whatever they chose. Ernst & Young pointed to the nine-day fortnight initiative as a major contribution to business development, forays into new fields and the expansion of all aspects of their current range of activities.

new idea happen? Is the organisation willing to support and implement the steps for action required?

● Do you get into trouble from time to time for doing things that exceed your authority? What is the organisational response to those who exceed their authority or remit?

● Have you managed to keep at it when something you were working on looked very likely to fail? What is the organisation's response to failure – blame or learning? Are processes for dealing with failure fully institutionalised?

● Do you have a network of friends, sponsors and supporters at work you can count on for support? What is the organisation's response to the creation of unofficial and ad hoc project and venture teams and groups?

● Can you share responsibility for your ideas with a team? Is the organisation prepared to accept responsibility for ventures and initiatives generated in these ways?

● Are you prepared to give up some salary in exchange for the opportunity to try out ideas, if the rewards for success are adequate? What is the organisation's approach to rewarding individuals and groups for new initiatives? Are these rewards valued? Are these rewards fairly and evenly distributed in all cases?

Apart from establishing common knowledge and understanding of the present position, such an approach ought additionally to inform staff recruitment and management development policies. This is so that the organisation gains staff who are happy to work with the confines, space and opportunities actually given, and so that staff know and understand what they are letting themselves in for in advance of committing themselves to the organisation and its preferred ways of working.

● Developing creative capacity

It becomes clear that discipline and commitment are required in order to harness creativity and commitment for effective and profitable organisation purposes. Organisations that adopt this approach have therefore to create the space and conditions in which creative and committed people are attracted, recruited and retained for long enough for their ideas and energy to be used effectively.

Lessem (1987) identifies four phases which organisations must be prepared to provide for and accommodate, as follows:

● *A solo phase*: during which the vision is being formulated, in which individuals work on projects and ideas.

● *A network phase*: during which individuals begin to share their ideas with trusted friends and supporters.

● *Bootlegging phases*: when informal teams and groups are formed around the idea.

● *Formal phases*: when official project teams, departments, divisions and functions are set up to carry the idea forward.

In each of these phases there is a need for organisation colloquy in creating the time, space, resources and conditions in which these forms of activities can take place. This additionally reinforces the point that fostering creativity and dynamism is an organisational commitment; and creating and developing the capability and willingness to work in these ways is a difficult part of managerial expertise.

It is additionally essential to know and understand that ideas have the greatest chance of success where there is a good fit and empathy between the individual or group proposing it, the marketplace and the collective organisational attitudes. The evaluation required in this context is discussed below.

Individual fit

- Are you personally involved in getting the idea off the ground? Is the organisation prepared to back you?
- Do you like and understand the potential customers? Does the organisation like or understand the potential customers?
- Do you have experience in this type of business? Does the organisation have experience in it?
- Are the tasks required ones that you are prepared to carry out? Is the organisation prepared to let you carry them out?
- Are the people to be engaged people you will enjoy working with? Is the organisation comfortable with engaging them?
- Has the idea fired your imagination? Do you believe in the project or service? Does the organisation believe in the product or service? (See Management in Focus 15.6).

Fit with the market

- Is there a real customer need? Does the organisation understand the precise nature of that need?

MANAGEMENT IN FOCUS 15.6

BRITISH AIRWAYS AND GO

In 1994, faced with increasing competition from the fledgling low-cost airlines, British Airways (BA) created its own low-cost subsidiary, which it called Go. Go had all of the strength and structure, route networks and aircraft fleet size that would enable it to gain a fully viable presence in the low-cost sector. It was to operate from a hub at London's Stansted airport and consequently would not be competing directly with BA's branded networks and core routes.

The demand for low-cost route networks had already been demonstrated, and this continues to the present day. However, the Go venture failed. BA never fully believed in it as a part of its range of products and services, and ultimately decided to concentrate on their existing high-brand, high-quality flag carrier operations. BA sold Go to easyJet in 1998.

Operationally, there was no reason why the Go venture should not have been successful. Internally, it was the lack of collective organisational belief that caused it to fail.

- Can you get a price that gives you good margins? Is this price acceptable to the organisation?
- Will customers believe in this product or service coming from your company?
- What are the cost-effective ways of getting the message, the product and the service to the customers? Is the organisation prepared to invest in this?
- Does the product or service produce a customer benefit that is clearly much greater than what is currently being produced? (See Management in Focus 15.7).

Fit with the organisation

- What are the reasons to believe that the organisation will be good at the business or venture?
- Does the business or venture look profitable? Will it lead to larger markets and higher growth? Is the organisation capable of accommodating these?
- What are the immediate and enduring opportunities, consequences and implications for the organisation? Is the organisation prepared to accommodate these?
- Does it fit the organisation culture? (see Management in Focus 15.8).

Fit with supply side

- Where are the necessary resources to come from? How much will these resources cost?

MANAGEMENT IN FOCUS 15.7

VIRGIN FINANCIAL SERVICES

From a business and organisational point of view, one of Virgin's most controversial ventures was into financial services.

The evaluation of the proposal to enter the financial services market was conducted with the standard Virgin approach. In particular, there had been a series of scandals concerning the mis-selling of pensions and endowment policies, and it was this that led Virgin into the market. It determined to develop niches offering the best value products, supported by the highest levels of service – exactly the approach taken to all its ventures.

The financial services sector collectively disparaged the Virgin proposal. Financial services products were sold not bought. The Virgin brand would be stretched to breaking point. Virgin had no expertise in the complexities of personal finance.

When it became clear that the Virgin financial services products were successful, attracting 1.2 million customers in their first year, the rest of the industry was forced to change its outlook and approach.

The company had entered into this market on the basis of 'fit with actual market demands and expectations', rather than narrow concentration on product design. It has consequently established a foothold in this market, by concentrating on what the market demanded and expected, rather than adopting a product-led approach.

MANAGEMENT IN FOCUS 15.8

PUBLIC SERVICE PROFESSIONS

Those entering into the public service professions of medicine, nursing, teaching and social work do so because of a commitment to serve, and deliver their expertise to the best of their abilities in response to the demands of those who are ill, disadvantaged and requiring education.

In the overwhelming majority of cases, those delivering these services do so from the point of view of an absolute professional discipline and commitment.

Consequently, the reforms of the health, education and social services institutions have found little 'fit' or sympathy with the professional staff. These reforms have been, and remain, cost-driven and aimed at narrow performance targets – waiting lists and death rates in hospitals; grades of pupils and students in schools; while performance targets for social services have never been fully defined.

There is therefore a conflict of interest in professional and organisational priorities which has led to losses of expert professional staff, and the inability to recruit the next generation in sufficient volumes. At the core of this is the lack of organisational fit with what is being proposed and implemented.

- Are the suppliers prepared to do business with us? What are their terms of business?
- Where are the potential hold-ups on the supply side? Can we accommodate these?
- Are we going to be dependent on one supplier? Are there alternatives, and if so, will they be prepared to do business with us?
- Will the supplies be guaranteed, or are we faced with having to compete on price, regularity or assurance with others?

In particular, existing organisations already taking these supplies may seek to buy up sufficient volumes to preclude others from becoming involved. Existing organisations may also put pressures on suppliers not to do business with potential entrants into the market. Thus assuredness of capability and willingness on the supply side is essential if particular initiatives are to be successful (see Management in Focus 15.9).

Developing creative expertise

Effective development of creative expertise requires recognition and resourcing as an organisational priority, and is then integrated into substantial organisational and management development activities and programmes.

The priority, as stated above, is to produce a body of managers capable of expert, creative and critical thinking. This in turn becomes a key part of the basis of expertise in judgement, analysis and decision making. This expertise is required at strategic, operational and individual levels.

MANAGEMENT IN FOCUS 15.9

CLOTHING AND GARMENTS

The mass-market, medium-quality clothing and garment manufacturers and retailers were, for many years, hampered by the customs and norms of the fashion industry. These customs meant that there was a time lag of between 6 and 12 months in getting new designs to mass markets. The fashion industry made this work to its own advantage by ensuring that new designs were sold on an exclusive basis to celebrities, and subsequently on a near-exclusive basis at haute couture fashion houses. Only then would the designs be released to the mass market.

Initiatives by Milliken Inc. in the United States and Matalan in the UK changed this for good. Milliken had an excellent and effective process of turning new designs into mass-market clothes in 80 days. By engaging in consultations with its factory managers, and re-posing the question as: 'What will it take to reduce this process to 24 hours?', Milliken was able to totally restructure its supply side to fit with both its own new demands, and the consequent expectations of the markets that new designs would now be available in 24 hours rather than 80 days.

Matalan adopted a similar approach. However, as a retailer only, Matalan had to find suppliers, both in the UK and elsewhere, that were prepared to work to a 24-hour new product development target once the designs were published. Both Matalan and Milliken had subsequently to change the processes again after the decision of leading designers and high-fashion houses to publish their designs on the Internet. This reduced the new product to market timescale from the 6–12 months noted above, or the 80 days of Milliken, to 24 hours.

Milliken and Matalan had therefore to ensure that supplies of cotton, thread and other materials were effectively advanced by anything up to 12 months if they were to be able to take advantage of these developments.

At strategic levels, creative and dynamic thinking, judgement and evaluation are used to clarify organisation direction and priorities, the viability of products and services, and assessment of new markets and opportunities. They inform particular decisions relating to investments and returns, initiatives and proposals (see Management in Focus 15.10).

At operational and individual levels, creativity is required in response to organisational, environmental, product and service issues that are certain to arise. Functions and activities find themselves faced with product and service resource changes and pressures, and these can be as wide and diverse as follows:

- cancellations, or sudden and urgent upturns and orders, of products and services
- loss or increases of product and service delivery capacity
- losses of staff and expertise; demands for changes in staff expertise and its application.

How individual managers respond to these issues is a reflection of their own resourcefulness, creativity and dynamism, and the ways they make effective use of

MANAGEMENT IN FOCUS 15.10

OUTSOURCING

Creative and dynamic approaches to outsourcing initiatives result in fully informed views of whether or not proposals are right for the particular organisation in its given set of circumstances. Based on full organisational and environmental analysis, the context for the outsource decision is known, understood and agreed. The decision to outsource or not is then taken. If the decision is not to go ahead, then there is a body of knowledge and understanding as to why this was the case; whatever was to be outsourced has then to be managed in-house.

If the decision is to go ahead with the initiative, then a series of opportunities, drives, hurdles and barriers have to be addressed. These issues are tackled from the point of view of identifying the desired outcomes and, working from this position, identifying the time and resource demands and constraints that have to be addressed in the given context in order to produce the results desired.

The particular issues vary between organisations and outsource relationships. It is usual to have to consider in full detail: contract management; organisation/outsource liai-

son; product and service levels; emergency responses and crisis management; and standards of conduct on the part of both organisations in their dealing with each other. The outcome of creative and dynamic approaches to management development in this set of circumstances ought to be a full knowledge and understanding of the nature of the relationship being entered into, specific demands for products and services, and the development of a fully confident and enduring professional relationship that is based on real activities rather than organisational expediency.

their managerial knowledge, skills and expertise in response to each event as it occurs (see Management in Focus 15.11).

Creativity, development and rewards

Many conventional organisations and professional and occupational career paths do not lead in the direction of the combination of freedom, creativity and discipline sought by intrapreneurs and the organisations that can accommodate them. Above all, formal promotion systems are much too rigid to cater for the natural, and often indirect, course of organisation, business and individual development that the approach implies. Traditional reward systems are also too restrictive to compensate for the risks involved, the developments that may arise, and the rewards on offer. Most promotional and reward systems are still based on the recognition of advancement through the ranks rather than advancement of organisational product and service performance. The need therefore is to develop a situation where rewards are related to collective and individual achievement, rather than rank orders and hierarchies. In many cases, this is a major hurdle for organisations to have to overcome. It is additionally the case that even where performance, profit and development awards are on offer, the softer aspects of

MANAGEMENT IN FOCUS 15.11

THE DIVERSE NATURE OF RESPONSES: EXAMPLES

- *Mitsubishi*: the Mitsubishi company changed and diversified itself away from making military aircraft, and into shipping, banking and car production, through investment in retraining and redeploying the staff rather than laying them off.
- *Sanyo UK*: Sanyo UK created a negligible staff absenteeism rate by ensuring that everyone who fell ill was visited by a member of staff from the company bearing a gift of flowers or chocolates. The company expressed sympathy, and hoped that it would not be long before the individual was back at work.
- *Otikon*: Otikon, the Danish hearing-technology company, provided a free and high-quality restaurant to encourage people to get to know each other, meet and understand each other, and from this to develop ideas, ventures and initiatives that would be of value to the company and its customers.

Developing creative and dynamic capabilities in managers at all levels therefore has a great range of pay-offs. It additionally enlarges and enhances both individual and collective expertise in facing anything that may occur, as shown above.

Many organisations are starting to see the benefits of ensuring that this is integrated into management development activities centred on project work, secondments and placements. From the organisation's point of view, this is becoming recognised as a key feature and benefit of mentoring, coaching and sponsorship activities.

reward are lacking – the aspects of status, recognition and esteem. Organisations have therefore to be prepared to develop their intrinsic, as well as extrinsic, approaches to reward management. If these problems are not addressed, this simply leads to frustration on the part of those with these qualities. Another result of this is under-performance on the part of the organisation, which is not maximising the talents, creativity and inherent commitment of the individuals that it is employing.

This is more complex than first appears. On the one hand, individuals have clearly to be recognised for the individual contribution that they make. On the other, if one key part of management is about achieving things through people then, ideally at least, all contributions need recognition as referring to their part of the whole achievement of the organisation; and there is therefore a fundamental requirement for an equality of recognition and reward. This is not always easy for those with high levels of creativity, expertise, innovation and commitment to recognise. Organisations therefore require processes and policies that are capable of accommodating all of these divergent (often conflicting) requirements, without departing from the path of a fundamental equality and fairness of treatment, nor from having to resort to rewarding people 'under the counter' in order that perceptions of unfairness do not become apparent.

● Conclusions

Fostering creativity, dynamism and commitment require organisational resourcing and strategic backing; this must be an enduring or strategic commitment. Very great care must be taken over the attraction, recruitment and retention of those individuals exhibiting these characteristics so that they can be developed into high value and expert members of staff. It is therefore essential to be clear about the characteristics of the individuals who can be developed in these ways, and made effective within given organisation settings. Organisations additionally have to know and understand the opportunities and consequences of employing persons with these capabilities.

The characteristics, qualities and creative drives identified as being essential within individuals are:

● commercial insight and market and environmental awareness and understanding
● personal strength of character and persistence in the approach to business matters and issues
● professional, occupational and creative stamina and staying power
● innovative and creative approaches to problems and the development of creative faculties
● the ability to manage and direct change in all aspects of the work, including processes and procedures
● the capacity for analysis
● the ability to organise, direct and control activities
● a clear understanding of the profit motive
● the ability to network, to animate people and to enable others to perform their jobs effectively and successfully.

Organisations wishing to engage these people must have the following characteristics:

● the ability to recognise the talents and potential of individuals and to harness these in mutually beneficial and profitable activities
● the ability to learn and develop more quickly than the rate of organisational change
● the ability to learn and develop as the result of all activities, including mistakes and errors
● the capacity to provide intrinsic and extrinsic rewards reflecting both organisational profit and individual capabilities and expectations.

The overall purpose is the creation of an organisation and environment where business activities and talented individuals can come together for the generation of successful, dynamic and profitable business activities. Effectively implemented, these approaches ensure a much greater clarity and focus upon strategy, policy, direction and priorities, and on the demands of markets, products and services. These approaches also influence: culture, attitudes and values; staff management; and leadership, cohesion, and collective and individual motivations and drives.

CRITICAL THINKING, ANALYSIS AND EVALUATION

1. Why do so many talented and creative individuals quickly become frustrated with their first management positions?
2. How should an organisation manage an enthusiastic and committed individual who keeps producing ideas which the organisation keeps turning down?
3. Identify the value and shortcomings of brainstorming as a creative and dynamic activity.
4. Identify the components present in any 'organisation immune system' that keeps turning down new ideas. From this, identify a creative and dynamic approach to removing the immune system itself.

DEVELOPING MANAGEMENT SKILLS AND EXPERTISE

INHERITANCE SUPERMARKETS LTD

Inheritance Supermarkets Ltd is a leading national retail chain. As well as selling the usual range of groceries, the company has recently extended its product range to include white goods, clothing, financial services, and books and CDs. The company additionally sells a branded range of retail pharmaceuticals, which are very profitable in terms of income per product sold.

The company used to hold a dominant position in the country's retail sector, but this has been declining for many years. Overall profitability and market share have fallen sharply, and this had led to talks with both other supermarket chains and venture capitalists about the possibility of buy out or takeover. To date, however, nothing has come of these talks.

Meanwhile, the company is doing what it can to try to restore its overall position, and to return towards the advantageous position that it used to enjoy. The company went back to assess its core range of grocery and foodstuff products. A full and extensive product and service analysis conducted over a period of seven months produced the following written comments on the monthly progress and sales of fresh food, fruit and vegetables and other perishables.

- *January*: fresh food sales are 49 per cent of what has been planned because of factory, warehouse and regional distribution centre backlogs.
- *February*: fresh food sales are 46 per cent of what is planned and this is because of the build-up of backlogs during the winter bad weather. It is likely that fresh food sales will be 20 per cent below what is planned for the month.
- *March*: total shipments continue to decline with overall sales at 50 per cent of plan, a 4 per cent increase from February. The company continues to have acquisition, production and distribution difficulties. There is a backlog of orders currently running at £500,000 per month. Part of the backlog is as the result of shipments and deliveries being withheld due to the bad weather.
- *April*: sales continue to decline due to a continuing product, market and distribution failure. The present advertising and marketing campaign has not led to increases in sales. Fresh foodstuffs now being offered at reduced prices on their

sell by dates now run at between 25–30 per cent. It is possible that some of the fresh produce can be shipped abroad to foreign operators on the mainland of Europe.

- *May*: sales continue to lag as reported in April. There is a slight improvement (0.5 per cent). Product acquisition and delivery backlog amounts to £560,000. All costs to date are in line with the latest forecasts; the only exception is an unseasonal demand for ice cream where there will be an overrun of £350,000. Acquiring, distributing and delivering the ice cream also has given problems due to a shortage of refrigerated transport.

- *June*: declining sales volumes, and the costs incurred, are now incorporated into the business plan for the coming year. Distribution continues to run at a backlog; and acquiring fresh products from suppliers is also a problem. Sales are at 52 per cent of plan.

- *July*: some of the cost calculations on acquisition, production, distribution and delivery were made in error; in particular there were accounting errors at head office. One group of costs priced the collection, delivery and distribution of lettuces at £2.50 per item. This figure was not checked. The present computerised stock management, acquisition and delivery system gives a period of three days only to be able to collect produce from suppliers, get it on to the shelves and sell it before its best-by date.

Questions

1. Identify the problems and barriers faced by Inheritance Supermarkets Ltd. Identify an order of priority for beginning to tackle these problems and barriers.
2. Identify as precisely as possible the outcomes desired, once it is determined to tackle these problems and barriers.
3. Identify the ways in which these problems might be addressed; identify also the opportunities, obligations and consequences that might have to be faced and accommodated.

Chapter sixteen

Culture

'The Body Shop is a tribe, a movement. It is a revolution in business.'
Anita Roddick, founder and Chief Executive, The Body Shop (1996).

'The Wimbledon spirit used to be worth 30 points a season. We would look at the people that we were playing against, international stars, household names, the lot. And I would say to Vinnie Jones, "This lot don't fancy it today. We're going to win easily" – and usually, we were right. We would beat the big clubs because we had spirit.'
John Fashanu, ex-footballer, interview, *Talk Sport* (1999).

'We have a maverick culture here. Anyone can do what they like. There are no rules.'
Kenneth Lay, President and CEO, Enron.

Chapter outline

- Introduction
- Pressures on organisation culture
- Internal pressures
- The cultural web
- Cultural influences
- Models of organisation culture
- Other aspects of organisation culture
- Culture management
- Conclusions

Chapter objectives

After studying this chapter, you should be able to:

- understand the sources and effects of cultural and behavioural pressures in organisations

- identify the steps necessary in order to be able to manage effectively these cultural and behavioural factors

- understand the relationship between what is to be done, and how it is to be done

- understand the consequences of not attending to the behavioural aspects of management.

● Introduction

If strategy, policy and direction are concerned with what organisations do, then organisational culture is about how they do it. The culture of an organisation is the basis for its management style, and individual and collective attitudes, values, behaviour and beliefs. It is therefore essential that the ways in which things are required to be done are clearly established, and accepted by all concerned. Distinctive standards of behaviour and attitudes must be established, rather than be allowed to emerge – neither must these be tolerated where they are legally, socially and morally unacceptable.

It is essential also to recognise the influence of different aspects of work layout, the working environment, and management style on the behaviour of organisations. The main points are as follows:

● Technology has influence on work arrangements and groupings, physical layout and the nature of the people employed.
● Structure and hierarchy influence personal and professional interactions, personal and professional ambitions and aspirations.
● Rules, regulations and systems influence attitudes and behaviour (positive or negative) depending on how they are drawn up and operated and on their particular focus.
● Leadership provides the key point of identity for everyone else, and from which people establish their own perceptions of the organisation's general standards.
● Management style influences the general feelings of well-being of everyone else, and sets standards of attitudes and behaviour as well as performance.
● Managerial demands and the ways in which these are made influence attitudes and behaviour also.
● Hierarchical and divisional relations and interactions influence the nature of performance, attention to achievement and the value placed on achievements; this also applies to functional activities.

Organisation culture is based on the following corporate and social issues:

● *History and tradition*: the origins of the organisation; the aims and objectives of the first owners and managers, and their philosophy and values; the value in which these are currently held; the ways in which they have developed.
● *Nature of activities*: historical and traditional as well as current and envisaged; this includes reference to the general state of success and effectiveness, and to the balance of activities – steady-state, innovative, crisis.
● *Technology*: the relationship between technology and the workforce, work design, organisation and structure; alienative factors and steps taken to get over these; levels of technological stability and change; levels of expertise, stability and change.
● *Past, present and future*: the importance of the past in relation to current and proposed activities; special pressures (especially struggles and glories) of the past; the extent to which the organisation 'is living' in the past, present or future, and the pressures and constraints that are brought about as the result.
● *Purposes, priorities and attention*: in relation to performance, staff, customers, the community and environment; and to progress and development.
● *Size*: and the degrees of formalisation and structure that this brings. Larger organisations are much more likely to have a proliferation of divisions, supervisory

structures, reporting relationships, rules, processes and procedures. This tends to cause communication difficulties, interdepartmental rivalries and problems with coordination and control.

● *Location*: geographical location: the constraints and opportunities afforded through choosing, for example, to site activities in urban centres, edge of town or rural areas. This also includes recognising and considering prevailing local, national and sectoral traditions and values.

● *Leadership and management style*: the stance adopted by the organisation in managing and supervising its people; the stance required by the people of managers and supervisors; the general relationships between people and organisation and the nature of superior–subordinate relations.

Organisation culture may be:

● designed or emergent
● strong or weak
● positive or negative
● cohesive or fragmented.

It is especially important that culture is designed, shaped and reinforced by those in top and senior positions. This involves setting standards of attitudes, values, behaviour and performance to which everyone is required to subscribe as a condition of employment. Statements of policies and procedures are produced so that everyone knows where they stand; and these are enforced when attitudes, behaviour, commitment and performance fall short in any way. Organisations with strong, positive and designed cultures are not all things to all people; and this needs to be made clear at recruitment and selection processes.

If organisation culture is allowed to emerge, the result is that people think, believe, behave and act according to their own priorities and the pressures of their peers; and this leads to the tendency to pursue their own agenda.

Organisations that allow this to happen succeed only if the aims and objectives of the staff, and interest groups, coincide absolutely with their own. When this happens, staff set their own informal procedures and sanctions; and it is a short step from this to bullying and victimisation. Organisations faced with emergent cultures invariably have staffing problems of some kind. When this happens, the characteristics of culture have to be identified and tackled (see Management in Focus 16.1).

● Pressures on organisation culture

Pressures on organisation culture exist both inside and outside the organisation. Organisations must respect the attitudes, values and ethics of the places where business is to be conducted; this includes reference to social and religious customs. External social and cultural prejudices may also have to be taken into account (see Management in Focus 16.2).

Local working practices and customs, expectations of hours of work and ways of working, have to be considered. In some places, activities close down for several hours during the day; in others people expect to start and finish work early. In some cases also, people are expected to socialise outside working hours as a condition of their employment (see Management in Focus 16.3).

MANAGEMENT IN FOCUS 16.1

CHARACTERISTICS OF CULTURE

Both in designing culture and in remedying the problems of emergent cultures, attention needs to be paid to each of the following areas to ensure that culture becomes strong, cohesive, positive, inclusive and designed. Culture is:

- *Learned*: rather than genetic or biological.
- *Shared*: members of groups and organisation share culture.
- *Continuous*: cumulative in its development and past on from one generation to the next.
- *Symbolic*: based on the human capacity to symbolise, to use one thing to represent another.
- *Integrated*: a change in one area will lead to a change in another.
- *Adaptive*: based on human qualities of adaptability, creativity, innovation and imagination.

- *Regular*: when participants interact with each other, they use common language terminology and recognised and accepted forms of behaviour.

Cultures has:

- *Norms*: distinctive standards of behaviour; the ways in which people interact with each other; relationships between, and within, ranks and hierarchies; the general patterns of behaviour, familiarity, habits, dress and speech.
- *Dominant values*: advocated by the organisation and expected by participants.
- *Philosophy*: policies concerning beliefs and standards of performance, attitude, behaviour and conduct. Organisational philosophy gives the cornerstone for establishing what is rewarded, punished and sanctioned.
- *Rules*: the formal rules that underline the constitution of the organisation; the informal rules that govern the interaction of individuals on a daily basis. The rules and procedures enforce what is rewarded, and especially what is punished and sanctioned.
- *Organisational climate*: conveyed by the physical appearance and layout of the organisation, and reinforced through the ways in which staff interact with each other and with the outside world.

Each of these characteristics is additionally a point of enquiry and potential influence when managers seek to change, develop and enhance organisation culture overall.

Physical distance affects culture and cohesion. The inability to see and meet with others, for example when work is being carried out in a foreign location or one remote from the main organisation, has effects on the structuring and ordering of tasks and activities, relationships among the staff at the location, and relationships between the location and head office. It also affects decision-making processes, and the attitudes and approaches to local problems and issues. Those in remote locations, and especially the person with overall responsibility and control, are likely to experience feelings of isolation from time to time and may need to be supported if the overall effectiveness of that part of the organisation is to be sustained (see Management in Focus 16.4).

MANAGEMENT IN FOCUS 16.2

HUMAN PREJUDICES

It is important to recognise that 'prejudice' – the subjective and unfounded attitudes adopted towards particular people, products and services – are a fact of human existence and behaviour. Most prejudices are harmless. For example, people who choose only to wear blue clothing are exhibiting a form of prejudice, as are those who always vote for a particular political party. Supporting a football club is a form of prejudice, as is always using the same supermarket for grocery shopping.

Prejudices against particular members of the community are abhorrent, however, and unacceptable in organisations. It is repugnant, and also illegal, to treat people with less respect on grounds of gender, race, disability, membership/non-membership of a trade union or spent convictions for a criminal offence. It is also ethically and morally abhorrent to treat people differently and with less respect on the grounds of age, sexual orientation, marital status, physical appearance, the way they

speak or the place in which they live. It is both abhorrent and illegal to allow bullying, victimisation, harassment, and physical and verbal assaults.

Organisations that allow repugnant forms of prejudice invariably suffer from low morale, and declining levels of output. Organisation cultures become weak and divided, as people gang up on the particular oppressed individual or group; and as those who are being oppressed seeks the means to fight back.

MANAGEMENT IN FOCUS 16.3

NISSAN UK

Headquarters staff at Nissan UK in north-east England used to meet regularly on Thursday and Friday evenings. This was expected by the company on the basis that meeting in a social atmosphere encouraged personal and professional understanding; it additionally gave the opportunity to sort out organisational problems away from the pressures of work.

One member of staff objected to this. This person, a lady in her early thirties, considered that her work commitment ended when she left the office. She had other priorities in her life, and especially had to return home early in the evening in order to feed her children.

Nissan first encouraged her to participate; then when this did not work, she was disci-

plined. The lady complained to ACAS and then to the UK employment tribunal system. Nissan initially defended the case; however, at the point at which the case was to be heard, the company proposed a settlement which was acceptable to all.

The company's managerial and administrative staff continue to meet on Thursday and Friday evenings.

MANAGEMENT IN FOCUS 16.4

FLEXIBLE WORKING

Maintaining a collective corporate identity is an enduring problem for those managers responsible for flexible and non-standard patterns of work. Whether these are related to irregular hours, working in remote locations or telecommuting, the core need is to ensure that everybody is instilled with collective, cohesive and positive attitudes and values in their relationship with the organisation.

It is therefore a priority for managers faced with these issues to ensure that they visit and meet with their staff as often as possible, and where this is not possible, to ensure that they speak to them on the telephone. This is preferable to regular e-mails; where e-mails are used, important and urgent issues must always be followed up with telephone calls, and meetings where possible.

Additionally, where flexible staff do attend at the organisation's headquarters or premises, they must be given the opportunity to meet and socialise with their colleagues, so that a personal, as well as occupational identity is developed.

Psychological distance has also to be managed. Psychological distance is likely to exist as a feature of physical distance even if there is a full range of electronic and telecommunications available. It is also present to a greater or lesser extent between the organisation and the communities in which it works, and the interaction of organisational attitudes, standards and values with those of the localities must also be considered. The relationship with the community has also to be considered from the point of view of the economic contribution made by the organisation in the provision of work. This is a responsibility for all organisations; it is a critical responsibility when the organisation is the largest single or dominant employer in the area.

Within organisations, psychological distance is reinforced by status symbols and trappings, perks and benefits, office location, and the employment of personal staff such as secretaries, personal assistants and staff officers.

The organisation may go into a given location for commercial advantage but with preconceived ideas or prejudices (which may either be positive or negative). The organisation may bring with it a particular reputation (again, positive or negative), either about itself or the sector which it represents and within which it operates. There may be wider questions of prejudice, fear and anxiety to be overcome as the organisation tries to live up to (or live down to) its reputation. Areas that have had bad experiences of multinational activities in the past for example may be anxious about the next influx.

All organisations have to work within the laws of their locations. Laws exert pressure on production methods, waste disposal, health and safety, marketing and selling, contractual arrangement, staff management, human resources, industrial relations and equality (or otherwise) of opportunity and access, community relations, organisational and professional insurance, and the reporting of results; each of these in turn affects the behaviour and priorities of the organisation.

Pressures are compounded when the organisation operates in many countries and under diverse legal codes. Balances have to be found in these cases to ensure that, as far as possible, everyone who works for the organisation does so on terms that transcend the varying legal constraints. Organisations are therefore obliged to set absolute standards that more than meet particular legal minima. Moreover, the phrase 'we comply with the law' invariably gives the message that 'the only reason that we set these standards is because we have to' and that the organisation has therefore been pressured into these standards rather than achieving them because it believes that they are right. It calls into question not just the organisation's attitude to the law, but also its wider general attitudes, values and standards (see Management in Focus 16.5).

Ethical pressures arise from the nature of work carried out and from the standards and customs of the communities in which the organisation operates. There are also general ethical pressures on many activities that are covered by the law; examples of these pressures are given in Management in Focus 16.6. Again, the ideal response of any organisation is to put itself beyond reproach so that these pressures are accommodated and leave the way clear to developing productive and harmonious relationships with all concerned.

Internal pressures

The internal pressures on organisation culture and cohesion are as follows:

- The interaction between the desired culture and the organisation's structures and systems. Serious misfit between these leads to stress and frustration, and also to customer dissatisfaction and staff demotivation.
- The expectations and aspirations of staff, and the extent to which these are realistic and can be satisfied within the organisation. This becomes a serious issue when the nature of organisation changes and prevailing expectations can no longer be accommodated. Problems also arise when the organisation makes promises that it cannot keep.
- Management and supervisory style, the extent to which this is supportive, suitable to the purpose and generally acceptable to the staff.
- The qualities and expertise of the staff, and the extent to which these divide their loyalties. Many staff groups have professional and trade union memberships, and continuous professional development requirements and career expectations, as well as holding down positions and carrying out tasks within organisations. In many cases – and especially when general dissatisfaction is present – people tend to take refuge in their profession or occupation, or their trade union.
- Technology and the extent to which it impacts on the ways in which work is designed, structured and carried out.
- Working customs, traditions and practices, including restrictive practices, work divisions, specialisation and allocation, unionisation and other means of representation; and the attitudes and approaches adopted by both organisation and staff towards each other – flexible and cooperative, adversarial, degrees of openness.
- The extent to which continuity of employment is feasible, or conversely, uncertainties around future prospects for work and employment. This includes degrees of flexibility, the extent and prevalence of employee and skills development, learning sub-cultures and the wider attitude of both staff and organisation to this. It also affects reward packages.

MANAGEMENT IN FOCUS 16.5

THE INDEPENDENT'S GLOBAL SWEATSHOP

Sweatshop labourers in some of Britain's small garment factories are routinely paid less than the minimum wage but are too frightened to complain, the Low Pay Commission has been told. Evidence to the Commission from the textile workers' union in 1999 said that workers fear reprisals if they ask for the legal minimum wage (£3.60 an hour at that time, and now £5.05). Most are scared of losing their jobs, and some have suffered physical abuse. 'The workers have told us that non-payment of the minimum wage is common practice in every company they know,' the National Union of Knitwear, Footwear and Apparel Trades told the commission.

The union has brought tribunal cases on behalf of several workers, all of them Asian. The lowest pay it found was about £1.50 per hour. The union says that because small garment factories are usually found in Britain's ethnic minority communities, workers often speak little English and, although they know their rights, they do not always know how to demand them.

One woman who was sacked because she asked her boss for the minimum wage told the union:

Many women are scared, especially those who have worked for the same employer for 10 years or more and have even more to lose. I told my friend to come forward, but she said that because her husband is out of work she cannot risk losing her job.

Union officers took *The Independent* on a tour of Leicester's garment factories, where 80 per cent of the manufacturing units employ fewer than 20 people. Reporters saw blocked fire exits, machines without safety guards and workers sewing garments behind padlocked doors. In a former typewriter factory that contained dozens of small garment units, it was reported that work stopped for the day when health and safety inspectors were expected. Off each damp, dark stairwell, groups of workers were huddled over antiquated machines amid piles of cloth and debris. Some of the workers said they were making goods for big high-street stores and were earning less than £3.60 an hour. Haroun Khan said he made jeans and leggings for a well-known store at rates as low as £2.50 an hour. During a quiet period earlier that summer he had been laid off without pay. 'There is no guard on my machine and when a needle flies out anything could happen,' he said. 'I told the boss there was supposed to be a guard. He said he knew what I meant but he didn't do anything. I'm thinking of avoiding factories in the future.'

He and several others confirmed that they were paid piece rates and their bosses simply divided their weekly earnings by £3.60 to come up with a fictional number of working hours for their pay slips. In many cases, no record was kept of what hours they worked.

Source: Fran Abrams *The Independent*, 27 September 1999.

● Internal approaches and attitudes to the legal and ethical issues that arise, the extent of genuine commitment to equality of opportunity and access for all staff; whether or not different grades have different values placed on them, standards of dealings with staff, customers, communities, suppliers and distributors.

MANAGEMENT IN FOCUS 16.6

EXAMPLES OF ETHICAL PRESSURES

Points for attention in relating ethics and culture are as follows:

- *Activities*: most activities carry some form of commitment, and other commitments are imposed on the staff by organisations. For example, medical staff have commitments to their patients, community services staff have commitments to their customers, and public servants have commitments to their clients.
- *Sectors*: there is a universal duty not to supply shoddy goods and service, but rather to provide products and

services of integrity. Some sectors have additional problems with this – for example, tobacco, alcohol, armaments and medical research.
- *Waste disposal*: the onus is clearly on organisations to make adequate arrangements to clear up any mess made by their processes. Some areas and countries have lower standards for this. Organisations assess the convenience of easier dumping of rubbish and balance this against absolute standards of right and wrong and any loss of reputation that

might occur in the future if its waste leads to some form of contamination.
- *Equal opportunities, staff management, industrial relations and health and safety*: high standards of practice in each of these areas are marks of respect and care to staff, customers and communities.
- *Results reporting*: results reporting should be done in ways that can be understood by anyone who has an interest or stake in the organisation, and indeed anyone else who would like to know how it is performing.

- The presence of pride and commitment in the organisation, its work and its reputation; standards of general well-being; the extent of mutual respect.
- Communication methods and systems, the nature of language used, the presence/absence of hidden agendas.
- Physical and psychological distance between functions, departments, divisions and positions in the organisation and its hierarchies, as discussed above (see Management in Focus 16.7 and Figure 16.1).

Cultural influences

Hofstede (1980; 2003) carried out studies that identified cultural similarities and differences among the 116,000 staff of IBM located in 40 countries. He identified basic dimensions of national cultures and the differences in their emphases and importance in the various countries. The four dimensions were.

- *Power distance*: the extent to which power and influence is distributed across the society; the extent to which this is acceptable to the members of the

MANAGEMENT IN FOCUS 16.7

THE CULTURAL WEB

The cultural web is an alternative way of looking at the internal pressures upon organisation culture. People draw heavily on points of reference which are built up over periods of time and which are especially important at internal organisational level. The beliefs and assumptions that comprise this fall within the following boundaries:

- There are routine ways that members of the organisation behave towards each other and that link different parts of the organisation and comprise 'the way that things are done'. These, at their best, lubricate the working of the organisation and may provide distinctive and beneficial organisational competency. However, they can also represent a 'take for granted' attitude about how things should happen which can be extremely difficult to change.

- The rituals of organisational life such as training programmes, promotion and assessment point to what is important in the organisation, reinforce 'the way we do things around here' and signal what is actually valued.

- The stories told by members of the organisation to each other, to outsiders and to new recruits, embed the present organisation in its history and flag up important events and personalities.

- There are symbolic aspects of organisation such as logos, offices, cars and titles, or the type of language and terminology commonly used.

- The control systems, measures and reward systems emphasise what is actually important and focus attention and activity.

- Power structures are also likely to be associated in so far as the most powerful groupings are likely to be the ones most associated with what is actually valued.

- The formal organisation structure and the more informal ways in which the organisation works are likely to reflect these power structures, and again to delineate important relationships and emphasise required levels of performance.

society; access to sources of power and influence; and the physical and psychological distance that exists between people and the sources of power and influence.

- *Uncertainty avoidance*: the extent to which people prefer order and certainty, or uncertainty and ambiguity; and the extent to which they feel comfortable or threatened by the presence or absence of each.

- *Individualism–collectivism*: the extent to which individuals are expected or expect to take care of themselves; the extent to which a common good is perceived and the tendency and willingness to work towards this.

- *Masculinity–femininity*: the distinction between 'masculine' values – the acquisition of money, wealth, fortune, success, ambition, possessions – and the

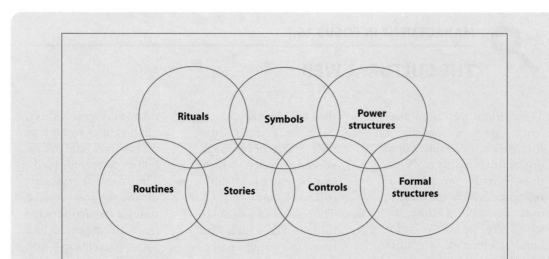

Figure 16.1 The cultural web

'feminine' ones of sensitivity, care, concern, attention to the needs of others, quality of life; and the value, importance, mix and prevalence of each (see Management in Focus 16.8).

Informal elements and sub-cultures

Sub-cultures exist in all organisations. They relate to membership of different groups and vary between these – for example, in the degree of openness of dealings between members. Sub-cultures become more destructive when they operate contrary to absolute standards. Forms of this are:

- *The canteen culture*: whereby the shared values adopted are those of groups that gather away from the work situations and in such places as the washroom or canteen.
- *Elites and cliques*: whereby strength and primacy is present in some groups at the expense of others. This leads to over-mightiness. It affects operations when the elites and cliques are able to command resources, carry out projects and gain prestige at the expense of others; to lobby effectively for resources at the expense of others; and to gain favour at the expense of others.
- *Work regulation*: whereby the volume and quality of work is regulated by the group for its own ends rather than those of the organisation; when groups set and work to their own targets which are at variance with those of the organisation.
- *Informal norming*: whereby individuals are pressurised to adopt the attitudes and values of those around them rather than those of the organisation. This occurs most often when the organisation's own norms are not sufficiently strong or structured enough to remove the local or group pressure.

MANAGEMENT IN FOCUS 16.8

CULTURE'S CONSEQUENCES IN ACTION: THE FROZEN FOOD INDUSTRY

A company based in London owned a frozen food factory in north-west England. Over a period of years, the factory developed a reputation for poor employee relations and low productivity. Whenever production deadlines were not met, or whenever there was a collective dispute or grievance, the head office in London always responded by threatening to close the factory down.

This process went on for a period of 12 years. The first time the threats were made, they were taken seriously, and productivity improved for a period of years. However, the problems continued and the company's response remained the same, and so people began not to take the threats seriously. The collective view of the workforce was summarised as: 'One day you will probably close us down anyway, because that is clearly your attitude towards us; the threat therefore has no potency. In the meantime, it is clear that you are treating us with disrespect and contempt.'

Until the announcement of the factory closure was made, nobody from the head office with any authority went up to see the problem for themselves. No meaningful communication took place. Everything was carried out by telephone, fax or memorandum. This all took place at a time when the frozen food industry was growing at a rate of 11 per cent per annum.

● *Power distance*: because power was located far away from the factory, the staff themselves had no ability to influence their own destiny; crucial decisions were taken without reference to their contribution.

● *Uncertainty avoidance*: eventually, the presence and repetition of the threats became a 'certainty'; the staff also created their own 'certainty' by moving to the assumption that they would be closed down anyway.

● *Individualism–collectivism*: the staff were dealt with by head office as a collective; no attention was paid to individual needs, wants, hopes, fears and aspirations.

● *Masculinity–femininity*: the company exhibited all of the adversarial and confrontational 'masculine' traits, rather than assessing the situation from the point of view of the end result required, and engaging a collective and inclusive consensus.

● *Culture of fear*: whereby, invariably as the result of threats, bullying and victimisation, a culture is created in which people are frightened to use their own initiative, take any actions that are not precisely regulated, or participate in decision-making processes, for fear that they will subsequently be held personally responsible for anything that goes wrong.

● *Culture of blame*: whereby organisations and their managers blame particular individuals or groups when things go wrong.

● *Personality cults*: whereby sub-cultures are formed around the powerful, dominant or expert personality of a particular individual.

● *Elite groups and teams*: often constituted for a particular purpose, elite groups and teams can develop a collective belief of infallibility and immortality (see Management in Focus 16.9).

Models of organisation culture

The various models of organisation culture are summarised below.

Power culture

Power culture is where the one key relationship that exists is between each member of staff and the person who weals power and influence. Power cultures depend on the figure at the centre, the source of power. All the other players draw their strength, influence and confidence from this centre and require its continued support to ensure prosperity and operational viability. The relationship is normally terminated when there is a loss of confidence on the part of the person at the centre

MANAGEMENT IN FOCUS 16.9

THE UK POLICE SERVICE

In recent years, the UK police service in all parts of the country has suffered a series of mistakes and errors. Many of these mistakes and errors can be put down to the inability to set and maintain overall standards in all aspects of police work. The informal elements and sub-cultures have therefore become dominant in specific situations. For example:

- In the north of England, a woman police constable suffered serious sexual harassment, resulting on three occasions in assault. The particular police force refused to listen to her complaint. It eventually settled at employment tribunal,

paying her £300,000 in damages.
- An anti-terrorist unit pursued and shot the wrong person. Despite having procedures to follow, which would have resulted in checks being made in advance of the individual being confronted and shot, the collective behaviour that drove the response to real and perceived terrorist threats took over. The subsequent inquiry took years to resolve.
- A police sergeant from the Asian community was vilified for trying to establish a community relations liaison function. When he pointed out

that all that he was doing was creating something that was already available to the white and Afro-Caribbean communities, he was disciplined and then transferred to other duties. The police force eventually paid him £250,000.

Each of these events occurred despite the very strong perceived and assumed culture of commitment to service held by the public at large; and the very strong collective and cohesive culture assumed by members of the police force as a whole; and in spite of the fact that policies and procedures exist to ensure that these things can never happen.

of power in those who work for him/her. Individuals generate power cultures when they attract those who have faith in them and who wish to be involved with them.

The main problem that a power culture must face is that of size. As it grows and diversifies, it becomes difficult for the person at the centre to sustain continued high levels of influence. There is also the problem of permanence, of what happens when the person at the centre of power passes out of the organisation. In situations where they have generated the ideas, energy, identity and strength of the situation, a void is left when they leave or die.

The structural form of the power culture may be seen as like a spider's web (see Figure 16.2). The main relationship of the subordinates is with the centre.

People/person culture

The people/person culture exists for the people in it – for example, where a group of people have decided that it is in their own overriding interest to band together and produce an organisation for their own benefit. This may be found in certain research groups, university departments, family firms, and companies started by groups of friends where the first coming together is generated by the people involved rather than the matter in hand. The key relationship is therefore between people, and what binds them is their intrinsic common interest. Hierarchy and structure may evolve, but these too will be driven by this intrinsic common interest (see Figure 16.3).

Task culture

Task cultures are to be found in project teams, marketing groups and marketing-oriented organisations. The emphases are on getting the job completed, keeping customers and clients satisfied, and responding to and identifying new market opportunities. Such cultures are flexible, adaptable and dynamic.

They accommodate movements of staff necessary to ensure effective project and development teams and continued innovation, and concurrent human activities such

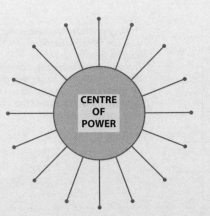

The **key relationship** is with the centre or source of power, hence no joining lines between the 'spokes'

The **key issue** is the continuation of confidence and reciprocity between the two.

Figure 16.2 Power culture + structure: the wheel

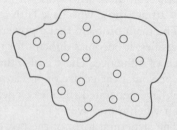

The **key relationship** is between the people; what binds them is their **intrinsic** common interest. Hierarchy and structure may evolve incidentally; they too will be driven by this intrinsic common interest.

Figure 16.3 People/person culture + structure: the mass

as secondments, project responsibility and short-term contracts. They are driven by customer satisfaction. They operate most effectively in prosperous, dynamic and confident environments and markets. They may also generate opportunities and niche activities in these, and create new openings. Their success lies in their continued ability to operate in this way (see Figure 16.4).

Role culture

Role cultures are found where organisations have gained a combination of size, permanence and departmentalisation, and where the ordering of activities, preservation of knowledge, experience and stability are both important and present.

The key relationship is based on authority and the superior–subordinate style of relationships. The key purposes are order, stability, permanence and efficiency.

Role cultures operate most effectively where the wider environment is steady and a degree of permanence is envisaged.

Other forms may also be identified.

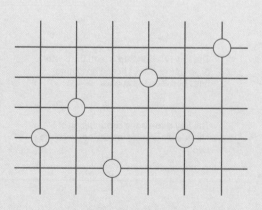

The **key relationship** here is with the task. The form of organisation is therefore fluid and elastic.
The **structure** is often also described as a MATRIX or GRID; none of these gives a full configuration -the essence is the dynamics of the form, and the structure necessary to ensure this.

Figure 16.4 Task culture + structure: the net

Focal elements

This is where the organisation identifies one key element as its cultural base. These are to be found in such areas as safety and learning cultures, whereby the particular point – safety or learning, for example – is placed at the centre of the organisation's commitment to standards. Examples of safety cultures are Western airlines and the oil industry, where everything is designed, built, structured and organised so that accidents and disasters cannot happen. Examples of learning cultures are to be found across all sectors and are instigated by companies as integral to continuous change and improvement, drives for flexibility and dynamism, the development of potential and quality, and organisation behaviour transformation (see Figure 16.5).

Distinctive models of organisation culture are very seldom found in isolation. In practice, most organisations (except for the very small) have features of each. Some conclusions may be drawn however. Whichever the dominant culture, the main concerns are:

- relationships between people, hierarchies, authority, reporting, attention to task and interaction during work
- standards, of behaviour, attitudes and performance; of integrity, honesty and openness; of mutual respect and regard
- values and shared values, and the basis on which these are established; the gaining and maintenance of commitment; the creation of a strength and identity of purpose
- management and organisation style that is suitable both to productive and effective work, and to underpinning the standards and values that ensure that this can take place
- expectations and aspirations, ensuring that what the organisation offers is clearly understood at the outset by all who come to work in it and reconciling these with those of the people concerned

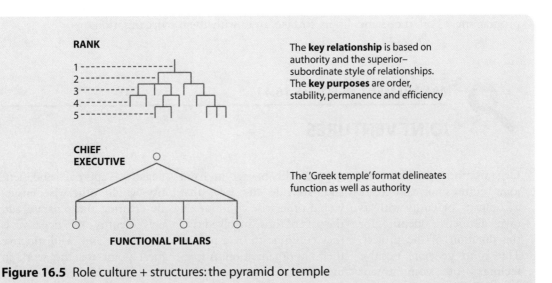

Figure 16.5 Role culture + structures: the pyramid or temple

- being positive and dynamic rather than negative, emergent and inert
- working within the pressures and constraints present in particular situations, locations and types of work; and devising means by which these two can be reconciled with organisational purposes, aims and objectives
- establishing universal interest in the success and future of the organisation; and reconciling and harmonising the divergence of interests, personal and professional aims and objectives within the organisation's overall purposes
- establishing a strength of identity between staff and organisation, a common bond, pride and positive feelings in belonging to the organisation, and a team, group and organisation spirit (see Management in Focus 16.10, 16.11 and 16.12).

MANAGEMENT IN FOCUS 16.10

IDENTITY

A telecommunication giant ran a series of culture change programmes for all its people. The purpose was to generate a new feeling and high degree of identity and commitment among those working for the company in the wake of recent privatisation, restructuring, job losses and redundancies.

Senior staff were flown to locations in Spain, Portugal and the South of France for a week to be put through their programme. For the same purpose middle and junior management and supervisory staff attended two-day programmes at 2, 3 and 4-star hotels around the UK. Skilled, semi-skilled, unskilled, operative and clerical staff attended half-day or one-day programmes at village halls, colleges and company training centres.

At the end of the programme each member was given sets of papers and handouts to take away with them and these were packaged in distinctive bags with the company's logo printed on them.

Consultants and trainers who carried out the work in the village halls and training centres reported that most people left the bags behind. Those who took them with them invariably turned them inside out before leaving the venue, so as not to be identified with the particular organisation.

MANAGEMENT IN FOCUS 16.11

JOINT VENTURES

Organisations involved in joint ventures normally create a company or entity with its own distinctive identity for the duration of the project. This is to generate positive feelings of commitment towards the matter in hand and override the view that would otherwise continue on the part of those involved that they continue to be a part of their old organisation. A fragmented and disordered – and negative – approach and identity would otherwise ensue. By creating the separate and new identity, the negative is overcome and a distinctive focal point for the work in hand is established.

MANAGEMENT IN FOCUS 16.12

MERGERS AND TAKEOVERS

Mergers and takeovers are normally extremely attractive from the point of view of generating short-term share price advantages. Almost invariably however, less attention is paid to how the newly merged organisation is to operate in the future. In particular, staff coming from the previously independent organisations, have to be steered and guided through the transition period in which the culture, values, attitudes and identity of the previous organisation are translated into a new and positive identity with what now exists. This is not always easy to achieve, and it is rarely considered by those steering mergers and takeovers. Failure to do so however, means that people will constantly hark back to the good old days before the merger or takeover; and they become even slower to accept and internalise new ways of working, and new patterns of behaviour and ways of working that now have to be followed, or to bond with colleagues from other organisations involved.

● Other aspects of organisational culture

Other features of organisational culture may be distinguished:

- *Relationships with the environment*: including the ways in which the organisation copes with uncertainty and turbulence; the ways the organisation seeks to influence the environment; the extent to which it behaves proactively or reactively.
- *History and tradition*: the extent to which the organisation's histories and traditions are a barrier or a facilitator of progress; the extent to which the organisation values and worships its histories and traditions; key influences on current activities and beliefs; the position of key interest groups – for example, trade unions.
- *The internal relationship balance*: the mixture and effectiveness of power, status, hierarchy, authority, responsibility, individualism, group cohesion; the general relationship mixture of task, social factors and development.
- *Rites and rituals*: these are the punctuation marks of organisation operations. They include: pay negotiations; internal and external job application means and methods; disciplinary, grievance and dismissal procedures; rewards; individual, group, departmental and divisional publicity; training and development activities; parties and celebrations; key appointments and dismissals; and the socialisation and integration of people into new roles, activities and responsibilities.
- *Routines and habits*: these are the formal, semi-formal and informal ways of working and interaction that people generate for themselves (or which the organisation generates for them) to make comfortable the non-operational aspects of working life. They develop around the absolutes – attendance times, work requirements, authority and reporting relationships – and include

regular meetings, regular tasks, forms of address between members of the organisation and groups, pay days, holidays and some trainee development activities.

- *Badges and status symbols:* these are the marks of esteem conferred by organisations on their people. They are a combination of location – near to or away from the corridors of power for example; possessions – cars, technology, personal departments; job titles – reflecting a combination of ability, influence and occupation; and position in the hierarchy's pecking order.

The effects of rites, rituals, routines, habits, badges and status symbols all lie in the value that the organisation places on them and the value in which they are held by the members of staff. There is no point in offering anything or undertaking any form of cultural activity if a negligible or negative response is received. In general therefore, these forms of culture development both anticipate people's expectations and seek to reinforce them and to meet them.

Stories, myths and legends

All organisations have their fund of stories, myths and legends. The nature and content of these represent and reflect the current state of organisational culture and well-being (see Management in Focus 16.13).

MANAGEMENT IN FOCUS 16.13

STORIES, MYTHS AND LEGENDS: EXAMPLES

- 'I knew I'd made a mistake, and I knew that the senior consultant was in a towering rage. I could hear him coming. So I borrowed a patient's dressing gown, wrapped it around me so that my uniform was not showing, and sat on a commode next to one of the beds until he had gone.' Staff nurse, south-eastern general hospital (2000) on inter-professional relations.
- 'We took an incredible risk going into the airline business.' Richard Branson, keeping up the adventurous image of the Virgin Group; in fact the venture was meticulously planned and the subject of extensive investment before Virgin Atlantic ever flew.
- 'McKinsey consultants used to be brilliant, creative and interesting – they were eccentrics. Now they all look the same, say the same, and have the same thing to offer – whether or not this is what the client requires.' Tom Peters (2000) *Masters of the Universe*, Channel 4, on the development of McKinsey Management Consultants since his departure.
- 'Everybody is harking back to the good old days. They speak and reminisce fondly of bygone times, a golden era – in fact, an era that never was.' *John Major: The Autobiography* (1998), Harper Collins.

● Culture management and attention to culture

Both the actual culture and the perceived ideal are subject to constant development. With this in mind, the best organisations therefore pay this constant attention. There are some basic assumptions here.

People can, and do, change if it is in their interests to do so. People resist change when they perceive or understand that it is not in their interests. All changes in standards and behaviour therefore require to be presented as being in the best interests of those affected; where this is not the case, people still need to know and understand clearly what is to be expected of them, so that they can then choose whether or not to remain with the organisation.

Culture can be changed and developed. There are too many examples where this has happened to think otherwise. Nissan UK transformed a population of ex-miners, shipbuilders and steelworkers into the most productive and effective car company in the UK. Toyota at Derby is following suit with former railway staff. British Airways transformed a bureaucratic nationalised monopoly into a customer-orientated multinational corporation. British Steel transformed itself from a loss-making national corporation, riddled with demarcation and restrictive practices, to a profitable, effective and flexible operator, before merging with Koninklijke Hoogovens to form the Corus Group.

Culture should be changed and developed. The constant development of operations, technology, markets, customer bases and the capabilities of the human resource make this inevitable. Current ways of working and equipment, and current skills, knowledge and qualities serve current needs only. The future is based around the developments and innovations that are to take place in each of these areas. Therefore, the culture must itself develop in order that these can be accommodated.

Culture change can be long and costly, especially where people resist. It is certainly true that where stability has existed for a long while, change is traumatic at first – and therefore costly in terms of people's feelings and possibly also in terms of current morale. It is made easier for the future if new qualities and attitudes of flexibility, dynamism and responsiveness are included in the new form and if this reinforced through ensuring that people understand that the old ways are now neither effective nor viable.

Culture change need not take forever. Indeed, people who are told that there are to be lengthy periods of turbulence lose interest and motivation. The reality of change and development can be quickly conveyed through critical incidents – the gain or loss of a major order, the collapse of a large firm in the sector, the entry of a new player into the sector, radical technological advances and so on. Once this is understood, the attitudes, behaviour and orientation of the staff are given emphases in particular directions and the general positioning of their aspirations, hopes and fears is changed.

● Conclusions

Effective organisation cultures are positive and designed rather than emergent. They must be capable of gaining commitment to purpose, the ways in which this is pursued and the standards adopted by everyone (see Management in Focus 16.14). Cultures are a summary and reflection of the aims and objectives, and the values held. Where neither are apparent, different groups and individuals form their own aims and objectives and adopt their own values; where these are at variance with overall purpose, or negative in some way, they are dysfunctional and may become destructive.

For this to be effective, a strong mutual sense of loyalty and acceptance between organisation and people is essential. Employees exert positive effort on behalf of the organisation, making a personal as well as professional or occupational commitment. The reverse of this – the organisation's commitment to its people – is also essential. A strong sense of identity towards the organisation and its purposes and values is required, and this happens when these are clear and positive. Any commitment made by people to organisations (or anything else) is voluntary and personal – and can be changed or withdrawn. The best organisations produce cultures that are capable of generating this. They create the desire among their people to join, remain with and progress, recognising their mutuality of interest and the benefits available to everyone.

The conclusion of this is an organisation culture that has the following elements:

● *A positive aura*: one to which people can subscribe and identify with confidence, pride, feelings of well-being; which in turn encourages positive views of the organisation and its work; positive and harmonious working relationships.

● *Shared values and standards*: capable of being adopted and followed by all concerned; this includes attention to high standards of integrity and morality; mutual concern and interest; and equity and equality.

● *High levels of individuality, identity, motivation and commitment*: coupled with high levels of group identity and mutual respect and regard.

● *Organisation and management style*: that is supportive of everyone involved (whatever the style, whether autocratic or participative) and which concentrates on results and output, effectiveness and quality of performance and also on the development and improvement of the people.

● *Regular flows of high quality information*: that reflect high levels of respect and esteem for the people on the part of the organisation.

Again, these can provide a useful point of reference for those concerned with the general well-being of the organisation, not least when it becomes apparent that things are going wrong.

MANAGEMENT IN FOCUS 16.14

EXCELLENCE AND CULTURE

Without exception the dominance and coherence of culture proved to be an essential quality of the excellent companies [the 62 American companies studied by Peters and Waterman]. Moreover, the stronger the culture, and the more it was directed to the market place, the less need there was for policy manuals, organisation charts or detailed procedures and rules. In these companies, people way down the line know what they are supposed to do in most situations because the handful of guiding values is crystal clear.

Source: T.J. Peters and R.H. Waterman (1982).

Much of this is clearly concerned with setting high standards and creating a positive general environment and background. This is to be seen in the context that where these elements are either not present or not attended to, or where the converse is present – a negative aura to which people do not subscribe, a lack of shared values, or an unsupported management style, for example – there is no identity or common purpose. People seek refuge in groups or in their profession or technical expertise. Absenteeism and turnover increase, performance declines. There begins to be an ever-greater concentration on self, on individual performance, often at the expense of that of the organisation. Interpersonal and inter-group relationships also suffer.

Both the positive and negative feed off each other. Striving for a positive and ideal culture tends to reinforce the high levels of value placed on the staff and the more general matters of honesty and integrity. Similarly, allowing the negative to persist tends to mean that relationships will get worse, aims and objectives become ever more fragmented or clouded, and organisational purpose ever more obscured.

CRITICAL THINKING, ANALYSIS AND EVALUATION

1. Outline the benefits and drawbacks of offering status symbols – for example, personal offices, car parking spaces, job titles – as marks of progress. What steps should be taken to ensure that overall benefits prevail and not the drawbacks?
2. What steps should organisations take to maintain and develop their culture in periods of (a) rapid expansion, and (b) rapid shrinkage?
3. What does the work of Hofstede indicate about cultural similarities and differences? Why are some multinational organisations so much more successful than others when operating away from their main locations and country of origin?
4. What changes are required in skills, knowledge, attitudes and behaviour for all groups of staff when moving from an archetype role culture to an archetype task culture? Produce an outline culture change programme to achieve this, indicating the timescale that you are prepared to allow for this change to take place.

DEVELOPING MANAGEMENT SKILLS AND EXPERTISE

TAYLOR ENGINEERING LTD

Taylor Engineering Ltd was a light engineering company producing components for the motor manufacturing sector. Staff management was generally good; employee relations were good also, though there were minor disputes and grievances form time to time, especially in the production departments.

In the design section, however, employee relations, attendance, output and quality of work were all excellent. There were 30 staff working in four teams. Each team was well structured, and the section as a whole were tightly knit, cohesive and got on very well at a personal as well as professional level. The dominant personality was Martin Briggs, aged 40, and an excellent designer.

The design manager, Maureen Tucker, was proud of the record of the design section, and would boast about it to anyone who would listen. Maureen walked the whole section on a regular basis and kept in close touch with all the staff. The staff thought that she could sometimes be a bit overbearing and interfering; but they always met her requests. In particular, her regular requests for overtime had never been a problem – anyone who wanted it could have it; and Martin would share it out on an equitable basis acceptable to all the staff.

Big changes in motor car designs across the industry entailed considerable design changes, and above all, streamlining and simplification. While this would result in increased work for the company as a whole, there was a clear prospect of reductions in the numbers employed in the design section. Redeployments elsewhere would undoubtedly be possible, and one or two might opt for early retirement; but it did seem that there would have to be at least one compulsory redundancy. The last person in was Louisa Horton, a graduate engineer and designer who had been with the company for two years.

Maureen spoke to Martin, and then to Louisa. All the staff felt that the section was bound to pick up extra work when the new designs became widespread across the car industry. Their view was that it was better to keep a good and cohesive team together even if things were a bit quiet at the moment. Good designers were difficult to attract to the motor car industry, which was not presently fashionable or desirable to many graduates.

Formal discussions were engaged, involving Maureen, Martin, Louisa and the company HR manager. These discussions went on for a month without agreement. At the end of the month, Louisa received her redundancy notice, and the rest of the design section walked out.

Questions

1. On the basis of what you are told, define the culture of Taylor Engineering Ltd. Where do the priorities for collective culture development appear to lie?
2. What actions do all managers need to be able to take in the effective management of dominant personalities such as Martin Briggs above? Why is this often so difficult? What problems can and do arise as the result of failing to deal effectively with strong personalities?
3. What other factors need to be taken into account when seeking a strong, positive and cohesive culture in organisations such as Taylor Engineering Ltd?

Chapter seventeen

Perceptions, attitudes, values and beliefs

'You don't have to be mad to work here but it helps.'
Workplace notice.

'High levels of pay can be very rewarding. However, when everything
else about the job is wrong, they act as a shackle.'
Jenny Hirschkorn, *Daily Telegraph* (23 March 2000).

'This book is dedicated to all those who can spot a good chap as soon as
they walk into the room. And to all those who suffer as the result.'
C.T. Goodworth, *Recruitment and Selection*, John Wiley (1997).

Chapter outline

- Introduction
- Perceptions
- Comfort and liking
- Inference
- Elements of perception
- Personal mapping and constructs
- Other influences on perception
- Attitudes and values
- Formation of attitudes
- Beliefs
- Socialisation
- Conclusions

Chapter objectives

After studying this chapter, you should be able to:

- understand the main behavioural aspects and features with which managers have to deal

- understand and be able to influence behaviour and attitudes

- understand the source of shared positive attitudes and values

- understand the source of negative and divisive attitudes and values, and be able to identify steps required to influence them

- understand the general basis of human behaviour in organised situations.

● Introduction

The purpose of this chapter is to introduce the more nebulous aspects of human behaviour with which managers have to be concerned. It is therefore necessary to deal with the main elements of perceptions, attitudes and values in turn. Each of these is then developed from the particular point of view of management requirements and understanding.

● Perception

Perception is a primary human activity, the process by which people manage their views of the world by limitation. Perception is essential because of the vast amount of information, signals and cues with which the senses are constantly assailed. The total is not capable of assimilation because it is constantly changing and developing, and because of the constant nature of human activity. A process of some sort is therefore clearly necessary by which this is first limited and then transformed into something that is useful and usable.

The processes by which individual and collective perception are developed are both learned and instinctive. Some perception comes from the senses – sight, hearing, touch, taste and smell. Some comes from instinct – one's view of what is edible is clearly coloured by how hungry one is. Some comes from socialisation and is based on levels of understanding of what is expected of individuals in particular situations (see Figure 17.1). Some comes from civilisation, and an understanding and awareness of the norms of particular parts of society. This gives rise above all, to moral and ethical codes by which behaviour is regulated. Perception also forms the basis for concepts of fashion and desirability and the need for achievement (see Figure 17.2).

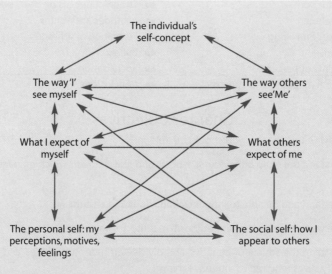

Figure 17.1 The basis of interpersonal perception
Source: Rogers (1947)

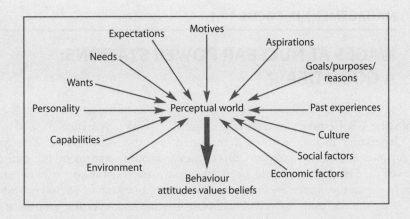

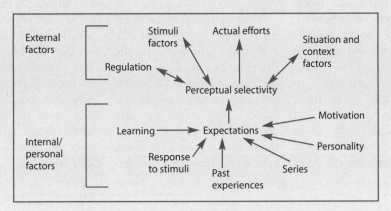

Figure 17.2 Relationships between perception, behaviour, attitudes and values

Source: from Huczynski and Buchanan (2003)

Perceptions are heavily influenced by media and business activity. Marketing is directed in a large part to the formulation of positive and acceptable impressions. Measures of success and failure are determined by key and influential figures as much as by product and service performance. Much human resource activity is taken up with influencing people's perceptions of others as they interact in work situations. Control functions are desirable in order that organisations may understand the state of their status and progress. Primary activities such as manufacturing or service provision must be undertaken in such a way that those conducting them understand to a considerable extent at least what is being done, how and why (see Management in Focus 17.1).

Comfort and liking

Comfort and liking occur when elements and features accord and harmonise with each other. Instant rapport is achieved when initial perceptions – strong characteristics, halo

MANAGEMENT IN FOCUS 17.1

WAGES AT NUCLEAR POWER STATIONS: A GOOD DEAL?

In the 1960s the UK Central Electricity Generating Board built nuclear power stations in remote parts of the UK. Many of the staff, especially the technical, semi-skilled and unskilled personnel, were to be drawn from rural, coastal and often remote communities. Stations brought additional income and work to these areas.

The first attempts to recruit people from these communities consisted of offering a high salary (about £18,000 at present levels) in return for which the staff concerned would work rosters determined by the station directorate. Hours would be flexible and extensive time off in lieu would be afforded to those having to work nights, weekends and public holidays.

Take-up of this arrangement was so low that the company returned to the drawing board. It came up with a basic wage of £10,000 per annum (also at present values) and extensive and complicated rostering arrangements that required overtime, shift pay, attendance, inconvenience and call-out allowances. The total to be earned by the staff concerned was to be between £15,000 and £18,000 provided that the overtime and so on continued to be forthcoming. Without exception the demand for jobs in the communities involved exceeded supply, in spite of the fact that the offer was worse than the original. But the perceptual barriers were overcome and those involved felt themselves to be getting a better deal. This was the reason for the success of the latter approach.

effects – coincide, meet expectations and lead to an initially productive relationship. This is developed as people become more familiar and knowledgeable about each other and about situations and circumstances.

The greater the continuing coincidence, the greater the harmony and accord, and the more flexible the boundaries of this become. For example, if the initial impression is that someone is a 'smoker', this may lead to discord; if the relationship then develops in strong and positive ways the smoking becomes less and less relevant and easier to accommodate.

Discomfort and dislike occur when the elements are in discord. This is usually founded in strong and contradictory initial and continuing impressions. For example, in response to a job advertisement, a beautifully prepared and overtly substantial CV may arrive, but at an interview the individual turns out to be scruffy; discomfort and dislike occur because expectations are not met. To the unwary the person has turned from a potential employee into someone to be got rid of as quickly as possible. In practice, everyone has contradictory characteristics and those with whom they come into contact have to reconcile these in order to build up a comfortable picture (see Management in Focus 17.2).

MANAGEMENT IN FOCUS 17.2

PERPETUAL ERRORS

The sources of error in person and situational perception include:

- not collecting enough information
- assuming that enough information has been collected
- not collecting the right information
- collecting the wrong information
- assuming that the right information has been collected
- seeing what we want and expect to see; fitting reality to our view of the world (rather than the reverse)
- looking in others for what we value in ourselves
- assuming that the past was always good when making judgements for the future
- failure to acknowledge and recognise other points of view
- failure to consider situations and people from the widest possible point of view
- unrealistic expectations about levels of comfort and satisfaction
- confusing the unusual and unexpected with the impossible

The remedies are to:

- understand the limitations of personal knowledge and perception; that this is imperfect and that there are gaps
- decide in advance what knowledge is required of people and situations, and set out to collect it from this standpoint
- structure activities where the gathering of information is important – this should apply, for example, to all interviews, research activities, questioning, work organisation, use of technology
- avoid instant judgements about people, however strong and positive, or weak and negative the first impression may be
- avoid instant judgements about organisations, whether as customer or employee
- build expectations on knowledge and understanding rather than halo effects, stereotypes and self-fulfilling prophecies
- ensure exchanges and availability of good quality information
- ensure open relationships that encourage discussion and debate and generate high levels of understanding and knowledge exchange
- develop self-awareness and understanding among all staff
- recognise and understand the nature of prevailing attitudes, values and beliefs – and prejudices
- recognise and understand other strong prevailing influences – especially language, nationality, culture and experience.

Inference

People constantly have to make inferences and assumptions, either because they do not have enough knowledge about a particular situation, or because there is so much knowledge available that they simply cannot accommodate it all (see Figure 17.3).

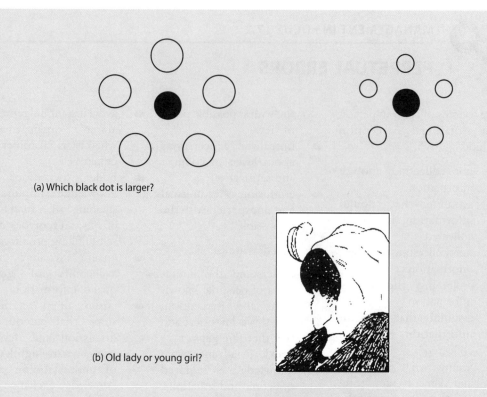

(a) Which black dot is larger?

(b) Old lady or young girl?

(c) Water flowing up and down?
Source: C. Escher/Cordon Art©

(d) A farmer was asked how many animals he had on his farm.
'Well,' he replied, 'I have 233 heads and 843 legs. Work it out from that'.

Figure 17.3 Perception: illustrations

Extreme forms of inference are jumping to conclusions and 'gut reactions' – in which quantum leaps are made about the outcome of something from a limited range of information available. In each case individuals select those elements before them with which they are familiar and place their own interpretation of the likely or 'logical' (sic) outcome on the basis of their knowledge and understanding of what happened before when these elements were present. The range of misunderstandings possible is virtually limitless. Out of six elements present, there may be three with which the individual is familiar; or this may be three out of ten, three out of 40, or three out of 100. In each case it is the familiar three which form the basis of judgement (see Management in Focus 17.3).

Elements of perception

The key elements and characteristics of perception are discussed in the following sections.

The halo effect

The halo effect is the process by which a person is ascribed a great range of capabilities and expertise as the result of one initial impression or overwhelming characteristic. This impression or characteristic may be either positive or negative; and the negative characteristic is often referred to as 'the horn's effect'. For example, a person with a strong handshake is perceived to be strong and decisive; a person with a weak handshake is perceived to be soft and indecisive.

MANAGEMENT IN FOCUS 17.3

JUMPING TO CONCLUSIONS AND GUT REACTIONS

- The old school tie: if from the same school, familiar and positive; if from a different school, subject to instant interpretation.
- You play golf; I play golf; therefore you are like me.
- You play golf; I play golf; I am a successful manager; therefore you are/will be a successful manager.

- Football has hooligans; you like football; therefore you are a hooligan.
- Mick Jagger has long hair; you have long hair; therefore you are like Mick Jagger.
- Men with beards are hiding something; Richard Branson has a beard; therefore he is hiding something.
- He has a firm handshake; I have a firm

handshake; therefore I like him.
- Kim Philby was a member of the establishment; he worked in the establishment; therefore, he could not possibly have been a Soviet spy.
- All Marks & Spencer products are good; Marks & Spencer sell apples; therefore, Marks & Spencer apples are good apples.

Stereotyping, pigeonholing and compartmentalisation

It is a short step from the halo effect to developing a process of stereotyping, pigeon-holing and compartmentalisation. This occurs at places of work where, because of a past range of activities, somebody is deemed to be suited for particular jobs for the future. This may both enhance and limit careers, activities and organisation progress depending upon the nature of the compartmentalisation. In any case it gives specific and limited direction. For example, people who have worked overseas for a multinational corporation for a long time may have difficulty getting a job back at Head Office because they have been pigeonholed as 'an expatriate' and may be perceived to have difficulties should they be required to conform to the Head Office norms and practices.

Self-fulfilling prophecy

Self-fulfilling prophecy occurs when a judgement is made about someone or something. The person making judgement then picks out further characteristics or attributes that support that view and edits out those do not fit in (See Management in Focus 17.4).

Perceptual mythology

Perceptual mythology occurs where myths are created by people as part of their own processes of limiting and understanding particular situations. A form of rationale emerges, usually spurious.

For example, people will say such things as 'I can tell as soon as someone walks in the door whether they can do this job,' or 'I always ask this question and it never fails,' or 'I never trust people in white shoes/white socks/with moustaches/with tinted glasses' – in order to give themselves some chance of understanding and therefore 'mapping' the person who stands before them.

MANAGEMENT IN FOCUS 17.4

SELF-FULFILLING PROPHECY

- If you want people to be trustworthy, trust them. If you want people to accept responsibility, give them responsibility (R. Semler: *Maverick*).
- People will behave as they expect those in charge would behave in the same situation. The *Herald of Free Enterprise*

sank because the staff perceived that it was important to set sail in spite of the fact that the bow doors were not closed. When the ship turned over the hunt was for scapegoats, not mistakes. (*Brass Tacks*, BBC2, 1989).
- Many universities have

adopted systems of numbered exam papers. This is so that those who mark the papers see what is actually written rather than what they expect to see written by particular students to whom they can put a name and therefore a set of perceptions.

People also use phrases such as 'in my opinion' and 'in my experience' for the same general reasons. Others use lines of argument such as 'X did this and it worked, so we should do it and it will work for us,' or 'it happened like this in 1929 and so this is the way to do it now,' or, more insidiously, 'we had to do things like this in my day and it never did us any harm and so this is how it has got to be done now.'

On a broader scale, industries publish league tables of company performance by business volume, business value, wage and salary levels, numbers employed and so on. These are then used to justify and explain a range of other issues of varying degrees of relevance and substance. Companies for example say 'we are sixth in the league,' or 'we are in the same boat as the rest of the industry,' or 'we are no worse than anyone else' without attaching any rationale to any of the points made. This develops a comfort zone which, in many cases, leads to feelings of complacency, immortality and infallibility.

Above all, this part of the process illustrates the difficulties involved. On the one hand each of the examples given in this part is flawed at best and spurious at worst. On the other hand, people have to limit their intake of information so that they can at least form some kind of general understanding. The key lesson at this stage is therefore to know and understand the limitations present.

Personal mapping and constructs

Personal mapping is the process by which people, situations, activities, images and impressions are placed into the individual's personal view of the world. This information is broken down into constructs or characteristics which may be categorised as follows:

- *Physical*: by which the people's qualities are inferred from their appearance, racial group, beauty, style, dress and other visual images.
- *Behavioural*: whereby people are placed according to the ways in which they behave, or the ways in which they are assumed to behave.
- *Role*: whereby assumptions are made about people because of the variety of roles they assume, the different situations in which they assume these roles, their dominant role or roles, and the trappings that go with them.
- *Psychological*: whereby certain occupations, appearances, presentations and images are assumed to be of a higher value than others.
- *Situational*: whereby collective and individual confidence increases as the result of becoming familiar with physical and psychological environments, and the ways in which the environment works. Repetition of patterns of behaviour, forms of address, and ways of working also contribute to situational perception.

Personal mapping and constructs enable individuals to arrive at a view of the world with which they are comfortable. People additionally need this comfort at their places of work in terms of the roles they are asked to carry out, identity with the organisation itself, and familiarity with the ways of working and with collective and individual standards of conduct.

Attribution

Attribution is the explanation put by individuals on behaviour or activities. Attribution may be:

- *Rational*: 'you burnt your hand because the plate was hot.'
- *Pseudo-rational*: 'he is a bully at work because he has a difficult home life.'
- *Empathetic*: 'in her place I would have done the same thing.'
- *Mythological*: 'this was how we always used to do it and it worked then.'
- *Insidious*: 'he is a bully at work; he has a difficult home life; and therefore, I am not going to do anything about his bullying.'
- *Excusing*: 'he is an expert and so is entitled to behave like a brute.'
- *Fearful*: 'he is an expert so I do not know how to approach him, therefore I will not approach him.'
- *Inert*: 'I must be even-handed in dealing with complaints, disputes and grievances.'

Whether rational or not, attribution gives people a point of reference for their actions and for those of others. It also helps in the attaining of comfort and satisfaction, enabling people to explain – to themselves at least – why they continue to work in particular occupations, ways and situations, or with particular people.

● Other influences on perception

The following more general influences may also be distinguished.

Emotions

Feelings of anger, antagonism, mistrust and disregard emphasise the tendency to reject. At the very least therefore, any such feelings present or potentially present in a given situation are to be recognised at the outset and at least neutralised where possible.

The greatest of all emotional barriers in organisations is pride. Nobody likes to lose face or to have it made plain that they were wrong. Nor do others wish to be associated with someone who is forced to be seen as defeated, to back down, or to climb down from a given position.

This is especially important in understanding the conduct of workplace disputes and grievances. It is important in understanding why projects that are plainly doomed to failure are nevertheless allowed to proceed.

In each case the alternative – withdrawal – is an admission of failure. It is seen as such and is therefore unacceptable from a variety of points of view.

Visibility

Visibility is the cornerstone of managerial effectiveness, style and communication. It greatly helps in the generation of confidence, familiarity and interaction. It underlines levels of honesty, trustworthiness and straightforwardness. It helps develop both professional and personal relationships among those involved.

There are therefore both general and specific benefits to be gained from an effective face-to-face relationship.

Physical visibility reinforces perceptions of proximity, intensity and confidence. Proximity is the process of empathising with those people who are physically met with most often; and continued visibility develops both intensity of relationships and confidence in relationships. Proximity, intensity and confidence are diluted where there is a lack of physical visibility and identity. Misunderstandings, disputes and grievances occur much more often where there is a lack of visibility.

Comparison

Some comparisons are precise and exact – this glass is fuller than that; she is better qualified than he is for example. Others are less so and may be based on a range of opinion – informal or otherwise – expectation and prejudice. Some comparisons are valid, others not.

Comparisons have the value of helping to meet the expectations of people in certain situations. If one company has a bigger percentage pay rise than another staff tend to be happy. If the pay rise is less, staff tend to be unhappy. Organisations therefore tend to seek out and emphasise those comparators that present them in their best light.

The standpoint from which the comparison is made is also to be considered. For example, the statement that bankers earn more than teachers is valid only if a simple comparison of earnings is being considered. It does not prove or disprove that one job is better or worse than the other. For other aspects therefore, other equivalent comparators have to be identified and addressed.

First impressions

First impressions count. First impressions are plainly misleading – prima facie you must know less about someone after 30 seconds than after 30 minutes. Yet overwhelmingly the converse is highly influential and this should be understood.

First impressions are formed as the result of physical appearance, dress, manner, handshake and initial conversation. The impact is therefore very strong. It is however essential to recognise the limitations, or else a one-dimensional view of the individual is formed and everything which is contrary to that single dimension, or which indicates complexities and other dimensions and qualities is edited out (see Figure 17.4).

This is a useful (but by no means perfect or complete) means of compartmentalising the cues and signals which are present when coming into any situation or into contact with someone for the first time. There are certain to be contradictions and contra-indications. It is essential to recognise and understand this in order to understand, in turn, the impact and influence of first impressions.

Expectations

Meeting people's expectations is an organisational priority; and fulfilment of expectations is a key feature of individual motivation. In general, people are happy if their expectations are met, are delighted if their expectations are exceeded, and are unhappy if their expectations are not met.

People have different expectations as they go about their different roles and functions. Organisations have to be able to identify and meet people's expectations in terms of:

● staff management
● customers, clients, and product and service end-users

People	Service
• appearance, dress, hair, handshake • voice, eye contact • scent, smell • disposition (positive, negative, smiling, frowning) • establishing common interest/ failure to do so • courtesy, manner • age	• friendliness (or lack of) • effectiveness • speed • quality • confidence • value • respect • ambience • appearance
Objects	**Organisations**
• design • colour/colours • weight • shape • size • materials • purpose, usage • price, value, cost	• ambience • welcome • appearance • image and impression • technology • care • respect for others • confidence • trust

This is a useful (but by no means perfect or complete) means of compartmentalising the cues and signals which are present when coming into any situation or into contact with someone for the first time. There are certain to be contradictions and contra-indications. It is essential to recognise and understand this in order to understand, in turn, the impact and influence of first impressions.

Figure 17.4 First impressions

- suppliers and others who depend on the organisation for their own business activities
- shareholders and others with financial interests in the organisation
- communities, and the range of their expectations of particular organisations.

Knowing and understanding, as precisely as possible, the expectations of each of these key groups is essential if overall harmony is to be maintained. Knowing and understanding that expectations are not being met for some reason does at least give managers and organisations knowledge and advance warning of where problems are likely to arise.

Defence mechanisms

People build perceptual defences and blockages against people or situations that are personally or culturally unacceptable, unrecognisable, threatening or incapable of assimilation. Perceptual defence normally takes one or more of the following forms:

- *Denial*: refusal to recognise the evidence of the senses.
- *Modification and distortion*: accommodating disparate elements in ways which reinforce the comfort of the individual.
- *Change in perception*: from positive to negative or from negative to positive,

often because a single trait or characteristic becomes apparent which was not previously so.

- *Recognition but refusal to change*: where people are not prepared to have their view of the world disrupted by a single factor or example. This is often apparent when people define 'the exceptions to the rule'.
- *Outlets*: where the individual seeks an outlet (especially for frustration or anger) away from its cause. For example, browbeating a subordinate offers a sense of relief to someone who has previously been browbeaten by the person next up the pecking order.
- *Recognition thresholds*: the higher the contentiousness or emotional content of information, the higher the threshold for recognition (i.e. the less likely it is to be readily perceived).
- *The use of the messenger*: organisations use external consultants and experts to deliver messages that are known, believed or perceived to be unacceptable if they come from within the organisation. Perceptual credibility is therefore given to proposed initiatives and ventures, and also to the negative aspects of business process re-engineering, if delivered by somebody who is not a member of the particular organisation.

Adaptation

People's adaptation processes are constantly in action. When people exhibit strong and conflicting characteristics, the general response on the part of the rest of the world is to reject or mistrust them, as accommodation and acceptance require an understanding of the limitations of perceptions at the point of meeting and dealing with them.

Inclusion is a part of the process which comes out in the 'preconceived idea' and 'prejudged case'. This process of inclusion occurs when a situation arises to which the individual can bring, or include, different familiarities and experiences. The situation is then reconstructed using these past experiences, in order to jump to conclusions and solutions.

Exclusion is the process by which anything that does not fit in with a preconceived idea or prejudgement is excluded.

It is possible through the observation of an individual's activity and behaviour to infer that person's attitude. It is not possible to know it for certain; and if this is the overriding requirement of the moment, further action must be taken in this regard to overcome these inferences and gain a true picture.

The adaptation process is constantly in action. People over-respond to someone who is polite if the last six others that they have met have been rude. The person driving home in a rush from work and likely to be late may fear the wrath of his or her partner; if the hurry results in a car crash, the driver immediately feels lucky to be alive; the feelings of the waiting partner change from anger to anxiety and then relief.

There is also the question of 'construct reconciliation' to be addressed. Examples of this include reconciling the brilliant performance of actors with their dull off-stage personalities; the image of the radical politician or religious leader on the public stage with one's experience of that person as next door neighbour or travelling companion; the children's matinee idol who refuses to sign autographs.

In general, a grasp of the basic principles of perception on the part of those in managerial roles at least enables the questioning of certain supposed 'rules' and 'facts'. It should be part of the process of generating a healthy scepticism and genuinely enquiring mind, when faced with such perceptual 'absolutes' (see Management in Focus 17.5).

● Attitudes and values

Attitudes

Attitudes are the mental, moral and ethical dispositions adopted by individuals to others and the situations and environments in which they find themselves (see Management in Focus 17.6).

The following elements are present in attitude formation and development:

- *Emotional*: feelings of positivity, negativity, neutrality or indifference; anger, love, hatred, desire, rejection, envy and jealousy; satisfaction and dissatisfaction. Emotional aspects are present in all work as part of working relationships with other people, reactions to the environment, and the demands placed on particular occupations.
- *Informational*: the nature and quality of the information present and the importance that it is given. Where this is known or widely understood to be wrong or incomplete, feelings of negativity and frustration arise.
- *Behavioural*: the tendency to act in particular ways in given situations. This leads to the formation of positive attitudes where the behaviour required can be demonstrated to be important or valuable, and to negative attitudes where the behaviour required is seen as futile or unimportant.

MANAGEMENT IN FOCUS 17.5

ADAPTATION

A passenger survey was carried out by one of the world's leading airlines. The survey questionnaire was given to passengers to fill in during long-haul flights to be handed in at the end. It covered the service offered by the cabin staff, range of goods on sale, quality of food, comfort of accommodation and general feelings about the flight.

Because the survey was carried out on the actual flight, the airline received only average feedback when everything had gone more or less smoothly. The feedback was highly negative when small things had gone wrong. Twenty minutes discomfort in flight was reported as a major negative implying a threat to life and limb. Lack of instant response to demand for service was regarded as sloppy and symbolic of a poor attitude. One item in the food offered would colour the entire perception of food quality – especially if this was poor or not to the liking of the individual passenger.

The results were based on the constant adaptation of the passengers in respect of each occurrence rather than their wider perceptions and feelings of satisfaction. The survey was therefore useless in terms of evaluating the overall quality of the flight and levels of service.

MANAGEMENT IN FOCUS 17.6

CONVEYING REAL ATTITUDES (1): EXAMPLES OF LANGUAGE USED

- *These people*: different and inferior groups, classes, tribes and families. It is a favourite phrase of politicians describing groups that they would rather not have to deal with (such as the poor, the homeless the socially disadvantaged).
- *Workers, workforce*: always used by directors. A variation of this is to be found in the Annual Report: 'Staff are our most valuable resource.'
- *'If you don't want this job there are x million unemployed who do'*: this phrase is never used in a satisfactory, or productive, or harmonious situation; the question of whether the person has a low level of value simply does not arise.
- *'We conform to legal requirements; we meet legal minimum standards; we meet particular directives'*: this is used where the organisation concerned is hiding behind the letter of the law rather than assuming absolute responsibility for its own activities.

- *Past experience*: memories of what happened in the past affect current and future feelings.
- *Preconceptions*: especially where those coming to work in the organisation have past histories as customers, clients or users of its facilities. These are key issues when going to work in education, health, social services or the travel industry; they require addressing at the outset of employment through effective induction programmes.
- *Visibility, proximity and intensity*: these are reflected in attitudes that cause people to deal with present problems rather than the most important issues, and to value staff with whom they interact everyday, above those working elsewhere.
- *Influence of over-mighty and over-influential individuals and groups*: this leads to attitudes that particular groups and individuals may not be approached, or managed, or directed, because of the power and influence that they are known or perceived to wield.
- *Specific influences*: especially those of peer groups, work groups and key individuals – managers and supervisors. These also include family and social groups; and may also include religious and political influences.
- *Defence*: once formed, attitudes and values are internalised and become a part of the individual. Any challenge to them is often viewed as a more general threat to the comfort of the individual.

Values

Values are the absolute standards by which people order their lives. People need to be aware of their own personal values so that they may deal pragmatically with any situation. This may extend to marked differences among individuals or between an individual and demands of the organisation. Conflicts of value often arise at places of work; anything to which people are required to ascribe must recognise this and, if it is to be effective, must be capable of harmonisation with the values of the individuals. Individual and shared values may be summarised as follows:

- *Theoretical*: where everything is ordered, factual and in place.
- *Economic*: making the best practical use of resources; results orientated, the cornerstone of people's standards and costs of living.
- *Aesthetic*: the process of seeing and perceiving beauty; relating that which is positive and desirable or negative and undesirable.
- *Social*: the sharing of emotions with other people.
- *Integrity-related*: matters of loyalty, honesty, openness, trust, honour, decency, concern for the truth.
- *Political*: the ways and choices concerning the ordering of society and its subsections and strata.
- *Religious and ethical*: the dignity of humankind, the inherent worth of people, the morality – the absolute standards – of human conduct; this includes specific beliefs and requirements of particular religions.
- *Prejudicial*: individual and collective preferences for colours, clothing, design, cars are all subjective influences on values, and contribute to feelings of conformity. These are legitimate subjective elements, and not at all to be confused with repugnant gender, racial and other social prejudices.

Attitudes and values are affected by the overall quality of organisational, professional and occupational relationships, and by relationships between staff and managers. Continuing experiences and interactions develop attitudes both positively and negatively. Attitudes are underpinned by the presence of specific rules, regulations and other limitations, and the ways in which these are enforced.

Attitudes and values are additionally reinforced by overall cultural cohesion, and the levels of identity with others involved in the work, and in the organisation overall.

Attitudes are also affected by general levels of confidence and comfort; and attitudes are reinforced by the ways in which individuals and groups within the organisation are treated and valued overall (see Management in Focus 17.7).

Formation of attitudes

The elements indicated are adopted by individuals in their own unique ways to form their own distinctive attitudes. The main processes that are involved are as follows:

- People's propensity to accept rather than reject those of the group (including the organisation) to which they seek to belong; they have a high degree of potential compliance.
- Their perception of the future relationship as being productive, effective, profitable and harmonious. People do not willingly enter a situation if they have no expectational perception of this; the greater the likelihood of this being achieved, the more willing and likely people will be to enter situations; and people will avoid situations where these elements are neither present nor apparent.

MANAGEMENT IN FOCUS 17.7

CONVEYING REAL ATTITUDES (2): SYMBOLS AND DIFFERENTIALS

Job titles

A. Typist, clerk, worker, operative.
B. Assistant manager, manager.
C. Crew, gang, cast.

Status

Hourly, clock, salary, levels and nature of supervision, industrial relations, management style, job titles, location, manuals and procedures.

Trappings

Cars, car phones, personal computers, offices, personal assistants, personal departments, staff officers, furniture and furnishings, personal facilities (fax, toilet, lift).

Behavioural differentials

Forms of address, separate canteens, designated car parking spaces, executive dining rooms, workers canteens, location by floor.

Procedural differentials

Dependent upon: occupation, job title, department, division, location, etc.

The cover-up/openness syndrome

Dealing with mistakes and errors, scapegoating, use of (and failure to use) phrases such as: 'we have made a mistake'; or: 'I was wrong'.

Dress codes

Dress allowances, the use of uniforms, overalls; universality or differential.

Address codes

Referring to staff by first and last names, job titles and rank.

- Relating past experience to current and future situations, relationships and environment; positive experiences tend towards the formation of positive attitudes, and negative experiences tend towards the formation of negative attitudes.
- Availability and completeness of information; availability includes access and clarity; completeness includes reference to key and critical gaps, and also to the value and usefulness of that which is available.
- The general state of organisational well-being, the general state of the individual, and the relationship and interaction between the two.
- Other pressures, including the views of peers, co-workers, superiors, subordinates, family and friends, as well as economic, social, legal, moral and ethical pressures. These are likely to include sweeping generalisations, prevailing received wisdom, opinions and prejudices (opinions formed without full reference to available facts), coming from all from the variety of sources indicated.
- Any myths and legends present in the particular group or situation. For example, the statement that 'the person who holds job x or sits in office y always gets promoted first/never gets promoted at all' puts behavioural and psychological pressures on each situation.
- Other environmental aspects, especially management style and communication forms that are known, believed or perceived to contribute to the general organisation climate (see Management in Focus 17.8).

MANAGEMENT IN FOCUS 17.8

CONVEYING REAL ATTITUDES (3): MANAGERIAL JOB ADVERTS

- '. . . you should be self-motivated, imaginative and able to persuade and influence at all levels . . .'
- '. . . our innovative and proactive approach in all areas of HR means we are introducing new policies and systems . . .'
- '. . . the competitive salary is pitched at a level attractive to the highest calibre individuals and you will receive the excellent company benefits you would expect from a leading financial services organisation . . .'
- '. . . you must be a professionally qualified graduate with at least five years relevant experience . . . creative, commercially driven and self-motivated, you are capable of designing and implementing original solutions to business issues . . .'
- '. . . highly visible, highly challenging and highly rewarding, this position requires at least five years experience in a significant personnel function, gained in a fast-moving environment . . .'

It is very difficult to pin down any precise quality actually required. Each of those indicated in these job advertisements is open to purely subjective interpretation, spurious justification and rationale. The perception and attitude generated is therefore that the organisation is entirely free to appoint whomsoever it wishes, regardless of the true demands of the situation.

Each part of the process is present in the promotion and development of all attitudes, though the mix varies between particular situations and individuals. The mix also changes as people come into and go out of organisations and their groups. Also, when seeking to move, individuals may need (or perceive themselves to need) to change their attitudes in order to stand any chance of being successful. The attitude may change again, depending on whether or not they were able to make the move, and if they did, whether or not this was successful (see Figure 17.5).

Beliefs

Beliefs are the certainties of the world. They may be:

- *Absolute*: based on such things as mathematical fact, night following day, mortality and taxation.
- *Near absolute*: based on seasonal changes, the continuous development of knowledge and awareness, the continuous technological and social development.
- *Acts and articles of faith*: based on the certainty of God, and often underpinned by religious allegiance and by following the teachings of those who pronounce in the name of God; this may also extend to the adoption of social and political creeds.

Positive	Negative
• Equality of opportunity and treatment • Saying what is meant, meaning what is said • Identifying and solving problems • Clarity of purpose • Unity of purpose • Reward for achievement, loyalty and commitment • Openness of management style • Particular standards set at outset • Absolute standards for everyone • High and equal value placed on all staff • Recognition of every contribution • Pride in the organisation • Identity with the organisation • High levels of esteem and respect for staff • Clarity of communications • Harmony • High quality information	• Inequality of opportunity and treatment • Expediency • Victimisation, scapegoating • Lack of clarity • Fragmentation of purpose • Rewards based on favouritism and in-fighting • Remoteness and distance of management style (both physical and psychological) • Standards allowed to emerge • Different standards for different groups, departments, divisions and individuals • Different levels of value placed on different staff groups • Lack of recognition • Lack of pride in the organisation • Lack of identity; rejection of identity • Low levels of esteem and respect; variations in levels of esteem and respect according to occupation, department, division and function • Lack of clarity of communications • Hostility • Low quality information

Figure 17.5 Influences on attitudes: summary

- *Other strong ethical and moral standpoints*: relating to honesty, trustworthiness, right and wrong.
- *Strong illusions and perceptions of order, permanence and stability*: often founded on long steady-state factors.

Beliefs are the psychological cornerstone of the lives of people. They provide the foundations and framework upon which people order and structure the rest of their lives. They are internalised to the heart and soul of the individual, providing the basis for other attitudes, values and chosen behaviour.

Forcing and imposing belief changes on people is very traumatic for those who are to be affected. During religious persecutions, the willingness of people to die for their beliefs indicates the strength of this. Many people would rather lose their lives than their beliefs.

From an organisational behaviour point of view it is clearly possible to make the rational case that, as there is no such thing as an eternal organisation, there is therefore no question of individuals believing in it. However, individuals may create a relationship very akin to belief, especially if they work in the same situation for a long time and the relationship is mutually productive, effective and harmonious. Any change in this (especially sudden change) is therefore in turn akin to the trauma indicated above. Moreover, people internalise particular aspects of the organisation, coming to believe (or nearly believe) in the proclaimed standards of honesty, trustworthiness, high ethical and moral standpoints. In these cases, when it becomes apparent that these are illusory the same degree of trauma is felt (see Management in Focus 17.9).

● Socialisation

Socialisation is the process by which individuals are persuaded to behave in ways acceptable to their society, family, social groups and clubs. This also applies to work organisations and their groups, departments, divisions and functions. Effective socialisation results in compliance and conformity with the values, beliefs, attitudes, rules and patterns of behaviour required. While this does not necessarily mean that the individual must adopt everything to the point of total faith and commitment, successful integration only occurs if people can at least acknowledge and respect these as boundaries and constraints within which they can work and operate.

For this to occur the group's attitudes, values, beliefs, behaviour and rules must be capable of being accepted by the individuals that seek or are required to join. They tend therefore to reflect the prevailing customs of the wider society and be in harmony with general ethical and social pressures.

On the other hand, socialisation should also leave enough space, latitude and freedom for individuals to express themselves in the given setting. Too much restriction leads to frustration. At the other extreme, a lack of clear understanding of these standards leads to lack of focus and purpose, leaving the individual in a void – and this can be just as harmful and stressful as over-restraint.

Socialisation takes place from the moment of birth. It is conducted in the early years by parents and family, schools and colleges, religious institutions, sports and leisure clubs. By the time individuals arrive in work they therefore have been subject to a great variety of pressures and influences. The problem for organisations lies in their ability to build on this and create conditions that are both acceptable to individuals and ensure that productive and effective work can take place.

MANAGEMENT IN FOCUS 17.9

BANK OF CREDIT AND COMMERCE INTERNATIONAL (BCCI)

BCCI collapsed in 1991, after a long history of allegations of fraud and participation in the laundering of drug money and the profits of illicit armaments' deals. The scandal was so extreme that most of the staff working in the Bank simply shut it out. They could not accept that their organisation could possibly be corrupt in this way. When the closure of the Bank occurred, following the removal of great volumes of its money and assets, many of the staff went into (and remain in) deep shock that this could have happened – to them.

Organisation	Individual
• Productive effort	• Comfort
• Effective workforce	• Warmth
• Effective individuals	• Belonging
• Effective groups	• Contact
• Continuous development	• Success
• New talents and energies	• Fulfilment
• Work harmony	• Achievement
• Expectations	• Professionalism
• Job proficiency	• Expectations
• Professionalism	• Rewards
	• Training and development

The lists represent two sides of the same coin. Organisation socialisation is designed and devised to bring them together, match them up and harmonise the pressures. Some of these pressures are convergent, others divergent; all must be integrated and interrelated as far as possible.

Figure 17.6 Social needs

This problem is greater with mature employees who may arrive at an organisation after experience in many others. They will therefore have formed their own ideas about high standards, best practice and optimum ways of working, and this in turn leads to the need for effective orientation at the outset of the new job. Where an employee comes to a new organisation after a long stay in a single place of work, the problem is greater still because the new employee's only recent (possibly only other) point of reference is the place that they have just left. For whatever reason, positive or negative, such people are coming into a new situation for the first time in a long while and great care is needed to ensure that they settle in quickly and effectively. This also applies to those returning to work after long periods of absence – because of previous job loss or family commitments for example.

Effective organisation socialisation processes tackle this by addressing the organisation's own needs from the point of view and perspective of the individual. By bringing comfort and warmth to the situation the organisation engages positive feelings in the individual. By setting its standards and expectations out clearly at the start, it leaves new staff members in no doubt about the expectations placed upon them and the ways in which they are to use their talents and qualities. This also generates the beginning of a relationship based on mutual respect and a sense of identity (see Figure 17.6).

This underlines the importance of adequate and effective induction and orientation programmes. Too many organisations and their managers still neglect this, believing orientation to be a waste of time that cuts into their other priorities; or else they have simply never learned to see it as an investment, the return on which is a committed and effective employee – and if this is really successful, much of the process is achieved over a relatively short period of time.

● Conclusions

All managers must know and understand perceptions, attitudes and values, and the ways in which each are shaped and influenced. This is for two reasons:

- so that they understand and acknowledge their own perceptual approaches
- so that they understand and acknowledge those of the people with whom they come into contact, especially staff, but also superiors, peers, suppliers, customers and clients.

Forming and nurturing the required attitudes and values clearly requires a broad knowledge and understanding of all the factors and elements indicated. If this is to be effective, the following must be present:

- Identification of the required attitudes and values, together with the reasons why these are desirable and ensuring that they are capable of being supported and adopted by all those concerned.
- Taking positive steps to reinforce them in the ways in which the organisation and its departments, divisions and functions operate, and penalising any shortfall.
- Recognising the effects of all training and development activities on attitudes and values, whatever the training and development is overtly concerned with. Attitudes and values are shaped, developed and reinforced by all learning activities, as is the general mutual relationship and commitment between organisation and individual.

It is also necessary to recognise that attitudes, and especially negative attitudes, emerge whether or not they are shaped and influenced by the organisation. Where the organisation has no influence on attitudes, these are formed by other pressures, especially peer, professional and social groups.

Positive attitudes help to provide a harmonious and open working environment, and increase general levels of motivation and moral. Negative attitudes tend to reinforce any stresses and strains – poor working relationships, lack of trust and value.

Attention to workplace attitudes, especially at the induction stage helps employees to adopt and find the place required of them in their environment. It helps to provide a clear mutual understanding between organisation and employee, and is one of the cornerstones of the working environment. Above all, as organisations strive for ever-greater levels of flexibility and responsiveness, building these characteristics as positive and valuable attitudes is essential.

CRITICAL THINKING, ANALYSIS AND EVALUATION

1. To what extent have the initial impressions that you formed about your current colleagues and/or organisation remained the same? To what extent have these altered and why?
2. Identify the basis on which Michael O'Leary, the Chief Executive of Ryanair, is held in such high esteem. What may cause this perception to change?
3. How do the behavioural aspects of fire safety and emergency drills affect staff attitudes?
4. To what extent can shared values be stated to be genuinely present at your organisation/college/university? What are the reasons for this? What steps does

the particular institution take to ensure that everyone has the same basic attitudes and values; what further steps could be taken?

DEVELOPING MANAGEMENT SKILLS AND EXPERTISE

YVON CHOUINARD: THE MAN FROM PATAGONIA

Take a young person and ask them to name the man behind their favourite fashion label. Many will offer Ralph Lauren, Calvin Klein or Tommy Hilfiger. But an increasing number of young people will tell you about a balding, weather-beaten 68-year-old French-Canadian called Yvon Chouinard.

Now ask a class of ambitious business-degree types to nominate a corporate chief executive they admire. Richard Branson, Michael O'Leary and Bill Gates are all obvious choices. But some will also opt for Chouinard. And who was it that inspired an ever-increasing number of young city dwellers to head for the hills in pursuit of the wilderness experience? Again, Chouinard's your man. Ask an environmental activist who helps fund their activities . . . well, you get the picture.

Yvon Chouinard is little known in the UK, but in the United States he is an icon. As the founder and head of Patagonia, the brand that ignited the craze for technical outdoor clothing – clothes that are all about functional simplicity – he can claim to be one of the most influential fashion forces of recent years. But his appeal goes far beyond that of an expert marketeer of fancy pants. Chouinard is perhaps unwittingly the point of convergence for any number of lifestyle trends – a reluctant guru of fashion, business and lifestyle. And ironically the more successful he becomes, the more he tortures himself over what he has created. He may be a hero but he is a complex and unwilling one.

Chouinard was born in 1938 and lived in Maine until he was seven when his parents moved to Burbank, California. Speaking only French-Canadian, the young Chouinard became something of a loner, spending much of his time surfing. An interest in falconry led him to climbing which became his major passion. By the early 1960s he was roughing it at Yosemite National Park's legendary Camp Four – to this day, the place that any rock climber dreams of pitching his tent. Chouinard pioneered a number of routes up Yosemite's celebrated peak El Capitan and the valley's other massive rock faces. In doing so, he became a hero of the emerging beatnik climbing scene – reading Jack Kerouac, listening to jazz and delving into Zen Buddhism. Along the way, he supported himself as a blacksmith, producing climbing hardware on a portable forge. An ice axe he designed in 1968 became a permanent exhibit at New York's museum of modern art.

Yet Chouinard was already concerned about the effect of his sport on the environment. Aged 19, he had revolutionised climbing by creating pitons that could be removed from the rock rather than just left to rust. Throughout the 1970s and 1980s the Patagonia label grew and grew. It became the leading name in outdoor clothing and started to find its way into urban fashion. In 1986, he started to contribute 1 per cent of sales or 10 per cent of pre-tax profits, whichever was the larger, to a wide range of environmental groups, many of them small, local projects. And still Patagonia kept growing. By 1991, sales had reached $100 million.

Then recession hit hard. Chouinard had to lay off 120 of his 620 staff, many of them friends. This set back caused him to have a radical rethink. He began to remodel the company. He began to formulate an idea of sustainable development – natural organic growth. He still limits the Patagonia range and encourages customers only to buy what they absolutely need.

After an environmental audit of the company's production, Chouinard started making fleeces out of recycled plastic bottles. In 1996, he decided to use only organic cotton in Patagonia clothes even though this added 25 per cent to the production costs. Sales dropped 20 per cent but he held steady, even loaning money to organic growers to keep them in business. Everything in the worldwide chain of stores was checked for environmental impact. If he is a man with a moral mission, he also has a faith that what he does will be repaid in profits and that the corporation can be a force for good. 'If you want to change government,' he says, 'change the corporations and government will follow. To change corporations, change the consumers. Perhaps the real good that we do is to use the company as a tool for social change.'

Patagonia's sales now stand at around $200 million. Chouinard it seems can do no wrong, with the Patagonia model being used by any number of companies who have realised that brand honesty and environmentally responsible production can translate into long-term security and profitability. 'If you focus on the goal and not the process,' says Chouinard, 'you inevitably compromise. But for me, profit is what happens when you do everything else right. A good cast will always catch a fish.'

This is not enough for Chouinard of course. He is still tormented by the company's success. Patagonia now reaches an audience far beyond the active outdoors types. The Patagonia zip-up jacket is part of a uniform for many young Brits and much of the range has been widely copied. Yet he has a strangely ambivalent attitude to those who use his products for the purpose for which they were intended.

'Part of the process of life is to question how you live it,' he explains. 'Nobody takes the time to do things right. With mountain climbing, people are only interested in reaching the top of the peak so that they can tell others that they did it.'

There is a discrepancy here. The Patagonia catalogue is a glorious call to the wild. Can he really blame stressed-out city dwellers for trying to get a bit of fresh air, especially if he allows them to look good and keep warm doing it? Chouinard proposes that the great American wildernesses should be the preserve of a dedicated few, yet his company encourages an exodus of the many. If the surf is crowded and the rock face cluttered, then Patagonia has had a big hand in making it so.

So the question arises: if Chouinard believes that we are consuming ourselves to destruction then why does he dedicate his life to making thermal underpants? It is a matter of compromise and Chouinard acknowledges his own weaknesses.

'We are an incredibly damaging species and we are pulling all these other beautiful species down with us. Maybe ought just to get out of here. You do what you can. Then, even if you are burning petrol to get there, you just have to say "forget it, let's go surfing".'

Chouinard's contradictions reflect those of our age. We want to heal the planet while stocking up with as many consumer goods as our credit cards will allow. We want to be outdoors but only if we get there in an air-conditioned, four-wheel drive and stay in rose-covered cottages with modern central heating. Chouinard is a contradictory hero for contradictory times but he is still a hero.

Source: Nick Compton, *Orange* magazine, Spring, 2000.

Questions

1. Identify and discuss the conflicting attitudes present. In your view, which are the dominant attitudes and values of the Patagonia company, and what are the effects of these on its performance?
2. How does the company develop the attitudes and values of customers in its dealings with them?
3. What potential for damage to the company is there in the divergent attitudes exhibited by Yvon Chouinard?

Chapter eighteen

Communication

Cary Grant: 'I can't find out a thing. I have asked the great man's accountant, his lawyer,
his partner, and his secretary, and none of them will give an answer.'
'Why haven't you asked the great man himself?'

'Pay attention to the direction signage.'
Instruction at the entrance to BBC Headquarters,
Wood Lane, London – requiring visitors to 'follow the arrows.'

'A picture paints a thousand words.'
Anon.

Chapter outline

- Introduction
- Communication structuring
- Communication policies and priorities
- Principles of effective communication
- Non-verbal communication
- Barriers and blockages
- Reinforcement
- Use of media
- Realpolitik
- Organisation toxicity
- Assertiveness
- Negotiations
- Conclusions

Chapter objectives

After studying this chapter, you should be able to:

- understand how communication processes work, and what makes them successful or otherwise

- understand some specific approaches that aid effective communications

- understand where barriers and blockages to communications may arise, and take steps to overcome them

- understand how communication processes are manipulated and corrupted, and why these occur.

⬤ Introduction

The issue of communication is vital for the successful functioning of any organisation. All organisations normally establish formal mechanisms and processes of vertical and lateral lines or channels of communication to provide the means by which information – facts, ideas, proposals, emotions, feelings, opinions and problems – can be exchanged. They also normally create integrating activities such as groups, committees and other meetings, and the means of consultation and participation to improve the all-round quality and understanding of this information.

Effective communication is based on: volumes, quality and integrity of information; the integrity of information systems; the ways in which information is presented and delivered; and the overall integrity of the wider situation.

Communications and information feed the quality of all human and operational relations in organisations. Good communications underline good relations and enhance the general quality of working life, motivation and morale. Bad or inadequate communications lead to frustration and enhance feelings of alienation and lack of identity and unity.

⬤ Communication structuring

Communications may be:

- *One-way*: information presented to particular target audiences that does not seek, or allow for, responses. General information may be presented on websites or in the media. Advertising is also generally one-way communication, although it does seek to build and reinforce product, service and brand awareness and identity.
- *Two-way*: two-way communication is the ability to engage in active and productive discussion, consultation, participation and involvement. Two-way communication is the basis of all effective staff management and employee relations, as well as customer, client and supplier liaison, and dealings with shareholders and backers.
- *Downward*: some downward communication is essential because overall standards and direction have to be communicated from those responsible to those who have to carry things out. Written rules, procedures and handbooks also require the backing and support of top managers. To be effective, downward communication requires active participation and consultation (see below).
- *Upward*: upward channels of communications are those that provide access to top management for the rest of staff. Their effectiveness is enhanced or limited by:
  - organisation culture that sets the boundaries of openness, integrity and honesty
  - physical and psychological distance between top managers and the rest of the organisation
  - attitudes of top managers to the rest of the staff.
- *Lateral*: between different professional and occupational groups and locations, departments, divisions and functions. In many cases, this is especially hard to manage because of in-built and historic barriers that exist between:

-    primary functions, administration and headquarters
-    doctors, nurses, ancillaries and managers (healthcare)
-    air crew, ground crew and headquarters (airlines)
-    managers and backers (dot.coms and telecommunications)
-    production and sales, or production lines and maintenance (factory work)
-    sales staff, branch managers and headquarters (retail).

Effective communication is underpinned by written documents, and by policies, procedures and practices governing standards of attitudes, behaviour and performance; the management of conflict and specific issues such as customer, client and supplier management, public relations and other aspects of organisation presentation.

Channels of communication may be formal, institutional or informal:

●   *Formal*: the hierarchies, systems, procedures and committee structures established to underpin management style and organisation effectiveness (see Figure 18.2 and Management in Focus 18.1).

●   *Institutional*: less formal channels that nevertheless carry both validity and influence – e.g. professional, occupational and managerial cluster groups, work improvement groups, quality circles (see Management in Focus 18.2).

●   *Informal*: ad hoc gatherings, scribbled notes and the grapevine (see Management in Focus 18.3).

● Communication policies and priorities

Communication policies are based on the extent to which organisations and their managers are prepared to engage in consultation, participation and effective committee work.

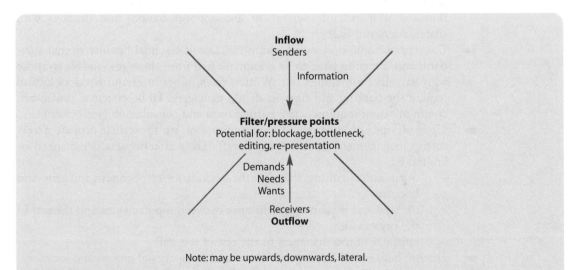

Figure 18.1 Principles of communication

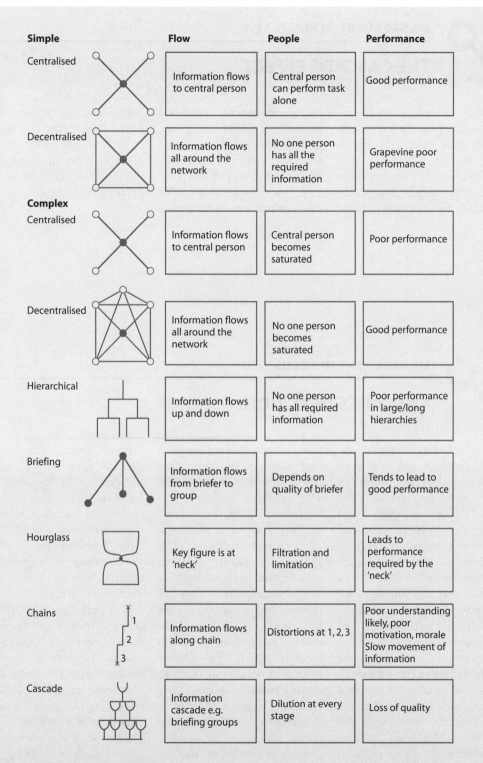

Simple		Flow	People	Performance
Centralised		Information flows to central person	Central person can perform task alone	Good performance
Decentralised		Information flows all around the network	No one person has all the required information	Grapevine poor performance
Complex				
Centralised		Information flows to central person	Central person becomes saturated	Poor performance
Decentralised		Information flows all around the network	No one person becomes saturated	Good performance
Hierarchical		Information flows up and down	No one person has all required information	Poor performance in large/long hierarchies
Briefing		Information flows from briefer to group	Depends on quality of briefer	Tends to lead to good performance
Hourglass		Key figure is at 'neck'	Filtration and limitation	Leads to performance required by the 'neck'
Chains		Information flows along chain	Distortions at 1, 2, 3	Poor understanding likely, poor motivation, morale Slow movement of information
Cascade		Information cascade e.g. briefing groups	Dilution at every stage	Loss of quality

Figure 18.2 Chains of communication

MANAGEMENT IN FOCUS 18.1

THE CASCADE EFFECT

This is attractive to hierarchies. Those at the top delude themselves that it works as an effective communication mechanism. It takes its name from the cascade appearance caused by pouring champagne into the top glass of a pyramid of glasses. The pouring is continued until the wine overflows and eventually fills all the glasses of the pyramid (see Figure 18.2). The effect of this – both for champagne and for communication – is the same. The quality of both is lost and there is a good measure of wastage by the time the bottom of the pyramid is reached.

MANAGEMENT IN FOCUS 18.2

CASCADES IN ACTION: FORD UK

This problem of communication cascades arose at Ford UK at the beginning of the twenty-first century. For years, the company had struggled with the problems of institutionalised racism: above all, the knowledge, perception and belief that it was very difficult for members of ethnic minorities to gain promotions to managerial and supervisory positions. Over the same period of time, the company's US head office in Detroit had been fed assurances that the situation was improving. The company described itself as having 'the best race relations policies in the business', yet this did not prevent increasing numbers of complaints being upheld over the period 1987–2000.

In late 2000, Ford took the decision to scale down car production at its UK Dagenham plant, and to concentrate only on engines at that location. The result of this was industrial uproar, led by the company's trade unions. Allegations of racism were re-stated. The government also became involved in consultations with the company to see if the effects on employment could be mitigated.

Only at that point, did the company Chief Executive, Jacques Nasser, come over to the UK from Detroit to see the problem at first hand for himself. The widely held conclusion was that most of the problems would have been resolved much more satisfactorily if only senior officials from head office had come over earlier.

The effectiveness of the direct approach and the ineffectiveness of the cascade or chains of communication method were stated by Dale Carnegie as follows: 'The only thing that should ever be passed on is simple messages. Otherwise, if you want someone to know something, tell them directly'.

MANAGEMENT IN FOCUS 18.3

GRAPEVINE

All organisations have a grapevine – consisting if gossip, half-formed opinions and general chatter about the present state of affairs.

The grapevine is an impor-tant indicator of general organisational well-being. If it is concerned with personal gossip and the mythical activ-ities of individuals, all is more likely to be well than if the primary topic of conversation is the future state of the organisation, uncertainty over job and work security, and spreading of rumours about redundancies.

Consultation, participation and involvement

Organisations consult with their staff on the implementation of decisions and poli-cies. The purpose is to ensure that everyone understands what is required of them, and why, and to give them a full understanding of a particular situation. Consul-tation also reflects the need for mutual confidence and unity of purpose among everyone in the organisation. Effective consultation, participation and involvement helps to ensure that what is proposed has been well thought out and tested, as well as providing a means for staff input (see Figure 18.3).

Genuine consultation also helps to ensure that any flaws in decision-making processes or the implementation of particular proposals may be raised. However well or thoroughly an issue has been overtly thought through, it must be capable of wide general scrutiny and examination.

Committees

Committees are constituted for a variety of reasons. From the point of view of communication, it is essential that they enhance both quality and value rather than act as a blockage. To ensure this, the purpose, scheduling, size, composition, agenda, control and recording must be managed. The ultimate test of the value of any committee is its output. If this is not forthcoming, then alternative means should be found to tackle the issues that the committee or committee system is supposed to face.

Committees may be used to render inert something that is threatening to a partic-ular vested interest. They are used to filter and edit information. They are used to draw the teeth of lobbies or pressure groups – and to advance particular desired points of view. In many cases, there is a pecking order. Committee membership may be subject to patronage or favour. Membership of certain committees is often the mark of status or achievement.

Committees should therefore be constituted for a purpose, and when this purpose is satisfied, they should be disbanded. They satisfy human needs of association, belonging, participating and contributing; it is important that they do this in the context of advancing the total quality and effectiveness of the organisation.

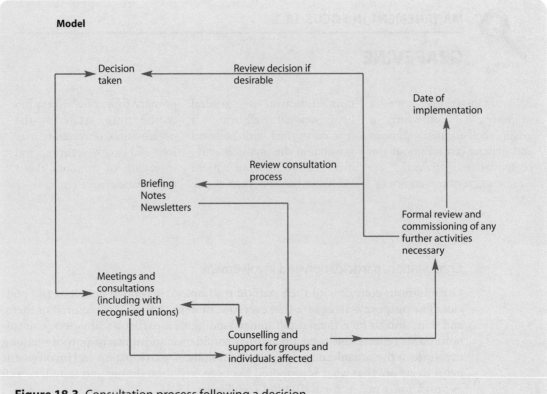

Figure 18.3 Consultation process following a decision

⬤ Principles of effective communication

Communication is at its most effective when it is delivered face to face, allowing for discussions and questions. Effective communication is underpinned by written documents, rules and procedures as above. It is additionally normally the case that core messages at least, have to be repeated many times (this is a key lesson from brand building and product and service awareness from the advertising industry).

- *Language*: of sender, receiver, and anyone else who may read or listen to it. The greater the clarity of language, the greater the likelihood that what is transmitted will be received and understood; and the reverse – when language is not clear – always dilutes effectiveness. It also leads to feelings that things are being hidden or not stated fully.
- *Conciseness*: in which everything that needs saying is stated simply and directly. This is not to be confused with lack of full coverage or leaving things out.
- *Precision*: language that addresses points directly reinforces total confidence in the communication. Language that is not direct tends to reinforce any feelings that may be present of dishonesty or mistrust (see Management in Focus 18.4).
- *The positive/negative balance*: people respond much more actively to positive communications. Where negative messages have to be transmitted, these

MANAGEMENT IN FOCUS 18.4

LANGUAGE BARRIERS

Forms of words and phraseology are used extensively to give off coded messages and to reinforce the real agenda that is being followed. Examples are as follows:

- With the greatest respect, I respect your views, I am sure that you/he/she is a person of great integrity

    = you are wrong, you are talking rubbish, I don't value you at all.

- We will take all steps, we are doing everything possible, we are complying with the law, we are complying with specific regulations

    = we are doing as little as possible in the circumstances, we are doing the least we can get away with in the circumstances, you cannot touch us.

- We do not have the resources/money/staff/equipment

    = we do not want to do it, we are not going to do it.

should be done with the same clarity and precision; at least then bad news is quickly, clearly and completely understood.

The selection of the correct media is essential and many communications go wrong because the wrong choice is made. The basic rules are as follows:

- Say what needs to be said; write what needs to be written; make best use of all the senses of those affected and media available.
- Say what needs to be said and confirm this in writing.
- Operate on a fundamental basis of openness, honesty, integrity and trust in terms of access to, and provision of, information.
- Use e-mails and written documentation only for giving general information, or to reinforce what has already been said.

Non-verbal communication

Non-verbal communication gives an impression of people to others without saying or writing anything. It also reinforces what is being said or written. It also tends to give the real message – the non-verbal message is usually much stronger. The main components that must be understood are:

- *Appearance*: this includes age, gender, hair, face, body shape and size, height, bearing, national and racial characteristics, clothing and accessories. Each of these items and their combined effect have great implications for: interviewing, public images, creating impressions, advertising public relations, salesmanship, presentation, design brand, marque, layout, comfort and familiarity.
- *Manner*: indicating behaviour, emotion, stress, comfort, formality/informality, acceptability/unacceptability, respect/disrespect.

- *Expression*: expression, especially facial expression, becomes the focus of attention and that is where people concentrate most of their attention.
- *Eye contact*: regular eye contact demonstrates interest, trust, concern, affection and sympathy. The depth of expression in the eyes generates deeper perception of feelings – anger, sorrow, love, hatred, joy.
- *Pose*: this is either static or active, relaxed, calm, agitated, nervous or stressful. It reinforces the overall impression conveyed. Different parts of the body – especially arms and legs – are used for expression, emphasis, protection and shield.
- *Clothing*: especially in work situations, clothing provides an instant summary of people. Technicians are instantly recognised by their overalls, police and traffic wardens by their distinctive uniforms, and so on. Many organisations whose staff deal regularly and consistently with the public insist either on a dress code or the wearing of a uniform – it helps to reinforce organisational image and the trust and confidence of the public.
- *Touch*: this reinforces a wide range of perceptions. Consider the difference between different people's handshakes and the impressions that these convey. Touching also reinforces role and sex stereotypes – the chairman/chairwoman banging a fist on the desk, the woman meticulously arranging her clothes.
- *Body movement*: this may be purely functional and fulfilling certain requirements for example, cleaning the car. Movements may be exaggerated, conveying anger or high emotions; languid, conveying comfort, ease or indolence; or sharp and staccato, conveying forcefulness and emphasis.
- *Position*: this reinforces formality/informality, dominance/dependency, superiority/subordination. People use position to enhance feelings of control and influence. For example, people may face each other across a large desk – this conveys a sense of security and defence to the person whose desk it is and a barrier to be crossed by the other. Chat show hosts sit without tables and ensure that their guests do not have recourse to this prop either. This puts the professional at an advantage and ensures that the guest is sufficiently alien to the environment to be subservient to the host.
- *Props and settings*: props and settings are used to reinforce impressions of luxury and formality. They are designed to ensure that whatever happens does so to the greatest possible advantage of the instigator. They either reinforce or complement perceptions and expectations, or else they contrast perceptions and expectations, so that the person coming into the situation is impressed for whatever reason.
- *Discrepancy*: this occurs where the body conveys one message while the spoken or written text convey others.
- *Social factors*: people are conditioned into having preconceived ideas and general expectations of particular situations. For example, people do not generally attend promotion panels or job interviews unshaven or dressed informally. There is no rationale for this other than the expectations of society and the general requirement to conform.
- *The other senses*: other aspects of non-verbal communication include the use of scent and fragrance, the use of colour and coordination of colours, matters of social and ethical importance and expectation, design and use of materials.
- *Listening*: listening is both active and passive. Passive listening may be no more than awareness of background noise; it may also be limited to a general aware-

ness of what is going on. Active listening requires taking a dynamic interest in what is being received. While the message is received through the ears, it is reinforced through eye contact, body movement and pose, and through the reception of any non-verbal signals that are given by the speaker.

- *Reinforcement:* non-verbal communication tends to reinforce: relative and absolute measures of status, value, importance and achievement; relative and absolute measures of authority, power and influence; confidence and well-being; and psychological barriers.

Barriers and blockages

Communication barriers and blockages arise either by accident and negligence or by design. Barriers arise by accident where the choice of language, timing or method of communication is wrong though people act with the best of intentions. In these cases, those involved ought simply to step back from the situation and rectify it as quickly as possible.

Negligence is where barriers and blockages are allowed to arise by default. In such cases, communication dysfunctions are either not acknowledged or, if they are acknowledged, are nevertheless not tackled.

It is the case however, that people within organisations create barriers and blockages in order to further their own ends.

Information becomes a commodity to be bought and sold, to be corrupted, skewed and filtered in the pursuit of the sectoral interest in question. This is endemic throughout the mid to upper echelons of the military, civil and public service institutions, multinational companies and other multi-site organisations with large and complex head office institutions where an active and negative form of realpolitik exists (see Management in Focus 18.5).

Within this context the following barriers can be identified:

- *Departmental, divisional, hierarchical and functional boundaries:* blockages are compounded when either expertise or information held in one department is used as a bargaining chip, or else filtered out in the department's own interest.

MANAGEMENT IN FOCUS 18.5

ERROL FLYNN

'Errol Flynns' are so called because they exhibit all the characteristics of the great film star. In organisational terms they are glamorous – blue-eyed persons, clearly favoured, on upward career paths, with histories and track records of successes. They attract followers and courtiers. They have a series of triumphs (real and overwhelmingly imaginary) which gain organisational recognition. They are their own best publicists.

Above all, their greatest characteristic is to be, in organisational terms, just the right side of the drawbridge as it comes up – to escape their own disasters by the skin of their teeth.

- *Language*: use of bureaucratic and imprecise phrases acts both as a barrier to effective communication and as fuel to the fires of any inherent discontent.
- *Distance*: both physical and psychological. Physical distance acts as a barrier when people working away from particular locations simply do not receive information. The filtering, editing and presentation of information also reinforces any other psychological barriers (e.g. status, hierarchy, modes of address) that may be present. Also, some managers put up physical barriers between themselves and the rest of the world in the form of secretaries, switchboards and information-filtering systems.
- *Trappings*: some trappings exude fear. For example, the person who has a car parking space, two personal assistants and a personal washroom puts up psychological barriers to communication with more junior staff. The junior, in turn, is both physically and psychologically discouraged from making any approach.
- *Control mechanisms*: where requests for specific information (e.g. output figures and costs) are requested in forms that are either inappropriate or may be taken and used for purposes other than that for which they were originally produced. The problem is compounded when those who are required to produce such information do not fully understand the purposes or standpoint from which it is being requested (see Management in Focus 18.6).
- *Confidentiality*: which becomes a barrier when it is used as a means of attracting or acquiring status rather than for operational effectiveness. Confidentiality should normally be limited to technological advances, marketing initiatives and research, development and pioneering inventions, and people's personnel files.
- *Lack of visibility or access*: which leads to feelings and perceptions that problems and issues cannot quickly be resolved.
- *Information systems*: combinations of communications, people and technology all have imperfections and therefore the potential to be a blockage or barrier. Information technology especially acts as a barrier where there is a lack of training for the staff, a lack of full understanding of the systems capabilities, where there are different and incompatible systems and formats present, and where not all staff have access.
- *The nature of the work*: the greater the intrinsic interest of the work, the greater the volume of reasons that the staff have for being there, the greater the likelihood that there will be effective communications. Where work is boring and alienating there is normally a more general background of lack of respect and trust. Problems are compounded where there are extensive and complex rule and regulation books and committee management structures (see Management in Focus 18.7).

⬤ Reinforcement

Reinforcement acts as a barrier where it and the given message are at variance. In these situations, the reinforcement is always that which is received and believed. It is damaging in each of the following cases:

- Where what is said is positive, but where the reinforcement is negative. The most common form of this is in the use of positive language, but without underpinning the communication with absolute commitments or objectives.

MANAGEMENT IN FOCUS 18.6

THE NEED TO KNOW

'The need to know' barrier occurs where organisations decide that information is to be given in different ways – or that different information is to be given – to different groups and individuals. It is a process of limiting the availability of information. On the face of it there is some sense in this – most organisations have far too much information to issue for any one person to understand, analyse and internalise.

The barrier arises from the reasoning behind 'the need to know'. As long as this is for operational reasons, it is sound. Otherwise, the message given is one of:

● A lack of capability to understand what is being said, and especially that the organisation (or an individual superior) does not think or believe that the subordinate has this capability.

● Lack of value or different levels of value placed on different groups of staff, especially those who are excluded from the 'need to know' list.

● Access: in order to be privy to certain information it is necessary to have reached a particular level of the organisation. Communication therefore becomes a trapping of personal status and importance.

● General disrespect: operation of this form of approach to the giving of information displays an overall view of lack of respect to those affected.

● Psychological distance: again, this emphasises the differences and divisions that exist in the organisation and between its functions, departments, divisions and individuals.

Operating a 'need to know' approach also leads to distortions in the presentational style and use of information media. What is issued is for the purposes of the issuer rather than the receiver, emphasising distance and supremacy rather than imparting valuable and useful information.

More generally, any restriction on information leads to reductions in the capabilities of those who need to take decisions and make judgements. Even if operated from the highest and most positive standpoint, this approach is restricting in this way.

This lack is the reinforcement and is that which is believed, acted upon and reacted and which becomes the focus for analysis.

● Where what is said is negative, but where the reinforcement is positive. However, this works well when, for example, the message is that 'We are in a crisis and we have to get out of it, and this is how we are going to go about it.'

● Where what is said is unclear and so is the reinforcement (see Management in Focus 18.8).

● Use of media

Media and message should reinforce each other. When the format and language is not appropriate, this is a barrier to effective communication. This applies to the

MANAGEMENT IN FOCUS 18.7

RULES AND REGULATIONS

Rules and regulations create barriers in all situations because they order and restrict people's activities. The problem arises when rules and regulations are:

- Too long and too complex, consisting of volumes of procedures that are designed to cover every possible eventuality or foible. This increases perceptions of restriction and negativity. It also indicates a more general negative view of the people concerned: if they need this amount of regulation, they are regarded as potentially lazy or dishonest.
- Written in language that is not simple and direct. The impression of restriction is compounded by the use of particular phraseology that seems to leave those in superior positions free to impose any restriction or interpret the rules as they see fit. While recourse to grievance procedures is always available to staff affected in this way, this requires energy and commitment on their part. It is also in itself very negative and consumes resources that could be better used elsewhere.
- Operated unevenly, where standards vary between different managers, supervisors, departments, divisions and functions. Some of this will be the fault of the individuals concerned, but often it is due to the nature and complexity of the rules themselves and the ways in which they have been written and applied.
- Contradiction: the more complex the set of rules, the more likely contradictions are to exist. In these cases again, time and energy is spent on resolving individual issues when they do arise and in working out which of the conflicting rules is to be applied in the circumstances.

spoken and written word and to any visual or pictorial information. Communication depends on recognising the needs of the receiver as well as the objectives of the presentation. Distortion occurs when one or the other is not properly dealt with. It is especially prevalent in the presentation of:

- statistics and trends, where figures and performance are taken in isolation or used out of context; answers to questions, where the answer produced is not related to the question asked
- strong, visual and pictorial images that are used to project a narrow view that is at variance with the wider picture
- discussion and debate that are not genuine but conducted from the point of view or vested interest of the protagonist
- essential information that is put out in ways that ensure that not everyone can gain access (e.g. through e-mail and intranet systems)
- different media that are used by vested interests to advance and promote their point of view to best advantage (see Management in Focus 18.9).

MANAGEMENT IN FOCUS 18.8

LANGUAGE AND MESSAGES

Negative

The use of words such as 'but', 'only', 'never'.

Negative	Positive
It is excellent but it is very expensive	It is excellent and it is very expensive
He/she is only a secretary	He/she is a secretary
You will never get to the top unless . . .	You will get to the top if or by . . .

Acronyms

Two people engaged in a construction industry research project conducted a positive, happy and ostensibly productive conversation around the acronym WIRS. Only when one party wrote up a note at the meeting did it become apparent that at the core of the conversation was the construction sector's 'whole industry research strategy'. The other party had thought that it was about the workplace industrial relations survey.

Over praising

Over-praising always gives a negative message because it reflects, either a lack of sincerity or a lack of understanding on the part of the praiser. The only exception to this is where the subordinate has resolved a crisis or problem for the supervisor which could not otherwise have been achieved.

Ambiguity

This often occurs because of the simple human failing to order the thoughts before speaking or writing – for example, school teacher to class: 'Watch the board while I go through it.'

There may also be punctuation errors:

- She said, 'she didn't mind what I did'.
- She said, she didn't mind what I did.
- 'She', said she, 'didn't mind what I did'.

Or errors of emphasis:

- *Long* may you run.
- Long *may* you run.
- Long may *you* run.

Confusion

The word 'solutions' means different things to management consultants, information technologists, chemists, doctors and nurses.

Dishonesty

More insidiously phrases such as 'there are no redundancies planned at present' and 'there are no plans for reorganisation at present' give off a dual meaning – what is not said is whether there are future plans, and how long the present actually lasts. Reinforcement in these cases centres around 'at present'.

More generally, the usual justification offered by managers and supervisors for over-emphasis on negativity to the exclusion of all forms of positive language is to the effect that 'if my staff do not hear from me, they know they are doing a good job'.

Problems are compounded where the delivery, either written or oral, is accidentally or deliberately unclear. This also applies to the visual, when the images used are at variance with the overall message.

There are problems where one of the protagonists has to put on some form of show for the benefit of someone else who is assessing him or her, and where this assessment is based on reasons other than organisational effectiveness. The organisation may require particular managers to present information in ways that are deliberately unclear and may reward them for this. More junior members of staff may respond to something in a strident or controversial manner in order to gain a reputation among their peers, or to bring themselves to the attention of those in authority for their own future advancement.

There are also issues where there is a party line to be followed and where the presentation needs do not match with this easily. A trade union for example, may have great sympathy with an organisation's need to restructure. It may have to reconcile this with its own need to be seen to be representing the interests of its members. This is compounded if the restructuring has effects and implications for their long-term future – especially redundancy, retraining or redeployment. The union may therefore be forced into a position of opposition in spite of its own careful analysis of the situation.

● Realpolitik

Realpolitik, or organisation politics, affects both the quality and the content of communications. As stated above, information can become a commodity to be guarded, filtered and fed into systems, including the grapevine, for managerial or departmental advantage as well as (or rather than) in the organisation's best interests. In these circumstances cluster groups and networks become the places where real messages get around the organisation. Managers are also known to make informal contacts in other parts of the organisation or other departments than their own (the equivalent of having their own spy network). Managers will also tend to gather information just in case they missed something that might be to their advantage (or the absence of which might be to their disadvantage).

Messages lose their effect if, and when, they raise expectations but nothing subsequently happens. This is, above all, where action is promised but not forthcoming,

MANAGEMENT IN FOCUS 18.9

USE OF MEDIA

Those with influence, power and authority choose the media that they believe they can use to best advantage.

This is especially true of political debate. For example, one party persists with the view that 'Not enough resources or priority is being given to a particular area (for example, roads, education, health, social services and social security).' The other party counters this by saying that 'More resources are being spent in this area than ever before.'

This is reinforced by the production of statistics, again for the end being pursued. On the question of health for example, one party will say that 'Waiting lists for treat-ment are longer than ever.' The other counters with: 'We are treating more patients than ever before.' Each produces statistics to back up its point of view.

The result is a stalemate. It is compounded by the over-whelming impression given that:

- There are only two possible points of view to hold – the one or the other indicated.

- Aligning others to the point of view depends upon their own vested interest, personal and political preference and conviction.

These distorted forms of debate and discussion take place in all organisations from time to time. The protago-nists again either take refuge in their own vested interest, seeking statistics to underpin it, or else produce counter-arguments to the opposing point of view. No productive debate and discussion takes place. This dissipates any feel-ings of shared commitment and involvement, reinforcing the differences between vari-ous departments, divisions, functions, groups and indi-viduals. It is compounded where one view is seen to be that of the organisation as a whole, or where the protago-nist gains advantage or favour as the result of holding or presenting a particular point of view.

when promises are made but not kept, and when people's opinions and views are asked for but then ignored. In each of these cases, if there is no intention of taking the action people are hoping for, it is best to give a clear and unambiguous statement of what is to occur rather than engaging in spurious consultative and participative efforts. These will in any case be construed as such at the time, and will colour people's opinions about any such activities in the future.

Other forms of dishonesty and duplicity should also be recognised. The first is where information is sought from members of staff for one ostensible purpose and is then used against them for others. A common version of this is to ask people during selection and appraisal interviews what they think their weaknesses are and then to use these as excuses not to appoint or to develop or to give pay rises. This also occurs in forms of organisation-speak, whereby messages that are delivered are couched in terms such as: 'There are no plans at present to close/make redundant/sell off,' 'We are considering a range of options,' and 'Training and development and excellent prospects are available to the right person.' Such phrases are always subject to sceptical scrutiny.

The volume of information issued may also itself be a barrier. This happens where one is told more than one wishes to know about a particular subject, or where one receives huge swathes of written information that is both incomprehensible and unusable in the form in which it is presented.

● Organisational toxicity

Organisational toxicity and toxic communications exist in organisations that have themselves become dishonest or corrupted for some reason. Essentially, all organisations have communication agendas as follows:

- stated and primary, where what is said is precisely what happens
- secondary and hidden, in which messages are given out dishonestly, using lack of clarity to distort and undermine what is being said.

Secondary and hidden agendas are forms of organisational toxicity. Toxic communications demotivate and demoralise staff, and ultimately dissipate the volume and quality of organisational effort and effectiveness. Where this happens, clusters of staff endlessly debate the general state of the organisation. High levels of disciplinary problems and grievances exist. There are complicated and duplicated sets of rules and procedures. The problem is reinforced by physical and psychological distance, and remoteness between managers and their staff.

The results are as follows:

- *Blame and scapegoating*: the organisation finds individuals to carry the can for its corporate failings. Sales departments get the blame for falling profits. Personnel get the blame for disputes and grievances. Individuals are blamed for specific failures (for example, the failure of a particular promotion campaign, the failure of work restructuring). They are often also named in this respect and their failure publicised around the organisation.

  A more insidious version exists whereby the scapegoat is not official but word is allowed to get around the grapevine and the organisation does nothing to deny the rumours or rehabilitate any individuals that are so named.
- *Communication as a weapon*: communications are targeted so as to cause maximum damage to particular individuals, groups, departments and divisions. This reinforces any culture or perception of blame and scapegoating that may be present. Information is fed, both officially and unofficially, into the hands of powerful and influential groups and individuals, in the hope and expectation that this will be used to the detriment of the departments or individuals targeted.
- *Secrets*: secrets are used as bargaining chips, and as forms of corporate or institutional blackmail, again with the purposes of getting powerful and influential groups and individuals to come round to a particular way of thinking.
- *Elites*: elites and specialist groups use the means and methods of communication at their disposal to reinforce the belief and perception of their excellence and infallibility.

The result of this is that those who wish to wield any influence have to become toxic communicators. Toxic communicators take active responsibility for, and become actively involved in, corrupting communications and information for their own ends.

It is clear from the above, that once an organisation and its practices are corrupted in these ways, toxic communication quickly becomes the organisation's way of life. It is a short step from this to concentrating the whole of collective and individual efforts on fighting internal battles rather than tending to products and services.

● Assertiveness

Assertiveness and assertive communications are important because nothing can be effective unless it is well thought out, its effects are understood in advance, and the message is delivered clearly and directly to the recipients.

Assertiveness and assertive communications seek to deliver honest, complete, clear and direct messages as follows:

- *Language*: clear, simple and direct; easy for the audience to understand and respond to; the words used are unambiguous and straightforward; requests and demands are made in a clear and precise manner and with sound reasons.
- *Aims and objectives*: precise and clear, considered in advance, recognising the effect that the message is likely to have on the recipient.
- *Delivery*: in a clear and steady tone of voice, or where written in a well presented and easy to read format. The use of voice is always even, neither too loud nor too soft, and does not involve shouting, threatening or abuse.
- *Persistence and determination*: where problems or issues are raised by the recipient, the sender sticks to the message, aims and objectives; assertive communicators do not become side-tracked; they answer any problems that are raised without diverting from the main purpose.
- *Positive and negative*: the general thrust of the message is always clear and apparent; this does not vary, whether the overall tone is positive or negative. This approach is especially important in handling general staff problems – especially matters concerning grievances and discipline.
- *Face and eyes*: the head is held up. There is plenty of eye contact and steadiness of gaze. The delivery is reinforced with positive movements that relate to what is being said (for example, smiles, laughter, nodding, encouragement; or a straight face when something has gone wrong).
- *Other non-verbal aspects*: the body is upright; hands and arms are open (in order to encourage positive responses and productive transactions; there is no fidgeting or shuffling; there are no threatening gestures or table thumping, or other displays of other forms of behaviour (see Management in Focus 18.10).

● Negotiations

Effective negotiation requires the application of communication skills in addressing and resolving individual and collective problems. It requires undertaking discussions with a view to establishing agreements, and arranging and delivering what is agreed. All managers should be able to do this. The keys initially are:

- knowing what you want from the situation, and the requirements of the others involved
- knowing what you do not want from the situation, and what others involved also do not want

MANAGEMENT IN FOCUS 18.10

USE AND VALUE OF ASSERTIVE COMMUNICATIONS

Assertive communications are designed to ensure clarity and integrity of message, as stated in the text above. They are additionally designed to neutralise behaviour that is:

- *Aggressive*: characterised by shouting, swearing, table thumping, arguments (cross transaction). The matter in hand is lost as the aggressor strives to impose his or her point of view. Winning the argument becomes everything.

- *Hostile*: where the main emphasis is on the personalisation of the matters in hand. Often also characterised by shouting and table thumping, the outcome is normally a personal attack (sometimes in public, on an individual or group.

- *Submissive*: characterised by saying or doing anything that the other party wants so that the aggressor will finish the argument or transaction and go away.

- *Inconsistent*: characterised by according people different levels of quality and value, having different standards for individuals and groups. Conversely, this may involve treating an individual or group in different ways according to mood or the environment for example.

- *Non-assertive*: characterised by the inability of people to put their message across. This is either because they are not sure what to put across, or else have not used the correct words or media.

- knowing what is acceptable, and unacceptable, both to yourself, and also to the other parties.

The elements of successful negotiations are based on:

- having the authority to make and deliver the agreement
- paying attention to detail
- having the resources to deliver and implement the agreements
- attention to the ability of everyone concerned to make sure that it continues to work.

It is also important to consider:

- the question of setting precedents – implications for future dealings along similar lines
- internal and external pressures – especially pressures from subordinates, superiors and backers
- the opportunities and consequences of agreeing to something; and the opportunities and consequences of not making an agreement
- what is open to negotiation and what is not.

The negotiating process has three elements:

- *Substance*: the matter in hand.

- *Process*: how it is to be addressed and resolved.
- *Presentation*: how the end result is to be perceived and received.

Negotiations may be conducted from two positions:

- that those involved trust each other to do their best by the particular situation and to resolve a particular matter in ways acceptable to all concerned
- a basic lack of trust – managers do not trust staff members or their representatives; and staff and their representatives do not trust their managers or the organisation's owners.

In many situations therefore, negotiations are an integral part of the process of managing conflict. It is essential therefore that both negotiating expertise and understanding of the demands of the environment are present.

Where there is a basis of mutual trust, matters can be discussed openly and honestly with a view to resolving them. Where this basis does not exist, the following approaches have to be taken:

- The opening position is always stated on the basis that it will be rejected.
- There then follows a process of counter-offer and counter-claim with each party working its way gradually towards the other.
- The content of the final agreement is usually clearly signalled before it is made as is the basis of what is genuinely acceptable or otherwise.
- Serious disputes occur when one side is determined not to settle or where there is genuine misunderstanding or misreading of the signals.
- Settlements are normally couched in positive terms in relation to all concerned to avoid the use of words such as 'loss', 'loser', 'climb down' and 'defeat' which have negative connotations, and which tend to store up resentment for the future and polarise attitudes.

Behavioural aspects of negotiation

The following must be understood:

- *The distributive effect*: opportunities and consequences of settling with one group at the expense of others.
- *Integrative drives*: opportunities and constraints of settling everything to the satisfaction of all involved.
- *Influencing attitudes*: in which attitudes are formed, modified and developed as follows:
  - confrontational, where the parties are motivated to defeat the other or win them over to their own point of view
  - individualistic, in which the parties concerned pursue their own self-interests without any regard for the positions of others
  - cooperative, where each party is concerned about the others, as well as its own position
  - collusive, where the parties concerned form a coalition in which they pursue a common purpose, possibly to the detriment of other groups within the organisation or of the organisation as a whole
  - use of language, which may be confrontational or cooperative
  - the formality–informality balance, especially the need for informal systems

of communication between the parties involved where formalised procedures are presenting barriers.

- *Individual and collective expectations*: based on what people know, understand, believe and perceive that they are likely to gain from a particular situation. Serious misunderstandings occur when individuals and groups have either been misinformed or else have failed to grasp the fact that substantial changes in a particular situation have led to radically altered expectations.

These processes must be understood and engaged according to the demands of the particular situation (see Figure 18.4).

Negotiations are required in resolving:

- Issues between staff and management in the pursuit of individual and collective grievances, and also concerning pay rises and improvements in terms and conditions of employment. In traditional UK organisations, this process is known as collective bargaining.
- Disputes between organisations and their customers.
- Interdepartmental issues: addressing, managing and resolving misunderstandings; gaining cooperation and agreement.
- Internal issues: handling discipline, grievance, disputes and dismissals, resolving personal and professional disputes.
- Customer and client relations: handling and managing complaints.
- Contracting agreements on the supply and output sides, and in the engagement of temporary, specialist and subcontracted staff.
- Gathering resources, especially where this is known, believed or perceived to be a competitive or distributive issue.
- Managing barriers and blockages, especially resolving crises and hold-ups on the supply and distribution sides.
- Managing the concerns of stakeholders and influential figures.

Conclusions

Effective communication is vital for the successful functioning of any organisation. It follows that all managers must be effective communicators, and that all organisations must have effective formal methods, mechanisms and processes of communication, and suitable and effective means of making sure that what they wish to say is transmitted effectively.

Effective communication is dependent on the volume, quality and accessibility of information; the means and media by which it is transmitted and received; the use to which it is put; its integrity; and the level of integrity of the wider situation.

Understanding and being able to apply the rules, principles, skills and techniques indicated are universal managerial skills. They result in the ability to produce effective communication capable of being received, accepted and acted upon or responded to. All levels of communication should be monitored. Remedial action where communication is poor or ineffective should always be taken. Concentration on barriers and blockages to effective communication should be designed to reinforce the need for clarity of purpose and language. As many channels of communication as possible should also be used, each giving the same message, so that the message received is complete and not subject to editing, interpretation or

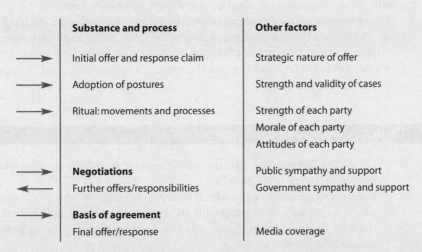

(a) Steps in the negotiating process

Substance and process	Other factors
Initial offer and response claim	Strategic nature of offer
Adoption of postures	Strength and validity of cases
Ritual: movements and processes	Strength of each party
	Morale of each party
	Attitudes of each party
Negotiations	Public sympathy and support
Further offers/responsibilities	Government sympathy and support
Basis of agreement	
Final offer/response	Media coverage

Each of these activities must be undertaken in these circles.
Each of the other factors must be acknowledged and understood.

(b) Process operation

Offer   Area of agreement   Claim

A	B	C	D
Low			High
Management			Staff/union

The collective bargaining process: offers between A and B rejected by staff; between C and D instantly accepted by staff; claims between A and B instantly accepted by managment; between C and D rejected by management; B–C is basis for negotiated settlement; normal first offer is around A, which leads to instant rejection; normal first claim is around D, but engages the process.

Figure 18.4 The negotiating process

distortion. Wherever toxic, expedient or dishonest communications take place, it should always be clearly understood that the wider message received by those at whom the communication is aimed will always be read as such.

Organisations and their managers are therefore responsible for creating the conditions in which effective communications can take place, and ensuring that their managers understand the full effects of what they say, write and present. It is therefore essential to understand the broad context, as well as being able to apply specific skills and techniques.

CRITICAL THINKING, ANALYSIS AND EVALUATION

1. Of all the barriers to effective communication, which in your view are the hardest to overcome and why?
2. For an organisation with which you are familiar, produce a communication strategy that addresses the problems you know to exist, and that takes positive steps to conquer them. How will you know whether your strategy has been successful or not?
3. Discuss the view that because of the nature of organisational hierarchies and the differing aims and objectives of those within them, effective communications are not possible within organisations.
4. Identify the main strengths and weaknesses of television, radio and newspaper news and current affairs coverage. What lessons may be learned from this by organisations and their managers?

DEVELOPING MANAGEMENT SKILLS AND EXPERTISE

'WHO WANTS TO KNOW? WHO NEEDS TO KNOW?'

Recently, 752 employees at a Thames Valley computer chip manufacturing company took strike action over the company's proposals for major restructuring, and organisational reform. Because of declining prices in the sector, and the consequent effect on profit margins, the company had called in management consultants who had proposed:

- 230 redundancies
- a restructuring of the workforce in order to allow for maximum flexibility of working
- transferring a further 200 staff from permanent status to 'as and when required' – i.e. only employed when production demands required.

The staff, with the full support of their trade union (the AEEU), accordingly went through the full legal process required, and then called an official strike.

The independent Advisory Conciliation and Arbitration Service (ACAS) initiated regular contact with the parties during the strike. Neither side was initially prepared to ask for its direct involvement. After seven weeks of strike action however, both sides accepted an invitation to a series of informal meetings, aimed at breaking the deadlock.

Management reiterated their argument that declining world markets, cut-throat pricing policies and successive years of reducing profit margins had made it necessary to restructure the organisation in order to keep the company competitive. Surplus labour had been identified and, while the lay-offs and restructuring were regretted, there was little that could be done to alleviate this.

The AEEU rejected the company's arguments. The union stated that management had accepted the consultant's proposals purely because they had been forced to pay heavily for them, and that they had not consulted on these proposals, either with the staff or with anyone else. They also contended that pushing the staff down the path of confrontation had simply compounded the losses. Customers were being lost on every day that the strike was going on. The union declared itself prepared to cooperate on a wider consultation. It stated that it fully understood the company's basic position, and the problems of the business environment. However, it was not prepared to accept any compulsion, either in the matters of redundancy or in the move to fully flexible working.

After full and frank exchanges of views over four days, agreement was reached that compulsory flexible working and redundancies would be withdrawn pending consultation with the unions and staff as a whole. This discussion would be subject to a strict timetable. At the end of this, if no agreement was reached, management would take whatever action they then deemed necessary. A timetable for transition to fully flexible working would also be agreed, and that this would be extended to new staff joining the organisation in the future.

As the result of this, the union balloted the staff on the agreement that has been reached. The staff voted by a four to one majority to accept the decision and arrangements were made for a full return to work the following day. Most staff were in any case anxious to get back to work, because they were in the situation where bills were not being paid; and it was also getting extremely close to Christmas.

Questions

1. What communications should have been put in place to ensure that this situation never arose in the first place?
2. What communications now need to be put in place; how should these be managed; how should they be delivered and by whom?
3. What communication processes should be established, in order to be certain that the problem is not going to blow up again over the foreseeable future, and over the particular period of the consultations?
4. On the basis of what you have been told in the case study, identify the effects of this failure to communicate effectively on:
a) business profitability and effective activity
b) staff relationships.

Chapter nineteen

Organisation technology, structure and design

'Rubbish in – rubbish out.'
Universal comment on the dysfunctional relationship
between computers and their human operators.

'Every time something goes wrong, people blame technology –
machine failures, systems failures. Anything but look at their own structures in fact.'
Peter M. Senge, *The Fifth Discipline*, Century (1998).

'Everything that can be invented, has been invented. We have all the technology possible.'
Howe M. Weiss, US Presidential Adviser, 1898.

Chapter outline

- Introduction
- Technology
- Expertise
- Effects of technological advances
- Organisation design and structure
- Organisation structures
- Spans of control
- Core and peripheral organisations
- Federations and virtual organisations
- Structures and expectations
- Conclusions

Chapter objectives

After studying this chapter, you should be able to:

- understand the complexity of the relationship between organisation design and technology

- understand the pressures that technology brings to bear on the activities of organisations, and understand some of the steps that may be taken to address these pressures

- understand the opportunities and constraints present in particular organisational forms

- understand the need to develop and advance the structure and design of organisations.

Introduction

Organisation structures reflect the aims and objectives, and the size and complexity of the undertaking, the nature of the expertise and technology to be used, the desired quality of the working environment, the desired management and supervisory style, and means of coordination and control. Whatever arises as the result must be flexible and dynamic and responsive to market and environmental conditions and pressures. It must provide effective and suitable channels of communication and decision-making processes, and provide also for the creation of professional and productive relationships between individuals and groups. Departments, divisions and functions are created as required to pursue aims and objectives, together with the means and methods by which they are coordinated and harmonised.

The history of organisation design and development indicates that structures are easier to put in place than to change, dismantle or rearrange. Long-standing organisations give the illusion of permanence to both staff and customers. Staff become accustomed to their positions, and base their hopes and aspirations for the future on opportunities that are apparent within the structure. Many organisations have traditionally consciously provided career paths through the structure and this becomes one of the attractions to stay rather than seek opportunities elsewhere. Customers become used to dealing with a particular department or official, and if they have problems the structure traditionally provides a clear point of reference as to who should address these issues.

Pressures of economic turbulence and change, increased competition, diminishing resources and technological and expertise advances have all combined to cause a rethink of the ways in which organisations should be structured. The problem is to reconcile the qualities of flexibility, dynamism and responsiveness, and the technology and expertise present, with the need for permanence, order and stability. This is the context in which the question of organisation structure and design should be seen.

Technology

All organisations use forms of technology and equipment in pursuit of their business, and this has a critical impact on the nature, design, structure and conduct of work. Technology also has implications for compartmentalisation, functionalisation and specialisation. Departments and divisions are created around the equipment used – whether for production, communications, information or control. It impacts on the physical environment – particular processes determine the layout and format in which work is conducted and the proximity of individuals and groups to each other. It therefore becomes a factor to be recognised in the creation of supervisory and managerial functions and activities.

Again, there is an historic background. Forms of technology and equipment were used in the construction of the great buildings, temples and monuments of the ancient world. Most of this was unmechanised, often requiring armies of people to move heavy blocks of wood and stone into place. Roman war galleys – fighting ships – used slave-driven banks of oars for propulsion and direction and to manoeuvre into fighting positions. In each of these cases a basic technology existed and was exploited – but using human rather than mechanised energy to make it effective. In each case also, the task requirements meant that forms of organisation were required; and while in many cases the labour force was composed of slaves, these nevertheless had to be sufficiently interested, motivated and directed to ensure that the product or output was both effective and of the required quality.

From a strategic point of view, it is essential to consider:

- *Approaches to production*: scientific management and its effects on production and behaviour; studies of groups in different working situations; the use of work groups in production.
- *Levels and types of technology*: the effects of the size, scope and scale of operations; the use of production lines; the effects of mechanisation and automation on individuals and groups; and the additional need to maximise and optimise returns on investment on technology.
- *Organisational requirements*: the maximisation/optimisation of production; attention to standardisation, quality, speed, reliability and consistency of output.
- *Human and behavioural implications*: boredom and alienation; health and safety and occupational health; stresses and strains; job and task division.
- *Identifying specific opportunities*: for example, flexible working, outsourcing and subcontracting.

Organisations require production, service and information technology and equipment. This may be largely manual or mechanised, requiring human expertise, energy and inputs to make it effective and productive. Or it may be largely automated, designed to produce products and deliver services to uniform standards of quality, appearance and performance.

In the latter case, the human input is often largely combined to switching the process on and off and monitoring (watching) the output flow. This has direct consequences for job and work design. Automation includes production robotics and computerised manufacturing, as well as commercially-driven technology-centred services such as finance, travel and telecommunications.

Organisations additionally require the following technology:

- *Support function technology*: included computer-aided design, desk-top printing and publishing, purchasing, stock room, storage and ordering systems.
- *Information systems*: for the input, storage, retrieval, output and presentation of data in ways suitable to those using it; and for the production of data for purposes of control, monitoring, evaluation and decision making.
- *Specialised systems*: for example health equipment includes scanners, monitors, emergency equipment, laser technology for surgery and healing, heart, lung, organ and pulse monitoring equipment.
- *Generic systems*: off-the-shelf computerised production and information systems that are of value to a wide range of organisations and activities.

● Expertise

The effective management of expertise requires addressing and reconciling the following aspects:

- The scientific management and organisation of activities demands the standardisation and ordering of work in the interests of efficiency, speed and volume of output.

- Outputs of the scale and scope of production may dictate that the flow, mass and (to an extent) batch types of activities require this standardisation.
- Professional and technical staff require variety, career development and the opportunity to progress and enhance their work and expertise.
- Everyone, in any occupation, has basic human needs of self-esteem, self-respect and self-worth.

The specific effects of developments, improvements and automation of technology, seen in isolation, are:

- to remove any specific contribution made by operators to the quality and individuality of production, whether real or perceived
- to dilute or remove understanding of the production processes used and to remove any direct individual contribution that is made
- to de-skill operations – operators become button pushers, machine minders and (when breakdowns occur) telephone users summoning specialist assistance
- to create a feeling of distance – alienation – between the work and the people who carry it out
- to create frustration, which occurs either when equipment is available but the expertise to use it is not, or when the equipment is not available but the expertise is – or when both are available but the organisation chooses not to use them.

The result is again to underline feelings of low self-esteem and worth and to encourage boredom and dissatisfaction – and sow the seeds of conflict (see Management in Focus 19.1).

Effects of technological advances

It is essential to understand that technological advances bring both opportunities and consequences for organisations and their managers.

Pay, at whatever level it is set, does nothing to alleviate any boredom or monotony inherent in the work itself, though it may make it more bearable in the short to medium-term. In many cases also, bonus systems are not within the control of the individual operator. Operators may work to their full capacity, only to see their bonus lost because of factors further down the production process.

Technological advance additionally brings the threat of insecurity and job loss. It may also require extreme working conditions, including extremes of temperature and noise, discomfort, and lack of human content and contact.

Low status and esteem is generated through feelings of being 'only a cog in the machine'. This leads to feelings of futility and impotence on the part of the operator. It is from this that feelings of hostility towards the organisation start to emerge. This also leads to increases in strikes, grievances and disputes (see Management in Focus 19.2).

Adversarial and confrontational styles of work supervision also contribute to alienation and dissatisfaction. This style of supervision tends to perpetuated even by those who have been promoted from among the ranks of operators. This is partly because it is all that they know and partly because of the pressure to conform that is exerted by the existing supervisory group. It is also apparent that supervisors themselves become alienated because of pressures from their managers and also because of feelings of hostility towards them from the workers.

MANAGEMENT IN FOCUS 19.1

ALIENATION

Alienation is the term used to describe the feelings such as:

- *Powerlessness*: the inability to influence work conditions, work volume, quality, speed and direction.
- *Meaninglessness*: the inability to recognise the individual contribution made to the total output of work.
- *Isolation*: which may be either physical or psychological. The physical factors arise from work organisation that requires people to be located in ways that allow for little human interaction or feelings of mutual identity and interest. The psychological factors are influenced by the physical. They also include psychological distance from supervisors, management and the rest of the organisation.

- *Low feelings of self-esteem and self-worth*: arising from the lack of value (real or perceived) placed on staff by the organisation and its managers.
- *Loss of identity with the organisation and its work*: the inability to say with pride: 'I work for organisation x.' This is reinforced by the physical and personal commitment made by the individual to the organisation in terms of time, skill and effort which does not bring with it the psychological rewards.
- *Lack of prospects, change or advancement for the future*: feelings of being stuck or trapped in a situation purely for economic gain.
- *General rejection*: based on adversarial, managerial and supervisory styles and lack of meaningful

communications, participation and involvement. This is increased by physical factors such as poor working conditions and environment.

- *Lack of equality*: especially where the organisation is seen or perceived to differentiate between different types and grades of staff to the benefit of some and detriment of others.

Alienation is the major fundamental cause of conflicts and disputes at places of work. It is potentially present in all work situations. Those who design and construct organisations need to be aware of it in their own particular situations and to take steps to ensure that ideally it can be eliminated or at least kept to a minimum and its effects offset by other advantages.

Approaches to the problems of dissatisfaction and alienation have taken three basic forms:

- attention to the work
- attention to the working environment
- attention to the people.

Attention to the work

Attention to the work has taken a variety of forms, including

MANAGEMENT IN FOCUS 19.2

THE KORNHAUSER STUDIES

Enduring effects on collective and individual morale and well-being were identified by the Kornhauser studies, the results of which were published in 1965. In many cases, feelings of dissatisfaction, alienation, and lack of involvement and purpose led to enduring mental health problems.

Arthur Kornhauser studied car assembly workers at Ford, General Motors and Chrysler at Detroit in the United States. A major conclusion was that basic assembly line work led to job dissatisfaction, which in turn led to low levels of mental health. This became apparent in the low self-esteem of the workers who also exhibited anxiety, life dissatisfaction and despair, and hostility to others.

- Job enrichment and enlargement, in which operators have their capabilities extended to include a range of operations. In some cases this has meant becoming responsible (with a group of others) for the entire production process in autonomous work groups.
- Job rotation, in which operators are regularly rotated around different work stations and activities making a different contribution to the whole.
- Empowerment, in which operators accept responsibility for their own supervision of quality control as well as for the work itself.
- Flexible patterns of work, related both to individual needs (the work–life balance) and to the opportunities for maximising technological output.
- Autonomous work groups, managing their own schedules of production and service delivery, limited only by absolute deadlines required.
- Shift patterns, in which evening, twilight and school hours opportunities are added to standard day and night shift type working.

Each of these also partly addresses some of the psychological and behavioural aspects of dissatisfaction and alienation (see Management in Focus 19.3).

Attention to the working environment

Attention to the work environment is a critical issue. It stems from the recognition that people bring their full range of needs to work with them, and that the more of these that are met, the lower the levels of personal dissatisfaction likely to arise. Basic and adequate levels of comfort are required. The opportunity to sit down at the workstation should always be offered unless it is impossible for overriding operational reasons. Temperature is to be controlled and extremes of heat and cold avoided or managed. Good-quality furniture, decor and furnishings in all places of work reinforce the perceptions of value that organisations place on their staff; bad quality or decrepit furnishings and tatty decor tend to lead to low feelings of perceived value (see Management in Focus 19.4).

MANAGEMENT IN FOCUS 19.3

PRODUCTION LEVELS IN THE ELECTRONICS INDUSTRY

Handy (1996), relating his observations of an electronics manufacturing firm, stated:

> Production went up only slightly but, more important from their point of view, quality was very high without the need for quality control experts, absenteeism and turnover went down to low levels, production flexibility was greatly increased and the job satisfaction of employees was higher.

It is essential to know and understand that effectiveness of resource utilisation is not just measurable through production and service output. As stated above, quality enhancement, removing the need for quality control experts, and reductions in absence and turnover, all contribute towards the overall cost effectiveness of production and service activities.

Attention to the people

The main features include the following:

- Setting absolute standards of honesty, integrity, expectations of performance, quality of output, attitudes, values and ethics to which all those coming to work must aspire and conform.
- Recognising that problems are inherent in all jobs, and organising the work on

MANAGEMENT IN FOCUS 19.4

ATTENTION TO THE WORK ENVIRONMENT: MARS CONFECTIONERY

A former Mars manager recounts the tale of Mr Mars visiting a chocolate factory in mid-summer. He went up to the third floor where the biggest chocolate machines were placed. It was very hot. He asked the factory manager why there was no air conditioning. The factory manager replied that it wasn't in his budget and he had to make budget. Mr Mars acknowledged that this was indeed true – all managers need to keep within budgets. Mr Mars then asked the maintenance people to get all the factory manager's furniture, and other things from his office, and put them next to the big hot chocolate machine. A Mars under-manager said: 'the guy figured out that it was probably a pretty good idea to air condition the factory sooner rather than later. Mr Mars told him that once that had been completed he could move back to his office at any time he wanted.'

Source: Peters and Austin (1986) *A Passion for Excellence*, Harper and Row.

the basis of a philosophy of fairness and evenness that requires everyone to share in the problem areas and unattractive tasks.

- Setting absolute organisational standards for managing the staff. These are based on high levels of integrity, support, equality, training and development. Pay and reward levels tend to be high in return for high-quality work. Pay and reward methods are honest, clear and unambiguous. Communications between organisation and staff, and the information flows in general, are regular, continuous and open.
- Ensuring that everything that is done contributes positively to the quality and volume of work required.
- Designing and ensuring a quality of work environment that supports the output required and provides good standards of comfort and harmony, as well as integrating technology, operations and output.
- Providing equal opportunities for everyone, whatever their patterns, occupations, hours and locations of work.

In all cases, the desired outcome is the reconciliation of organisational and operational drives on the one hand, with the technology and equipment that are to be used – and the ways they affect the staff – on the other. The ability to do this stems from a recognition and understanding of the influences of the technology, both operational and behavioural.

Organisation design and structure

Organisations are designed and structured in order to:

- ensure efficiency and effectiveness of activities in accordance with the organisation's stated targets
- divide and allocate work, responsibility and authority
- establish working relationships and operating mechanisms
- establish patterns of management and supervision
- establish the means by which work is to be controlled
- establish the means of retaining experience, knowledge and expertise
- indicate areas of responsibility, authority and accountability
- meet the expectations of those involved
- provide the basis of a fair and equitable reward system.

The general factors affecting organisation design and structure are:

- The nature of work to be carried out and the implications of this (unit, batch, mass and flow scales of production all bring clear indications of the types of organisation required, as do the commercial and public service equivalents); job definitions; volumes of production; storage of components, raw materials and finished goods; the means of distribution, both inwards and outwards; and the type of support functions and control mechanisms.
- Technology and equipment: the expertise, premises and environment needed to use it effectively; its maintenance; its useful lifecycle; its replacement and the effect of new equipment on existing structures and work methods.
- Capability and willingness to integrate the work and shift patterns required with managerial and supervisory priorities.

- The location of the organisation; its relationships with its local communities; any strong local traditions – for example, of unionisation (or not); particular ways of working; specific activities, skills and expertise.
- Aims and objectives strategy; flexibility, dynamism, responsiveness, or rigidity and conformity in relation to staff, customers and the community; customer relations; stakeholder relations.

●● Organisation structures

Organisations may be structured in various ways.

- *Tall structures*: in which there are many different levels or ranks within the total (see Figures 19.1 and 19.2). There is a long hierarchical and psychological distance between top and bottom. Tall structures bring with them complex reporting relationships, operating and support systems, promotion and career paths, and differentiated job titles. Spans of control (see below) tend to be small. The proportion of staff with some form of supervisory responsibility tends to be high in relation to the whole organisation.
- *Flat structures*: in which there are few different levels or ranks within the total. Jobs tend to be concentrated at lower levels. There is a short hierarchical distance between top and bottom; this may reduce the psychological distance or it may not. Lower-level jobs often carry responsibilities of quality control, volume and deadline targets. Spans of control tend to be large. Career paths by promotion are limited; but this may be replaced by the opportunity for functional and expertise development, and involvement in a variety of different projects. Reward structures may not be as apparent as those offered alongside progress through a tall hierarchy. Reporting relationships tend to be simpler and more direct. There is a reduced likelihood of distortion and barriers to communications in a flat structure than in a tall one simply because there are fewer channels for messages to pass through.
- *Centralised structures*: in which centralisation is generally an authority relationship between those in overall control of the organisation and the rest of its staff. The tighter the control exerted at the centre, the greater the degree of centralisation. Even if an organisation conducts a wide range of activities in many different locations, so that most of the staff work far from head office and most of the work is carried out in remote locations, top management may nevertheless retain tight control over the ways in which activities are conducted.
- *Decentralised structures*: in which the role and function of the centre is to maintain a watching brief, to monitor and evaluate progress, and to concern itself with strategic rather than operational issues. The operations themselves are designed and allocated in accordance with overall aims and objectives, and the departments, divisions and functions are given the necessary resources and authority to achieve them. The advantages of decentralisation are:
  - It speeds up operational decisions, which can be taken at the point where they are required, rather than every matter (or a high proportion) having to be referred back to head office.

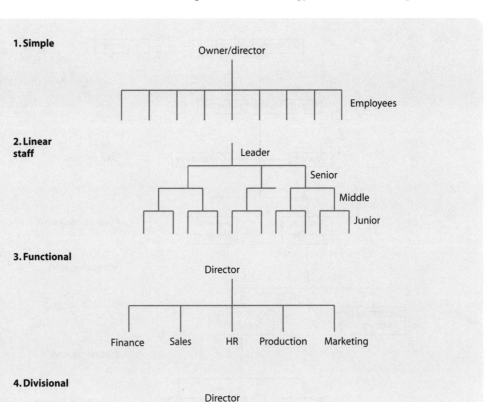

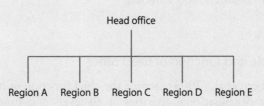

Figure 19.1 Organisation structures

– It enables local management to respond to local conditions and demands, and to build up a local reputation for the overall organisation.

– It contributes to organisation and staff development through ensuring that problems and issues are dealt with at the point at which they arise. This helps organisations to identify and develop potential for the future; it also contributes to motivation and morale, as well as expertise development.

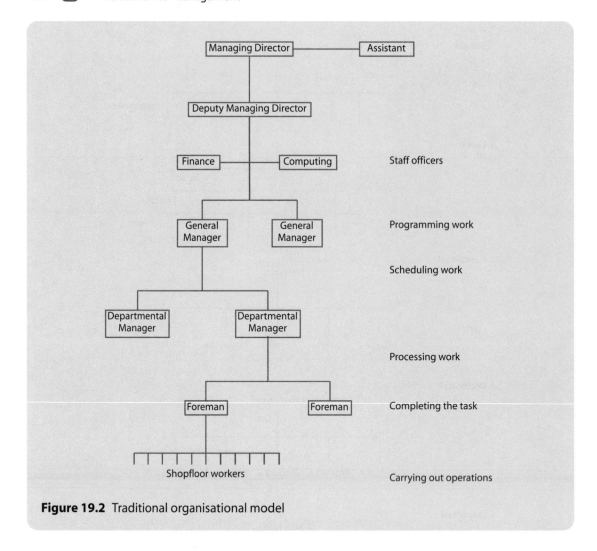

Figure 19.2 Traditional organisational model

The role and function of head office

Mintzberg et al. (2003) identify the chief function of head office as relating and integrating organisational activities at all levels and functions with the pressures and constraints of the environment, and with 'ideology' (see Figure 19.3). Ideology is a combination of cultural and social pressures, related to preferred ways of working and the managerial and supervisory style chosen.

Head offices in all but the simplest structures have the responsibility for planning, coordinating and controlling the functions of the rest of the organisation; of translating strategy into operations; and of monitoring, reviewing and evaluating performance from all points of view – volume, quality, standards and satisfaction.

In large, complex and sophisticated organisations – public, private and multinational – the head office is likely to be physically distant from the main areas of operations, and this brings problems of communications systems and reporting relationships. Equally important, however, is the problem of psychological distance and

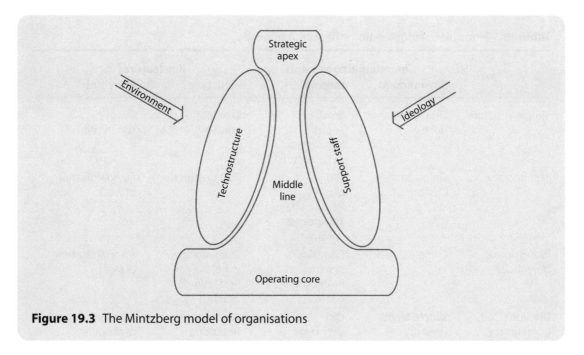

Figure 19.3 The Mintzberg model of organisations

remoteness. This occurs when the head office itself becomes a complex and sophisticated entity, which often leads to conflict between personal and organisational objectives, in-fighting, and concentration of resources on head office functions rather than operational effectiveness. This is exacerbated when jobs at head office are, or are perceived to be, better careers and more likely to lead to personal opportunities than those in the field. In many cases the head office becomes so remote that it loses any understanding of the reality of activities. Cocooned by the resources that it commands for its own functions, it preserves the illusion of excellence and dynamism often in the face of overwhelming evidence to the contrary (see Management in Focus 19.5).

⬤ Spans of control

The term 'spans of control' refers to the number of subordinates who report directly to a single superior, and for whose work that person is responsible.

Spans of control are defined in a broad to narrow spectrum. The narrower the span, the greater the number of supervisors required by the organisation in total. A workforce of 40 with spans of control of 4 (1 supervisor per 4 staff) needs 10 supervisors (see Figure 19.4). The same workforce with a span of control of 10 only needs 4 supervisors. If the principle is then developed as a hierarchy, it can be seen that in the first case additional staff are needed to supervise the supervisors. If the broader span is adopted in larger organisations, layers of management and hierarchy can be removed. An organisation of 4000 staff would remove about 800 managers and supervisors by changing its spans of control from 4 to 1 to 8 to 1 (see Figure 19.5).

Table 19.1 Principles of organisation structure: a summary

	Operational constraints		Key features	
	Environment	Internal	Structure	Activities
Simple structure	Simple/dynamic Hostile	Small Young Simple tasks CEO control	Direction + strategy	Direct supervision
Technocracy	Simple/static Conformist	Old Large Regulated tasks Technocrat control	Technostructure	Standardisation of work
Professional bureaucracy	Complex/static	Complex systems Professional control	Operational expertise Professional practice	Standardisation of skills
Divisionalised bureaucracy	Simple/static Diversity Hostile	Old Very large Divisible tasks Middle-line control	Autonomy Reporting relationships	Standardisation of outputs Sophisticated supervision
Ad hocracy	Complex/ dynamic Committed	Often young Complex tasks Expert control	Operational expertise	Mutual adjustment
Missionary	Simple/static Committed	Middle-aged Often 'enclaves' Simple systems Ideological control	Ideology Standards	Policy, norms, standards
Network organisation	Dynamic Committed	Young Reformed	Operational expertise Technostructure	Networking

Source: Mintzberg (1979), Johnson and Scholes (1994)

The matter does require additional consideration however. Narrow spans of control normally mean a tighter cohesion and closer working relationship between supervisor and group. They also give greater promotion opportunities. There are more jobs, more levels and more ways of moving up through the organisation, and this may be a driving force for those within it and one of their key expectations.

On the other hand, the complex structures created by narrow spans of control tend to act as barriers and blockages to communications – the greater the number of levels that messages have to pass through, the more likely they are to become distorted and corrupted.

MANAGEMENT IN FOCUS 19.5

IBM

In 1992 IBM declared the highest-ever corporate loss in business history and John Akers, the Chief Executive Officer, was forced to resign.

The basis of the problem lay in the organisation's utter faith in its own excellence and infallibility. This was promulgated by head office in support of the company's main thrust of activities: mainframe computers and business operation systems. This was in spite of the fact that the emphasis of the computer world had switched to personal computers – for both business and private use.

Belatedly, during the 1980s, the company started to develop its personal computer division, but sales were disappointing (due to the long lead times on delivery and the high prices charged), and the market continued to be dominated by those organisations that took the fast-moving consumer goods approach to computer sales. These companies produced equipment that was compatible with IBM business systems, and effectively removed IBM from the market as the supplier of hardware.

The company failed to respond. It had been lionised in the 'Excellence' studies. It was a huge, multi-billion-dollar corporation. Its technology and expertise were respected and held in awe the world over.

Unfortunately, this awe was a mark of technological respect that was no longer being translated into the levels of sales necessary to support such an organisation. In particular, the company was slow to respond to the personal computer and software markets.

The crisis arose because the organisation, and its head office, had lost direction and contact with its markets. To date, the company restructuring has taken over ten years; alongside this, it has been necessary to institute flexible and dynamic attitudes and values, designed above all to make sure that such a crisis can never happen again because of the centralised, institutionalised – and cocooned – nature of executive management.

On the face of it there is therefore a trade-off between the effectiveness of the organisation and the satisfaction of staff expectations through the availability of promotion channels. Assuming that the effectiveness of the organisation is paramount, means must be sought to enable expectations to be set and met in ways that contribute to this. The absolute effectiveness of the promotion channels must therefore be measured in this way, and where necessary different means of meeting staff expectations found.

Attention is then to be paid to operational factors. These are:

- The ability of management to produce results with spans of a certain size.
- The ability of the subordinates to produce results within these spans; in general, the greater the level of expertise held, the less direct supervision is required.
- The subordinates' expectations of relative autonomy; for example, professional and highly trained staff expect to be left alone to carry out tasks as they see fit, while other types (for example, retail cashiers) need to be able to call on the supervisor whenever problems, such as difficulties with customers, arise.
- The expectations of the organisation and the nature and degree of supervision

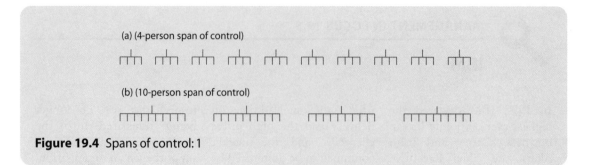

Figure 19.4 Spans of control: 1

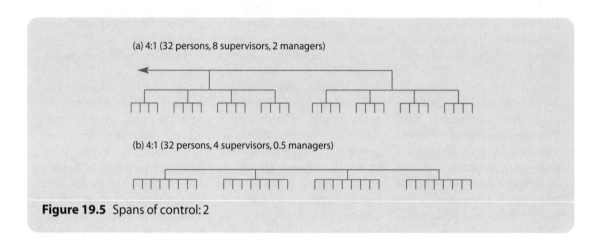

Figure 19.5 Spans of control: 2

necessary to meet these, or the ability of the staff concerned to meet these without close supervision.

- Specific responsibilities of supervisors in some situations, where the supervisor has a direct reason for being there other than to monitor the work that is being carried out. The most common examples are related to safety – for example, on construction sites and in oil refineries – and, in shops and supermarkets, to handle customers' queries and complaints.

- The nature of the work itself, the similarity or diversity of the tasks and functions, its simplicity or complexity.

- The location of the work: whether it is concentrated in one place or in several different parts of one building or site, or whether it is geographically diverse. Sub-spans are normally created where the location is diversified, even if ultimate responsibility remains with one individual, and boundaries of autonomy are ascribed to one person and group in the particular location.

- The extent of necessity and ability to coordinate the work of each group with all the others in the organisation, to coordinate and harmonise the work of the individuals in the group and to relate this again to the demands of the organisation.

- The organisation's own perspective – the extent to which it believes that close supervision, direct control and constant monitoring are necessary and desirable.

Hierarchies

Spans of control create hierarchies. These reflect the level, quality and expertise of those involved, and also the degree of supervision and responsibility of those in particular positions. These are underpinned by job titles that indicate both levels of position held in hierarchy and also the nature and mix of expertise and responsibility.

Problems with hierarchies

The main issue is reconciling the need to divide and allocate work efficiently and effectively without creating blockages and barriers that the process of division tends to create.

It is certain that there will be divergence of objectives. For example, the marketing department may be asked to create marketing initiatives with which it has no sympathy, or it may create marketing initiatives at variance with the products, style and image of the organisation. It may seek to enhance its own reputation, and yet perceive that to pursue organisation objectives may be detrimental to this.

If one of the functions of hierarchy is to provide career paths, then these may be blocked by long-serving officials in particular jobs; or the organisation may create vacancies which are filled either by people who do not yet have the required expertise or, where this is recognised by the organisation, by outsiders. Sudden departures in particular may leave a void which it is impossible to fill in the short term and which is then likely to lead to loss of departmental or organisation performance. In these cases outsiders may be brought in, again tending to lead towards frustration for those already in position.

Units and divisions tend to pursue their own aims and objectives as part of the process of competing for resources, prestige and status rather than the overall purpose of the organisation. Similarly, individuals pursuing career paths take whatever steps are necessary to get on to the next rung of the ladder; and again this may be detrimental to overall requirements.

Specific responsibilities are not always apparent. Things may not get done because nobody knows quite whose responsibility the matter in question is, or everyone involved thought that it was somebody else's area of operation. This is also a problem with the organisation's customers and clients, who may find it difficult to gain contact with the person specifically responsible for dealing with their problem.

Hierarchies can be very difficult to move once they are established. They may continue to exist in a given form after the purpose for which they were specifically created has been served. They often hinder the organisation development process and may act as a barrier to the introduction of new technology, project activities and culture and behaviour change.

Those responsible for the creation of organisation structures have therefore to recognise that whatever is done must be capable of satisfying the organisation's purposes and reconciling these with the problems and difficulties inherent. Any organisation form that arises must be capable of flexibility and responsiveness as well as creating order and stability.

● **Core and peripheral organisations**

These forms of structure are based on a total reappraisal of objectives and activities with the view to establishing where the strategic core lies, what is needed to sustain this and where, when and why additional support and resources are required.

The essential is the core. The rest is the peripheral and may be seen as a shamrock or propeller (see Figure 19.6). Peripheral elements can take the following forms:

● Professional and technical services and expertise, drawn in to solve problems; designed and improved work methods and practices; manage, change and act as catalysts and agents for change. All of these functions are conducted by outsiders on a contracted basis. Areas include marketing, public relations, human resource management, industrial relations, supplies, research and development, process and operations management and distribution.

● Subcontracting of services such as facilities and environment management, maintenance, catering, cleaning and security. These are distinctive expertises in their own right, and therefore best left to expert organisations.

This form of subcontracting is now very highly developed across all sectors and all parts of the world as organisations seek to concentrate on their given expertise and minimise areas of non-contributory activity.

Organisations now identify operational pressures much more accurately, and arrange work patterns in which staff are retained to be available at peaks (daily, periodical or seasonal) and are otherwise not present. This has contributed to both the increase in part-time, flexible and core hours patterns of employment, and to the retention of the services of workforce agencies, who specialise in providing particular volumes of expertise in this way. Some organisations have additionally created patterns of outworking (often home working), in which staff work at alternative locations including home, avoiding the need for expensive and extensive facilities. This also

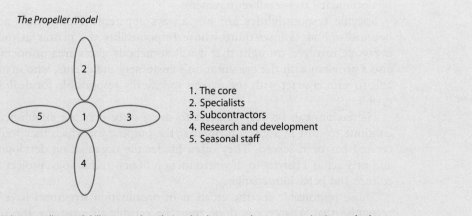

The Propeller model

1. The core
2. Specialists
3. Subcontractors
4. Research and development
5. Seasonal staff

Note: the propeller model illustrates the relationship between the core organisation and other specialists who come to work for it.

Figure 19.6 Core and peripheral: the propeller model

enables those involved to combine work with other activities – parenting, study or working for other organisations. For this, people may be paid a retainer to ensure their continued obligation of loyalty, and may be well paid, even overpaid, to compensate for periods when there is no work. They may be retained on regular and distinctive patterns of employment – normally short time or part time.

The benefits lie in the ability to maximise resources and optimise staff utilisation. Rather than structuring the workforce to be available generally, the requirement for expertise and the nature of operations are worked out in advance and the organisation structured from this point of view. All activities that are to be carried out on a steady-state daily basis are integrated into the core. The rest are contracted or retained in one of the forms indicated.

Federations

Federations are extensions of the core and peripheral format (see Figure 19.7). Federations tend to be more or less regularised between organisations with their own specialisms that are then harmonised and integrated in the pursuit of overall stated objectives. Within this, each organisation has its distinctive identity and full autonomy to pursue and conduct other work as long as it meets its obligations and makes its contribution to the federation.

The capability to operate within federations in these ways has driven the outsourcing phenomenon. The outsourcing of call centre and customer services activities in financial services, and of manufacturing in the garment industry, has attracted the greatest overall attention. However, many organisations use the opportunities to outsource support functions, for example HR activities and accounting, catering, cleaning and security, and the manufacture of specialist components.

The main problem lies in integrating, coordinating and controlling the relationships and activities required of each contributor. The critical factors are ensuring mutuality of interest, continuity of general relationship, communications and harmony. The reporting relationship is based on a combination of work contract (or contract for services) and measures of integrity, rather than on a bureaucratic or legal/rational format.

Operationally, the critical factors are meeting volume and quality requirements and deadlines. A much simpler and clearer form of direction and purpose is likely to emerge as a result and this is focused on performance overall rather than procedures and functions.

The likelihood is therefore that organisations will seek to simplify all of their features as they become involved in this form of activity. As well as clarifying purpose, it also frees up resources that otherwise have to be used in accommodating staff and their equipment, supporting rules and procedures and the sub-functions that operate them.

● Structures and expectations

Reference has already been made to the need to match people's expectations with the opportunities that the organisation can offer. The traditional way of making progress through the ranks of organisations is well understood and has hitherto been a strong driving force, especially for those in administrative, professional and

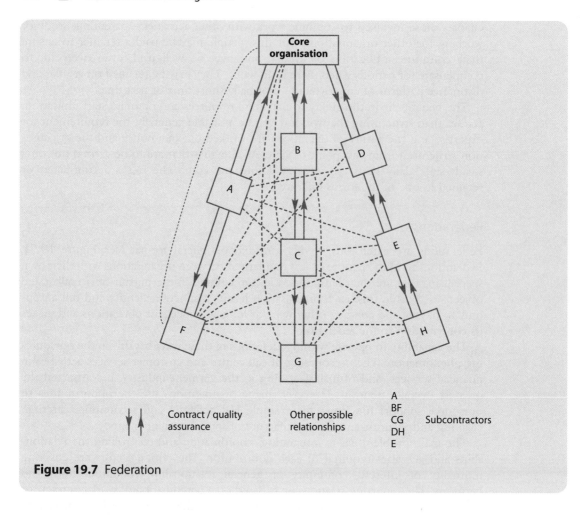

Figure 19.7 Federation

technical grades. This has also opened up expectations for those in less skilled, front-line and clerical jobs. As organisations increase spans of control, and drive towards simpler forms, federations, reduced hierarchies and scalar chains, there are fewer of these avenues available and competition for each position becomes greater. There is also therefore likely to be an increase in the quality of candidates from which to choose as each seeks to maximise his or her chance of gaining the particular position.

On the one hand therefore, there is a great opportunity for organisations to choose excellent, high-quality staff for key positions. On the other, there is the question of what to do with those who do not achieve these positions, bearing in mind that this may affect a large number of staff and lead to wider general dissatisfaction.

The matter is partly resolved by ensuring that expectations are set at realistic levels at the outset. The nature of avenues available is to be made clear, whether these are based on promotion or variety, development, location and project work. The rewards to be gained through the pursuit of each should also be made clear. Organisations must also recognise that if these are higher for one path than for others, then individuals will gravitate towards this in preference to the others.

Structure and career development

In terms of organisation structure, the purpose is to translate the combination of expectations and desire for advancement that the individual brings with the prospects that the organisation can offer into a productive and positive relationship. For this to happen the position of each should be clearly established at the outset. There is no point in the organisation expecting loyalty and long service of an individual who anticipates rapid progression through the ranks, if these channels are not open to all or are very restricted. Similarly, there is no point in the individual expecting this form of progression if the organisation has made it quite clear that this is not available and that progress is based on variety and development rather than promotion through the ranks.

Organisations have therefore to establish the basis on which variety and progress is to be offered, what they expect of their staff in this context and where they place value on them.

Other points may usefully be made. Programmes of organisation and professional development must be seen as leading to goals and objectives. Staff who are given training and development normally expect to be able to practise their new skills and qualities and to attain some reward or enhancement as the result. In very few cases at present can organisations be certain that people have reached the absolute pinnacle of their potential, education, training or development, and that they can therefore be certain that they have a particular niche for a long period of time. Even if this is the case, the niche is invariable subject to pressures of continuous improvement and development, and this again places obligations on the long-term post holder. Successful people at all levels both raise their own expectations and have raised expectations placed on them by their organisation.

Structure and reward

A traditional driving force of the promotion path was normally that increased pay, salary and therefore standard of living accrued as the result of progression upwards through the hierarchy. This was also a means of ensuring general measures of organisation talent and potential development, as well as meeting the staff's general expectations of enhancement. It was also seen to reward loyalty and commitment.

Today, two assumptions are regularly challenged. The first is that those at the top of the hierarchy should receive greater rewards than those lower down (see Management in Focus 19.6). The second is that this is the only way of developing and rewarding loyalty and commitment.

Certainly, adequate means of reward have to be established. The organisation structure must be capable of doing this so that the contribution of everyone is seen to be valued. Once the connection is removed between rank and reward however, opportunities become available to assess this on the basis of whatever is of absolute value to the organisation – whether this is loyalty, output, professional development, invention, creativity or whatever.

The overriding concern is to ensure that rewards are targeted, paid out for achievement, give satisfaction and meet expectations. Rewards are not ends in themselves. People expect both continuity and improvement. In steady-state and rank-structured organisations especially, people forgo measures of instant or short-term reward in return for the continuity and enhancement that they expect in the longer term. In more turbulent organisations, the expectations are for shorter term and enhanced levels of reward.

MANAGEMENT IN FOCUS 19.6

REWARDS

There are lessons to be learned from many sectors. The best-paid people in the entertainment sector are the entertainers themselves. Professional sports men and women earn more than tournament and competition managers and promoters.

In many cases labourers on construction sites earn more than site managers and supervisors. This is partly because of the hours that they have the opportunity to work and partly also because supervision is likely to be divided between several persons.

Productivity and output bonuses are often made available to factory and retail workers, enabling them to earn more than those on equivalent or higher (but non-front-line) grades.

This has implications for promotion and development structures. People do not wish to lose money as the result of change (especially promotion), except where this is known to be a short-term disadvantage and that the prospects over the long term are greatly improved.

Rewards must also meet basic expectations and be seen to be placing adequate levels of value on the efforts of the staff. A mail-order company based in Stoke-on-Trent, UK, asked its telesales staff to promote a distinctive range of kitchen products as part of their general workload. The initiative was highly successful and the 22 women involved sold a million pounds worth of products. The staff received a letter from the managing director of the company thanking them for their efforts. Enclosed with the letter was a small bar of chocolate. All of the staff felt insulted by this gesture; none found it to be an adequate expression of their efforts. Most said that they would rather have received nothing than such a slight gesture and token. The whole approach was perceived by the staff to be disrespectful and to belittle and denigrate their efforts.

● Conclusions

There are obvious complexities in trying to create and maintain organisational stability and durability in the face of changing expertise and technology. It should be clear that problems are certain to arise when managers try to adapt the changing circumstances to the present organisational form, rather than seeking to create and maintain something that is capable of responsiveness and adaptation, as well as imposing its particular way of doing things on the environment and markets that it serves.

Approaches such as flexible working, multi-skilling, removal of demarcation lines, hot-desking and virtual organisation have all been attempted in particular situations, with varying degrees of success. However, all too often, these fall into the trap of being perceived as 'quick fixes', and consequently:

- are seldom given enough time to work
- are seldom fully thought out, especially with reference to the behavioural aspects
- are seldom fully evaluated in terms of what they are expected to achieve.

It is consequently essential that the behavioural aspects of structure, technology and design are addressed. As stated above, loyalties become divided – managers and others on career paths, as well as those with technological or professional expertise, find themselves retreating into the perceived safe world of group loyalties and occupational identity, rather than addressing the real problems that organisations as a whole have to face. Such problems are very often compounded when top management of organisations take on consultants' recommendations without assessing the full implications. The pressure to do this is compounded if the particular consultancy is highly branded or extremely expensive.

There are also problems if career, professional and occupational paths are seen to be threatened. The groups of staff affected use their positions of influence to block developments in structure, design and technology, and this can lead to serious organisational dysfunction. Problems that arise in this way are then compounded if the organisation's top managers seek to impose changes by threat or force, rather than returning to the drawing board.

It is also essential that those responsible for designing and structuring any organisation recognise that these problems and issues are certain to become very much more central to its future success and effectiveness. The speed of technological change renders present production, service and information output obsolete much more quickly; and the pressures are compounded, not eased, if a mechanistic approach is taken. This means that organisations must be designed to accommodate advances in technology and expertise, rather than considering them as professional, occupational or culture shocks. This requires a recognition and assumption by organisations of the broadest possible scope and scale of their responsibilities, and the creation of structural conditions that enable this to take place successfully and effectively. Investment in the structure and design of organisations is as essential as that required in expertise and technology.

CRITICAL THINKING, ANALYSIS AND EVALUATION

1. Discuss the view that truly rewarding and satisfying work is impossible to achieve because of the constraints placed on all occupations and organisations by technology and equipment.
2. Identify the opportunities and constraints placed on organisations by:
    a) the establishment of formalised clocking-on procedures
    b) the removal of formalised clocking-on procedures.
3. What are the likely effects on the functional effectiveness of those affected by:
    a) a reduction in the number of levels in a hierarchy from 12 to 3 with no redundancies
    b) a reduction in the number of levels in a hierarchy from 12 to 3 with redundancies?
    What broader problems does this cause? What structural features should be created within organisations to keep these effects to a minimum?
4. Outline the main structural issues to be addressed when establishing a core and peripheral or federated working relationship.

DEVELOPING MANAGEMENT SKILLS AND EXPERTISE

CALL CENTRES

Call centres are in danger of becoming dark, satanic mills of the twenty-first century as the industry gains a reputation for sweatshop practices and assembly line methods. Centres already exist where staff sit in tiny pens and cubicles with high screens around them, or else in assembly line rows. A report by the Merchants Group in 1997, said that: 'in a survey of 106 call centres, morale was low, stress levels high, and absenteeism was running at 5 per cent, compared with the national figure of 3.5 per cent.'

Early in their development, call centres became a victim of their own success, with response far outstripping projections. High stress levels were caused by the sheer volume of calls, wrongly forecasted levels of success, heavy pressure on achieving targets, and inadequate and cramped working conditions.

The call centre industry continues to expand rapidly. It employs about 200,000 people, and this is predicted to rise to 5 million in the next three years. Recent research by Incomes Data Services (IDS) into pay and conditions in call centres shows that their rapid growth has led to rising pay settlements, intense competition for staff, and high levels of turnover (up to 25 per cent per annum in some cases), and these are all attributed to competition between centres and the intensity of work. The speed of growth in the call centre industry has meant effective management strategies are often left behind. Organisations are not properly structured, and little consideration has been given to the enduring effects on morale, output, performance and profits of the relationship between staff and technology. Centres that do not invest in training, development and organisation design are bound to suffer from high rates of absenteeism, poor performance and increases in labour turnover, according to the Chartered Institute of Personnel and Development.

Jim Parle, business personnel manager at Halifax Direct, which has 800 staff, agrees that stress is a symptom of poor management but argues that call centres are no different to any other working environment. He adds:

> Of course, there are pressures when an operation is based on bottom-line cost figures, but it is important to balance the customer's needs with appropriate working practices. You have to start from a premise that no one works a seven-hour day, and allow time for breaks, feedback, team meetings and training.

The industry has consequently gained for itself a reputation as a high-stress area. However, there is some evidence that the environment is changing. In the words of Phil Harris, sales director of the CallCentric consultancy:

> Until recently, call centres were driven by productivity and keeping the costs as low as possible. Activities were largely functionalised so that people got bored or felt they were being driven to achieve numbers. The focus on productivity is giving way to a realisation that it costs a lot to win new customers. Staff therefore have to become more highly valued because they maintain the relationship with existing customers.

Far-removed from the assembly line image, Autobar, a catering wholesaler which handles 6000 calls a day, encouraged a fun environment for its call centre teams, and this included cartoons on the walls, and comic team identities such as the sharks and the bears.

Phil Harris forecasts that it will take five years for call centres to be perceived as career opportunities rather than short-term jobs at low wages. Some organisations are already introducing NVQs and job gradings so that staff can see that there is a career ladder.

Call centre work varies enormously. It ranges from telesales and marketing to technical assistance and emergency response. Before setting up a call centre, companies should be certain that they have the capability, technology, expertise, and structure of organisation; and this has to be related to capability and effectiveness in forecasting the projections of workload.

Source: Adapted from One Minute Briefs, *Management Today*, February 1999.

Questions

1. Comment on the view expressed that 'staff can see that there is a career ladder'. What form of career ladder is required in this industry in order to make career paths attractive to those coming into it?
2. Why do people get bored with this form of work? What can, and should, be done to alleviate this? To what extent do the 'cartoons on the walls' alleviate the sense of boredom and alienation a) in the short-term; b) in the long-term?
3. Comment on the statement above that 'It will take five years for call centres to be perceived as career opportunities'.
4. This case is adapted from information produced several years ago. In what ways, if at all, has the call centre industry changed over the period?

Chapter twenty

Human resource management

'Human resource management is far too important to be left to
personnel professionals. All managers need to be able to do it.'
Peter Drucker.

'We cannot have the monkeys running the zoo.'
Frank Bormann, labour relations director, Eastern Airlines (1984).

'Better managed staff are happier, more motivated and more productive;
and well managed companies often attract better staff than their competitors.'
Mike Walmsley, Parker Bridge, *Evening Standard* (24 November 1998).

Chapter outline

- Introduction
- Strategic approaches to HRM
- The principle of equality and fairness
- Attraction, recruitment and retention
- Maintenance functions in HR
- Employee relations
- Conclusions

Chapter objectives

After studying this chapter, you should be able to:

- understand the importance and value of human resource management as a universal part of management expertise

- understand the contribution made by effective recruitment, selection, retention and reward activities

- understand the importance and value of establishing and managing effective workplace relations

- understand the direct relationship between effective staff management practices, and sustained profitable and effective output.

● Introduction

The concept and basis of human resource management (HRM) has moved from welfare concerns and a moral or enlightened attitude to the staff and workers of organisations, through highly structured and highly staffed corporate and department personnel functions, to 'resource management', where it currently rests.

The purpose of HRM is to provide the basis for staff management, employee relations and personnel practices required by the organisation. This is so as to be able to fit work to people and fit people to technology, producing effective and profitable products and services. This in turn enables maximisation and optimisation of return on what is normally the largest single fixed cost that organisations incur.

● HR strategies

To achieve these goals effectively, organisations require clear and well-understood HR strategies. These strategies are set in the overall context of core foundation or generic positions adopted (see Chapter 8 above), which forms the basis for the structure, composition and expertise of the workforce. HR strategy is then implemented and delivered through the adoption of one of the following positions in relation to the staff:

- *Unitarism*: this assumes that the objectives of all involved are the same or compatible, and concerned only with the well-being of the organisation and its products, services, clients and customers. The most successful unitary organisations (e.g. McDonald's, Virgin, IMG) set very distinctive work, performance and personal standards, to which anyone working in the company must conform. This is also inherent in the Japanese approach to the management of the human resource.
- *Pluralism*: admitting a variety of objectives, not all compatible, among the staff. Recognising that conflict is therefore present, rules, procedures and systems are established to manage it and limit its influence as far as possible. This is the approach taken especially in public services, local government and many industrial and commercial activities, where diverse interests have to be reconciled in order that productive work may take place.
- *Radicalism*: the view that commercial and industrial harmony is impossible until the staff control the means of production and benefit from the generation of wealth. Until very recently, this was a cornerstone of the philosophy of many trade unions and socialist activists in industry, commerce and public services.
- *Conflict*: the basis on which staff are to be dealt with is one of mistrust, divergence, irreconcilable aims and objectives; disparity of location; divergence and complexity of patterns of employment and occupations, among professional, technical, skilled and unskilled staff. In such cases as this, the HR strategy will be devised to contain the conflicts, to reconcile differences, and to promote levels of harmony as far as possible.
- *Conformity*: where the diversity of staff and technology may be (and often is) as great as in the above scenario, but where the HR strategy rather sets standards of behavioural and operational aims and objectives that in turn require the different groups to rise above their inherent differences.

- *Consensus*: where the way of working is devised as a genuine partnership between the organisation and its staff and their representatives The consensus position in HR is rare in all but the simplest and smallest of organisations (and may not exist even in these).
- *Paternalism*: in which the organisation accepts responsibilities for providing staff comfort and support in return for known, understood and assured ways of working, including flexible responses when pressures on the organisation are heavy.

Whichever the approach adopted, this must be known, agreed and implemented by all managers whatever their department, division or function. This then forms the foundation and standpoint for the conduct of all HR and personnel activities (see Figure 20.1).

⬤ The principle of equality and fairness

Whatever the size, location or activities of the organisation, all staff must be treated equally and fairly. As well as being a legal requirement, this is a fundamental prerequisite for the creation of organisation and operation effectiveness. Managers and organisations must first overcome the tendency to compartmentalise people by race, gender, religion, marital status, disability, age, location, postal address, non-essential qualification, school background, club membership, hobby or interest. They must take the opposite standpoint, isolating the qualities essential and desirable to carry out a job. They must view people in terms of their potential as staff members, as contributors to the success and prosperity of the organisation. Without this, true equality of opportunity cannot exist.

There is also a question of basic human decency that requires that all people be treated the same. This is a social as well as organisational concern. For organisations, all activities, management styles, policies, practices and procedures, publications, advertisements, job and work descriptions, and person specifications are written in ways that reinforce this. This emphasises, formulates and underlines the required attitudes and beliefs.

These standards are based on operational capabilities alone. Anyone, including managers, who adopts a negative approach or attitude to equality of opportunity, or who victimises, harasses or bullies members of their staff, must be subject to organisation discipline.

Offering equality of opportunity to all sectors of the workforce is both cost effective and profitable. By concentrating on (discriminating against) certain sectors of the population on operational grounds, organisations greatly limit their prospects either of making effective appointments or of maximising the human resource.

The lead therefore comes from the top of organisations and the attitudes filter down to all the staff. Organisational equal opportunities policies must be clear, unequivocal and easily understood by all concerned. They must be valued and adopted at all levels and in all sectors and departments. A genuine adoption of the principle of equality for all constitutes excellent marketing to the human resource of the organisation. Staff are known to be valued for their capabilities. It also underlines any high moral or ethical stance taken in other business and organisational activities.

Area of work	Strategy and direction	Personnel operations
Work design and structuring	Principles, approaches, departmentalisation, organisation structure	Job descriptions, work patterns, work structuring
Staff planning	Systems appraisal, design commissioning	Systems usage
Recruitment and selection	Standpoint (grow your own, buy in from outside)	Training of recruiters and selectors, recruitment and selection activities
Induction	Policy, content, priority	Delivery
Use of agencies and external sources of staff	Principles, circumstances	Contacts and commissions
Performance appraisal	Purpose, systems, design, principles, aims and objectives	Systems implementation, training of appraisers and appraisees
Pay and rewards	Policy, levels, mix of pay and benefits, package design	Assimilate individual staff to policy
Occupational health	Policy, content, design of package	Operation of package in conjunction with functional departments
Equality	Standards, policy, content, context, ethics	Policy operation, monitoring of standards, remedial actions
Industrial relations	Standpoints (conflict, conformist), representation	Negotiations, consultation, participation, staff communications
Discipline	Policy, procedure, practice, design, standpoint	Implementation of policy and procedure, support for staff, training of all staff
Grievance	Policy, procedure	Implementation of policy and procedure, training of all staff
Training and development	Priority and resources	Activities, opportunities, accessibility
Dismissal	Standards of conduct, examples of gross misconduct	Operation of disciplinary procedures, operation of dismissal procedures, support and advice

Human resource management is divided into strategic and directional activities; and personnel activities. The role and function is:

• policy, advisory, consultative, supporting, a point of reference
• personnel practitioner and expert
• establisher of policy content
• establisher of standards of best practice
• creator of personnel activities
• monitor/evaluator of personnel activities.

Figure 20.1 Human resource management summary

Managing diversity

The management of diversity is concerned with ensuring that people from a wide range of backgrounds, ethnic origins, social groups and occupational disciplines are brought together and harmonised into an effective and productive workforce. Effective diversity management seeks to bond and maximise the strengths inherent in the absolute standards set by the organisation, and the different knowledge, understanding and expectations brought by those from a variety of different backgrounds.

Diversity management takes the fundamental premise of equality of treatment and opportunity a stage further. Diversity management concentrates on ensuring that everyone gets the same treatment and opportunities, rather than identifying and separating out those whose career paths and opportunities may be hindered, then removing the obstacles faced by these particular groups.

Overall workforce cohesion is further reinforced by the business opportunities that this form of employment practice brings (see Management in Focus 20.1).

To be fully effective however, diversity management needs to be fully institutionalised as a corporate commitment and priority in strategic HRM. Diversity is an investment on which both immediate and enduring returns are demanded. Once the decision is taken to go down this route, this then becomes a key factor in organisation development and the creation of an effective positive and cohesive culture and set of values.

Diversity should also apply across the board, to all levels of staff regardless of occupation, location, length of service or hours worked.

A strategic and institutionalised approach to diversity additionally reinforces the knowledge and understanding that the best person for the job will get it; and this results also in management time and energies being concentrated on effective product and service outputs, rather than dealing with individual cases, grievances and disputes brought by those who feel that they are not being treated fairly on the basis of gender, ethnic origin, social background, age or disability.

Pay, renumeration and reward

Effective systems of payment or reward must meet a variety of purposes and considerations. They must reward productive effort, expertise and outputs, in whatever terms these are measured. They must provide an adequate level of income on a regular basis for those receiving it. They must motivate and encourage. They must meet the expectations of those carrying out the work. They must be fair and honest to all concerned.

If rewards are based on targets, then the targets must be achievable. If rewards are based on quality of performance, performance must be measurable in some way. Specific payment systems such as commission, bonuses or merit increments should be clearly understood by all concerned. The criteria by which performance is to be measured must be clearly spelled out. As long as objectives and targets are met, payment must be made.

For some occupations, this is very straightforward. The sales executive working to a commission based on sales volume or income from sales has a clear ready-reckoner against which he/she will be paid.

MANAGEMENT IN FOCUS 20.1

EQUALITY AND DIVERSITY MANAGEMENT

The Chartered Institute of Personnel and Development (CIPD) states:

> Managing diversity is based on the concept that people should be valued as individuals for reasons related to business interests, as well as for moral and social reasons. It is recognised that people from different backgrounds can bring fresh ideas and perceptions which may make the way work is done more efficient and products and services better.

The business benefits identified are as follows:

- improved customer satisfaction and market penetration by employing and supporting a diverse workforce whose composition reflects that of the local population
- a diverse workforce brings a range of skills and approaches to generic problems and issues
- effective diversity management improves the supply of staff, promotes confidence between staff and organisation, and reduces costly discrimination cases.

For example:

HBOS invited members of Manchester's Chinese community to apply for work within the bank. In the past, the company had few customers and staff from this community. Bilingual posters were placed in the main Chinatown advice centre in the city asking whether people were interested in working for the bank. This eventually led to the employment of six Chinese people by the bank in the Manchester area. A consequence of the policy has been increased business from the Chinese community at large, because of greater cultural recognition and improved language capability.

Over the period since 1998, HBOS has increased the proportion of employees from ethnic minorities from 4 per cent to 6.4 per cent nationally. Increases in some localities are even higher, for example, from 9 per cent to 27 per cent in Keighley.

HBOS' diversity programme is also about women, older workers and people with disabilities. The com-pany uses a diversity team which includes a disability manager and an equal opportunities advisor.

Sources: CIPD (1999) *Managing Diversity*; N. Merrick (2001) *People Management*, CIPD; M. Marchington and A. Wilkinson (2002) *People Management and Development*, CIPD.

For others, it is not so clear. Performance-related pay schemes for office, administrative, clerical, executive and professional staff have often fallen short of expectations because the criteria against which performance was to be measured were never made clear or fully understood by those concerned. In such cases, the scheme actually demotivates those affected, and falls into disrepute and discredit.

Those devising payment systems must also understand the motivations and expectations of the job holders, and either meet these as far as possible or else accept the consequences of not meeting them. In general terms, these factors will consist of: a level of income; consistency, stability and security; and a match between achievement and reward. Workforces have become used to annual pay rises to compensate for the loss of purchasing power due to inflation. Professional, clerical and managerial staff expect to receive incremental rises in addition to this.

Bad or unvalued payments and reward systems cause instability and labour turnover. A major consequence of a bad system is extreme demotivation and demoralisation. This is true for whatever is wrong with the scheme – if objectives are not achievable, or if they are achievable but the rewards are not forthcoming, or if the pay or pay rise does not meet expectations.

Finally, it must be remembered that while all payment systems should aim to provide recognition, rewards, incentives and motivation to the job holder, no amount of money will make a boring job interesting, but merely more bearable. Similarly, it is possible to offer intrinsic benefits in inherently interesting or fulfilling jobs, where there may be constraints on a reward package based purely on salary.

Components of a wage, salary or reward package

The following elements are required:

- *Payment*: annual, quarterly, monthly, four-weekly, weekly, daily. Commission, bonus, increments, fees. Profit, performance and merit-related payments.
- *Allowances*: attendance, disturbance, shift, weekend, unsocial hours, training and development, location and relocation, absence from home.
- *Benefits*: loans (e.g. for season tickets), pension (contributory or non-contributory), subsidies (on company products, canteen, travel), car, telephone/car phone, private healthcare, training and development, luncheon vouchers.
- *Chains of gold or super-benefits*: school holidays (teachers); cheap loans (banks); free/cheap travel (railway, shipping, airlines); pension arrangements (for older or longer-serving staff).
- *Economic rent*: high rates of pay for particular expertise (especially scarce expertise or that which is required at short notice).
- *Work/life and rewards*: in which people who have to balance work demands with outside pressures accept a given level of pay in return for flexible working arrangements.
- *Performance and profit-related pay*: in which bonuses are delivered in return for meeting performance criteria, particular targets, and collective and individual profit and output levels.
- *Specific incentives*: related to particular occupations, partly reflecting people's expectations and partly reflecting performance.

This is very complex, and the mixes adopted by organisations in the devising and implementation of reward strategies for different staff categories cover a variety of aims and purposes in response to particular situations. The overall general objective is, however, to address the following:

- *Expectations*: all systems must meet the expectations of the job holder to a greater or lesser extent if they are to be effective at attracting and retaining staff in the required occupations.
- *Motivation*: within the constraints illustrated above, all payment and reward motivates to a greater or lesser extent; the levels of reward offered to particular job

holders also carry implications about the nature, complexity and commitment to the work in hand that is required on their part.

- *Mixes of pay with other aspects*: much of this also relates to expectations; for example, in the UK the offer of a company car to professional and managerial staff is still very attractive, in spite of the diminishing tax advantage.
- *Occupational aspects*: part of the reward package may include the provision of specialist or expert training and equipment.
- *International variations*: these relate to the mix of payment and other benefits in the total reward package. In the UK, there is a wide variety of components; in Switzerland, on the other hand, only 2 per cent of managers receive a company car, preferring instead (collectively) a higher level of salary.

Attraction, recruitment and retention

The ability to attract, recruit and retain staff is based on a variety of factors, including:

- the relative attraction of the organisation and the work offered, the organisation's wider reputation, together with perceptions formed by more general contacts with it, e.g. through media coverage or as a customer
- the location of the organisation; this refers both to the place of work, and also to ease and convenience of transport and access
- the relative value and worth of the occupation, both to the individual and also to the organisation
- the relative perception in which the organisation and the work are held.

Assessment of these factors indicates the overall attractiveness or otherwise of the organisation and the work. This has then to be related to the rewards on offer as follows:

- the material rewards on offer, salary/pay/wages and other benefits
- the intrinsic rewards on offer, including responsibility, autonomy, opportunities for progress and development
- reflections of personal value, including status, esteem, rank and job title, each of which is important to some people in particular sets of circumstances
- recognition factors on the part of the individual, the organisation and society at large
- the fit between the particular occupation and the management style with which the work is directed.

This is therefore clearly complex. It needs to be based on good levels of expert knowledge of each of the factors indicated above. Full assessment of these factors indicates why people want to carry out their occupation for the particular organisation, and the advantages and barriers relative to this. It is additionally necessary to see the nature of the rewards on offer relative to people's professional and occupational demands and expectations (see Management in Focus 20.2).

A full and detailed evaluation is therefore required. In particular, it is never enough simply to throw money at the problems. It is also not enough to guess at the other issues; each has to be evaluated in relation to the given set of circumstances.

MANAGEMENT IN FOCUS 20.2

ATTRACTION, RECRUITMENT AND RETENTION IN THE NATIONAL HEALTH SERVICE

In the twenty-first century, the UK National Health Service is facing severe shortages of professional medical staff.

In terms of intrinsic rewards, these occupations are held in the highest possible public esteem. Caring for health, curing illness and giving the opportunity for life in the future are absolute priorities for everybody.

In terms of extrinsic rewards, wages and salaries paid to doctors and specialist staff are often very high. Yet despite increased funding of the NHS in recent years, wages and salaries paid to nurses and related professions (e.g. midwives, physiotherapists) continue to decline in real terms.

There is a strong vocational element normally present in all those who seek to go into these professions. However, this has not prevented a decline in the numbers of people from within the UK wishing to enter these professions in the Health Service. The reasons stated are as follows:

- divergence of objectives between healthcare professionals and the managers of healthcare institutions
- adversarial management styles, reinforced by short-term and unconsidered politically driven changes in direction
- the collective and individual stress that is caused by uncertainties in budgets, technology, equipment and facilities provisions
- property and living costs and charges in many locations, meaning that those wishing to work in particular locations cannot afford to live there.

Sources of staff

Potential staff exist everywhere, limited only by qualifications, capability and willingness to work in the organisation. Organisations recruit them through advertising in newspapers and trade press, using agencies and specialists, and through local and professional word of mouth. Recruiting people with specialist or scarce expertise may additionally require such approaches as 'executive search'. Advances in international education, together with the opportunities afforded by technology, have led some organisations either to establish specialist services overseas, or to recruit staff from abroad to come and work in the UK.

Ideally, a mix and diversity of sources of staff will be used, in order to ensure the maximum possible opportunity of gaining the best people for the job, and gaining a wide range of approaches and perspectives.

Some posts within organisations will attract both internal and external candidates. The priority here is to reconcile the issues relating to:

- the need to offer opportunities for development to staff already working within the organisation on the one hand, and to prevent the organisation from becoming too inward looking on the other
- attracting fresh talent and perspectives as mentioned above, while reconciling

this with the fact that external expertise has to be capable of being harnessed and delivered within the culture and operational constraints of the particular organisation.

Where there are serious skills gaps and staff shortages, managers should not only resort to specialist agencies and overseas initiatives. They should also be prepared to reconsider the ways in which the work is divided up, to see if it possible to alter the approach to meeting the objectives. In some cases, this will be possible; in others, not. However, this approach should be adopted as a key part of the staff planning process; thus even if no restructuring is possible, at least it will have been fully considered.

Wherever staff are drawn from, they need to be given the best possible opportunity to demonstrate their capability and willingness to do the job in the ways demanded by the organisation. Where there is a field of candidates for particular positions, all must be given the same fair and equal opportunity to demonstrate their capabilities. Consequently, recruitment interviewing, selection testing, personality tests and other specific requirements must be structured in order to be fair to everyone involved (see Management in Focus 20.3).

The overall purpose of adopting rigorous approaches to attracting, recruiting and retaining expert, qualified and committed staff is required at a variety of levels; again, organisations and their managers need to be clear about which approach they are adopting. The approaches are as follows:

- to fill positions
- to develop an extended working relationship
- to provide opportunities; and to take advantage of the opportunities created when new people come into the organisation
- to concentrate on people who, all things being equal, will stay for a long time
- to concentrate on people who, all things being equal, will stay for a given and understood period of time.

There is nothing intrinsically right or wrong with any of the above approaches. It is however necessary for managers and organisations to be clear about which of these approaches are being targeted (see Management in Focus 20.4).

To attract, recruit and retain of staff is, from time to time, a competitive process. Competitive pressures arise as a result of:

- new employers opening up in the particular locality
- existing employers moving from the particular locality, so that spouses and dependants of particular groups of staff also have to move
- increases in wages and salaries within organisations in the same sector
- increases in wages and salaries within professional and occupational groups in the same sector
- changes in transport access and egress availability (see Management in Focus 20.5).

Retention of staff is based on ensuring that the factors and elements present in the attraction part of the process are delivered in practice. Retention is most effective when the position of building a relationship, as outlined above, is adopted. This leads to the formation of 'a psychological' contract, in which the nature and level of staff obligations and commitments to the organisation, and vice versa, are clearly understood. Retention is enhanced further by the opportunities that the organisation provides for career, professional, occupational and personal enhancement and development; by increases in

MANAGEMENT IN FOCUS 20.3

BABIES!

A public authority interviewed two candidates for a middle management post. One candidate was a woman in her late twenties; the other, a single man of 33.

The woman was interviewed first, the man the following day. When the man went in for the interview, he found himself confronted by a panel of three. One of the members was the senior manager for whom he would be working if successful, another was an HR officer, and the third was a representative of the public authority.

After 20 minutes of the interview, the member of the public authority asked: 'Tell me, when are you going to leave your job, and go away and have babies?'

It was immediately clear that, contrary to both legal and statutory requirements and also best practice, this particular individual had asked the same question of the woman. She therefore insisted that the other candidate was asked exactly the same question in exactly the same way.

The news quickly travelled around the organisation. It reinforced perceptions of a fundamental lack of strength and equality in selection processes. More generally, it is the sort of story that becomes embedded in organisational mythology; and this can lead to persons from particular groups within the workforce into thinking that they will never have further opportunities within the organisation.

material levels of rewards; and by placing high and ambitious levels of product and service output requirements on the staff. Retention capability is always diluted when these elements are not present or when the organisation fails to deliver them (see Management in Focus 20.6).

Induction

The purpose of induction is to get the new member of staff to be as productive as possible, as quickly as possible. This consists of matching the organisation's needs with those of the individual as follows:

- *Setting the attitudes and standards of behaviour required*, ensuring that new employees know what is expected of them, and that they conform to these expectations and requirements. It is most important that the organisation assumes absolute responsibility for this, rather than allowing employees to set their own standards, or for these to emerge by default.
- *Job training and familiarisation*, mainly to do with the ways of working required by the organisation, and ensuring that these are matched with the new employee's expertise. The required standards and methods of work must be established.
- *Introductions* to the new team, work colleagues, and other key contacts as part of the process of gaining confidence, understanding and mutuality of objectives required for the development of effective working relationships and environment.

MANAGEMENT IN FOCUS 20.4

WORKING IN THE PRIVATISED SOCIAL CARE SECTOR

At the end of the twentieth century, many social care organisations and institutions in the UK were privatised.

When these institutions were run by public authorities, staff working in them had to have minimum qualification levels. There were national agreements that ensured that staff with these qualifications received relatively high levels of minimum salary.

When the institutions were privatised, the requirement for qualifications was abolished. This led to the privatised institutions no longer employing qualified staff. Instead, they concentrated on employing unqualified staff at, or near, the national minimum wage.

On the face of it, this was an efficient and effective cost-cutting exercise. However, the following lessons have subsequently been learned:

- In many cases, it has proved impossible to attract, recruit and retain staff to work in these institutions on this basis.
- The convenience of being able to attract unqualified staff from within particular localities has worked effectively only where the intrinsic quality of the work has been maintained, and where this has been supported and underpinned by a positive and participative managerial and supervisory style.
- The privatised institutions have consequently had to spend a large proportion of the money saved on salaries in ensuring a steady flow of short-stay staff. This is in contrast to the experience of the public authorities, who found that qualified staff who were properly rewarded would normally stay for a long time.

- *Familiarisation with the environment*, premises, ways of working and particular obligations on the part of the employer; ensuring that new employees understand their position in this environment; emergency procedures and health and safety.

Commitment is vital. Many organisations go to much trouble to ensure that the process is adequately and effectively completed, recognising the returns on an excellent and well-resourced induction process in the production of a highly motivated and committed workforce.

The induction process will have been started in general terms by any vague impression that the new employee has picked up of the organisation. This will have been further reinforced if, for example, he or she has been a customer or client of it. Any correction of these impressions must also be addressed as part of the induction process, which will also be reinforced by the ways in which the selection process is conducted.

Performance measurement and appraisal

Performance measurement is conducted for the organisation, departments, divisions, groups and individuals. To be effective and successful, it must be conducted as follows:

MANAGEMENT IN FOCUS 20.5

GETTING TO WORK

A large multinational corporation used to have its head offices in the centre of London. For the administrative staff especially, this was convenient. Although they did not live in the centre of London, bus, train and underground networks were plentiful and almost universally used.

The company decided to relocate to the edge of London, and commissioned a brand new headquarters building.

There was an immediate problem of transport to and from work. For many staff, the new building was much closer to their homes; however, because the transport networks were not present, this was more than offset by the need to drive to work. When the new offices opened, the road network quickly became clogged up, and this led to people in practice taking longer to get to work than previously when they were using public transport.

It also became clear that the centre of London had been a good focal point, drawing in people from all parts of the surrounding suburbs and home counties. The new location (on the west side of London) meant that the pool of labour was now much more restricted, and also subject to competition from other local employers. There was an additional pressure based on the fact that many staff were not prepared to forgo some of the benefits of working for a large multinational organisation in return for the convenience of not having to travel on an overcrowded road network.

- pre-set and pre-agreed aims and objectives, priorities, performance targets and deadlines for achievement
- a process of regularised formal reviews, combined with a continuous and participative working relationship
- concentration on a combination of measuring and evaluating achievements, together with establishing what is to be done for the future.

Within this framework, particular organisational appraisal schemes may seek to: provide merit pay awards; identify potential, training and development needs, job–person mismatches, organisation development prospects, and poor and sub-standard performance; and be a vehicle for other remedial action.

Appraisal schemes fall into disrepute for the following reasons: that they are not believed in or valued; they do not contribute to the wider success of the organisation; they are bureaucratic or mechanistic; that it is the scheme and its paperwork that are seen as important, and not the process that should be completed; that the reviews are too infrequent, or (in practice) missed altogether; and that what is promised in them (e.g. pay awards, training, promotion) is not delivered in practice.

They also suffer from performance criteria being identified in general terms only. This leads to inconsistency in application and unfairness (and perceived unfairness) in the award of merit pay rises and places on training courses; while at the other end of the spectrum, individuals may be picked up for poor performance on the same uneven basis.

There is, and must be, a basis of mutual understanding, openness, trust and honesty inherent in the process if it is to succeed. If staff are asked to declare short-

MANAGEMENT IN FOCUS 20.6

KAREN WELLS

Karen Wells joined a large hospital in the south-east of England as a personnel assistant straight from college. She was impressed by the welcome that she received. She went through an extensive induction course and looked forward to starting work in earnest.

After a few weeks however, frustration began to set in. She went back to the job advertisement. The job advertisement had promised: 'A lively working environment; hands on personnel experience; the opportunity to become involved in all aspects of human resource management work. Professional training and development will be available to the right person.'

As the weeks and months went by, Karen found her frustration greatly increasing. She was employed on clerical and filing duties. Because she could type, this quickly became a secretarial post. She was regularly asked to provide tea and coffee for meetings. She sometimes sat in on these meetings and occasionally took minutes but was not allowed to participate.

After six months, she confronted her supervisor with her concerns. She was told: 'After the induction course, we did not know what to do with you. All the HR work is covered and so there is no opportunity for you there. We are pleased that we have found you a clerical job.' On the specific point about training and development, she was told bluntly: 'You are not the right person and so training and development is not available to you.'

After this, Karen reviewed her situation. She looked again at the job advertisement which had also stated: 'Starting salary up to £16,000'. Karen had started on £11,000. When she had mildly questioned this at the time, she had been told that it was normal practice and not to worry.

Karen Wells left the hospital after ten miserable months; and she now works for a major clearing bank.

comings in their recent performance, and if this is then used as a stick with which to beat them, they will simply not do it.

It follows, therefore, that there is a necessary body of skills and knowledge required of the manager in the conduct of effective performance appraisal. Communication, articulation, target and objective setting, counselling, support, trust, dependency and assertiveness are all clearly necessary. These qualities will also be required to be translated into dealings with frustrated and recalcitrant employees in particular situations.

Finally, the control of the appraisal process must always rest with the manager, and while agreement of objectives with the member of staff is desirable, this should never be at the expense of a diluted or sub-standard performance.

Maintenance factors in human resource management

The basis of this part of HRM is that the staff require maintenance in the ways equivalent to other aspects and resources of the organisation if its operations are to be maximised and optimised.

Job and work development

This is designed both in terms of the formation of attitudes and standards at the workplace to which employees are required to subscribe, and of the division, regulation and allocation of the work itself. Both are undertaken with the intention of generating a greater measure of positive commitment and a reduction of workplace alienation. This may involve job rotation and progression schemes, as well as project work, secondments, and fixed-term and action-learning type placements. Related to this is the ever-increasing obligation on employees to maintain and improve their skills, knowledge and technical expertise in the interests of continuing organisation effectiveness, profitability and prosperity. On the other hand, the expectations of those at work have also changed, and part of the job design process increasingly includes improving the quality of working life.

Creative approaches to employment patterns

This involves a much greater awareness and willingness on the part of organisations to relate the hours of work that they offer to the non-work commitment and aspirations of potential staff members. This means having regard to the use of flexitime, annual hours and other flexible work patterns; job sharing; working away from the organisation and especially allowing staff to work at home and providing them with the means and workstations to do so; and the devising of shift patterns especially to fit around those with primary responsibility for looking after young children. More widely, organisations may offer career breaks – extended periods of time off for employees to go to do other things. Organisations may also offer 'returner schemes' pitched primarily at those who have had lengthy periods of time out of work, usually for the purpose of bringing up a family; the returner scheme tackles the issues of familiarisation, confidence building and personal and professional comfort that are the concerns of anyone coming into any job after a lengthy break. Such schemes also provide specific job training and re-training as necessary and desirable. Organisations may also underline their commitment to these creative approaches through the provision of nursery facilities for very young children, canteen facilities that are open all day so that all work patterns are accommodated, and through the adoption of general ways of working and general attitudes at the workplace that place the same intrinsic value on all members of staff regardless of their own particular pattern of work.

Stress

Stress may be either positive or negative. It essentially consists of the amount of pressure present in a given situation in which the individual has to work. The sources of stress are occupational, role, organisational, hierarchical, social and personal; stresses on the individual result from an imbalance of these. There is, in particular, a growing awareness of the links between work stress and other illnesses such as nervous exhaustion, executive and professional burn-out, heart conditions and high blood pressure. The manager's role in this is therefore threefold: to recognise it as an issue; to prevent stress among staff; and to recognise it in him or herself and take steps to limit it.

Good occupational health schemes thus have a recognition of stress and the ability to treat its symptoms and manifestations as central features of health provision. The ability of organisations to accept and recognise the condition, to treat it where it occurs and, above all, to engage in practices and a style of management that prevent it from arising as far as possible is an essential contribution to the maintenance of the human resource.

Occupational health

Organisations are increasingly assuming responsibility for the good health of their staff and taking positive steps and making interventions that are designed to ensure this. This approach entails determining that the employee is fit and healthy when he or she first starts work and that this continues throughout the period of employment. For those who have persistent or regular time away from work there may be assessments by company medical staff as well as the employee's own doctor. This may also require the employee to take medical treatment at the behest of the organisation, as a precondition of continuing to work for it. Occupational health schemes at the workplace are, in the best cases, particularly strong and valuable in the early diagnosis of job-specific illnesses and injuries. They also provide a valuable general source of medical knowledge by which the organisation may assess the overall state of their workforce's health.

Particular matters related to the workplace have come to the fore and gained recognition and currency. Major issues of which any manager should be aware are:

- stress, its causes and effects and techniques for its management, as discussed above
- repetitive strain injuries (RSI) which are caused by continuous use of certain muscles or the carrying out of certain activities – for example, continuous keyboard working and process work
- back injuries caused either by bad lifting practices or a continuous bad back posture
- the effects of VDU screens on eyesight
- industrial and commercial heating and lighting and the relationship between these and eye strain, coughs, colds and other minor but recurrent ailments
- smoking, both active and passive, and the effects of it on all staff, both in relation to health and also more general concerns of its offensive odour (see Management in Focus 20.7)
- alcohol abuse (see Management in Focus 20.7)
- HIV and AIDS, and their implications for particular workplaces and occupations.

Employee relations

Employee relations – or industrial relations, employment relations, staff relations – is the system by which workplace activities are regulated, the arrangement by which the owners, managers and staff of organisations come together to engage in productive activity. Employee relations (ER) concerns setting standards and promoting consensus, and is additionally about solving problems and the management of conflict (see Management in Focus 20.8).

MANAGEMENT IN FOCUS 20.7

ORGANISATIONAL APPROACHES TO TOBACCO, ALCOHOL AND DRUGS

These are dealt with because they are current, high-profile and contentious issues.

Organisations should make clear the stance to be adopted on each, giving a clear lead to managers and staff. Whatever the outcome it should reflect organisational requirements, and not simply be allowed to evolve unmanaged. Organisations may set any standard that they wish on each of these issues (provided that they also conform with the law).

Organisations that wish to exclude smoking from their premises may do so. In the implementation of this, they should consult with staff, and offer counselling and support to those who have to fundamentally change behaviour. They will follow the consultation process and timescale referred to elsewhere.

Staff who have addiction problems should be supported by organisations; they should be offered counselling, rehabilitation and reference to medical authorities except in the rare cases where this is impossible.

There is a moral as well as an operational imperative in this, which is increasingly being recognised as part of the organisation's total commitment, ethical stance and wider obligations to its staff. Levels of support for members of staff through programmes and periods of treatment will be directed at both treating the matter in hand and rehabilitating staff, getting them back into productive and effective work.

ER in practice

It is usual to define a broad framework for ER as a relationship between:

- government, which legislates for ER and workplace practice in many areas, and which influences all organisational ER in its role as dominant employer and in the management of public services
- employers, in discharging their enduring responsibilities to staff; and in conducting and developing their relationships with the staff in accordance with the provisions of the law
- employees and their representatives, including trade unions, in ensuring that required standards of behaviour, probity and performance are carried out within the constraints of the particular situation (see Management in Focus 20.9).

ER developments

The historic complexity of ER, and the expense and stress incurred, has caused many organisations to seek alternative, more effective approaches.

Many organisations have actively redrawn the relationship between staff management practices and ER in terms of integration with, and contribution to, overall organisational performance. As well as being concerned with employee terms and conditions, and the state of the working environment, many organisations now

MANAGEMENT IN FOCUS 20.8

PROBLEM SOLVING IN EMPLOYEE RELATIONS

A strategic approach to specific ER matters will be adopted by organisations and their managers. As well as briefings for staff, and training for managers in ER skills and knowledge, organisations will take an approach to the management of workplace conflicts based on answers to the following six sets of questions.

- What is the likelihood of a dispute occurring? If it does, how long might it last? What are the wider consequences to ourselves, and to our staff?
- If it does occur, can we win it? What are the consequences of winning it? What are the consequences of losing it?
- If it does occur, what costs are we going to incur? As well as finan-

cial cost, what of the questions of PR, media coverage and local feelings in our community? Is this a price worth paying?

- What happens when it all settles down? How will we interact and work with the staff afterwards? How long will any bad feeling last? What are the wider implications of this?
- What other ways are there around the matter or dispute in hand? Are we able to use these? What are the pros and cons of going down these alternatives, vis-à-vis a dispute?
- What are the behavioural and psychological aspects that surround this issue? If we win, what will be the effects

on the workforce? And on managers? Are there questions of morale to be considered? If we lose, would loss of face be important? How could we save face, if that were to arise? What would be the response of the workforce and its representatives?

From consideration of the matter in hand this way, and by establishing the answer to these issues, the answer to the critical question emerges: 'Why are we seeking, entering, or preparing to enter, into this dispute?'

This approach will form the basis of any strategic consideration of any conflict, or potential conflict, whether global, organisational, departmental, or divisional; or at team, group or individual level.

negotiate and consult with staff representatives and recognised trade unions on a much wider range of issues, including:

- productivity and service delivery issues, including attention to quality and customer satisfaction
- organisational operating expenses, engaging consensus and cooperation in how best to manage these
- the design and implementation of technology changes and upgrades
- the opening up of new markets, products, services and locations.

This represents a shift away from adversarial and conflict-based approaches to ER. It reinforces any notions that may be required of a genuine consensus and cooperation; this in turn has led to much greater levels of participation and involvement on the part of the staff in many organisations.

MANAGEMENT IN FOCUS 20.9

THE DONOVAN COMMISSION

Part of the remit of the Royal Commission on Trade Unions and Employers' Association (the Donovan Commission of 1965–67) was to define for the first time what the real roles of unions were. In summary, the findings were that unions:

● bargain for best possible wages, terms and conditions for members

● lobby for an improved share in national wealth for members

● influence government policy and legal frameworks on behalf of members

● lobby for social security for all

● lobby for full employment, job security, better wage levels and

cheap housing for the poor

● bargain nationally, regionally, locally and industrially, for organisations and individuals

● represent members at disputes and grievances and for any other reason according to need.

Source: Donovan (1968).

Problem solving

It remains true that a substantial part of organisational ER practice is concerned with resolving problems, disputes, grievances and disciplinary issues. These issues arise as the result of:

● genuine misunderstandings
● negligence
● personality, professional and occupational clashes
● determination to engage in conflict.

Historically, these matters used to be resolved through reference to lengthy and complicated procedures. The provision of procedures, together with ensuring adequate representation, remains a statutory duty. However, many organisations and their managers have come to know and understand that if matters can be resolved without recourse to formal procedures, this is more productive and less stressful for everyone concerned. This in turn has led to a much greater emphasis on management development and training in the field of ER, with specific reference to the following:

● problem solving and resolution
● disputes and grievances management
● correct ways to conduct disciplinary hearings.

This is underpinned by organisations producing comprehensive staff handbooks, in which all duties and obligations are clearly set out. Such staff handbooks ensure that everyone knows and understands what constitutes minor misdemeanours, major problems, and serious and gross misconduct (the penalty for which will always normally be dismissal).

The onus is therefore shifted on to managers to resolve problems when they do arise, and to create the conditions and relationships in which matters are raised early and resolved quickly without the need to resort to formal procedures.

It does however remain true that many organisations still conduct ER in more traditional ways. It is not always easy to shift managerial or collective staff attitudes, and not always possible without more extensive organisational restructuring. It remains the case however that where adversarial ER does exist, there is a much greater organisational expense inherent in its management and conduct, leading to a much greater proliferation of disputes, grievances and disciplinary matters.

Conclusions

Staff management, human resource management, and employee relations strategies and policies must be designed to work in harmony with the interests of the organisation, rather than those of HRM and ER specialist functions. Many organisations are coming increasingly to the view that HRM is a strategic rather than operational issue; and that this, in turn, means that day-to-day HRM issues are tackled and resolved by the particular line managers and supervisors involved, rather than being referred to specialist functions.

There is clearly a pressure for this strategic approach to be developed and enhanced. With the increased complexity of organisational structure, uncertainties of markets, and the continuing need for the development of expertise, a strategic approach to HRM is much more likely to make a long-term and enduring contribution to organisational effectiveness through following this agenda, rather than through concentrating on specific issues and minutiae in functional departments and divisions. The strategic HR role also requires specific attention to establishing, maintaining and developing the required organisational management style and culture, and to engaging management development programmes in support of this. Staff development, expertise and technological training are also much better managed from a strategic point of view. Finally, the procedures that underwrite the required and desired human resource management style and strategy are much more likely to be effective if they are written from a strategic, rather than an operational, point of view.

CRITICAL THINKING, ANALYSIS AND EVALUATION

1. What are the problems with long-term staff planning activities, and how might these be overcome?
2. What are the key areas of HRM which managers from all disciplines need to be aware of, and why?
3. Discuss the view that those on very high wages and salaries (e.g. sports and entertainment stars, top managers and directors of companies) work for job satisfaction, while those on very low wages (e.g. bar and waiting staff, food fryers and cleaners) work purely for the money.
4. If an organisation consciously adopts an adversarial approach and attitude to its staff, what costs and charges (both overt and hidden) are incurred as a direct consequence?

DEVELOPING MANAGEMENT SKILLS AND EXPERTISE

GREETHAM BOROUGH COUNCIL

The staff of Greetham Borough Council Social Services Department have returned from their Christmas break to find out that the department is to be broken up and that the following services are to be privatised:

- care of the elderly
- childrens' services
- care of the disabled.

All of the residential and daycare establishments in these services are to be sold to the highest or preferred bidders. The Council will guarantee a certain volume, frequency, density and value of clients for a period of seven years to those who are awarded the contracts. In addition, the department's personnel and human resources management function is to be sold to Ulvaeus, the Swedish management consultancy firm, and these services are then to be bought back by the Council over an initially contracted period of 12 years.

The staff have been notified that consultation will begin immediately. Discussion of specific issues concerning all those staff affected is also to start immediately because the Council wishes to have the whole situation resolved by the time of the local elections on 1 May.

Greetham is a large metropolitan borough in the northern part of the UK, and was once part of a rich and prosperous city. However, unemployment rose to 35 per cent in the early 1980s when the dockyards, car factories and military establishments on which it had depended were closed down. This created extensive and extreme social problems, deprivation, dependency culture, crime and an 'alternative economy'. On one estate of 9500 households, there was virtually full unemployment. This has now been alleviated to some extent through the attraction of inward investment. There are assembly factories, call centres, freight forwarding and some financial services. However, many of the jobs are either low paid or unskilled.

Many of the social problems continue. The consensus among experts and professional people working in these areas is that the problems are certain to continue until massive investment is poured in to enhance the quality of life, the living environment, schools, and recreation and leisure services, as well as long-term mass job creation.

There is great affinity between individual clients and members of staff on the ground and at the frontline. However, the Council as a whole has a poor reputation for high council taxes and charges and inadequate service volumes. Moreover, the last round of privatisations led to investigations into corruption allegations against two elected members and the chairman of a local building company, though all were subsequently acquitted.

The present round of privatisations has therefore to be considered very carefully, and a strategic approach drawn up. Of especial concern are the following:

- the morality of trading in services for at-risk, vulnerable and deprived clients
- the quality of care, service and support available over the medium to long term

- career paths and opportunities available to those who transfer over to new employers in the services themselves when they are privatised
- career paths and opportunities available to those who remain behind once the services are privatised
- strategic and operational staffing issues
- presentational factors, especially concerning the client groups, their relatives and the community at large
- long-term costs, charges, benefits and responsibilities
- other potential opportunities, problems and consequences.

Questions

1. What are the main immediate and enduring HR, ER and staff management concerns that have to be addressed in response to the above list of concerns?
2. Identify the nature of investment in HR expertise that is required if the proposed changes are to be effective in terms of service delivery:
   a) immediately
   b) for the foreseeable future.

Chapter twenty one

Leadership and management

'I am the leader. Therefore I must serve.'
Winston Churchill, on becoming Prime Minister in 1940.
The Gathering Storm, Allen and Unwin (1947).

'Being made captain of Pakistan was the proudest moment of my life.'
Imran Khan, cricketer.

'One does not manage people, one leads them.
One does not manage change, one leads and directs it.'
Peter Drucker, *Management Challenges for the 21st Century*, Harper Collins (2000).

Chapter outline

- Introduction
- Definitions and priorities
- Leadership in practice
- Traits and characteristics
- Leadership types
- Leadership styles
- Contingency theories
- The complexities of leadership
- Measures of success and failure
- Conclusions

Chapter objectives

After studying this chapter, you should be able to:

- understand the range, scale, scope, expertise and responsibilities of being placed in a position of leadership

- understand the importance of carrying out the leadership function in any management job or occupation

- understand and be able to develop the particular traits and qualities required in order to be an effective leader

- understand the consequences of bad, ineffective or negligent leadership.

● Introduction

The context in which leadership expertise is required of managers is as follows:

- It is becoming increasingly essential to be able to legitimately assign responsibility, authority and accountability to those in charge of organisations, and those who head individual departments, divisions and functions.
- It is increasingly difficult, and in some cases impossible, to sustain the expense incurred of having large and complex hierarchical and bureaucratic systems for the coordination and control of organisations.

Employing and assigning those with expertise in leadership, and developing the traits, characteristics and qualities required, is therefore a clear alternative to the bureaucratic approach. Employing people with leadership expertise in key and critical positions and functions therefore reduces expense; it additionally leads to clearer lines of authority and accountability, resulting in increased output that is delivered more quickly and with fewer problems and barriers.

Leadership is therefore the core of all managerial and supervisory activities. This is more clearly observable in some areas than others – political leaders and chief executive officers are self-evidently 'in charge'. However, all those in managerial positions have a leadership function; and all those in leadership positions have managerial responsibilities. These are:

- to give vision and direction
- to energise
- to set and enforce absolute standards of behaviour, attitude, presentation and performance.

In this context, the key role and function is having the combination of expertise, commitment and personality required to see things through to completion. It is additionally essential that leaders surround themselves with expertise that they themselves do not have so that any gaps in their own shortcomings are filled.

● Definitions and priorities

Definitions

Some useful definitions are:

- A leader is someone who exercises influence over other people (Huczynski and Buchanan, 2004).
- Leadership is the lifting of people's vision to a higher sight, the raising of their performance to a higher standard, the building of their personality beyond its normal limitations (P.F. Drucker, 1999).
- A leader is: 'cheerleader, enthusiast, nurturer of champions, hero finder, wanderer, dramatist, coach, facilitator and builder' (Peters and Austin, 1986).
- The leader must have infective optimism. The final test of a leader is the feeling you have when you leave their presence after a conference. Have you a feeling of uplift and confidence? (Field Marshal Bernard Montgomery, 1957).

- Leadership is creating a vision to which others can aspire and energising them to work towards this vision (Anita Roddick, 1992).
- There is a need in all organisations for individual linking pins who will bind groups together and, as members of other groups, represent their groups elsewhere in organisations. Leadership concerns the leader themselves, the subordinates, and the task in hand (C.B. Handy, 1996).
- Leadership can be described as a dynamic process in a group whereby one individual influences others to contribute voluntarily to the achievement of group tasks in a given situation (G.A. Cole, 1994).

Priorities

In order for leaders to be successful and effective, they have to be able to combine their expertise, authority and character so as to be able to:

- get optimum performance from those carrying out the work in whatever terms that is defined
- adopt an overview and long-term perspective, and deliver this alongside attention to detail whenever required (see Management in Focus 21.1).

Other areas of enduring priority are concerned with ensuring continuity, development and improvement in those carrying out the work; monitoring and evaluating both the work and those involved; and taking remedial action where necessary. It is essential to relate the skills and capacities of all those involved to the work itself. This is a key part of motivating and encouraging the staff, and promoting positive, harmonious and productive working relations. There is also a concern in seeking continuous improvement in all aspects of the work environment; and providing opportunities for continuous development and enhancement for everyone involved.

MANAGEMENT IN FOCUS 21.1

WINSTON CHURCHILL

Winston Churchill, the UK Prime Minister during the period 1940–45 of the Second World War, provided identity and inspiration to the British population at a time of enduring national crisis.

Many of Churchill's military commanders complained of his constant meddling and interference in both the strat- egy and tactics used. The commanders took the view that they were employed as experts in the particular field, and so should be allowed to get on with the job.

Those employed in key and critical positions need to be sufficiently expert themselves to be able to respond to detailed questioning. From the leader's point of view, it is much better to be accused of interference, meddling and over-attention to detail, and to have the character and capacity to 'back-off', than it is to be accused of remoteness, distance and unapproachability.

Leadership in practice

Leaders are expected to deliver and achieve what they set out to do, or else to provide a clear explanation as to why this was not possible, and what they now intend to do as the result. Leaders have specific responsibilities and accountability, in the following areas:

- *Results*: results are measured in terms of what was intended and the actual outcomes; how and why these were achieved; how they were viewed at the time and subsequently by posterity; and whether this represented a good, bad or indifferent return on the resources and energy expended in their pursuit.
- *Inspiration*: in order to achieve success, leaders must be able to motivate, inspire and energise. In order that people follow, and resources are attracted to the cause, this is normally translated into a simple, direct and positive statement of what the leader is going to do, how and why this is to be achieved, and the benefits that this will bring to others as the result. They must be capable of inspiring others – it is no use having a good idea if people do not recognise it as such.
- *Hard work*: for all this to occur leaders must have great stores of energy, enthusiasm, dedication, zeal and commitment. They have to inspire and energise people and resources in pursuit of the desired ends. They also set the standards for their followers – in normal circumstances, hard work cannot be expected of others if the leader is not also prepared to put this in.
- *Honesty*: people follow leaders either because they believe in them or because it is in their interest to do so (or for a combination of the two). Leaders who fail to deliver are normally rejected or supplanted. Leaders who say one thing and mean another will not be trusted, and people continue to work for them only until they can find something else.
- *Responsibility, authority and accountability*: leaders accept their own part in triumphs and successes, and also disasters and failures (see Management in Focus 20.2).

Traits and characteristics

There have been a great many studies of leaders, directors and managers from all walks of life and all parts of history. By studying a range of leaders and managers from a variety of situations and background – for example, sport, politics, the military, exploration, religion and business – it is possible to infer and draw conclusions about the reasons for, and causes of, their successes or failures. Their contribution can be assessed and analysed together with the other elements and factors present.

Attempts to identify the traits and characteristics present in successful leaders are largely inconclusive, in that none identify all the attributes necessary to lead, direct or manage in all situations. However, the following are more or less universal:

- *Communication*: the ability to communicate with all people with whom the leader comes into contact – regularly, continuously and in ways and language which those on the receiving end will be able both to understand and to respond to.
- *Decision making*: the ability to take the right decisions in given situations, to take

MANAGEMENT IN FOCUS 21.2

LEADERSHIP

Peters and Austin (1986) identified a long and compre- hensive list of factors present in a 'leader'; and they con- trasted this with the mirror attributes of the 'non-leader'.

Leader	Non-leader
Carries water for people	Presides over the mess
Open door problem solver, advice giver, cheerleader	Invisible, gives orders to staff, expects them to be carried out
Comfortable with people in their workplaces	Uncomfortable with people
No reserved parking place, dining room or lift	Reserved parking place and dining table
Manages by walking about	Invisible
Arrives early, stays late	In late, usually leaves on time
Common touch	Strained with 'inferior' group of staffs
Good listener	Good talker
Available	Hard to reach
Fair	Unfair
Decisive	Uses committees
Humble	Arrogant
Tough, confronts nasty problems	Elusive, the 'artful dodger'
Persistent	Vacillates
Simplifies	Complicates
Tolerant	Intolerant
Knows people's names	Doesn't know people's names
Has strong convictions	Sways with the wind
Trusts people	Trusts only words and numbers on paper
Delegates whole important jobs	Keeps all final decisions
Spends as little time as possible with outside directors	Spends a lot of time massaging outside directors
Wants anonymity for him/herself, publicity for the company	Wants publicity for him/herself
Often takes the blame	Looks for scapegoats
Gives credits to others	Takes credit
Gives honest, frequent feedback	Amasses information
Knows when and how to discipline people	Ducks unpleasant tasks
Has respect for all people	Has contempt for all people
Knows the business and the kind of people who make it tick	Knows the business only in terms of what it can do for him/her
Honest under pressure	Equivocates
Looks for controls to abolish	Looks for new controls and procedures
Prefers discussion rather than written reports	Prefers long reports

Straightforward	Tricky, manipulative
Openness	Secrecy
As little paperwork as possible	As much paperwork as possible
Promotes from within	Looks outside the organisation
Keeps promises	Doesn't keep promises
Plain office and facilities	Lavish office, expensive facilities
Organisation is top of the agenda	Self is top pf the agenda
Sees mistakes as learning opportunities and the opportunity to develop	Sees mistakes as punishable offences and the means of scapegoating

Peters and Austin additionally state: 'You now know more about leaders and leadership than all the combined graduate business schools in America. You also know whether you have a leader or a non-leader in you manager's office.' Source: from Peters and Austin, *A Passion for Excellence: The Leadership Difference*, Harper and Row (1986).

responsibility and be accountable for them, and to understand the consequences of particular courses of action. Part of this involves being able to take an overview or strategic view of particular situations, to see the longer term and to take a wider general perspective. This is sometimes called 'the helicopter view'.

● *Commitment*: both to matters in hand and to the wider aspects of the organisation as a whole. This includes an inherent willingness to draw on personal, as well as professional, energies and to bring qualities of enthusiasm, drive and ambition to the particular situation.

● *Concern for staff*: respecting, trusting and committing oneself to them; developing them, understanding them and their aspirations and reconciling these with the matters in hand. Staff should be treated on a basis of equality and confidence.

● *Quality*: a commitment to the quality of product or service so that, whatever the matter in hand, customers receive high value and high satisfaction, and the staff involved receive recognition for their effort.

● *Values*: leaders bring a given set of values with which others will identify, and to which they will commit themselves. These values are founded in personal integrity and the establishment of high absolute standards of conduct and performance required and demanded. Values are then additionally developed and enhanced through levels of respect accorded to all members of staff.

● Leadership types

The following different types of leader may be distinguished:

● Traditional leaders, whose position is assured by birth and heredity. Examples of this are the kings and queens of England (and of other places in the world).

This form of leadership may also be found in family businesses, where child succeeds parent as the chief executive or chair.

● Known leaders, whose position is secured by the fact that everybody understands it, at least in general. Kings and queens are examples again. Priests are known to be leaders of their congregations. Aristocrats are known to be masters and mistresses of their own domains. It is known also that they will be succeeded by one from their own estate when they die or move on.

● Appointed leader, whose position is legitimised by virtue of the fact that they have gone through a selection, assessment and appointment process in accordance with the wishes and demands of the organisation and the expectations of those who will now be working for them. This invariably carries a defined and formalised managerial role in organisations.

● Bureaucratic leaders, whose position is legitimised by the rank that they hold. This is especially true of military structures and is reinforced by the job titles used and their known position in the hierarchy – corporal, captain, major, general. It is also to be found in more complex and sophisticated, commercial and public organisation structures. This also normally implies managerial responsibilities.

● Functional or expert leaders, whose position is secured by virtue of their expertise. This form of leadership is likely to be related to particular issues – for example, the industrial relations officer may be a junior functionary who, however, becomes the acknowledged leader, director and problem solver wherever industrial relations problems arise, and whatever the rank or status of other people involved.

● Informal leaders, whose position is established by virtue of their personality, charisma, expertise, command of resources, but not formally legitimised by rank, appointment or tradition. This position may also be arrived at by virtue

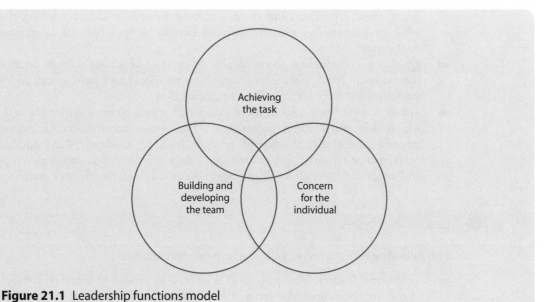

Figure 21.1 Leadership functions model

of some other activity for which they are particularly responsible – for example, local trade union representative.

- Charismatic leaders, whose position is secured by the sheer force of their personality. Many great world leaders (good or evil) have (or had) this – Napoleon, Adolf Hitler, Winston Churchill, Margaret Thatcher, John F. Kennedy. In the business world, charismatic leaders include Richard Branson (Virgin), Anita Roddick (Body Shop) and Michael O'Leary (Ryanair) (see Management in Focus 21.3).

Leadership styles

The rationale for studying management styles is that employees will work better for managers who use particular styles of leadership than they will for others who employ different styles (see Table 21.1 and Figure 21.2).

MANAGEMENT IN FOCUS 21.3

CHARISMA: IDENTITY – AND REJECTION

It is very easy for people to identify with someone who holds a position of influence and who has a strong, dominant or forceful personality:

- J.F. Kennedy based both his election campaign and the years of his Presidency on his personality – his charm, his freshness, his vitality, his appearance and looks – rather than his expertise and potential for running the country.
- Adolf Hitler had great personal presence with which he generated both pride and identity among the German nation of the 1920s and 1930s at a time of national bankruptcy.

- Margaret Thatcher fought the 1979 General Election in the UK, not on the basis of detailed and well analysed policies, but rather on the slogan 'I will make Britain great again'.

Identity can quickly turn to rejection:

- The USA has had great cultural and national problems in reconciling the glamour and the martyrdom of J.F. Kennedy with subsequent revelations about his private life, the activities of the rest of the Kennedy family, and possible Mafia connections.

- The entire civilised world has turned against Hitler and everything that he built following the brutality of the way in which his armies fought the Second World War and the great evil perpetrated in the concentration camps.
- The validity and extent of Margaret Thatcher's political legacy to the UK is coming under increasingly heavy scrutiny. Nearly 20 years after the end of her prime ministership however, it is still very difficult for some members of her political party to question or criticise the results that she delivered.

Table 21.1 Leadership and management styles

Autocratic (benevolent or tyrannical)	Consultative/participative	Democratic/participative
1. Leader makes all final decisions for the group.	1. Leader makes decisions after consultation with the group.	1. Decisions made by the group, by consultation or vote. Voting based on the principles of one person, one vote; majority rules.
2. Close supervision.	2. Total communication between leader and members.	2. All members bound by the group decision and support it.
3. Individual member's interests subordinate to those of the organisation.	3. Leader is supportive and developmental.	3. All members may contribute to discussion.
4. Subordinates treated without regard for their views.	4. Leader is accessible and discursive.	4. Development of coalitions and cliques.
5. Great demands placed on staff.	5. Questioning approach encouraged.	5. Leadership role is assumed by chair.
6. Questioning discouraged.	6. Ways of working largely unspecified.	
7. Conformist/coercive environment.	7. Leader retains responsibility and accountability for results.	

There are caveats however. Any management style must be supported by mutual trust, respect and confidence existing between manager and subordinates. If these qualities are not present then no style is effective. There must be a clarity of purpose and direction in the first place – and this must come from the organisation. Participation can only genuinely exist if this clarity exists also – it cannot exist in a void. Leadership and management styles must also be suitable and effective in terms of cultural and environmental pressures, as well as personal, professional and occupational acceptability.

These factors are interrelated (see Figure 21.2). Account must also be taken of the fact that where a leadership style is to be truly democratic, the decisions and wishes of the group must be accommodated, whatever is decided and whether this is 'right' or 'wrong' in terms of the demands of the work and the pressures of the wider environment (see Management in Focus 21.4).

Blake and Mouton (1986): The Managerial Grid

The managerial grid is a configuration of management styles based on the matching of two dimensions of managerial concern – those of 'concern for people' and 'concern for production/output'. Each of these dimensions is plotted on a nine-point graph scale and an assessment made of the managerial style according to where they come out on each (see Figure 21.3). Thus, a low score (1–1) on each axis reflects poverty in managerial style; a high score (9–9) on each reflects a high degree of balance, concern and commitment in each area. The implication from this is that an adequate, effective and successful managerial style is in place.

The 9–9 score is indicated as the ideal by Blake and Mouton; it reflects a desired position of equal concern for people and task, and the need for continuous improvement.

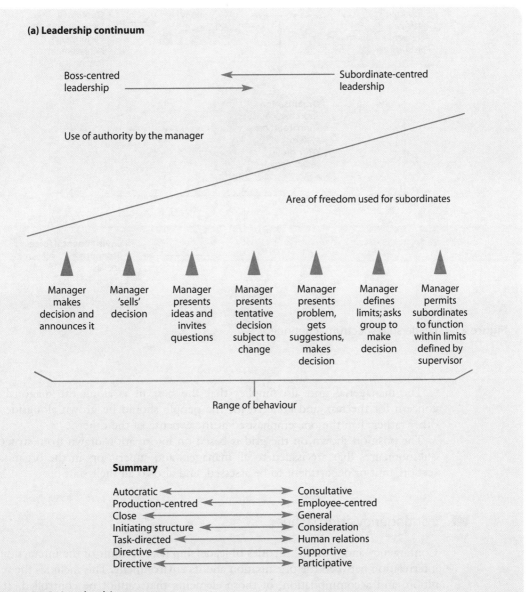

(a) **Leadership continuum**

Boss-centred leadership ⟶ ⟵ Subordinate-centred leadership

Use of authority by the manager

Area of freedom used for subordinates

| Manager makes decision and announces it | Manager 'sells' decision | Manager presents ideas and invites questions | Manager presents tentative decision subject to change | Manager presents problem, gets suggestions, makes decision | Manager defines limits; asks group to make decision | Manager permits subordinates to function within limits defined by supervisor |

Range of behaviour

Summary

Autocratic ⟷ Consultative
Production-centred ⟷ Employee-centred
Close ⟷ General
Initiating structure ⟷ Consideration
Task-directed ⟷ Human relations
Directive ⟷ Supportive
Directive ⟷ Participative

Figure 21.2 Leadership spectrum

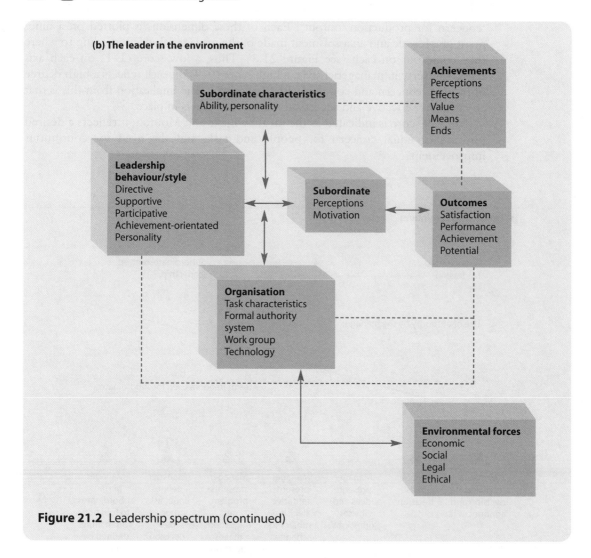

(b) The leader in the environment

Subordinate characteristics
Ability, personality

Achievements
Perceptions
Effects
Value
Means
Ends

Leadership behaviour/style
Directive
Supportive
Participative
Achievement-orientated
Personality

Subordinate
Perceptions
Motivation

Outcomes
Satisfaction
Performance
Achievement
Potential

Organisation
Task characteristics
Formal authority
system
Work group
Technology

Environmental forces
Economic
Social
Legal
Ethical

Figure 21.2 Leadership spectrum (continued)

The managerial grid also implies that the best fit is along the diagonal line: concern for the task and concern for the people should be grown alongside each other rather than the one emphasised at the expense of the other.

The position shown on the grid is based on information drawn from structured questionnaires that are issued to all managers and supervisors in the organisation section, unit or department to be assessed, and also to all their staff.

Contingency approaches

Contingency and 'best fit' theories of leadership take account of the interaction and interrelation between the organisation and its environment. This includes the recognition, and accommodation, of those elements that cannot be controlled. It also involves recognising that those elements that can be controlled and influenced must

MANAGEMENT IN FOCUS 21.4

LEADERSHIP STYLE: A MILITARY EXAMPLE

'You cannot expect a soldier to be a proud soldier if you humiliate him. You cannot expect him to be brave if you abuse him. You cannot expect him to be strong if you break him. You cannot ask for respect and obedience and willingness to assault hot landing zones, hump back-breaking ridges, destroy dug-in emplacements if your soldier has not been treated with respect and dignity which fosters unit and personal pride. The line between firmness and harshness, between strong leadership and bullying is a fine line. It is difficult to define, but those in authority who have accepted a career as a leader of men must find that line. It is because judgement and concern for people and human relations are involved in leadership that only people can lead and not machines. I entreat you to be ever-alert to the pitfalls of too much authority. Beware that you do not fall into the category of a little man, with a little job, with a big head. In essence, be considerate, treat you subordinates right and they will literally die for you'.

Source: General Melvin Zais: quoted in Peters and Austin: *A Passion for Excellence*, Harper and Row (1986).

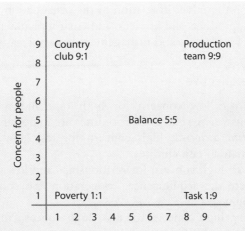

Other styles identified are:

- **9-1**: the country club: production is incidental; concern for the staff and people is everything; the group exists largely to support itself
- **1-9**: task orientation: production is everything; concern for the staff is subordinated to production and effectiveness. Staff management mainly takes the form of planning and control activities in support of production and output. Organisational activity and priority is concerned only with output.
- **5-5**: balance: a medium degree of expertise, commitment and concern in both areas; this is likely to produce adequate or satisfactory performance from groups that are reasonably well satisfied with working relations.

Figure 21.3 The managerial grid

be addressed in ways that vary in different situations: that the correct approach in one case is not a prescription to be applied to others. There is a constant interaction between the leader's job and the work to be done; and between this and the general operations of the organisation in question. It is also necessary to vary the leadership style according to the changing nature of the situation.

Fiedler (1961) used the contingency approach to identify situations where directive and prescriptive styles of leadership and management worked effectively. Directive and prescriptive styles could be engaged where the overall situation was very favourable to the leader; where the leader was liked, respected and trusted by the group. Tasks needed to be clearly understood, easy to follow and well defined. The leader needed to have a high degree of influence over group members in terms of reward and punishment. Additionally, the leader had to enjoy unqualified support from the organisation.

Directive and prescriptive styles of leadership and management were also effective from the point of view of achieving results where the situation was unfavourable to the leader. Where leaders were disliked, distrusted and disrespected by the group, where they had low degrees of influence over rewards and punishments, and where the leader did not always enjoy the full backing of the organisation, concentration on tasks and outputs, together with a knowledge and understanding of the nature of leadership, meant that standard and understood levels of achievement were possible.

Reddin (1968) developed the contingency approach by identifying dimensions of appropriateness and effectiveness on the one hand, and inappropriateness and ineffectiveness, on the other, in relation to the organisation, nature and composition of work groups, products and services, and environmental pressures. Reddin presented a spectrum of leadership and management behaviour as shown in Figure 21.4.

Appropriate, effective

- *Bureaucrat*: low concern for both task and relationships; appropriate in situations where rules and procedures are important.
- *Benevolent autocrat*: high concern for task, low concern for relationships; appropriate in task cultures.
- *Developer*: high concern for relationships and low concern for tasks; appropriate where the acquiescence, cooperation and commitment of the people is paramount.
- *Executive*: high concern for task, high concern for relationships; appropriate where the achievement of high standards is dependent on high levels of motivation and commitment.

Inappropriate, ineffective

- *Deserter*: low concern for both task and relationships; the manager lacks involvement and is either passive or negative.
- *Autocrat*: high concern for task, low concern for relationships; the manager is coercive, confrontational, adversarial, lacking confidence in others.
- *Missionary*: high concern for relationships, low concern for task; the manager's position is dependent on preserving harmony and there is often a high potential for conflict.

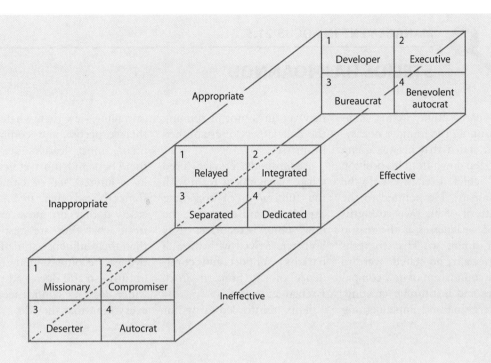

Purpose: The middle set of boxes identifies the four archetype leaders of Reddin's theory. These archetypes may then be translated into *appropriate, effective* or *inappropriate, ineffective* personal types.

Figure 21.4 W. Reddin: leadership and management behaviour

● *Compromiser*: high concern for both tasks and relationships; manager is a poor decision maker, expedient, concerned only with the short term.

The contingency and best fit approaches to leadership draw attention to the specific requirement and priority to be effective in the given organisation, environment, and present and evolving set of circumstances, as well as drawing attention to the critical need for an effective style. The question therefore arises as to whether or not individual leaders are capable of varying their style in response to demands, or whether it is necessary to appoint leaders with particular styles at which they are expert, according to the precise nature of circumstances and demands (see Management in Focus 21.5).

The consequence is that leadership is therefore in turn itself becoming more specialised and compartmentalised. In this context, it is usual to identify different types of leader, and the balance of their expertise and effectiveness, as follows:

● *Pioneer*: pioneers and pioneering leaders establish and create new products, services, brands, ventures and markets. Pioneers have a clear vision of what is possible, and through their commitment, energy, enthusiasm and ambition, they use their expertise to create and energise whatever is proposed, and see it into existence, effectiveness and profitability. Pioneers may however become ineffective once a particular venture is established, secured and viable.

MANAGEMENT IN FOCUS 21.5

STELIOS HAJI-IOANNOU

In early 2005 Stelios Haji-Ioannou, the founder of easy-Jet, stated that he was going to step down from his position of chief executive of the company. He pointed to the pattern of his own strengths and weaknesses as the reason for doing so. His strengths especially, he stated, were in the foundation of new companies and instituting, creating, energising and implementing new ventures, not in running the daily affairs of established businesses.

Accordingly, easyJet hired a top management team with the full range of corporate experience and expertise; the new chief executive, Ray Webster, arrived with the full backing, support and confidence of the London Stock Exchange.

This reinforced a major prevailing view that, whatever their expertise and commitment, most leaders are at their best and most effective in a limited set of circumstances; and that in many cases, if they do move away from what they are best at, then their influence and effectiveness become diluted. This in turn can and does lead to a wider loss of confidence in everything that they do.

- *Transformational*: transformational leaders undertake major initiatives and ventures on behalf of organisations that require 'transforming' in some way. Often appointed purely to see the particular initiative through, transformational leaders must be able to assimilate and become authoritative, comfortable and familiar in a new organisational setting very quickly and effectively.
- *Second in command*: all organisations need a 'second in command', a deputy CEO: someone to take the place of the overall leader whenever he or she is not present for any reason, and to act as a sounding board, confidant, reflector and analyst at top organisational levels. The second in command has to have strength of character and expertise in order to be able to debate, argue – and disagree when necessary – with people who are more senior; and additionally to deliver that own expertise in ways credible and acceptable to powerful and expert personalities (see Management in Focus 21.6).
- *Corporate*: corporate leaders are appointed to serve the interests of primary and dominant stakeholders; and this normally means the shareholders and their representatives. Problems arise when the returns to shareholders are not made for some reason. Problems additionally arise when someone who has been successful in one industry or company, and is engaged on that basis, subsequently encounters problems in the new organisation.
- *Strategic*: strategic leaders are engaged because of their capability in seeing and envisioning the direction that a company or organisation ought to take over the medium to long term. The key need for strategic leaders is the ability to engage the quality and standing of expertise required to translate the vision and strategy into action and achievement.
- *Operational*: operational leaders are those who provide clear leadership and direction to those who work for them, when working to a clear remit given to

MANAGEMENT IN FOCUS 21.6

FROM NUMBER TWO TO NUMBER ONE

There are sufficient examples of where an excellent deputy has not made the transition successfully to the top job to draw attention to the differences between the two.

The person in charge is ultimately accountable to all stakeholders, and responsible for delivering the results desired and demanded. This is very different from acting as a sounding board during the process of ensuring that the results are delivered, or from ensuring that conditions are being met for entering into a specific venture, or range of products and services.

The person in charge is the standard bearer and point of identity of the company or organisation; and the deputy is not. Anyone who moves up from second to first has to create an identity and focus for themselves, in exactly the same way as someone who is appointed from outside the organisation.

Many deputies use their elevation and new position to introduce pet schemes, projects and ventures that they have nurtured under the previous regime but which have so far been rejected. Such schemes and ventures require the same degree of rigour and evaluation as under the previous regime.

Many former deputies fail to appoint an adequate deputy of their own; this results in not having the capabilities and character close by, as confidant, sounding board and evaluator, that the new number one used to provide so effectively.

Many former deputies know, believe or perceive that they are themselves on trial, under pressure to deliver early and high-profile results. Everything then becomes concentrated on producing a triumph, whether or not this is in the longer-term best interests of the organisation and its stakeholders.

them by the organisation. The best operational leaders do not normally make fully effective pioneers or creators. Indeed, to be effective in a Chair or CEO role, corporate leaders normally have to have been given a clear remit or set of targets or directions by those who appointed them, especially shareholders.

- *Problem solver and crisis leader*: problem solvers and crisis leaders are appointed to get an organisation out of a mess. Problems and crises may relate to stock market, product or service performance; or to scandals, negligence or incompetence. The key here is the ability to master the brief, and additionally to be able to address and resolve the particular problem, while at the same time restoring morale and reputation. The organisation has to be left strengthened by the actions of the leader in this context; it is no use solving one problem but leaving others (see Management in Focus 21.7).

Complexities of leadership

All of the above indicates a range of complexities in the whole field of leadership. Understanding the complexities of leadership therefore in turn requires full consideration of *assumptions* and *roles*.

MANAGEMENT IN FOCUS 21.7

FRANK LORENZO: CRISIS LEADER OR HATCHET MAN?

For very many years, Frank Lorenzo enjoyed a great reputation as a labour and employee relations troubleshooter. He would be hired by companies at times of staffing crises to come in and sort the matters out.

Frank Lorenzo built this reputation on, above all, handling strikes and labour disputes in the airline industry. He handled major crises at Eastern Airlines and Braniff, the internal and international US carriers. He would identify where the sources of power and influence lay on the employees' side; and he would then set out with the specific intention of targeting the key figures involved. The purpose of this was to break the power and influence of the unions and staff representative bodies involved.

His approach was based on crisis leadership through a direct and often aggressive approach to the problems described to him by the company; and this invariably meant seeking out and confronting the most powerful and influential individuals and groups on the staff side.

In terms of handling the given crisis, Frank Lorenzo normally succeeded. However, the legacy left behind invariably caused enduring operational as well as labour relations problems. As the result of his actions, Eastern went bankrupt – and Braniff went bankrupt twice. To his death, however, Frank Lorenzo remained the crisis leader of choice in much of corporate USA.

Assumptions

Leaders act in the name of the particular organisation, department or function. They therefore have a degree of power, influence, authority, responsibility and accountability. This is to be used in the pursuit of effective leadership performance. It may be enhanced, diminished or withdrawn by the organisation at any time (in Western organisations, this is usually but not always as the result of some form of consultation or appraisal of performance).

Leaders must be acceptable to all those with whom they come into contact. This applies both inside and outside the organisation. The range and complexity of relationships that they must develop are dependent on this.

Leaders have clearly defined tasks, activities and functions. The effectiveness of leaders is dependent additionally upon their qualities of flexibility, dynamism and responsiveness; and their honesty, trustworthiness and integrity, as explained above.

Leaders must have a working knowledge and understanding of the tasks being carried out by everyone for whom they are responsible. This does not mean being a technical expert; it does mean knowing and understanding in full detail the pressures under which every member of staff is operating, and every task that has to be carried out. For example, managers who have secretaries cannot always type, but they must understand what typing is, how long it takes, what is an acceptable level of performance, what is an acceptable level of presentation, what is the best and most suitable machinery on which typing is to take place – and so on; this extends to all spheres of activity. Where there is no such understanding dysfunction always occurs (see Management in Focus 21.8).

MANAGEMENT IN FOCUS 21.8

NEW APPOINTMENTS

Whenever anyone is appointed to a position of leadership, authority or responsibility, their first priority must be to become as familiar as possible, as quickly as possible, with the staff, activities and the operating environment. This should always form the basis of leadership and managerial induction programmes, and it ought also to form a key part of management training and development schemes.

This approach additionally gives an early opportunity for those freshly appointed to begin to develop wider relationships within the organisation, and to know and understand how particular operating pressures interact with each other to produce effective performance.

Leadership roles

The main leadership roles are as follows.

- *Figurehead*: the leader acts as the human face of the department, division or organisation to the rest of the world. For senior managers, politicians, public figures and other charismatic leaders, this is straightforward, and the effect is often enhanced by stage management and presentation techniques (see Management in Focus 21.9).

MANAGEMENT IN FOCUS 21.9

LESSONS FROM THE NAZI ERA

Nobody would ever have heard of Adolf Hitler if he had not managed to secure the backing of the German military establishment and civil service, and the endorsement of the then Chancellor of Germany, Hindenburg. This backing had been achieved and secured through the presentational expertise of Josef Goebbels, a propaganda and publishing expert. It was further developed when the rising Nazi party was able to secure the services of Leni Riefenstahl, a German film director, who made 'Triumph of the Will' about the 1934 Nuremberg rally. Between them, the propagandist and film director were able to refine and deliver the Nazi vision of Germany in ways that no other politician had so far achieved, and in a format that would be favourably received by the mass population.

When war broke out in 1939, the UK Prime Minister was Neville Chamberlain. He resigned in 1940 to be replaced by Winston Churchill. Churchill quickly realised that his own vision and utter dedication would not be enough. He accordingly spent extensive periods of time learning voice projection and the art of being filmed in particular situations. A Pathé news crew was with him at all times. Newsreel films were shown in all cinemas throughout the country. Churchill's radio broadcasts were put out at times when it was known that there would be mass audiences available, and when they were unlikely to be disrupted by bombing.

At departmental, divisional and functional level, managers and supervisors act as figureheads in dealings with others. This requires attention both to the merits of particular cases or arguments, and the effectiveness of presentation and delivery. The key to being an effective departmental or divisional figurehead is extensive preparation, and the development of high-quality communication skills.

● *Ambassador*: leaders act as advocate, cheerleader and problem solver on behalf of their department, division, organisation and staff. Again, for high profile public leaders this is straightforward (see Management in Focus 21.10).

Every high profile public figure playing this role requires expert briefing and preparation, as well as sound knowledge and understanding of the particular situation into which they are going. This must also apply to organisation, departmental and divisional supervisors and managers when they have to carry out these functions.

● *Servant*: this view of leadership and management is based on the premise that the manager is the ultimate supporter or servant of staff, product and service output and quality, and markets, customers and clients (see Figure 21.5).

MANAGEMENT IN FOCUS 21.10

LESSONS FROM LEADERS IN THE TWENTY-FIRST CENTURY

● *Stelios Haji-Ioannou (easyJet)*: Stelios Hadj-Ioannou normally appears in public upon request. Whether this is to address specific problems or complaints about the easyJet airline, or to offer opinions about other things, he takes the view that this enhances the profile and reputation of his company. Since 1999, his company has featured in the television documentary series *Airline*. The series is so popular with viewers that it continues to run to this day.

● *Richard Branson (Virgin)*: Richard Branson has had to counter adverse criticisms of the quality of some of his activities – especially railways and financial services. On each of these occasions, he uses the media to acknowledge the problems, to gain general positive publicity for the Virgin Group – and to act as the company's general cheerleader.

● *Anita Roddick (Body Shop)*: Anita Roddick was forced to take an active part in educating the stock market when both brokers and media analysts failed to understand the basic business premise of the Body Shop – long-term security and viability (and therefore owner value), rather than short-term share price advantage.

Each of these examples illustrates the point of view from which the ambassadorial role may be seen. In each of these cases, the contribution is positive, addressing the specific issues as well as enhancing general profile and value.

The manager or supervisor is placed at the bottom point, prima facie supporting and serving the workforce rather than sitting on top of it.

Figure 21.5 The inverse pyramid

- Maintenance: this role requires:
  - daily maintenance: attending to problems and issues as they arise
  - preventative maintenance: continuous improvement of the work, working environment, and procedures and practices, and attending to staff development; also
  - breakdown maintenance: handling crises, blow-ups and storms in a quick and effective manner.
- *Role model*: leaders, managers and supervisors set the style, standards, attitudes and behaviour for those who work for them. If leaders show qualities of commitment, enthusiasm, energy and honesty, these may be expected and are likely to arise in subordinates (see Management in Focus 21.11).

MANAGEMENT IN FOCUS 21.11

DISASTERS AND THE MODEL OF LEADERSHIP

In 1987 the *Herald of Free Enterprise*, a car and passenger ferry operating between the ports of Dover, Calais and Zeebrugge sank outside Zeebrugge harbour, Belgium, with the loss of 200 lives. The cause of the disaster was water rushing in through the bow doors, which had been jammed open and had not closed before the ship put to sea. The inquiry into the tragedy described the ship's owners, Townsend Thoresen, as a company 'riddled with the disease of sloppiness'. Nobody had thought it important enough to check or ensure that the doors were closed before the ship set sail. The report of the subsequent inquiry stated clearly that staff had behaved in ways that they thought were expected of them by the organisation's top managers, and as they thought that those managers would behave if they themselves had been faced with the crisis.

● *Ringmaster*: in their own particular spheres, all managers and supervisors are ringmasters. This is quite apart from any particular knowledge or aptitude for the task in hand.

The role elements indicated here are essential to successful and effective leadership and direction at whatever level. The individual who is to be an effective leader has an overwhelming responsibility to adopt these roles and the responsibilities inherent within them. It is also incumbent upon the person concerned to develop any of the qualities required in which he or she is not proficient.

● Measures of success and failure

The performance of those in leadership positions is assessed in simple terms against whether or not they delivered what they set out to achieve, and the reasons for that. The broader approach to the assessment of performance of those in leadership positions relates to the key questions of confidence and complexity.

Confidence

Those who appoint others to leadership and managerial positions are normally confident at the outset that they have got the right person for the job; and following appointment, the development of mutual confidence is essential. Once those in leadership and managerial positions have lost the confidence of the people who appointed them, they normally leave.

For example, the CEO of a publicly quoted company must maintain the confidence of the world's stock markets, or else the share price falls. If this cannot be reversed and the share price continues to fall despite the activities and directions proposed by the CEO in question, that person will normally leave. This may also occur as the result of a bad set of company figures, either for a period or on a more continuous and long-term basis.

Confidence may also be lost among other backers and stakeholders. The leader in question may lose the respect and regard of the staff – as the result of some dishonest, expedient or unjustifiably punitive action for example.

Leaders may lose the confidence of the markets in which business is conducted. This occurs for example, if a product is launched during their tenure that subsequently fails commercially, has a bad image or which is shown to be unsafe or dangerous.

The converse of this is 'leaving a void'. This is where the confidence and identity of the organisation are fully integrated with the leader. Any question of the leader departing is therefore viewed with great alarm. For example, commentaries on the Virgin Group always include questions about 'What happens to the organisation if anything happens to Richard Branson?'

Confidence is only maintained through honesty and integrity. Where the leader (of anything) is caught lying, the clear, instant and unambiguous message given out is that 'He/she is a liar.' Any subsequent dealing or transaction with such individuals is therefore invariably prefixed by questions about the extent to which they may be trusted. This is in turn exacerbated during briefings for those who are to be involved with them along the lines of 'Don't believe a word they say' and 'Get something in writing and get their signature.'

Complexity

Measures of success and failure will also address the question of what else was achieved during a particular period of office. The direction taken may have opened up a great range of subsequent opportunities, and a part of the assessment will relate to the extent to which these were exploited.

This is also to be seen in the complexity indicated. The hard targets may be achieved for example, but only at the expense of the soft – the destruction of staff relations, motivation and morale. Conversely a superbly integrated and supportive group may be built but never actually produce anything of substance. The targets that were set may turn out to have been unmeasurable, hopelessly optimistic or far too easy. In the latter case in particular, it is both easy and dangerous to indulge in an entirely false sense of success.

The legitimacy of the objectives and performance targets must also be generally and constantly questioned. To return to the hard examples quoted above – claims about increases in output, profit and cost effectiveness by x per cent should always be treated with scepticism. They assume that the basis on which the percentage is calculated is legitimate and valid. They assume that this constitutes the best use of organisation resources. They assume (this especially applies to public services) that adequate and effective activity levels can be maintained.

It should be clear from this that the setting of organisation performance targets is a process capable of rationalisation and must be founded on the understanding of general organisation requirements. In the particular context of leadership, it should be clear also that ultimate responsibility for success or failure in achieving these targets rests with the leader.

It is also clear that leaders are made and not born. People can be trained in each of the qualities and elements indicated so that (as with anything else) they may first understand, then apply, then reinforce and finally become expert in the activities indicated. This is to be understood on the same basis as aptitude for anything else however. Not everyone has the qualities or potential necessary in the first place. There is nothing contentious in this – not everyone has the qualities or potential to be a great chef, racing driver, nurse or labourer, and in this respect leadership is no different.

● Conclusions

In business, commercial and public service sector organisations, leadership is that part of management that provides the vision, direction and energy that gives life to policy, strategy and operations. It provides everyone involved – above all, the staff, but also suppliers, customers and community groups – with a point of identity and focus, a personification of the organisation with which they themselves are involved or with which they are dealing. Problems always occur when the leader, for whatever reason, is either unwilling or unable to accept the full responsibilities of the position. These problems are compounded when it becomes known, believed or perceived that the leader is acting without integrity, and is seeking to blame either circumstances or other people for organisational, strategic and operational shortcomings. In these cases, staff only remain in employment so long as they believe it is in their interests to do so; this invariably leads to the early loss of high-quality staff. Problems also arise when leaders accept their responsibilities to one group of stakeholders in preference to others – this is a serious problem in large public and multinational corporations when senior managers discharge their responsibilities to shareholders, political interests, and the drives of boards of directors and governors, at the expense of staff, suppliers, customers and clients.

Those who aspire to leadership positions must therefore be prepared to accept that there are certain qualities that go with the job – above all, enthusiasm, ambition, clarity of purpose, energy and direction – and must be prepared to develop these as the condition of employment in these positions. It is also important to recognise that this part of management development cannot be achieved except through a period of long-term, prioritised, intensive and demanding training, supported with periods of further education undertaken either at a university or through the private sector. It is impossible to develop leaders purely on the basis of single or isolated short periods of training, unsupported by activities at the workplace. Moreover, it must be stressed again that the best practitioners of a particular trade, profession or occupation do not necessarily make the best leaders and managers of groups in those fields; assessment for leadership and management potential must be carried out on the basis of the ability to observe the fledgling qualities required, rather than existing professional and technical expertise.

It is clear that this part of management development is going to become very much more important in the future. Organisations are certain to value much more highly the all-round capabilities and willingness to accept responsibility on those whom they place in top positions. In the medium to long term, the ability to satisfy dominant shareholder or political interests is certain not to be enough.

CRITICAL THINKING, ANALYSIS AND EVALUATION

1. What are the key attributes of a good leader? Give examples that illustrate these. To what extent can an effective leader lead in any organisation or situation? To what extent is their effectiveness limited by the constraints in which they find themselves?

2. To what extent may the last three UK Prime Ministers be considered successful? Identify the criteria and means by which they are judged and state whether or not you think these are valid and reliable.

3. What is the role of organisational leadership in a crisis or disaster?

4. Devise a leadership training programme for junior managers and supervisors with aspirations to become more senior. This should be of 6–12 months duration. It should indicate aims and objectives, content, learning methods and the means by which success/failure would be judged and evaluated.

DEVELOPING MANAGEMENT SKILLS AND EXPERTISE

THE ANNANDALE WATER COMPANY

After several years of extremely profitable activity, decisions are needed on the future direction of Annandale Water Ltd, a company located at Annandale, just north of Carlisle, inside the Scottish borders. It has its own springs from which it takes both its name and its main product: an exclusive, highly branded bottled water, Annandale Natural Mineral Water. This is bottled in distinctive green (still) and royal blue (sparkling) bottles. It is sold as a luxury and exclusive item to the following main markets:

- the weddings industry at Gretna, which is only six miles away, and which forms 40 per cent of turnover
- two exclusive City of London catering companies, which use Annandale for their very top clients, and form 25 per cent of turnover
- direct sales from the bottling plant at Annandale, which accounts for 10 per cent of turnover
- Harrods and Fortnum and Mason in London, which take the rest between them (25 per cent of turnover).

However, while turnover has risen at an average 10 per cent per annum for the past five years, profit margins have sharply and suddenly declined. Last year, on a turnover of £30 million, profits were down to £700,000; the previous year, on turnover of £28.2 million, profits were exactly £2 million.

The company employs 80 staff – 40 on bottling, packaging, quality assurance and the visitor centre; 25 on sales and client and customer liaison and support; and 15 on transport. It has a fleet of ten 40-ton articulated trucks, 15 smaller delivery vans, and 17 cars for speedy and responsive deliveries.

The company makes three deliveries per week to London, and also operates a policy of 'instant response' to special requests from Harrods, Fortnum and Mason, and the catering companies.

There is a board of six directors and a chief executive, and an administration and finance staff of five. All of the staff are based at Annandale.

The company has recently called in consultants to study the problem. The consultants conducted a SWOT analysis, and their findings were as follows:

- Strengths: exclusive image, distinctive appearance, good reputation, reliable service, strong local market.
- Weaknesses: transport costs to other markets, vagaries of the motorway network, problems with the railways, unpredictability of the passing trade, loss of Harrods' royal seal.
- Opportunities: further promotions in Scottish markets, further inroads into other perceived exclusive outlets.
- Threats: declining profit margins, clearly indicated increased distribution costs, competition from other bottlers, increased quality available at supermarkets.

In addition to this, one member of the team of consultants suggested going into supermarket supply as a way of extending the product reach. This suggestion was rejected out of hand by the board of directors, because they did not want to destroy their exclusive image. However, this did at least lead to further considerations of what other lines the company could go into. Some of the suggestions that they came up with were:

- diversification into the supply of other luxury goods, including shortbreads, cheeses, hams, and branded Scottish clothing
- starting local home-delivery services in the immediate area around Annandale and the Scottish borders
- extending the bottled water range, to include a selection of 'hints of' products (i.e. bottled water that has a 'hint of' orange, lemon, grapefruit etc.)
- developing relations with tour operators to try to establish a more secure turnover base from visitors to the company
- cutting costs through reducing the transport fleet and frequency of deliveries to London.

The company directors discuss these and other ideas at some length, without coming to any conclusions. They then turn to the company CEO, Martin Court, for his opinions.

Questions

1. Where do the key leadership responsibilities lie in this case?
2. What are the options open to the company; and what part should Martin Court play in deciding which options to accept, and which to reject?
3. What other factors need to be taken into account when moving on from the present position?

The Body Shop

The culture of The Body Shop has always been strong, positive, passionate and inclusive. From the outset, the core value of the company was to keep any damage to the environment to an absolute minimum, and to recycle anything and everything if at all possible. In the early stages of the company's existence, the staff would sell their own clothes if the customers wanted to buy them.

To date, there has been no significant cultural shift from this position and from the company's values. However, as The Body Shop expanded, it became necessary to employ managers in the shops and for different functions. The question became one of maintaining the strength of culture, while at the same time ensuring that the company remained commercially viable. Anita Roddick states:

> With managers in place running the shops, I wanted to know more about the industry. I thought I could learn from the big boys in the business, so I bought all the trade magazines and started going to conferences and presentations given by people like Revlon and Estée Lauder, always sitting at the back in the hope that I would not be noticed. But what they were selling, and the ways they were selling it, was the antithesis of my own beliefs, and it did not take them long to realise that I was an alien. I did not speak the same language as these people, I did not even look like them – all the other women were in silk and furs while I was in jeans. It seemed to me that there was not a single truly creative spark to be found in the cosmetics industry, and that the real creativity came from the perfume houses. They were the gentlemen of the industry; the others were the cowboys who simply provided the vehicles to sell perfumes. So I switched my curiosity, visited the perfume houses, talked to the perfumiers, and learned from them. I loved the fact that many of them were small family businesses with a long history and their own culture, and that the skill of testing fragrances through smell had been handed down through generations.
>
> My favourite perfume shop was Culpepers, the herbalists. I thought their stores were dreamy with a wonderful sense of style, a great smell and terrific presentation. The Body Shops were rag-bags by comparison, we didn't look as if we knew one herb from another. I also envied the fact that Culpepers had the best sites in every town.
>
> I think what really separated us from stores like Culpepers during our gestation period was our burning enthusiasm. There was a tangible sense of euphoria in every Body Shop. Maybe we were amateurs and maybe we did not look serious, but we were mad keen and excited by what was going on and we were changing constantly – we just love change.

It took time for us to develop a distinctive style and identity: we weren't even sure if we would end up selling skin and hair care products. It was certainly what we wanted to do; but on some trading days, as much as 60 per cent of our turnover came from sundries and nick-nacks. The certainty and confidence that we could survive by selling our own products only came later.

Sources: A. Roddick (1992) *Body and Soul: The Body Shop Story*, Ebury Press; www.anitaroddick.net; www.thebodyshop.com.

Questions

1. Identify the basis of The Body Shop culture; from this, identify the key lessons that need to be learned by managers in all organisations.
2. How is it possible to maintain positive and collective culture and shared values when expanding into different countries of the world?
3. Identify the key areas of The Body Shop in which communications have to be successful and effective. What obligations does this place upon the present management of The Body Shop?
4. Where do the key priorities for human resource management for The Body Shop lie on the basis of what is stated above?

Part four

Management
in action

●　Introduction

The clear drive for the future in organisational practice is towards the employment of fewer and much more expert managers; this is because most organisations simply cannot afford the overheads and other expenses involved in employing complex chains of supervision, communication and administration, as well as management.

If this is to be the case, then managers are going to need environmental, strategic and organisational behaviour expertise, as already covered. They are also going to have to be capable of exercising the authority, responsibility and influence that are certain to come with fewer managerial positions and consequently greater autonomy. Increasingly therefore, managers in all positions within organisations are going to have to be leaders. This involves taking, accepting and discharging responsibility for the performance and standards in their own sphere of activities without recourse to the support systems that hierarchies and complex structures provide – and without the dilution and dissipation of responsibility and accountability that very often occur as the result of the presence and operation of such hierarchies.

If there is to be a much greater concentration on the leadership aspects of management, then some key leadership roles and priorities have also to be discharged. The ability to motivate and energise, to maximise and optimise output and commitment, both immediately and for the future, in the face of declining resource levels, is a primary capability. So is the ability to create, energise, harmonise and make productive work teams and work groups; and this is increasingly going to require the capability to integrate those who come from different locations, nationalities and ethnic groups (see 'Managing diversity' in Chapter 20). The other key aspect is the physical presence required of those in genuine positions of leadership; historically this can be contrasted with remote, distant and absent styles of bureaucratic and process-orientated management.

Those in leadership and management positions therefore need to develop their own form of presence and presentation. Peters and Waterman (1982) refer to this as 'managing by walking about', and the advantages of being physically present and the disadvantages of not having a presence still hold good. Where there is regular physical presence and access, problems can to be spotted earlier and dealt with before they become serious. Managers retain and develop current and continuous first-hand knowledge and understanding of what is going on at the frontline of activities. A much greater mutual confidence and cohesion is generated between workforce and managers or leaders, who become much more approachable on any matter at all. It also makes it much easier to get to the roots of conflict, arguments and disputes, and again, to resolve these before they get out of hand.

This part of management has to be delivered in relation to everything so far covered. Effective management in action requires all of the knowledge, understanding and expertise indicated in Part 1; strategic capability, and the marketing, financial, product and service knowledge and understanding indicated in Part 2; and the knowledge, understanding and expertise in collective and individual human behaviour addressed in Part 3. In particular, those in leadership positions must have all of this knowledge, understanding and expertise in its broadest context so as to be able to deliver the results required, and discharge their specific responsibilities.

Chapter twenty two

Management, influence, power and authority

'With power comes responsibility.'
Charles de Gaulle, French President, 1945.

'Authority flows from those who know.'
Anon.

'In a time of turbulence and change, it is more true than ever that knowledge is power.'
J.F. Kennedy, US President, Inaugural Address, 1961.

Chapter outline

- Introduction
- Sources of power
- Centres of power in organisations
- Power and influence relationships (realpolitik)
- Hierarchy
- Delegation
- Conclusions

Chapter objectives

After studying this chapter, you should be able to:

- understand the sources of power that exist within organisations, and the responsibilities and consequences imposed on managers as a result

- recognise unacceptable use of power and authority, and take steps to ensure that it is nipped in the bud as soon as it becomes apparent

- recognise the necessity for effective managerial authority, and understand sources of this, and how it is built up

- recognise the potential for power bases within organisations, and take steps to ensure that these are managed in the interests of all concerned, and of the organisation overall.

Introduction

Influence, power and authority are present in all organisations, and all managers have measures of influence, power and authority.

- Influence is exercised where a person, group or organisation changes the attitudes, values, behaviour, priorities and activities of others.
- Power is the capability to exercise influence in these ways.
- Authority is the legitimisation of the capability to exercise influence and the relationship by which this is exercised.

Influence, power and authority have responsibilities; those who wield influence, power and authority are normally accountable for their actions and results.

Power and influence are to be seen as positive and negative. The positive occurs where power and influence are used to energise, enhance and develop productive and profitable activities. The negative is where they are used to block or diminish activities, to limit the ability of others to succeed through the capability to restrict resources, money or information for example, or to bully, victimise and harass.

Influence, power and authority are themselves limited by organisational structures and methods of behaviour. Authority is normally given out for a limited range of activities or people only, and the extent of influence and the ability to wield power are therefore also limited. Authority also normally impersonalises – that is, someone who acts with authority does so in the name of the organisation and not in a personal capacity. The need to exercise authority will be founded on both personal and professional judgement; the actions carried out are in ways prescribed by the organisation.

Leaders and managers have to be able to exercise power, influence and authority in the best interests of everyone concerned, and to use responsibility based on integrity and judgement. Leaders and managers need to know and understand where the boundaries of their power, influence and authority actually lie, and where those boundaries ought to lie (see Management in Focus 22.1).

Sources of power

There is a range of sources of power and influence present in all organisations. These are as follows:

- *Physical and coercive power*: the power exerted by individuals because of their physical size and strength, the force of their personality, and their appearance. Physical and coercive power are used to dominate situations, influence the outcome of meetings and decisions. Large and dominant organisations exert their own equivalent of physical power in the pursuit of market or sector domination, in the ability to select their own preferred range of prices to determine the ways in which markets will operate, and in their ability to command staff expertise and resources. Physical power is also used by individuals to intimidate, bully and victimise others.
- *Traditional power*: whereby the ability to command influence derives from accepted customs and norms. Traditional power is present in the hereditary principle whereby the office or position is handed down from parent to child; for example, kings and queens and the aristocracy, family businesses, and (less

MANAGEMENT IN FOCUS 22.1

HARASSMENT AND INEQUALITY CLAIMS IN THE CITY OF LONDON

In recent years, there has been a large increase in the volume of claims made by employees working for top UK and international organisations in the city of London. The majority of these claims have come from women employees, and there have also been claims from members of ethnic minority groups.

These claims have been founded on facts, beliefs and perceptions that female members of staff and those from ethnic minorities have been treated unfairly in relation to their white male colleagues. This has led to accusations of refusal, on the grounds of gender and ethnic origin, to give opportunities, bonuses and rewards.

Where the authority of the organisation was clearly and firmly established, and managers were held actively accountable, few cases have come about. Where the cases have been settled in favour of those who brought them, managers and others awarding the bonuses apparently had the power to do as they pleased, without accepting any responsibility for the consequences. There was additionally a fear of reprisals from white male staff if they were not awarded bonuses when female staff and those from ethnic minorities were.

Each issue in this example illustrates some of the ways in which power, authority and influence are wielded. Those in positions of responsibility certainly had the choice to use their position to ensure that people were treated fairly. The organisations could also have supported this ethos. Instead, the overwhelming impression is that they chose to use their financial power to pay for the consequences of unfair approaches, rather than ensuring that they used their authority to give everyone a fair deal.

frequently at present than in previous times) in areas such as dock working where the child took the parent's job.

- *Expert power*: based on the expertise held by an individual or group and the demand for this from other parts of society. The power and influence that stems from highly prized expertise is dependent upon the volume and nature of demand, the location of the experts and their willingness to use their skill. Expertise comes in the form of professional and technical skills, knowledge, aptitudes, attributes and behaviour. It also includes situational and social knowledge.
- *Charismatic power*: charisma is the effect of one personality on others, the ability to exert influence through force of personality. It is also the ability to inspire high levels of confidence and identity among other people. Charisma is found in all parts of society, and all departments, divisions and functions in organisations. Hitler, Napoleon and John F. Kennedy all had charisma; iconic organisational figures such as Richard Branson and Anita Roddick have charisma based on the combination of their appearance, public presentation, and commitment to their organisations. Charismatic power and influence normally have to be manufactured. Those who have the power of personality

normally know and understand this; it is however essential that those people know and understand both the extent, and the limits of their charisma (see Management in Focus 22.2).

● *Resource power*: this is the ability to influence others through the command of resources. This may be beneficial and positive – the giving and allocating of resources to enable someone else to succeed, the result of which is a feeling of well being towards the resource giver. Or it may be negative, threatening or coercive, based on the ability to limit or cut off particular resources if the receiver does not behave in certain ways.

Resource power is closely related to *reward power*, which is the ability to influence behaviour and activities by offering rewards for compliance and acceptance. The extent of influence exerted in this way is dependent upon the nature and volume of rewards and the extent to which these meet the needs of

MANAGEMENT IN FOCUS 22.2

CHARISMATIC POWER: *THE DAY OF THE JACKAL*

Frederick Forsyth's best-selling novel *Day of the Jackal* begins with a vivid picture of the execution of Lieutenant Colonel Jean-Marie Bastien-Thiry on 11 March 1963.

Bastien-Thiry was a leading member of the OAS, the secret army organisation that opposed independence for Algeria, and conducted a savage civil war both in Algeria and against those in the French government who wished to give it up. To Bastien-Thiry, its loss would be 'even graver than that of Alsace-Lorraine', the provinces whose seizure by Germany in 1870 had been a major cause of the First World War.

Despite passionate resistance, De Gaulle pushed Algerian independence through after the referendum of 1 July 1962. Seven weeks later, as he was being driven with his wife in an unarmoured Citroen DS through a Paris suburb, the OAS opened up with machine guns, raking his car and the nearby cafe.

Bastien-Thiry was not at the scene, but was arrested on his return from a scientific mission to the United Kingdom. He was brought before a military tribunal on 28 January. During the trial, which lasted until March 4, he accused De Gaulle of genocide against the European population of Algeria, and compared himself with the German officers who had attempted to assassinate Hitler in 1944. He also claimed that he had not attempted to kill De Gaulle but merely to capture him for trial by the OAS. He and two others were condemned to death. The sentences on the others were commuted to life imprisonment, but not Bastien-Thiry's. The president gave four reasons: the colonel had ordered an attack on a car carrying an innocent woman; he had endangered nearby civilians; he had brought foreigners into the plot; finally, while prepared to spare those who had fired on him and put themselves in danger, the general would not forgive the man who directed events from a distant place of safety.

Forsyth recounts how, the night before his execution, the colonel assured his lawyers that he was perfectly safe. 'No squad of Frenchmen,' he laughed, 'will raise their rifles against me.'

But as Forsyth says, he was wrong. The self-proclaimed hero-patriot's last vision was a squad of Frenchmen preparing to raise their rifles.

those over whom influence is sought. The other side of this is the *power to punish*. Again, the extent of the influence exerted depends upon the nature of the punishment being threatened and whether this is felt to be important by those affected (see Management in Focus 22.3).

- *Legal, rational and position power*: this is the limitation, ordering and direction of power and influence in the name of organisations. This form of power is based on the setting of rules, procedures, regulations and norms for each job, role, department, division and sector, and for the individuals who carry out the work. It is based on certain principles:
  - the right and duty of organisations to establish what they consider to be the best ways of working
  - the managerial prerogative: the establishment of persons in positions of command, responsibility and accountability to ensure that these are put into practice
  - the willingness of subordinates to accept direction and the right of superiors to expect this
  - duties of care placed on organisations by legal, social and ethical pressures that means that they will seek to operate in efficient, effective and profitable ways without being punitive or coercive (see Management in Focus 22.4).

MANAGEMENT IN FOCUS 22.3

AUTHORITY AND IMPERSONALISATION: NAZI CONCENTRATION CAMPS 1935–45

The Nazi regime in Germany (1933–45) established concentration camps for the Thousand Year Reich. Originally conceived as a harsh and extreme penal regime, the concentration camps quickly had their roles expanded as follows:

- to house and re-educate dissidents and those who held views contrary to those of the establishment
- to house and hold hostage the families and friends of dissidents
- to remove undesirables (for example, homosex-

uals and the disabled) from society at large
- to exterminate inferior races and populations (Poles, Slavs, Gypsies, and above all Jews).

People were sent to camps for fixed periods or for life. A total of 300 camps were constructed and operated over the period. Most of the camp commandants and administrators were bureaucrats, civil servants working for ministries in certain locations and following career paths. The guards were either soldiers or members of the prison service.

All involved had power and influence over the lives of the inmates. Above all, they all had authority to act in the name of the State, in the terms of the Nazi empire. However, those directly responsible were only able to carry out their punishment and extermination duties once their victims had been completely dehumanised and impersonalised.

This, in essence, is why the horrors lasted for so long and affected so many. It was because the camps were run by instruments of the state and acted with its authority.

MANAGEMENT IN FOCUS 22.4

LEGAL, RATIONAL AND POSITION POWER AND AUTHORITY IN PLACES OF WORK

In the UK, there are three tests of legal, rational and position power as follows:

- *The master–servant relationship*: it is held that all working relations are based upon the ability of one person – the master – to direct and order the work of others – the servants – as he or she sees fit. This is often now called the managerial prerogative. Masters are required to take good care of their servants. Work and workplaces must be safe and not detrimental to personal health. The work may be hard but not punishing. Servants are expected to work hard and to the best of their capabilities. They may not be worked to death, disease or illness. Masters may exert discipline and servants are required to accept it, provided that this is positive and not punitive.

- *The wage–work bargain*: once people are hired by an organisation they must be paid (whether or not they actually carry out

any work) according to the terms offered. The work carried out must also reflect expectations. For example, a secretary who has been told that he/she is to receive a salary of £12,000 per annum, payable in instalments of £1000 per month, must receive this and may expect to be asked to carry out secretarial duties (as distinct from carpentry for example) in return. Both salary and duties may be varied by mutual agreement. Training may be necessary or desirable if this occurs, and may be requested by either or both parties. If no agreement is forthcoming then the relationship may be changed and alternative work offered or sought within the organisation. If the original work has ceased or diminished and no alternative is available, the organisation and the employee may sever the relationship in accordance with the law and the organisation's own procedures.

- *Fairness and reasonableness*: organisations and their employees are required to act fairly and reasonably at all times. This especially is the test that is applied by courts and tribunals when adjudicating on employment law cases brought before them. This is because required standards of behaviour and demeanour vary between organisations. For example, attitudes and relationships between staff are different on a building site from those at a high fashion and exclusive clothes shop; the forms of dress required for work in the fields in winter are different from those in a public relations company. The question of fairness and reasonableness is always considered from this point of view.

These factors constitute the absolute boundaries of legal, rational and position power and authority in UK organisations.

● Centres of power in organisations

Each department, division, function and group always has its own power base to a greater or lesser extent. This power base is both structured and limited by a range of organisational and environmental circumstances (see Figure 22.1).

Organisations and their managers additionally have to be aware of the existence of: vested interests, pressure groups and lobbies; over-mighty individuals and departments; and the structures of relationships, and the sphere of influence that they develop.

Vested interests, pressure groups and lobbies, both internal and external, bring their own point of view to bear on particular proposals and activities. For example, work groups may lobby for improved facilities for themselves, arguing that many people have already left the group because it lacks proper amenities, and that they are difficult to replace. Pressure is then exerted on the organisation to consider the request and if necessary re-allocate and re-prioritise resources in order to comply.

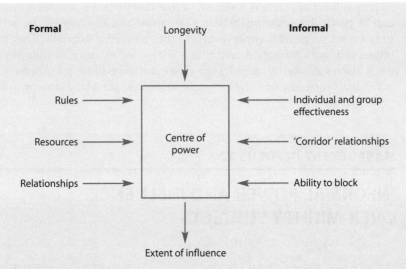

Longevity: people, groups and institutions become behaviourally both strong and influential when they have been in place for a long while. This has implications for needs and demands for change, reorganisation and restructuring.
Blocking: this is the power to prevent things from being done. It exists in most situations and is a combination of resource and reward restriction and work prioritisation. It is also the ability to call upon other resources and influences to ensure that the blocking process is effective.
Corridor diplomacy: this occurs when a route that will bypass problems has to be negotiated when the formal procedures of the organisation have been exhausted. Power and influence are used between the parties concerned on an informal basis to try and explore other means of resolving the issue.
Success and failure: a run of successes may lead to individuals or groups becoming acknowledged as experts, enabling their influence to grow. Conversely, a series of failure is likely to lead to loss of influence, whatever the absolute standard of the expertise present.
Group energy: this is the ability of the group as a whole to influence things, both positive and negative. The latter is particulary prevalent; groups can become very effective in dissipating the energies of those who come to them. For example, those dealing with bureaucracies and who are constantly handed on from one person to the next depend a great deal of energy in this and may well give up altogether if the goal is not important or if some other way of achieving it can be found.

Figure 22.1 Factors relating to the centres of power

Externally, organisations are subject to public pressure groups wherever they contemplate engaging in activities that are, or are perceived to be, detrimental to the environment (for example construction, infrastructure projects and waste disposal always have to cope with this).

Pressure groups may also arise among shareholders and other stakeholders as the result of, or in response to, proposed sets of activities; or conversely, they may propose or attempt to influence these sets of activities themselves. Pressure groups may also consist of cluster groups of managers, supervisors, technical and professional experts; specialist groups; trade unions and employee representatives.

Over-mighty subjects and over-mighty departments wield great levels of influence and autonomy in certain conditions. They exist in locations physically removed from head office and the main directorate, where a large measure of independence of operation is granted. Over-mighty departments occur where, for operational reasons, they are required to act autonomously. Over-mighty subjects arise where, again for operational reasons, they are required to act in the name of the organisation in all aspects of work. The issue is compounded when the over-mighty subject or division is stationed overseas from the organisational head office, and in particular situations where the nature and delivery of the service is given only broad or general supervision by the managing officials. This may again be influenced by organisation tradition – where for example, a long-serving individual is always allowed to air his/her views and have these taken into account. Such individuals then become the target of lobbyists (see Management in Focus 22.5).

MANAGEMENT IN FOCUS 22.5

INFORMAL POWER AND INFLUENCE: OVER-MIGHTY SUBJECTS

In sixteenth-century England the Tudor kings and queens were burdened with what came to be known as their over-mighty subjects. These were the land-owning nobility whose support the monarch required to keep the peace in outlying parts of the country and who, if support was not forthcoming, constituted a real threat to the monarch's position. This support was therefore generated by hiving off parcels of land, local ruling rights and general autonomy to these nobles, in return for their continuing support to the Tudor dynasty. The kings and queens went on regular progressions throughout the country to try to ensure that the bargains that had been struck were adhered to. In practice however, great areas of the country were effectively the personal fiefdoms of these nobles.

The same situation exists in many organisations today. Effective control of large parts has often to be left in the hands of particular individuals. The relationship is normally based upon the organisation conceding large measures of autonomy and freedom of action to the individual, who in return addresses and pursues the organisation's interests in the particular area. As well as location however, organisations often become dependent upon these individuals in key critical and functional divisions and areas.

Relationship structures and spheres of influence are created by individuals, groups and departments both to serve themselves and to act in the name of the organisation as a whole. A number of elements affect relationship structures and spheres of influence:

- *Mutual interest groups and alliances* occur between individuals, groups and functions to try and exert wider pressures on their organisations. This occurs for example, where one of these has failed and where there is a widely perceived need for particular changes or activities to be undertaken.
- Relationships are affected by the extent and prevalence of *other means of interaction, participation and involvement.* This includes departmental and group staff meetings, work improvement groups, quality circles and project groups. It may also include pioneering activities, research and development functions where those involved are drawn from across the organisation.
- *External consultancies, agencies and statutory bodies* may be cited or called in to support particular points of view. For example, consultants carry great influence when organisations engage in restructuring operations; changes in working practices may lead to health and safety experts being called in; in some cases, trade unions exert influence when the restructuring of work and changes to working practice are being considered.
- *Isolation and inclusion* may be either physical or psychological. Inclusion may be used to ensure that specific individuals and groups support (or oppose) particular ideas, proposals and initiatives. Isolation is used to ensure that specific groups and individuals have as little influence on proposals as possible.

● Organisational politics (realpolitik)

Organisational politics exists in all organisations, and influences the relationships between groups, divisions, departments and functions, and individuals.

Those involved seek initially to ensure that their position is legitimised within the organisation both in terms of functional outputs and in terms of influence on direction. In practice, this is then developed, in many cases, to try and influence the orders of priority, and to try and influence any position of dominance and dependency to the advantage of the particular group or individual.

Orders of priority

Orders of priority refer to the position of each individual group or department in relation to the organisation as a whole. This is the organisational pecking order; and it is established as the result of a combination of factors: the respect and regard held for the group or individuals by the organisation's top management; demands for resources, and the ability to command these; the extent of the group or department's influence on organisation output; the extent of its influence on internal ways of working; the size of the group and the nature of the expertise that it wields; its physical location; and the nature and quality of its leadership, output and results, both in absolute terms and in those required and valued by the organisation (see Management in Focus 22.6).

MANAGEMENT IN FOCUS 22.6

THE ROLE OF THE PERSONAL ASSISTANT

In many organisations, senior managers have personal assistants, and these are courted by those wishing to gain influence for some reason. In particular, the personal assistant (PA) to a chief executive normally exerts great informal influence. The PA is used as the manager's personal resource and as a sounding board and critic for possible and proposed courses of action. The PA therefore becomes an exerter of influence as the levels of mutual trust and confidence grow, and the relationship is reinforced if the judgement of the PA is shown to be sound.

PAs become the focus for lobbies and support from elsewhere in the organisation because they can (or are perceived to) provide a route to the sources of power. They have low status but high influence. They also become a source of quality information both for the manager for whom they work and also potentially for the rest of the organisation.

Dominance and dependency

Dominance and dependency define the overall extent to which some groups are able to influence, direct and dominate the courses of action of others, and the benefits and consequences that arise as the result. The key areas of dominance and dependency are as follows:

- Captive markets are dominated by their suppliers and providers and this brings responsibility in terms of level, volume, quality and frequency of supplies and service, and the prices that can be charged – and the prices that *should* be charged.
- Staff and workforces are dominated by their employers; the potential for this increases at times of increasing unemployment, causing some organisations to take a more expedient view of the working relationships.
- Locations may be dominated by a single employer or industrial, commercial or public service group, and this brings with it responsibilities in terms of corporate citizenship, as well as the local dependency for employment.
- Individuals may dominate an organisation or work group through the combination of their expertise, force and strength of personality and charisma.
- Experts may dominate in particular situations, especially when their expertise is urgently or highly required, or prized. This leads to the ability to charge at very high levels (economic rent); experts may also choose to limit or filter their expertise, or else to prioritise those with whom they have dealings.
- Owners and controllers of rare supplies, raw materials and specialist information may, from time to time, exert undue influence at specific points during the relationship (see Figure 22.2).
- Resources, especially finance, command and control, are in many cases a dominance–dependency issue. This especially occurs where organisations require their staff, managers, departments, divisions and functions to bid against each other as part of the allocation process. This is always morally questionable and

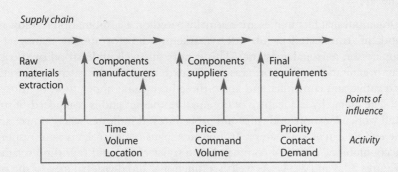

Figure 22.2 The supply chain and points of influence

operationally inefficient. Those involved nevertheless have to engage in bidding activities in the particular environment and context. For some groups, this brings the need for alliances and other forms of support.

Dominance–dependency also exists as a consequence of physical and psychological distance. Those in remote locations find themselves powerless to influence the course of events; this is compounded when organisations have preconceptions about particular locations based on prejudice, rather than strategic and operational assessment (see Management in Focus 22.7).

MANAGEMENT IN FOCUS 22.7

BRANDED CLOTHING AND SPORTS GOODS

For some time, there has been a general concern about the disparity between the wages of those who produce branded sports goods and clothing in the emerging world, the prices charged by retailers in Western Europe and North America, and the salaries paid to the sports stars who wear and use the products.

One Christmas a consignment of branded children's tracksuits had to be recalled because the stitching was faulty, causing the clothes to fall apart. The branded goods company offered unconditional refunds to the customers. This approach was conducted with maximum publicity, and the company enhanced its reputation.

However, no publicity was given to the company's subsequent dealings with the factory in Viet Nam where the clothes were made. Questions about this aspect were either diverted, or else answered in the most general of terms (e.g. 'We have solved our supply side problem').

This example illustrates the different ways in which power and influence are wielded. The company was unable to dominate the retail side, and so had to actively manage the relationship. Because of its dominant position vis-à-vis the suppliers, the company was able to do as it pleased. On the supply side therefore, in the short term the problem was solved. In the longer term, a substantial amount of resentment has inevitably been stored up.

Hierarchy

Organisational hierarchies are normally based on a combination of rank and function and this is reflected in job titles (marketing director, quality manager, production supervisor, personal assistant). This is normally well understood by those in particular organisations. The process is clouded by job titles such as secretary, officer, executive and controller and again these have to be understood by those involved.

The hierarchy is a feature of organisation design and is composed of structure, job and work allocation, and rules and procedures. It indicates where power and influence lie and its extent and nature. It indicates spans of control, areas of responsibility and accountability, chains of command (the scalar chain) and reporting relationships (see Figures 22.3 and 22.4). As well as a functional and divisional map of the organisation, the hierarchy is a representation of the nature and limits of power and influence.

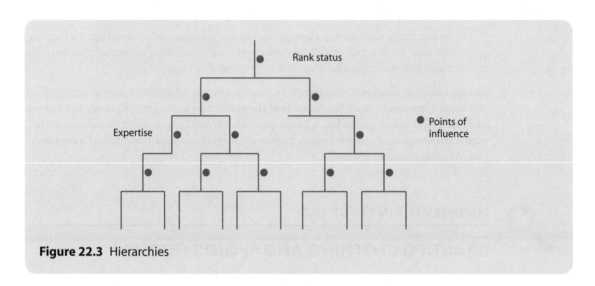

Figure 22.3 Hierarchies

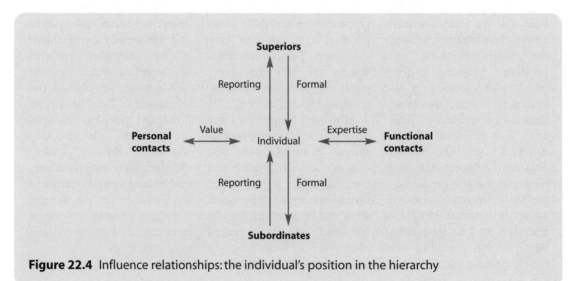

Figure 22.4 Influence relationships: the individual's position in the hierarchy

Status

Status influences the perceptions of power relationships in organisations. It is also a reflection of general perceptions of influence. Status is a reflection of the rank or position of someone (or something) in a particular group. Relative status is based on the inter-relationship of each position. Status is based on the importance and value ascribed to the rank by the organisation and individuals concerned, and on the esteem and respect that accrue as a result of holding the given rank. Status is also based on the ambition, self-esteem and self-worth of the rank holder – the ability to say with pride 'I hold job x' or 'I work for organisation y.'

Status is reinforced by the trappings that go with the rank held – personal office, expensive furniture, car, mobile phone, expense account; and by the volume and quality of items such as these.

It is also reinforced by the responsibilities of the rank held – size of budget, numbers of staff, performance requirements. It is also often enhanced by the physical location of those concerned: for example, whether their office is in the 'corridors of power' (that is, the same area as those of the top managers). In wider social circles it may also be reinforced by perceptions of glamour or excitement that are assumed to exist in certain occupations – for example, show business, publishing, travel.

The components of status may thus be represented as in Figure 22.5.

Status and rank are closely related. It is additionally essential to note that both status and rank can be used both with and without responsibility (see Management in Focus 22.8).

Friendships

Friendships influence power relationships in organisations where people who have positive feelings for each other also work together. A part of the way of working then becomes the desire to support the friends to ensure that they derive some of the benefits that are to accrue from particular courses of action. The use of friendships

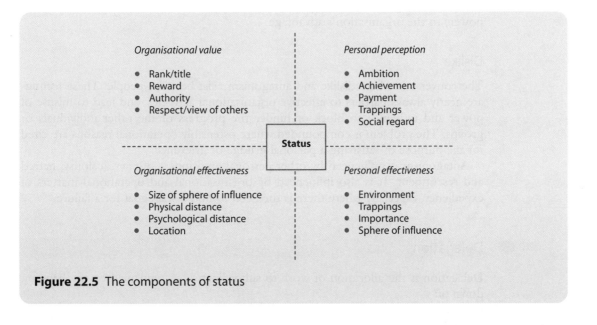

Figure 22.5 The components of status

MANAGEMENT IN FOCUS 22.8

MEDICAL RESEARCH

A young university academic produced a pioneering piece of medical research. This work called into question the value of a hitherto generally accepted treatment for a particular condition. The work was substantial and thorough, and was widely lauded among the researcher's peers.

However, the university Pro-Vice-Chancellor in charge of research took a very different view. He had made his reputation in developing the hitherto generally accepted treatment. The Pro-Vice-Chancellor consequently harassed the researcher, taking steps to ensure that funding was cut off, and that no further work would be done in this area. He additionally started to pick on the individual, using his position and status for leverage.

The researcher complained to the university authorities. The consequence was that the Pro-Vice-Chancellor was warned three times by senior HR staff. He took no notice. At one of the hearings, when asked why he was persisting in this attitude, he replied: 'Because I can'.

The matter was not resolved formally. It was resolved informally when the researcher agreed to pursue different activities in return for 'decent treatment' by the university authority. The Pro-Vice-Chancellor had simply used his rank and status to behave in this way, and so was able both to flout expert advice, and also de facto break the law.

More generally in these cases, where powerful and influential individuals do not come into line, organisations normally have to either pay for their actions through compensation, or else to absolve themselves of responsibility through coming to individual settlements, each of which again normally involves financial considerations.

and personal contacts to resolve problems and address issues is a general feature of the informal organisation. It represents the ability to use personal influence (referent power) to the organisation's advantage.

Dislike

The converse is where dislike and antagonism exist between people. These feelings are nearly always barriers to effective organisational activities, and lead to misuse of power and influence to block or hinder the progress of the other individuals or groups. The problem is compounded where ostensibly operational reasons are cited for the purpose of satisfying a personal grudge or grievance.

Antagonism is influenced by other personal emotions – of envy, jealousy, hatred and resentment. It is also influenced by organisational and operational matters of expediency, especially where there is the need to find a scapegoat for a failure.

● Delegation

Delegation is the allocation of work to subordinates, accompanied by the handing down of:

- Authority in the given area to carry out the work and to make requests for equipment, materials and information; to act in the name of department, group or superior in the given area.
- Control over the process by which the work is to be carried out. Delegation thus normally involves relaxing a part of the process of work supervision. Activities taken in pursuit of the task are normally left entirely to the subordinate.

There is an effect on the wider issues of responsibility and accountability. Overall responsibility, especially to the wider organisation, normally remains with the superior. Any problems arising, especially questions of failure or ineffectiveness, therefore remain a matter between the superior and the rest of the organisation. However, this is invariably accompanied by discussions between the superior and subordinate. Where such problems do arise, to apportion blame to the subordinate when dealing with the wider organisation leads to loss of morale and accusations of scapegoating.

Effectiveness

For effective delegation to take place, strong mutual trust, respect and confidence must exist. On the part of the superior, this is based on respect for the capabilities, motivation and commitment of the subordinate and the fact that he or she is interested in the work and wishes to pursue it to a successful conclusion. On the part of the subordinates, this is based on an understanding that they will receive support and backing in their efforts to get the work done, help with any problems and a proper assessment of the end results. This is always enhanced where a strong and effective reporting relationship is already established and mutual trust and confidence are already in place. This is in turn influenced by the relationship between the task to be delegated and the staff available to carry it out. The greater the control the superior has over this, the more likely that confidence and trust are present and the greater the willingness of the superior to cede the required measure of control.

For both, work is likely to be successful only if expectations are clearly set out at the commencement of work. This is reinforced wherever possible with the establishment of proper, measurable, deadlined objectives. The subordinates can then be given enough autonomy over the process to see that the work is done (see Management in Focus 22.9).

Misuses of power and influence

It remains the case that, in practice, both individuals and groups misuse the power and influence that they have. The main areas of misuse are as follows:

- *Favouritism*: promoting an individual's career, prospects and advancement because of a personal liking and at the expense of others.
- *Victimisation*: the converse of favouritism – the blocking or reduction of someone's career prospects and advancement.
- *Lack of manners*: calling out rudely to people, abusing and humiliating subordinates in public.
  Lack of respect: treating subordinates with contempt, giving individuals dressing downs in public, or conducting discipline in public.

MANAGEMENT IN FOCUS 22.9

EMPOWERMENT

Empowerment is a form of delegation that gives measures of control and responsibility to employees over their work, work processes and working lives. The concept of empowerment is based on the view that people seek as much personal satisfaction and fulfilment as possible from all situations, that this includes work situations, and that responsibility and control lead to increased levels of satisfaction.

Empowerment is attractive to organisations, because by vesting these elements in front-line operative and other traditionally 'non-responsible' jobs, levels of supervision and management can be reduced. Expensive senior staff are no longer needed in current volumes. Complex and sophisticated supervisory practices, structures and controls can be simplified, thereby cutting down on overheads, non-productive processes and efforts, and numbers of staff not actively engaged in primary output.

It is attractive to the staff (as long as the process is honest) because increased responsibilities are normally expected to lead to increased reward and benefit levels, and to increased prospects and opportunities. Potential may be identified that either the organisation or the individual may wish to develop. New levels and ranges of interest may become apparent.

Harvester

The following example illustrates the point.

Harvester, the UK restaurant chain, took steps to empower its restaurant and kitchen staff. The chefs decided what the menus for each week were to be and how often these were to be changed. They also became responsible for ordering the necessary levels and quality of stock, ensuring that supplies were delivered, chasing up any quality defects, and making sure that food was stored according to legal and best professional standards. They were responsible for ordering patterns, purchasing new kitchen equipment and ensuring that the kitchen and associated areas were clean. They dealt with the food and premises inspections and inspectors, and implemented any necessary changes.

The restaurant staff (i.e. waiters and waitresses) became responsible for all aspects of the eating area. They were required to clean and polish the tables, put flowers and candles out, and see that the restaurant was clean, tidy and welcoming. They would greet customers, show them to their seats, take and process orders. At the end of the work period, they were to clean the restaurant area, check for security and close it down and lock up.

Both chefs and restaurant staff would handle any customer complaints directly, according to the nature of the complaint; rather than going through sophisticated managerial processes, these would be dealt with at the front line.

The company was therefore able to remove the differentiated, non-productive (or largely non-productive) jobs of head waiter, restaurant manager, work supervisor and general manager. Chefs and waiting staff were given large initial pay increases in return for accepting these ways of working.

The organisation adopted methods of supervision and control based on a roving and mobile area manager system (area managers would visit each of their sites at least once a week), a flexible but agreed budgeting system that enabled the staff to make a large range of decisions, and an emergency/problem-solving 24-hour hot-line to the area management.

- *Bullying and harassment*: overwhelmingly by superiors of subordinates. This is usually found in the following forms: racial abuse; sexual harassment (especially of female staff by males); bullying of the disabled by the able-bodied; religious manias and persecutions (for example, bullying people because they belong to another religion); acting upon personal likes and dislikes – especially where the dislike is based on a perceived threat to the security of the senior's position.
- *Scapegoating*: the need to find someone to blame for the superior's errors.
- *Inequality of opportunity*: promoting or not promoting staff on the basis of gender, race or disability.

Each of these misuses can, if not checked, lead to serious problems. At present, about 150,000 individual cases arising from the misuse of power are referred to ACAS and the employment tribunal system of the UK each year.

The problem is compounded by the fact that managers and supervisors who misuse power often do not see that they are acting improperly. In many cases, they state that they act in these ways because this is how they were treated when they were in more junior positions. Other managers state that they only act in these ways because they think that it helps to get the job done. It is however clear that many managers and supervisors do indeed know that they are doing wrong. Whether it occurs by accident or design, this is an organisational problem and needs to be stamped out wherever and whenever it is found (see Management in Focuses 22.10 and 22.11).

MANAGEMENT IN FOCUS 22.10

GORDON'S FURNISHING LTD

Simon Baker was employed by Gordon's Furnishing Ltd as a payroll clerk. He analysed time sheets and the electronic clocking on and clocking off procedures.

One day, Simon rang in sick. However, he came in to the office after hours to meet with his supervisor, Charlotte Black. Simon was heavily bandaged, and he explained that he had been beaten up near his home by two of the staff. He stated that the reason for the beating was because he refused to fiddle the hours worked by some of the members of staff.

Charlotte Black knew that fiddling went on; she also knew that Simon's rigorous approach had helped to reduce the problem.

Charlotte took the matter to her manager, Rachel Whittington. Rachel told her to ensure that Simon went 'a bit easier' on the time sheets; a rigorous crackdown would lead to a full internal investigation, and the company could not afford the loss of staff.

This example illustrates the direct contrast and conflict between doing what is expedient, doing what is comfortable, and doing what is right. In the end, nothing was done; and the full extent of the problem only came to light many years later when a takeover bid for the company was launched, and the due diligence process unearthed time-sheet and clocking-on fiddles to the tune of nearly £500,000.

MANAGEMENT IN FOCUS 22.11

STRIKES AND DISPUTES

Strikes and disputes may be used as each of the following:

- enhancement of charisma, authority and influence by the strike leaders
- rites and rituals in pay bargaining processes
- trials of strength between staff and managers
- trials of strength between organisations and strike leaders

- safety valves
- additional holidays
- catalysts for change, as well as for the resolution of grievances.

Where physical or psychological isolation occurs, groups may engage in strikes and disputes in order to draw attention to themselves, as part of a drive for gaining influence and being taken more seriously. Those involved

also perceive that taking these forms of action may cause attitudinal changes on the part of those with whom they have the dispute. This can clearly be an extremely dangerous tactic – while it may increase their influence, there is always the possibility that senior managers will simply close the organisation down altogether.

● Conclusions

In all organisations, everyone involved recognises to some extent the nature and prevalence of particular forms of power, authority and influence, and the ways in which these are wielded. People also recognise the presence or absence of integrity in organisational approaches to managing the different power and influence bases that are present. Above all, they understand the extent of their influence in the given situations, and become especially disillusioned when they know that the management of influence is based on expediency rather than integrity.

The integrity of the organisation as a whole, and its managerial practices in particular, form the basis of the effective management of the different sources of power and influence. It is essential therefore that a full understanding of the true extent and nature of power and influence is established by those responsible for the strategy and direction of the particular organisation. This can then be translated into managerial authority so that this part of organisation management and activity is addressed effectively.

This is especially a problem when authority is devolved to those working in remote locations, or as a result of their distinctive expertise. It is for example very difficult for some health authority managers to confront expert surgeons and other medical practitioners, especially where these people have extremely powerful and dominant personalities. It is very difficult for head office managers to exercise full authority over those who work in remote locations or in the operational field, and this is often compounded by the lack of a full understanding of what the exact nature of this authority should be. The result, in each case, is that there is great potential for the particular individuals to run their part of activities as their own fiefdom, and for effective accountability and responsibility to be diluted or lost. Once problems such as these arise, they become extremely difficult to redress. Indeed, in some cases the situation may only be bought under control as the result of a scandal or disaster.

CRITICAL THINKING, ANALYSIS AND EVALUATION

1. Taking one group of which you are member (social or work), identify the ways in which you influence the others, and the ways in which they influence you. What conclusions and inferences can you draw from this?
2. What steps should organisations take to limit and control the potential for undue influence of:
   a) managers
   b) experts
   c) those working in remote locations?
3. What are the advantages and disadvantages of hierarchical management structures in terms of the ability to manage power and influence, and to determine where authority lies?
4. If a company commands 75 per cent of the total market in which it operates, what responsibility does this influence bring with it? To what extent do these responsibilities remain the same, and to what extent are they changed, for a company that commands 50 per cent of the market; 30 per cent of the market; 1 per cent of the market?

DEVELOPING MANAGEMENT SKILLS AND EXPERTISE

TROUBLE AT FIRMLINE PLC

Paul Hewson, Firmline's Chief Executive, was reading the result of a strike ballot held at the company's main factory. The ballot paper had asked the staff whether they were willing to take all-out strike action against the company's final offer on pay conditions and restructuring. Staff had voted by 90 per cent to conduct strike action.

With such a clear majority, there seemed little doubt that all production of Firmline's car body parts would be halted, with effect from the end of the following week. With a currently full order book, this would mean delivery delays to customers, and this in turn would trigger penalty clauses for missing agreed deadlines. Moreover, as a major supplier to Ford, Nissan and Toyota, the last thing that the company needed was to get a bad reputation among such powerful customers.

Paul Hewson called together a crisis management committee. This consisted of Heather Platt, strategic planning director, Peter Davis, production director, and Dennis Gaffen, marketing and sales director.

The committee met and decided that there were three strategic options:

● engage in discussion with the staff and representatives, with a view to seeking compromise

- denounce the strike proposal, and make it clear that the company would not compromise
- denounce the strike proposal, and warn that if it went ahead, the entire workforce would be dismissed and new staff be recruited.

They debated each of the three options but came to no clear conclusions. As the meeting was breaking up, Heather Platt, the strategic planning director, said: 'We could take advantage of the situation to de-recognise the trade unions, and reconstruct the workforce. I know this will lead to delays, but customers will understand, and the shareholders will be delighted.' As she developed her theme, it was clear that both Peter and Dennis were coming round to her point of view. The meeting broke up shortly afterwards.

Paul Hewson returned to his office, and discussed the matter over a cup of coffee with his secretary, Joan Campbell. Joan had worked for the company for 25 years, and understood it better than most.

She listened to what he had to say and then replied: 'You are assuming that we can get the staff with the necessary expertise and attitudes from anywhere. You should know that the workforce has skills developed over many years that are unique in this industry.' Paul shook his head and did not reply.

Meanwhile, staff representatives were meeting in the work's council office. They were all jubilant at the ballot outcome, for it seemed to them that after years of meek acceptance, their members were at last willing to take a stand against Firmline's strident management approach. They speculated on the terms of any new offer that could be made by the management side.

For the rest of the day, both the Chief Executive and the work's council chairman fielded a series of questions from journalists. The Firmline dispute was major national news because it might become the biggest private sector strike for many years. The factory employed 3500 people, and was the largest single employer in its location in the West Country.

The next day, the morning papers were full of articles on the dispute. The *Daily Telegraph* condemned 'high and mighty union officials attempting to fight the class war all over again'. The *Financial Times* commented that:

> the company's pay offer of 5 per cent seems reasonable, given the 2.5 per cent inflation currently. It is ambitious, however, to tie that in with moves towards fully flexible working, and changes in production processes, that would effectively mean that the staff could be requested to work whenever the company saw fit.

The Sun said: 'This is madness. It should end. The workers should be grateful for any job – especially when it pays a basic minimum of £350 per week.'

After they had reviewed the press coverage, Paul and his colleagues met and agreed a further press statement as follows.

Press release

Firmline Plc

Firmline Plc regrets this campaign of misinformation by union officials has produced a ballot result that threatens the survival of the company. As only 30 per cent of employees actually belong to a union, fewer than half of all staff have voted for a strike. We therefore insist that the strike is called off. Should the strike take place, the company's senior management would take whatever action it deems necessary.

Those who go on strike will be deemed to have broken their contracts of employment, and may be dismissed. The company will employ security agencies to ensure that those who do want to get to work can do so. Should the strike go ahead, the company also undertakes to de-recognise two trade unions, the AEEW and the TGWU.

The company's position is non-negotiable. Whatever action the staff take is therefore their responsibility and not that of the company'.

Media commentators expressed surprise at the severity of the message. Particularly anxious were the local ITV station, and regional evening newspaper. However, these both accepted assurances given by Paul Hewson that the strike would evaporate in the face of such a threat, together with the extremely generous pay offer.

Staff representatives received no direct communication from Paul Hewson and his colleagues. The first notice that they had therefore of the company's intended line was when they read the evening paper. Staff throughout the factory abandoned their posts to look for union or management officials to clarify the situation. Coverage in the press only aggravated the situation, and the result was a total of 2500 staff hours lost during that afternoon. By now there were plenty of journalists around, and plenty of Firmline staff prepared to talk to them.

It began to become clear that the workforce felt that they had been exploited over the previous five years. They believed that the company's top management had deliberately used a period of uncertainty about employment as an excuse for undermining the pay and conditions of manufacturing staff and their supervisors. One member of staff expressed this as follows.

> First we were told about the value of de-layering the management. This was supposed to give us more responsibility, but all it did was to give us twice the work and hassle. Then came empowerment, which was intended to provide job enrichment, but all we got was more paperwork and longer working hours. At the same time, top management pay has moved ahead, and the ten senior managers of this company have managed to double their pay in the past three years.

For the rest of the week, little activity took place in the West Country factory. The official strike was still nearly two weeks away, but there was little sense of urgency to complete work before then, either from the staff themselves or from supervisors. In fact, the threat of mass sackings had united factory managers, supervisors and staff; the common enemy was the crisis management team, headed by Paul Hewson.

The following day, in the local newspaper, the company's figures for the present year were published as follows:

Firmline Plc Company accounts – Current year

Profit and loss account	£m	Balance sheet	£m
Revenue	120	**Fixed assets**	32
Materials	(44)	Stocks	46
Labour	(40)	Debtors	26
Gross profit	36	Creditors	(38)
Overhead	29	**Net current assests**	34
Interest	5	**Assests**	66
Operating profit	2	Loans	50
Tax	0.5	Share capital	10
Dividends	3.5	Reserves	6
Retained profit	(2.0)	**Capital**	66

Questions

1. Where do the sources of power and influence in this situation actually lie? Where should they lie?
2. What responsibility is being accepted and acknowledged by each of the participants in this situation, for the situation itself?
3. What are the advantages and disadvantages of wielding power and influence in these ways?
4. Produce a set of recommendations designed to:
    a) resolve the situation as described
    b) ensure that, as far as is reasonably practicable, the situation never arises again.

Chapter twenty three

Corporate governance

'All I ever want to do is my best for everyone.'
Terry Leahy, CEO, Tesco

'The only duty of a company is to make money.'
Milton Friedman.

'By definition, risk takers often fail. So do morons.
In practice, it is often difficult to sort them out.'
Scott Adams.

Chapter outline

- Introduction
- Standards of conduct and behaviour
- Managing shareholders' interests
- Managing other stakeholder interests
- Working within the law
- Setting and maintaining standards of probity and integrity
- Managing dishonesty
- Establishing clarity in rewarding top and senior managers
- Conclusions

Chapter objectives

After studying this chapter, you should be able to:

- understand the range and complexity of corporate governance

- understand critical leadership and management priorities in setting and maintaining standards of probity, integrity and behaviour

- understand distinctive roles and functions ascribed to particular individuals

- understand the direct relationship between corporate probity and enduring effective performance.

Introduction

Corporate governance is the term used to describe the constitution, processes, actions and priorities by which organisations are led, directed and developed. It refers to the policies and practices that are present and in use. Studies of corporate governance specifically identify key responsibilities and expertise required of those in top, senior and key positions; and each of these sets examples for everyone else in the organisation to follow.

Behind this overtly simple and straightforward assertion lies a complexity of leadership and management expertise, and a critical priority for those in top, senior and key positions (see Management in Focus 23.1).

MANAGEMENT IN FOCUS 23.1

GUINNESS

The case for active and prescriptive corporate governance first became clear in the UK at the time of the Guinness trial. During the late 1980s, it became clear to regulatory authorities in the finance industry and stock markets that the Guinness company was taking active steps to enhance its share price. Ernest Saunders, the Chief Executive, and some of his colleagues were tried and convicted in 1990 of buying up shares to reduce the share volumes on the stock market, and therefore increase the price and value of those shares remaining available for sale and purchase elsewhere.

This practice was, and remains, illegal. When the matter came to light, it caused the following problems:

- an impression that the company was unwholesome, which affected the sales of the beer (whose quality had not changed)
- a wider perception that this was going on in many other organisations and that the only thing that Guinness had done wrong was to get caught
- loss of shareholder confidence in the overall strength, integrity and direction of the company
- a wider general perception away from the stock exchange that top and senior managers, directors and key executives had no interest in the running of companies and organisations as trading entities, but only in taking profits from dividends and share options.

Mr Saunders and his colleagues were duly tried and convicted. However, the cases of Enron, Marconi and Barings, among others that have occurred subsequently to the Guinness case, have made it clear that problems at the top of organisations are very far from over.

Moreover, Mr Saunders and his colleagues have gone through a series of appeals against their convictions; and still remain engaged in litigation. To date therefore, the case has been hanging over the Guinness company for nearly 20 years, and this is set to continue for the foreseeable future. This, apart from anything else, is very damaging and destructive to the collective morale of those who continue to work at the company, and remains an enduring specific problem that has to be addressed by those presently engaged in its direction.

The Guinness case and others like it imply and illustrate a wide and complex set of issues for organisations and their top and senior managers to tackle. These issues are as follows:

- standards of conduct and behaviour
- managing shareholders' interests
- managing other stakeholders' interests
- working within the law
- setting and maintaining absolute standards of probity and integrity
- managing dishonesty
- establishing clarity in rewarding top and senior managers.

At the heart of these issues are fundamental questions of collective culture, conduct, behaviour and performance. The priority is to be absolutely clear that staff will take their lead from the ways in which top and senior managers conduct themselves. Conduct at the top of the organisation establishes the absolute standards of right and wrong present. In particular, there is the fundamental issue of what is and is not tolerated de facto. If there is any question of wrong behaviour and actions being tolerated, these behaviours and actions quickly become 'not wrong'; and it is a further short step to these behaviours and actions becoming 'right'. The damage becomes most deeply embedded when the perpetrators of these behaviours and actions gain known and understood rewards; for example, they may be promoted away from the scene of their wrongdoing, or else handsomely paid off and allowed to leave the organisation.

Standards of conduct and behaviour

Top and senior managers set the standards for the conduct and behaviour of the organisation as a whole; functional managers, section heads and supervisors do the same for their own people. The immediate issues are as follows:

- If top management set lax standards, there is ultimately little point in those lower down the organisation trying to set high ones.
- If top management set high standards, then the extent to which these are absolute in practice is a direct reflection of what happens when those lower down the organisation allow standards to slip.

Managing shareholders' interests

The priority in managing shareholders' interests is communication. Shareholders and their representatives need to know and understand the nature of returns on offer, the conditions under which returns are possible, and any changes in conditions likely to affect these returns. This is so that shareholders and their representatives understand where top management is taking the organisation, and why, in terms of financial returns. It also provides shareholders and their representatives with a key point of reference in their dealings with top management; ultimately, if they do not like what top management are doing, shareholders' representatives will replace them.

● Managing staff interests

EU regulations on equality of treatment, working time, wage levels and consultation have caused all organisations to take a much broader view of their responsibilities to their staff. The overall effect has been to demand much greater knowledge and transparency about pay, and terms and conditions of employment; this has led in turn to a greatly increased propensity to make claims to courts and tribunals when collective and individual pay and terms and conditions are known or believed to be wrong for some reason. Defending claims is expensive, stressful and time consuming. Legal cases can lead to wider adverse publicity, and this can, and does, lead to loss of confidence in the integrity of the organisation as a whole (see Management in Focus 23.2).

● Managing other stakeholder interests

Top and senior managers have a clear commitment to all those who come into contact with the organisations, especially those whose immediate and future well-being is at stake.

MANAGEMENT IN FOCUS 23.2

THE CASE OF PAULA GRAHAM

Paula Graham worked as a senior purchasing manager for a large multinational manufacturing organisation, which she had joined straight from school. She had managed to get herself on to an accelerated promotion programme, and by the age of 25 she was in charge of purchasing operations for the whole of Western Europe. Between the ages of 28 and 35, Paula took a career break and had three children.

Paula returned to the organisation at the age of 35. However, she now found that opportunities were being denied to her. She took this up with senior managers, only to find that their attitude towards her had now shifted. The organisation had restructured

during her absence and she no longer enjoyed the influence or range of activities, though she retained her job title of senior international buyer.

Paula pursued these issues through the organisation's grievance processes; however, the matters remained unresolved. Accordingly, she took the company to an employment tribunal. The case attracted a lot of publicity, especially in relation to the conduct and behaviour of top and senior managers towards both Paula herself and towards UK staff from ethnic minorities and indigenous staff in countries where activities were being carried out.

The tribunal case eventually proved sex discrimination and

Paula was awarded £250,000. The outcome caused one major shareholder to seek the replacement of three directors; another major shareholder withdrew its funds altogether. This led in turn to a further restructuring of the organisation; the restructuring process has to date been going on for over five years and shows no signs of completion. The effect has been to reduce both turnover and profit margins, and increase operating expenses. While many of the problems were nothing to do with Paula Graham's case directly, the fact that the matter came out into the open was the reason why all of the other inquiries were opened, and why loss of confidence ensued.

Suppliers and contractors, especially those whose existence depends on large, understood and regular volumes of work from a particular organisation, have a moral as well as commercial right to be told of actual and potential plans for the future. In particular, they are entitled to know of any plans to restructure the supply side, or take key or critical orders elsewhere.

Top and senior management have a responsibility to ensure that products and services produced and delivered are of value to the particular markets and communities served. This responsibility is a combination of providing work for people, keeping the environment clean and tidy, and managing waste and effluent.

Managing waste and effluent itself is a specific corporate responsibility and falls into the following categories:

- ensuring safe dispersal of everyday rubbish such as paper, packaging, food and canteen waste
- ensuring safe management of production processes that produce particular hazards, toxins and otherwise dangerous effluent
- ensuring so far as is reasonably practicable that noise, heat, light and dust pollution, and fumes from transport fleets are kept to a minimum
- ensuring that confidential waste in the form of staff, customer and supply records are disposed of with absolute security (see Management in Focus 23.3).

Probity and integrity

It follows directly from all of the above points that responsibility for setting and maintaining absolute standards of probity and integrity rests at the top of the

MANAGEMENT IN FOCUS 23.3

THE DE VERE GRAND HOTEL, BRIGHTON

In January 2006, the national media broke the story that the De Vere Grand Hotel, a five-star hotel that was one of the most famous and prestigious in the UK, had put staff, customer and supplier records, including financial details, out for dispersal in skips.

In particular, the hotel was faced with having to defend and justify the breach of confidentiality which had arisen. Customers' bank and credit card details, visit schedules and comings and goings were now in the public domain. Staff files and records were similarly now out in the open. Order numbers and purchase agreements and arrangements, and charging policies towards suppliers, had also been found.

The company was unable to answer questions about why these records had not simply been shredded. This was a simple matter of trust, and the direct responsibility of those at the head of the company. Substantial compensation had consequently to be paid to staff and suppliers; in addition, some suppliers used information about others to renegotiate more favourable conditions. Many staff received compensation for breach of trust and confidentiality. To date however, no top or senior member of staff has been disciplined as a result of these errors.

organisation. Probity and integrity in corporate governance are concerned with the ways in which responsibilities and obligations are identified, accepted, met and discharged.

There is again a clear choice open to top and senior managers; and again, whatever is chosen becomes de facto an active choice with direct consequences for the future conduct of the organisation. The options are as follows:

● Setting standards which are fully transparent, open and honest, and which can stand detailed scrutiny from any quarter. In theory, this is the ideal position. In practice, the culture, behaviour patterns, norms, values and past history of the organisation may simply not allow for this to happen. It may also not be acceptable to powerful and influential groups and individuals, shareholders and other stakeholders.

● Full and active compliance with the law and wider sets of responsibilities and obligations. This involves using the full range of communication and consultation processes to deal with all stakeholder groups in answering questions about conduct and performance as accurately and comprehensively as possible.

● Passive compliance, in which standards are set to comply with the law and other regulations and statutory instruments.

● Sectoral compliance, in which top managers discharge their obligations to the perceived and understood standards of openness, or otherwise, that prevail in the rest of the sector.

● Stretching the rules, which may be necessary from the point of view of meeting shareholder and stakeholder expectations in responses to crises and emergencies; or which again may reflect the norms and cultural perceptions of how matters are conducted in the given sector.

● Criminal intent, in which top and senior managers conspire among themselves to break the rules in order to gain advantages either for themselves or for a particular group of stakeholders or, rarely, for the organisation as a whole (see Management in Focus 23.4).

● Managing dishonesty

In theory, the standards of probity and integrity chosen reflect the fact that 'either the organisation is honest or it is not'. In practice, within the cultural constraints and the nature of organisation conduct indicated above, it is rarely that simple. However, the active choice of a position and the consequences are absolutes.

A key test of the strength and integrity of corporate governance, and of the top and senior managers responsible, is the response to dishonesty. Dishonesty potentially exists in all areas of human activity, and organisational and managerial practices are no different.

Dishonesty in organisations is potentially present everywhere. This potential covers macro-organisational issues relating to misrepresentation of assets, finances, performance and profitability, ranging through to micro issues concerning the fiddling of time sheets, expenses and the use of the phone and Internet access for private matters, and petty pilfering.

Again, there is a clear absolute; and again, there are certain to be constraints linked to cultural issues and practices. For example:

MANAGEMENT IN FOCUS 23.4

PETER NICHOLL ON LEADERSHIP

Introduction

The purpose here is to identify the main challenges for the leadership of all organisations in the twenty-first century. The starting point is to make the direct link between the two words: 'challenges' and 'leadership'. Leaders in any organisation always face plenty of challenges. Anyone who is not prepared to deal with challenges should not take up leadership roles.

Thriving on challenge

The key characteristic of a leader is therefore someone who thrives on challenge. This does need to be seen in context however. In some cases, people look for challenges everywhere and can end up creating challenges that are neither necessary nor desirable; and this is counter-productive. Additionally, it is possible to find people who enter an organisation, create disruption and then make their reputation through dealing with the chaos that they have caused. However, even in the most steady-state of organisations, things can always be improved; and in these cases, the key is still to identify and prioritise those aspects – challenges – that have to be faced.

Prioritising

A key part of the leadership expertise is to be able to anticipate those challenges and issues that are going to have to be tackled. Anticipating and dealing with them before they become serious matters is the best course of action. Clearly, this is not always possible however, and so recognising them early when they do become apparent is next best.

These challenges and issues have then to be put into a manageable form. This means prioritising, structuring and resourcing those activities that have been identified and seeing them through to their conclusion. It means confronting and dealing with powerful and influential stakeholder and staff groups. It means tackling financial aspects from the point of view of what is possible in the given set of circumstances, rather than from the point of view of some utopian ideal. It also means facing external and internal pressures as these become apparent.

Dealing with awkward people

The leadership response to dealing with awkward people, from wherever they come, can be broken down into two basic approaches:

- vilifying them and ignoring their concerns
- addressing their concerns and, where necessary, negotiating a form of agreement or coexistence that is acceptable to all.

Each has its place. However, vilifying people is normally counter-productive, as is ignoring them. It is also overwhelmingly the case that when people do raise concerns they are genuine concerns and so need to be treated with respect.

It is therefore essential to be able to break the particular issue down as follows.

- Who is attacking you, and why?
- What are their motivations?
- What issues are they using? Is it a single issue or a range of issues?
- Are there issues on which you can, and should, offer something in return?
- What are their intended outcomes?

Another key part of leadership expertise is the ability to evaluate the issues for importance, substance and influence. It is essential to be able to stand firm on the key issues, and to explain why. It is essential additionally to be able to command the media, channels of communication, and other points of contact as and when required, so as to be able to explain the particular point of view effectively.

Taking action

Leaders have to be action oriented; this applies to those in leadership positions in all organisations, in all sectors. Taking action means that some things will go well, and on other occasions mistakes will be made. No leader is successful every time. It is essential however to learn, and learn quickly, from mistakes. It is also essential to study and evaluate the performance of other leaders in other sectors, and from this to analyse and evaluate the reasons why they were successful in some sets of circumstances, and less so in others. Many people in top positions have learnt lessons from such diverse examples, areas and individuals in the political, sports, business and religious sectors. Again, this is a key commitment that those who aspire to leadership positions must make; anyone who is not prepared to do this should not be present in a leadership position.

Crises and emergencies

All leaders are faced with crises and emergencies from time to time. How these are dealt with is a mark of key leadership expertise and effec-

tiveness. It is essential to study the different ways in which crises and emergencies are handled and dealt with by different individuals overtly facing similar situations. It is also essential to ensure that the lessons from each situation are fully analysed and evaluated. Again, it is necessary to ensure that the lessons and approaches of the widest possible range of examples are studied; this is more effective still where overtly similar situations led to very different outcomes.

Working relationships

Those in leadership positions must be able to establish effective working relationships with:

- external stakeholders and influence groups
- the top management team of the organisation in question
- the staff of the organisation.

In each case, the absence of an effective working relationship can ruin the overall effectiveness of the leader's contribution. It is especially vital, where the leader is on a fixed period appointment only, that these relationships are generated early and made as effective as possible within the first month or two of appointment. Again, this requires involvement rather than distance; staff especially are going to have no

discernible relationship or identity with the leader if the leader does not make himself or herself known and understood to everyone on a face-to-face basis. This is then reinforced in each of the above cases through delivering results, developing the interests of the organisation, and enhancing its performance and effectiveness.

Delegation

No leader can do everything. None have expertise in all of the areas in which they going to have to be involved. Reference was made above to the need for effective relationships with the top management team; the basis for effectiveness is strongest when the leader is personally able to select that team. This is not always possible; nevertheless the top management team and the leader must be able to work effectively together. Deadlines must be set and adhered to. Reporting relationships must be fully effective. Regular meetings are required at which all major issues can be thrashed out.

It is essential to recognise that delegation requires that the leader retains overall responsibility and accountability for outcomes. Delegation is not an absence of responsibility, nor is it a way to abdicate responsibility or accountability for failure. All effective teams hold a fully shared accountability; and this must be a pivotal responsibility and priority of all of those in leadership positions.

Additionally, there is a practical issue here. Managers who do not delegate simply get swamped by the weight of detail and variety of issues in which they must become involved. There are simply not enough hours in the day to be able to deal with everything that is the legitimate area of concern of those in leadership positions. It is essential therefore to have good systems, information flows, reporting relationships as discussed above, and communications. Full effectiveness has to be based on a foundation of full trust, integrity, and mutuality of interest.

Reference was made above to challenges. The main challenges faced by those in organisation leadership positions are to be able to:

- establish their own authority
- cope with change and uncertainty
- deal with the wide range of stakeholders who have an interest in what the organisation does
- take a fully developmental view of the organisation (in the case of large organisations, this means especial reference to globalisation, regionalisation and expansion)
- learn from all sectors and organisations
- harness technology productively (many organisations harness technology unproductively, or else become blinded by the brand value, modernity, or capacity of the technology without reference to what it can, and should, do for the organisation)
- establish good internal

processes, with especial reference to planning, budgeting, information systems and forecasting
- choose good staff and subordinates
- encourage and reward initiative, excellent performance, targeted performance and advancement; and deal effectively with poor performance
- deal with stress (this means in turn the ability to identify those areas where stress is occurring, the reasons for this and taking steps towards ensuring that its effects are minimised)
- identify potential and develop a fund of expertise for the future.

Source: P. Nicholl (2005) *Leadership and Management in the Twenty-first Century*, Central Banking Publications.

- if an organisation truly reported the absolute volatility of markets, this might cause total collapse in confidence, leading to loss of shareholder backing and customer bases
- if an organisation was fully open about staffing difficulties, this could lead to the best staff seeking jobs elsewhere, thereby compounding the problem
- if an organisation fully admitted to flaws in production, service and information technology, then this again might lead to questions about confidence and security.

At the micro level, if time and resources are being wasted by petty pilfering and fiddles, this too has to be managed in such ways so as not to be counter-productive, while at the same time ensuring that the required standards are upheld. For example:

- Most organisations take an absolute view that downloading Internet material on political extremism, pornography, or incitement to terrorism and violence constitutes gross misconduct.

●　Pilfering and fiddles can be managed out by ensuring that expenses are reimbursed on the production of receipts only.

At the micro level, the largest single issue arises from known, believed and perceived inequalities of treatment when seeking to enforce individual and collective honesty and conformity; these problems occur when staff in some departments, divisions and functions, and above all, with different ranks and status, are seen to get away with things that would not be tolerated elsewhere (see Management in Focus 23.5).

MANAGEMENT IN FOCUS 23.5

FALMERS FOODS LTD

Falmers Foods Ltd are located in central southern England. The company makes ready meals, pot noodles and instant soups for the branded goods companies in their sector, and for supermarket own brands.

The company had a spate of petty vandalism, the most serious of which was that bits of waste food, cigarette ends and ring pulls were turning up in the products. This matter was extensively covered in local news media, and Falmers determined to put a stop to it.

An investigation was held in full accordance with procedures and the perpetrators were caught. They were disciplined, again in full accordance with procedures, and dismissed.

Immediately after the dismissals, two shift leaders were disciplined. They also were charged with contaminating products by putting sweepings and other waste from the factory floor into products in order to 'bulk up'

the volumes produced; they were additionally charged with failing to supervise the staff who had already been dismissed.

The two shift leaders were disciplined in accordance with procedures; both were found guilty. One, a man in his early fifties, was transferred to an administrative job that carried a pay rise and company car. The other was transferred to security, again with a pay rise.

This led to outrage among the production staff. There were calls for the reinstatement of their dismissed colleagues; and calls also for industrial action.

While nothing ultimately came of either call, the affair lasted nine weeks. It was very damaging to morale, and caused a 20 per cent drop in production over the period.

Additionally, this affair caused detailed scrutiny of the whole way in which the company conducted its affairs. Local press and television stations conducted their own investigations. It became

apparent that the problem was symptomatic of a wider malaise, sloppiness and laxity. The top management of the company rarely visited the factory concerned, and one admitted to knowing nothing of the problems until he saw the television reports.

The organisation continued to decline, and the factory and assets were sold on to a competitor some months later.

The overall lesson is therefore that everyone who works for the organisation, as well as its key stakeholders and the wider community form a general perception of the attitude of the organisation to dishonesty. As long as equality is present and the status quo is known, understood and maintained, there are seldom problems. If, however, there something should trigger an investigation for any reason, the overall attitude to dishonesty will always become apparent; and this does, in many cases, lead to much more serious consequences.

● Rewards for top and senior management

Wilkinson (1992) stated that the greater the divide in rewards between those at the top and bottom of particular societies, the greater the instability of those societies. This applies equally to organisations: the greater the divide between the highest and lowest salaries, the greater the likelihood that the organisation is under-performing, unstable or at risk in terms of its ability to sell products and services on a long-term and enduring basis.

The issue of pay and rewards for top and senior managers again centres on the combination of perception and transparency referred to above. The law concerning the publication of annual reports demands that the salaries and rewards of directors are published; this does not however apply to those in top and senior executive and general management positions. It is therefore entirely at the organisation's discretion as to whether it chooses to publish further information in this area.

There is the question of how much top managers, directors and senior executives ought to be paid, and what they are being rewarded for. In practice the answer to this again de facto entails the acceptance of and discharge of responsibility. The alternatives are:

● Integrative rewards based on the ability to satisfy the demands of all stakeholders.
● Distributive rewards based on the ability to satisfy one group of stakeholders but not all. This relates invariably to the ability to satisfy the financial interest that delivers enhanced share values, earnings per share and assured dividend values.

Each position reflects the reasons why the top and senior management were appointed, and the extent to which they have any discretion in varying their brief. There are additional questions of timescales, outcomes and results to be factored in (see Management in Focus 23.6).

The structure of rewards is also critical. The pay of top and senior managers is normally based on a combination of salary, bonuses and share options; it is also increasingly usual to provide a pension and a severance payment.

Severance payments are often controversial. As well as rewarding failure (see Management in Focus 23.6), there is also the issue of change in status or ownership of the organisation. The severance payment may be so high as to make it the over-riding interest of top managers to engineer a takeover or change of status in order to work themselves out of a job.

If payments are made for results, there is the question of standpoints to be addressed. At the core are the needs and wants of the organisation's stakeholders, customers and staff. There is the issue of how the results are delivered, as well as the results themselves. For example:

● Short-term share advantages can normally be bought by outsourcing or contracting out specific functions, thereby reducing the ratio of payroll as a percentage of capital employed.
● Short-term market advantages can be bought or indicated as the result of product and service flooding and dumping.
● Short-term stock market interest can be bought as the result of engaging top brand consultants such as McKinsey or Bain.

Each of these eventualities has to be considered in terms of what is right for the long-term future of the organisation, as well as addressing the immediate financial

MANAGEMENT IN FOCUS 23.6

EXECUTIVE REWARDS IN ACTION

A Chief Executive Officer was brought in to complete the restructuring of a multinational pharmaceutical company that was one of the largest such companies in the world. Following a spate of mergers and acquisitions, productivity, profit margins and turnover were now being affected by virtue of the fact that there were no common standards for producing and delivering products and services.

The new Chief Executive was appointed on a salary of £900,000 per annum. In addition he was given share options to the value of £2 million, and was promised a bonus of £1 million each year that productivity, turnover and profit rose by more than 10 per cent.

Recognising the difficulties, he managed to negotiate for himself a severance payment of £22 million should things not work out, and the Board dismiss him.

At no stage did the Board of Directors of the company ever give a rationale for the structuring of the salary package, or for the size of the severance package. It also appeared that they had not considered that, under the terms specified, the new Chief Executive would be much better rewarded for failure than for success.

This case emphasises the need for specific expertise, understanding and involvement on the part of everyone concerned with the ordering and direction of all organisations. It is not enough simply to 'pay the market rate'; indeed, the phrase 'market rate' is seldom backed up with hard data, comparisons or rationale. In the most extreme of cases, this general and insubstantial approach reinforces any perceptions that might be present that those at the top of organisations are being over-paid for passive rather than active involvement.

concern. Each has a critical bearing on the ways in which top and senior managers are going to conduct themselves, and the objectives that they are going to pursue.

Each of the above areas of expertise forms the basis for corporate governance, and the structuring, ordering and direction of organisational activities.

These areas of expertise additionally form the basis for the key tasks and functions of:

- the Board of Directors
- conducting strategic and operational audits
- establishing a staff management style
- managing negligence and incompetence
- managing stock market relationships
- ensuring a succession of top management
- dealing with regulatory bodies.

The role and function of the Board

Within the given context, the primary role and function of the Board is to carry out the wishes and intentions of the owners of the organisation – the shareholders in the case of private organisations, and the government and its instruments in public services. This appears simple and straightforward. Complications set in, however, in a variety of ways; it is in managing within the constraints of these complications, as well as in response to specific issues, that directors, and top and senior managers prove their worth and value.

In many cases, the remit of the shareholders may only be defined in the most general terms. For example, shareholders and their representatives may wish to see 'significant growth', 'a 10 per cent return on investment per annum', or 'merger and acquisition activity to the value of £90 million'.

The remit of public service bodies can, and does, change rapidly in response to political drives and initiatives. Change is fuelled further by constant changes in the composition of the Cabinet, central and local government political institutions, and policy makers. Boards are therefore faced with a continuous process of revision of priorities, accelerating some initiatives, cancelling others, and gathering and organising resources in pursuit of the present range of ideas.

The primary role and function therefore has two clear standpoints from which it is to be delivered. One is responsiveness, in which the Board takes the remit, however generally given, and does its best to see that this is achieved. The other is to use the remit as the basis for a dialogue, the purpose of which is to ensure that there is much greater clarity of purpose, and that the remit is the best use of organisational resources or (in public services) public funds. Boards must be satisfied that whatever they are being told to do is capable of being achieved in the given set of circumstances; if it is not, they must be clear about the other actions that shareholders and political influences might have to consider if the remit is to be achieved.

The result ought to be to get directors and top and senior management actively involved in implementation processes; the outcome is, or should be, that they have a direct and vested interest in the success or failure of what is proposed. From this, a series of sub-roles and sub-functions become apparent, and have to be accepted and discharged as a direct consequence. These sub-roles and sub-functions are as follows:

- directing the audit process
- strategic and operational audit
- staff relations and management style
- stock market relations
- succession of top management
- working with regulatory bodies
- specific issues
- crises.

Directing the audit process

All organisations in every sector are required to produce annual reports and accounts, and it is increasingly usual to produce interim statements also. Annual reports provide an accurate reflection of the trading and operating position during the period in question, and this is supported by statements made by top and senior managers. The financial figures have to be audited and signed off by the auditors. It is essential therefore that the Board has an effective working relationship with the auditors. This ideally needs to be a partnership; and full mutual confidence must always exist. In particular, each party must have the confidence to raise specific issues when required. Specific issues that can and do come up are:

- profit warnings
- likely and potential revenue shortfalls or (in public services) budget shortfalls
- gains and losses in market share and changes in the nature of market activity
- factors likely to affect share values and earnings per share
- requests for investment in the future which may affect dividend volumes adversely because of the need to retain a proportion of the profits
- managing the consequences of previous decisions (see Management in Focus 23.7).

Strategic and operational audit

Strategic and operational audit requires that directors, top and senior managers satisfy themselves on a continuous basis that the priorities, direction and activity of the organisation remain effective and profitable. This requires reference to the core foundation or generic position adopted; it is also necessary to know and understand, and accept the consequences of, any changes in this position. There are specific issues that directors and top and senior managers need to address:

- moves into new markets, products and services
- investments in new product, service and information technology
- organisational re-branding and restructuring
- specific initiatives, including market expansion, going overseas/international/ global, and merger and acquisition activities.

MANAGEMENT IN FOCUS 23.7

UNIVERSITY COLLEGE LONDON HOSPITAL (UCLH)

The new University College London Hospital (UCLH) was opened in May 2005. Built under a private finance initiative, the hospital was delivered on time, within budget, and providing the full set of medical and surgical facilities originally included in the project specification.

However, the audit process quickly found some serious consequences which had not been hitherto considered. High on the list of priorities was the need to manage within the given set of financial calculations; and because all the equipment was new, depreciation and equipment usage charges were very high. Additionally, interest payments on the private finance initiative funding also had to come out of operating budgets.

In September 2005, those responsible for the direction of the UCLH Primary Care Trust, the hospital's management body, warned of an operating deficit of £6 million for the present year; this deficit was certain to become very much worse in subsequent years unless the question of budget volume, consumption and usage was addressed. Those responsible for the financial management of the hospital sought to have the basis of budget calculations changed in order to minimise the charges.

It quickly became clear that delivery of the project had been seen in isolation from the need to be able to operate, deliver and manage the services that it was subsequently to provide.

If the specific priority is to act effectively in the interests of the shareholders and owners, then whichever of the above is proposed must be capable of delivery against the following drives and priorities:

- meeting return on investment demands, based on the most detailed forecasting and extrapolation data available
- assessing effects on present ranges of activities, with especial reference to whether funds are going to be taken away from present activities to support new ventures
- assessing effects on the immediate viability and profitability of the organisation, because each of the above requires investment in some form
- likely and possible effects (positive and negative) on the wider reputation of the organisation.

The outcome of strategic audits is a clear knowledge and understanding of the effects of particular initiatives on the immediate and enduring strength of the organisation, on present ranges of activities, and on prospects of remaining profitable.

Directors and top and senior managers need to have data available which they can use to inform and support their considered point of view in these issues, and to ensure that shareholders and owners' funds are being used in ways that secure an immediate and enduring return on investment (see Management in Focus 23.8).

Staff relations and management style

Between 50 and 70 per cent of an organisation's fixed costs and enduring obligations

MANAGEMENT IN FOCUS 23.8

STRATEGIC AUDIT IN THE AIRLINE INDUSTRY

- 'Everything that we do is in the name of delivering the lowest possible fares for passengers. We drive out cost at every point possible. It is really that simple. And it is very, very exciting.' Michael O'Leary, Chief Executive Officer, Ryanair.
- 'Selling tickets, filling planes and operating a flight timetable is essentially mundane. It is a simple process; it is not rocket science. So you get

top and senior managers in this company and others going into new routes, areas and initiatives, not because the company needs it, but to bring some excitement into their otherwise humdrum corporate lives.' Unnamed director, unnamed international airline.

The key lesson is commitment and involvement. Commitment and involvement are

related to the nature of responsibility given and accepted in the name of managing shareholders' funds. The two examples underline the point that the best directors and top managers have a full personal, professional and active involvement in the core of the particular business. It is equally clear that others use shareholders' funds to make a name for themselves, to satisfy personal whims and preconceptions, and to bring some excitement, as described above.

relate to the staff. It follows therefore that the return on investment on the employment of staff must be maximised and optimised as far as possible. Directors and top and senior managers need a clear and detailed view of whether this is happening or not, and the conditions under which it is being attempted. This means that directors and senior managers need to know and understand what the present management style is, what it is delivering, what it is supposed to deliver, and where the differences lie. They need to be aware of the present state of employee relations, staff morale and commitment; and whether all this is delivering what it is supposed to deliver, and where the problems lie (if any) and their causes.

Directors and top and senior managers need to know and understand the effects on returns on investment, turnover and profit margins of strikes, disputes, absenteeism, staff turnover, accidents and disasters. Audits of strategic management and employee relations conducted by top managers need to relate collective staff performance to business effectiveness. Where there are problems, directors and top managers need to be able to provide clear direction for what the organisation as a whole proposes to do about these matters; and where necessary, they need to be able to make effective interventions themselves (see Management in Focus 23.9).

Stock market relations

Stock markets and their allies in the business and financial media like to know who they are dealing with, and what these individuals are seeking to achieve for their companies and organisations. If directors and senior managers do not actively engage in relations and communications with stock markets and the media, the latter will start to make assumptions about them; these assumptions may, or may not, be accurate.

Stock market and business media relationships are based on the following:

- managing perceptions
- informing and communicating
- responding to rumours.

Managing perceptions is the most straightforward aspect, providing positive and open communications on the range of issues that is the legitimate concern of stock markets and the media. Stock markets need, and like, to have access to directors and top managers, and so the priority is to ensure that this happens. Perceptions of uncertainty creep in when access is restricted.

The need to manage perceptions ought also to inform a broader communication strategy. The overall purpose of communication strategies from the point of view of top and senior managers ought to be to ensure that there is the fullest possible knowledge and understanding of what they are seeking to achieve; this then informs the basis on which stock markets buy, sell and trade in shares, and the clients to whom they recommend the shares.

In practice, all organisations have to accept that they will be the subject of rumours. Rumours abound in every aspect of business practice and cover: scandals, strikes, mergers and acquisitions, departure and arrival of key figures, plant and premises closures, and opening up new markets.

The priority is to be able to respond quickly and positively. This requires expertise in grasping the essentials of unfolding situations very quickly. This has then to be related to giving the fullest possible information, without compromising the organisation's approach to what is or may be in hand; and with the sure and certain

MANAGEMENT IN FOCUS 23.9

MARSTONS DEPARTMENT STORES LTD

Marstons Department Stores Ltd is a top-brand and very prestigious chain of six luxuriously appointed stores. In recent years, faced with declining sales and increased competition from mainstream supermarket chains for its products, the company has employed a succession of sales directors to turn the problems around.

The first of the new appointments decided that the staff were 'too comfortable' sitting at their sales desks, rather than actively engaging in conversation with shoppers. He therefore directed that staff must approach shoppers and ask them what they were looking for, and this must be followed up with a direct sales pitch. This director left after four months, and was replaced by another from the cosmetics industry. This director decided that, because cosmetics were a 'vanity' and 'indulgence'

product, all of the stores' products could be sold on this basis. Staff therefore went through intensive training programmes, the outcome of which was a standard sales patter designed to appeal to people's vanity, indulgence and sense of self-worth. Again, a direct sales effort was to be engaged, rather than simple presence on the shop floors.

This person lasted 11 months, and was then replaced by someone from the Internet industry. This person had demonstrated growth in his previous company, an online retailer, of 40 per cent per annum (admittedly starting from a very small base). He decided that the staff uniforms were too staid and traditional; and so these were replaced with high-quality tracksuit tops and jogging bottoms. A new young image would be presented, and older members of staff encouraged to take

jobs in the stock rooms and back offices.

Sales, turnover and profitability continued to decline; the past year's audited figures have showed a loss for the first time in the company's 120-year history. This has resulted in the sales director tendering his resignation, and this has been accepted. His severance payment is equal to that of his predecessors: a pension of £120,000 per annum, and lump sum of £250,000.

The lesson here is to ensure that directors, top and senior managers do not come in with preconceived ideas and assumptions about the staff. What is stated here also clearly implies that these particular directors were much more interested in stamping their mark on the organisation than in making it profitable.

knowledge that anything that is not covered will be addressed and assessed by the stock market in their own ways anyway (see Management in Focus 23.10).

Succession of top management

Persons in all functions, at every level of an organisation, come and go; directors and top and senior managers are no different. There are some particular issues that have to be addressed however, and those are the direct and active responsibility of top managers themselves.

If an overriding concern is the fundamental stability and security of the organisation, then this has to be delivered in spite of the comings and goings at top and

MANAGEMENT IN FOCUS 23.10

A MERGER IN THE CHEMICALS INDUSTRY

A merger was proposed between two large and very influential companies in the international chemical industry. All was settled. The lawyers and accountants were happy. Due diligence was satisfied. Compatibility of cultures, technology, communications and operating priorities was assured. Consultation with staff, including the subject of harmonisation of terms and conditions of employment, was already well in hand. Stock markets were kept informed of progress at every stage, and their view was that this was a 'model merger', a blueprint for everyone else to follow.

Then suddenly the merger fell through. No reasons were given and communication suddenly went silent. Then a journalist picked up on the rumour that the Chief Executives of the two independent companies had been unable to agree on who was to have which office. One of the offices looked out towards the edge of the city and into the countryside; the other faced the opposite direction with extensive views over the city centre only.

It gradually emerged that this was indeed the case; the merger had fallen through because the two Chief Execu-

tives were unable to agree who was to have which office. This merger would have created a company worth £100 million.

The key lesson is that every single issue has to be satisfied; and that things can and do go wrong because of the smallest of personal issues.

However, Williams and Anning (2006) point out a serious issue: that if one of the Chief Executives had given way on this issue, attention would be drawn each time he gave way on subsequent and strategic operational issues.

senior management levels. Those presently in position therefore need to know and agree who they want to succeed them when the time comes; ideally, each position should have a shortlist of two or three in case the first choice either does not want the job or is not available.

This has to be related to the facts of notice periods, departure and severance. When people in leadership or key positions give notice of intention to leave, in practice they normally depart either on the spot, or else very soon afterwards. There is a practical and perceptual problem with having people in charge of business while they are working their notice; they are clearly no longer committed to the present job, but rather looking forward to the new one. From all points of view therefore, it is better that they leave as soon as possible; and this underlines the need to have a good field of potential candidates who can be approached very quickly when the situation arises.

This in turn, however, raises a number of issues which have to be dealt with in this aspect of organisational management practice.

Confidence

Whoever is, or is likely to be, appointed needs to have the full confidence of all of the rest of the remaining Board members. He or she need to be able to gain the confidence of owners, shareholders, backers and political interests very quickly.

Sources of top staff

As with staff at all levels, a decision is required about whether to bring in outsiders, or grow the next generation of top managers internally. The same arguments hold good for top staff as for staff at all levels, relating to the need for fresh ideas from outside, balanced with maximising opportunities for internal candidates who show that they have commitment, expertise and ambition. With this in mind, there are a host of opportunities for the development of top and senior staff. Many universities and business schools run executive development programmes, and these are normally related to the assumption of some executive responsibilities. Some organisations get potential high fliers appointed as directors or non-executive directors of other organisations. Others take a project management approach to developing top managers so as to ensure that they get potential candidates as deeply immersed as quickly as possible in all aspects of executive practice.

Loss of confidence

If a top manager loses the confidence of colleagues, backers or the stock market, or if a potential high flier fails to shape up, then the only way forward is to remove that person either from the top management team, or from the executive development programme.

Loss of confidence arises from a variety of sources. New organisation owners may simply want to bring in their own top team. Stock markets and shareholders' representatives may change their mind about someone's capabilities or ability to continue to deliver results. There may be a personal or professional difference of opinion that results in a major row or falling out. It may be that a top team member changes his or her mind about the strength of present organisation strategy and direction. In each of these events, the only way to resolve it is to remove the particular individual (see Management in Focus 23.11).

Working with regulatory bodies

All organisations are overseen by a combination of government, statutory and non-statutory bodies that exist to ensure compliance with the law and with industry and sector specific regulations and practice. Most sectors additionally have their own codes of conduct and practice, which are implemented and overseen by a combination of regulatory and sector-specific bodies.

The keys to effective working relations with regulatory and other statutory bodies are as follows:

- commitment on the part of top and senior managers to implement and deliver what is demanded of them by the particular bodies
- commitment on the part of top and senior managers to do what is right in the circumstances
- developing mutual confidence and trust so that everyone knows and understands that what is being demanded on the one hand, and what is to be implemented on the other, is to ensure the best possible standards of conduct, behaviour and performance.

MANAGEMENT IN FOCUS 23.11

FLEMMINGS PLC

Flemmings Plc supplies high-quality glassware from all over the world to the top-brand and exclusive department store and boutique sector in the UK. The Director of Operations and Deputy Chief Executive is Harry Jordan.

The company has a long tradition of loyalty to and from its staff. Harry Jordan's view however is that many staff are kept on well beyond their useful period of employment; it would be a good thing to have a cull throughout the company of everyone over the age of 55, replacing these people with young, bright and dynamic individuals.

This reputation has earned him enduring contempt within the organisation, and the stock market and media press regard him as a larger than life character.

The company Chief Executive eventually took the bull by the horns, telling Harry Jordan that he would have to change his attitude to the staff. In order to improve his image, Harry Jordan agreed to stand in for the Chief Executive, and to present gold watches to three old and long-serving company employees at a formal dinner.

When they realised who was to present the gold watches, the three employees refused to come up and receive them.

This story was widely covered in the stock market and financial press, and also made the national television news. Because of the way that the story was covered, satirising Harry Jordan's approach to his staff, he was forced to resign.

The lesson here is to emphasise the fact that top managers do leave organisations very quickly; and so it is necessary to have a pool of named individuals who can be targeted at short notice, as discussed above. If such a pool is not available, a void will be left, which can be just as destructive as the presence of an ineffective or, as in this case, controversial figure.

Specific issues

All organisations and sectors have issues specific to themselves which have to be addressed. This underlines the need for effective induction and active involvement on the part of directors and top and senior managers; and it also reinforces the point that what works in one place or organisation cannot simply be replicated elsewhere. There are additional matters that ought to be integrated into all top and senior management practice as follows:

- the ways in which activities are conducted and staff and working relations implemented and developed
- the management of waste and effluent, and other environmental impacts (waste and effluent disposal, heat, light and noise pollution)
- discharging duties to all stakeholders
- managing within the constitution or framework of the organisation.

Crises

All organisations face crises from time to time. The key is to ensure that this is acknowledged (rather than denied) by top and senior management, and that processes are in place:

- to anticipate events so that their impact is minimised if and when they do occur
- to respond to events when they occur in ways that are designed to get the organisation back on track as quickly as possible, and to deal with the fall-out openly and effectively
- to create processes that manage collective confidence when crises occur (in times of trauma and emergency, everyone needs to know what is being done to put things right and move things on, and so there is an absolute duty to ensure that this happens).

Conclusions

The purpose here has been to outline and develop the nature of corporate governance as a whole, and to indicate the key areas in which expertise is required of those in top and senior management positions. Examples of some of the ways in which this expertise is applied, and the opportunities and consequences present, illustrate the points.

The ability to use this expertise is both enhanced and limited by the overall ambition, constitution, composition and priorities of the particular organisation.

Additionally, there are cultural issues to be considered. Especially, courses of action acceptable in one organisation or industry may not be acceptable in others. There is the wider question of how expertise ought to be applied; a priority for those aspiring to top management positions is to be able to learn quickly and accurately the right ways of doing things, and to discharge responsibilities in the given organisation and situation.

Many of the constraints indicated are imposed by regulatory bodies. Regulatory bodies are statutory organisations, constituted for the purpose of regulating both generic issues and industry-specific issues. Directors and top and senior management need to establish the relationships desired and demanded with regulatory bodies to ensure that specific compliance issues are addressed, and to see that particular problems are dealt with in accordance with any specific demands.

Directors and senior managers also normally appoint non-executive directors. Non-executive directors have a (supposedly) independent role in ensuring that specific duties and obligations are discharged effectively, and that problems are identified and resolved. Non-executive directors have the additional very precise role of ensuring that everything that is proposed and implemented relates to core organisation purpose, and is capable of being conducted within the confines of the standards, policies and priorities of the organisation.

Effective corporate governance additionally ensures that there is an ability to respond to serious issues and crises when they do occur. In particular, failure to respond to crises quickly and effectively always calls into question wider matters of confidence in the organisation and its products and services as a whole. The capability to respond effectively is a function of clarity of purpose, honesty and integrity, and strength of overall organisation culture. The inability to respond to crises again calls into question the expertise and commitment of top and senior management, and the confidence in which they are held.

The whole question of corporate governance has been raised in recent years as a result of crises and scandals in particular organisations, as stated above. As a result, there is now a much sharper focus on the roles, function, expertise and commitment of those in top, senior and executive positions. While this focus has not resolved the problems altogether, it has resulted in a much clearer understanding of what directors and top and senior managers ought to be doing for their organisations, and how they ought to be conducting themselves.

CRITICAL THINKING, ANALYSIS AND EVALUATION

1. Identify the problems and issues involved in legislating to ensure that each of the areas indicated is carried out.
2. If a chief executive officer moves from a hospital to a supermarket chain, what must this individual do first, and why?
3. Identify the responsibilities that top managers have to staff when declaring an organisational loss for the first time.
4. Identify the responsibilities that top managers have to all stakeholders when managing the development of a crisis such as the oil terminal fire in Hemel Hempstead in January 2006.

DEVELOPING MANAGEMENT SKILLS AND EXPERTISE

FAIRFAX ENGINEERING PLC

'You can keep your target-setting scheme. We are not using it,' said Fred Sykes, Chief Executive Officer of Fairfax Engineering. Addressing the main Board of Directors, he thumped the table to make his point. 'We at Fairfax Engineering are too busy making money to waste time filling in forms.' As everyone around the head office conference table was aware, Fairfax Engineering, although one of the smallest companies in the group, was one of the most profitable. Originally a family firm, it had been taken over two years earlier in order to acquire more capital for development plans, and it was still very much a law unto itself.

Fred Sykes stormed out of the Board meeting and went back to his office. He felt pleased. The Board of Directors would not dare to push him around, not with the profits that he was making – and certainly not with his reputation in the industry, for being an excellent innovator, developer of markets and driver of change.

The success of Fairfax Engineering was generally agreed by the staff to be due to the dynamic leadership of Fred Sykes, and morale in the organisation was high. Sales had increased by at least 10 per cent per annum for the last five years. Costs were kept to a minimum, and the staff were earning excellent salaries, including profit-related bonuses. Fred Sykes rarely had complaints from any of his staff. He expected them to get on with their work without interference; and they in turn appreciated the amount of freedom that they were given. He was considerably shocked therefore when he went to open his e-mails. One of his brightest and most successful engineers had complained about his strident ways to the group managing director, threatening to take the company and the group to an employment tribunal.

Questions

1. On the basis of what is stated here, identify the strengths and shortcomings of the corporate governance present.
2. What is the balance required between ensuring that independent companies and divisions are free to operate within a group structure, and the need for control and direction from the centre?
3. Identify what needs to be done and why in order to build an effective working relationship between Fred Sykes and the group's main Board of Directors.
4. What, if anything, is the role of a non-executive director in this situation?

Chapter twenty four

Teams and groups

'Team working is vital. Everyone knows their role and responsibility.'
Barbara Gordon, BA cabin crew member.

'We needed to play as a team. We needed to bat, bowl and field as a unit.'
Michael Vaughan, England Cricket Captain, after reclaiming the 'Ashes', 2005.

'We should celebrate our individuality and our differences.
That is what gives strength to the whole department.'
Andrew Scott, Director, Management Studies Centre,
University College London (January 2001).

Chapter outline

- Introduction
- Purpose
- The creation of effective teams and groups
- Issues facing work groups
- Group factors and characteristics
- Group leadership
- Group cohesion
- Sources of potential group stresses and strains
- Group development
- High performing teams and groups
- Conclusions

Chapter objectives

After studying this chapter, you should be able to:

- understand the behavioural and operational features and constraints of group work

- understand the management priorities in the ordering and direction of groups

- understand the universal problem areas that arise in the management of groups

- understand the key processes that have to be used if effective groups are to be constituted.

● Introduction

Workplace teams and groups are gatherings of two or more people that either exist already, or else are drawn together and constituted for a purpose which is understood and accepted by all those involved, and where there is a clear understanding that the group will serve wider organisation requirements, as well as the interests of those involved. It is usual to define workplace teams and groups as follows:

● *Formal groups*: constituted for a precise purpose. Formal groups normally have rules, regulations and norms that support the pursuit of that purpose. They also normally have means and methods of preserving and enhancing their expertise. There are also likely to be means and methods that enable people to move in, contribute and move out of a given group.
● *Informal groups*: where the purpose is less precise but still clearly understood and accepted by all involved. A card school falls into this category, as does a Friday night gathering of friends and colleagues at the bar.
● *Psychological groups*: viewed from the point of view that membership is dependent upon people interacting with each other, being aware of each other, and perceiving themselves to belong.
● *Peer groups*: in which those of the same rank, status, occupation or profession gather together to debate matters of value and interest to themselves.
● *Professional and occupational groups*: which draw and bind themselves together in pursuit of a distinctive set of professional and occupational values. This includes membership of professional bodies (e.g. British Medical Association, Chartered Management Institute); and also membership of trade unions (e.g. Royal College of Nursing, Transport and General Workers Union).
● *Committees*: all organisations constitute committees, working parties and other meetings for the purpose of addressing problems, issues, procedures and processes.
● *Project groups and teams*: constituted for specific purposes, normally resulting in the delivery of a specific initiative or 'project' after a given period of time.
● *Other teams and groups*: constituted for specific purposes, including client liaison, supplier liaison, work improvement and quality assurance, and staff development; examples are joint consultative committees, joint negotiating committees and works' councils.

All organisations have different titles for the teams and groups that they constitute. However, it is essential to realise that each of the above areas has to be addressed in some way or another. From this point of view, organisations and their managers need to know and understand how to constitute effective teams and groups.

From the above, it is possible to identify an initial set of general group characteristics. These are as follows:

● collective interest in, and commitment to, the stated purpose of the group
● the ability of each member to communicate with every other member of the group, regardless of rank, status or position within the wider organisation
● the ability to generate a collective identity based on a combination of the circumstances and environment in which members find themselves
● shared aims and objectives.

Purpose

Whatever the constitution or structure of the particular group, there needs to be a core purpose, set of targets, aims and objectives, and a pattern of progress. Especially in the creation of new teams and groups, the opportunity for demonstrable early progress and initial successes must be present. Failure to make this available normally leads to immediate demoralisation; members will begin to disassociate themselves from both the group and the work if failures persist and if successes are not forthcoming.

Groups may be constituted formally for specific purposes or to carry out a continuing remit. For example, a group constituted as a disciplinary panel has a formal set of rules and procedures to which it must work, even if it only hears one case. Formal committees have rules and procedures to underpin their effectiveness in serving a continuing purpose.

Teams and groups may be given a degree of permanence and additional purposes if the delivery of their specific task is seen to lead to other opportunities.

All teams and groups need to be wound up and disbanded when either their purpose is served and there is no prospect of developing this into further effective activities, or when it is clear that they are neither effective nor suitable in carrying out the given purpose.

Membership of work groups gives individuals the following opportunities:

- distinctive work roles within which they can be comfortable and happy, and which satisfy their feelings of self-esteem
- establishing a self-summary and self-concept which can be presented both to others in the work group and to the world at large
- contribution to productive, positive, profitable and effective activities, which in itself leads to satisfaction and feelings of personal success and raised levels of self-esteem
- the ability to fulfil personal aims and ambitions which normally have to harmonised and entwined with those of a particular organisation
- wider feelings of general comfort, familiarity and contribution within the organisation.

In practice, people are members of many different groups at places of work. People additionally carry out divergent and sometimes conflicting roles according to membership of specific groups. In some cases, it is not always easy to reconcile work, professional or personal concerns with the demands of specific groups (see Management in Focus 24.1).

Group responsibility

The best workplace teams and groups accept responsibility for the work carried out, and the ways in which targets are met. There is therefore responsibility for both processes and outcomes. While the group is in existence, it is essential to be aware of the nature of responsibility present, and the ways in which it is delivered. For example:

- Peer pressure may act as a force for good in ensuring collective commitment to purpose. However, it may also be used to bully and coerce people into doing things that they would not otherwise do.

MANAGEMENT IN FOCUS 24.1

ROLE CONFLICT IN WORK GROUPS

Publishing

Stefan Ekstrom used to work for an international firm of management consultants. His last assignment was to produce proposals for the restructuring of a large magazine, newspaper and book-publishing company. Stefan was then hired as Chief Executive by the publishing company to implement his own proposals.

The Board of Directors of the publishing company had been perfectly happy with Stefan's proposals. However, now that he, and therefore they, were to be responsible for the implementation of these proposals, he quickly ran into difficulties. Especially there were two key proposals

which were now seen not to fit. These were:

- the divestment of television listings magazines, which sold well but which Stefan's initial investigations had deemed to be declining
- the integration of business publications and men's publications into one division.

Stefan's position as CEO quickly became untenable and he was forced to leave after six months.

The role conflicts that ought to have been addressed were as follows:

- Stefan's role as consultant was very different to that of CEO; and

specific difficulties were enhanced when it became clear that Stefan actually intended to carry out his proposals.

- The Board of Directors was happy and comfortable in their collective role of engaging and supporting the consultancy initiative. However it became clear that they had then been expecting to implement the proposals in their own preferred ways rather than having to work in a reconstituted group, which included the person who had originally developed the proposals.

- The group may use relationships within the organisation in order to gain influence or resources. The group's purpose may be compromised, however, if the providers of influence or resources then uses the group to further their own aims and objectives.
- Groups may be constituted for a stated purpose. It then quickly becomes clear that those who constituted the group have done so because they wish for a particular outcome.
- Individual members may use the group as a shield and abdicate personal responsibility for a given set of outcomes (see Management in Focus 24.2).

The creation of effective groups

Tuckman (1965) identifies four stages as follows:

- *Forming*: the coming together of the individuals concerned; beginning to learn about each other – personality, strengths, capabilities; assessment of the group

MANAGEMENT IN FOCUS 24.2

GROUP RESPONSIBILITY

Handy (1998) states that 'Groups take riskier decisions than the individuals that comprise them would have done if they had been acting independently.' They behave more adventurously.

Fear of non-conformity also contributes to this. When a newcomer joins a group, he/she is normally willing and eager to accept its norms and rules. A range of research underlines this.

The Milgram experiments of 1974 were based on the question: 'Would you torture someone else simply because you were told to do so by a person in authority?'

The experiments involved volunteers acting as 'teachers' of those trying to learn word pairs. If the subject got the pairs wrong the 'teacher' administered an electric shock. The shocks increased in intensity, the greater number of mistakes made.

In fact, no electric shocks were administered, but the volunteer 'teachers' believed they were. They nevertheless pressed the switch that supposedly gave the shocks when directed to do so by someone 'in authority'.

Defiance only occurred when the subject was first encouraged to protest by 'rebellious elements' drawn from among the other group members. Little defiance was exhibited by volunteers working alone.

Philip Zimbardo (Zimbardo et al., 1973) created a simulated prison to observe the impact that the adoption of roles had on individual and group behaviour.

The group of volunteers were divided into two subgroups, prisoners and warders.

Within a very short space of time each adopted the expected, desired or inferred behaviour of their role. Thus the warders became aggressive, domineering, even bullying and violent. The prisoners at first became cowed and submissive. Later they sought ways of escaping. After 36 hours one prisoner left the experiment suffering from a nervous breakdown and three more followed during the next three days. Others promised to forfeit their fees for taking part in the experiment if only they would be released.

purpose; introduction to the tasks, aims and objectives; initial thoughts around rules, norms, ways of working and achieving objectives; initial social and personal interaction; introduction to the group leader/leadership; acquiring and setting resources; constraints, drives and priorities.

- *Storming*: the first creative burst of the group; energising the activities; gaining initial markers about its capabilities and capacities and those of its members; creating the first output and results; mutual appraisal and assessment of expertise and process. Initial conflicts tend to become apparent at this stage, together with the need for means for their resolution. Opportunities and diversions may also become apparent. Conflicts between group and personal agendas start to emerge.

- *Norming*: the establishment of norms – the behavioural boundaries within which members are to act and operate; the establishment of rules and codes of conduct that underline and reinforce the standards set by the norms. By doing this the group provides itself with means of control and the basis of acceptable and unacceptable conduct, performance and activities.

For rules and norms to be effective they must be clear, understood and accepted by all. They must be capable of doing what they set out to do. They must reinforce the mutuality, confidence and integrity necessary to effective group performance.

● *Performing*: the addressing of matters in hand; attacking the tasks to be carried out; getting results; assessing performance. This includes attention to group effectiveness and cohesion, as well as absolute performance measures – the two are invariably entwined.

There are further elements to be added as follows:

● *Re-forming*: which takes place if, for any reason, the group is ineffective in either processes or task delivery. Re-forming may also occur if it becomes clear that, even for the most positive of reasons, the group is not now right for the purpose originally intended.

● *Rejuvenation*: the process of adding fresh expertise and resources to particular groups once the need is demonstrated. Rejuvenation may take place because individual members withdraw for some reason (e.g. they leave the organisation), and so are replaced by others. Rejuvenation may also occur as the result of an organisation deciding that it needs to re-energise a moribund group.

● *Ending*: all teams and groups ultimately have a finite useful life. Some teams and groups come to an end after the performance of one task (as with the disciplinary example above). Other groups may have a life only for the duration of a particular project or initiative; and others still may lose their legitimacy as the result of organisational, technological and expertise changes.

Owen (1985) identifies the need for groups that have had a long constitution and clear remit to celebrate their achievements and mark the parting of the ways of the members. Owen states that from an organisational point of view, this marks a clear indication that the task is achieved and the work is done; and from the member's point of view, it marks a parting of the ways as the people involved now go on to new activities.

This is to be seen as a process rather than a linear progression, a series of steps and stages. For example, early successes in the life of the group may strictly speaking come under the heading of 'performing' but are nevertheless essential to the gaining of mutual confidence, trust and reliance that are integral to effective 'forming'. Regarding this as a process also underlines the need for attention to the behavioural as well as operational aspects (see Management in Focus 24.3) – especially group maintenance.

● ## Issues facing work groups

The main issues facing all work groups are as follows:

● *Atmosphere and relationships*: the nature of relationships; closeness, friendliness, formality and informality.

● *Participation*: the nature and extent to which participation is to be allowed, restricted and restrained; and the extent to which participation is allowed, restricted and restrained because of clear roles within the group, and also in spite of clear roles within the group.

MANAGEMENT IN FOCUS 24.3

FOUNDATION OF CORPORATE AND COLLECTIVE NORMS

People seek to belong to peer groups wherever they congregate; this includes in organisational and corporate surroundings.

The tendency towards exclusivity exists in open-ended and corporate situations where people come and go. The formation of groups is influenced by the fact that fellow workers have been thrown together from the start in overtly unnatural mixes. At a large cocktail party groups will drift together and apart without constraints but in a company people with different backgrounds and views are forced to work together and form groups. The bigger the company and the wider the range in social attributes of individuals, the better the chances are that there will be numerous groups with tight-knit and defensive norms.

Where both formal and informal norms coexist as they do in companies the informal norms transcend the formal. This leads to what has been called 'shadow organisation' in which the apparent management structure is actually superseded in importance by the mesh of group-norm dictates.

Individuals will go to extreme lengths to live up to (or down to) the expectations placed on them by others, even doing things that in other circumstances they recognise as going counter to their own best interests, their characteristics, their normal standards of ethics and behaviour. They can persevere in this behaviour however with the easy rationalisation that 'everybody else is doing it'.

Norms-imposed habits are lasting. Even when the original members of a group have disappeared and/or the norms themselves have lost their original purpose, there will be strong norm remnants unthinkingly respected by new members. Negative norms cannot be changed unless the norm follower is made aware of their existence, because most people respect and go along with the norms quite unconsciously; this is reinforced by pressures to conform.

The priority issue facing all teams and groups at the outset is to ensure that aims and objectives are clarified, and that everyone involved understands and accepts them. Means and methods of communication and decision making have then to be agreed. It also needs to be made clear at the outset how personal and professional conflict, and disagreements are to be handled and resolved. The performance of individuals and the group as a whole has to be measured and evaluated.

The nature of the leadership of the group has to be addressed, clarified, understood and agreed. If one person is to be in charge at all times, this must be made clear; if the leadership is to be rotated, this also must be understood and agreed.

Addressing these issues at the outset provides a strong basis for the development of mutuality of interest and positive and professional working relationships. Attention can then be given to ensuring that the conditions for creating effective work groups are met and the potential for ineffectiveness is kept to a minimum (see Table 24.1).

Table 24.1 Characteristics of effective and ineffective groups

Effective groups	Ineffective groups
Informal relaxed atmosphere	Bored or tense atmosphere
Much discussion, high level of participation	Discussion dominated by one or two people
Tasks, aims and objectives clearly understood	Discussion often irrelevant, unstructured and away from the point
Commitment of members of the groups to each other	No common aims, objectives and purposes
Commitment of members of the groups to the tasks, aims and objectives	Members do not value each other's contribution nor do they listen to each other
Members respect each other's views and listen to each other	Conflict is allowed to develop into open warfare; it may also be suppressed
Conflict is brought out into the open and dealt with constructively when it arises	Majority voting is the norm; pressure is put on minorities to accept this
Decisions are reached by consensus; voting is only used as a matter of last resort	Consensus is neither sought nor achieved
Ideas are expressed freely and openly; rejection of ideas is not a stigma	Criticism is embarrassing and personal
Leadership is shared as appropriate, and is divided according to the nature of the tasks; ultimate responsibility, authority and accountability rests with the designated group leader	Leadership is by dictat and is issued by the group leader only
The group examines its own progress and behaviour	The group avoids any discussion about its behaviour

Source: from D. McGregor, *The Human Side of Enterprise*, Harper and Row, 1970.

● Group factors and characteristics

The main factors that affect the cohesion, behaviour and effectiveness of groups are outlined below.

Size

The size of the group relates to both the numbers of people involved and the nature of their involvement. Some authorities have tried to identify optimum size for work groups. This has to be seen in the context of the nature of the task to be carried out – if a particular process needs two people then this is the optimum size in the circumstances; if a process needs 15 people, then 15 is the optimum (see Management in Focus 24.4).

MANAGEMENT IN FOCUS 24.4

GROUP SIZE

Creating the right group size requires that a wide range of factors is addressed. There are some absolutes: the size of a tennis doubles team is two; of a rugby team, 15. In work situations the technology used may determine that a group size is three, eight, 30 or whatever.

In general terms there is a balance involved between size, contribution and participation – the larger the group, the greater the range of expertise and quality is drawn in, but the lesser the chance of full participation by individual members.

Larger groups also have a greater risk of splitting into sub-groups (either formal, based on the work, or informal, based on workstation location, friendship, establishment of common bonds and interests). Total group identity may then become diluted. The interaction between the sub-groups becomes a barrier to the progress and achievement of the full group. The sub-groups themselves create their own barriers – especially if they have become constituted around the distinctive expertise of members. If this is in high demand by the rest

of the main group, the sub-group establishes its own filter and priority systems based on its preferences and criteria.

Smaller groups are less susceptible the sub-grouping effect. They may however develop a group identity so strong that it leads to a belief that the group is infallible and indispensable.

The size of any group therefore has clear implications, both for its management and leadership and also for participants if these pitfalls are to be avoided.

Leadership of teams and groups

Whatever the size or remit of the particular team or group, those in leadership positions are directly responsible and accountable for creating the conditions, relationships and processes in which work can be produced effectively, and in which those involved are both comfortable and productive.

Morale and satisfaction are monitored through the study of absenteeism, accidents, member turnover and the ability to attract, retain and develop new talent. They are established and developed through a full understanding of the tasks and activities to be carried out, and fulfilling the expectations of group members.

Group ideology is normally based around concepts of participation, involvement and recognition of the value of the contribution that each member makes. It is underpinned by norms and rules. Individuals may also choose to belong to a group (or seek to join it) because of its strong and distinctive ideology. Some organisations – for example, The Body Shop and Nissan – also attract people because of their strong commitment to the environment or product and service quality.

Team and group spirit must be positive and harmonious, and capable of acceptance by all. Individuals have their own reasons for belonging to groups in addition to professional, occupational and intrinsic membership value; where group spirit is either negative or not present at all, individuals revert to professional and occupational (rather than group or organisational) identity.

Conformity and loyalty are normally expected of individuals who join groups. Conformity and loyalty are at their strongest and most effective where individual aims, objectives and values are capable of being harmonised and integrated with those of the group. Conformity is reinforced by:

- *Physical identity*: including the wearing of uniforms.
- *Social identity*: the use of particular modes of address, manners, and approaches to each other by group members.
- *Emphasis on the positive*: in which the standards, attitudes and values to which individuals are required to conform are positive.
- *Regimentation*: in which the standards, attitudes and values to which individuals are required to conform are imposed from above.

All teams and groups need to know and understand environmental pressures and changes; and other factors that they cannot control. Groups have to be able to respond to changes; resources can be – and often are – reduced, direction and priorities are changed, and results are suddenly required much more quickly than previously envisaged, yet the groups still need to operate effectively. They may also have to work effectively if the leadership is changed and if a new leader is imposed.

● Group cohesion

Cohesive groups are most likely to be achieved if attention is paid to: the division, allocation and structuring of work; the creation of a behaviourally suitable working environment; and the installation of a leader or manager who is aware of the pressures and potential problems, and acceptable to the rest of the group.

Effective division of work ensures that individual and collective capabilities and expertise are used to greatest effect. It also includes enabling people to follow their personal and professional preferences wherever possible, as long as this can be offered to everyone. Unpleasant, mundane and routine tasks are also to be shared out on a basis of equality.

The creation of a suitable environment depends on the availability of technology and equipment, and physical proximity if at all possible. Difference of location is a physical barrier to group identity and therefore effectiveness. This difference may be a matter of yards, or thousands, or hundreds of miles.

A productive environment can be created only if these points are first recognised and then underpinned with adequate and effective methods and systems of communication. If the environment is not managed effectively, those involved will begin to form their own sub-groupings, alternative cultures, and unofficial sets of values (see Figure 24.1 and Management in Focus 24.5).

● Sources of potential group stresses and strains

A key part of the effective leadership and direction of groups and teams is recognising where things can, and do, go wrong. Those in leadership positions therefore require active and continued attention to the following:

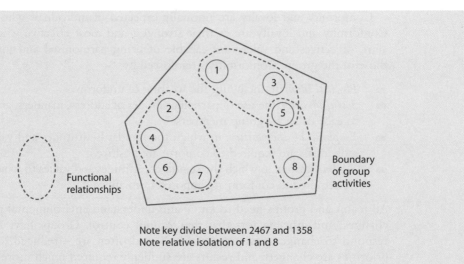

Functional relationships

Boundary of group activities

Note key divide between 2467 and 1358
Note relative isolation of 1 and 8

Figure 24.1 Group cohesion: sociogram of an eight-person group

MANAGEMENT IN FOCUS 24.5

CANTEEN CULTURES AND NETWORKING

These terms are used to describe the non-formal, unofficial (and often unwanted) ways in which groups think, behave and act. They derive from unofficial meetings and interactions between members (for example in the works or office canteen) where the real views, aspirations, attitudes – and prejudices – of those involved are nurtured and developed.

It is to be found in response also to the symbols and labels used – the managers' dining room, the officers' mess, the workers' cafeteria – and also 'the old school tie', 'one of us/not one of us'. These clearly differentiate between different grades and classes of staff. This reinforces group identity among those so labelled. It also presents exclusions and barriers to those who do not carry the particular label.

The canteen culture is often a very powerful organisational force, especially when negative. Ways of working and patterns of behaviour are derived and developed according to the wants of the groups involved rather than the needs of the work groups of which they are also (invariably) members.

This culture is also used as a form of networking by people who wish to gain access to particular work groups, departments, projects and activities. They use these informal channels rather than those devised by organisations if they perceive that these constitute the best and most certain routes of success and acceptance.

- The nature and mixture of the personalities involved, and the nature of activities that are engaged in with the purpose of reconciling these.
- The nature and mixture of the expertise and talent that is brought to the group

by its different members. This is especially important where some members of the group have expertise that is either rare or of high price/high value.

- The nature and mix of other and more general strengths and weaknesses that each of those involved brings to the group.
- Means and methods of communication, consultation and participation; the availability of good-quality information. Stress and strain is created when these are either inappropriate, inaccurate, dishonest or incomplete.
- Changes in group composition and membership; changes in influence of particular members as the task unfolds; the bringing in of new members; the phasing out of those whose part of the task is done.
- Levels of confidence, trust, respect and regard held by each member of the group towards the others and their positions in the group.

Attention is constantly required to the nature of the working environment, and this includes ergonomic factors, technology, location and design of workstations, and the physical distance/proximity that exists between group members. It also includes extremes of temperature, climate, discomfort, danger and location.

Attention is required to the form of management style adopted, and its continued suitability to the situation and task in hand. In particular, leadership and management style must be concerned with the suitability of the means of communication, nature of decision-making processes, levels of performance and how these are achieved. It is additionally the case that leadership and management style must be able to operate effectively in relation to matters outside the group's control.

Other symptoms of group and team malfunction are as follows:

- Poor performance in which deadlines are missed, output is sub-standard and customer complaints increase.
- Members reject responsibility for their actions and for those of the group. They become involved in lobbying and seek to blame others for these shortcomings. The group breaks up into sub-groups, and elites are created within it. Individuals claim rewards and bonuses for team efforts. Scapegoating and blame occurs, with destructive criticism and dismissive behaviour towards others, both inside and outside the group.
- Becoming involved in grievances with other group members; increases in the numbers of these; personality and personal clashes; overspill of professional and expert argument into personal relationships.
- Increases in general levels of grievances, absenteeism and accidents; moves to leave the group.
- Lack of interest in results, activities, plans and proposals of the group.
- General attitude and demeanour that exists between group members; the general attitude and demeanour of individuals within the group; lack of pride and joy in the group; moves to leave the group again; difficulties in attracting new members to the group.
- The presence of an individual or sub-group that is known, believed or perceived by the rest of the members to be holding them back from greater achievements and successes. It is a very short step from this attitude to the presence of bullying, victimisation and harassment.

Some of these are clearly specific to group activities and functions. Others are more general symptoms that should be considered in the group context as part of the continuing monitoring of its effectiveness. For the person concerned with identifying and assessing trouble and potential problems, each symptom can be taken as a starting point for the process of tackling problems (see Management in Focus 24.6).

⬤ Group development

The creation and formation of effective teams and groups is not an end in itself. To remain effective, cohesion, capabilities and potential must be maintained and developed. This takes the following forms:

- Infusions of talent from outside, bringing in people with distinctive qualities and expertise to give emphases and energy to particular priorities and directions.
- Infusions of new skills, knowledge and qualities from within through the identification of potential among existing members and having them receive training and development, and targeted work that has the purpose of bringing out the latent expertise.

MANAGEMENT IN FOCUS 24.6

THE 0.5 PER CENT RULE

The 0.5 per cent rule is the rule that states that 99.5 per cent of people are penalised for the misdemeanours of the other 0.5 per cent. Rules and procedures are created with the stated purpose of standardisation of behaviour without reference to the fact that most people behave as they should all of the time.

For example when someone steals something, everyone on the premises is subject to searches and security checks. When someone is seen to be late arriving for work, sophisticated clocking in and signing in procedures are devised.

The certain result of this is the alienation of all of those who do not steal and who do turn up on time. If there is a problem with an individual, it is a problem that must be addressed as an individual issue.

There are knock-on effects both ways also. The more sophisticated the set of rules, the greater the length of time spent on them through consultative, joint negotiating and other group management and industrial relations activities – and the greater the consequent waste of organisational resources. Conversely, if individual problems are dealt with on an individual basis by managers as and when they arise, all the time, energy and resources that would otherwise be wasted is freed up for other things. If the manager in question is doing his/her job properly, misdemeanours happen only rarely and are dealt with quickly when they do arise.

Either approach underlines the levels of respect and regard in which the staff are held. The greater the amount of this type of regulation and procedure, the lower the level of respect and regard. Above all, the converse is true: the fewer such rules and regulations, the greater the level of respect and regard in which the staff are held. In the latter case the staff are treated as adults and are much more likely to respond as such when required. The approach also requires that the general malcontent or criminal is dealt with on an individual basis. Rules are no substitute for judgement in any circumstances.

- Attention to group processes when it is apparent that these are getting in the way of effective task performance, and attention to task performance when it is apparent that this is ineffective.
- Attention to the relationship between team and task. This may involve using a good team to carry out a difficult or demanding task, or using the difficult and demanding task to build a good and effective teams. From either standpoint, the results will only be fully effective if the task achievement is within the capabilities of the group. As long as this is so, the rewards of success are likely to contribute greatly to overall group performance, well-being and confidence among members.
- Attention to team roles, both to build on strengths and to eliminate weaknesses. This is likely to involve reassessing what the requirements and priorities are, and reassessing the strengths and weaknesses of each individual. It may lead to reallocation or rotation of roles and infusions of new talent, either from within or without.
- Attention to team roles and expertise from the point of view that different qualities, expertise and capability are likely to be more or less important at different phases of activity. This may lead to infusions again, or to the buying in of expertise on an 'as-required' basis (for example, using consultants). It may also involve the recognition that members of the group may need to be let go once they have made their particular contribution, and that there will be a time when the group itself has come to the end of its useful life.

The core of effective group work is the ability to use the talents and expertise of everyone involved to deliver the results required within the constraints and opportunities of group norms, mutuality of interest and respect, and the pressures of the operating and external environment. All aspects of group development must concentrate on these as core issues if enduring high levels of output and productivity, and mutuality of interest are to be maintained (see Management in Focus 24.7).

● High performing teams and groups

The characteristics of high performing teams and groups may be summarised as follows:

- They have high levels of autonomy, the ability to self-manage and self-organise. This includes team responsibility for self-regulation and self-discipline. It encourages the fast and effective resolution of problems and a commitment to dealing with issues before they become problems.
- There are clear and unambiguous performance targets, capable of achievement and related to overall organisation purpose; these should be understood, accepted and committed to by all concerned.
- They take full responsibility for all aspects of production and output process, quality assurance, customer relations and complaints. Issues and problems are identified and addressed by the particular team so that improvements can be made directly without going through sub-processes and procedures.
- Job titles do not include references to status, differentials or trappings, or other elements of psychological distance.

MANAGEMENT IN FOCUS 24.7

FADDISH APPROACHES TO TEAM AND GROUP DEVELOPMENT

'Teams that play together, work together' is a mantra familiar to many managers. This has led the unwary to engage in a variety of team-building exercises, including paint-balling, mountaineering, staff nights out and even corporate holidays. These activities are only ever effective if they are structured into a regular programme of events, conducted during working hours, and integrated with hard business, organisation, group and individual development activities.

In isolation, the mantra itself is false. In practice, teams that play together do not normally work together. On corporate paint-balling and other events, people adopt roles different to those at work; the ways in which they behave in these roles may be uncomfortable and unacceptable to the others involved. This in turn can, and does, lead to wider perceptions and beliefs that particular individuals are unsuitable overall for membership of the team, however good they may be at their job. This can additionally lead to individuals being identified as being suitable for specific organisational roles on the basis of their effectiveness and success at mountaineering.

All team-building exercises require clear aims and objectives, boundaries, and pre-stated constraints and confines around patterns of behaviour, especially those which would not normally be exhibited at places of work.

- Team-based reward systems are available and payable to everyone who contributed, based on percentages of salary rather than occupational differentials.
- There is an open approach: to environment layout (no individual offices, trappings, barriers or other factors of physical and psychological distance); self-commitment for the whole team; open communication systems and high-quality communications; open approaches to problems and issues; open airing of grievances and concerns – these are usually very few in such circumstances, so that when they do arise full attention is paid (see Management in Focus 24.8).
- High performance teams require autonomy as stated above; this has to be supported through a 'federal' relationship with the core organisation, operating systems and reporting relationships. These relationships are based on monitoring, review and evaluation of production and output targets and other task-based indicators. The general management style must be supportive rather than directive, bureaucratic or administrative.

Additional requirements and conditions are as follows:

- Fast and easy access to maintenance and support staff to ensure that equipment breakdowns are repaired as soon as possible and that production levels can be kept as high as possible for as long as possible.

BRITISH AIRWAYS' CABIN CREW

British Airways' cabin crew deliver a high and clearly defined standard of service on all flights. This is in spite of the fact that, because of different shift patterns and working arrangements, very few individual members of the cabin crew remain in post on an extended basis.

The level of service is therefore dependent upon extensive and continuous staff training. The result is that, by the time any staff go to work on airliners, they know and understand their roles and the rules by which they are required to abide, and are expert at the tasks to be carried out.

Once assigned to a flight, the members of staff meet up with their cabin services director, who is responsible for all activities on board the airliner, other than flying the plane.

The staff arrive three hours before the flight is due to depart. Under the direction of the cabin services director, all the members then introduce themselves. Specific tasks and duties are then allocated. The longest-serving member of the cabin staff has first choice, and all duties are allocated and chosen on the basis of relative length of service. This is clearly known and understood by everybody; anyone who is not happy to work in this way is not allowed to become a member of BA cabin staff.

Once the staff arrive on the airliner, each has a clear set of tasks and duties to perform, both while the plane is on the ground and subsequently when it is in flight. As stated above, each member of staff has been fully trained and drilled in the conduct of each task and duty, and also in the attitudes and presentation required towards the passengers.

In order for this to be effective, heavy and continuing investment is required in the training and development of all members of cabin crew staff. This is further underpinned by the fact that many of the staff have always dreamed of working as cabin crew, and so the job is something that they have always wanted.

In this part of their activities, British Airways sets the highest possible standards of conduct, behaviour and performance; this in turn has established, and continues to establish, the norms for customer service and presentation throughout the airline industries of the world.

- Full flexibility of work, multi-skilling and interchangeability between task roles. Roles are assigned according to people's behavioural strengths.
- Continuous development of skills, knowledge, qualities, capabilities and expertise; continuous attention to performance quality and output; continuous attention to production, quality, volume and time; continuous attention to high levels of service and satisfaction.
- High levels of involvement, confidence, respect and enthusiasm among group members, towards both each other and the work.
- Attention to equipment and technology to ensure that this is suitable and capable of producing what is required to the stated and expected standards of volume, quality and time.
- Simple, clear and supportive policies and procedures covering organisational rules and regulations, human resource management and discipline, grievance and disputes.

- Continuous monitoring and review to ensure that the intended focus and direction is pursued and that group activities are in accordance with this (see Management in Focus 24.9).

Conclusions

Everybody belongs to groups. To be effective in working situations, it is essential that there is as great a measure of mutual trust, respect, identity, cohesion and clarity of purpose, understood and accepted by all, as is possible in the circumstances. It is also essential that attention is paid to the human values – the shared values – necessary for its effective functioning as a working group.

The critical nature of the relationship between the leader and the group should therefore be apparent. It is essential that the leader establishes both clear patterns of work and an environment in which the mutuality of interest and respect can be assured. This is the cornerstone on which cohesion and effectiveness are founded. Without it, there can be

MANAGEMENT IN FOCUS 24.9

MANAGING HIGH PERFORMANCE AND EXPERT GROUPS

All organisations seek to develop work groups to their maximum potential and capability. This however, is not an end in itself. Problems arise in managing the following:

- highly expert and dedicated groups
- groups that enjoy high levels of autonomy
- groups that include strong, dominant, arrogant and aggressive personalities
- groups that are known, believed and perceived to be very successful (and with those that have a long history of failure, demotivation and lack of output)

- groups that enjoy high levels of favour, prestige and status.

The potential for problems lies in the perceived inability of managers to deal with group members on the basis of equal status and prestige, whatever the rank of the manager. Problems are compounded when the group's managers are not present all of the time, and are located away from the group's place of work. Psychological distance may also be reinforced by group professional and occupational attitudes of contempt towards managers; this is a form of bunker mentality and group think, and needs to be addressed.

In these situations, all managers must establish and develop visibility and a physical presence. This is instituted by 'managing by walking around' the location of the group. It is reinforced by establishing a series of regular staff meetings that all group members must attend. Barriers have to be broken down so that the group learns that its expertise, prestige and value have still to be delivered in the total context in which it was created in the first place. The physical presence also institutes, develops and reinforces the ties between the group and the rest of the organisation.

no secure basis for group development, or for the progress and enhancement of the expertise of individual members (see Management in Focus 24.10).

If this cohesion does not exist, individual members will only use the group as long as it remains in their interests. Their performance and contribution declines, and they will move on as soon as it becomes apparent that they have no further personal interest, respect or value for the group and its activities.

Effective groups therefore require a combination of early and continued operational successes together with a mutually enhancing and developing personal and professional respect among the members. All group activities that are proposed must be considered from each of these points of view. If something is contemplated or planned which can be seen to have potential for a damaging or divisive effect on the group then, where possible, that initiative should be abandoned or re-positioned in order to ensure that everybody receives some form of benefit. Where it is not possible to abandon the initiative or proposal, then recognition of the likely effects on group cohesion must be acknowledged and understood. Steps can then be taken to remedy the situation as early as possible, and from the point of view of understanding and pre-planning, rather than surprise.

It is also particularly important that attention is paid to the rewards (both financial and non-financial) that are available to group members. Ideally merit, performance and profit-related financial rewards should be paid on the basis of fairness and evenness, and the current prevailing wisdom is that all members should receive an equal percentage of their salary in these cases. Where for some reason it becomes necessary or right and proper to pay an individual above and beyond the rewards available to the rest of the group, the reasons for this should be made plain to everybody. If these are honest and straightforward, then they will be understood. If they are not, then the leadership and direction of the group is always called into question.

Finally, it is necessary to understand that all groups come to an end. They either outlive their useful life, or else the leadership changes, or the nature of the task and work activities changes to such an extent that the requirement for the group as presently constituted no longer exists. It is essential to manage this end phase, to avoid feelings of loss and deprivation on the part of members. As stated above, many organisations provide wakes and other celebrations at the end of particular group functions, projects or periods of activity. Even if such events are not arranged, acknowledgement of the group's contribution must be formally made. This enables everyone involved to recognise for themselves that a particular period of work has come to en end, and to have this publicly acknowledged. People are then able to move on within themselves to the next part of their working life.

CRITICAL THINKING, ANALYSIS AND EVALUATION

1. What are the major disadvantages of committee work and how can these best be overcome?
2. What lessons ought to be learned by all organisations from the British Airways' cabin crew example (Management in Focus 24.8 above)?
3. Identify the main reasons why canteen cultures arise and the steps that organisations should take for dealing with them.
4. Identify the main roles and functions of group leaders. What are the best ways of:
   a)   identifying these
   b)   training individuals to be effective group leaders?

MANAGEMENT IN FOCUS 24.10

STRUCTURING INDIVIDUALS INTO EFFECTIVE TEAMS

Belbin (1986; 1992; 2002) proposes the means by which the capabilities and characteristics of individuals can be identified and then harmonised with those with different characteristics and expertise, forming effective, productive and eventually high-performing, teams.

Belbin isolated the characteristics and capabilities of individuals (see Figure 24.2 below).

The value of this approach is to demonstrate the need for a wide range of tasks and activities in all team and group working situations. Whatever the matter in hand, there is a need for: creativity; activity; questioning, analysis, evaluation and judgement; attention to detail; and completeness of work.

Type	Symbol	Typical features	Positive qualities
Company worker	CW	Conservative, dutiful, practicable	Organising ability, practical common-sense, hard-working
Chairman	CH	Calm, self-confident, controlled	A capacity for treating and welcoming all potential contributors on their merits and without prejudice. A strong sense of objectives
Shaper	SH	Highly strung, outgoing, dynamic	Drive and readiness to challenge inertia, ineffectiveness, complacency or self-deception
Plant/creative genius	PL	Individualistic, serious-minded, unorthodox	Genius, imagination, intellect, knowledge
Resource investigator	RI	Extroverted, enthusiastic, curious, communicative	A capacity for contacting people and exploring anything new. An ability to respond to challenge
Monitor-evaluator	ME	Sober, unemotional, prudent	Judgement, discretion, hard-headedness
Team worker	TW	Social orientated, rather mild, sensitive	An ability to respond to people and situations, and to promote team spirit
Completer-finisher	CF	Painstaking, orderly, conscientious, anxious	A capacity to follow through to perfection

Figure 24.2 Effective teams
Source: R. M. Belbin (1986)

DEVELOPING MANAGEMENT SKILLS AND EXPERTISE

CANYON PICKLES LTD

Canyon Pickles Ltd is a specialist supplier of pickles, herbs, spices, sauces and other condiments to the food industry. The company has two distinctive approaches - it sells packaged products to the supermarket retail and food wholesale sectors; and it sells specialist products to order and by contracted agreements with restaurants, pubs and bars.

The company employs a sales force of ten to deal with the supermarket, wholesale and retail side of the operations, and a sales and client liaison team of 20 to deal with the restaurant and specialist part of the business. Each team is paid a combination of salary and performance related bonus; and bonus targets are regularly met, and usually exceeded by both teams.

Working relations are generally good between and within the two teams, and the team that serves the restaurant sector especially is very tightly knit. However, there are troubles from time to time over productivity and performance. In particular, one of the most enduring grumbles is that those on the supermarket team feel that they have to work a lot harder for their money than those who deal with the restaurants. The restaurant side of the business has additionally come to be seen as much more glamorous by the company and many within it, since it gained a long term contract with the producers of television shows, including *Ready Steady Cook* and *Saturday Kitchen*.

Accordingly, the company has decided to take on a further six persons for the restaurant team. When the jobs are advertised, all ten members of the supermarket team apply.

Questions

1. On the basis of what you are told, evaluate the basis of the cohesion and strength of each team.
2. On the basis of what you are told, how are you going to investigate the reasons for the evident dissatisfaction of the supermarket team?
3. Make recommendations for possible courses of action open to the company; and evaluate the opportunities and consequences of each.

Chapter twenty five

Management and motivation

'The wishbone will never replace the backbone.'
Ron Saunders, Manager, Manchester City Football Club, 1973.

'I have a dream.'
Martin Luther King, the Lincoln Memorial in Washington DC, 1963.

'To turn the dream of First Tuesday into reality, I worked 100 hours a week
non-stop for three years. I had no other life – it was all First Tuesday.
That's what it took to turn the dream into reality.'
Julie Meyer, interview for *Management Today*, May 2000.

Chapter outline

- Introduction
- Definitions
- Initial conclusions
- Major theories of motivation
- Motivation, achievement and rewards
- Motivation and incentives
- Frustration
- Conclusions

Chapter objectives

After studying this chapter, you should be able to:

- understand the major theories of motivation, and their relationship to human behaviour and work performance

- understand the conditions that have to be in place if long-term commitment to work is to be sustainable

- understand the steps that need to be taken when low levels of motivation and morale are present

- understand and be able to apply specific lessons, with the objective of raising levels of commitment and morale.

Introduction

Motivation is a reflection of the reasons why people do things. All behaviour has a purpose (often several). All behaviour is therefore based on choice – people choose to do things that they do. Sometimes this choice is very restricted (sink or swim for example). Sometimes again, it is constrained by the law (for example, stopping the car when the traffic lights are red). And again, it is constrained by the norms and processes of society – for example, people tend to wear smart clothes to a party where they know that everybody else will be well dressed. In each case however, there is a choice, though the propensity and encouragement and direction to choose one course of action rather than the other in the examples given is strong, if not overwhelming.

Definitions

Huczynski and Buchanan (2003): a combination of goals towards which human behaviour is directed; the process through which those goals are pursued and achieved; and the social factors involved.

Luthans (1992): motivation is a combination of needs, drives and incentives. Motivation is defined as 'a process that starts with a physiological or psychological deficiency or need that activates behaviour or a drive that it is aimed at a goal or incentive'.

Mullins (2005): the underlying concept of motivation is some driving force within individuals by which they attempt to achieve some goal in order to fulfil some need or expectation. Mullins also distinguishes between extrinsic motivation related to tangible rewards such as money, and intrinsic motivation related to psychological rewards such as the sense of challenge and achievement.

Some key factors begin to become apparent.

Initial conclusions

Workplace, occupational and professional motivation is a process. This process is based on a combination of driving forces. On the one hand are internal drives from within the individual, related to what the organisation can provide to satisfy these drives. On the other hand, there is a commitment to the organisation on the part of the individual, which entitles the organisation to expect that the individual will deliver his or her expertise in the ways it requires and in its best interests, over an extended period of time. Motivation is therefore a combination of mutuality of interest, capability and willingness.

Many organisations mistake motivation for incentives. Organisations offer incentives – directly targeted rewards – which they then expect to deliver an enduring commitment. Incentives provide specific rewards for short-term achievement only; and if the organisation's only tool to motivate staff is the provision of incentives, then incentives have to be made available for every activity (see Management in Focus 25.1).

Goals and ambitions must be present, realistic and achievable if satisfaction is eventually to occur. Problems arise when the goals set are too low (leading to

MANAGEMENT IN FOCUS 25.1

MOTIVATION AND INCENTIVES IN THE CENTRAL BANKING SECTOR

The central banking sector is composed of the national banks of the countries of the world, together with over-arching bodies, including the International Monetary Fund, European Central Bank, and World Bank.

Across the whole sector, there is a structural difficulty in attracting, recruiting and retaining persons of expertise.

Highly qualified staff come to work in the central banking sector and then, attracted by the much higher salaries on offer, move to the commercial banking sector.

The sector as a whole has therefore recently begun to concentrate incentives on what is a wider issue of capability and commitment. Incentives were traditionally provided to

support the attraction part of the process rather than to contribute to retention. Until recently, few organisations in the central banking sector concentrated their recruitment effort on targeting the characteristics and ambitions of those who wanted to work in the sector. Only belatedly has a wider and more positive approach been adopted.

feelings of frustration), or too high (leading to the constant lack of achievement). They must also be acceptable to the individual concerned – in terms of self-image, self-worth, and self-value – so they are likely to be positive and based on the drive for improved levels of comfort, capability and well-being. They must also be acceptable (or at least not unacceptable) to the society and environment in which the individual lives and works, and capable of being harmonised and integrated with them.

A critical part of the motivation process lies in the nature and levels of recognition accorded to the achievement of particular goals. The need for recognition is therefore a drive. Individuals pursue goals that are of value to them; it is therefore essential that organisations match their objectives to those that are important to their staff.

The components of achievement are the anticipated and actual rewards that the fulfilment of a particular goal brings. High levels of achievement consistently occur where real rewards completely match those that are anticipated – and where they are greater than expected. Low levels occur where the anticipated rewards are not forthcoming; this devalues the achievement. High or complete achievement is normally seen and perceived as successful. Low achievement or failure to achieve is seen and perceived as – a failure (see Management in Focus 25.2).

Additional issues

Additional issues now become apparent.

People need success. They therefore tend to aim their sights at what they know they can do or think they can do – or think that they may be able to do – so that success is forthcoming. Genuine successes, victories and triumphs enhance feelings of self-esteem and self-value; failures diminish them.

MANAGEMENT IN FOCUS 25.2

ACHIEVEMENT MOTIVATION THEORY: D.C. McCLELLAND

McClelland (1971) identified relationships between personal characteristics, social and general background, and work achievement.

Persons with high needs for achievement exhibited the following characteristics:

- They have task rather than relationship orientation.
- They prefer tasks over which they have sole or overriding control and responsibility.
- They need to identify closely, and be identified closely, with the successful outcomes of their action.
- They require task balance: the task has to be difficult enough on the one hand to be challenging and rewarding, to offer the chance to demonstrate expertise and good results, and

gain status and recognition from others. On the other hand it needs to be moderate enough to be capable of successful achievement.

- High achievers seek risk balance, in which the individual seeks to avoid as far as possible the likelihood and consequences of failure.
- Feedback is needed on the results achieved to reinforce the knowledge of success and to ensure that successes are validated and publicised.
- They need progress, variety and opportunity.

Need for achievement is based on a combination of:

- intrinsic motivation: the drives from within the individual
- extrinsic motivation: the drives, pressures and

exp-ectations exerted by the organisation, peers and society.

The need to achieve is also influenced by education, awareness, social and cultural background, and values. One potential problem was identified in relation to the appointment of high achievers to highly responsible managerial and supervisory positions. Because the higher achievers tended to be task rather than relationship driven, many did not possess (or regard as important) the human relations characteristics necessary to get things done through people, nor did they understand that they would need to develop these if they were to be successful in the future.

Source: D.C. McClelland (1971) *Human Aspects of Management*, John Wiley.

People need rewards, both extrinsic (money, trappings and status) and intrinsic (self-esteem and value). Rewards must be valued by the individual receiving them, and also by the wider society, organisation, occupation and profession.

People need to be accepted, recognised and valued by others. This value arises through a combination of pursuing things that the individual knows or perceives will be valued by those around them (as stated above) and of seeking out those who will value the achievements for themselves.

People need to develop and improve. If satisfaction is not forthcoming in one field, individuals are likely to lose interest and find something else to pursue. As well as matters of comfort and well-being, improvement includes broadening and deepening experience and variety of life (including working life). It also includes developing new skills, capabilities and interests with the view to pursuing personal potential as far as possible.

As well as being workplace drives, these are wider social and behavioural needs, wants and desires. Each is influenced, developed and conditioned by societies and organisations, and groups within them. Each is based on more fundamental human needs, as follows:

- *The need and instinct for society and belonging*: this is a reflection of the need for esteem, warmth and respect. More fundamentally, it is the need to belong, to interact and to have personal contact with those with whom the individual has identity, respect, liking and love. It also includes being drawn to those who have similar hopes, aspirations, interests and ambitions.
- *The need to be in control*: this is the ability to influence the actions and feelings of others, and to influence the environment, to make it comfortable and productive in response to the particular needs, wants and drives. Control is a function of purpose – the organisation and arrangement of particular resources (including other people) for given reasons.
- *The need to progress*: this is a reflection of the capacity to develop, to enhance knowledge, skills and capability. It includes:
  - economic drives for better standards of living, quality of life and enhanced capacity to make choices
  - social drives to gain status, respect, influence and esteem as a result of enhanced capability and economic advantage
  - personal drives reflecting ambition and the need to maximise/optimise the potential to achieve
  - opportunistic drives, the identification and pursuit of opportunities that may become apparent and attractive to the individual
  - invention and creativity, the ability to see things from various points of view and create the means by which quality of life can be enhanced.

Development, adaptation and creativity are also features of the needs for survival, society and control. They are a reflection of the extent to which the individuals are able to influence their ability to survive, belong and control their environment.

Except at the point of life and death, when the instinct for survival is everything, these needs constitute parts of the wider process of adaptation and interaction. At given moments therefore, some needs will be stronger than others – there is no linear progression from one to the next.

⬤ Major theories of motivation

Rensis Likert: System 4

Likert's contribution to the theories of workplace motivation arose from his work with high-performing managers: managers and supervisors who achieved high levels of productivity, low levels of cost and high levels of employee motivation, participation and involvement at their places of work. The work demonstrated a correlation between this success and the style and structure of the work groups that they created.

The groups not only achieved high levels of economic output, and therefore wage and salary targets, but were also heavily involved in both group maintenance activities and the design and definition of work patterns. This was underpinned by a supportive style of supervision and the generation of a sense of personal worth, importance and esteem in belonging to the group itself.

Likert identified four styles or systems of management, as follows:

- *System 1*: Exploitative Authoritative, where power and direction come from the top downwards and where there is no participation, consultation or involvement on the part of the workforce. Workforce compliance is thus based on fear. Unfavourable attitudes are generated, there is little confidence or trust, and low levels of motivation to cooperate or generate output above the absolute minimum.
- *System 2*: Benevolent Authoritative, which is similar to System 1 but which allows some upward opportunity for consultation and participation in some areas.

In both Systems 1 and 2, productivity may be high over the short run when targets can be achieved through a combination of coercion and bonus and overtime payments. However, both productivity and earnings are demonstrably low over the long run; high absenteeism and labour turnover are also manifest. In System 2, the basis of collective involvement can be developed through engaging a more consultative style.

- *System 3*: Consultative, where aims and objectives are set after discussion and consultation with subordinates; where communication is two-way and where teamwork is encouraged at least in some areas. Attitudes towards both superiors and the organisation tend to be favourable, especially when the organisation is working steadily. Productivity tends to be higher, absenteeism and staff turnover lower. There are also demonstrable reductions in waste, improvements in product quality, reductions in overall operational costs and higher levels of earning on the part of the workforce.
- *System 4: Participative*, where three basic concepts have a very important effect on performance. These are: the use by the manager of the principle of supportive relationships throughout the work group referred to above; the use of group decision making and group methods of supervision; and the setting of high performance and very ambitious goals for the department and also for the organisation overall.

Abraham Maslow: a hierarchy of needs

Maslow (1960) presented a hierarchy of needs which explained different types and levels of motivation that were important people at different times. The hierarchy of needs works from the bottom of the pyramid upwards, showing the most basic needs and motivations at the lowest levels and those created by, or fostered by, civilisation and society towards the top of it (see Figure 25.2).

The needs are as follows.

1. *Physiological needs*: for food, drink, air, warmth, sleep and shelter; basic survival needs related to the instinct for self-preservation.
2. *Safety and security needs*: protection from danger, threats or deprivation and the need for stability (or relative stability) of environment.
3. *Social needs*: a sense of belonging to a society and the groups within it, for

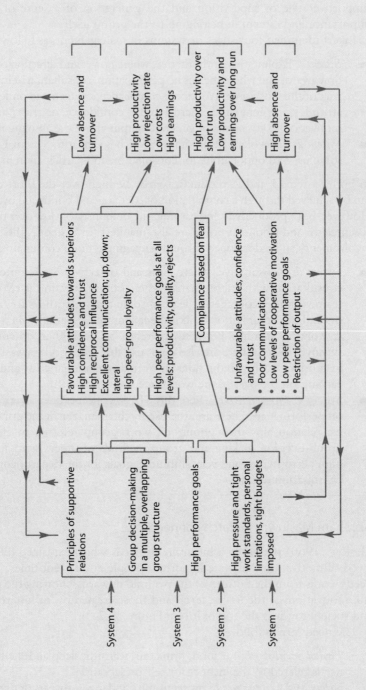

Figure 25.1 System 4
Source: Likert (1961)

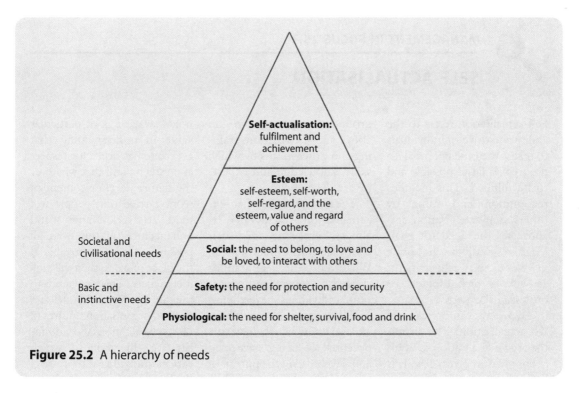

Figure 25.2 A hierarchy of needs

example, the family, the organisation, the work group. Also included in this level are matters to do with the giving and receiving of friendship, basic status needs within these groups, and the need to participate in social activities.

4. *Esteem needs*: for self-respect, self-esteem, appreciation, recognition and status both on the part of the individual concerned and the society, circle or group in which he or she interrelates; part of the esteem need is therefore the drive to gain the respect, esteem and appreciation accorded by others.

5. *Self-actualisation needs*: for self-fulfilment, self-realisation, personal development, accomplishment, mental, material and social growth and the development and fulfilment of the creative faculties (see Management in Focus 25.3).

Two-factor theories

Herzberg (1967) identifies two sets of factors affecting workplace motivation as follows:

- those factors that lead to extreme dissatisfaction with the job, the environment and the workplace
- those factors that lead to extreme satisfaction with the job, the environment and the workplace.

The factors giving rise to satisfaction he called motivators. Those giving rise to dissatisfaction he called hygiene factors (see Figure 25.3).

The motivators he identifies are: achievement, recognition, the nature of the work

MANAGEMENT IN FOCUS 25.3

SELF-ACTUALISATION

Self-actualisation refers to the ability and drive of individuals to realise their full potential, to progress as far as possible and to be fulfilled. This includes recognition and value by others. Self-actualisation also addresses the need for challenge, responsibility and pride in work and achievement, as well as technological or professional expertise.

Two views can be taken of self-actualisation. The first is that self-actualisation is available only to the very few. It is limited by the inability to develop sufficient qualities and capabilities for this to take place. This is due to the limitations of the social back-ground of many people and above all, of education, training and other means by which skills, knowledge and expertise are developed.

The second view is that self-actualisation is achievable by almost everyone in their own particular circumstances. Whatever the limitations created by society and education, individuals nevertheless exhibit a range of capabilities and qualities which have the potential of being harnessed and developed in the pursuit of highly rewarding lives in their own terms. Self-actualisation is therefore an individual and not an absolute process.

The latter view currently holds sway. It is of particular value in understanding that everyone has needs for respect and esteem; and that whatever the nature, level or content of work carried out, people will tend to seek variety and enhancement if this is at all possible. If it is not possible at the place of work, they will seek it elsewhere. This view tends to militate against traditional and classical organisation features of task specialisation and administrative hierarchies, which expect individuals to restrict their capabilities, work as directed and operate machinery and systems, rather than develop and use their capabilities and talents to the full.

itself, level of responsibility, advancement, and opportunities for personal growth and development. These factors are all related to the actual content of the work and job responsibilities.

The hygiene factors or dissatisfiers are: company policy and administration; supervision and management style; levels of pay and salary; relationships with peers; relationships with subordinates; status; and security. These are factors that where they are good or adequate will not in themselves make people satisfied; by ensuring that they are indeed adequate, dissatisfaction is removed but satisfaction is not in itself generated. On the other hand, where these aspects are bad, extreme dissatisfaction was reported by all respondents (see Management in Focus 25.4).

The work of Herzberg and McGregor has tended to encourage attention to such factors as:

- good and adequate supervision which encourages and extends the workforce rather than restricts it
- job satisfaction, which can often be increased through work restructuring, job enrichment and job enlargement programmes
- the setting and achieving of targets and objectives based on a full understanding of what they are and why they have been set.

MANAGEMENT IN FOCUS 25.4

THEORY X AND Y

McGregor (1970) developed the two-factor approach by identifying two distinctive sets of assumptions made by managers about their staff, as follows:

- *Theory X*: in which people dislike work and will avoid it if they can; they would rather be directed than accept responsibility; they must be forced or bribed to put out the right effort; they are motivated mainly by money, which remains the overriding reason why they go to work; their main anxiety concerns personal security, and is alleviated by earn-

ing money; people are inherently lazy and require high degrees of supervision, coercion and control in order to produce adequate output.

- *Theory Y*: in which people wish to be interested in work and, under the right conditions, will enjoy it; they gain intrinsic fulfilment from work; they are motivated by the desire to achieve and to realise potential, and to work to the best of their capabilities; they will accept the discipline of the organisation and also impose self-discipline.

Effective work motivation was therefore seen as a managerial responsibility. The core of this responsibility lay in understanding the collective attitudes of the organisation and designing approaches to motivation and incentives around this. Organisations that adopted a largely Theory X approach could not expect long-term, enduring high levels of production and output; organisations that adopted the Theory Y approach required much greater levels of investment in the behavioural, as well as operational, side of enterprises.

Some organisations have also concentrated on removing the dissatisfiers or hygiene factors to ensure that causes of intrinsic dissatisfaction with the workplace and its environment are minimised (see Management in Focus 25.5).

MANAGEMENT IN FOCUS 25.5

ABSENTEEISM

Absenteeism is a feature of the general level of satisfaction or otherwise at the place of work. The greater the level of dissatisfaction, the higher the level of absenteeism.

This translates as follows: for every 100 members of staff, every percentage point of absenteeism requires an additional person employed. Thus 5 per cent absenteeism requires

105 members of staff to do the work of 100; or conversely it takes 105 days to do 100 days work.

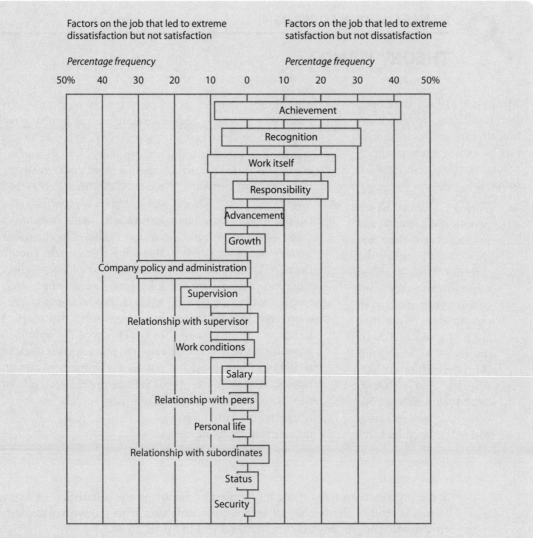

Figure 25.3 Two-factor theory
Source: Herzberg (1967)

In order to manage the two-factor approach to motivation effectively, attention is essential in the following areas:

- A management style, attitude and approach to staff that is based on integrity, honesty and trust, whatever the nature, limitations or technology concerned in the work itself. A suitable quality of working environment must also be ensured.
- General factors of status and importance that ensure that every member of staff is respected, believed in, treated equally and given opportunities for change, development and advancement within the organisation.
- Effective and professional operational relationships among members of staff

that in turn promote profitable and successful activities across the entire organisation. This includes recognising the existence of barriers and potential conflicts between departments, divisions and functions and taking steps to provide effective counters to these.

Pay and reward levels must meet expectations, as well as providing adequate levels of income so that individuals feel secure in both life and work. There are collective, cultural and social requirements to increase pay and reward levels; it is also becoming increasingly accepted that there is a moral responsibility on organisations to share the fruits of their success (e.g. through profit and performance-related pay). However, it is also necessary to recognise that high levels of pay do not make work more interesting or worthwhile – though they do certainly make it more bearable, especially in the short-term.

Administrative support and control processes and mechanisms must be designed, to make life easy for those working at the front line while at the same time providing the necessary management information. This particularly refers to the nature and effectiveness of the roles and functions of corporate headquarters and the relationships between these and the front line operations.

The work itself must be divided up fairly. There is particular reference here to those parts of the work that are looked upon with disfavour but which nevertheless must be carried out adequately and effectively.

People need to be confident in the security of their occupation. This ensures that people are employed on a continuous basis as far as that is possible. At the same time steps have to be taken to ensure that there is a steady and open flow of information, so that when changes do become necessary the staff concerned are forewarned and able to respond positively (see Management in Focus 25.6).

Expectancy theories

The expectancy approach to motivation draws the relationship between the efforts put into particular activities by individuals, and the nature of the rewards that they expect to get for these efforts (see Figure 25.4).

This is compounded however by other factors – the actual capacities and aptitudes of the individual concerned on the one hand, and the nature of the work environment on the other. It is also limited by the perceptions and expectations that the commissioner of the work has towards the person who is actually carrying it out. There is a distinction to be drawn between the effort put into performance and the effectiveness of that effort – hard work, conscientiously carried out does not always produce effective activity; the effort has to be directed and targeted. There has also to be a match between the rewards expected and those that are offered – a reward is merely a value judgement placed on something offered in return for effort, and if this is not valued by the receiver it has no effect on their motivation.

Effective approaches to motivation, based on the expectation–effort–reward mix are based on a combination of: recognising personal, professional and occupational ambition; recognising the opportunities and constraints of the situation; establishing performance levels that satisfy both organisational drives and the need for individual achievement (see Figure 25.4).

The expectancy approach may additionally be re-stated as motivation–achievement–reward. Drives for particular goals are enhanced by the capability to

MANAGEMENT IN FOCUS 25.6

GRAHAM LUCAS

Graham Lucas is in charge of a section involved in heavy production engineering. The safety officer, Jim Stevens, has been trying out various types of safety equipment. Jim Stevens keeps a close watch on the staff and periodically tells them how to carry out their duties. The staff object to this, and complain loudly that they are not guinea pigs, and that their work is being interfered with. Stevens then complains to Lucas that the staff are uncooperative. Lucas however, thinks that this problem must be sorted out by Stevens and consequently does nothing about it. As a result, Lucas is called into the department head, and is told that Stevens has complained to top management that there has

been a lack of cooperation and would he, Lucas, see that in future his staff cooperate with Stevens and follow his instructions. Moreover, should job losses be required, if they did not follow Stevens' instructions, then Lucas' department would be among the first to be required to make cuts.

The key lesson here is relating motivation and commitment to whatever is required to the broader situation. One the basis of what is stated, all of this could have been avoided if:

- the reasons for Stevens' involvement had been made clear
- the reasons why it was necessary to engage the staff had been made clear

- staff had actively participated in the whole process, rather than merely being ordered to respond to a series of instructions.

It is also clear, on the basis of what is stated here, that both expense and stress have been incurred as the result of not taking a broader perspective. Further expense and stress is additionally certain as the result of positions becoming more entrenched, rather than acknowledging the true state of the problem. All of this is damaging to collective motivation and morale, and this becomes increasingly difficult to re-engage as the position develops.

achieve them and the rewards that are to accrue as a result. To be fully effective, this requires matching the rewards that are, and may be, on offer with what is valued by individuals. The value that individuals place on particular rewards varies between, and within, professions and occupations. However, one or more of the following must normally be engaged:

- *Economic reward*: monetary pay for carrying out the job, for special achievement, responsibility and accountability; expected to continue and improve in line with the relationship between organisation and individual, in terms both of current and future occupations and of loyalty and commitment. Economic rewards meet the needs and expectations of individuals, and also reflect the value in which they are held by the organisation.
- *Job satisfaction*: intrinsic rewards attained by individuals in terms of the quality of their work, the range and depth of expertise used and the results achieved.
- *Work content*: the relative contribution to the output of the organisation as a whole and the feelings of success and achievement that arise from this. As stated

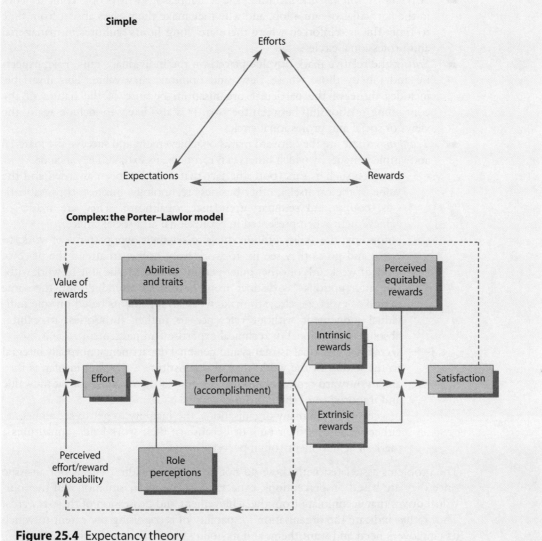

Figure 25.4 Expectancy theory
Source: from Luthans (1992)

elsewhere, operating a small part of the production process or administrative system tends to be limited in its capability to satisfy this part of the requirement for achievement.

- *Job title*: certain job titles give images of prestige as well as a description and summary of what the work is, and the respect and esteem in which it is held by the individual and his or her peers and social circles.

- *Personal development*: the extent to which the individuals' capabilities are being used (or limited in their use), and the extent to which alternative means of achievement and reward may become apparent through the development of both current and new expertise.

- *Attendance and absence*: including the actual reasons why people come to work in the particular organisation, and why they make themselves absent from time to time; this is reinforced where there are 'long hours' cultures in managerial and professional circles.
- *Status*: the relative mark of value placed on the individual's rank, role, expertise and job by those whose views and opinions they value. This invariably includes those of the particular organisation, because of the nature of the continuing relationship between the two. It is also likely to include again, the views of social and professional circles.
- *Trappings*: these are the outward marks of achievement and success, the material and visible benefits by which others can recognise its extent. They include:
    - benefits: such as cars (both the fact that a car has been awarded and the value of the car itself), other business technology, business trips, sabbaticals, course and seminar attendance, healthcare. They are marks of achievement when presented in professional and social circles.
    - autonomy: the ability of individuals to set their own patterns of work; to come and go as they see fit, to work from home; to attend the place of work at weekends or other quiet periods in order to be able to work without interruptions (as distinct from having to attend during the same period as everyone else); to make work arrangements based on sole individual judgement without reference to higher authorities; to exhibit absolute professional or technical expertise and judgement
    - secretaries, personal assistants and personal departments: normally integral to the nature of the work, they also constitute a trapping insofar as they are an outward representation to the rest of the organisation of the value and importance of the individual's work
    - inaccessibility: in many organisations, the inability to get to see someone, either because of their rank or because of their work loads, constitutes a mark of achievement (often perverse).

The problems associated with these do not lie in their validity. This is not an issue since they are based on perceptions, expectations, the wider situation and the individual drives that accumulate from the achievement and possession of these rewards. They rather indicate the organisation's capability of recognising the extent to which its employees need and want them, and its ability to satisfy them in these ways.

It is the responsibility of all organisations to find means of giving recognition, giving opportunities for growth and advancement, and measuring achievement. This extends to front-line production and service activities as well as professional occupations. It involves taking a broad and enlightened view of what the whole purpose of the work is. Advocates of efficient but alienative traditional production and service methods point to the reductions in unit costs that are achieved by these, but usually fail to recognise the consequences of that alienation – absence, turnover, disputes and grievances and the additional levels of supervision that go with these. Above all, such approaches take no account of the resources base needed to compensate for these negative activities.

Argyris (1957; 1997) stated that the priority in managing people's expectations was to get them to move from a state of passive acquiescence to active involvement. Transition from passivity to activity occurred as a part of growing up and education, so that by the time individuals were ready for work, they required active rather than passive engagement.

Workplace motivation was therefore directly related to personality development. The inference is that highly structured and formalised organisations are therefore fundamentally unsuitable places in which to work. There is a fundamental lack of harmony – or congruence – between the needs of the individuals and the drives of the organisation. This tends to get worse as the organisation becomes more sophisticated and as its rules, procedures and hierarchies grow – and as the individuals concerned themselves seek to progress. This leads first to restriction, then frustration, and finally to conflict. Frustration and the potential for conflict are greatest at the lower levels of the organisation, where the ability to work independently is most restricted. It is also apparent where people at any level of the organisation and of any level of professional or technical expertise (or lack of it) believe themselves to be restricted in their potential to achieve by unnecessary and unproductive rules, procedures and systems.

From whatever point of view the matter is considered, the relationship between such an organisation and people is fundamentally unsound. The conclusion is that organisations create the conditions for disharmony and unproductiveness themselves by placing so many limitations on the potential and drives of their people. Staff apathy and lack of effort are the inevitable results of this approach to structuring and organising work. Effectively therefore, people are expected to behave in these passive and negative ways (see Management in Focus 25.7).

MANAGEMENT IN FOCUS 25.7

TAYLOR'S DEPARTMENT STORE

Lillian Charles recently took over as section head at Taylor's department store. One of the sales assistants in Lillian's section is Paul Newbury. Paul Newbury has been with the company for two years. His sales figures are not the lowest in the section, but are usually among the bottom three. The previous section head was not very enthusiastic about him and had told Lillian: 'Paul Newbury is all right, but he is not one of the best people. He lacks any enthusiasm in the job. His time-keeping is also not good.' Paul kept his sales area tidy. He was good at handling the stock and re-ordering processes. However, he always appeared to be slow. Lillian noted that he arrived late once or twice; and when she tackled him about his time-keeping, he stated that it was always difficult to rely on public transport (his train journey to work took 45 minutes).

Paul Newbury's manner with customers has always been satisfactory; although Lillian did once note that he seemed impatient with a customer who could not make their mind up about a particular item.

The result was that Lillian became aware of a 'general issue' around Paul's motivation. She thought that if he would only liven up a bit, he would make a much more useful contribution both to his own sales, and also to the section's general working.

The key lesson here is to illustrate the relationship between the work and effort required, in the context of organisation institutionalisation. On the basis of what is stated, it is very difficult to know what, if anything, could be done to move Paul Newbury from a state of passive acquiescence to active engagement.

Motivation and classification

Schein (1971;1990) identified the relationship between motivation and commitment, and 'a classification of humankind', as follows:

- *Rational economic*: people are primarily motivated by economic needs. They pursue their own self-interest in the expectation of high economic returns. If they work in an organisation they need both motivation and control. As they intensify their pursuit of money they become untrustworthy and calculating.

  Within this group, however, there are those who are self-motivated and have a high degree of self-control. This is the group that must take responsibility for the management of others. They also set the moral and ethical standards required.
- *Social*: people are social and gregarious beings, gaining their basic sense of identity from relationships with others. People will seek social relationships at the place of work and part of the function of the work group will be the fulfilment of this necessity. The role of management in this situation is therefore greatly concerned with mobilising the social relationships in the pursuit of operational effectiveness and drawing a correlation between productivity and morale. It must also take an active interest in the development of the work group.
- *Self-actualisation*: people are primarily self-motivated. They seek challenge, responsibility and pride from their job, and aim to maximise the opportunities that it brings. They are likely to be affected negatively by organisational and management style, external controls, scarcity of resources and other pressures. They will develop their own ways of working, and objectives and integrate these with the ones established by the organisation.

  The inference is that this is strongest among professional, technical, skilled managerial staff. However, all work groups have tended towards higher levels of motivation and morale when given a greater degree of autonomy at work.
- *Complexity*: people are complex and sophisticated. They have 'varieties' of emotions, needs, wants and drives driven by personal circumstances, interactions and adaptation. They have many differing, diverse and contradictory motives that vary according to the matter in hand and the different work and social groups in which they find themselves. They will not fulfil every need in any one situation, but rather require a variety of activities in order to do this. They respond to a variety of stimuli according to needs and wants at a given moment. Schein's view of 'complex man' in organisations is that there is a psychological contract, based on mutual expectations and commonality of aspirations. It is therefore a psychological partnership.

The psychological partnership

The psychological partnership is based on the following motivations:

- to seek out particular types of work, to follow a particular career, to work in particular sectors, occupations, trades, professions and crafts
- to apply for specific jobs, with specific employers, to complete the application process and to subject oneself to the recruitment and selection processes
- to accept job offers, to accept the salary/occupation/prospects mixes of particular organisations
- to turn up for work on the first day

- to turn up for work on the second day and to continue turning up on a daily basis; and to start and continue to produce effective and successful work on behalf of the organisation
- to earn a living, and to both ensure and increase one's standard of living
- to progress, develop and advance
- to have physical and occupational variety; and to apply skills and expertise in a range of situations, and problems and issues (see Figure 25.5).

Some job titles are, in themselves, demeaning and dissatisfying. Titles such as typist, dustman, operative (and their politically correct alternatives of clerical assistant, refuse executive, crew person) are issued by organisations as marks of status as much as occupational indicators.

Job enrichment, job rotation, job enlargement and empowerment activities have to address all aspects if they are to be effective. If carried out successfully, motivation and commitment can be generated in any staff or occupational group, whatever the working situation, provided that the behavioural satisfaction aspect is also addressed.

It is also to be noted that the converse is true – that where jobs and occupations are not effective, productive and satisfying, demotivation and demoralisation occurs whatever the interests inherent in the particular profession may be.

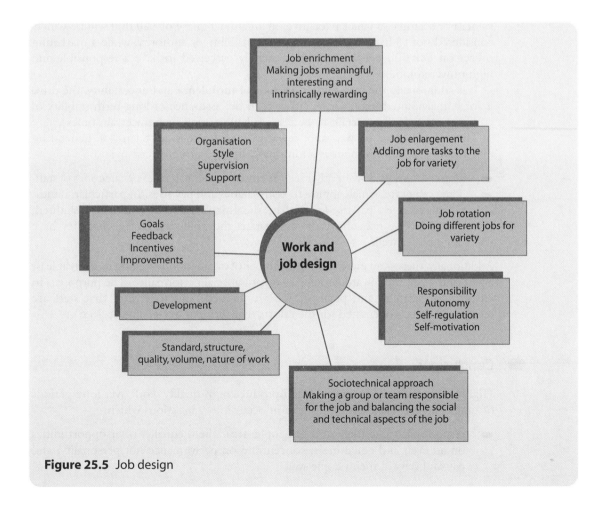

Figure 25.5 Job design

Motivation, incentives and money

As stated above, a clear distinction needs to be made between motivation and incentives. Incentives are delivered in return for achieving specific targets; motivation is a broader process.

Nevertheless, monetary rewards and other material benefits are important in ensuring the levels of commitment required of the staff. Wages and salaries are paid by organisations to individuals to reward them for bringing their expertise and efforts, and delivering these effectively. Financial rewards must therefore reflect:

- the specific levels of expertise brought by individuals, and the ways in which they are required to apply it
- the duration, quality and intensity of effort
- the effectiveness of individual performance, and the effectiveness of overall performance
- the locations where performance is required.

Monetary and financial rewards additionally reflect the value that organisations place on individuals and their expertise, and the value placed by individuals on their own expertise.

There is a strong perceptual relationship between pay and job importance and value. For example, a Chief Executive on an annual salary of £20,000 will be widely considered not to have a great deal of responsibility or authority, while a marketing officer on £80,000 per year will be generally perceived to have a responsible and high-powered job.

It is additionally the case that, in periods of turbulence and uncertainty, the drive is for higher immediate rewards, rather than the assurance of long-term stability of employment (which is certain to be less available during such uncertain times).

The effectiveness of pay and rewards management in terms of generating motivation and commitment is additionally limited or enhanced by:

- Comparisons made with other sectors employing similar types or categories of staff.
- The going rate, which applies to both salaries and pay rises. In particular, if individuals receive a pay rise lower than 'the going rate', they tend to feel slighted; if they receive rises above the going rate, they will tend to feel that they have done rather well.

Additionally, there is an increase in the number of organisations seeking to tie in at least a part of the pay and reward package to organisational performance. The purpose is to ensure that strategy and performance are aligned, and to ensure that staff are recognised and compensated for the efforts that they put in (see Figure 25.6).

Conclusions

Highly motivated and committed staff produce high-quality work over long periods of time. The highest levels of motivation occur in organisations which:

- respect and value their staff as people; treat them equally; offer opportunities on an even and equal basis; concentrate on performance not personality; and pay and reward their people well

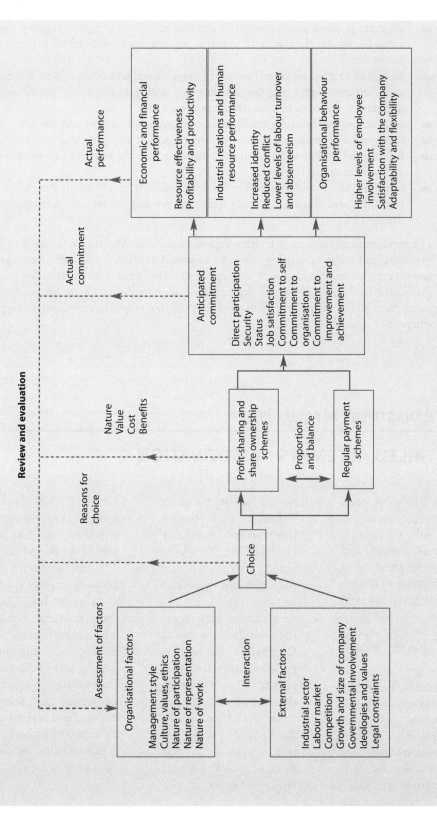

Figure 25.6 The relationship between pay and performance

- generate positive and harmonious culture; take early action to remove negative attitudes where they start to emerge; reward contributions to organisational performance
- recognise that everyone has personal, professional and occupational drives, aims and objectives that require satisfaction; and take steps to harmonise and integrate these with organisational purposes
- balance the key behavioural features of expectation, effort and reward
- recognise and reward achievement, development and progress
- balance the attention given to the work in hand, the workings of work groups, and individual performance
- recognise the prevalence and influence of those elements that, if right, tend to motivate; and those that, if wrong, tend to demotivate (see Management in Focus 25.8).

The fundamental concern is to have capable people on the staff who want to work. The best and most rewarding jobs in the world can be – and are – destroyed by negative styles and attitudes of management. The most overtly mundane jobs in the world can be – and are – transformed and made excellent by positive and supportive styles of management and by offering respect, value and recognition where it is possible.

MANAGEMENT IN FOCUS 25.8

FAILED ATTEMPTS AT MOTIVATION

Each of the following cases demonstrates the need to understand fully the nature and process of human and workplace motivation, and above all the futility of throwing money at problems and the dangers of failing to recognise the broader aspects that have to be understood:

- At the end of the twentieth century, the Allied Irish Bank gave an additional week's holiday to every member of staff who took no time off for sickness during the previous year. Once people had had a day's sickness, they would therefore tend to take at least another five working days to ensure that they did not miss out anyway.
- At about the same time, the Batchelor's Food Company initiated a policy which stated that anyone who was more than ten minutes late for work would lose half a day's pay. The result was that anyone who was more than ten minutes late – whether at the start of the day or returning after lunch – would simply take the rest of the period off.
- Early in the twenty-first century, public professions in the UK – especially teaching, medical and social care – are having great difficulties gaining new staff because the wider conditions of service are known, believed and perceived to be so poor that they place a lack of value on those who work in them.

Demotivators	Motivators
• Management/supervisory style	• Value
• Administrative overload	• Respect
• Length of chains of command	• Esteem
• Attention to procedures rather than output	• Responsibility
• Bad communications	• Progress
• Lack of respect/value/esteem	• Achievement
• Status/importance based on rank rather than achievement	• Communications

High levels of motivation are indicated by the following:

● low levels of absenteeism
● low levels of turnover
● low levels of accidents, sickness and injury
● few disputes, personality clashes, inter-departmental wrangles
● open approach to problems; early recognition of and attention to potential problems
● active participation in consultation, organisational initiatives, suggestion schemes.

In each case, these are reinforced by open and participative styles of management; ready access to organisational, functional and personal information; and clear and simple systems and procedures.

Low levels of motivation are indicated by:

● high/increasing levels of disputes and grievances; high/increasing levels of disciplinary cases and the use of disciplinary procedures
● high/increasing levels of accidents, sickness and injury
● high/increasing levels of absenteeism and turnover
● steady decline in quality and quantity of performance over the medium to long term, a trend that is reinforced by concentrating on procedures and systems rather than output, and by the proliferation of new systems, procedures and monitoring and support functions.

These are the initial indicators of high and low levels of motivation. The key areas to address when assessing levels of staff motivation and morale are:

● the level and nature of identity that the staff have with the organisation; the extent to which status, esteem and rewards are issued for productive output as distinct from adherence to procedures
● the ability to offer fulfilment, recognition accomplishment to all levels and grades of staff.

Everyone has basic needs for: a sense of belonging, self-respect and self-worth; the respect and value of others; and for growth, development and progress. Initial enquiries in this area are, therefore, to be made along these lines, and these are the key features to address where problems are found to exist.

CRITICAL THINKING, ANALYSIS AND EVALUATION

1. Why do some top sports stars, on huge salaries, become demotivated and unwilling to perform to the best of their capability? What lessons are there in this for managers in other situations?
2. Identify the motivating and demotivating effects that different performance-related pay schemes can have on people in organisations.
3. Outline the motivating and demotivating effects present in:
   - job sharing and enrichment programmes
   - twilight shift working
   - nightshift working.

   What other factors do organisations have to be aware of when employing people under these conditions?
4. Identify the reward package that you would put together for:
   - hospital nurses
   - double-glazing salespeople
   - call centre operatives
   - factory production workers.

   What motivators have you addressed, and what demotivators have you addressed, and why?

DEVELOPING MANAGEMENT SKILLS AND EXPERTISE

BORTON BOROUGH COUNCIL

Drumcree Ltd is a top-quality outward-bound centre situated on the shores of Loch Lomond in Scotland. It runs courses for people from all walks of life, including parties from schools and colleges. Its top-brand, flagship course, however, is for management development. This is very expensive. Drumcree take groups of no more than ten, and put those managers who come on the courses through a series of physically demanding and mentally gruelling exercises. The purpose of this is to identify the character and determination necessary to be a top manager in a large and sophisticated or complex organisation. Everyone who goes on these courses is assigned a personal tutor. The activities are recorded on video, and the Drumcree staff write extensive and detailed reports for the delegate's employers at the end of the courses. For this, Drumcree charge £3000 per delegate for a week's course.

Borton Borough Council sent seven of its staff on this flagship course. All had been identified as high fliers, potential senior management material. All were in middle-ranking executive posts, and ready to take the next step up the career ladder. They were:

- Anna Johnson, 32, from the Education Department
- Bob Friend, 37, from Corporate Personnel
- Caroline Hicks, 38, from the Highways Department
- Dev Desai, 35, from the Planning Department
- Eric Ameoli, 33, from the Social Services Department

- Faisal Ahmed, 39, from the Careers Department
- Gillian Francis, 30, from the Public Relations Department.

It was an important course for Borton Borough Council, and also for those attending. It would not only develop their leadership skills, and identify the character and determination necessary to succeed. All seven had been short-listed for a senior corporate policy job in the Education Department, and their assessment on this course would be a key feature of the decision to appoint. Accordingly, the staff at Drumcree were asked to prepare a special programme that would require the equal commitment of all seven if it were to be completed satisfactorily.

All of the delegates knew each other by sight, having met briefly at management meetings. They were all physically fit enough to undertake the activities. Indeed, the physical demands at Drumcree made on its delegates were never particularly arduous. It did however, set great store in placing delegates in unfamiliar and stressful situations.

The seven travelled from Borton to Drumcree Ltd on the Sunday. That evening, they received a full briefing from the Drumcree staff. They met their personal tutors, all of whom had been members of either the military, police or emergency services. The course had been prepared especially for Borton Borough Council by Austin Layard, the Centre's founder and Chief Executive. He had spent 20 years designing and delivering courses for this kind of client. The brief was understood, the objectives agreed. That first evening, the group had its first short exercise, moving a heavy log up a muddy slope. During the exercise, Bob slipped and fell down the slope, and lay writhing in agony. The exercise was abandoned, and they all trooped back to the centre disappointed. A doctor was called to see Bob, and his ankle was heavily strapped.

Layard and the remaining six met later. Layard said to them: 'This is a bit of a nuisance. The course was specifically designed for seven of you. Now that we have only six, I do not know what we should do'.

The other six went into a brief huddle, then emerged and replied to Layard: 'We will carry out the course. Your staff will be present at all times, so if there is anything that we genuinely cannot do, we can simply abort the particular exercise.'

After a short discussion, it was agreed that the course would proceed as planned, but without Bob.

The remaining six completed all the exercises designed for them. On many of them, there was considerable stress and strain placed on individuals, because they were one person short. However, as the week wore on, they got used to the idea that they were short-handed, and completed everything without any help from the course tutors. At the end of the course, they returned to the centre for the debrief. Layard spoke to them:

> You are, without doubt, the best group that we have ever had on one of these courses. We did not think that the seven of you would be able to complete it – indeed, we were told by your employers to make sure that you could not. The fact that the six of you have managed so well is a tribute to the character, determination and willingness in the face of adversity on the part of every one of you. I am very proud to have had you along. The reports that we will be sending back to Borton will be the best that we have ever written.

There was a short silence. Then Anna spoke, 'Where is Bob?'

Layard replied, 'Oh, he's gone. Fortunately there was nothing too much wrong with his ankle. The doctor had a look at it on the Monday morning. He pronounced it nothing more than a sprain. Bob caught the next train home, saying that he was going to have the week off.'

The others were briefly disappointed. However, such had been the development of their team spirit and group cohesion, that they thought little of it, and went off to celebrate a successful week.

The following Monday they returned to Borton Borough Council. A week later, they were summoned by David Griffiths, the Personnel Director of the Council, for the announcement of the Corporate Senior Officer post in education. Griffiths looked round at them all and then said, 'I am delighted to be able to tell you that we have appointed Bob Friend to this senior post. I am sure you will all want to congratulate him on this marvellous achievement.'

Questions

1. On the basis that successful completion of the outward-bound course was supposed to be a key determinant of the Senior Officer appointment, produce a logical, rational and honest explanation for the decision.
2. What are the likely effects on the motivation, morale and commitment of the other six?
3. Discuss the reasoning and validity of using this form of activity as an assessment of motivation and commitment.

Chapter twenty six

The management of conflict

'The right decision from every other point of view can often be wrong politically.
This causes conflict.'
Anthony Jay.

'Lessons will be learned.'
Universal conclusion to inquiry reports,
designed to head off further conflicts.

'If I had an argument with a player we would sit down for 20 minutes and decide I was right'
Brian Clough, former football manager.

Chapter outline

- Introduction
- Levels of conflict
- Competition
- Conflict as warfare
- Sources of conflict in organisations
- Symptoms and causes of conflict
- Strategies for the management of conflict
- Conclusions

Chapter objectives

After studying this chapter, you should be able to:

- understand the potential for conflict in all human situations, and how to recognise this

- understand different strategic approaches to the management of conflict, once it becomes apparent that this exists

- understand the organisational and managerial steps that need to be taken in order to ensure that a productive working environment is not disrupted

- understand the expense of allowing conflict to develop

- understand and be able to apply particular remedies to specific situations.

Introduction

Conflict or the potential for conflict exists everywhere where two or more people are gathered together. It is inevitable that people will have differences and disagreements. The nature of differences and disagreements is enhanced and sharpened by the nature of organisational settings, where departments, divisions, functions, groups and individuals pursue their own agenda, activities and priorities. When their agenda, activities and priorities do not accord with those of others, or are not capable of harmonisation, organisational conflict exists.

Levels of conflict

The following levels of organisational conflict may be distinguished:

- argument, discussion and debate
- competition
- warfare.

Argument and competition may be either positive, healthy and creative or negative, unhealthy and destructive. Warfare is always destructive.

The nature, symptoms and causes must be understood, and these then become a focus for management action in striving for productive and harmonious places of work.

Conflict may be positive and beneficial, capable of being harnessed for the greater good, and contributing to organisation effectiveness. Conflict is also clearly negative and destructive in many forms.

Argument, discussion and debate

Argument, discussion and debate are essential if progress is to be made. They need to be structured and orderly so that everything is concentrated on the matter in hand, rather than a competition between the personalities involved.

They take place between two or more groups or people and bring about (whether by accident or design) a better quality, more informed and better balanced view of the matter in hand. Provided that it is positive, the process of argument and debate leads to a better understanding also of the hopes, fears and aspirations of other group members. It also identifies gaps in knowledge and expertise. These can then be remedied, either through training or the inclusion in the debate of persons with the required expertise. The process helps in the building of mutual confidence and respect. It also encourages individuals to dig into their own resources, expertise and experience and to use these for the benefit of all concerned. It helps to build group identity. It leads to a better quality of decision making and understanding and acceptance of the reasons why particular directions are chosen.

Argument, discussion and debate become unproductive if they are not structured. People must be clear what they are debating. Otherwise they will inevitably argue about different things. At the very least this leads to group dysfunction and disharmony in the particular situation. The essence is therefore to be able to set out the desired aims and objectives of the discussion and to have available, as far as possible, all necessary information.

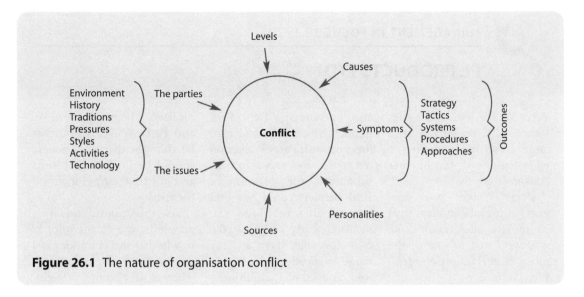

Figure 26.1 The nature of organisation conflict

The form of argument must be one that allows people to express strongly held views without sowing the seeds of potentially deeper and divisive differences. Attention is therefore paid to the behavioural as well as structural side. An atmosphere of trust and confidence must be created if this is to be successful. Persons have to be supported in their views even if the group eventually decides to go in different directions.

Failure of argument, debate and discussion processes does not necessarily lead to more serious strife, though this may (and does) happen from time to time. The relationship is neither linear nor one-way. For example, a serious conflict that has recently come into the open may be managed and made positive through a continuous airing of the matter in debate and discussion. Where voices are raised and feelings run high in debate, this is not a problem as long as the group situation can accommodate this effectively and relationships return to normal after the event (see Management in Focus 26.1).

Competition

Competition exists between individuals and groups and within organisations. It also exists between organisations. It can be either positive or negative, healthy or unhealthy. At its best, competition sets standards for all to follow – whether within the organisation or within the entire sphere within which it operates. On a global scale, the standards of production, quality and managerial practice of certain organisations are held up as models to which the rest of the world should aspire. Some sectors arrange their organisations into league tables, thus shining a competitive light on some aspects of the activities carried out.

The nature of competition

This may either be:

- Closed or distributive, where one party wins at the expense of others.

MANAGEMENT IN FOCUS 26.1

PL PRODUCTS LTD

Peter Walker joined the sales force of PL Products Ltd, a large company marketing a wide range of fast-moving consumer goods.

Peter Walker was very good at his job, and less than six months after training, he was appointed to one of the most important sales areas. He continued to be very successful, but sometimes it appeared that he did not get on very well with the other staff on the team.

The sales director was thinking of promoting him, and arranged for Paul Bennett, the area manager, to meet up with Peter Walker on his route, and report on his suitability for promotion. Paul Bennett could not find him on his route. However, he had clearly made all the calls for that day: a large range of products had been sold, and he had additionally collected many more orders.

Because he had missed him, Paul Bennett called at Peter Walker's house. Arriving at 3.30 pm, Paul Bennett was surprised to see him mowing his lawn. The two men spoke, and Peter Walker stated that he thought that sales people should be judged on results and not on the time spent on the road.

At this point, the two people have a clear choice as to whether this continues as a debate and argument, or whether it becomes a fight. The outcome now depends on the attitudes adopted by each to the particular situation, and the steps that they wish to take to resolve it.

- Open or integrative, where there is scope for everyone to succeed.
- Collaborative, where the boundaries of operations of each party can be set to ensure that everyone has a fair share of 'the cake' – i.e. whatever is being competed for. The competitive environment may be dominated by one party or a few large parties who each take what they want from the situation, and whatever is left over is to be disputed among the remaining players.
- Based on either positive or negative attitudes; competition is only genuinely fruitful in the long term if it is based on positive attitudes.

Competition is more likely to be successful and effective if it is open, if the rewards for competing effectively are available to all. Competition is likely to degenerate into conflicts where, for example, competition for resources or accommodation is closed and one party is to succeed at the expense of the others.

The purpose of competition

This needs to be carefully managed. Competition between groups is much more likely to degenerate into conflict or warfare if a competitive relationship is simply encouraged without adequate structure and without due consideration of the purpose and of the people involved. Competition between individuals within groups is also likely to become disruptive if this is the case.

For competition to be positive and productive a number of conditions must exist. The rules of the competition must be fair (and be seen to be so) to all concerned.

They must be understood and accepted by everyone. The rewards of competing must be available to all involved, and be given to those who succeed. The competitors' destinies must be in their own hands – they are to succeed or fail by their own efforts and not by the arbitrary decision of persons elsewhere.

The rules must be adhered to and groups who cheat should be punished, not rewarded for finding alternative means to the given end. Those in charge of the situation should have considered all alternatives and have arrived at the conclusion that this form of approach is the best way of achieving the stated goal.

Competitive relationships exist best within organisations where attention is positively given to standards, creativity, the nature of the groups and the purpose of creating the situation. The aim is to bring out the best in everyone concerned, to improve performance and efficiency, and to set absolute standards for activities, and from this to form a base from which improvements can still be made. If these elements and rationales are not present, then organisations should consider alternative means of achieving their purposes. A negative competitive approach is likely to lead to interdepartmental strife, especially where the form of competition is closed.

Conflict as 'warfare'

Warfare exists where inter-group relations have been allowed to get out of hand, where the main aims and objectives of activities have been lost, and where great energies and resources are taken up with fighting the corner, reserving the position and denigrating other departments and functions.

The potential for conflict also exists between organisations and their external stakeholders – shareholders and backers, customers and clients, suppliers, and the communities in which they operate. The basis of conflict management with external stakeholders lies in providing constant, adequate and effective communications at all times; this is underpinned through the provision of clear points of reference within the organisation so that external stakeholders can get in touch whenever they wish, and especially at times of crisis or emergency.

Sources and causes

Resources

Internal organisation warfare is often centred around resource questions and issues. It emerges when departments and individuals perceive that those who have control over resources are susceptible to non-operational approaches. They are also perceived to have their own reasons for issuing resources to particular departments – for example the availability or potential for achieving triumphs, and thus gaining favour and acceptance.

Influence

Competition for power and influence is also apparent. A multiple agenda is normally pursued. Particular groups and individuals present their achievements in the best possible light. This takes various forms and is designed to ensure that:

- Real achievements are recognised.
- Achievements are presented in ways acceptable to the sources of power and

influence (for example, chief executive officers, top managers, particular shareholders and stakeholders, the community at large).

- The group is likely to receive patronage and that there are rewards to be gained by both the patron and those who come within their ambit.
- The group's results are presented as major achievements, the best possible return on resources and expertise put in.
- The department or individual is presented as having high value and expertise, and so eligible for higher favours and good jobs; this department or person can be relied upon to produce 'the right results'.
- The results are related (where possible or desirable) to questions of organisation success.

This presentation also has a shadow or counter-presentation that:

- Shows other departments and individuals in unfavourable light.
- Denigrates the skills, expertise, qualities and achievements of others.
- Steals the achievements of others or attaches the presenter to their coat tails.
- Identifies any slight disagreement as a major barrier to progress.
- Apportions blame for failure to others.

Divide and rule

Warfare is the normal outcome of management styles based on divide and rule. It is superficially attractive because it breaks a whole entity down into component parts – following the argument that, for example, a tonne of bricks may not be lifted by one person, but each individual brick may be and so the tonne is eventually shifted.

The analogy is false and so is the premise on which it is based. Dividing the whole into small chunks in this way causes energy to be expended by the individuals and groups on fighting their own corner rather than bonding to the common cause. To finish the analogy, the individual brick becomes the centre of attention rather than the use to which they can all be put.

Organisations and their managers that practise divide and rule therefore create battlefields on which the wars for resources and prestige are to be fought. The rules of combat are normally simple – winning is everything, and the losers may expect to lose influence, prestige, resources and possibly also their jobs. The process is normally further complicated by the 'dividers and rulers': victories and triumphs are handed out in non-rational (more non-rational) ways that are primarily designed to ensure that everyone is 'kept on their toes' and 'takes nothing for granted'.

This is compounded again by clandestine meetings, denigrations and denouncements involving individuals and groups in relation to each other and the organisation's top managers in its dealings with some groups.

Struggles for supremacy

In struggles for supremacy, alliances are formed between different parties and so factions grow up. These may be overt or clandestine. Groups seek a fifth column – sources of influence in the departments that hold power, sources of information in the departments with which they are working. Promises of reward are made to be delivered when victory is achieved; this comes in the form of promotion, increased pay, prestige work or a prestige location for the next job.

Resources and expertise are gathered together. This especially includes information of a nature and quality that can be used to enhance one's own cause and damage the others. Public relations, presentational and lobbying skills are also required to ensure that what is done and achieved is seen in the best possible light by those with influence.

Struggles for supremacy can, and do, turn nasty. Organisations coerce their staff to behave in particular ways, and dire warnings of the penalties for non-conformity are given. Trade unions and staff groups also use threats and coercion to ensure that their members stay in line (see Management in Focus 26.2).

Sources of conflict in organisations

Differences in attitudes, values and belief cause conflict. This occurs most often when the demands of the organisation and the standards, expertise and ethics of its staff are at variance.

For example, hospitals are required to work within management and administrative budgets, and this often means that the medical work has to be prioritised and

MANAGEMENT IN FOCUS 26.2

REIGNS OF TERROR

Reigns of terror have been used by rulers, emperors, kings and queens throughout the ages as a means of keeping their subjects in check. The idea on which it is based is that if subjects live in a constant state of fear, this will prevent them from taking up arms and rebelling against those with power and authority. Indeed, they will be too frightened to do anything that does not clearly conform lest it be construed as rebellion.

A direct parallel may be drawn with organisational behaviour and associated managerial practices. Reigns of terror are a form of divide and rule in which dissidents and non-conformists are marginalised (and sometimes sacked). Once these have been removed however, the leadership looks for other marginal groups, and if none are apparent they will be created anyway. Everyone therefore becomes at risk.

Again, the idea is superficially attractive along the 'keeping everyone on their toes' lines. The result is normally that indicated above – everyone is too scared to do anything and therefore production, output and morale all collapse.

Almost all reigns of terror ultimately fail. Caligula, Nero, Robespierre and Danton were all themselves assassinated during their own reigns of terror. Persecution of early Christians by the Romans went a long way towards ensuring the survival of the Catholic Church. In turn, the persecution of the Catholic Church of its own dissidents in the fifteenth, sixteenth and seventeenth centuries helped to ensure the survival and success of the Protestant Reformation. The Nazi Empire – the Thousand Year Reich – lasted 12 years only (1933–45) and it used every organ of state in its reign of terror.

There are therefore clearly lessons to be learnt by managers who are tempted by the divide and rule approach, and by organisations which encourage it.

ordered to keep within these financial targets. On the other hand, doctors and nurses have an absolute professional commitment to treat all those who come to them to the best of their ability.

There is also the relative commitment to the profession and the organisation. Conflict occurs when the individual is required to choose between the demands of the profession and those of the organisation where these cannot be reconciled. Operational factors have also to be considered – the balance of professional with managerial and administrative work for example, and the willingness of the individual to accept this.

This is, in turn, compounded by the attitudes inherent in the wider working relationship between organisation and individual. If this is largely positive and supportive, there is likely to be a greater willingness to take on peripheral and extraneous duties. If it is negative, the individual is more likely to retreat from the organisation and into the profession and find comfort among other members.

Conflict is also caused where the attitudes, values and beliefs of the organisation in general are not the same as those of the individuals who carry out the work. People may, from time to time, be asked to do something that is counter to their own personal beliefs. For example, they may be asked to lie on the part of the organisation (give a false excuse for the failure of a delivery for example), and then to sustain this in public at least. They may be asked to dismiss or discipline someone else in ways with which they have no sympathy. The result is that the organisation's continuing integrity is questioned (see Management in Focus 26.3).

● Symptoms of conflict

If the potential for conflict exists in every human situation, as indicated above, then the symptoms of conflict are potentially present also. The key is to recognise how the symptoms are presenting themselves, and then to take steps to ensure that the underlying problems are addressed.

The main symptoms of conflict in organisations are related to the quality of communications and relationships.

Poor communications between groups, individuals and the organisation and its staff lead to lack of clarity, and eventually to mistrust. People then develop the habit of looking for things that are, or may be, going wrong; and they then seek to secure their own position, on the basis of their reading of the particular situation.

This leads to increases in disputes and grievances, and professional and personality clashes.

If these matters are not addressed, then the symptoms of conflict grow into organisational maladies, including group-think, internal alliances, favouritism and victimisation (see Management in Focus 26.4).

● Forms of conflict

The main forms of conflict in organisations are as follows:

● Differences between corporate, group and individual aims and objectives, and the inability of the organisation to devise systems, practices and environments in which these can be reconciled and harmonised.

MANAGEMENT IN FOCUS 26.3

THE AUDITOR [1]

Robert Shaw worked as an auditor for a county council in the south-east of England. He was invited to the wedding of a colleague. He was very pleased for his colleague; he attended the church service and the reception and wished his colleague all the best for the future.

When he returned to work he was studying some papers that related to the colleague who had just got married. One of these concerned an invoice addressed to 'The Old Rectory' in the village where the wedding had taken place. Studying the papers closely, he found that the colleague

had indeed hired the person who lived at The Old Rectory to do some work for him shortly before he got married.

Robert brought this to the attention of the County Council Chief Executive. A full inquiry and investigation was launched. The accusation to his colleague was that he had presented the clergyman concerned with some work in return for conducting his marriage for free.

A month-long investigation was held. The following transpired:

- The person who lived at the Old Rectory was not

the clergyman but a management consultant who had been hired legitimately to carry out the work. He had been paid a fee of £400 for doing this.
- The clergyman's fee for conducting the marriage was £90.
- The County Council spent £15,000 on the investigation.
- Robert wondered whether he should feel ashamed of himself as the result of instigating this investigation and the way in which it had arisen.

MANAGEMENT IN FOCUS 26.4

THE NEED FOR VICTIMS

Many organisations, and their managers, find themselves in the position of 'needing victims'. This is an unacceptable aspect of organisation and managerial practice. In practice however, it is an extensive feature of large and complex multinational industrial, commercial and public service concerns.

In these cases, the organisation and/or managers seek 'victims' – those on whom all the misfortunes of the organisation or department can be blamed. These individuals become stressed and traumatised through the bullying, harassment and discrimination that occurs as the result, and either leave or are forced out.

It is true that, in some cases, victims do receive compensation. Invariably however, the problem continues to exist within the organisation once the victim has departed, for the organisation and/or its managers simply find other victims.

- Interdepartmental and inter-group wrangles, overwhelmingly concerned with either:
  - *territory*: where one group feels that another is treading in an area that is legitimately its own
  - *prestige*: where one group feels that another is gaining recognition for efforts and successes that are legitimately its own
  - *agenda*: where one group feels that it is being marginalised by the activities of the other
  - *poaching and theft*: where one group attracts away the staff of the other and perhaps also, its technology, equipment, information and prestige.
- The relative status awarded by the organisation to its different departments, divisions, functions, groups and individuals. This is to be seen in terms of:
  - *formal relations*: based on organisational structure and job definition
  - *informal relations*: based on corridor influence and possibly also personal relationships
  - *favoured and unfavoured status*: the means by which this is arrived at and what is means to those concerned, especially the relationship between head office and frontline activities
  - *the organisational pecking order*: and any other means by which prestige and influence are determined.

Conflict also arises from the changes in the status quo, both where people seek to alter their own positions and from changes that the organisation seeks to make. For example, when an individual or group suddenly loses power, then a void is left which all the others rush to fill. Conversely, an individual or group may suddenly find itself in favour (for many reasons: operational necessity, expediency, the possibility of a triumph for the favour-giver) and the others rush to do it down.

Individual clashes, both professional and personal, lead to conflict if the basis of the relationship is not established and ordered. For example, one individual sees that a point of debate is a personal attack or questioning of his or her professional judgement – 'a lively discussion' may be regarded by some people as the straight-forward airing of a point of view, by others as questioning their expertise and integrity. This is also often the reason why feelings of favouritism lead to clashes between the recipients (perceived or actual) of preferential treatment and the others around them. Bullying and scapegoating are also forms of individual clash, causing conflict between bully and bullied. This again may lead to conflict based either on support for the victim by others, or by others following the leader and setting upon the victim themselves.

Groups may be drawn into conflict as the result of a clash between their leaders or between particular individuals.

Role relationships have the potential to cause conflict. This is based on the nature of the given roles. For example, trade union officials are certain to come into conflict with organisations in the course of their duties – they are often representing the interest of members who have some kind of trouble or dispute.

There is potential for conflict in all role relationships, including those that are: senior–subordinate; internal–external; and inter-departmental, where individuals are acting in the name of their occupation.

Behavioural issues cause conflict; and people feel resentment when they understand that they are being slighted or disparaged (see Management in Focus 26.5).

MANAGEMENT IN FOCUS 26.5

CAUSES OF CONFLICT: FORMS OF LANGUAGE

A symptom of the existence of some of these causes is to be found in language forms. These proliferate as levels of inherent conflict rise. Some examples are given below:

- 'A plan exists' – means that something has once or twice been discussed; it is perhaps required; no decision has been taken; and no one should be surprised if it does or does not happen.
- 'With the greatest res-pect' or 'I respect your views' – normally means that the other person is thought to be talking or producing rubbish.
- 'I work too hard', 'I cannot leave things', 'I find it impossible to go home at night' – become the normal statement of weaknesses at appraisal interviews if the individual perceives that they will otherwise be penalised.
- 'You move in exulted circles' – normally means that the person being addressed has influence and prestige far beyond that which his or her level of perceived competence deserves.
- 'We did all we could' – usually indicates that one individual or group is going to make it absolutely clear that they were let down by others in a situation where some form of failure has occurred.

Other issues in conflict

The other issues are:

- vested interests and hidden agendas
- differentials
- levels of honesty and integrity.

Vested interests and hidden agendas

Hidden, secondary and parallel agendas cause conflict. These proliferate where overall aims are not well or tightly drawn; where they do not, or are not able to, accommodate those of the individuals involved; and where people feel that, even if they do the work well, they are not likely to receive due recognition. The parallel agendas therefore address these points: the need for individuals to progress, the need for recognition and the status and kudos that accrues as a result. At the very least, the organisation's purpose is diluted.

In pursuit of this, other activities start to emerge. The department or group concerned is likely to start to engage in other means of achieving its objectives – use of any negative or blocking power that it has available, restricting and prioritising its own output, choosing deadlines to its own greatest advantage.

Those involved may also come to see or feel that the real issue is to fight for resources and/or prestige and re-position their activities accordingly. This is especially true where lobbies are seen or perceived to succeed at the expense of others (see Management in Focus 26.6).

Differentials

The establishing of differentials causes conflict. Difficulties here include company cars, company parking spaces, personal computers and faxes, mobile phones and other technology (executive technology), the flexibility to work from home, personal secretaries and assistants, and differentiated office furniture. Conflict is caused when the allocation of these elements is done (or seen to be done) from a point of view of patronage, prestige and status rather than operational necessity.

This also enhances conflict and resentment where:

● People receive differentials who do not (overtly) need them, while those who do need them do not receive them (e.g. company cars for sales staff, and also for top managers).

● Some people on a given grade receive them, while others on the same grade do not.

● People on a given grade in one department or division receive them, while others on higher grades in other departments and divisions do not.

● Some people receive them (or some of them) because of operational necessity, while others on higher grades do not receive them either for operational necessity or for reasons of prestige.

MANAGEMENT IN FOCUS 26.6

THE AUDITOR [2]

As recounted above, Robert Shaw had reported his colleague to the County Council Chief Executive on the basis of a combination of perception and possibility that something was wrong.

An investigation was duly arranged and conducted. Nothing untoward was found. However, there had been a delay in the investigation; and the consequence was that the matter was now common knowledge throughout the County Council offices. Having engaged in the effort and expense of the investigation, there was pressure on the County Council to find things wrong. There was also a question of pride and integrity.

Accordingly, the County Council found that the individual who had got married had been sloppy in his activities, and had not taken sufficient steps towards ensuring that everything was conducted above board.

The particular individual replied that it was a pure accident that the consultant who had been engaged happened to live in a house called 'the Old Rectory'. His contention was that none of this would have arisen had the house had a different name!

The County Council persisted in its point of view. The individual was transferred away from his current duties to a role that was perceived as being less prestigious.

In this case, the 'lobby' was the County Council's top management team; and the focus of their lobby was the need to be seen to be 'doing something', as the result of having expended resources on an investigation.

Honesty and integrity

A key factor in the presence of conflict, and its resolution, is the level of honesty and integrity present. The greater the integrity of the situation – of the relations between groups and individuals and the relationship between the organisation and its staff – the greater the likelihood of the effective management of conflict. This includes hierarchical and reporting relations.

Human emotions, especially those of envy, jealousy, anger and greed, are brought into being when people are confronted with a situation in which they perceive themselves to be losing out. Fear and resentment flourish if the nature of the situation is such that those involved feel threatened by the success and prestige of others relative to their own position. The key to managing these emotions is founded in the honesty and integrity of the situation.

Groups and individuals all seek to improve their position in all circumstances. They seek the capability to do this through any means, channels and resources available. Organisations may either leave these open, remove them or close them down. If one group or individual pursues a channel successfully, others will follow. If this is not successful they will try other methods. Groups and individuals are attracted to where the rewards that come from the improved position are forthcoming.

The factors discussed above summarise the factors present in the causes of any particular conflict, and also indicate the main behavioural components of the conflict itself. Recognition of these therefore greatly contributes to an understanding of conflict itself and of some of the issues that have to be addressed if it is to be managed and contained, and if relations between groups and individuals are to be made positive and productive. A complex picture of the potential for conflict, its emergence and strength begins to take shape. This involves:

- the intensity of conflict, and whether the conflict is positive or negative
- the issues at stake, whether substantial or trivial, and whether positive or negative
- the source (or sources) of conflict
- the causes of conflict
- its symptoms.

To this may be added the following factors:

- *The parties to the conflict*: the simplest form of conflict involves two parties only. Much organisation conflict is more complex however.
- *The issues in dispute*: the strength of feeling that the parties involved have about the issues; the interests and agenda of those involved; the extent to which there is a hierarchy of contentious issues.
- *The dynamics of the conflict*: its causes; its sources of energy (see Table 26.1); the extent to which it is formalised; the extent to which it is personalised; the length of time it has been going on and is allowed to run on; the extent to which the eventual outcome is predictable; the range of possible outcomes.

At this point therefore, a basic conceptual framework exists for the understanding of conflict. It is important to know also that conflict, once it has been generated, is likely to feed off itself, gathering a life of its own if it is allowed to proceed unchecked (see Management in Focus 26.7).

Table 26.1 Sources of energy in conflict

The personalities involved	Expediency
The departments and functions involved	Need for triumphs, scapegoats and favours
The agenda of those involved	Relative necessity and compulsion to win
The organisational point of view	Wider perceptions of the dispute
The interests of those involved	Wider perceptions of the outcome
The presence and influence of third parties (for example, ACAS, the HSE, trade unions)	Alliances: the ability to call on outside support
Any absolute organisation standards, rules, regulations and practices involved	

MANAGEMENT IN FOCUS 26.7

THE START OF THE FIRST WORLD WAR

At first glance, there is no apparent relationship between the assassination of a middle-aged nobleman in Sarajevo, Bosnia, and the death of 15 million soldiers from France, Germany, Russia, Britain and so many other countries. However the two are indeed cause and effect.

The Archduke Franz Ferdinand of Austria was assassinated by a Serb in Sarajevo on 1 August 1914. Austria immediately took this as an act of war and mobilised to invade Serbia.

At this point the domino effect of alliances became energised. Russia declared that any attack on its ally Serbia, would constitute an act of war against itself. Because of a Franco-Russian treaty, France was drawn in as well. Austria sought help from its ally Germany, which sent a huge army across the Rhine and invaded northern France and Belgium. Britain, which had guaranteed the integrity of Belgium and had a long-standing 'entente' with France, declared war. Also quickly involved were the countries of the British Empire who rushed to the support of the motherland. Battle lines were drawn across northern Europe for most of the next four years.

The War took less than a fortnight to start. The cause was quickly forgotten. The conflict took on a life of its own and all that mattered was winning.

The outcomes of conflict

Everyone who enters into conflict needs to know and understand what they need and want to get out of it; and the minimum conditions under which they are prepared to settle. The following results are possible.

- win–win (the integrative relationship in which everyone is content)

- win–lose (the distributive relationship in which one side wins at the expense of the other or others)
- lose–win
- lose–lose

The ultimate outcome of the distributive process that occurs when the dispute escalates. In industrial relations terms this normally means recourse to strikes, lock-outs or arbitration. This is the result of both sides becoming entrenched. In these cases a rational solution between the two parties is unlikely.

A victory for one side may eventually be gained internally if a dominant–dependency relationship can be called into play. From a workforce point of view, this occurs mostly where the staff have control of output (for example, as used to happen with newspapers). The organisation's normal standpoint in these cases is economic – the necessity for staff members to be paid.

Arbitration may also be called upon to resolve disputes between individuals, especially those involving the superior–subordinate relationship. Many such cases lead to job losses and to accusations of victimisation and prejudice, and are resolved only through the courts and employment tribunals.

In all but integrative cases, the behavioural outcome is as important as the substantive. People do not like to be defeated. Neither do they like to have been seen by others to have been defeated. A large part of the distributive process therefore covers the need to find suitable forms of words to address questions of wounded pride and loss of face that would otherwise occur. The great benefit of going to arbitration in these cases is the ability to present the outcome as an independent or outsider view, and therefore acceptable.

Table 26.2 Operational and behavioural outputs of conflict

Operational constraints	Behavioural
Dysfunctional elements	Loss of face
Inefficiency	Wounded pride
Squandering of resources	Triumphalism
Loss of productive effort	Scapegoating
Customer complaints	Humiliation
Customer loss	Loss of faith
Loss of confidence	Loss of integrity
Loss of trust	Loss of morale
Loss of morale	Loss of confidence
Loss of performance	Loss of trust

Several of these items occur in each column. The purpose is to draw the relationship in terms of business performance as well as organisation behaviour.

Strategies for the management of conflict

Thus far it is established that the potential for conflict is present in every human situation, and that organisations are no exception. Indeed, much of what has so far been discussed clearly applies to a variety of areas (for example, families social groups, guides and scouts troops). Many of the issues that are present throughout society are emphasised and concentrated when they are present in work organisations, and are compounded by the ways, structures, rules and regulations in which these are constituted.

The first lesson therefore, lies in the understanding of this. The second lesson is to recognise that, if attention is paid only to the symptoms, overload is placed on the existing systems of the organisation, as indicated above.

From this, in turn, there derives the need to adopt strategic (rather than operational) approaches to the management and resolution of conflict. These should be based on a framework designed at the outset that should:

- recognise the symptoms of the conflict
- recognise the nature and level (or levels) of conflict
- recognise and understand the sources of conflict
- investigate the root causes of the conflict
- establish the range of outcomes possible
- establish the desired outcome (see Management in Focus 26.8).

MANAGEMENT IN FOCUS 26.8

THE AUDITOR [3]

Robert Shaw had simply reported what he thought was a possible misdemeanour. Given his role as auditor, it seemed rational that such matters should be investigated. The overall outcome, in all such cases, would always be that either something was amiss and the investigation was justified; or that, following investigation, nothing was found to be amiss.

However, because of the way that the matter had been handled to date, positions were entrenched.

Robert's colleague now instituted a grievance procedure. The grievance was heard by a panel constituted for the purpose. It found that there was no substantive case to answer; however, the particular individual had indeed been sloppy and should have been more careful. The individual now requested to return to his former duties, and he was promised this whenever a suitable vacancy arose.

However, both parties now needed a victim. The County Council began to call Robert's judgement into question. His colleague refused to have anything to do with him.

Both the County Council and the individual were now seeking ways to get themselves off the hook from their own particular point of view. The colleague needed an outlet for what he felt was his righteous anger. The County Council could not be seen to be making mistakes of this kind. However, nobody in the case ever clearly established their desired outcome; consequently no effective steps were taken to resolve the matter to anyone's satisfaction. The result was simply to ensure that resentment and the potential for conflict continued to exist. Work had been disrupted, as had personal and professional relationships.

Effective strategies for the management of conflict are dependent upon the following:

- Attention to standards of honesty and integrity in order to ensure that people have a sound understanding of the basis on which the relationship between themselves and their department, division or group and the organisation as a whole is established. This is brought about by absolute commitment by the organisation and those responsible for its direction and its top managers. It is translated into the required management activities by those responsible for the direction and supervision of the rest of the staff.
- Attention to communications to ensure that these meet the needs of receivers and that what is said or written is simple and direct, capable of being understood, honest and straightforward.
- Attention to the hopes, fears, aspirations and expectations of all those who work in the organisation. Much of this is based on empathy and mutual identity and commitment – and can be dissipated by compartmentalising and differentiating between staff groups.
- Attention to the systems, procedures and practices of the organisation, the ways in which these are structured and drawn up, and the ways in which they are operated. This especially means attention to equality and fairness of treatment and opportunity; the language and tone of the procedures themselves; and the training and briefing of managers and supervisors in their purposes, emphases and operation. This also normally means the presence of sanctions for those who do not operate these systems with integrity.
- The establishment of organisational purposes common to all those present in the organisation, with which they can all identify and which transcend the inherent conflicts of objectives. This is the approach most favoured for example, by Japanese companies in their operations in Western Europe and North America. All organisations however, need their own operational approaches which can be applied in their own situations (see Management in Focus 26.9).

⬤ Conclusions

The key to the effective management of conflict lies in recognising that it exists at the three levels of argument, competition and warfare. From there, it is essential that the conditions are created that allow for constructive, open, honest and often heated debate, without this escalating into competition – proving oneself right and someone else wrong – or warfare – going to extreme lengths to demonstrate or prove a point. It is equally essential that all people are given the opportunity to voice their considered professional, occupational and personal informed opinion when required to do so, without fear of reprisal. It is extremely damaging, both to morale and effectiveness if the honest expression of opinion leads to an individual as being thought of as awkward or 'not a team player'.

Conflicts based on prejudice, preconception and misperception are not to be tolerated either. Everyone has prejudices – supporting a football club, or preferring one brand of baked beans over another, for instance. However, prejudices based on race, gender, occupation, ethnic origin, place of origin, religious background, sexuality and age are not to be tolerated. If they are proved, in every case the perpetrators

MANAGEMENT IN FOCUS 26.9

OPERATIONAL APPROACHES TO THE MANAGEMENT OF CONFLICT

The operational approaches used by organisations normally take the following forms:

- Rules, procedures and precedents should be developed to minimise the emergence of conflict and then, when conflict does occur, to minimise its undesirable effects.
- Organisations should ensure that communications are effective in minimising conflict; bad communications may cause conflict or magnify minor disputes to dangerous proportions.
- Sources of potential conflict can be separated geographically, structurally or psychologically (for example, through the creation of psychological distance between functions and ranks).
- Arbitration machinery may be made available as a strategy of last resort.
- Confrontation may be used to try and bring all participants together in an attempt to face them with the consequences of their action.
- Benign neglect: this is the application of the dictum that 'a problem deferred is a problem half solved'. This can normally only be used as a temporary measure while more information is being gathered or a more structured approach is being formulated.
- Industrial relations operations can be used to contain and manage of conflict; these include consultation, participation, collective bargaining and negotiating structures.

Whichever is used, each requires careful assessment as to its suitability for the situation. Each approach is then to be designed and implemented with the particular demands of the situation in mind. The choice of a single approach used piecemeal is never effective. More generally, each of these approaches is fraught with problems, if not adequately designed and implemented, and if the process is not managed.

must be dismissed. If this does not happen, it sends a clear signal to the rest of the organisation that this form of behaviour is tolerated, and this becomes the defining point of a total lack of organisational integrity. Where preconceptions and misperceptions have been allowed to occur, it is essential that these are changed. It is the continuing responsibility of top management as well as divisional, departmental and section heads to ensure that they know as much as possible about the human, occupational and professional interactions. Only thus can they fulfil their obligation to create conditions that ensure any conflict is nipped in the bud as soon as professional and occupational argument and debate are seen to be getting out of hand.

It is also essential to recognise the extent and prevalence of conflict that is based on the abuse of rank, or professional or occupational status, when these forms of power, influence and authority are used to get something done that is illegitimate. It is a very short step from this to bullying, victimisation and harassment. This is personally, socially, occupationally and professionally destructive, as well as being morally repugnant. And it is endemic throughout organisations. A survey carried out by the University of Manchester Institute of Science and Technology (UMIST), the Institute of Management, and the Trade Union Congress (TUC) in the year 2000 published its results in March 2001. Among other things, it found that:

- One person in two suffered some form of stress or dysfunction as the result of workplace conflict over the course of their working lives.
- One person in four had suffered direct or indirect bullying over the previous five years.
- At the greatest risk were professionally or occupationally qualified staff – especially nurses, teachers, social workers, financial advisers, bank cashiers, computer operators and secretaries. For example, one teacher in every six complained of stress caused by conflict, bullying, victimisation or harassment in the previous five years; for nurses, the figure was one in every four.

Almost without exception, organisations and their senior managers did nothing to respond to these findings. Health and education authorities were particularly crude in their attitude, and their response was summed as 'professionally qualified staff have to get used to a range of pressures, and conflict is always present. Robust organisational and managerial attitudes are therefore certain to prevail.' The same attitudes were found in the banking and oil industries, as well as the police service.

Conflict causes stress – organisational, occupational, group and personal. This, in turn, has a knock-on effect on organisational performance and output. Productivity falls, customers and clients are not served properly, and long-term profitability and effectiveness is damaged. There is also a professional and occupational marketing factor to be taken into account: those professions or occupations that come to be known, believed or perceived to suffer from stress and conflict have the greatest difficult in recruiting the next generation of staff. Moreover, it is increasingly expensive for organisations to accept the presence of stress and conflict without doing anything about it, because the levels of damages paid in compensation to those who are able to demonstrate or prove negative effects on their mental or physical well-being have risen sharply in the past few years. Many cases also attract extensive media attention, and this too has an adverse effect on the presentation and confidence of the particular organisation in the public eye.

In support of managing conflict, it is essential that there are clear grievance and disciplinary procedures, and that these are supported by full staff and management training. All procedures should be in writing, state to whom they apply, and how, when and where they are to be used. Standards of required attitudes, behaviour and performance must be clearly stated. Especially when serious conflict exists, staff must have instant recourse to a named, senior and influential official, to whom they can talk without fear of reprisals. If this is managed effectively, it goes a long way to ensuring that organisational conflict is kept to an absolute minimum, and indeed that it only arises as the result of genuine misunderstanding.

CRITICAL THINKING, ANALYSIS AND EVALUATION

1. Outline and discuss the benefits and drawbacks of referring every single dispute or argument to arbitration.
2. Choosing an organisation with which you are familiar, outline the extent and

prevalence of conflict present, and the causes and symptoms. What approaches should those responsible be taking in order to reduce their effect?

If the organisation you have chosen has little conflict, identify and evaluate the actions and management style already present.

3. Identify, as fully as possible, the potential for conflict in:

   a) a joint venture arrangement between large companies and subcontractors for a major engineering project

   b) a transition from individual offices to an open-plan arrangement

   c) a transition from demarcated jobs to fully flexible working.

   Outline a strategy for the management of each of these situations.

4. Comment on the language used in the quotes at the start of the chapter. What attitudes can you infer from each?

DEVELOPING MANAGEMENT SKILLS AND EXPERTISE

CHANGE AND TRANSFORMATION AT THE BBC

In October 2004, the BBC appointed Mark Thompson as its Director General (or chief executive). A journalist by trade, Thompson moved from reporting into the corporate media hierarchy, and over a ten-year period had worked for independent and satellite broadcasting companies, as well as for the BBC. He had been Chief Executive of Channel 4 since December 2001.

The BBC employs approximately 23,000 staff in all of its activities. It also commissions programmes, books, magazines and periodicals from outside sources. The BBC has regional offices, newsrooms and programme centres and studios in many parts of the UK.

In December 2004, Mark Thompson announced that up to 1800 BBC staff would be moved to Manchester to dilute the London influence, and to ensure that the corporation continued to serve all parts of the UK on an even basis.

In early 2005, Thompson produced a blueprint for the future of the BBC that required substantial job losses. The BBC had been heavily criticised for its reporting of the war in Iraq, and its general attitude to political issues in both the UK and the USA. There was also a widespread belief among political circles that there was a tendency to aggression on the part of some interviewers when interviewing government and opposition politicians.

The BBC's Charter is due to be renewed in 2006.

Implementing change

In March 2005, Thompson announced that there would be 6000 job losses. Having relocated 1800 staff away from London, he then announced that a high proportion of redundancies would come from the different regional offices.

At the same time, Thompson announced that the BBC was no longer to compete with independent, commercial or satellite channels in 'ratings wars'. Ratings wars are essential to the well-being of independent, commercial channels because these directly reflect the amount of advertising revenue that can be raised. A public service broadcaster such as the BBC has no direct need to be involved in ratings wars as long as its sources of revenue are assured.

The BBC consequently has a unique relationship with the government, upon which it depends for its continued ability to raise 'assured' money through the collection of the licence fee. On the other hand, the government has always sought to maintain the impression that it does not meddle in the affairs of the BBC; that the licence fee enables the Corporation to remain independent rather than a being mouthpiece for, or reflector of, government priorities and pressures.

Events

'I cannot see how the BBC will deliver all Thompson's promises about new services after ditching so many staff,' stated an official from BECTU, the broadcasting trade union. The clear implication from the broadcasting union was that the BBC would become ever more dependent on programmes produced by independent production companies, rather than those made internally. This is likely to be reinforced by the fact that, although the job losses are to be phased in over three years, in practice it is very difficult to keep to such a schedule, once people know that they are to lose their jobs.

The use of technology is also expected to reduce job requirements. However, the BBC's record in the implementation of new technology has been uneven. When the Corporation introduced its electronic news production system, it took five years to eliminate the teething troubles. The BBC's electronic accounting system still fails to work evenly, deleting invoices at random and generating hundreds of queries.

Other parts of the technology and production aspects of the BBC have already been sold off. This includes the sale of theatre and graphics technology to Siemens, the German engineering company, for £150 million. Some of the broadcasting technology is to be sold to TF1, the French national broadcaster for £100 million.

The money from these sales is to be used to invest in the 'digital future of television'. Announcing these savings, Thompson stated that:

> The commitment to digital was a key demand of the government in return for Charter renewal; in addition, the government expects to make a cash windfall for themselves on the sale of space for digital, satellite and cable broadcasting in the future.

However, there is a problem because not enough digital television sets are being produced for retail sale and consumption. Moreover, there is no clear commitment (although there is an understanding) that those sets presently on sale will be able to pick up a digital set of BBC channels when the broadcasts do finally go digital.

At this time of change and uncertainty, the BBC has also faced adverse media coverage as the result of its continued hiring of perceived high-value presenters at a time when many in the Corporation are losing their jobs. Recent figures to draw this criticism have included Piers Morgan, Johnny Vaughan and Graham Norton, all of whom are on very high salaries, fees and commissions, out of proportion (to date) with their contribution to the Corporation. This also applied to Angus Deayton, who was sacked in 2001 after revelations about his private life.

Thompson has however told programme makers that they must put forward explicit plans for progress, innovation, enhancement and development. Imitation programmes will not now be commissioned. 'Reality' and 'fly-on-the-wall' programmes will be subject to scrutiny by the Corporation's top management before they are commissioned. There is to be a return to substantial and in-depth coverage of current affairs. In addition, BBC3 and BBC4 especially are to be used to develop pioneering comedy, drama, research, arts and performance programmes and series.

Questions

1. Identify the sources of power and influence, the potential for conflict, and the range of possible outcomes in any conflicts that may occur.
2. Identify any incremental steps that may usefully be taken to try and manage the potential for conflict.
3. Identify the specific vested interests present and what they may contribute to:
    -   the escalation of conflict
    -   the resolution of conflict.

Chapter twenty seven

Management in practice

'Beware of rashness, but with energy, and sleepless vigilance, go forward and give us victories.'
Abraham Lincoln (1865).

'No epilogue, I pray you; your play needs no excuse. Never excuse.'
William Shakespeare, *A Midsummer Night's Dream*.

'People like to work for a good guy, but they will only take it for so long,
especially if they do not get their bonuses.'
Ricardo Semler, *The Maverick Solution*, BBC (1997).

'You can ask me for anything you like except time.'
Napoleon.

Chapter outline

- Introduction
- Managerial roles
- Attitudes and values
- Setting goals
- Managing by walking about
- Wait a minute
- Control
- Time
- Interpersonal skills and
  assertiveness
- Continuous performance
  assessment
- Realpolitik
- Conclusions

Chapter objectives

After studying this chapter, you should be able to:

- understand the complexity of managerial performance

- understand the need for constant development of managerial skills and qualities

- understand and be able to apply specific skills and points of enquiry to generate
  problems

- understand the opportunities, problems and consequences of undertaking particular
  courses of action, or particular approaches to issues and problems

- understand the need for review and evaluation of every activity.

● Introduction

The purpose of this chapter is to bridge the gap between the acquisition of the skills, knowledge and aptitudes required of the manager and an understanding of the complexities and application problems in functional terms, so as to combine them to generate effective and successful managerial performance.

● The managerial role

Managers require an understanding of both the principles and practice outlined thus far and the qualities necessary to put them into effect in ways suitable to the function, operation and nature of the situation in which they have to work.

The manager is the department's figurehead, symbol and representative. As such, an image and identity is generated for the department in the whole organisation and with anyone else with whom he/she comes into contact. Managers represent their departments at meetings; they carry the hopes and aspirations of the staff at all times in all dealings with the rest of the organisation. It is their role and duty to fight the department's corner and to ensure that the interests of both department and staff are put forward and represented. Depending on the nature of the department in which they are working, this function may involve belonging to a wide range of professional associations, cluster groups and functional lobbies, and being an effective operator in all of these.

Managers must have a decision-making capability that is suitable to the purposes of their department. Again, this involves drawing on capacities and capabilities and using them in ways suitable and effective in their own particular situation. In particular, part of this decision-making faculty must include an effective problem-solving method (see Figure 27.1). Again, the precise configuration of this will vary from situation to situation but essentially must address the basic process of: identifying and defining the problem; assessing its causes; considering the variety of approaches that are possible and feasible in the situation; and deciding on appropriate courses of action.

Effectiveness in any managerial position requires both understanding and capability in these areas. If these are present there are additional benefits in terms of the creation of identity and pride among departmental staff. Finally, decision making constitutes a critical part of the backcloth that is in any case necessary to manage effectively in any work situation.

● Attitudes and values

Forming and nurturing the 'right' attitudes is an essential part of the managerial task, and any manager or supervisor must have a full grasp of this and be able to do it. If enthusiasm is infectious, so is negativity; it is very easy to have a demoralised workforce very quickly if certain matters are not picked up. In both multinational and public and health services, this is manifest in the 'canteen culture', and has been partly responsible for engendering and perpetuating negative and undesirable attitudes. The overall purpose must be that everyone is happy, harmonious and productive on the organisation's terms and those of the manager and department in question. A clear and positive lead must therefore be given, and clear and positive attitudes engendered and formed.

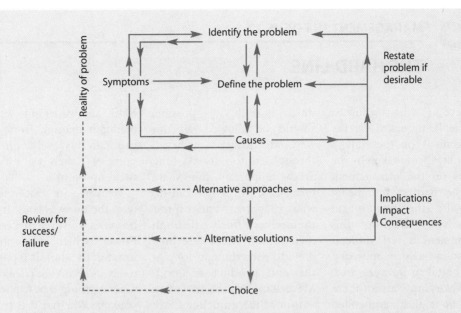

Purpose: to ensure that a rigorous and disciplined approach is recognised and understood as being necessary in all situations, and that such an approach is adopted.
Points for consideration throughout the process must also include: the context and nature of the process; when it is occurring; where it is occurring; why; its impact on the rest of the organisation, department or division; the extent to which it can be avoided; the extent to which it can be controlled; the consequences and opportunities of not tackling it (which is always a choice).

Figure 27.1 A problem-solving model

Negativity, therefore, is to be avoided. Prevention of such attitudes is achieved through adequate and well-designed induction and orientation programmes so that every employee is given a positive set of both corporate and departmental values, a clear identity with the organisation and its purposes, and confidence in the rest of the staff. Ultimately, people wish to feel good about the organisation and department for which they work.

Curing bad attitudes is harder. In isolated or extreme cases, people who do not wish to work for the particular organisation will be dismissed. In large or complex organisations they may be moved somewhere with a view to reforming their attitudes and getting a positive response from them. Marks of envy must also be dealt with; office executives who wish for the sales persons' cars should be informed that, without the efforts of the sales force, there would be no office job. Similarly, professional and technical experts may feel a much stronger loyalty and commitment to their expertise than to the organisation that actually employs them to use it. In general departmental managers will address such matters either at the point at which they first assume their post, or when new members of staff come into the department. They thus set standards of attitude and conformity to which all are to aspire in the pursuit of the goals of the department. One manager's view of such 'ground rules' is given in Management in Focus 27.1.

MANAGEMENT IN FOCUS 27.1

THE HARD LINE

I believe in as hard a line as possible being taken by the management on the staff, a harder line being taken by the owners on the management and the hardest line being taken by the owners on themselves. Creating this environment is very difficult and so a strong approach must be taken in every area. The working atmosphere must be tightly controlled and be all-pervasive or it will not work. This seems contradictory to the 'kind' approach of Maslow or Rogers. I think it is necessary however if their dreams of what people are capable of are to be achieved.

The vital ground rules must be ascertained (no more, no less) and then they must be stuck to absolutely rigidly. The Japanese conformity approach should be made to look weak, when it comes to the ground rules. On the other hand, once these rules are adhered to, as

much flexibility as possible should be allowed. In this way individuality is achieved through conformity. As long as the important things are taken care of, people can do what they want and express themselves freely through their jobs. I don't care how they do something as long as the end product is good. Mavericks who can work within the guidelines are welcome and a great source of creativity and inspiration.

It may be possible to summarise the ground rules into simply one thing. You must keep to your agreements. This encourages the development of the person's integrity, their ability to make choices and their sense of responsibility. It then gives us the opportunity to ask them to agree to what we really want, i.e., be at work at 8.00 a.m. If they agree to this, we will hold them to it, precisely two minutes past 8.00 is not

8.00, and providing we can maintain enough front (and maintain this level of integrity ourselves) then we will pull them up on it.

Reasons are not relevant (e.g. the bus was late). It then becomes a matter of Personal Power, which we want to foster in the staff. It is possible to act as if you are responsible for everything that happens in your life whether it is true or not. Doing this eventually means it will end up as being true, in your reality. It is possible to look ahead and manipulate the environment. If you expect traffic then you can leave earlier. If they were paid £100,000 just for turning up on time, they would be there. This principle can be applied to everything we want, and although it may seem strange, in the long-term it will benefit the individual as much as us.

Source: David Scott, *Artisan Group Ltd Business Plan*, 1993.

Setting goals

It is essential that all departments have clear aims and objectives, and that all staff understand what they are and why that particular part of the organisation aspires to achieve them. It is invariably a feature of departments that malfunction, and staff who are demoralised or demotivated, that they are not clear about this purpose or about the requirements and directions of the part of the organisation for which they work.

Such aims and objectives should be stated in writing so as to give high levels of credibility and to serve as visual reminders to all concerned. They should also be positive, and reflect both aspirations and achievement. They should be 'personal' and be drawn up in ways with which everyone in the department can identify. They must be challenging and motivating and reflect the theme of constant improvements and achievements wherever possible. They must be prioritised; they will not all be instantly achievable but will set a progression and configuration of the value of the work of the department. They must also be realistic without introducing measures of complacency or inefficiency.

Objectives must be measurable; this includes those established for managers and supervisors. This involves reducing any qualitative objectives wherever possible to a series of quantifiable measures. Where this cannot be expressed it is often nevertheless possible to break an objective down into useful, specific and more controllable sub-objectives. For example, where phrases such as 'a matter of urgency' or 'as soon as possible' are used, these should be replaced with particular timescales or deadlines; the phrases quoted bind nobody to anything in reality and will be read as such by those involved. Above all, goals, aims and objectives that are established must be clearly understood and valued by everybody. They must seek to combine the capacities and talents of everyone concerned in productive and effective effort and to reconcile the divergent and often disparate reasons that individuals within a department have for being there. Management in Focus 27.2 gives model goal and objective formulations.

Managing by walking about

Managing by walking about (MBWA) enhances visibility, and also creates opportunities for productive harmony, early problem and issue resolution, and improvements in communications.

MANAGEMENT IN FOCUS 27.2

OBJECTIVES: AN EXAMPLE

A social service or welfare objective may be (and often is) written as follows.

To promote the social well-being of groups with physical, mental and environmental handicaps, to enable them to function, as far as possible, as a community and within the community of their choice.

This is wrong. It is imprecise and unintelligible, and draws people away from it rather than to it. It is written in 'politician and bureaucrat-speak', and is thus full of opportunities for interpretation, and will be read as such.

This approach is also wrong, therefore, unless what is actually desired is a clouding, rather than clarification of the issues raised. Assuming that clarity is what is wanted, the matter should be treated thus:

In regard to each group of clients, the establishment of the following facilities and services .... by .... (a stated deadline).

Everyone is clear where they stand. Those working in the service have targets; the client group has expectations. There are included: performance achievement targets, measures of success or failure, and the basis of an operational review in relation to 'service' objectives.

In behavioural and perceptual terms, the manager who is 'visible' is seen as approachable and acceptable. This will be reinforced when the manager, while walking about, takes active steps to approach the staff members, to get to know them, and to understand their jobs, their problems and their concerns. More specifically, MBWA underlines the essential qualities of trust, openness, honesty and integrity, as well as visibility. It fosters a communication forum and informal meeting point between manager and staff that demonstrates the manager's care and concern and enables small concerns to be brought up and dealt with on the spot before they become big issues. Such behaviour is an essential cog in the process of continually appraising the performance of staff. It enables any misunderstandings on the part of anyone concerned to be raised and rectified quickly.

Such behaviour also fosters the quality of empathy in the manager or supervisor, and gives a full general knowledge and background to the hopes, fears and aspirations of those who work in the department. This is an essential prerequisite to the process of motivating the staff successfully.

Such behaviour reduces both the physical and behavioural barriers between the manager and staff. The closed door, large desk and executive trappings are not only physically imposing; they also present a perceptual barrier that the subordinate has first to overcome because they reinforce the differences in rank and status between the two: MBWA dilutes these.

Related to MBWA is the need to lead by example, to set absolute standards. Good managers are always present whenever there is a crisis or emergency. Managers gain and improve their respect among their staff through their willingness to lead by example. Mark McCormack of IMG goes out with sales executives and consultants to demonstrate his own ability and preferred style in closing deals. Richard Branson of the Virgin Group regularly serves drinks and meals on his scheduled airline flights. Both also make a point of regularly telephoning those staff whom they have not seen during the week. Not only are they demonstrating their own willingness and capacity, they are also setting an example to, and for, their staff, and keeping an active eye on the day-to-day operations of their organisation. It is also excellent general marketing among both staff and customers.

MBWA is an essential tool for the manager and one that must be in constant use. If it is not, the staff will develop their own patterns and ways of working, their own means of problem and issue resolution, and control will pass out of the hands and office of the manager. In more sophisticated or complex organisations where there is a global, off-site, or other 'arm's length' supervision or direction mode, there should be an individual designated to act in the manager's stead, maintaining the visible face of the organisation and its management, taking the day-to-day decisions and resolving minor and operational issues before they become major crises.

Wait a minute

All managers should have a mechanism in some shape or form that constitutes a 'wait a minute' facility. This will be present in the formulation of policy or direction, the taking of decisions, and the implementation of strategy. At departmental and other junior levels the purpose is to ensure that no inconvenient operational precedent is being set by taking a particular line to resolve what may seem a simple one-off problem. 'Wait a minute' is not an abdication of decision-making ability or of decision making itself. It need not take a 'minute'. It is simply to ensure that what is to be done has been questioned from every conceivable angle. It is more generally part of the monitoring, review, and early and late warning systems that should be integral to all aspects of the manager's task. The presence of a 'wait a minute' facility does not of itself ensure that the right decision is taken, but it does at least afford a moment's further consideration. If this is all that is necessary to confirm that what is being done is truly for the good of the organisation and the fair and equitable treatment of the staff concerned, it is a moment well spent. Management in Focus 27.3 considers three situations where 'Wait a minute' could usefully be used.

● Control

All managers must have control mechanisms that are suitable to the department or unit concerned, and that relate to the staff, resources and operations that are carried out within in it. This must apply even where the work in hand is of a professional, administrative, technical or qualitative nature. The overall function of control involves setting desired standards and measuring actual performance against them; from this, analyses of differences between the two will be made and remedial action will be taken where necessary. It follows from this that objectives must be fully understood by all concerned, so that involvement in the control of the work neces- sary and any remedial action that becomes apparent is adopted and understood by all concerned.

The methods and mechanisms to be used will therefore be department or task specific; they will also be linked to and in harmony with the overall methods adopted by the organisation. They must reconcile the necessity to produce clear results with the need to be flexible and objective in operation and economical and simple. Presentation of control information in ways that everyone can understand and have regard to is essential. It is necessary not only to indicate differences and deviations from required performance but also to provide the means of establishing the causes of these: where failures are occurring, why this is so and what to do about them. Within this context managers will draw up and use their own control methods. These will include:

- *Forecasts:* based on the resources – staff, financial and technological – available, and relating to the outputs that the organisation requires.
- *Budgets:* for all the activities within the manager's sphere, covering such matters as staff, production, outputs, operational costs, administration, other over- heads, cash and daily expenditure and possibly also an overall department reconciliation of these matters.
- *Management information systems:* including the gathering and promulgation of information within the department and the reconciliation of this with desired levels of performance; these also provide a vehicle for the manager's contribution to the information systems and requirements of the organisation.
- *Reporting systems and relationships:* designed to highlight any deviations and problems immediately, and to identify means by which such situations may be remedied; in any case, they should be able to provide information that can be used on an organisational basis for future planning and direction setting.
- *Job and work design:* to ensure that work is allocated so as to ensure effective

MANAGEMENT IN FOCUS 27.3

WAIT A MINUTE

● Nike, the sportswear corporation, tried to devise a global travel policy for their staff. In particular the focus was on who should travel first class, business class or economy class on the world's airlines. Should this be based on: the distance travelled, the part of the world to which the executive was travelling, the length of the journey, or the volume or value of business to be conducted?

● The Ceramics Industry Training Board summoned a meeting of junior field executives to its head office in Harrow, North West London.

The junior executives were from all over the UK and overnight hotel accommodation was arranged for them. The meeting was unproductive and wasteful because two executives based in London were unable to attend. Because they lived in London no accommodation was found for them. On the day in question they were unable to travel because of a terrorist bomb. They also felt discriminated against, and slighted, by accident of their location in London.

● John Stevens, an official with an international bank at their London office, asked to be able to take two years' annual leave back-to-back (a total of two months) to visit friends and relatives in Australia. His request was granted. Mary Phelps, an official in an equivalent position and with longer service at the same bank, put in the same request for the back-to-back leave to visit friends and relatives at Ullapool in Scotland. She underlined the request by stating that it would take longer for her to get to her destination than for Stevens to get to his.

long-term organisational, departmental and individual performance; and that the bad or unattractive parts of the work are evenly shared out. This is likely to require attention to the ability to attract and retain staff, and to the design of effective (and often flexible) working patterns.

● *Feedback*: part of the control process is the communication process that keeps the departments informed of progress on a continuous basis. There is a control function inherent in the nature and content of feedback that is given; part of this may also be achieved through any performance appraisal scheme that is in place.

● *Conflict resolution*: part of the purpose of having control methods and procedures in place must be to ensure that conflicts or disputes between members of staff are resolved as quickly and effectively as possible.

● *Control methods and means*: these should be integrated into the general review, monitoring and process assessment that should be in place in all departments. To be fully effective, they require full understanding on the part of all concerned – the manager, the staff and those other departments and units with whom they interact; they should also mirror the aims and objectives of the departments if they are to be fully effective. Management in Focus 27.4 gives examples of the problems a manager may have to field even when events are outside his or her control.

● Time

Time at the workplace may be divided into: productive time; non-productive, stoppage or downtime; maintenance time; and wasted time. From this, priority, crisis, wastage, overload and underload can be identified, and a time–resource–energy dimension put on each. The purpose is to ensure that what happens in reality accords with what managers think happens. Other dimensions and variables will also be included. These include the complexity and difficulty of the task in hand, the importance of it, the urgency of it, and the frequency of it. The value of what is done, whether derived or implicit, will also have a time configuration to it. What is therefore required is an attitude of continued questioning of time usage based on the premise that anything and everything can always be improved and made more efficient and effective (see Management in Focus 27.5).

In order to maximise or optimise time usage, certain steps can be taken. The first is for the manager to be aware of the time issue. Part of the process that arises from this is:

● to set priorities for the department
● to set a pattern of delegation of tasks and activities
● to produce suitable and effective work schedules

MANAGEMENT IN FOCUS 27.4

AN AIRLINE MANAGER WORKING IN THE MIDDLE EAST

This manager regularly fields questions from powerful and influential people in his region. Problems handled have included the following:

● Why the daughter of a diplomat had to wait 20 minutes for an orange juice on her flight back to London.
● Why packages and parcels carried by a

worldwide courier organisation had to go through security screening and not straight on to the aeroplane.
● Why it took two hours for a particular cargo to be cleared from the airport by customs.
● Why Europeans have to go through the full immigration procedure

upon arrival in countries of the Middle East.

The point that each of these items has in common is that they are all outside the manager's control. They are nevertheless raised by customers and clients of his firm and he must therefore either deal with them or else find someone else to provide a suitable and adequate answer.

MANAGEMENT IN FOCUS 27.5

WASTE OF MANAGERIAL TIME

A report published jointly by the UK Industrial Society and the BBC at the end of the twentieth century drew the following main conclusions.

Managers spend up to 20 per cent of their time or the equivalent of one whole day per five-day working week in meetings. Furthermore, they spend up to a third of their working time on paperwork, routine and administration. The main time wasters identified were interruptions from colleagues, handling telephone calls that a junior or subordinate should have fielded, and dealing with untargeted bureaucracy and memoranda. The main operational cause of hold-ups was found to be computer problems and system failures.

The stark conclusion to be drawn from this is that managers represent an overpaid niche of the workforce, in relation to the quality of their output. Operations, contributions and key results require better targeting and better definition; another need is for an understanding on the part of the organisations and their top executives of what outputs are required from their subordinates and how these are to be achieved.

Further studies carried out by the Chartered Management Institute, Chartered Institute of Personnel and Development, and Department of Trade and Industry state that the knowledge and understanding of so much time being wasted in these activities was having a seriously adverse effect on the morale of many junior and middle management staff. A further conclusion was that at no previous time had managers felt under so much 'pressure to perform', and that this was in many cases compounded by a lack of knowledge or understanding of what 'perform' actually meant. Many organisations consequently continued to resort to requiring attendance for long hours, whether or not productive work was being carried out.

- to continuously assess the work in hand against time constraints, as well as against constraints placed by other resource implications.

Next the manager should identify those things that waste time. These may consist of:

- long, unnecessary or habitual meetings, or those which are procedural rather than executive in content
- interruptions and the nature of these in his or her work
- idle conversations and unnecessary bureaucracy, reporting systems and record keeping
- the balance of travelling time against effective business conducted
- task allocations – especially the allocation of the easy tasks which should be conducted on a basis that leaves those of high capacity and quality to carry out key, critical or other activities that match their capabilities, not filling up their work schedules with items that are could be done by less qualified personnel.

The manager should also be aware of creative approaches to time management in terms of machine, equipment and plant usage; working patterns and shift arrangements; personal planning; the setting and maintenance of deadlines; and giving clarity of purpose to meetings. There are opportunity costs of time usage, and especially time wastage, that can never be made up. All managers and their departments should have a system of time measurement that is suitable to its purpose; and that encourages efficiency and effectiveness of performance in regard to this resource.

⬤ Interpersonal skills and assertiveness

Everyone has interpersonal skills. For managers, these constitute a tool that is essential to them in the pursuit of their daily occupation. They are instrumental in creating and reinforcing the management style adopted. They are part of the process of MBWA and the visibility that goes with this. They reinforce messages of honesty, openness and trust. They have implications for general levels and states of communication within the department, conducting meetings and handling public presentations.

The first and most important thing that a manager's use and application of his or her interpersonal skills will represent is the degree of trust and confidence in the staff and the basis on which they are to be treated. Overall it sets the tone and tenor for the whole department and its way of working. Managers will therefore apply their interpersonal skills in the following ways. They will never criticise members of staff either in public or on a personal basis when the problem is related to work. If there is a personal issue that requires managerial activity and concern, this will be conducted in private and remain a matter between the manager and the individual. If it is necessary to criticise somebody's work performance, then it must be done in a clear and straightforward way, with the emphasis upon remedy rather than apportioning blame. Effective criticism is always constructive; the end result must be to reinforce the importance of the individual as a member of the department. If it is possible, such criticism should be reinforced by finding areas of work to be praised at the same time. In this way also, the work remains at the centre of the concern.

It follows from this that praise should be extended where it is due. It is a powerful form of recognition and a universal motivator. Every manager should avoid only dealing with staff when there are negative concerns. Praise makes the individual concerned feel identity, respected and important. It should be handed out whenever and wherever due, and it should be conducted in public.

Managers also use interpersonal skills to instil pride and enthusiasm for the job, the work and the department. The best managers inspire and generate pride and enthusiasm by the ways in which they behave in relation to the department's work and the people carrying it out. It is the manager's job to instil this feeling and to promote this attitude among the staff, and the interpersonal relationship with the staff is instrumental in this.

All work should be a matter of enthusiasm; and a matter of enjoyment as well as fulfilment. Again, the interpersonal skills of the manager are instrumental in creating this background (see Management in Focus 27.6).

Other qualities of leadership that become apparent through the use of interpersonal skills include the courage of the manager concerned, job knowledge, self-control and self-discipline, a sense of fairness and equity, standards of personal conduct and behaviour that reflect the standards required in the department, and a sense of humour. It is also a reflection of the interpersonal qualities of the manager that ensures that the correct and appropriate standards of dress, language and

MANAGEMENT IN FOCUS 27.6

DR VASILIY PETROV

Dr Petrov, a physicist, came to the UK as a refugee from the Balkans crises of the 1990s. He was an expert in his field, and soon gained employment in the research laboratories of a large multinational company. He was considered to be a brilliant researcher but very eccentric.

One day, a junior member of the research staff who was known to dislike Dr Petrov, reported to the director of research that he had seen Dr Petrov stealing sweets from the local Woolworths. Later that day, Dr Petrov was seen eating the sweets in his office; and there was a large pile of packets of sweets on his desk.

This kind of allegation destroys any joy of work, and the interpersonal and professional relationships necessary to sustain this. Managers faced with this kind of issue need to tackle both parties separately and immediately. A clear standard needs to be established as a basis for 'telling tales' (some of which will be legitimate, others not). Disciplinary sanctions must be available, and enforced immediately, upon any member of staff making false allegations.

manners are established. This is particularly important in departments and units where dealings with the public are an everyday feature.

The purpose overall must be to establish an adult and assertive means of interaction within the department (see Management in Focus 27.7). The prime purpose of the manager's interpersonal skills and approach in the situation is the promotion of effective work, for without it actual standards will always fall short of the ideal. These interpersonal factors are an essential and integral part of this promotion.

Interpersonal skills are important when giving negative messages too; just because the message is negative, there is no reason for this to have any lasting effect upon the motivation and morale either of the staff member who is to receive the negative message or of the department at large. If it is necessary to deny someone a request, this should always be done quickly; the reason for the negative response should be made clear and should be the truth. The manager should never hide behind phrases like 'it's not company policy'. The reason given for the negative response should always be operational; and it should be clearly and unequivocally communicated.

The end result of all this is that the staff and manager know where they stand in relation to each other, and that the interpersonal skills applied and relationship generated support this. This provides the basis for effective work transactions and ensures that disputes and misunderstandings are kept to a minimum.

It also ensures that when these do occur they can be quickly and effectively remedied without lasting effect and, above all, negative consequences for the department as a whole. The particular issues are:

● *Discipline*: establishing absolute standards of behaviour and performance based on both ordinary common decency and absolute organisational demands; and ensuring that when disciplinary procedures are invoked, matters are dealt with quickly, fairly and effectively.

MANAGEMENT IN FOCUS 27.7

ASSERTIVENESS IN ACTION: MANAGERIAL AND PROFESSIONAL DEMEANOUR

The following is a summary of how to apply the principles of assertive behaviour and communication.

Language	Assertive language is clear and simple. It is easy for the hearer or receiver to understand. The words used are unambiguous and straightforward. Requests and demands are made in a clear and precise manner, and with sound reasons. Weasel words, political phraseology, ambiguity and 'get-outs' are never used.
Delivery	Assertive delivery is in a clear and steady tone of voice. The emphasis of the delivery is on important and crucial words and phrases. The voice projection that is used is always even, and neither too loud nor too soft. Assertive delivery does not involve shouting, threatening, or abuse, at any time or under any circumstances; nor does it resort to simpering or whining.
Face and eyes	The head is held up. There is plenty of eye contact, and a steadiness of gaze. The delivery is reinforced with positive movements that relate to what is being said (e.g. smiles, laughter, nodding; or a straight face where something has gone wrong).
Other non-verbal aspects	The body is upright (whether standing or sitting). Arms and hands are 'open' (in order to encourage a positive response or transaction). There is no fidgeting or shuffling, nor are there threatening gestures or table thumping; or other outward displays of temper.
Situational factors	Assertive delivery is based on an inherent confidence, belief in and knowledge of the situation, and the work that is done. Openness, clarity, credibility, and personal and professional confidence, all spring from this. Any clarity of purpose or delivery will inevitably be spoilt through having to operate from a weak position or one which is not fully known or understood. In such cases, important issues are either clouded or avoided altogether. In extreme cases the people involved often interact aggressively or angrily in order to try to compensate for this basic lack of soundness, clarity or understanding. Assertive behaviour is also the best foundation for effective negotiations and problem-solving activities. The approach taken is the determination to get to the bottom of the particular matter in hand and to resolve it to the satisfaction of everyone. Where in practice it becomes necessary to resort to more expedient means, there is invariably resentment somewhere at the outcome.

- *Dismissal*: ensuring that offences such as vandalism, violence, theft, fraud, bullying, victimisation, discrimination and harassment are dealt with fairly and effectively; and that when these are proved, the perpetrators are dismissed.
- *Grievances*: handling and resolving issues rather than institutionalising them; ensuring that the full facts of the case are covered; and ensuring that everyone understands what outcome has been reached and the reasons for this.
- *Health and safety*: creating and maintaining the conditions whereby a healthy and safe working environment exists; taking remedial action where unsafe practices and unhealthy aspects are found.
- *Occupational health*: above all paying attention to stress, repetitive strain injuries, and the causes of these; recognising the potential for their existence; addressing and remedying working practices when these are found.

In each of these cases, it is essential that managers understand that there are procedures to be followed, and that failure to do so normally constitutes a breach of a employment law. Managers must therefore ensure they have a full knowledge of the relevant laws, and are expert in their application (see Management in Focus 27.8).

● Continuous performance assessment

It is implicit in much of the above that the manager must be able to assess and judge the levels and quality of performance in the department and to measure it against the required standards, taking remedial action where necessary at the relevant level. If there is a shortfall at departmental level the manager may need to conduct a range of activities to find out why this is so in order to establish what response is needed. Such activities may consist of, for example, a walk-through of the processes and procedures of the organisation or department; an observation or sampling of departmental activities, harmony and cooperation; or the assessment and identification and remedying of blockages, again either in processes, procedures or the operations themselves.

At team level it may be necessary to systematically examine the workings of the team in question to assess where performance is falling down, and what is causing the problem. From this, a more accurate compartmentalisation and definition of the cause under one or more of the headings of attitude, conflict, processes, procedures, communication, decision making and interrelations should be possible. Furthermore, such an approach may clearly reveal the problem area so that a remedy can be applied in the interests of reforming and recreating a positive and productive team.

At the individual level a twofold approach is necessary. One is to ensure that those in the department receive organisational feedback on the nature of their work, praise for good performance and quick and effective remedy for any shortfall. The organisation's formal appraisal methods may in any case require this and may use these methods as the means of allocating training, development, secondment, the next move and pay rises. In all these cases it will be important to the members of staff that such appraisal is carried out in accordance with expectations and generally effectively.

The other part of the approach to the individual here concerns the general monitoring of the department's work by the manager concerned. Performance will actually be continuously assessed as part of the manager's 'leadership' role in the department. If this is done effectively, the manager will know the state and the performance of the

MANAGEMENT IN FOCUS 27.8

OFFICE STAFF PRACTICES, 1852

1. *Godliness, Cleanliness* and *Punctuality* are the necessities of a good business.
2. This firm has reduced the hours of work, and the Clerical Staff will now only have to be present between the hours of 7 a.m. and 6 p.m. on weekdays.
3. Daily prayers will be held each morning in the Main Office. The Clerical Staff will be present.
4. Clothing must be of a sober nature. The Clerical Staff will not disport themselves in raiment of bright colours, not will they wear hose, unless in good repair.
5. Overshoes and top-coats may not be worn in the office, but neck scarves and headwear may be worn in inclement weather.
6. A stove is provided for the benefit of the Clerical Staff.
7. No member of the Clerical Staff may leave the room without permission from Mr Rogers. The calls of nature are permitted and Clerical Staff may use the garden below the second gate. The area must be kept in good order.
8. No talking is allowed during business hours.
9. The craving of tobacco, wines or spirits is a human weakness and, as such, is forbidden to all members of the Clerical Staff.
10. Now that the hours of business have been drastically reduced, the partaking of food is allowed between 11.30 a.m. and noon, but work will not, on any account, cease.
11. Members of the Clerical Staff will provide their own pens. A new sharpener is available, on application to Mr Rogers.
12. Mr Rogers will nominate a Senior Clerk to be responsible for the cleanliness of the Main Office and the Private Office, and all Boys and Juniors will report to him 40 minutes before Prayers, and will remain after closing hours for similar work. Brushes, Brooms, Scrubbers and Soap are provided by the owners.
13. The New Increased Weekly Wages are hereunder detailed:
    Junior Boys (to 11 years) 1/4d
    Boys (to 14 years) 2/1d
    Juniors 4/8d
    Junior Clerks 8/7d
    Clerks 10/9d
    Senior Clerks (after 15 years with owners) 21/-d

The owners recognise the generosity of the new Labour Laws but will expect a great rise in output of work to compensate for these near Utopian conditions.

department on a current and continuing basis. Issues will be remedied before they become problems, and problems addressed before they become crises.

The final part of this activity is a continuous measure of performance against targets and objectives, the criteria against which the success or otherwise of the department will be assessed. Part of this requirement, therefore, is to see the department in this way and to be able to measure and judge its performance along these lines.

Realpolitik

This is the art of survival in the organisation in which the manager is working (see Management in Focus 27.9). It requires knowledge and understanding of the nature of the particular 'jungle' in question. From this managers will devise their own methods and means of becoming an effective and successful operator therein. They must be able to survive long enough to do this. It follows that they must understand and be able to work within the formal and informal systems of the organisation and to establish their place in them. Especially in the informal system they may need to find their own niches and from there go on and develop networks and support within the organisation. Large, complex and sophisticated organisations have series of 'cluster groups' determined by profession, location and status, and people in such situations must discover those that are suitable and make sure that they are involved in them to their advantage. They will develop a keen 'environmental' sense. This comprises:

- the ability to spot straws in the wind, indicating possible changes, developments, innovations or crises
- recognition of the departments and individuals where actual power and influence truly lie
- sources of information within the complexities of the organisation
- 'managerial antennae' which are finely tuned to perceive any shifts in the other aspects or across the environment in general.

Managers will assess their own position in the pecking order, the competition for power and influence, and the qualities that they bring to the organisation's internal political situation. They will assess their own strengths and weaknesses in it, and the capabilities and capacities that are required in order to be effective and professional operators in the given situation.

They will identify where the inter-group frictions (and sometimes hostility) lie and assess the reasons for them. From this standpoint they will similarly assess the position of their department in the whole, and look to be able to lobby for support and influence where they are most likely to get it in the pursuit of these interests.

They must adapt their managerial style to the situation. For example, a highly open and task-orientated approach is not likely to work in a bureaucratic set-up. By adopting it anyway, because of preference, the manager would simply throw away any advantages held and the political positioning necessary in order to

MANAGEMENT IN FOCUS 27.9

'AFTER THE STAFF MEETING'

'. . . so I went to the leader, and I asked him to build me a wall for my back, so that when the knife came, I would be able to see it. And he agreed, and he built me my wall; but he left a hole in it, just in case . . .'

Source: *Minisaga* (Pettinger, 1988, unpublished).

operate in the environment. This would also impinge upon both the work and effectiveness of the department and its own regard in the organisation. (Consider Management in Focus 27.10.)

Other factors that affect the political and operational environment in the organisation are as follows. There may be a question of role ambiguity, either among departments or staff, where particular lines of activity, authority, job and task boundaries are not clearly delineated. There may also be more general problems in this area relating to lack of clarity of aims and objectives where departments are unsure of their remit and consequently operate in a void. Furthermore, departments may use this lack of clarity to push their own boundaries outward and build or extend their empires. Lack of clarity in the fields of performance and output standards also relates to this and leads to interdepartmental wrangles and conflicts based upon the consequent inevitable shortfall in performance and the necessity to draw attention away from that which relates to the department of the manager in question and towards other departments.

Throughout the operational environment there will also be various agenda that are to be followed. Departments and their managers have secondary and hidden agendas, especially to do with the advancement of a particular course of action but also, more generally, in the promotion of the department or its manager in the pecking order of the organisation. Departments may engage in unhealthy, negative competition that has nothing to do with the pursuit of effective operations, but rather negatively encourages success at the expense of other departmental failures. It becomes a drive for power and influence in itself, motivated by the need to gain the ear of the chief executive or to increase other spheres of influence.

The situation may be exacerbated by bad and inadequate communications and communication systems so that people find things out via the grapevine or other vested interests; in such situations especially, trade union officials prosper and flourish. There is a consequent increase in the numbers of disputes, including those between departments, and in those disputes and grievances that get put on a formal basis and go either to arbitration or to the top of the organisation for resolution. Rules and regulations in such situations become the end and not the means to an end. Where such situations are allowed to persist over long periods of

MANAGEMENT IN FOCUS 27.10

THE CHOICE OF MINISTERS

Machiavelli wrote that 'the first opinion formed of a ruler's intelligence is based on the quality of the men he chooses to be around him. When they are competent and loyal he can be considered wise, when they are not the Prince is open to adverse criticism.'

The prince has 'an infallible guide for assessing his minister: if the minister thinks more of himself than of the prince, seeking his own profit rather than the greater good he will never be a sound minister nor will he be trustworthy.'

Source: Machiavelli, *The Prince*.

time, bureaucratic superstructures are devised and additional staff and procedures taken on and adopted, and such interdepartmental and organisational wranglings become institutionalised and part of the ways of working.

In such situations also information becomes a critical resource to be jealously guarded and to be fed out in the interests of the information holder rather than the organisation. Impurities are fed into information systems by vested interests and those seeking increased power and influence for themselves and their own unit or sector at the expense of others. In such situations, over-mighty subjects prosper, also at the expense of others (as do designated officials such as union representatives). Manager must therefore recognise these components and vagaries of the work environment; and must be able to work their way around them, accommodate them, and where necessary, tap into them and feed into them in the pursuit of their own effective performance.

● Conclusions

The issues raised and discussed in this chapter are those common to all situations – projects, operations, industrial, commercial and public services sectors. Whether or not they are formally written into organisation strategy, policy and direction, each has to be addressed on a daily basis. It is essential therefore, that all managers ensure that they have their own ways of establishing specific standards in each of these areas, and uphold them.

The managers' performance in the eyes of their subordinates is underpinned by their determination to know and understand the field of operations in which they are working, even if they have no professional or occupational expertise in it. Preaching perfection, it is the bounden duty of all managers to ensure that they know as much as possible about the field of activities as a whole, as well as the pressures and constraints on every activity for which they have direct responsibility, and the professional and occupational boundaries for which they are ultimately responsible. Cohesion of managerial activities with professional and occupational operations is essential if long-term effective organisational performance is to be sustained. This does not always happen – indeed, in some organisations, the overwhelming impression is that management and activities run parallel to each other, with very little direct contact. The public services sector has an enduring reputation for this; indeed, many school head teachers and hospital ward managers can go for weeks without any direct contact with those to whom they are ultimately answerable. However, this is not a unique feature of the public sector – many multinational and multi-site industrial and commercial organisations run in exactly the same way. For example, a large oil company decided that it was going to undertake a programme of strategic change. Consultants were hired, and an outline strategy agreed. The consultants found that a key perception of those working as oil engineers in the field was that they did all the work, while head office spent the money. Accordingly, proposals were drawn up to make sure that nobody spent more than three years at head office without doing at least six months in the field somewhere in the world. The same year, the company reported a 0.5 per cent decline in annual profits, even though turnover had risen by 7 per cent. The company's top managers flew to a hotel in South America to discuss the implications. The consultants were paid off, and the change programme was dropped.

It is essential that all managers have a visibility and integrity of style and personality. This applies whether the manager is autocratic, democratic or participative (there is no reason at all why autocrats should not also be honest). Participation and consultation should never be used as an excuse for sitting on the fence. Many managers use their overtly participative style as an excuse to avoid taking decisions or confronting awkward problems and individuals. Once the staff know, believe or perceive that a manager's style is solely concerned with the abdication of responsibility, a 'hands-off' approach, the position becomes very difficult to retrieve.

It is stated elsewhere in the book that key qualities underlining all effective managerial performance are enthusiasm, ambition, dynamism, flexibility, responsiveness, and the acceptance of responsibility and accountability. To these must be added a willingness to be wrong and to admit mistakes, a willingness to put things right, and characteristics of integrity and truthfulness. It is important to recognise however, that such approaches are not always welcome in organisations. Political systems, the demands of top managers and other corporate boundaries often make it extremely difficult to accept responsibility without being made a scapegoat for a particular failure. It is important to recognise that – however necessary it may therefore be in the short term or as long as the prevailing culture remains unchanged to adopt the rules of the organisation's realpolitik – in the long term, a lack of such approaches will destroy integrity, professionalism and working relationships. It is a very short step from this to steep declines in organisational, departmental and managerial performance.

CRITICAL THINKING, ANALYSIS AND EVALUATION

1. You are a departmental manager. You have just returned from your lunch to find that one of your staff has had a very bad accident and been taken to hospital by another member of the group. What immediate actions are you going to take and why?

2. Why is it very difficult to maintain the long-term integrity of organisational and superior–subordinate relationships?

3. There still exists a widely held view that the performance of managers is largely down to 'common sense'. If this is the case, why are so many mistakes made at the day-to-day performance sharp end?

4. Two members of your staff come to see you, each requesting the following day off. Operational pressures mean that you can only let one of them have the time off. Outline the strategy for the negotiations that you are going to undertake. What alternatives are available to you? What are the advantages and consequences of each approach?

DEVELOPING MANAGEMENT SKILLS AND EXPERTISE

AUTUMN PUBLISHING LTD

The Autumn Press Ltd is a printing establishment that employs a labour force of 400 people. Of these, 15 per cent are women, and they are concentrated at the finishing ends of the works – the binding department. There are also about 40 men in the department. Anthony Thompson is the binding department manager.

Anthony's deputy is Ted Adam. Ted has been with the company for 28 years and has worked his way up by experience rather than by any technical or scholastic achievement. He does not have any formal management or technical qualifications. Ted relies heavily on Jack Phillips, his deputy, for technical advice as he is not familiar with the most modern machines recently installed in the department.

Jack was recruited five years ago on Ted's personal recommendation after qualifying at the local technical college. He is a good member of staff and a very able administrator, but he drinks a lot. On many occasions, he has come into the works heavily drunk and Ted would take him home. At times, he has not come back to work for days immediately after pay day. And when he did return, he presented medical certificates to cover the days he had been absent. Anthony Thompson has questioned Ted about this, but all that Ted has said is that 'Jack has a lot of domestic pressures', and Anthony has not so far followed these up.

One morning, Angela, one of the women members of staff, approached Ted for permission to see a friend off to Rome from the local airport. Ted refused as the work she was doing would have to be delivered at noon that day. Angela was annoyed and said, 'You won't let me have two hours off, but if it were Jack, he would be taken away home in your car and would remain at home for days.' She picked up her handbag and went off to the airport. The result was that the work was not completed on time, and now Anthony Thompson has the customer – a large national bookshop chain – on the telephone demanding compensation.

Questions

1. How should Anthony Thompson going to resolve the immediate situation? Why should he take these actions?
2. How should he aim to resolve the broader situation, bearing in mind that he has rather allowed it to slide for a long period of time?
3. What general lessons are there to be learned from this situation in developing effective managerial performance?

Chapter twenty eight

Management for the present and future

'I would rather have a general who was lucky than one who was good.'
Napoleon.

'The harder I practice, the luckier I seem to get.'
Arnold Palmer, top professional golfer.

'The exclusively competitive commercial ethics should be replaced by cosmopolitan approach made up of guts and competitiveness, brainy organisation, heartfelt co-operation and transcendent unity. It is a long and arduous path to follow but one well worth pursuing.'
R.S. Lessem, *The Global Business*, Prentice Hall International (1986).

Chapter outline

- Introduction
- Clarity of purpose and direction
- Core and peripheral business activities
- Dominant stakeholder drives
- Economic and social demands and pressures
- Investment
- Mergers and takeovers
- Customers and clients
- Staff management
- Structures and cultures
- Management and organisation development
- Conclusions

Chapter objectives

After studying this chapter, you should be able to:

- understand the opportunities and constraints that are likely to be placed on organisations as they develop themselves and their markets

- understand the need for a managements style driven by staffing, strategic and operational demands, rather than those of hierarchy, rank and status

- understand the need to develop expertise in the knowledge and understanding of customers, clients, consumers and end-users

- understand and internalise the need for continuous professional, occupational and organisational development.

Introduction

It was stated in Chapter 1 that the primary concern of management is to make best use of scarce resources in a changing and uncertain environment, to cope with change and uncertainty. From that point of view, managing in the future is likely not to be all that different from managing at present and in the recent past.

It is certain, however, that a much greater understanding is required of what 'coping with change and uncertainty' actually means. Effective managers are going to be required to lead and direct change, to create structures and cultures that accommodate this, to do it profitably and effectively in the long term, and from the genuine point of view of the organisation's enduring best interests and those of all its stakeholders. This is certain to apply to all managers, whatever their level of responsibility, seniority or occupational position. Organisations can no longer afford the expense of large and sophisticated bureaucratic and administrative structures; the consequence is that long-term effectiveness, profitability and viability are only possible if this approach is adopted universally (see Management in Focus 28.1).

MANAGEMENT IN FOCUS 28.1

'WE ARE DOING ALL WE CAN'

In the latter years of his term in office, Ronald Reagan, President of the United States, used this phrase as a catch-all for whenever he was asked awkward questions by the media about particular issues. The phrase was coined for him in a whispered aside by his wife, Nancy, when he was stuck for an answer on the Gulf Crisis of 1984. It was subsequently adopted as the public relations mantra, and survives to this day. In organisations, this is not enough.

An example is Ford UK, whose Dagenham plant had been known to have problems of inter-racial strife since the mid-1980s. The company produced procedures and sent managers on racial awareness training courses over the period 1985–99. This did not prevent problems from becoming very much worse. In 1994, 1996 and 1999 there were riots at the plant, generated by the continued perception that the company tolerated racial strife; and in 2003, the plant ceased producing cars, concentrating on engine production only.

It subsequently became clear that this was symptomatic of a wider organisational malaise. In 2006, the Ford Corporation announced that it was to close 14 factories, losing 30,000 jobs in the process. This was to ensure its ability to optimise production capacity for the medium to long-term future in the context of the present and envisaged state of the automobile market.

Clearly, the company had not done all it could to address either the institutional staff management issues or the wider questions of delivering high-quality products profitably in the evolving market and environment. Effectively, it took the company over 20 years to face the issues that were its core concerns.

Clarity of purpose and direction

The aim of all organisations is required to be long-term effectiveness and profitable existence in a turbulent and competitive world. Lack of expertise in strategic management and organisational behaviour has meant that this has all too often become lost in the pursuit of short-term gain, or satisfaction of the financial interest alone. In these cases this clarity has been replaced by:

- the hiring of high-branded consultancies, leading in many cases to a hype in the share price in the short-term in spite of the fact that the consultant's remit and prescription had not yet been agreed
- the use of parallel communications, using management speak and professional babble to give an impression of direction and clarity (see Management in Focus 28.2).

MANAGEMENT IN FOCUS 28.2

MANAGEMENT SPEAK AND PROFESSIONAL BABBLE: EXAMPLES

These phrases are used by senior managers and on behalf of corporations to avoid explaining in detail their actions to the media, staff interests, customers, lobbies and other legitimate vested interest and stakeholder groups. They are designed to give the overwhelming impression that the precise mysteries of the organisation and its activities are well under control, but that to explain these in detail is clearly unproductive, as nobody would understand them.

- '*We must tighten our belts*': meaning that trading or operational conditions are bad. Invariably how exactly the belts are to be tightened is never fully explained – or justified.
- '*We must hit the ground running*: meaning that the time has come for action. How this action is to be engaged or implemented is never made clear.
- '*We must keep our eye on the ball*': usually a response to criticism, or an apparent imperfection.
- '*We must work smarter, not harder*': normally an exhortation for front line staff to indeed work harder so that non-productive corporate lifestyles may be maintained.

- '*We must think outside the box*': an encouragement to creative thinking (which is wholly laudable), but normally issued by organisations that stifle creativity, especially in the places where it is most needed.
- '*We will achieve synergies or economies of scale*': a phrase extensively used by directors and top managers in their dealings with the media; somehow the media always fail to follow up and to ask where, how and why more is to be produced using the same or a reduced resource base.

Beyond this, there is a regular failure to carry out full market, production, customer and client assessments. This in turn leads to:

- Fashion-based drives – for example, we must have a website, we must have every office/school/airliner equipped with computers and other portable technology – as ends in themselves.
- Hiring strategy consultants and accepting their findings unquestioningly and blindly.
- Sending staff on irrelevant professional, management, occupational and organisational development programmes without relating these to the needs of the organisation or the individuals concerned.
- Concentrating on peripheral rather than core issues (see Management in Focus 28.3).

Core and peripheral business activities

All organisations and their top managers must understand where their core activities lie. It is very tempting to draw attention and resources away from the core business, and to concentrate on exciting overseas adventures, thereby giving the illusion of globalisation. This varies between organisations. In some organisations the core business may not be clear even to top managers. Core business has to be assessed from the point of view of the following:

MANAGEMENT IN FOCUS 28.3

HIGH-PROFILE PERIPHERAL ISSUES: EXAMPLES

- *Supermarkets and department stores*: as companies within these sectors achieve high-profile UK reputations, market positions and familiarity, they seek to differentiate themselves by calling attention in annual reports and press releases to overseas expansion and globalisation. This is dangerous if it is overdone because it calls into question the organisation's commitment to its core market in the UK. In some cases the strategy can backfire – for example Marks & Spencer in its annual report for the year 2000 drew attention to its global reputation and continued expansion on mainland Europe; this was abruptly turned around in March 2000 when it announced the closure of all its non-UK operations.

- *The National Health Service*: the UK NHS has concentrated all its efforts on managing specific statistics – reducing waiting lists and according priority treatment to some diseases. The core of the problem is the lack of staff, facilities, equipment and investment; no substantial improvement will occur in the services that it provides until it increases pay and status for front-line medical staff, and enhances their terms and conditions of employment.

- what attracts
- what sells
- what makes money
- why this mix should be so.

Attention is needed in each of these areas, not just to the narrow issue of 'what makes money'. From the point of view of attract/sell/make money, core business has also to be seen in terms of enduring customer and client reputation, and brand loyalty and identity (see Management in Focus 28.4).

● Dominant stakeholder drives

In industry and commerce, this refers to the desired priorities of shareholders' representatives, other financial interests, backers, and powerful and influential figures who drive their organisations into their own preferred core business. In public services the dominant stakeholder is government, which sets performance priorities and targets according to political need; there is a divergence here from the majority stakeholder – the public – whose interest is in having high-quality, enduring, good-value public services. In the not-for-profit sector, many large charities now take the view that in order to provide the best possible service for their client groups, it is necessary to engage in fully commercialised fundraising activities; in these cases the core business becomes the conducting of marketing campaigns.

Primary and support functions need to be balanced in terms of resource consumption. Resource allocation depends on what the organisation values and rewards in terms of output and what it does not, and on the effectiveness of administration. In

MANAGEMENT IN FOCUS 28.4

CORE BUSINESS IN THE TWENTY-FIRST CENTURY

Many organisations have found themselves diverted away from focusing on core business by media, public relations and stakeholder pressures. They have consequently found themselves over-committing to peripheral or unfashionable business in the pursuit of media coverage. Many organisations have created their own websites on the basis that they perceived that they had to have one regardless of any contribution that it would make to long-term effectiveness, profitability and viability.

In an attempt to redress the balance, Porter (2000) wrote:

At the end of the day there are no new business models or paradigms. There is no virtual industry. There are no easy rides, quick fixes or absolute certainties. Nothing can be fixed through public relations alone. There are no virtual markets. There is only competition – the pursuit of real customers for real businesses who are going to avail themselves of products and services at prices they are willing to pay.

Source: M.E. Porter (2000) Competition in the Twenty-first Century, *Harvard Business Review*, January/ February.

many cases administration and bureaucracy become dominant elements. Where this is taken to an extreme and organisations are dominated by their support functions, their 'core business' is effectively to provide career patterns for individuals within them.

● Economic and social demands and pressures

Managing economic and social demands and pressures requires constant attention to the broader competitive environment. This is one reason why undertaking and using the Five Forces model (see Chapter 8) is so vital. This especially involves taking the broadest possible view of:

- *Threats of entry*: where new rivals or key players may conceivably emerge from; for example, 'If we can set up there, there will come a time when others can set up here.'
- *Threats of substitution*: an example of this is the sourcing of textile manufacture all over the world by Western companies; while this may not always be wholesome or ethical or enduring, it provides immediate cost pressures on those who would complete with the particular sector. The alternative view of this form of sourcing is to determine to pay Western prices for imports from the emerging world as The Body Shop does with the crops it purchases to manufacture its cosmetics.
- *Threats of re-entry*: from players that used to conduct activities in an area or sector, but have withdrawn for the time being. This especially applies to the re-entry of airlines into mothballed routes; re-entry of defence electronics companies into commercial and consumer products; re-entry of private hospitals into emergency and urgent surgery (this is going on at present by arrangement with the National Health Service in the UK, and may become a services that is purchased universally over the long-term).
- *Threats from suppliers*: these become a problem when new players can command greater access to suppliers, thanks to initial investment levels and willingness to pay. This may lead to supply auctions, which some existing players may not be able to afford.
- *Threats from customers and clients*: these arise when product and service levels decline; where the existing is superseded by the same thing at better price, quality and value; where the existing is replaced by something altogether new.

It is also essential that the macro environment is continuously analysed and evaluated. This is so that as broad a view as possible of likely and potential, and unlikely, change is always kept fully in mind. Organisations and managers that do this are much less likely to suffer from foreseeable if unlikely events such as:

- the energy crash in California 2000 and 2001
- the stock market uncertainties of March 2001
- the possibility of a 'bird 'flu' epidemic from 2006 onwards
- the water crisis that threatens parts of the UK and much of Western Europe and North America
- the financial crisis facing the UK NHS, and healthcare and public services elsewhere in the Western world.

The organisations and industries worst affected by such events are those that become so used to their environmental conditions that they come to regard them as certainties; these organisations and industries therefore have no response when things do change. The consequence in turn is that assumptions, forecasts and projections then take on a life of their own, based on historic stability, and the perceived 'certainty' of the sector's durability.

Investment

The traditional – almost cultural – view of investment concerns the placing of finance and other resources into a situation or venture, in the expectation of more or less certain and predictable returns. This is founded on the widely held behavioural aspect of placing money in individual deposit accounts, on which a rate of return is guaranteed or predicted. Even though this is less certain than in the past, and returns tend to be lower, the psychological drive to look at all investments from this point of view remains very strong, and this still applies to industry, commerce and public sector investments. For the future, however, a much more active managerial expertise and responsibility in this area is essential.

Investment in production, service and information technology must be undertaken on the basis that it may be necessary to discard systems overnight in order to remain competitive and effective, because new equipment is now available to competitors. Appraising potential investment in technology therefore requires that as full a projection as possible is available as to whether competitive activities around price, quality, output and retention of market share would be sustainable should alternative technology suddenly become available. A key part of the management of investment in industrial, commercial and public service situations thus inevitably requires a continuous and active 'what if' approach – so that managers keep a close and constant focus on answers to questions such as:

- What if this technology becomes obsolete overnight?
- What if we have to replace a particular system at short notice?
- What if a competitor gains access to technology that can produce the particular product or service in a quarter of the time?

Greater expertise in forecasting a projection is required overall. This applies especially in those sectors that operate under mega-project conditions, where the true costs and returns on activities may not be realised for many years. Several current and recent high-profile examples of this in the UK must cause a radical re-think of how projections and forecasts are carried out (see Management in Focus 28.5).

This also applies to investment in production, service and public sector technology by individual organisations and departments. This requires a much greater projected understanding of density and frequency of usage, speed and convenience of product and service, and quality enhancement and insurance, as key elements of assessing returns on investment.

Mutuality of interest and confidence between the core stakeholders – financiers, backers, venturers, contractors, political interests, suppliers, subcontractors, clients and end-users – must be ensured as far as possible. Ideally this should also extend to peripheral stakeholders – lobbies, vested interests, social and pressure groups, and the media. If this is not possible among the core group, serious consideration ought to be given

MANAGEMENT IN FOCUS 28.5

PROJECTIONS FOR COSTS AND REALITY: THE WEMBLEY STADIUM PROJECT

The Wembley Stadium development in north-west London had the purpose of producing a state of the art, high-prestige and iconic facility for the UK football association and football industry. The original projections for this venture quoted a project cost of £250 million. This was also guaranteed to be self-funding by the perceived enduring appeal of top-class football as mass entertainment. Proposals to make the stadium more universally attractive by including athletics facilities were rejected. The original projection was produced in September 1999. When the project was returned to the drawing board in January 2001, the estimated cost had risen to £660 million.

Work commenced in 2003. It quickly became clear that the cost was going to rise again; and a 'final' figure of £870 million was established. The project would be completed in March 2005.

The project was not completed in March 2005; nor was it completed by March 2006. The March deadline had been agreed with the contractors so that the facility would be available for the FA Cup Final the following May.

The need for high-profile prestige and iconic developments remains. However, cost and deadline projections have also to be agreed with a much greater measure of accuracy and understanding if project work like this is to be produced more effectively.

to the enduring viability of what is proposed, because it is unlikely that results can be achieved where there is not full confidence or mutuality of interest; this becomes all the more certain where there is a known, believed or perceived conflict of interest.

Investment in technology projects and expertise has therefore to be viewed as a sunk cost from a managerial point of view – one on which there may not be any direct or apparent returns. This flies in the face of the widespread current behavioural need to make simple the calculation of return on investment. It should be apparent that, preaching perfection, this is not possible in absolute managerial terms. Moreover, the return on investment is in every case the subject of personal and professional evaluation and these judgements may quite legitimately vary (see Management in Focus 28.6).

Investment in expertise is dependent at the outset on whether staff are valued as assets or liabilities, and the basis on which this is calculated. This also varies in each case; and is likely to vary within organisations according to:

- The nature, relative and absolute expertise of particular staff in different functions.
- The ease or otherwise with which they can be replaced or transformed through retraining and redeployment.
- Specific industrial, commercial and public service advantages (and liabilities) that they bring. This is particularly true of highly capable and well-known key figures in industry and commerce (e.g. Michael O'Leary at Ryanair, Alex Ferguson at Manchester United). It also applies to public services (e.g. Magdi Yacoub, Robert Winston in health services; Peter Hall in town planning).

MANAGEMENT IN FOCUS 28.6

PRIVATE FINANCE INITIATIVES

The private finance initiative, together with partnering arrangements and public–private partnerships, represents a political drive by the UK government to attract private funds and expertise into the creation and management of public facilities and services.

To date the Home Office (prisons), the Department of Transport, Environment and the Regions (roads, railways and bridges) and local government (care of the elderly and at-risk members of society) have all commissioned projects that are to be conducted under the private finance initiative. In essence they are to be designed, built, owned and operated by the private sector. Investing companies fund the costs of the project; and when it is completed, the companies are either paid a lease, or else allowed to recoup their costs through charges to the end-users.

The aims of government were to attract short-term finance and expertise to accelerate and enhance the facilities available for the long-term provision of public facilities.

The aims of the private companies involved were founded on the capability to attract short-term capital injections, to take up spare capacity in their organisations, and to ensure guaranteed rates of return.

Clearly some harmonisation of these aims and objectives is possible. However, the overwhelming political drive has ensured that most ventures have been inadequately constituted, and that returns have been measured in narrow political terms, with only secondary reference to the quality and durability of the projects, ventures and services. This has led, in almost every case documented, to a poorer quality of project and service delivery, greater costs to the public purse, and reduced total quality of project and service.

This is clearly a double-edged sword; individuals remain assets so long as they deliver their expertise in ways compatible with the priorities of their organisation, and there may be a loss of confidence on the part of key backers and stock markets should such a figure suddenly move on. On the other hand, no organisation should be dependent upon an individual, however great his or her expertise, for its future survival.

Investment in expertise is also required at the 'all staff' level. This consists of underwriting whatever steps are necessary to ensure that effective, productive and positive conditions are created, maintained, enhanced and improved so that high-quality industrial, commercial or public service output may be maintained. It is also essential to ensure these conditions include the capability and willingness to transform when required.

Mergers and takeovers

All this is reinforced when considering the enduring managerial responsibilities in mergers and takeovers. Investment in mergers and takeovers requires managerial attention to the reasons behind the findings of two surveys carried out in 1996 and

1998 by the Institute of Management and Industrial Society. These found that 87 per cent of such ventures do not work fully or at all in the long-term. The reasons for this were found to be exactly those considered elsewhere:

- lack of attention to behavioural and cultural aspects
- an assumption that these would simply fall into place once the financial deal was completed (see Management in Focus 28.7).

As a precondition any particular venture, a lack of attention to the long-term staff management, management style, human resource and industrial relations issues would have to be remedied. So too would a failure to require, or to understand the need for, a long-term and sustainable staff management strategy.

The surveys also found a lack of precise definition of what synergies or economies of scale were projected or forecasted and the nature of investment necessary to achieve them. This especially referred to technological incompatibility; again it was found that problems of cultural fit and the need for culture transformation were not properly considered, and change programmes were not sufficiently well thought out or costed.

Mergers or ventures were designed to satisfy short-term financial demands, shareholder interest and the reactions of the media and stock markets, rather than to ensure long-term enduring customer satisfaction in terms of their relations with the new merged organisation.

Those in senior positions with strategic responsibilities are therefore required to understand and acknowledge the full range of concerns when seeking opportunities and enhancements in this form of investment. It is also incumbent upon those in departmental, divisional and functional positions to understand the pressures that mergers and takeovers bring with them, especially if it is known, believed or perceived that overwhelming attention has been given to the narrow financial interest.

MANAGEMENT IN FOCUS 28.7

THE SMITHKLINE BEECHAM AND GLAXO WELLCOME MERGER

The merger of SmithKline Beecham and Glaxo Wellcome was first mooted in 1998. If successful, it would have been the largest-ever merger between two companies anywhere in the world, and would have created the world's fifth largest company. The first attempt foundered because the 12 most senior figures involved could not agree who was to do what job in the newly merged company.

The merger was finally completed in September 2000. To this day, there remain problems with the divisionalised and functional structure; these have yet to be fully resolved. Some senior executives have left; others have been required to take on jobs that they initially had no desire for. The company is able to operate in this way, ultimately, because it can afford to do so.

This may be contrasted with the proposed takeover of the Superdrug chain by the German company, Risparti. Superficially attractive at first, the venture was called off by Risparti on the grounds of 'a lack of cultural fit'.

⬤ Customers and clients

Developments in the management of customers and clients have caused organisations to look much harder at every aspect of product and service delivery, marketing and presentation. This means addressing the following continuously:

- Competing with whom? Who are our strategic competitors? Who are our competitors in particular given locations? What causes customers to use them? What causes customers to use us and why? What causes customers to return to us? What causes customers to leave us?
- Competing for what? Which part of the customers' spending priorities are we targeting? What proportion of the customers' disposable income are we targeting? Are these real needs, perceived needs or wants?
- Assessing the speed, access and quality of input, raw materials and other sources, and the positive and negative contribution that each makes to the total quality of products and services. This is conducted alongside the recognition that, even if what is done today is satisfactory and acceptable to customers and clients, other organisations may see different opportunities and perceive better and higher-value ways of doing things that could cause people to look elsewhere, once their expectations had changed.
- Assessing the habits and behaviour of the customer and client bases. This means continued attention to perceived convenience and value, especially where there is heavy dependence upon convenience rather than loyalty.
- Assessing rather than assuming the benefits that customers and clients gain from products and services, and making sure that these continue to match demand. This includes the 'relationship benefits' – the levels of satisfaction that are gained by customers and clients as a result of their identity with a particular organisation's products and services.
- Understanding the causes of increasing levels of satisfaction on the part of customers and clients, and from this taking action to ensure that this is maintained and enhanced.
- Understanding the causes of decreasing levels of satisfaction on the part of customers and clients, and from this either taking action to remedy this, or else understanding that if no action, or the wrong action, is taken, then loss of customers will occur if there are adequate alternatives. This especially applies to:
  - Companies such as Marks & Spencer: for many years, Marks & Spencer attracted adverse media coverage concerning its decline in financial performance, when it came to be believed and perceived that customers' expectations were no longer being met.
  - Companies such as British Airways that have to tread a very fine line between overall convenience, market domination, premium prices and customer satisfaction. Again losses to low-priced good-value airlines have occurred on certain routes.
  - Local shops, pubs, restaurants and other public and commercial facilities that depend on an actively loyal customer base.
  - Public services: part of the enduring problem with UK public services in the twenty-first century is that the groups that they serve now have such low expectations that they anticipate trouble, inconvenience and lack of quality, and so they look for and find signs that reinforce these perceptions.

– Dot.com companies and those in the mainstream with commercial website activities: in these cases it is essential that the websites themselves are sufficiently consumer-friendly to attract and retain interest, are perceived as convenient, and are supported with levels of customer service at least equivalent to mainstream activities. Where any of this is not satisfactory, customers will simply revert to mainstream suppliers; this applies to business-to-business transactions just as much as to consumer-based activities.

In summary, this centres around developing product, service and marketing strategies, opportunities, priorities and activities on the basis of what is known – rather than merely believed or perceived – about customer, client and consumer demands, and fitting products and services to this. It is also essential to develop expertise in anticipating changes in the market and developing new products and services to meet future demands based on the fullest possible understanding of what customers, clients, consumers and end-users are likely to need and want.

● Staff management

Effective staff management in the future is certain to require the development of management styles based on openness and access to information, and basic honesty and integrity. This will be the case whatever leadership and management style is chosen – autocratic, participative, democratic, hands-on, hands-off or consultative. For there is no reason why any organisation, whatever the sector or nature of activity, should have a management style that emerges through trial and error rather than being consciously designed. There is quite sufficient management literature, training and expertise (together with examples of good and bad practice) around, to ensure that all those responsible for the design and direction of an organisation establish this from their own particular point of view.

Once this is established then it is possible to address the key elements of the working relationship, pay–work bargain, and quality of working life and environment to establish:

● What organisations and their managers require of their staff, why, when, where and how often.
● What staff require of their managers and organisations, why, when, where and how often.
● Whether this is practicable, feasible or possible in the particular sets of circumstances (see Management in Focus 28.8).

It is increasingly apparent that there are some principles of staff management to understand.

Rewards

While everyone values intrinsic rewards – esteem, value, achievement, personal, professional and occupational satisfaction – these only satisfy in the long term where the extrinsic rewards are also at least adequate. For example:

● Voluntary Service Overseas and other voluntary activities (e.g. charity work, caring for dependent relatives) only work because the nature of the relationship

MANAGEMENT IN FOCUS 28.8

DEVELOPING THE RELATIONSHIP BETWEEN STAFF AND THEIR ORGANISATIONS

The need for mutual respect is a lesson that many organisations never learn. It is also not always recognised from either the staff's or management's point of view.

One example was seen by a consultant engaged in drawing up a marketing plan for a small manufacturing company that produced souvenirs for the seasonal seaside trade. She had been asked to look at the prospects of business development because, while the seaside trade itself was booming, sales of the particular products to outlets were declining.

The consultant was working on her plan when she heard the company chief executive bawling out a member of staff. The chief executive, a man in his fifties, then came in to see her, rubbing his hands with glee. 'I always treat my staff like that,' he said with evident relish, 'it keeps them on their toes. Most of them are on a final warning.'

The marketing consultant put down her pen. She said to him, 'No marketing plan for this company will be ever fully effective until you agree to treat your staff with a great deal more respect.' The chief executive promptly dismissed the consultant and she did not get paid. At the end of the season, the company went into receivership.

Staff too may act antagonistically. One member of staff of a children's charity sought to enhance his income through constantly nagging for increases in allowances, evening shift and weekend work. He took out grievances aimed at pushing up these fringe areas of remuneration. Matters came to a head when the Chairman of the charity's governors asked him, almost as an aside, why he did not get another job as plainly he was dissatisfied with everything that he was doing.

---

is clearly understood and accepted as voluntary or social at the outset. Caring for dependent relatives is in any case becoming more of a social problem because of the real and perceived economic as well as personal stress that is placed on the carers.

- Public service jobs in healthcare, teaching and social work continue to offer high intrinsic reward levels. However, in UK public services at the start of the twenty-first century these are more than offset by the low and declining quality of working environment, shortages of staff and resources, and low pay – and a lack of political willingness to tackle these as core staff management issues.

High levels of pay and remuneration are required to compensate people as follows:

- Economic rent: reward for known, believed and perceived excellence or expertise (e.g. sports stars, entertainers, specialists in the stock market and financial services).
- Lack of wider social respect and regard (e.g. public service chief executive officers and top managers).
- Lack of work variety (e.g. factory, financial services); much of this work is still carried out in repetitive and tedious work patterns.

- Extreme working environments, or extreme levels of responsibility (e.g. railways, public transport, airline pilots and crews).
- Enduringly profit-effective and high-quality output of products and services.

Staffing problems occur where the relationship between rewards and work is not effective. These are compounded when the level of extrinsic reward is known, believed or perceived to be so low as to represent an overall lack of respect, value and esteem for the work itself; this is an especial problem in public service professional occupations. Problems are compounded when there is a great spread of rewards between the highest and lowest levels on offer within a particular organisation; staffing problems are reduced when the spread is narrow, and exacerbated when the spread is very wide.

Whether managers continue to organise staff and workforce structures on traditional or current lines, or whether they adopt more flexible patterns of approach, effective operations are dependent upon the following:

- Integrity of working relations, including management and staff hierarchies. Above all, attention must be paid to the human as well as operational problems of staff who work flexible hours, are away from the organisation location for extended periods, work from home, or have to be on call. The need for integrity applies to dealing with these staff as much as to those following regular patterns of attendance.
- Physical means of supervision, such as clocking in or logging on. These should be universally applied or else not used at all. This applies to factory and production staff as well as those in administrative and support functions. Those who work from home or in the field should never be made to log on or ring in if the rules do not also apply to their office or location-based colleagues.
- Paying people for their flexibility and willingness, as well as their expertise. Where it is necessary for staff to work unsocial hours (e.g. in financial services and other direct personal sales), or where they are expected to be fully responsive at short notice (e.g. in supply teaching, agency nursing, social care, ferry and airline crew replacements) this must be recognised and premium rates paid; many organisations also pay retainers for this.
- Managing by walking around, managing by ringing around, and any other means available for ensuring that continuity and visibility of relationship are maintained. Those who work in the field should be called into the office upon a regular basis; and part of the time spent on these occasions must include the opportunity for social interaction. This is both a consequence and responsibility of organising activities along these lines.
- Balance of primary and support activities. There is an ever increasing managerial need to look very hard at support functions in terms of overall cost, resource utilisation and consumption, contribution to operational effectiveness. This does not mean that administration and support are no longer necessary. It does mean that organisation systems and bureaucratic operations must be as simple, flexible and responsive as possible, and designed in direct support of the primary activities. This in turn means attention to the effectiveness of overall organisation culture, and individual, professional and occupational career paths, especially those provided by head and regional offices.

● Structures and cultures

The demand here is that top managers take a continuous, positive interest in the ways in which activities are carried out, in order to ensure that the organisation of staff continues to fit operational demands. Problems are caused when ranks and hierarchies work in favour of individuals and groups but cause blockages in operations and activities. It is therefore essential that questions of culture and structure change are addressed as part of any wider staff management strategy, and that these elements are related directly to organisational policy, priority, direction and performance.

A starting point for this is to look at structures and cultures from the point of view of how well they fit the strategy direction. The initial enquiry is to establish whether:

● structure, culture, strategy and staff management style clearly fit and match
● structure, culture, strategy and staff management style fit in some parts but not others
● structure, culture and staff management style do not match and fit with strategy direction at all.

One clear indicator of this is to assess what is rewarded and punished, and what is not.

This enquiry causes attention to be drawn to the whole relationship between behaviour, operations, activities and direction. This is often not considered or not addressed fully because:

● Its importance is not fully understood by directors and shareholders' representatives.
● There is a history of paying attention to 'the bottom line' rather than how the bottom line is achieved.
● It is not fully understood conceptually by top managers; or it is assumed that once direction is established, everything else will automatically fall into place.
● Top managers take the easy way out, preferring to rely on consultants' prescriptions, rather than tackling critical issues for themselves (see Management in Focus 28.9).

● Management and organisation development

The present view of management and organisation development is that in order to professionalise and make expert the practice of management, and develop the expertise of individual managers, there is a body of skills, knowledge, attributes and qualities that must be learned about and put into action.

In essence this consists of each of the areas covered in this book, together with a commitment to take an active interest in keeping abreast of future developments. Beyond this, management training and development is addressed through:

● Further and higher education: syllabus-based management teaching and learning programmes, ranging from Higher National Diploma certificates through undergraduate programmes; the main standard management educational qualification remains the MBA.
● On and off the job balance: in which those in supervisory and junior managerial positions, or those coming for the first time into managerial positions because of their functional expertise or work experience, follow courses in

MANAGEMENT IN FOCUS 28.9

NEW FADS

Structure, culture, strategy and staff management and integration often get handed on to consultants. This is all very well provided that a genuine brief is worked out with the consultants and is based upon full assessment of the situation. Many consultancy firms have taken advantage of this gap in organisational managerial expertise to sell off-the-shelf solutions such as:

● Business process reengineering, which is overwhelmingly taken to mean reductions in head count, de-layering, and increases in workload for the front line.

● Down-sizing, right-sizing, re-sizing, the outcome of which is normally a structured design suitable for the present rather than the future.

● Empowerment, normally resulting in pushing further responsibilities onto often overstretched front line staff.

● Synergies and economies of scale – concentrating again on a narrow economic gain rather than the broader context of behavioural aspects.

● Facilitation – guiding companies through extended programmes of change.

In many cases, this leads to a long-term relationship between consultants and client organisations. One way of looking at this is to consider 'the circular flow of consultancy'. This works as follows:

The fee levels charged by top brand consultancies make it behaviourally very difficult to turn down their recommendations. There is also a collective perception that if fee levels are very high, then the consultants must necessarily know what is best for the organisation. Many organisations and their top managers come, therefore, to depend on the consultants that they have hired.

Effectively, the process is: consultants are asked to come in; they provide an initial organisational assessment, leading to the conclusion that 'the organisation needs some work doing'; they then produce further investigations and a report to the effect that 'you need some more work doing'.

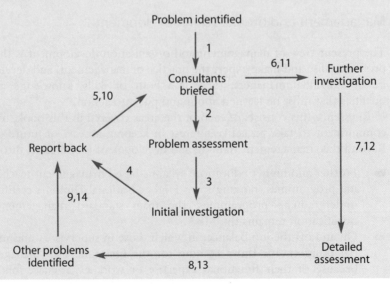

supervisory studies, certificates and diplomas in management, and take management modules and units as part of continuing technical and professional development. National Vocational Qualifications, especially at Levels 4 and 5, require the production of portfolios of practice and evidence that demonstrate understanding and application of this expertise.

- Short course provisions in areas of skills, knowledge, expertise and current affairs development, including seminar programmes and the activities of professional bodies.
- Project work, planned placements and secondments, supported by mentoring, coaching and counselling.

These approaches are generally well understood and represent, almost by common consent, the known ways in which the required body of knowledge, skill and expertise is imparted.

To this must be added the following.

- Common standards of integrity in all dealings. This is an active, collective responsibility as well as one placed on individual managers and supervisors. Moreover while this may stand to reason in theory, in practice many managers do not approach all their dealings from the point of view of this absolute standard. It needs to be clearly understood that customers, clients, suppliers and staff all come to know very quickly when the person or organisation with whom they are dealing is trustworthy, and when not. When the person or organisation is proved to be untrustworthy, given any choice in the matter, customers will move elsewhere if they possibly can.
- The need to develop a distinctive, positive and collective management style. This reinforces culture, values, attitudes and behaviour, and is reinforced by the approaches and activities of individual managers. It matters much less whether this is autocratic, participative or anything in between, than that it is common, open, honest and universally delivered.

The style, attitudes and behaviour of individual managers need to be developed along the above lines. Key priorities have to be:

- visibility
- openness of communications
- the building of the personal as well as occupational and professional aspect of relationships
- the ability to develop suitable long-term work group cohesion, expertise, performance (see Management in Focus 28.10).

There is a critical need for continuous professional development. Many professional and occupational bodies now demand this as a condition of continued membership. In any case part of the professional and personal responsibility of all managers is to keep abreast of developments in the whole field, to learn lessons as they become available, and to study and evaluate practice in other organisation sectors and locations. For example:

- One supermarket chain requires all its staff to go into competitors on a regular basis and to return with at least one example of what the competitor does better than it does; to return and say 'there is nothing we can learn from that competitor' is not acceptable.

MANAGEMENT IN FOCUS 28.10

BACK TO THE FLOOR

In practice it is very easy for managers to lose sight of the day-to-day operational details that contribute so much to the enduring effectiveness of products and services. This reinforces the need for visibility, access at all times and the practice of managing by walking around.

It also ensures that the overtly simple and straightforward details are not overlooked. The ideal is for managers to at least 'walk the job' as part of their own regular and enduring commitment to personal, professional and organisational development.

For several years, the BBC has produced a series of programmes entitled *Back to the Floor*. In these programmes, camera crews follow senior managers as they return to the front line of their operations and activities, and either shadow members of staff or else adopt specific operational roles in order to better understand the particular jobs that they are asking others to do. Organisations featured have included:

- Sandals, the exclusive holiday resort, tour operator and wedding package provider, in which the chief executive worked as a weddings coordinator
- Hamleys, the toy shop department store situated in the West End of London
- The London Borough of Southwark, in which the chief executive worked for a week as a housing assistant
- Galliford Property Services, in which the chief executive was forced to work in substandard building site and sales office conditions.

This approach is a development of the action-learning scheme pioneered by Reg Revans in the 1970s. Revans' view was that the most effective management and organisational development resulted from placing managers in unfamiliar operational situations, and meeting regularly in a support group to review progress. The action-learning sets or clinics were supported by expert facilitators, and full evaluation of the effectiveness and context of actions was undertaken. The *Back to the Floor* approach is excellent at drawing attention to internal operational details and priorities, and again is only effective if it is reviewed and evaluated fully.

Source: *Back to the Floor*, BBC Television 1997–2005.

- A dot.com travel agent, despairing at the lack of real customers, at last sent its staff into its high-street competitors to study the real demand of customers; it subsequently redesigned its approach and website to take account of these factors.
- A hospital reduced attacks on, and abuse of, its staff in its accident and emergency department by studying the management of long-stay customers and clients in airport lounges.
- A single location grocery store quadrupled its turnover in six months as the result of studying the range available at Tesco and Asda and increasing the perceived choice available to customers as well as convenience.

All of this is legitimate and effective as continuous professional development. It is as substantial as professional updates, technical studies and evaluation, and project work and secondment. Ideally continuous professional development should be planned and reinforced with the opportunity to put it into practice. Ultimately this is a matter of personal responsibility, whether or not it is actively encouraged by particular organisations.

Conclusions

As stated above, the key drive is towards managerial expertise in delivering performance and coping with change and uncertainty in whatever the context may be. Organisations and managers that blame environmental conditions for failings and shortcomings in their own expertise are therefore increasingly certain to get left behind by those that do not. All managers need to know and understand the effects of the following conditions, and to be able to operate effectively when they change:

- Fluctuations in interest rates, inflation, retail prices indexes, currency values and other economic factors that 'simply could not be predicted or foreseen.'
- Currency collapses or surges that make activities either too expensive to complete, or too expensive to contemplate.
- Turbulence in the global economy, especially competitive surges from different parts of the world.
- Changes in consumer demand and confidence caused by unfair trading practices on the part of manufacturers and service producers in areas of perceived cheap activities. (It should always be remembered that the first countries to be accused of this were Japan in manufacturing, the Gulf States and Norway in oil production, and Switzerland in banking and finance industry practices.)
- Resorting to public relations campaigns, rather than managerial enquiry, to counter commentaries by the media on organisation and sectoral shortfalls.
- The practice of taking refuge in perceived sectoral league tables; this leads to the excuse that 'we are doing no worse than anyone else in our sector,' or 'we are all beset by difficult trading conditions,' as a substitute for active managerial responsibility.

In practice there is enough management literature, training, development, understanding and awareness, in all sectors as well as overall, to ensure that each of these factors can be understood and accommodated. The most successful organisations in the long term are those that accept the constraints under which they have to operate, accept the potential for competitive and operational turbulence, and understand the factors outside their control within which they have to operate. In the future, the best managers are going to be those that take active responsibility for this, and continue to deliver high-quality, high-value, profitable and effective products and services, rather than those who take refuge in a ready-made list of excuses.

The most important lesson for all managers to accept is that coping with change and uncertainty, and achieving things through people, comes with a wide range of active responsibilities. Furthermore, the resources required for combining into productive, profitable and effective activities have to be gathered from a broader environment over which individual managers have very little control.

The purpose of this final chapter has been to illustrate the active steps that can be taken on a more or less universal basis, in order to ensure capability and expertise in coping with change and uncertainty, organising and directing people, and combining resources.

Above all, genuinely expert managers, those who accept and understand the constraints under which they have to work, and the expertise required as a result, are certain to become very much more highly prized in the future. As organisations come to query every more precisely, the actual added value of support functions and structures and hierarchies, managers who can deliver enduring customer, client, supplier and end-user satisfaction are certain to become most valuable commodities to organisations, and their expertise will be highly prized.

CRITICAL THINKING, ANALYSIS AND EVALUATION

1. Outline the ways in which you foresee the practice of management in public sector services changing over the next ten years.

2. A large children's charity has the opportunity to greatly enhance its profile through taking part in a television series about the exploitation of children in the emerging world. What factors should it take into account before it agrees to do so?

3. Outline a continuous professional development programme for a management trainee going to work in a hospital for the first time. What should be included in this and when? How are you going to measure it for success or failure? Repeat the exercise for someone going to work as a trainee site manager at a civil engineering company. Compare and contrast the conclusions to which you have come.

4. On what basis should managers be rewarded for their expertise in the future and why?

DEVELOPING MANAGEMENT SKILLS AND EXPERTISE

SEMCO

When I took over Semco from my father, it was a traditional company in every respect with a pyramid structure and a rule for every contingency. Today our factory workers sometimes set their own production quotas and even come in their own time to meet them without prodding from management or overtime pay. They help redesign the products, they make and formulate the marketing plans. Their bosses for their part can run our business units with extraordinary freedom determining business strategy without interference from the top brass. They even set their own salaries with no strings. Then again everyone will know what they are since all financial information at Semco is openly discussed. Our workers have unlimited access to our books. To show we are serious about this, Semco with the labour unions that represent our workers developed a course to teach everyone, including messengers and cleaning people, to read balance sheets and cash flow statements.

We don't have receptionists. We don't think that they are necessary. We don't have secretaries either, or personal assistants. We don't believe in cluttering the payroll with un-gratifying dead-end jobs. Everyone at Semco, even top managers, fetch guests, stand over photocopiers, send faxes, type letters and use the phone. We have stripped away the unnecessary perks and privileges that feed the ego, but hurt the balance sheet and distract everyone from the crucial corporate tasks of making, selling, billing and collecting.

One sales manager sits in the reception area reading newspapers hour after hour, not even making a pretence of looking busy. Most modern managers would not tolerate it. But when a Semco pump on an oil tanker on the other side of the world fails and millions of gallons of oil are about to spill into the sea he springs into action. He knows everything there is to know about our pumps and how to fix them. That's when he earns his salary. No one cares if he doesn't look busy the rest of the time.

We are not the only company to experiment with participative management. It has become a fad. But so many efforts at workplace democracy are just so much hot air.

The rewards have already been substantial. We have taken a company that was moribund and made it thrive chiefly by refusing to squander our greatest resource, our people. Semco has grown six-fold despite withering recessions, staggering inflation and chaotic national economic policy. Productivity has increased nearly seven-fold. Profits have risen five-fold. And we have had periods of up to fourteen months in which not one worker has left us. We have a backlog of more than 2,000 job applications, hundreds from people who state that they would take any job just to be at Semco. In a poll of recent college graduates conducted by a leading Brazilian magazine, 25 per cent of the men and 13 per cent of the women said Semco was the company at which they most wanted to work.

Not long ago the wife of one of our workers came to see a member of our human resources staff. She was puzzled about her husband's behaviour. He was not his usual grumpy autocratic self. The woman was worried. What, she wondered, were we doing to her husband?

We realised that as Semco had changed for the better, he had too.

Source: Ricardo Semler (1993) *Maverick*, Free Press.

Questions

1. Why has this approach to the management of a manufacturing company been so successful?
2. What lessons are there to be learnt from Semco by those who work in more traditional multinational organisations and public sector services management?
3. What commitments must be undertaken by Semco management to ensure that this management style continues to be profitable and effective?

The Body Shop

To be successful, any organisation must have strong and effective leadership, and The Body Shop is no different. The creation and growth phases of The Body Shop were closely identified with the personality of Anita Roddick, and to a lesser extent, her husband Gordon. By way of corporate identity, Gordon Roddick became company Chairman, and Anita Roddick Chief Executive.

The job titles made no difference. As Chairman, Gordon Roddick attended to the strategy, direction, finances and performance of the business; Anita Roddick took the position of charismatic figurehead. As figurehead, Anita's priority was as follows:

> You have to look at leadership through the eyes of the followers and you have to live the message. What I have learned is that people become motivated when you guide them to the source of their own power and when you make heroes out of employees who personify what you want to see in the organisation.

The leadership of the company is very distinctive and precise; and this distinctive approach has been used in recent years to ensure that, in Anita Roddick's own words:

> the leadership of a company should encourage the next generation not just to follow, but to overtake. The duty of leadership is to put forward ideas, symbols and metaphors of the ways it should be done so that the next generation can work out new and better ways of doing the job.

Until recently, both Gordon and Anita Roddick used to complain that their staff did not question them often enough. As with all companies and organisations, and especially those led by strong and dominant personalities, the need is to ensure that effective questioning, scepticism, and attention to detail are kept uppermost.

The leadership of The Body Shop remains based on a distinctive combination of charisma and capability. The company has never reinforced anyone's position through providing specific titles, trappings or status symbols; nor has it ever provided luxurious office, accommodation or other facilities for top and senior managers.

To remain true to the company's ideals and identity, the present and future generations of company leaders need to be able to broaden the reputation of The Body Shop, as well as ensuring business efficiency and effectiveness. Anita Roddick remarks:

Why are we always called naïve and innocent; why are we not just right? There are those who tend to the view that The Body Shop is nothing more than a passing business phenomenon, a flash in the commercial pan that will collapse and disappear even more quickly than it mushroomed around the world. The big mistake that they make however, is to equate our distinctive values with weakness and inefficiency. What they do not realise is that while The Body Shop is founded on principles generally alien to mainstream business, it nonetheless operates according to strict criteria in terms of marketing and customer care and motivation, and all the other elements that combine to make a successful retail business. It always amazes me that anyone can believe that The Body Shop can have grown from one shop to more than 700 shops around the world without being an efficient and well run business. The fact that we have grown with compassion, love and a sense of fun does not negate our business efficiency. Neither does the fact that we have never employed anyone from Harvard Business School or Procter & Gamble, have never had a marketing department, and have never paid for a single product-based advertisement. We are not a bunch of bleeding hearts who have somehow stumbled into a successful business. We know how to run a business. We do it differently, and we do it well.

At the micro end of the company's activities and leadership responsibilities, Anita Roddick's commitment and attention to detail were no less comprehensive. She used to visit each of the stores at least once every three months. She used to make it her business to ensure that, within the core values of the company espoused by the leadership, business efficiency and effectiveness were as tight as possible. When she used to visit the shops, she would deliberately seek out those staff who appeared bored, and enthuse them with the 'spirit' of The Body Shop. As company Chief Executive, Anita used to be meticulous in her attention to detail. She was always obsessed by cleanliness and tidiness and would be very fierce with the manager of any store who did not run a spotless ship. She states:

I have a really tight-fisted sense of housekeeping. When you start something off yourself, you are more likely to be worried about waste than those staff who were not there at the beginning when you were struggling to survive. We have never lost the sense of outrage we felt at the beginning of The Body Shop when we thought we were being misused, or our time and money were being wasted. Cutting down on waste is no more than good housekeeping. I will suddenly for example, have a blitz on paper wastage or office furniture. There was one time I stormed into the sundries department because they were not printing brochures on both sides of the paper and because they were using plastic folders instead of ordinary cardboard. I am also very bugged by carelessness – by people doing things like spilling coffee on the carpet at new offices. Coffee stains do not rank high on my list of global concerns, but it is a symbol, a metaphor for a whole way of thinking, a lack of housekeeping and a lack of care. We talk about being lean and green, but I can see a fat-cat mentality creeping in: the paper is wasted, the lights left on after meetings. What it comes down to is arrogance. We have to keep an eye out for that soft smug attitude which says we really think we are so brilliant, so successful, that anything we do is alright – that really infuriates me.

In early 2006, Anita Roddick suddenly announced that the Body Shop was to be sold for £638 million to L'Oreal, the French cosmetics multinational organisation. The sale would be beneficial to all. It would safeguard the brand, the presence, the ecological and environmental 'mission'. Above all it would safeguard the jobs of the staff who had worked so hard over many years to put the company onto the map, in order to establish, gain and ensure its (real and perceived) worldwide reputation for ethics, fair dealing and trading practices.

At the time of the sale, assurances were given by L'Oreal that there would be no dilution of the Body Shop brand. There would be no changes to the ways in which The Body Shop gained its supplies, dealt with its suppliers, or conducted its retail affairs. It was also considered to be a very good acquisition for L'Oreal, who would now gain an alternative international source of revenue and a foothold in the 'environmental' cosmetics and gifts markets – markets in which it had as yet no discernible or substantial presence. In terms of strategic and economic fit, advocates of the sale pointed to the fact that, for example, McDonald's owned 35 per cent of Pret A Manger, and this had done neither of them any harm in their own very different and distinctive markets. The question of the cultural and behavioural fit between The Body Shop and L'Oreal was avoided altogether. Neither was any attention given to the nature and quality of leadership and direction that would now be required to take The Body Shop on in the next phase of its existence.

The move was immediately controversial. Anita Roddick had criticised L'Oreal some years previously for being the one of the main proponents of the unacceptable face of the cosmetics industry – especially, selling its female customers an impossible and unwholesome image of womanhood and aspiration. This was compounded by subsequent pronouncements by Anita Roddick that she was bored with business, and that she was going to use the funds that she had raised from the sale of the company to pursue her goals of ecological and environmental revolution.

This led to many accusations that Anita Roddick had 'sold out' – that she had traded her dream, her (perceived) unique organisation purely for money.

Sources: A. Roddick (1992) *Body and Soul: The Body Shop Story*, Ebury Press; www.anitaroddick.net; www.thebodyshop.com.

Questions

1. Was Anita Roddick successful as leader of The Body Shop? By what criteria? What lessons are there for her successors?
2. Outline different approaches by which transition may be made from the leadership of a strong and successful organisation founder, to an enduring corporate viability?
3. Comment on the strengths and weaknesses of Anita Roddick's micro leadership and attention to detail. What conclusions can be drawn?
4. On the basis of this example, what are the key qualities required of all those who aspire to leadership positions, and other positions of responsibility and authority?

Bibliography and further reading

Adair, J. (1980) *Action Centred Leadership*, Sage.

Adair, J. (2000) *Great Leaders*, Arrow.

Adair, J. (2004) *Inspirational Leadership*, Arrow.

Adams, F., Hamil, S. and Carruthers, G. (1990) *Changing Corporate Values*, Sage.

Adams, S. (2000) *The Joy of Work*, Boxtree.

Ahlstrand, B. (1990) *The Quest for Productivity*, Cambridge University Press.

American Management Association (AMA) (2001) *Merger Activity in the USA 1985–1995*, AMA.

Andrews, K. (1980) *The Concept of Corporate Strategy*, Irwin.

Argyris, C. (1957) *Personality and Organisations*, Harper and Row.

Argyris, C. (1997) *Organisation Development in Three Dimensions*, Harper and Row.

Armstrong, M. and Baron, A. (1998) *Performance Management: The New Realities*, CIPD.

Ash, M.K. (1985) *On People Management*, MacDonald.

Baker, M. (1992) *Marketing*, Macmillan.

Bach, S. and Sisson, K. (2000) *Personnel Management: A Comprehensive Guide to Theory and Practice*, CIPD.

Belbin, R. (1986) *Superteams*, PHI.

Belbin, R. (1992) *Creating and Managing Effective Teams*, Gower.

Belbin, R. (2002) *Superteams* (2nd edition), Gower.

Bevan, J. (2002) *The Rise and Fall of Marks and Spencer*, Harper Collins.

Bickerstaffe, G. (1998) *Mastering Global Business*, FT Pitman.

Blake, R. and Mouton, J. (1998) *The New Managerial Grid*, Sage.

Boddy, D. (2004) *Introduction to Management*, PHI.

de Bono, E. (1984) *Lateral Thinking for Managers*, Pelican.

Bower, T. (2003) *Broken Dreams*, Harper Business.

Bowman, C. and Asch, D. (1994) *Strategic Management*, Macmillan.

Boxall, P. and Purcell, J. (2002) *Strategy and Human Resource Management*, Palgrave.

Boyatsis, R. (1982) *The Competent Manager*, Wiley.

Braun, E. (1999) *Technology's Empty Promise*, Earthscan.

Brech, E. (1984) *Organisations*, Longman.

Buell, V. (1990) *Marketing*, McGraw Hill.

Burnes, B. (2002) *Managing Change*, FT Pitman.

Burns, T. and Stalker, G. (1968) *The Management of Innovation*, Tavistock.

Caplan, D. and Norton, A. (1996) *The Balance Scorecard*, Harvard.

Carnegie, D. (1936) *How to Win Friends and Influence People*, Simon and Schuster.

Cartwright, D. (1958) *Studies in Social Power*, Institute of Social Research.

Cartwright, R. (2000) *Mastering the Business Environment*, Palgrave.

Cartwright, R. (2001) *Mastering Customer Relations*, Palgrave.

Cartwright, R. (2002) *Global Organisations*, Wiley.

Cassidy, J. (2001) *dot.con*, Penguin.

Cellan Jones, R. (2001) *dot.bomb*, Aurum.

Chattell, A. (1995) *Managing for the Future*, Macmillan.

Cheatle, K. (2000) *Mastering Human Resource Management*, Palgrave.

Christensen, C.R. (1987) *Business Policy and Corporate Strategy*, Irwin.

Christensen, C. Roland, Andrews, K.R. and Bowen, J.L. (1990) *Business Policy: Text and Cases*, Irwin.

Clark, E. (1988) *The Want Makers*, Corgi.

Cole, G.A. (1994) *Management: Theory and Practice*, DPP.

Confederation of British Industry (CBI) (2005) *Corporate Risk Management*, CBI.

Cooper, C. (1996) *Stress Management*, McGraw Hill.

Cornhauser, A. (1965) *Mental Health of the Industrial Worker*, Wiley.

Creaton, S. (2003) *The Ryanair Story*, Harper Collins.

Cruver, B. (2003) *Enron: A Story of Greed*, Harper Collins.

Daft, R. (2005) *Management*, South Western Press.

Davies, H. (2002) *The Eddie Stobart Story*, Harper Collins.

Donovan, D. (1968) *The Role and Function of the Trade Unions: A Royal Commission,* HMSO

Drennan, D. (1992) *Transforming Company Culture*, McGraw Hill.

Drucker, P. (1955) *The Practice of Management*, Heinemann.

Drucker, P. (1986) *The Effective Executive*, Warner.

Drucker, P. (1990) *Frontiers of Management*, Heinemann.

Drucker, P. (1993) *The Ecological Vision*, Transaction.

Drucker, P. (1996) *The Practice of Management*, Heinemann.

Drucker, P. (1999) *Management Challenges for the 21st Century*, Harper Collins.

Etzioni, A. (1964) *Power in Organisations*, Free Press.

Eyre, E. and Pettinger, R. (1998) *Mastering Basic Management*, Palgrave.

Farnham, D. (2000) *Employee Relations in Context*, CIPD.

Fayol, H. and Urwick, L. (1946) *The Principles of Administration*, Allen and Unwin.

Fiedler, F. (1961) *A Theory of Leadership Effectiveness*, McGraw Hill.

Fligstein, N. (2002) *The Architecture of Markets*, Princeton.

Fowler, A. (1999) *Induction*, CIPD.

Furnham, A. (1999) *The Psychology of Managerial Incompetence*, Whurr.

Gantt, H. (1919) *Organising for Work*, Harcourt Brace Jovanovich.

Gates, B. (1997) *Business @ the Speed of Thought*, Warner.

Ghoshal, S. and Bartlett, C. (1998) *The Individualised Corporation*, Heinemann.

Gilbreth, F. and L. (1916) *Fatigue Study*, Harper and Row.

Goldsmith, W. and Clutterbuck, D. (1990) *The Winning Streak*, Penguin.

Goldthorpe, J., Lockwood, D., Bechhofer, F. and Platt, J. (1968) *The Affluent Worker: Industrial Attitudes and Behaviour*, Cambridge University Press.

Goleman, D. (2003) *The New Leaders*, Little, Brown.

Goleman, D. (2005) *Working with Emotional Intelligence*, Vintage.

Gratton, L. (2000) *Living Strategy*, FT Pitman.

Greenberg, D. and Baron, J. (2003) *Behaviour in Organisations*, Prentice Hall International.

Griseri, P. (1997) *Managing Values*, Macmillan.

Griseri, P. (2003) *Management Knowledge*, Palgrave.

Groucutt, J. (2006) *Marketing Management*, Palgrave.

Groucutt, J. and Griseri, P. (2004) *Mastering e-Business*, Palgrave.

Guest, D. and Conway, N. (1998) *Fairness at Work and the Psychological Contract*, CIPD.

Guest, D., Michie, J., Sheehan, M., Conway, N. and Metochi, M. (2002) *Effective People Management*, CIPD.

Hamel, G. (2005) *Leading the Revolution*, Harvard.

Hamel, G. and Prahalad, C.K. (1999) *Managing for the Future*, Harvard.

Hammer, M. and Champy, J. (1994) *Re-engineering the Corporation*, Harper Business.

Handy, C. (1978) *The Gods of Management*, Arrow.

Handy, C. (1984) *The Hungry Spirit*, Penguin.

Handy, C. (1987) *The Future of Work*, Arrow.

Handy, C. (1994) *The Empty Raincoat*, Arrow.

Handy, C. (1996) *Understanding Organisations*, Penguin.

Handy, C. (1998) *They Did It Their Way*, BBC.

Hannagan, T. (1998) *Mastering Statistics*, Palgrave.

Harris, P. and Moran, R. (1991) *Managing Cultural Differences*, Gulf Press.

Harrison, R. (2000) *Employee Development*, CIPD.

Harvey Jones, J. (1990) *Making it Happen*, Fontana.

Hays, C. (2004) *Pop: Truth and Power at the Coca-Cola Company*, Arrow.

Heller, R. (2000) *Management*, Dorling Kindersley.

Heller, R. (2002) *The New Naked Manager*, Coronet.

Hendry, C. (1994) *Human Resource Management*, Butterworth.

Henry, J. (1992) *Creative Management*, OUP.

Herz, N. (2001) *The Silent Takeover*, Arrow.

Herzberg, F. (1967) *Work and the Nature of Man*, Harvard.

Hilton, C. (1948) *Be My Guest*, Harper Collins.

Hoffman, D. (2002) *Managing Operational Risk*, McGraw Hill.

Hofstede, G. (1980) *Cultures Consequences*, Sage.

Hofstede, G. (2003) *Cultures Consequences: Second Edition*, Sage.

Honey, P. and Mumford, A. (1986) *The Manual of Learning Styles*, Peter Honey Publishing.

Huczynski, A. and Buchanan, D. (2003) *Organisational Behaviour*, Prentice Hall.

Hutton, W. (1995) *The State We're In*, Cape.

Hutton, W. (1997) *The State to Come*, Vintage.

Hutton, W. (2002) *The World We're In*, Little, Brown.

Hutton, W. (2005) *The Productivity Report*, Vintage.

Industrial Society (1996) *Merger Activity in the UK*, Butterworth.

Institute of Management (1998) *Management Mergers and Acquisitions*, CMI Publications.

Jay, A. (1978) *Management and Machiavelli*, Harper Collins.

Jay, A. and Lynn, J. (1999) *The Complete 'Yes Minister'*, BBC.

Johnson, G. and Scholes, K. (1994) *Exploring Corporate Strategy* 3rd Edition, Prentice Hall.

Johnson, G., Scholes, K. and Whittington, R. (2005) *Exploring Corporate Strategy*, PHI.

Kanter, R. (1985) *When Giants Learn to Dance*, Free Press.

Kanter, R. (1990) *The Change Masters*, Free Press.

Katz, D. and Kahn, R. (1978) *The Social Psychology of Organisations*, Wiley.

Kennedy, C. (2000) *The Merchant Princes*, Sage.

Klein, N. (2000) *No Logo*, Harper Business.

Knott, G. (1999) *Financial Management*, Macmillan.

Kornhauser, A. (1965) *The Health of the Production Line Worker,* Harvard University Press.

Kotler, P. (2003) *Marketing Management,* PHI.

Kotter, J. (1996) *Leading Change,* Harvard.

Lawler, E. (1990) *Strategic Pay,* Jossey Bass.

Legge, K. (1995) *Human Resource Management: Rhetorics and Realities,* Macmillan.

Lessem, R. (1987) *Intrapreneurship,* Wildwood.

Lessem, R. (1989) *The Global Business,* Prentice Hall.

Likert, R. (1961) *The Human Organisation,* McGraw Hill.

Lockyer, K. (1992) *Quantitative Production Management,* Pitman.

Lockyer, K. (1996) *Project Management,* Penguin.

London Chamber of Commerce and Industry (LCCI) (1998) *Mergers and Takeovers in the City of London,* LCCI.

Lupton, D. (1999) *Risk,* Routledge.

Lupton, T. (1984) *Management and the Social Sciences,* Penguin.

Luthans, F. (1992) *Organisational Behaviour,* McGraw Hill.

Mabey, C., Salaman, G. and Storey, J. (1998) *Human Resource Management,* Blackwell.

Machiavelli, N. (1986) *The Prince,* Penguin Classics.

Mangold, T. (2001) *The Hunger Business,* Channel 4.

Maslow, A. (1960) *Motivation and Personality,* Harper and Row.

Mayo, A. (2000) *The Human Value of the Enterprise,* Nicholas Brealey.

McAlpine, A. (2000) *The New Machiavelli,* Wiley.

McClelland, D.C. (1971) *Human Aspects of Management,* John Wiley.

McCormack, M. (1983) *What They Don't Teach You At Harvard Business School,* Fontana.

McGregor, D. (1970) *The Human Side of Enterprise,* Harper and Row.

Mendzela, J. (2003) *Managing Change in the Central Banking Sector,* Central Banking Publications.

Milgram, S. (1965) *Some Conditions of Obedience and Disobedience to Authority,* Human Relations Publications.

Mintzberg, H. (1979) *The Structure of Organisations,* Prentice Hall.

Mintzberg, H., Ahlstrand, B. and Lampel, J. (2003) *Strategy Safari,* Prentice Hall.

Mintzberg, H. and D. Quinn, D. (2000) *Strategy,* Prentice Hall.

Monbiot, G. (2001) *The Captive State,* Penguin.

Montgomery, B. (1957) *Montgomery of Alamein,* Chatto and Windus.

Morita, A. (1987) *Made in Japan: The Sony Story,* Fontana.

Morton, C. (1994) *Becoming World Class,* Macmillan.

Moss Kanter, R. (1992) *The Change Masters,* Free Press.

Mullins, L. (2005) *Management and Organisational Behaviour,* FT Pitman.

Noon, M. and Blyton, P. (2002) *The Realities of Work,* Macmillan.

Ohmae, K. (1986) *The Mind of the Strategist,* Penguin.

Ouchi, W. (1981) *Theory Z,* Addison Wesley.

Owen, H. (1985) *Myth, Transformation and Change,* Free Press.

Owen, H. (1990) *Myth Transformation and Change,* Routledge.

Owen, J. (2003) *Hard Edged Management,* Kogan Page.

Packard, V. (1957) *The Hidden Persuaders,* Penguin.

Packard, V. (1960) *The Waste Makers,* Penguin.

Pascale, R. (1989) *Managing on the Edge,* Simon and Schuster.

Pascale, R. and Athos, A. (1983) *The Art of Japanese Management,* Fontana.

Payne, D. and Pugh, D. (2001) *Managing in a Corporate Environment,* Penguin.

Peters, T. (1986) *The World Turned Upside Down,* Channel Four.

Peters, T. (1989) *Thriving on Chaos*, Pan.

Peters, T. (1992) *Liberation Management*, Pan.

Peters, T. (1996) *The Tom Peters Seminar,* Dorling Kindersley.

Peters, T. and Austin, N. (1986) *A Passion for Excellence*, Harper and Row.

Peters, T. and Waterman, R. (1982) *In Search of Excellence*, Harper and Row.

Pettinger, R. (1999) *Managing Performance*, FT Pitman.

Pettinger, R. (1999) *Investment Appraisal: A Managerial Approach*, Macmillan.

Pettinger, R. (2002) *Managing the Flexible Workforce*, Wiley.

Pettinger, R. (2005) *Contemporary Strategic Management*, Palgrave.

Pinchot, G. (1984) *Intrapreneuring*, Sage.

Porter, L. and Lawlor, E. (2000) *Management and Motivation*, Harper and Row.

Porter, M. (1980) *Competitive Strategy*, Free Press.

Porter, M. (1986) *Competitive Advantage*, Free Press.

Porter, M. (1999) *Competitive Strategy and the Internet*, Harvard.

Pugh, D. (1986) *Writers on Organisations*, Penguin.

Randall, G. (1992) *Marketing*, Routledge.

Reddin, W.E. (1968) *Effective Leadership*, McGraw Hill.

Revans, R. (1967) *Action Learning*, Sage.

Rice, J. (2000) *Doing Business in Japan*, Penguin.

Roddick, A. (1992) *Body and Soul: The Body Shop Story*, Ebury.

Rogers, C. (1947) Observations on the Organisation of Personality, *American Psychologist*, vol. 2.

Scheen, B. (1988) *The Herald of Free Enterprise*, HMSO.

Schein, E. (1971/1990) *Organisational Psychology*, Prentice Hall.

Schiller, R. (2003) *The New Financial Order: Risk in the Twenty-first Century*, Princeton.

Schlosser, E. (2002) *Fast Food Corporation*, Harper.

Semler, R. (1993) *Maverick*, Century.

Semler, R. (2003) *The Seven Day Weekend*, Century.

Senge, P. (1992) *The Fifth Discipline*, Century.

Silbiger, S. (1996) *The Seven Day MBA*, Piatkus.

Simon, H. (1967) *Organisations and Management*, Harper and Row.

Sternberg, E. (1990) *Just Business*, Warner.

Storey, J. (2001) *Human Resource Management: A Critical Text*, Routledge.

Sun Tzu (2000) *The Art of War*, Free Press.

Sutton, C. (1999) *Strategic Concepts*, Macmillan.

Taylor, F. (1947) *Scientific Management*, Harper and Row.

Thompson, J. (2002) *Strategic Management*, Thomson.

Thurley, K. and Wood, S. (1983) *Industrial Relations and Management Strategy*, Cambridge University Press.

Torrington, D. and L. Hall, L. (2002) *Personnel Management*, Prentice Hall.

Trevor, M. (1992) *Toshiba's New British Company*, Centre for Policy Studies.

Trott, P. (2001) *Innovation Management and New Product Development*, FT Pitman.

Tuckman, B. (1965) *Group Development*, BPS.

Tyson, S. and York, A. (2000) *Essentials of HRM*, Heinemann.

Vroom, V. and Deci, E. (1990) *Management and Motivation*, Wiley.

Walker, J. (1992) *Human Resource Strategy*, McGraw Hill.

Warr, P. (1987) *Psychology at Work*, Penguin.

Weightman, J. (2002) *Managing People*, CIPD.

Wheeler, D. and Sillanpaa, M. (2000) *The Stakeholder Corporation*, FT Pitman.

Whittington, R. (2001) *What is Strategy, and Does It Matter?* Thomson.

Wickens, P. (1990) *The Road to Nissan*, Macmillan.

Wickens, P. (1998) *The Ascendant Organisation*, Macmillan.

Wilkinson, R. (1992) *Unhealthy Societies*, Routledge.

Williams, A., Dobson, P. and Walters, M. (1990) *Changing Culture*, CIPD.

Williams, A., Dobson, P. and Walters, M. (2000) *Managing Change Successfully*, Thomson.

Williams, T. and Anning, M. (2006) *Organisational Change*, UCL.

Winch, G. (1996) *Management Principles*, UCL.

Woodward, J. (1961) *Industrial Organisation: Behaviour and Control*, OUP.

Wright, M. (1990) *Financial Management*, McGraw Hill.

Zimbardo, P., Haney, C. and Banks, C. (1973) *A Study of Prisoners and Guards*, US Navy Research Publications.

Index